Massialot

The Court and Country Cook

ISBN: 978-1-948837-18-7

This classic reprint compilation was produced from digital files in the Google Books digital collection, which may be found at http://www.books.google.com. The artwork used on the cover is from Wikimedia Commons and remains in the public domain. Omissions and/or errors in this book are due to either the physical condition of the original book or due to the scanning process by Google or its agents.

The Court and Country Cook is a 1702 translation, compilation, and publication (London) of *Le Cuisinier roial et bourgeois*, written by Massialot and originally published in 1691, and *Nouvelle instructions pour les confitures, les liqueurs, et les fruits*, likewise written by Massialot and originally published in 1692.

Townsends
PO Box 415, Pierceton, IN 46562
www.Townsends.us

THE
Court and Country Cook:

GIVING

New and Plain DIRECTIONS
How to Order all manner of

ENTERTAINMENTS,

And the best sort of the
Most exquisite *a-la-mode* RAGOO's.

Together with

NEW INSTRUCTIONS
FOR
CONFECTIONERS:

SHEWING

How to Preserve all sorts of FRUITS, as well dry as liquid: Also,

How to make divers SUGAR-WORKS, and other fine Pieces of Curiosity;

How to set out a DESART, or Banquet of SWEET-MEATS to the best advantage; And,

How to Prepare several sorts of LIQUORS, that are proper for every Season of the Year.

A WORK more especially necessary for Stewards, Clerks of the Kitchen, Confectioners, Butlers, and other Officers, and also of great use in private Families.

Faithfully translated out of French into English by J. K.

London: Printed by *W. Onley*, for *A.* and *J. Churchill*, at the Black Swan in *Pater-noster-row*, and *M. Gillyflower* in *Westminster-hall*, 1702.

THE PREFACE TO THE READER.

Altho' the Shortness of Man's Life is imputed by some Persons, to his departure from the simple and frugal Manner of Living of our first Parents, and to the vast Quantities of exquisite Ragoo's and Sauces, that are continually coveted; it is certain, That this Practice cannot be justly censur'd, at least, without calling in Question the Conduct of Divine Providence, that has ordain'd so great a Variety of Things for the Use of Man; as long as he keeps within due Bounds, and does not neglect the particular Duties of his Calling: Not but that there is good reason to condemn the Luxury of some Princes of Antiquity, who not contenting themselves to furnish their Tables, at vast Expences, with every Thing, that was most rare and costly, in the other Parts of the World, but also extended their Magnificence, to the ordering of Pearls, of an ineftimable Value, to be serv'd up in Drink; whilst they were as hard-hearted towards others, as they were indulgent to themselves, and ignorant in Matters of Religion.

The Preface to the Reader.

However, since it is to be presum'd, That Men are now far remov'd from those exorbitant Disorders, as having their Understandings enlighten'd by Divine Revelation, and the Instructions given in this Book; would it not be deem'd, as it were a kind of Homage done to that liberal Hand, from which so many Largesses have been receiv'd, to know how to make use of them, after the most perfect manner? And admit it were so, that these Ragoo's may tend to the corrupting of the Body; may it not also be affirm'd, with as much Truth, That they serve to support it, and to remedy Nauseousness and Satiety, soon occasion'd by the Weakness of its Nature, or the Multiplicity of Business? Nay this Inconveniency often happens even in the use of the most delicious Meats, if not prevented by the grateful Variety, and unexpected Novelty of the Seasonings and Sauces.

Indeed, all Men are not endu'd with this discerning Faculty; which nevertheless, is a Ray of their Reason and Intellect. If credit may be given to the Relations of Travellers, there are some whole Nations, which are so far from understanding, in the least, how to raise an Appetite, by a due Preparation of Messes, proper for their Nourishment, that they are altogether ignorant of the Excellency and Nature of the most part of them; often preferring the most mean and ill-dress'd Meats, or eating them, after the most distasteful manner: So that upon the Whole, Neatness may only be said to Preside in *Europe*, where the best Ways of Seasoning and Dressing all sorts of Provisions, which that Continent affords, are well known; and where Justice is done, at the same time, to the wonderful Productions, caus'd by the happy Situation of other Climates. It must also be acknowledg'd, That the English and French are more especially well

vers'd

The Preface to the Reader.

vers'd in the Art of Cookery, as it will more fully appear, upon the perusal of the following Treatise.

The Author of this ingenious Work, assumes the Title of, *The Royal, or Court-Cook*; and not without good reason, in regard that the several Entertainments particularly describ'd by him, for the different Seasons of the Year, were all lately serv'd up, at the Court of *France*, or in the Palaces of Princes, and in the Houses of Persons of great Quality. In shewing how to prepare the respective Messes, of which all those Entertainments consisted, he explains the true Methods observ'd by the King's Officers, who were employ'd upon those Occasions; so that it may be justly affirm'd, That this Book contains all the most exquisite *à-la-mode* Ragoo's that are now in use.

Therefore the Reader will here meet with many sorts of different Messes, not so much as mention'd in any other Treatises of Cookery formerly printed, and others of a better Relish, prepar'd with a great deal more Art, as well as explain'd after a more clear and intelligible manner: Upon this account, nothing has been omitted, that might render the Meats more succulent and rich, and yet it must be confess'd, That no Particular is specified, but what may be easily put in Practice. If any Persons should happen to be in such Places, or Circumstances, as will not admit of the like expensive Entertainments; nevertheless these Directions may be often follow'd to very good purpose, by endeavouring at least, to come as near to them, as is possible: So that this Book will be also serviceable, even in Country-Houses, where there is only a small quantity of Provisions. Besides, that upon some particular Occasions, it will be expedient to make Entertainments, that surpass the ordinary rate of Expences; and then, as a Cook may be furnish'd with all sorts of

neces-

The Preface to the Reader.

necessary Provisions; so it is no less requisite, that he know how to make use of them to the best Advantage.

In this Book is also contain'd a very great number of common Messes, as of Chickens, Pigeons, and even of Butchers-meat, which may give a great deal of satisfaction, for indifferent Ordinaries; more especially, in the Country: And in short, it may be averr'd, That nothing has been omitted, which may contribute either to the Honourable Entertainment of a Person of Quality, or to the Assistance of the Officers employ'd in preparing it: Since without deviating from the best Ways, that are now in Use, a particular Description has been always given, of every Thing, that may serve for all kinds of Tables, except those of the meaner sort of Country-People, on which it would be needless to insist; because the Management of them may be easily perform'd, when that of the others above-mention'd, is sufficiently understood.

After having thus given an Account of the Design of this Book, and of the Usefulness and Certainty of the Instructions contain'd in it; our *Court* and *Country Cook* does not fear the Censure of malevolent Carpers, unless it were for divulging the Secrets of his Art, to oblige the Publick; which is a very pardonable Offence, considering, That the Advantage of the Common-wealth ought to be preferr'd before that of private Persons. It may happen, That in managing the Business several Ways, it may also be brought to good Effect, and therefore every Man is left to his liberty, to follow his own Method, which may tend to the same purpose; provided, that care be taken, to order the respective Messes, with all possible Neatness; to season them well, and to dress them according to Art.

It

The Preface to the Reader.

It was design'd to add here, what relates to those Officers, whose Business it is to look after the Deserts, that is to say, the Fruits, Sweet-meats, Comfits, Liquors, &c. But forasmuch as the present Volume has already attain'd to a sufficient Bulk, we have contented our selves only to touch upon some Articles, by the Way; viz. such as are proper for Intermesses, and others that serve for the garnishing of particular Dishes; referring the rest, to be treated of at large, in another Volume hereto annex'd, which is of no less Importance, and equally deserves a favourable Reception. It is also to be hop'd, That the *Court and Country-Cook*, will be as acceptable here, in an English Dress, as in that of his native Country; where three several Editions of his Work have been printed and sold, in a short space of Time: To that purpose, care has been taken to make a faithful and significant Translation of it, and for the greater benefit of the Reader, to annex a Table, explaining all the difficult Terms of Art, and French Words us'd throughout the whole Work.

A

A Table of the Entertainments and Instructions contain'd in this Book.

An Entertainment for the Month of January; the Table being furnish'd for twelve Persons, according to the Model of one made by the Order of the Duke of Chartres for Mademoiselle his Sister, Feb. 15. 1691. Page 1

An Entertainment for the Months of February and March, conformably to a Supper prepar'd for the Duke of Orleans, by Monf. L'anglois, March 28. 1690. 3

An Entertainment for the same Month of March; being the Duke of Orleans's Dinner, on Easter-day, March 26. 1690. 5

His Supper the same Evening, 6

A List of what may serve during the Months of January, February and March, besides the afore-mentioned Dishes, 7

The Potages, ibid.
Side-Dishes, ibid.
Roast-Meats, 8

An Entertainment for the Month of April, given by the Marqueß d' Arci to the Duke of Chartres, Apr. 10. 1690. 9

Another Dinner for the same Time and the same Persons, April 18. 1690. 10

Another Dinner for the Month of April, prepar'd at the Marqueß d' Arci's, for the Duke of Chartres and Mademoiselle, 11

A great Entertainment for the Month of May, in the same Year, made at Seaux by the Marqueß de Seignelay, for the Dauphin, the Duke and Dutcheß of Orleans, the Duke of Chartres, Mademoiselle his Sister and other Princes and Ladies of the Court, 12

Another Entertainment for the same Month of May, celebrated May 18. 1690. 14

An Entertainment for the Month of June, according to a Model

A Table of the Entertainments, &c.

Model of the ordinary Courses serv'd up at the French King's Table, 16

Another Entertainment for the same Month; made at Court for Monsf. de Livri Principal Steward to his Majesty; the Table being furnish'd for twelve Persons, 17

Another Entertainment prepar'd June 20. 1690. for the Cardinal d' Estrées and the Ambassadours, at the Table of the Grand Chamberlain and Surveyor to the French King, 18

A List of what may be serv'd up, besides the before-menmention'd Dishes, during the Months of April, May, and June, 19

Potages, ibid.
Side-Dishes, 20
Roast-Meats, ibid.

A great Entertainment for the Months of July and August, according to the Model of that, which the Marqueß de Louvois caus'd to be provided in the Castle at Meudon, for the Dauphin, the Duke and Dutcheß of Orleans, the Duke of Chartres, and the whole Retinue of the French Court, on the Festival of St. Lewes, Aug. 25. 1690. 21

Several other Entertainments made during the same Season for different Tables, 23 & sequ.

A List of what may be serv'd up, besides the above-mention'd Messes during the Months of July, August, and September, 26

Potages, ibid.
Side-Dishes, ibid.
Roast-Meats, 27

An Entertainment that may be made in the Months of October, November, and December, according to the Model of a Supper provided in the Duke of Chartres's Palace, Decemb. 1. 1690. 27

Another Entertainment, or Feast prepar'd at the Duke of Aumont's Palace, the Table being furnish'd for forty two Persons, Decemb. 27. 1690. 28

A Table of the Entertainments, &c.

A List of what may be ferv'd up, befides the above-mention'd Difhes, during the Months of October, November *and* December, 31
Potages, ibid.
Side-Difhes, ibid.
Roaſt-Meats, 32
A General Table of the Intermeſſes, ibid.
Entertainments on Fiſh-days, throughout the whole Year, 34
Potages on Fiſh-days, for the Months of January, February *and* March, 35
Potages on Fiſh-days, for the Months of April, May *and* June, 36
Potages on Fiſh-days, for the Months of October, November *and* December, 37
Side-Difhes of Fifh, for the whole Year, ibid.
——— ——— *for the fecond Courfe,* 40
A Lift of the Fifh-Sallets, 41
Divers Entertainments for Fifh-days, according to the Model of the Ordinary Courfes ferv'd up at the Duke of Chartres's *Table,* 41 & fequ.
Entertainments with Roots, conformably to the Duke of Orleans's *Dinner on* Good-Friday, *A. D,* 1690. 47 & fequ.
A Lift of the Sallets, for the Collation on the fame Day, 50
Inftructions in form of a Dictionary, fhewing how to drefs every particular Mefs, and how to ferve them up to Table, for the Side-Difhes, Intermeſſes and Roaſt-Meats, or otherwife, after the beft manner, 51 & fequ.
See the General Table of the Meſſes.

A TABLE *explaining all the Terms of Art and French Words us'd in this Treatise of Cookery.*

A.

ANdouille, a sort of Chitterling made either of Hoggs or Calves-guts; the former being stuff'd with Pork, and the other with Calves-chaldrons, Udder, &c.

Andouillet, minc'd Veal, with Bacon and other Ingredients rolled into a Pelt, *Andouillets* for Fish-days, are also made of Eels and Carps-flesh chop: small or pounded in a Mortar.

B.

Barbe-Robert, a particular Way of dressing Hoggs-ears.

Bards, thin broad slices of Bacon, with which Capons, Pullets, Pigeons and other sorts of Fowl are sometimes cover'd, before they are roasted, bak'd, or otherwise dress'd.

Beatilles, certain Tid-bits; such as Cocks-combs, Livers, Ghizzards and other Appurtenances of Fowls, of the same nature as Goose-gibblets; which are usually put into Pies, Potages, &c. There are also *Beatilles* of Fish, as Roes, Livers, &c.

Beccafigo, or *Fig eater*, a little Bird like a Wheat-ear, being a kind of *Ortolan*.

Beef a la mode, see the last Article of Beef in the body of the Book.

Biberot, minc'd Meats made of the Breasts of Partridges and fat Pullets.

Bisk, a rich kind of Potage, made of Quails, Capons, fat Pullets, and more especially of Pigeons roasted.

Biset, a sort of Stock-dove, or Wood-pigeon.

Blanc-manger, a kind of Jelly made of Calves feet and other Ingredients, with pounded Almonds.

Boucons, Veal-flakes roll'd up with thin Slices of fat Bacon and Gammon.

Bouillans, little Pies made of the Breasts of roasted Capons or Pullets, minc'd small with Calves-udder, Bacon, Herbs, &c.

Bourgeoise, as Veal dress'd *à la Bourgeoise*, i.e. after the Country-fashion: See the second Article of Veal in the Body of the Book, under the Letter V.

Bouton, a Dish of large *Bards*, or thin Slices of Bacon cover'd with a Farce and Ragoo, and bak'd between two Fires.

Braises, or Meat dress'd *à la Braise*, that is to say, either broil'd upon the live Coals, or bak'd in a Pot, Pan, or Campain-oven, between two Fires, viz. one underneath, and the other on the top of the Lid. This last Way of dressing Meat is much in vogue, and extremely heightens its relish.

Brochette, as Chickens fried and stew'd *à la Brochette*; for which particular Way, see the fifth Article of Chickens.

Brussles, or *Bursoles*, Stakes of

[b 2] Veal

A Table explaining the Terms of Art, &c.

Veal or other Meat, laid in a Stew-pan between thin Slices of Bacon, with the usual seasoning Ingredients, and bak'd between two Fires; pouring a Ragoo or Cullis upon them before they are serv'd up to Table.

Butter may be us'd in Sauces, after three several manners; that is to say, 1. *Natural*, or only melted without any alteration; 2. *Burnt*, or fried brown till it turns as it were to an Oil; 3. *Refined*, or clarified, by boiling, and taking off the Scum.

C.

Capitolade, a particular Way of dressing Capons, Partridges and other sorts of Fowl.

Casserole, a Stew-pan; also a Loaf stuff'd with a Hash of roasted Pullets, Chickens, or other Roast-meat, and dress'd in a Stew-pan of the same bigness as the Loaf: Also a kind of Soop or Potage of Rice, &c. with a Ragoo.

Cervelat, or *Cervelas*, a large kind of Sausage, well season'd and eaten cold in slices.

Ciboulet, a young Chibbol, a sort of little Onion.

Citrull, a kind of Cucumber of a Citron-colour.

Civet, a particular Way of dressing Chickens, Hares, and other sorts of Venison; first frying them brown in Lard, and afterwards stewing them in Broth. See the several Articles of *Civet* in the Body of the Book, under the Letter C.

Civette, or *à la Civette*, another manner of dressing Chickens; for which see the seventh Article of *Chickens*.

Compote, Fruit, or Meat stewed: For a *Compote* of Pigeons, see the fourth Articles of *Pigeons*.

Court-bouillon, a particular Way of boiling Fish, in Wine, Verjuice and Vinegar, with all sorts of Spice. For Carp dress'd in *a Demi-court-bouillon*. See the sixth Article of *Carp*.

Crepines, a sort of Farce wrapt up in a Veal-caul, call'd *Crepine* in *French*. For Capons-livers dress'd *à la Crepine*, or in a Veal-caul, see the first Article of *Livers*.

Croquets, a certain Compound made of a delicious Farce, some of the bigness of an Egg, and others of a Walnut; the former may serve for a Side-dish, and the others only for Garnishing.

Croutade, a peculiar manner of dressing a Loin of Mutton.

Cullis, a strained Liquor, made of any sort of Meat or other things pounded in a Mortar and pass'd thro' the Hair-sieve. These Cullises are usually pour'd upon Messes, either of Flesh or Fish, and into Pies, a little before they are brought to Table.

Cutlets, are made of the short Ribs of a Neck of Mutton or Veal, and take their Name from the *French* Word *Cotelette*, signifying a small Rib.

Cuvet, a kind of oval Dish.

D.

Dame Simonne, a particular Way of farcing Cabbage-lettice *à la Dame Simonne*; for which see the Article of Lettice.

Daube, a certain peculiar manner of dressing a Leg of Veal, as also of several sorts of Fish and Fowl;

A Table explaining the Terms of Art, &c.

Fowl; to find out which, recourse may be had to the General Table of the Messes.

Dauphine, as Veal-sweet-breads farced *à la Dauphine*, as it were for the Dauphin's Table. This Dish is explain'd in the first Article of *Veal-sweet-breads*.

Demi-court-bouillon, see *Court-bouillon*.

Douillet, as a Pig dress'd after a particular Way, call'd *au Pere Douillet*: See the fourth Article of *Piggs*. For Pigeons so order'd, see the last Article of *Pigeons* under the Letter P.

E.

Epigramme, as a Knuckle of Veal *à l' Epigramme*, a particular manner of dressing it.

Essence de Jambon, see *Gammon-essence*.

Estoufade, a particular Way of stewing Meat or other Things in an earthen Pan: For a Leg of Veal so dress'd, see the last Article of *Leggs*, in the Body of this Work, under the Letter L.

F.

Farces, are usually made of several sorts of Meat and Herbs chopt small and well season'd with Spice; in order to stuff any Joint of Meat, Fowl, or Fish: Of these Farces there is very great variety, and some are distinguish'd by particular Names, as *Godivoes*, *Mirotons*, *Poupetons*, *Salpicons*, &c.

Feuillantins and *Fleurons*, certain small Tarts or Puffs of fine Pastry-work, proper for Garnishing, fill'd with Sweet-meats; they serve for the garnishing of other Pies of a larger size, and are usually set among the Intermesses.

Filets, any sort of Butchers-meat, Fowl, or Fish cut into slices and dress'd in a Ragoo.

Filets mignons, large slices of Beef, Veal, or Mutton, spread over with a rich Farce, well roll'd up, and cover'd both underneath and on the top, with *Bards* or thin slices of Bacon; in order to be bak'd in a Stew-pan, between two Fires; and serv'd up with a good Cullis or Ragoo.

Fricandoes, a sort of *Scotch* Collops, made of thin slices of Veal well larded and farced, which are afterwards to be dress'd in a Stew-pan, close cover'd, over a gentle Fire.

G.

Galantine, as a sucking Pig serv'd up in *Galantine*; which remarkable manner of dressing is explain'd at large in the third Article of *Piggs*.

Gallimawfry, a kind of Hash; see a Shoulder of Mutton so dress'd in the Article of *Gallimawfry*, under the Letter G.

Gammon-essence, is made of thin slices of Gammon dress'd in a Stew-pan with a Ragoo and afterwards strain'd thro' the Hair-sieve; to be put into all sorts of Messes, in which Gammon is us'd: See the first Article of *Gammon*.

Gatoe of Soles, a particular Way of dressing them.

Gibelote, as Chickens dress'd *à la Gibelote*; for which see the tenth Article of *Chickens*.

Godard, or *à la Godard*, a particular Way of dressing a short Rib of Beef, described in the first Article of *Beef*.

Godivoe, a kind of delicious Farce

A Table explaining the Terms of Art, &c.

Farce made of Veal and several other sorts of Meats; or else of Carps, Pikes and other Fish, for Days of Abstinence.

Grenade, a Dish of larded Veal-collops bak'd in a round Stew-pan between two Fires, with six Pigeons and a Ragoo in the middle, and cover'd on the top and underneath with thin slices of Bacon.

Grenadin is made of a good *Godivoe*, or Farce laid upon thin slices of Bacon in a Baking-pan, with a hollow Place, to receive a Fowl cut into halves and dress'd in a Ragoo. *Grenadins* may be made of fat Pullets, Chickens, Pigeons, Partridges and all other sorts of Fowl.

Grillade, Meat broiled upon the Grid-iron.

H.

Haricot, a particular Way of dressing Mutton-curlets and several sorts of Fowl and Fish in a Ragoo, with Turneps; specified in the General Table of the Messes. Also a kind of *French Beans*.

Hatlets, a Dish of Veal-sweetbreads, Capons-livers and young Bacon, cut into small pieces and fried, with a little Flower, in order to be spitted on small Skewers, breaded, and broil'd or fried.

Huguenote, or *à la Huguenote*, a particular Way of dressing Eggs with Gravy: See the tenth Article of *Eggs*.

I.

Jacobine, a kind of Potage, with Cheese.

Intermesses, Courses set on the Table between other Dishes.

Julian, a very considerable Potage made of a Leg of Mutton roasted and put into a great Pot or Kettle with a good piece of Beef, a Fillet of Veal, a fat Capon, all sorts of Roots and some Herbs. Another sort of *Julian* is also prepar'd for Fish-days.

Jus lié, thick Gravy of Beef or Veal.

L.

Lardon, a small slip of Bacon proper for Larding.

M.

Marinade, pickled Meat, either of Flesh or Fish.

Matelotte, as Cucumbers dress'd *à la Matelotte*, or after the Seaman's Way; for which see the second Article of *Cucumbers*.

Mauviette, a kind of Mavis or Thrush.

Mazarine, or *à la Mazarine*, a particular Way of dressing several sorts of Fowl; more especially Pigeons and Chickens; for the latter, see the third Article of *Chickens*.

Menehout, or *à la Sainte Menehout*, a peculiar Manner of baking Meat cover'd with Bards or thin slices of Bacon; either in an Oven, or between two Fires: For a Loin of Mutton so dress'd, see the fifth Article of *Mutton*; for Piggs-petritoes, the last Article of *Piggs*; for fat Pullets, the third Article of *Pullets*; and for Pigeons, the seventh Article of *Pigeons*.

Menus-droits, or *Mine-droit*, a certain Dish proper for Intermesses, made of different Things; among others of an Ox palate, or of Stags flesh, cut into thin slices, and fried. See the Article of *Menus-*

A Table explaining the Terms of Art, &c.

nus-droits, under the Letter M.

Meringues, a sort of Confection made of the Whites of Eggs Whipt, fine Sugar and grated Lemmon-peel, of the bigness of a Walnut. They are proper for the garnishing of several Dishes.

Miroton, a kind of Farce made of Veal, Bacon, &c. or else of Fish, and dress'd several Ways; for which see the respective Articles in the Body of the Book under the Letter M.

Miroir, as Eggs dress'd *au Miroir*, that is to say, broken into a Plate full of Gravy, over a Chafing-dish, and afterwards ic'd with the red-hot Fire-shovel.

Mode, as Beef *à la Mode*, a particular Way of dressing it. See the last Article of *Beef*.

Morille, the smallest and most delicious kind of red Mushrooms.

Mousseron, a sort of white Mushroom.

N.

NAntilles, Lentils a sort of Pulse.

O.

OIl, a very rich *Potage* after the *Spanish* Way, made of Buttock-beef, part of a Fillet of Veal, a piece of a Leg of Mutton, and another of raw Gammon; as also Ducks, Partridges, Pigeons, Chickens, Quails, Sausages and a Cervelas; all fried brown and afterwards boil'd with all sorts of Roots and Herbs. Other kinds of Oils are also prepar'd for Fish-days, with Peas-soop, several sorts of Fish, Roots and Pulse.

Omelet, a kind of Pancake made of Eggs.

Ortolan, a delicate Fowl of an exquisite taste, about the bigness of a Lark.

Out-works, Courses of Dishes set on the out-side of the Table.

P.

PAins, i. e. Loaves, divers Messes proper for Side-dishes so call'd as being made of Bread stuff'd with several sorts of Farces and Ragoo's: See the respective Articles in the Body of the Book.

A la Parisienne, a particular Way of making Pies, after the Mode of the City of *Paris*.

Parmesan, Cheese brought from the City of *Parma* in *Italy*.

Petits-choux, i. e. small Coleworts; a sort of Paste for garnishing, made of fat Cheese, Flower, Eggs, Salt, &c. bak'd in a Pie-pan and iced over with fine Sugar: See the Article of *Cabbage* and *Coleworts*.

Petits-patez, little Pies.

Poleacre, or *à la Poleacre*, a particular Way of dressing Chickens and other sorts of Fowl.

Poor-man's Sauce, or *Carrier's Sauce*, a Sauce made of Shalot cut very small, with Salt, white Pepper, Vinegar and Oil of Olives.

Potage de Santé, i. e. *Health-potage*, a rich Potage made of the Broth of Buttock-beef, with a Knuckle of Veal and Mutton, boil'd again in a Pot with Capons, fat Pullets or other sorts of Fowl, proper for that purpose. *Potage de Santé* for Fish-day is likewise prepar'd, with chopt Lettice, Purslain, Sorrel, Beets, and other savoury Herbs first stew'd in an earthen Pot with Butter, and afterwards boil'd in Water.

Pot pourri, a Hotch-potch, or Dish

A Table explaining the Terms of Art, &c.

Dish of several sorts of Meat, as Ducks, young Turkeys, Leverets, &c. first larded and fried in Lard to give them a colour, and afterwards stew'd in Broth with white Wine, Pepper, Salt, a Bunch of Herbs, &c.

Poupeton, a particular Mess made in a Stew-pan, as it were a Pie, with thin slices of Bacon laid underneath; Pigeons, Quails, or other sorts of Fowl dress'd in a Ragoo in the middle, and a peculiar Farce call'd *Godivoe* on the top; in order to be bak'd between two gentle Fires. For Days of Abstinence, the *Poupeton* must be prepar'd with a good Fish-*Godivoe* and Sole-*Filets*, or others in a Ragoo, as also a fine Artichoke-bottom in the middle. See the Articles of *Godivoe* and *Poupeton*.

Poulets Mignons, a Dish of roasted Chickens larded and barded. See the eighteenth Article of *Chickens*.

Poupiets, are made of somewhat long and thin slices of Bacon, cover'd with Veal stakes of the same bigness, as also with a good Farce; in order to be roll'd up, and roasted on a little Iron-Spit, wrapt up in Paper.

Profitrolles, certain small round Loaves farced and set in the middle of several sorts of Potages: See the Article of Potages.

Prunes de Brignoles, Prunelloes.

R.

Ragoo, a high season'd Dish, after the *French* Way.

Ramequins, small slices of Bread-crum cover'd with a Farce made of pounded Cheese, Eggs and other Ingredients, and bak'd in a Pie-pan. They may be made of a round or square Figure, and serve, either for Out-works, or to garnish other Dishes.

Ramolade, a particular Sauce, made of Parsley, Chibbol, Anchovies and Capers, all chopt small and well temper'd in a Dish, with a little Pepper, Salt, Nutmeg, Oil, and Vinegar.

A la Reyne & à la Royale, certain peculiar Ways of dressing Meat, more especially Beef, as it were for the King and Queen's Table. There are also several Potages so call'd; for which see the respective Articles.

Rissoles, a sort of minced Pie made of Capons-breasts, Calves-udder, Marrow, Bacon, fine Herbs, &c. and fried in Lard to give it a fine colour. *Rissoles* may be also prepar'd, for Days of Abstinence, with a delicious Fish-farce, or even with white Mushrooms and Spinage.

Robert-sauce, a Sauce made of Onions, Mustard, Butter, Pepper, Salt and Vinegar.

Rocambole, a kind of small Garlick of the bigness of a Shalot.

Roulades, Veal-stakes, thin slices of Bacon and other slices of a Calves or a Sheep's Tongue, all cover'd with a particular Farce, roll'd up together, and boil'd in a Pot.

S.

Saingaraz, as Rabbets dress'd *à la Saingaraz*, that is to say, larded, roasted and put into a Ragoo of Gammon. Fat Pullets, Pigeons and Chickens may also be dress'd in the same manner. See the Article of *Rabbets*.   Sa-

A Table explaining the Terms of Art, &c.

Salmigund, a kind of Hotchpotch; or Ragoo of several sorts of cold Meats cut into pieces and stewed on a Chafing-dish, with Wine, Verjuice, Vinegar, &c.

Salpicon, a kind of Ragoo or Farce made of Gammon, Caponslivers, fat Pullets, Mushrooms, Truffles, &c. proper for large roasted Joints of Beef, Veal, or Mutton, more especially Leggs; making a Hole in them, taking away the Meat, and substituting this Ragoo in its room. See the Article of *Salpicon*, in the Body of the Book, under the Letter S.

Sauce, see *White Sauce*.

Souse, a certain compound Souse or Jelly made of Hoggs-Ears and Feet, boil'd in Water, and afterwards being cut into small pieces, stew'd in Vinegar and Sugar.

Spatula, a Spattle or Slice to stir Liquors or any sort of Butter.

Sur-tout, as Pigeons dress'd in *Sur-tout*; that is to say, farced, tied up, and every one cover'd on the Breast with a larded Veal-collop, in order to be roasted, wrapt up in Paper, and serv'd up in a Ragoo or Cullis. Partridges, Woodcocks and other sorts of Fowl may also be dress'd in this manner. See the eighth Article of *Pigeons*.

T.

Artre, or *à la Tartre*, a particular Way of dressing Chickens, after they have been breaded and boil'd upon the Gridiron.

Terrine, a very considerable Mess made of a Breast of Mutton cut into pieces, with Quails, Pigeons and Chickens, all stew'd in an earthen Pan call'd *Terrine* in French, cover'd with slices of Bacon on the bottom, and set between two gentle Fires.

Tourte, a Pie bak'd in a Pan, of which there are several sorts: See the Article of *Tourte*, under the Letter T, in the Body of the Book.

Truffles, a kind of Mushroom, or Puff, cover'd with a blackish Skin, without either Stalk or Root, which grows within the Ground, especially after great Rains.

V.

Ermicelli, i. e. *little Worms*; a sort of *Italian* Dish, made of very small thin slips of Paste, season'd with white Pepper, Salt and *Milan*-Cheese, well grated and put into Potage or Soop, with some other Ingredients.

W.

Hite Sauce, a Sauce made of blanched Almonds and the Breast of a Capon, pounded together; adding Cinnamon, Cloves, Ginger, Rose-water and Sugar.

A General TABLE *of the Meſſes, the particular manner of preparing which, is deſcribed at large in this Work.*

A.

ALMONDS, Paſtes made of them after ſeveral manners, *pag.* 51 & 52. Almond-milk, 52. Potage of Almond-milk, 52, 53. Almond-*Tourtes*, or Pan-pies, 53. Almond-cream, 93, 94. Green Almonds, how boil'd and preſerv'd, 54. Criſp Almonds, 53.

ANCHOVIES, 54, 55. Sauce made of them, 195, 244.

Andouilles, or Hoggs-chitterlings, 55. Veal-*Andouilles,* 56. Peas-potage made with them, 55, 56, 198.

Andouillets of Veal, 56. Of Fiſh, 57.

APRICOCKS, how to preſerve them green, 54.

ARTICHOKES, with white Sauce, 57. with natural Butter, *ibid.* fried, *ibid.* fried in Paſte, 58. with Cream, *ibid.* 59, 169. dreſs'd *a la Saingaraz,* 17, 58, 234. with Gammon-ſauce, *ib. a l'Eſtouſade,* or ſtew'd, 15, 58. iced, *ib.* 58. in an *Omelet* with Cream, 169. in Potage, 218. in Pies, 251. how to preſerve them, 58.

ASPARAGUS, with natural Butter, 60. in Cream, 15, 59, 169. in Gravy, 59. in a Sallet, 50, 59. with green Peas, *ibid.* in an *Omelet,* 169. in Potage, 215. in a Pan-pie, 261. The Way of preſerving them, 60.

B.

BASES, ſtew'd, 75.

BASIL, Pigeons with ſweet Baſil, 186.

BEANS, green Beans in Cream, 169. in an Omelet, *ibid. French* Beans, how to preſerve and dreſs them, 60.

Beccafigo's roaſted, 237.

BEEF, a ſhort Ribb of Beef, 61, 62. A great Side-diſh of a Buttock of Beef, 62. Beef *a la Royale,* 63. Other Side-diſhes of Joints of Beef, 62, 63. Beef-ſtakes rolled, 63. Beef-ſtake Pie, 65. Beef-*Filets,* with Cucumbers and otherwiſe, 64. Beef with Gravy, 65. Beef *a la mode, ibid.* with Pepper and Vinegar, *ibid.* Briſket-beef, *ibid.*

Biberot, of Partridges, 29, 173.

Biſets roaſted, 236.

Bisk of Pigeons, 67. of Quails, 68. of Capon and others, *ibid.* of Fiſh, *ibid.*

BISKETS, of *Savoy,* 66. other ſorts of Biſkets, *ibid.* 67.

Blanc-manger, for Intermeſſes, 68. of Harts-horn, 69. of divers Colours, *ibid.* Potage with *Blanc-manger,* 210.

BOAR, a wild Boar's Head for an Intermeſs, 136. A wild Boar roaſted, 238. A young wild Boar roaſted, *ibid.*

Boucons, 69.

Bouillans of Capons-breaſts, 70. *Bouton,* 70.

Braiſes,

A General Table of the Messes, &c.

Braises, 71. Veal or Beef-stakes dress'd *a la Braise*, 64. Neats-tongues, 164. Boucons, 70. *Brusoles*, 74. Quails, 231. Galantine, 191. Leggs of Mutton, 145. *Filets Mignons*, 123. Capons-livers, 150. *Poupetons*, 225, 226. *Mirotons*, 155, 156. Partridges, 174. Pigeons, 187. Chickens, 86.

BREAST of Mutton dress'd several Ways, 155, 162, 163. Parboil'd and afterwards fried, 26.

BREAST of Veal, 72, 211, 273. In a Ragoo, 27.

BROTH, fat, 71. Broth for white Potages, *ibid*. For brown Potages and Side-dishes, 72. For Break-fast, *ibid*. Jelly-broth, *ibid*. Fish-broth, 73, 74. Broth with Herbs and Roots, 74.

Brusoles, 74.

BURTS, or BRET-FISH, 75.

BUTTOCK of Beef for a great Side-dish, 62.

C.

CABBAGES, or Coleworts, Potages made with them, 76, 196, 199, 216, 218. A farced Cabbage, 76. Farced Cabbage for Fish-days, *ibid*. 122. How to make *Petits-choux*, i. e. *Small Coleworts*, 76.

CALVES-EARS farced, 111. Calves-chaldron fried, 20.

CAPONS, a Bisk of them, 68. Capon in a *Daube*, 107. In a Pie, 179. Roasted, 5, 237. A Capon-cullis, 101.

CAPONS-BREASTS, see *Tourtes*, *Rissoles* and *Bouilans*.

CAPONS-LIVERS, dress'd in a Veal-caul, 4, 149. With Mushrooms, *ibid*. With Gravy, 150. With Gammon, *ibid*. Bak'd between two Fires, *ibid*. Puddings made of them, 228. Tosts with Capons-livers, 255. A Pan-pie made of them, 257.

CARBONNADO'D Mutton, 163. *Cardoons*, for Intermesses, 77. With Parmesan, 28. Potages made with them, 205, 214, 217.

CARPS, dress'd with *Mousserons*, 78. In a *Daube*, *ibid*. Farced, 79. Larded with Eels flesh, *ibid*. In *Filets* with Cucumbers, *ibid*. In a *Court-bouillon*, 80. In a *Demi-court-bouillon*, 79. Boil'd upon the Grid-iron, 80. Potages made of them, *ibid*. Pies, 182. Hashes, 135. Carp-sauce and Cullis, 176.

CASSEROLES, for a Side-dish, 80. With Parmesan, 81. With Rice, *ibid*. Fish in a *Casserole*, 90, 114, 195, 244.

Cervelas, 59, 201.

CHEESE-CAKES, 82.

CHIBBOLS, or young Chibbols in a Pie, 181. In Potage, 218. With Eggs, 120. Chickens and other Fowls dress'd with Chibbols, 85.

CHICKENS, with Gammon, 82. Farced with Oisters, 83. Dress'd *a la Mazarine*, *ibid*. *A la Sainte Menehout*, *ibid*. With a Cray-fish-cullis, *ibid*. *A la Brochette*, 84. Farced, with a Mushroom-cullis, *ibid*. *A la Civette*, 85. With Garlick, *ibid*. In a Fricassy, *ibid*. *A la Gibelote*, 86. After other manners, *ibid*. 87. Bak'd between two Fires, 86. Boned, *ibid*. In *Filets*, 87. With Wood-cock Sauce, *ib*. With Gravy, *ib*. With Pike-sauce, *ib*. Chickens call'd *Poulets Migaons*, *ib*. *A la Saingaraz*, 234. Dress'd with *Truffles*. 87. Their Skins stuff'd with a Fish-farce, 131. *A la Polacre*, 18.

[c 2] CHIT-

A General Table of the Messes, &c.

CHITTERLINGS, see *Andouilles*.

CHOCOLATE, with Cream, 97. In a Ragoo, 109.

CITRULLS, Potage made with them, 217.

Civet, of Chickens, 88. Of a Hare and other Venison, 89.

Civette, Chickens dress'd *a la Civette*, 85.

COCKSCOMBS, farced in a Ragoo, 89. How to preserve them, 90.

COD FISH, 90.

COLEWORTS, see CABBAGES.

CALLOPS. See *Fricandoes*.

COLLY-FLOWERS, 91.

Compote of Pigeons, 6, 187.

Congers, in a Marinade, 37, 153.

Court-bouillon Shads dress'd in a *Court-bouillon*, 243. Pikes, 195. Carps, 80. Smelts, 244. Sea-ducks, 169. Turbot, 269.

CRAY FISH, in a Ragoo, 91. With white Sauce, 92. In a Hash, *ibid*. In a Pan-pie, 263. In a Sallet, 41, 92. Chickens or other sorts of Fowl dress'd with Crayfish Cullis, 83. Potage made of them, 92. And a Cullis, 83, 92.

CREAM, us'd in Sauces and Ragoo's, 4, 59, 124. Pistachoe-cream for Intermesses, 93. Cream after the *Italian* Way, 94. Almond-cream, 93. Pastry-cream, 94. Burnt Cream, 95. Burnt Cream, with Orange, *ibid*. Crackling Cream, *ibid*. Virgin-cream, 95. Fried Cream, *ibid*. Chocolate-cream, 97. Sweet Cream, *ibid*. White and light Cream, *ibid*. Cinnamon-cream, *ibid*. A Farce with Cream, 104, 143, 229.

Fricassies with Cream, 85. The *Filets* of a fat Pullet with Cream, 124.

Crepines, 98. A Farce *a la Crepine*, or in a Veal-caul, *ibid*. 232. Capons-livers dress'd in the same manner, 4, 149.

Croquets, two sorts of them, 4, 98. *Croquets* for Fish-days, 122.

CRUPPER, of Veal, 273. Of Mutton, 162.

CRUSTS farced, 205, 206, 222.

CUCUMBERS, Beef-*Filets*, with Cucumbers, 64. Salt-fish *Filets*, 245. Leg of Mutton and Cucumbers, 145. Farced Cucumbers, 99, 100. *A la Matelotte*, 100. In Potages, 205, 215. In a Sallet, 50, 100. How to preserve Cucumbers, 100.

CULLIS, white, 73, 137, 159, 182, 202, 212, 214. Green, 137, 215. Of Lambs-livers, 137. Of Partridges, 102, 173. Of Lentils, 103, 200. *A la Reine*, 201. Of Beef, 101, 206, 209. Of Gammon, 101. Capon, *ibid*. Partridges, 102. Duck, *ibid*. Large Pigeons, *ibid*. Of Pullets-breasts, *ibid*. A white Cullis for Fish-days, 103. Another sort for Fish-potages, *ibid*. A Cullis made of Roots, *ibid*. Mushrooms, 84, 104, 161. Carp, 104, 176. Crayfish, 92. A brown Cullis, 161. A Cullis of Pease, 104, 193. Of the Yolks of Eggs, 104, 203. Of Veal, 237. *Truffles*, 104.

CUTLETS, farced with Cream, 104. Larded, 105. In *Haricot*, *ibid*. Breaded and broiled upon the Grid-iron, *ibid*. Marinated, *ibid*.

D.

A General Table of the Messes, &c.

D.

A DAB or SANDLING marinated, 105. In a Court-bouillon, 105. In a Sallet, 41, 106. With white Sauce, 106. In Filets, with Anchovie sauce, ibid. In a Pie, ibid. 182.

Daubes, of Eel, 113. Carp, 78. Legg of Veal, 106. Green Geese and other sorts of Fowl, 107. Oisters, 167. Sea-ducks, 109.

DEER, several Ways of dressing it, 107. Roasted, 238.

DUCKS, with Oisters, 108. In a Ragoo, ibid. In Filets, ibid. With Turneps, ibid. A Duck-cullis, 102. Ducks in Potages, see Potage. In Pies, 179, 186. Roasted, 236.

SEA-DUCKS, in a Daube, 109. With Cucumbers, ibid. In a Court-bouillon, ibid. In a Ragoo, with Chocolate, ibid. In Haricot, 110. In a Pot-pourri, or Hotch-potch, ibid. Roasted, ibid. In a Pie, ibid. Sea-duck-potage, 111. Young wild Ducks in Potage, 16.

E.

EARS, Hoggs-ears with Robert-Sauce, 111. In Souſce, 246, 247. Calves ears, farced, 111.

EELS, farced, 112. Dress'd with white Sauce, ibid. With brown Sauce, ibid. Fried, ibid. 113. Broil'd on the Grid-iron, 113. In a Daube, ibid. In Potage, ibid. In a standing pie, ibid. 114. In a Tourte, or Pan-pie, 114.

EEL-POWTS, in a Ragoo, 114. In a Casserole-potage, ibid. In a Pie, 115. In other sort of Potage, ibid.

EGGS, with Orange-juice, 115. Farced, ibid. 116. With Tripe, 116. After the German Way, ibid. After the Burgundian Mode, 117. Fried in Hoggs-ears, ibid. With Bread, ibid. After the Swiß Fashion, ibid. A la Huguenote, 6, 117. After the Portuguese Manner, 118. Pistachoes, ibid. With Orange-flower-water, ibid. In Filets, ibid. After the Italian Way, 119. With Rose-water, ibid. With Sorrel-juice, ibid. With Verjuice, ibid. With Cream, 116, 119. In a Sallet, 120. With young Chibbols, ibid. Dress'd after several other Manners, ibid. 252. Counterfeit, or Artificial Eggs, 120, 121.

ESSENCE, of Garlick, 11. Of Gammon, 129, 267. Of Onions, 269, 270.

Estoufade, or stew'd Meat, 58, 146.

F.

FArces, 122. A Farce for Fricandoes, Croquets, Filets mignons, &c. 4, 63. With fine Herbs, 269. With Oisters, 83. With Cream, 104, 144, 229. Wrapt up in a Veal-caul, 242. A Fish-farce, 122.

Fawn, how to dress it, 107. Roasted, 238. Leg of a Fawn larded and breaded, 16.

Fennel, Pigeons dress'd with Fennel, 187.

Filets-Mignons, 123. Beef-Filets and others, with Cucumbers, 64. Fish-Filets, 245. Filets of Beef and Mutton, with Truffles, 64, 65, 124. Filets of Pike, 193, 194. Carp, 79. Smelts, 41. Whitings, ibid. In Sallet, ibid. Fish-

Filets

A General Table of the Messes, &c.

Filets in a Standing-pie, 182. In Pan-pies, 264. Perch-*Filets* dress'd several Ways, 176. Soles in *Filets*, 219, 24ᵉ, 246. Chickens, 87. *Filets* of a fat Pullet with Cream, 124. Of a fat Pullet marinated and fried, 211. Of a large Pullet, with *Ramolade*-Sauce, 230. *Filets*, with white Sauce, 124, 176. With Oisters, 124. With Gammon, ibid. Of Eggs, 118. With Cucumbers, 124.

FEET, Lambs-feet farced and fried, 122. Hoggs-feet *à la Sainte Menehout*, 192. Hoggs-feet in *Sousce*, 246. Sheeps-feet or Trotters farced, 266.

Fricandoes, farced, 75, 124. Larded, ibid. Of Sturgeon, 248.

FRICASSIES, of Pigeons, 187. Of Chickens, 85. With white Sauce, ibid. With Cream, ibid. Of Chickens, with Pike, 16. Of Tenches, 251. Of Tortoises, 254. With broiled Garniture, 28.

FRITTERS, made with Water, 125. Apple-fritters, 127. Milk-fritters, 126. *Blanc manger*-fritters, 126. Several other sorts of Fritters, 127.

FROGGS, Potages made of them, 223.

FRUITS, Pastes, or Marmelades made of them, 127. Fruits in Jelly, 128.

G.

Galantine, for an Intermess, 128, 191.
Gallimawfry, 128.
GAMMON, Essence, 129. A Gammon-*Pain*, 170. Gammon-pies, 129, 130. Gammon in a Ragoo, 130. Gammon in a Hash, 63, 169. In *Omelets*, 169. Gammon in a *Tourte* or Pan-pie, 258. Gammon in slices, 3, 130. A Gammon-cullis, 101, 130. Fish-gammon, 130. Gammon-sauce, 129, 230.

GARLICK, Chickens with Garlick, 85. A Leg of Mutton so dress'd, 24. Garlick-essence, 81.
Gatoe of Soles, 46, 246.
GEESE, roasted, 236. Green Geese in a *Daube*, 107. Farced, 212. Roasted, 236. In a cold Pie, 186.
Godivoe, of a *Poupeton*, 131. In a Pie, 180.
A *Godivoe* for Fish-days, 170.
GOOSE-GIBBLETS, 26, 131. In a Pan-pie, 132.
GRAVY, of Beef, 68, 132. Of Veal, 132. Of Mutton, ibid. Of Partridges and Capons, ibid. Fish, ibid. 133.
Grenade, 133.
Grenadin, 134.
Grillade, 134.
Gruel, 135.

H.

A HARE in *Civet*, 89. In a Pie, 185.
A *Haricot*, 136. Of Pikes, 194. Ducks, 108. Cutlets, 105. Sturgeon, 249. Sea-ducks, 110.
Haricots, or *French* Beans, how to dress and preserve them, 60.
Hashes, 135. Of Partridges, ibid. Carps, ibid. Cray-fish, 92. Tenches, 251. Gammon, 63, 169. Of Carps and other sorts of Meats, 135. Of Quavivers, 232.
Hatlets, 136.
HEADS, 136. Of Fish, 137. Of Pikes, 193. Of Salmon, 140. Of a wild Boar, 136. Lambs-heads, 137.

HIND,

A General Table of the Messes, &c.

HIND, how dress'd, 138. In *Civet*, 89. Roasted, 238. And in a Pasty, 175.

HOUGHS, of a Stag and a wild Boar, 199.

I.

ICES for several sorts of Things, 250.

JELLY, for the *Blanc-manger*, 68, 69. Jellies for Intermesses, 138. Of divers Colours, 139. Of Harts-horn, 69. Of Fruits, 128.

Jelly-broth, 72.

Intermesses, Dishes proper for them, 32.

JOINTS of Beef, 61, 62, &c *sequ.*

JUICE of Mushrooms, 161.

Julian, a sort of Potage, 14, 21, 45, 140.

K.

KID, for Side-dishes and Potages, 141. Roasted, 237.

KNUCKLE of Veal, in Potage, 26, 204.

L.

LAMB, a Quarter of Lamb roasted, 2, 141, 237. For a Side-dish, 162. Potage of Lambs-heads, 137. Other sorts of Lamb-potages, 137, 138. A Side-dish of Lambs-heads, 138. Lambs-feet farced, 122. Lamb in a Ragoo, 141.

LAMPREYS, a Side-dish of them, 141, 142. Lampreys in Potage, 142. In a Pie, 184.

LARKS, in a Ragoo, 142 In a Standing-pie, ibid. In a Pan-pie, ibid. In Potage, 7. Roasted, 237.

LEGGS of Mutton, farced, 143. A Leg of Mutton farced with Cream, ibid. Farced in its Skin, 144. *A la Royale*, ibid. Larded and bak'd in a Pot between two Fires, 145. With Succory and Cucumbers, ibid. With *Robert*-sauce, 146. Roasted and breaded, 5. In a Pie, 185. With Garlick, 24.

A LEGG of Veal in a *Daube*, 106. Farced, 146. *A l'Estoufade*, or stewed, ibid.

LEMMON - PEEL, how to preserve it dry, 147. In Tarts, 251.

LENTILS, a Cullis of them, 103, 104, 200. Potage, 200, 201. In an *Oil*, 201. In a Ragoo, with fine Herbs, ibid.

LETTICE, farced *à la Dame Simonne*, 147.

LEVERETS, larded, 148. After the *Swiß* Way, ibid. In Potage after the *Italian* Mode, ibid. In a Pie, 185. Leverets and Hares roasted, 237.

Liquor, of Veal, 73. Chickens, ibid. Capon, ibid. Strong Liquor of Herbs, 191.

LOAF, see *Pain*.

LOBSTERS, 151.

LOIN of Veal, half larded, 18. Larded with *Hatlets* and garnish'd with Marianade, 29. In a Ragoo, 272. In a *Court - bouillon*, ibid.

LOIN of Mutton, dress'd *à la Sainte Menehout* and otherwise, 163, 164.

M.

MACKAREL, 151. *Marinade*, 151. Of Chickens, 152. Of Pigeons, ibid. Of Par-

A General Table of the Messes, &c.

Partridges, ibid. Of the *Filets* of a fat Pullet, 211. Of Veal, 152. Of Cutlets, 105. Of Fish, 153. Of Oisters, 168.

MARMELADES, 127, 128. In Pan-pies, 174.

Mauviettes, farced, with Mustard, 28, 153. In Potage, 153. Roasted, 237.

Menus-droits, of an Ox-palate, 153. Of Venison, ibid. With Mustard, 247.

Meringues for garnishing, 153, 154. Pistachoe meringues, 154.

MILK, Almond-milk, 52. Potage of Almond-milk, ibid. 53.

Mirotons of several sorts, 154, & sequ. A *Miroton* for Fish-days, 156, 157.

Morilles, in a Ragoo, 157. With Cream, ibid. 160, 169. Fried, 157. Farced, 13. In Potage, 213. In a *Tourte* or Pan-pie, 262. In an *Omelet*, 169.

Mousserons, dress'd in a Ragoo, 158. In Potage, 213. In an *Omelet*, 169. How to preserve them, 161.

Mushrooms, 159. Common Mushrooms fried, 160. In a Ragoo, ibid. With Cream, ibid. 169. Breaded and bak'd, 160. Farced, ibid. In Potages, ibid. 161. In a Pan-pie, 262. How to extract their Juice, 161. And to preserve them, ibid. 162.

MULLETS, broil'd, fried and dress'd in a Ragoo, 158. In Standing-pies and Pan-pies, ibid.

MUSCLES, in a Ragoo, 158. In Potage, 159. In a Pan-pie, 265.

MUTTON, Cutlets, 104. A Fillet of Mutton, with *Truffles*, 124.

A Neck and Breast of Mutton, 155. A large Joint of Mutton roasted, 162. A Quarter of Mutton farced, ibid. Carbonnado'd Mutton, 163. A Loin of Mutton *à la Sainte Menéhout* and otherwise, 164, 165.

See LEGGS of Mutton.

N.

NEATS-TONGUES, bak'd between two Fires, 164. Dried, 165. Side-dishes of them, ibid. 166. A Neck of Mutton, 155.

O.

OIL, a sort of Potage for Flesh-days, 166, 212. An *Oil* for Fish-days, 167. Ringdove Potage in form of an Oil, 201.

OISTERS, 167. Fish dress'd with Oisters, 193. Water-fowl, with Oisters, 108. Oisters in a *Daube*, 167. Farced, ibid. 168. Marinated and fried, 168. In Potage, 196, 213, 224. In a Pan-pie, 255. A Farce with Oisters, 83.

OLIVES, Fat Pullets, and other sorts of Fowl with Olives, 168.

Omelets, with Cream, of several sorts, 169. A sugar'd *Omelet*, 168. A Gammon-*Omelet*, 169. Farced *Omelets*, 170.

Onion-essence, 269, 270. Onions with sweet Basil, 35.

Ortolans roasted, 237. In a *Tourte* or Pan-pie, 256.

P.

A General Table of the Messes, &c.

P.

PAins, of Gammon, 170. Partridge-*Pains*, 171. A Veal-*Pain*, ib. A *Spanish Pain*, 172. A Sole-*Pain*, 246. A farced *Pain*, for a Side-dish, 172. A farced *Pain*, or Loaf in Potage, 202, 203, 206, 211.

PALATE of an Ox in *Menus-droits*, 153.

PAN-PIES, see *Tourtes*.

PARTRIDGES, with *Spanish* Sauce, 172. In a *Biberot*, 173. In a *Daube*, 107. In a Hash, 135. In Pies, 177, 186. In *Marinade*, 152. In *Filets*, with Gammon, 173. With Olives, 168. Bak'd between two Fires, 174. In a *Grenadin*, 134. In *Sur-tout*, 174, 189. With Wood-cock-sauce, 173. With Pike-sauce, ibid. In Potages *à la Reyne* and others, 199, 200, 201, 202. Partridges and young Partridges roasted, 236.

PASTES, of Almonds, 51. Of Fruits, 127, 128. Syringed Paste, 52, 175. Paste for crackling Crust, 174, 175.

PASTIES, 175.

PEAS, green, in Cream, 59, 169. In a *Miroton*, 155. In Potage, 198. In a Poupeton, 225.

Petits-patez, or little Pies, after the *Spanish* Way, 184. Made of Fish, ibid.

PERCHES, with *Moufferons* and Cream, 175. In *Filets*, with Cucumbers, 176. With green Sauce, ibid. In *Filets*, with white Sauce, ibid. In Potages, 222.

PHEASANTS, with Carp-sauce, 175. In a hot Pie, 177. In Potage, 208. Pheasants and Pheasant-powts roasted, 236. In a cold Pie, 186.

PIES, or standing Pies hot for Side-dishes, 177, 178, *& seq.* Cold for Intermesses, 185, 186. After the *German* Way, 179. Of Larks, 142, 178. After the *English* Manner, 181, 182. Eel-pies, 113, 114. Plate pies, 180. A Pie made of Eel-powts, 115. Dabs, 106, 182. Wood-cocks, 177, 186, 276. Pike, 194. Quails, 178. Ducks, 179, 186. Carps, 182, 183. Boned Capon, 179. Young Chibbols, 181. Turkey-powts, 178, 186. Leg of Mutton, 185.

PHEASANTS, 177, 186, Thrushes, 178. *Godivoe*, 180. Fish-*Godivoe*, 182. Gammon, 129, 130. Rabbets, 185, 233. Hares and Leverets, 181, 182, 185, 186. Lamprays, 184. Sea ducks, 110. Mullets, 182. Green Geese, 186. Partridges, 177, 186. Pigeons, 178. Fat Pullets, 186. Chickens, 178, 179. Fillet of Veal, 180, 185. Roaches, 183. A Blood-pie, 180, 181. Wild Boar, 175. Teals, 186. Soles, 183, 184. Tunny, 184. Beef-stakes, 65, 185. Trout, 183. Turbot, ibid.

PIGEONS, in a Bisk, 67, 68. In a *Poupeton*, 131, 225. In standing Pies, 178. With sweet Basil, 9, 12, 15, 19, 22, 24, 29, 186. With Fennel, 17, 21, 23, 24, 187. Bak'd between two Fires, ibid. In Compote and in a Fricassy, 187. With Gammon, ibid. With *Truffles*, 188. *A la Sainte Menehout*, ibid. In *Sur-tout*, 188, 189. In a *Court-bouillon*, 188. Dress'd *au pere Douillet*, 190. With Gravy, ibid. In a *Marinade*, 152. In a *Grenadin*, 134. In a Cullis, 102. Roasted, 236. Stuff'd with a

[d] Fish-

A General Table of the Messes, &c.

Fish-farce, 131, 265. In Potages, 201, 205, 209.

PIG, a Sucking-pig farced, 190. Dress'd after the *German* Way, ib. 191. In *Galantine*, 191. Roasted, 237. *Au Pere Douillet*, 192.

PIGS-PETTITOES, *à la Sainte Menehout*, 192.

PIKES, with Oisters, 193. Dress'd four several Ways, ib. 194. With Sauce after the *German* Mode, 193. In *Filets*, marinated and fried, 193, 194. In *Filets* with white Sauce, 194. In *Filets*, with Cucumbers, ibid. In standing Pies, 194. In *Haricot*, with Turneps, ibid. In a *Court-bouillon*, 195. Farced, ibid. In *Casserole*, ibid. With Anchove-sauce, ibid. Roasted Pike, 196. For an Intermess, on Flesh-days, ibid. In Potages, ibid. In a *Tourte*, or Pan-pie, 264. A Sauce, or thickening Liquor for Pikes, 87.

PIKES-LIVERS, 264.

PILCHARDS, marinated, 153.

PISTACHOES, in Cream, 93. In a *Tourte* or Pan-pie, 263.

PLAICE in a *Casserole*, 197. Fried Plaice, ibid.

PLOVER, roasted, 236.

A la Polacre, Chickens so dress'd, 18.

POTAGE, of Almond-milk, 52, 53. Of *Andouilles*, with Peas, 55, 56, 198. *Andouillets*, 57. Artichokes, 218. Asparagus, 215. Of a Breast of Veal, 211. Of Cabbage, 75, 196, 199, 200, 216, 217, 218. Of a boned Capon, with Oisters, 213. Capon, with a Cullis of Lambs-livers, 5. Capon, with Cucumbers, 205. Capon, with Rice, 207. Capon, with Roots, 200. Of Cardoons, 205, 214, 217. Carps, 80. Young Chibbols, with Milk, 218. Of farced Chickens, 204, 205. Chickens, with green Peas-soop, 198, 205. Chickens, with Asparagus, 10, 215. Chickens, with Lettice, 11, 12, 215. Chickens, with Onions, 204. Chickens, with Turneps, 199. Chickens, with Cucumbers, 205. Chickens, with Succory, 211. Citrulls, with Milk, 217. Crabb-fish farced, 225. Crayfish, 92. Of Crusts farced with Partridge-breasts, 205, 206. Crusts farced with Lentils, 206. Crusts, farced with Gammon, ibid. Crusts stuff'd with Perches, and other sorts of Fish, 222. Of Cucumbers, 205, 215. Of Ducks, with Peas, 108, 109, 198. Ducks, with a Lentil-cullis, 108, 200. Ducks, with Turneps, 108, 199. Young wild Ducks, 16. Sea-ducks, 111. Of Eels, 113. Eel-powrs, 114, 115. Of Fennel, 216. Of Froggs, 223. Of Goats-bread, 214. Of green Geese, 12, 14, 198, 212. Goose-gibblets, 26, 131. Of Hops, 214. Of the Houghs of a Stag or wild Boar, 199. Potage after the *Italian* Way, 148, 212. Of Kid, 141. Of Lambs-heads, 137, 138, 198. Of Larks, 7, 31, 201, 208. Lentils, 200, 201. Farced Lettice, 215. Leverets, 148. Mackarel, 151. Marbled Potage, 215. Of *Marviettes*, 153. Melons, 217. Milk-potage, 135. With Yolks of Eggs, 155. Potage of *Morilles* and *Mousserons*, with Cream, 213. Muscadine-grapes, 217. Muscles, 159. Mushrooms, 160, 161. With Oisters, 196. Of Onions, 204, 205, 214. Parmisan, 81, 209, 210. Of Partridges, with a Cullis *à la Reyne* and otherwise, 201, 202.

A General Table of the Messes, &c.

202. Partridges, with brown Broth, 210, 211. Partridges, with Lentils, 200. Partridges, with Cabbage, 199. Of green Peas, 198, 216. Of Perches, 222. Of Pheasant-powts, with *Truffles*, 208. Of Pigeons, with a white Cullis, 205, 209. Pigeons with brown Cullis, 209. Pigeons, with Radishes, ibid. Pigeons, with Cabbage, 199, 200. Pigeons with Onions or Cardoons, 205. Pigeons, with Lentils, 200. Of Pike, 195, 196, 197. Of a fat Pullet with Roots, 200. Pullets, with Succory, 211. Pullets, with Rice, 207. Pullets with a brown Cullis, 211, 212. Of Purslain, 214. Of *Profitrolle*, 206, 207. *Profitrolle* for Fish-days, 223, 224. Of Quails, 231, 232. Quails, with a *Blanc-manger*, 210, Quails, with sweet Basil, 286, 203. Quails farced with Capons-breasts, 202, 203. Quails, with *Truffles*, 208. Quails in a *Bisk*, 68. Quails in form of an *Oil*, 201. Quails, *à la Reyne*, ibid. & 202. Quails, with Roots, 200. Of Quavivors, 222. With Radishes, 209, 214. *A la Reyne*, 201, 202. With Rice, 81. *A la Royale*, 224. Of young Ring-doves, with Turneps and Roots, 200. Ring-doves in form of an *Oil*, 201. Potage, with Roots, for all sorts of Fowl, 200. Of Salmon, 219. Potages *de Sainté*, 204, 213. Of Skirrets, 214. Of farced Soles, 219. Soles for Flesh-days, 220, 221. Of Spinage, 216. Of young Sprouts, 214. Of Sturgeon, 248. With Succory, 211. Of Teals and other sorts of Fowl, with Mushrooms, 208. Teals, with Turneps, 199. Of young Teals, with sweet Basil, 29. Of farced Tenches, 224, 225. Of Tortoises, both for Flesh and Fish-days, 221, 222. With *Truffles*, 208. Of Turbet, 219. Of young Turkeys with Succory, 12, 211. Young Turkeys, with Peas, 198. Young Turkeys, with Cucumbers, 205. With Turneps, 196, 199. Of *Vermicelli*, 207. Of Vine-buds, 216. White Potage, 201, 202, 212. Potage without Butter, 213. Without Water, 203. For other sorts of Potages, see *Bisks, Casseroles, Julians* and *Oils*.

Pot-pourri, 225.

Poupetons, 131, 225, 226. For Fish-days, 226.

Poupiets roasted and breaded, 226. Larded, ibid.

PUDDINGS, white Hoggs-puddings, 227. Black, ibid. & 228. Of Capons-livers, 228. Of Calves-livers, ibid.

PULLETS, a fat Pullet, with Olives, 168. After the *English* Way, 228, 229. Bak'd between two Fires, 15, 86, 230. Farced with Cream, 229. With Gammon-sauce, 230. In a Ragoo, with *Truffles*, 188, 230. *A la Saingarax*, 230, 234. *A la Sainte Menehout*, 22. After several other Manners, 230. Accompanied with a delicious Farce, ibid. In *Filets*, with Cucumbers, 64. With a Cray-fish-cullis, 230.

Q.

QUAILS, in a Bisk, 68. Quail-potages, of several sorts, 186, 200, 201, 202, 203, 208, 210, 231, 232. Bak'd or stew'd between two Fires, 231. In a hot Pie, 178. In a *Poupeton*, 131, 225. In a Ragoo, 231.

A General Table of the Messes, &c.

With sweet Basil, as Pigeons, 186. Large Quails and young Quails roasted, 236.

QUARTER, of Lamb, 141, 162. Of Mutton, 9, 162. Of Veal, 11, 272.

QUAVIVERS or Sea-dragons dress'd in a Ragoo, 232. In *Filets*, with Cucumbers, ibid. With white Sauce and Capers, ibid. In a Hash, ibid.

R.

R*abbets*, in a hot Pie, 233. Rabbets and young Rabbets in a cold standing Pie, 186. The same in a *Casserole*, 233. Young Rabbets, with white and brown Sauce, ibid. Old and young Rabbets in a *Tourte* or Pan-pie and otherwise, ibid. Young Rabbets, with Gammon-sauce, ibid. A la *Sairgaraz*, 15, 18, 234. Rabbets, roasted, 237.

Ramequins, 234.

Ramolade-Sauce, 41, 163, 188, 230.

RESTAURATIVE Broth, or Potage without Water, 203.

RIB (Short) of Beef, dress'd a la Godard. 61. After the *English* Way, ibid. With Cucumbers, ibid. Farced, 62. The *Filets* of a short Rib in its own Gravy, 25.

RING DOVES and young Ring-doves roasted, 236.

Rissoles, of Capons-breasts, 233, 235.

ROACHES, marinated, 235. Dress'd in a Ragoo, and after divers Manners, ibid.

ROAST-MEAT, for every Season, 8, 20, 27, 32. How to prepare and serve it up to Table, 235, *& seq.*

ROBERT-*Sauce*, 111, 146, 246, 453.

ROE-BUCK, order'd several Ways, 239. In a Pasty, 175. Roasted, 238.

ROOTS, Entertainments with Roots, 47.

Roulades of Veal, 239, 240.

S.

S*Aingaraz*, Meat dress'd in that manner, 17, 18, 21, 27, 234.

Sainte Menehout, Piggs-pettitoes so order'd, 192. A Loin of Mutton, 163. Pigeons, Chickens and other sorts of Fowl, *a la Sainte Menehout*. 83, 188. 229.

SALLETS of Fish, 41. With Roots and Herbs, 50.

SALMON, fresh for Fish-days, 240. In a *Casserole*, ibid. With sweet Sauce, and otherwise, 241. In a Ragoo, 240.

Salpicon, 241.

SANDLING, see DAB.

SAUCE, after the *Spanish* Way, 28, 172, 173. White Sauce, 85, 112, 194. Brown Sauce, 85, 112. Woodcock-sauce, 87. Pike-sauce, ibid. Sauce after the *German* Mode, 193. Anchove-sauce, 195, 244. Carp-sauce, 176. Gammon-sauce, 129, 230. Robert-sauce, 111, 146, 246, 453. Sauces for cold Meats broil'd upon the Gridiron, 163, 188. Sweet-sauce, 27, 247. Ramolade-sauce, 41, 163, 188, 230. Sauces proper for the Roast meat, 238. Green Sauce, 44.

SAUSAGES, of Pork, 241, 242. Of Veal, 242. Royal Sausages, ibid.

SCOTCH-COLLOPS, see *Fricandoes*.

SEA-DRAGONS, see QUAVIVERS.

SEA-

A General Table of the Messes, &c.

SEA-FISH, for Flesh-days, 267, 268.
SEASONING Ingredients, 62.
SHAD, roasted, or broil'd upon the Grid-iron, 243. In a *Court-bouillon*, Ibid.
SHEEPS-*trotters*, farced and with white Sauce, 266.
SHOULDER of Mutton, dress'd several Ways, 128, 146. In a Ragoo, 7. In Potage, 199.
SIMNELS, iced, 243, 244.
SMELTS, in a *Court-bouillon*, 244. Fried, with Anchove-sauce, ibid. Stew'd, ibid. In Potage, ibid.
Smelt-*Filets* in a Sallet, 41.
SNIPES, in a Ragoo, 244. Roasted, 236.
SOLES after the *Spanish* Mode, 244, 245. Fried, 245. In *Filets*, with Cucumbers, ibid. Farced several Ways, 219, 220, 245, 246. Sole-*Filets*, with a Lentil-cullis, 246. With a Caper-cullis, ibid. With *Truffles*, ibid. With *Robert*-Sauce, ibid. With Cray-fish, 83. Soles, with sweet Basil, 246. In a Marinade, 153. Sole - *Gatoes*, 246.
SORREL, in Cream, as Asparagus, 59, 169.
Souscé, for Intermesses, 246, 247.
SPINAGE, with Cream, 59, 169. In an *Omelet*, 169. In Potage, 216. In a Pan-pie, 261.
STAKES, of Beef or Veal rolled up, 63, 64.
STAGG, several Ways of dressing it, 247, 248. In *Civet*, 89. In a Ragoo, 248. In Pasties, 175. In Potage, 199. Roasted, 238. Cut into *Menus-droits*, 153.
STOCK-FISH, see COD-FISH.
STURGEON, dress'd *a la Sainte* *Menehout*, 248. In *Fricandoes*, or Collops, ibid. In *Haricot*, with Turneps, 249. In a *Court-bouillon*, ibid.
SUCCORY, a Leg of Mutton, with Succory, 145. In Potage, 211.
SUR-TOUT, Pigeons and other sorts of Fowl in *Sur-tout*, 188, 189.
SWEET-SOUR, Sauce, 247. Pie, or Tart, 250.

T.

TAIL-PIECE of Cod, in a *Casserole* and otherwise, 90. A Salmon farced, 240.
TARTS, a broil'd Peach-tart, 250. Of Cherries and other Fruits, 249. A Sweet-four Tart, 250. Apple-tarts and others, ibid. & 251. A Cream-tart, 94, 251. Plum-tarts, 174, 250.
TEALS, roasted, 236. In a Pie, 186. In Potage, 208.
TENCHES, in a Fricassy, 251. In a Hash, ibid. In *Casserole*, ibid. Farced, 224. In a Ragooe and otherwise, 251. Fried, in refined Butter, ibid.
Terrine, a Side-dish so call'd 155, 251, 252.
THRUSHES, in a hot Pie, 178. In a Ragoo, 252. In Potages, ibid. Roasted, 237.
TONGUES, Neats-tongues bak'd between two Fires, 164. Dried, 165. In a Ragoo, ibid. After some other Manners, ibid. & 166. Hoggs-tongues dried, 253. Sheeps-tongues dried, 254. Broil'd, 16. Dress'd several other Ways, ibid. Calves-tongues farced in a Ragoo, 252, 253. Other

A General Table of the Messes, &c.

Other Ways of dressing them, 252.

TORTOISES, in a Fricassy and otherwise, 254.

TOSTS, covered with a Wood-cock-farce, 235. With Capons-livers, ibid. With Veal-kidneys, ibid.

Tourtes or Panpies, of Almonds, 53, 54, 94. Artichokes of several sorts, 261. Asparagus, ibid. Of *Beatils*, 259. Fish-*Beatils*, 265. Beets, 250. Butter, 259, 260. Capons-breasts, 257. Capons-livers, ibid. Carps-roes and Tongues, 264. Chickens, 88. Coloured Pan-pies, 263. Of Crackling Crust, 175. Cray-fish, 263, 264. Eels, 114. Eggs, 262. Gammon, 258. Goose-giblets, 132. Lard, 260. Larks, 142. Lemmon-peel, 263. Marmelade, 174. Marrow, 260. *Mauviettes*, 256. Melons, 250. *Morilles* and *Mousserons*, 262. Mullets, 158. Muscles, 265. Mushrooms, 262. Neats-tongues, 258. Osters, 265. Orange, 263. *Ortolans*, 256. Of Perches, 265. Pigeons, 189, 190, 256. Pigeons stuff'd with a Fish-farce, 265. Pike, 264. Pike-livers, ibid. Pistachoes, 263. Pomegranates, ibid. Quails, 256. Rabbets, 233. Salmon, 264. Sheeps-tongues, 258. Smelts, 264. So'es, ibid. Sorrel-juice, 262. A *Tourte* after the *Spanish* Way, 256. Of Spinage, 261. A sugar'd *Tourte* or Pan-pie, 260. Of farced Tenches, 265. Tortoises, ibid. Truffles, 262. Veal-sweet-breads, 258, 259. Veal-kidneys, 259.

TROTTERS, 266.

TROUTS, broiled, ibid. Dress'd for Fish-days, 267.

TRUFFLES, in a *Court-bouillon*, 268. Broil'd upon the Coals, ibid. With Mutton-gravy and otherwise, ibid. In an *Omelet*, with Cream, 169. Filets and Ragoo's with *Truffles*, 64, 65, 188.

TUNNIES, in *Filets*, 268. In a Sallet, 41, 268. In a *Marinade*, 153. Broil'd upon the Grid-iron and otherwise, 268. In a Pie, 184. In a *Poupeton*, 226, 268.

TURBOT, in a *Court-bouillon*, 269. For Flesh-days, ibid.

TURKEYS, in a *Daube*, 107. Roasted, 236.

TURKEY-POWTS, or young Turkeys, farced with fine Herbs, 16, 269, 270. Dress'd with Onion-essence, 270. With Gammon-sauce, as Chickens, 82. In a *Salmigund*, as Wood-cocks, 275. In *Filets*, with Cucumbers, 270. Order'd several other Ways, ibid. In a standing Pie, 178, 186. Roasted, 236. In Potages, 198, 205, 211.

TURNEPS, in Potage, 196, 199. In *Haricot*, 110, 194, 249.

TURTLE-DOVES, roasted, 236.

V.

UDDER of a Calf, with sweet Sauce, 27.

VEAL, dress'd after the *Italian* Way, 271. *A la Bourgeoise*, 29, 271, 272. Scallop'd Veal, 125. Veal-cutlets, 104, 105. Veal-stakes roll'd up, 64. A Loin of Veal, 18, 272. A Quarter of Veal,

A General Table of the Messes, &c.

Veal, ibid. A Crupper of Veal, 273. A Breast of Veal in a Ragoo, ibid. Marinated Veal, 152. A Fillet of Veal in a Ragoo, 27. With Oisters, 32.

VEAL-CAULS, 98. A Farce wrapt up in a Veal-caul, ibid. & 242. Capons-livers dress'd in the same manner, 149.

VEAL-SWEET-BREADS, farced *a la Dauphine*, 17, 22, 274. Order'd after several other manners, ibid.

Vermicelli in Potage, 207.

Vinaigrette, or Vinegar and Pepper-sauce for Beef, 65.

W.

WAter-fowl, roasted, 236. Farced with Oisters, 108.

WHITE, as White Thickening Liquors and Ragoo's: See *Fricassy, Cullis, Sauce*, &c.

WHITINGS, in *Casserole*, 275. Farced, ibid. Whiting-*Filets* in Sallet, 41, 275.

WOOD-COCKS, dress'd in *Sur-tout*, 189. With Wine, 275. In a *Salmigund*, 275, 276. With Olives, 168. In Pies, 117, 186, 276. Wood-cock-sauce, 87. Wood-cocks roasted, 236. In *Sur-tout*, as Pigeons, 189, 276.

THE

THE
PREFACE
TO THE
READER.

Since this Work is not the firſt that has been ſet forth on the ſame Subject, there is no neceſſity of juſtifying the Deſign of it againſt the Cavils of malevolent and cenſorious Carpers, who are no leſs ready to debar Mankind of the Uſe of theſe ſorts of Dainties, than of that of Ragoo's and high-ſeaſon'd Meats, a juſt Vindication of which is inſcrib'd in the Preface to the *Court and Country-Cook*, equally oppoſing their erroneous Opinion, That theſe Dainties tend only to the impairing of the Health and the ſhortening of Humane Life: And indeed, nothing is more natural than ſuch an Apology, in this Caſe; not to make mention of Fruits, againſt the uſe of which, without doubt, no Objection can be made, as being the moſt innocent Productions of Nature. As for the reſt of theſe Varieties, when us'd with due moderation (which is always to be preſuppos'd) do they not afford almoſt innumerable Delights and Advantages; to deny which to the Exigencies of Mankind would be a ſignal Piece of Injuſtice, more eſpecially in regard that they are of ſo great energy in the comforting as well of healthful Perſons, as of thoſe that are ſick, or indiſpos'd?

[a a] This

The Preface to the Reader.

This is a Truth so well known, that the Use of Sweet-meats, is allow'd even in the most retired Families, and besides the peculiar Trade of Confectioners, there are many Persons of Quality, and accomplish'd Ladies, who sometimes divert themselves with making several sorts of Comfits. Therefore perhaps it may be objected, That there is no need of any new Instructions in a Matter that is so obvious; but if other Arts are daily improv'd, is there not ground to believe, that this may also be brought to farther Perfection? Which will be more plainly made manifest by means of this Treatise, wherein are contain'd several Methods of Preserving Fruits and other particular Circumstances, that are altogether new, and quite different from the common Practice, as also from what has been before written on this Subject by any Authors: For it may be suspected, That in laying down such imperfect Rules and Directions, (not to mention the unprofitable Repetitions us'd by them, on purpose to augment the Bulk of their Volumes) they had no other Design but to abuse the Publick; being fully resolv'd before hand, not to discover the Secrets of their Art.

Indeed, it is certain, That such a Discovery (as it ought to be expected here) cannot be really made by any Person, without doing himself a considerable Injury; in regard, that by reason of the easiness of making all sorts of wet and dry Sweet-meats, according to the Instructions that are given, the meanest House-keepers, or Chamber-maids might afterwards set up for Confectioners and Butlers, and perform the greatest Part of the Functions of those Officers: Hence it comes to pass, that so great a Number of Noble Families usually dispense with such Officers; and how many other Artists of the first Rank would be likewise disregarded, if the Oeconomy of that Northern Prince were in request, who having once caus'd his Desert

to

The Preface to the Reader.

to be dress'd, orders it to be carefully lock'd up in his Presence, in the Appartment, where he takes his Royal Repast, every time that it is serv'd up to his Table, which is as long as it lasts, and always keeps the Key in his Pocket?

Forasmuch as the Officers of the Mouth are employ'd to somewhat better purpose, in these Parts, it is here design'd to do them a Pleasure, by causing them to be instructed in every Thing that is most modern, generally receiv'd, and most curious, relating to the principal Part of their Employment, that is to say, the Art of Preserving Sweet-meats, treating of it as methodically, and with as much Perspicuity, as is possible. It is acknowledg'd, That if any Persons be desirous to attain to Perfection in this Art, and to comprehend all its abstruse Mysteries, with greater Facility, 'tis requisite, that they work for some time, under those that are Masters of it; so that by the means of frequent Practice, they'll soon understand, at a cast of the Eye, several Preparations, which cannot otherwise be well explain'd: Among these, the particular Way of making Sugar-plums, is more especially remarkable, as absolutely depending upon an habitual Exercise, and this Reflection affords Matter of Consolation, to Master-Confectioners and other Officers, who have laid out Money and spent a considerable time in acquiring their Skill, and who may perhaps take it ill, that the Grounds of their Art are so freely communicated to Persons, that may make use of it to their Prejudice.

However, if the Advantage, in this Particular redounds to the Publick, they themselves may also receive some Benefit, from the assistance of these Instructions, which may serve, as it were a Manual, for the refreshing of their Memories; so that it will be an easy matter for them to take notice in every Season, what is most proper to be Preserv'd and brought to

[a a 2] Table,

The Preface to the Reader.

Table, according to the Entertainments which are requisite upon several Occasions, and the particular Customs of Noble-mens Houses, in which they are entertain'd. If their Methods are not altogether conformable, in certain Articles, to that which is here express'd, nevertheless let them not reject it, till they have made a Tryal; and if after such an Experiment, they still have an Inclination to follow their accustomed Practice, they may be at liberty to continue it: Altho' it may be averr'd, That nothing is here deliver'd, but what has been confirm'd by Experience, with respect to the several Ways of Preserving the richest and most delicious sorts of Sweet-meats and Comfits.

The whole Work is concluded with different Models for Deserts, or entire Banquets of Sweet-meats, and a short Treatise of Liquors; the ordering of which, belongs likewise to certain peculiar Officers: But no notice is here taken of some other Circumstances relating to their domestick Concerns; such as the distribution of Bread and Wine, the care that ought to be taken of the Plate in their Custody, the particular manner of laying the Cloth, furnishing the Table, &c. Because the management of Affairs of the like nature is never committed to Novices, or Persons who are so ignorant, as to stand in need of any other Instructions in these Matters, than what their own Discretion, or their Masters Orders may readily suggest to them.

The

The Contents of the New Instructions for Confectioners.

Chap. 1. *Of the different Ways of Boiling Sugar; of the Choice of it; and of the Manner of Clarifying it,* Page 1

Chap. 2. *Of the Utensils and Instruments necessary for a Confectioner, and of their Use,* 6.

Chap. 3. *Of the Confectioners Employment throughout the whole Year, according to the Seasons of Flowers and Fruits,* 10

Chap. 4. *Of green Apricocks,* 16

Chap. 5. *Of ripe Apricocks,* 19

Chap. 6. *Of green Almonds,* 21

Chap. 7. *Several other Ways of preserving Almonds,* 23

Chap. 8. *Of preserv'd Cherries, as well dry as liquid,* 27

Chap. 9. *Of Strawberries and Rasberries,* 31

Chap. 10. *Of Gooseberries and Currans,* 32

Chap. 11. *Of Walnuts,* 36

Chap. 12. *Of Plums,* 37

Chap. 13. *Of Pears preserv'd dry and liquid,* 40

Chap. 14. *Of Peaches and Figgs,* 42

Chap. 15. *Of Apples,* 45

Chap. 16. *Of Bell-grapes and Muscadine-grapes,* 47

Chap. 17. *Of Quinces, and Marmelade made of them,* 49

Chap. 18. *Of Oranges and their Flowers,* 52

Chap. 19. *Of Lemmons,* 56

Chap. 20. *Of Cedres, Limes and yellow Citrons,* 61

Chap. 21. *Of Compotes for the whole Year,* 63

Chap. 22. *Of the Conserves of Flowers and Fruits,* 74

Chap. 23. *Of Marmelades,* 76

Chap. 24. *Of the Pastes of Fruits,* 81

Chap. 25. *Of the Jellies of Fruits,* 87

Chap. 26. *Of Biskets,* 90

Chap. 27. *Of March-panes,* 97

Chap.

The Contents of the New Instructions, &c.

Chap. 28. *Of* Meringues *and Macaroons,* 102
Chap. 29. *Of Pastils,* 104
Chap. 30. *Of the* Caramel *Sugar-work and candy'd Comfits,* 106
Chap. 31. *Of* Mosses, *and Sultanes,* 109
Chap. 32. *Of certain natural and artificial Flowers,* 110
Chap. 33. *Of Pies made of Crackling Crust and Puff-paste,* 114
Chap. 34. *Of Chesnuts and Mulberries, with some particular Observations upon several other sorts of Fruits,* 117
Chap. 35. *Of the Accidents that may happen to Sweet-meats, and of proper Means for the remedying of them,* 122
Chap. 36. *The Way of Ordering and setting out a Desert or other Regalio of the like nature, to the best advantage, with some Models of such Entertainments,* 125

The

The Contents of the New Instructions for Liquors.

Chap. 1. *Of the iced Waters of Flowers,* Page 1
Chap. 2. *Of the iced Waters of Fruits,* 4
Chap. 3. *Of Liquors that are proper for the Winter-Season,* 8
Chap. 4. *Of Hippocras and some other Liquors,* 10
Chap. 5. *Several sorts of Ratafiaz.* 13
Chap. 6. *Of the Syrups of Flowers,* 15
Chap. 7. *Of the Syrups of Fruits, &c.* 18

A TABLE

A T A B L E *explaining certain Terms of Art and French Words us'd in these Instructions for Confectioners.*

B.

Igarrade, a kind of great Orange.

Biscotin, a sort of Confection made of fine Flower, the Whites of Eggs, Powder-sugar, Marmelade, &c.

Blanquet, a sort of Pear.

C.

Aramel, the sixth and last Degree of Boiling Sugar: Also, a curious Sugar-work so call'd.

Cedre, a kind of Citron, or Lemmon.

Certoe, a sort of *French* Pear.

Compote, stewed Fruit, more especially Apples, Pears, Plums, &c.

D.

Auphine, as a *Compote à la Dauphine*, a particular Way of stewing Apples; as it were, for the Dauphin's Table.

Desert, a Banquet of Sweetmeats.

F.

Euillantins, certain small Tarts of the breadth of the Palm of a Man's Hand, fill'd with Sweetmeats.

I.

Ndigo, a Stone brought out of *Turkey*, commonly us'd by Dyers to die blew; as also by Confectioners, to give their Jellies, Pastes, Sugar-works, &c. a blew Tincture.

M.

Azarines, a sort of small Tarts fill'd with Sweetmeats.

Mirabolans, certain Plums, which are cold in the first Degree and dry in the second; serving to strengthen, purge and bind at the same time.

N.

Ompareil, a kind of small Sugar-plum.

O.

Rangeade, a cooling Liquor made of the Juice of Oranges and Lemmons, with Water and Sugar.

P.

Armesan, a sort of Cheese made at *Parma*, a City of *Italy*.

Pastille, a kind of odoriferous Sugar-paste, of which there are several sorts specified under that Article, in the Body of the Book.

Petit-choux, a kind of Paste, proper for garnishing and other uses made of Cheese, Flower, Eggs, Salt, &c. bak'd in a Pie-pan and ic'd over with fine Sugar.

R.

A Table explaining Terms of Art, &c.

R.

Atafiaz, a delicious Liquor made of Cherries, or Apricocks and other Fruits with their Kernels bruised, infus'd in Brandy; adding Sugar, Cinnamon, white Pepper, Nutmeg, Cloves, Mace, Ginger and some other Ingredients.

Rousselet, a kind of Russet-pear.

A la Royale, a particular Way of preserving Cherries as it were, after the Royal Manner.

S.

Siamoise; as *Amandes a la Siamoise*, a particular Way of preserving Almonds; explain'd under the first Article of that Fruit, Chap. 7.

Sultane, a kind of Sugar-work, made of Eggs, Powder-sugar and fine Flower.

Sur-tout, as Pistachoes in *Sur-tout*; that is to say, cover'd with Sugar and order'd after the same manner, as Almond-sugar-plums: See the last Article of Almonds, Pag. 26.

T.

Tambour, a kind of fine Sieve call'd a Drum, proper for the sifting of Sugar, &c.

Turning, a particular Way of paring Oranges and Lemmons: This Term of Art signifies to pare off the superficial Rind, or Peel, on the out-side very thin and narrow, with a little Knife, proper for that purpose; turning it round about the Lemmon or Orange, so as the Peel may be extended to a very great length, without Breaking.

Z.

Zests, certain Chips of Orange, or Lemmon-peel, cut long-wise, from top to bottom, as thin, as it can possibly be done: See the second Article of *Lemmons*.

A

A General TABLE *of the Sweet-meats, Comfits, Sugar-works, Fruits and other Matters contain'd in this Treatise of the Confectionary Art.*

A.

ACcidents that may happen to Sweet-meats, 122, 123, 124.

Almonds, how preserv'd green, 21, 22. A la *Siamoise*, 23, 24. Blown, 24. Iced, ibid. Crisp Almonds, 24, 25, 26. Gray, 24. Red, 25. White, ibid. Of a Gold-colour, 26. Almonds in *Compotes*, 64. Almond-paste, 82.

Amber-plums, preserved, 38.

Anis preserv'd and iced, 113.

Apples, green preserv'd, 45. *John-apples* and Pippins in quarters, 46. Apples in *Compots*, 70. 71. Paste of Apples, 84. Marmelade, 79. Jelly, 89.

Apricocks, green preserv'd, 16. 17. Par'd, 18. Ripe Apricocks, par'd, 19, 20. Apricocks preserv'd in half Sugar, 20. In Ears, ibid. In *Compotes*, 63, 64, 66. Marmelades of Apricocks, 77, 78. Pastes, 82, 83. Pastils, 105.

Aubicons, or Feaver-figgs preserv'd, 45.

B.

BArberry-conserve, 76.

Barley-sugar, how prepar'd, 122.

Bell-grapes, preserv'd liquid, 47. Dry, ibid. & 48. Par'd, 120. Jelly of Bell-grapes, 48. *Compotes*, 72. Paste, 86, 87, 120.

Bergamot-pears preserv'd, 41.

Biscotins, 96, 97.

Biskets made of Almonds, 90, 91. Of Chocolate, 92. Of Lemmons and Oranges, 92, 93. *Savoy*, or *French* Biskets, 93, 94. *Lisbon*-biskets, 94. Light iced Biskets, 95. Common Biskets, ibid. For Lent, 96. Crackling-biskets, ibid.

Boiling of Sugar, 1, 2. *& Sequ.* Smooth, 2. Pearled, ibid. Blown, 3. Feather'd, ibid. Crack'd, ibid. Caramel, ibid. & 4.

Broom-flowers, preserv'd, 112.

C.

CAndy'd Comfits, 106, 107.

Caramel-boiling of Sugar, 3, 4. A Sugar-work so call'd, 108.

Cedres, green in Sticks or in Quarters, 61. Ripe Cedres preserv'd, ibid. & 62.

Certne-pears preserv'd, 41.

Cherries, in Ears, 27. Preserv'd in half Loaf-sugar, ibid. In half Powder-sugar, 28. Liquid, ibid. Dry, with Strawberries, 29. In Bunches, ibid. Booted *a la Royale*, ibid. After the manner of *Tours*, ib. & 30. Cherry-cakes, 30. Cherries in *Compotes*, 65. In a Caramel-Sugar-work, 108, 109. Iced, 31. Conserves of Cherries, 74, 75. Marmelades, 77, 78. Jellies, 88. Pastes, 82.

Chesnuts, preserv'd, 118. In *Compotes*, 73.

Chips, see *Zests.*

Cinnamon, candy'd, 106, 107. In Pastils, 104.

Ci-

A General Table of the Sweet-meats, Comfits, &c.

Citrons, how preserv'd, and dry'd, 62. In *Zests*, or *Chips*, 63.
Clove-pastils, 106.
Comfits, made and kept throughout the whole Year, 10, 11, 12, &c. *sequ.*
Compotes, for the whole Year, 63, 64, &c. *sequ.* Of green Apricocks, 63, 64. Of ripe Apricocks, 66. Of green Almonds, 64. Of green Gooseberries, 65. Of Cherries, ibid. Of Plums, 67. Of Summer-pears, 68. Of other sorts of Pears, ibid. Of Pears stew'd in a Bell, 69. Of roasted Pears, ibid. Of Apples, 70. Of Apples *a la Dauphine*, ibid. Of farced Apples, 71. Of Peaches, ibid. Of Bell-grapes, 72. Of Quinces, ibid. & 73. Of Chesnuts, 73. Of Oranges and Lemmons, ibid. Of Rasberries, 66. Of Strawberries, ibid. Of Currans, ibid.
Conserves of Flowers and Fruits, 74, 75, &c. *sequ.* Of Orange-flowers, 74. Of Cherries, ibid. Of Currans, 75. Of Rasberries, ibid. Of Smallage, ibid. White Conserve, 76. Of Violets, ibid. Of Roses, ibid. Of Jessamin, ibid. Of Pomegranates, ibid. Of Barberries, ibid.
Crackling-crust, 114, 115.
Cream, or Rock-cream how made, 116. Boil'd Cream, 117.
Crisp Almonds, see *Almonds*.
Currans, iced, 31. What sort fit for preserving, 32. Liquid, 34. In Bunches, ibid. Jelly of Currans, 34, 35. *Compotes*, 66. Marmelades, 78. Conserves, 75. Pastes, 83.

D.

Eserts, how order'd and set out, 125.

E.

Mployment, of Confectioners throughout the Year, 10, 11, 12, &c. *sequ.*

F.

Aggots, of Oranges, 55. Of Lemmons, 60.
Fennel, candy'd, 107. Several Ways of icing it, 113.
Feuillantins, what, 117.
Figgs, preserv'd dry, 44. Green Figgs, 45, 119, 120. *Genoa*-figgs, or Feaver-figgs, 45.
Flowers of Oranges preserv'd, 52. Marmelade of them, 80, 81. Conserves, 74. Pastes, 86. Pastils, 104. Orange-flower-buds, 53. *Tuberosa*-flowers preserv'd, 111. Violet-flowers and others, ibid. 112. *Spanish* Broom-flowers, 112.
Fruits, in season every Month, 10, 11, 12, &c. *sequ.*

G.

Oose-berries, what sort to be chosen, 32. Green Gooseberries liquid, 33. Jelly of Gooseberries, ibid. *Compotes*, 65.
Grapes of several sorts, 47. Bell-grapes preserv'd liquid, ibid. & 120. Dry, 47, 48. Par'd, 120. Jelly of them, 48. *Compotes*, 72. Pastes, 86, 87, 120, 121. Muscadine-grapes liquid, 48. Dry, 49. Paste made of them, 87.

I.

Ellies, of Fruits, 87. Of green Gooseberries, 33. Of red Currans,

[bb 2]

A General Table of the Sweet-meats, Comfits, &c.

rans, 34, 35. Quaking Jelly of Currans, 35. Curran-jelly with a Tincture of Rasberries, ibid. After the Manner of the City of *Tours*, ibid. Jelly of Bell-grapes, 48. Of Cherries, 88. Of Rasberries, 89. Of Apples, &c. ibid. Of Quinces, 90. Other sorts of Jellies, ibid.

Jessamine-conserve, 76.

Inconveniences, happening to Comfits, 122, 123, 124.

Instruments, us'd in the Confectionary Art, 6, 7, 8, 9, 10.

Isle-verte-plums, preserv'd, 37.

L.

Lemmons, of several sorts, 56, 57, & sequ. Green *Indian* Lemmons preserv'd, 56. White Lemmons in Sticks, 127. In *Zests* or Chips, 58. In Slips, ibid. & 59. In Faggots, 60. Entire, ibid. *Compotes* of Lemmons, 73, 74. Marmelades, 80. Pastes, 85.

Limes and *Pomecitrons* preserv'd, 61, 62.

M.

Macaroons, 103, 104. March-panes, common, 97, 98. Other sorts, 98, 99. Royal March-pane, 99. Made of Orange-flowers, 100. Of Lemmon, ibid. Of Rasberries and other Fruits, ibid. Iced, 101. Suff'd, ibid. & 102.

Marmelades, 76, 77. Observations upon them, 81. Marmelade of Quinces according to the City of *Orleans*, 51. Other sorts, ibid. & 52. Marmelade of green Apricocks, 77. Of Cherries, ibid. & 78. Of Currans, ibid. Of Rasberries, ibid. Of Apricocks, ibid.

Of Plums, 79. Of Pears, ibid. Of Apples, ibid. Of *Sevil*-Oranges, ibid. & 80. Of Lemmons, 80. Of Orange-flowers, ibid. & 81.

Mazarines, a sort of Tarts, 117.

Meringues, a kind of Sugarwork, 102. In Pairs, ibid. Dry, 103. Pistachoe-meringues, ibid.

Models for Deserts, 126, 128, 130.

Mosses, a Sugar-work of divers Colours, 109.

Mulberries, preserv'd dry and liquid, 117, 118, 119.

Muscadine-grapes, preserv'd liquid, 48. Dry, 49. Paste of them, 87.

Muscadine-pears, preserv'd, 41.

N.

Nectarines, preserv'd, 44.

O.

Orange-pears, preserv'd, 41. Orange-plums, 37, 38.

Oranges preserv'd 52, 53, & sequ. *Sevil*-Oranges in Quarters and in Sticks, 53, 54. Preserv'd whole, 54. *China*-Oranges Entire or in Quarters, ibid. 121, & 122. Port-Oranges, 54. Sour Oranges, ibid. & 55. Oranges in Faggots, 55. In *Zests* or Chips, ibid. In Slips, 56. *Compotes* of Oranges, 73, 74. Marmelades, 79, 80. Pastes, 85. Conserves of Orange-flowers, 74. Marmelades, 80, 81. Pastes, 86. Pastils, 105.

P.

Pastes for Crackling crust, 114. Puff paste, 117. Pastes of Fruits, 81, 82, & sequ. Of green Apricocks, 82. Of green Almonds, ibid.

A General Table of the Sweet-meats, Comfits, &c.

ibid. Of Cherries, ibid. Of Currans, 83. Of Rasberries, ibid. Of ripe Apricocks, ibid. Of Plums, 84. Of Apples and Pears, ibid. Of roasted Apples and Pears, ibid. Of Peaches, ibid. Of Quinces, 85. Of Oranges, ibid. Of Orange-flowers, 86. Of Lemmons, 85. Of Violets, 86. Of Bell-grapes, 86, 87. Of Muscadine-grapes, 87.

Pastils of several sorts, 104. Of Cinnamon, ibid. White, 105. Of Orange-flowers, ibid. Of Apricocks, ibid. Of Violets, &c. ibid. & 106. Of Cloves, 106.

Peaches, green preserv'd, 42, 43. Ripe, 43, 44. In half Sugar and in Ears, 44. *Compotes* of them, 71. Pastes, 84.

Pears, preserv'd dry and liquid, 40. Blanquets, 41. Large Muscadines, ibid. Orange-pears, ibid. *Certoes*, &c. ibid. Musked *Bergamots*, ibid. In quarters and otherwise, ib. & 42. *Compotes* of them, 68, 69. Marmelades, 79. Pastes, 84.

Perdrigon, a sort of Plum, 37.

Pies, of Crackling-crust, 114, 115. Of Puff-paste, 117.

Pistachoes in *Sur-tout*, 26.

Plums, of several sorts, 37. Orange-plums, ibid. & 38. Amber-plums, 38, 39. Red Plums, 39. Preserv'd in half Sugar and otherwise, ibid. Pastes of them, 84.

Puff-paste, how made, 117.

Pyramids, of Cherries, &c. 109. A Model of Fruit-pyramids, 126, 128, 130.

Pomegranate-conserve, 76.

Q.

Quinces, the Nature of them, 49. Preserv'd liquid, 50, 121. Marmelades of Quinces, 51,
52. *Compotes*, 72, 73. Pastes, 85. Jellies, 90.

R.

Rasberries, iced, 31. Preserv'd dry, ibid. Liquid, 32. Other Ways of ordering them, ibid. What sort fit for preserving, ibid. *Compotes* of them, 66. Conserves, 75. Marmelades, 78. Pastes, 83. Jellies, 89.

Roses, in conserve, 76.

S.

Slips, of Oranges, 56. Of Lemmons, &c. 58, 59, 60.

Smallage-conserve, 75.

Sugar, several Ways of boiling it, 1, 2, 3, 4. The choice of it, 4. How to clarifie it, 5, 6. Barley-sugar, 122. Sugar-candy, how prepar'd, 107, 108.

Sultanes, a sort of Sugar-work, 110.

Strawberries, their Nature and Virtue, 31. Iced, ibid. How order'd, ibid. *Compotes* of them, 66.

Spanish Broom-flowers, preserv'd, 112.

T.

Tarts of several sorts, 117. *Tuberosa-flowers* preserv'd, 111.

V.

Violets, Conserves of them, 76. Pastes, 86. Pastils, 105, 106. Violet flowers, &c. Preserv'd, 111, 112.

Utensils, necessary for Confectioners, 6, 7, 8, 9, 10.

W.

A Table of the Waters, Syrups, Juices, &c.

W.

Wafers, how made, 116.
 Walnuts, the choice of them, 36. How preserv'd white, ibid. & 37.
 White Conserve, 76. White Pastils, 105.

Z.

Zests, or chips of Lemmons, 58. Of Sevil-oranges, 55. Of yellow Citrons, &c. 63.

A TABLE of the Waters, Syrups, Juices, and other Matters contain'd in the Instructions for Liquers.

A.

Anis-seed-water, 9.
 Apricock-water, 5. Ratafiaz, 15. Syrup, 19.

B.

Bell-grape-syrup, 20.
 Brandy, the Quantity requisite for Ratafiaz, 13, 14, 15.
 Burgundy-wine, 12.
 Burnt Wine and Brandy, ibid.

C.

Cherry-water, 4. Ratafiaz, 13, 14, Syrup, 18.
 Chocolate-water, 8.
 Cinnamon-water, 8, 9. Essence, 12.
 Clove-gilliflowers, fit for Syrup, 17.
 Clove-water, 10.
 Coriander-seed-water, 9.
 Curran-water, 5. Syrup, 19.

D.

Delicious sort of Wine, 12.

E.

Extraction of the Juices of Fruits, 20.

F.

Flowers, iced Waters made of 'em, 1, 2, 3, 4.
 Fruits in several iced Waters, 4, 5, 6, 7.

H.

Hippocras, of all sorts, 10, 11, 12. White, 11. Pale, ibid. Red, ibid. & 12. Made more speedily, 12. Without Wine, ibid.

I.

Iced Waters of Flowers, 1, 2, 3. Of Fruits, 4, 5, 6, 7. How to ice all sorts of Liquors, 4.
 Jessamin-water, 3.
 Jonquil-water, 2.
 Juices of Fruits, 20.
 Juniper-water, 10.

K.

A Table of the Waters, Syrups, Juices, &c.

K.
Kernel-water, 10.

L.
Lemmon-water, 6.
Limonnade, 6, 7.
Liquors, for the Summer, 4, 5, & sequ. For the Winter-season, 8, 9, 10.

M.
Mulberries, for Syrup, 18.
Mulberry-juice, 14.
Muscadel-Ratafiaz, 15.
Musk-rose-water, 3.

O.
Orangeade, 6.
Orange-flower-water, 2. Infus'd in Ratafiaz, 14.
Orange-water, 6.
Orleans-wine, 14.

P.
Pale Hippocras, 11.
Peach-water, 5.

Q.
Quince-syrup, 19.

R.
Rasberry-water, 5.
Ratafiaz, of all sorts, 13, 14. & sequ. Of Apricocks, 15. Of Cherries, 13. With a Tincture of Rasberries, 14. Muscadel, 15. White, 14.

Red Hippocras, 11.
Rosade, 8.
Roses, proper for Syrup, 16, 17.
Rose-water, 3.

S.
Strawberry-water, 4, 5, 6. In Ratafiaz, 14.
Sugar turn'd to Syrup, 20.
Syrups of Flowers, 15, 16. & sequ. Of Clove-gilliflowers, 17. Its Virtue, ibid. Of Roses, ibid. How long kept, ibid. Of Violets, 16, 17. Of Fruits, 18. & sequ. Of Apricocks, 19. Of Bell-grapes, &c. 20. Of Cherries, 18. Of Currans, &c. 19. Of Mulberries, 18. Its efficacy, ibid. Of Quinces, 19. Of Sugar, 20.

T.
Tuberosa-flower-water, 3.

V.
Violets fit to make Syrup, 16. When gather'd, ibid.
Violet-water, 1, 2.
Virginal-water, 7.

W.
White Hippocras, 11. Ratafiaz, 14. Water, 7.
Wine of Burgundy, 12. Burnt, ibid. Of Orleans, 14. Pale, 11, 15. Red, ibid. White, ibid.

NEW

4. Model of a Table for six Persons, furnished with one large Dish, and four small ones.

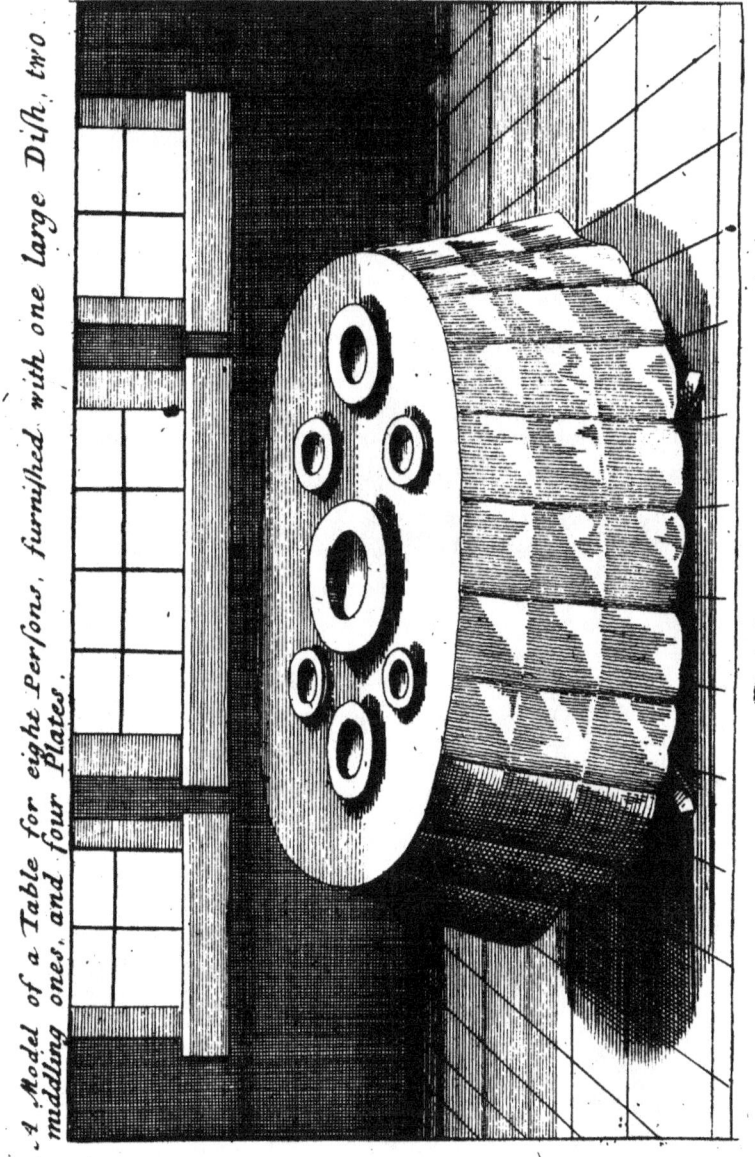

A Model of a Table for eight Persons, furnished with one large Dish, two middling ones, and four Plates.

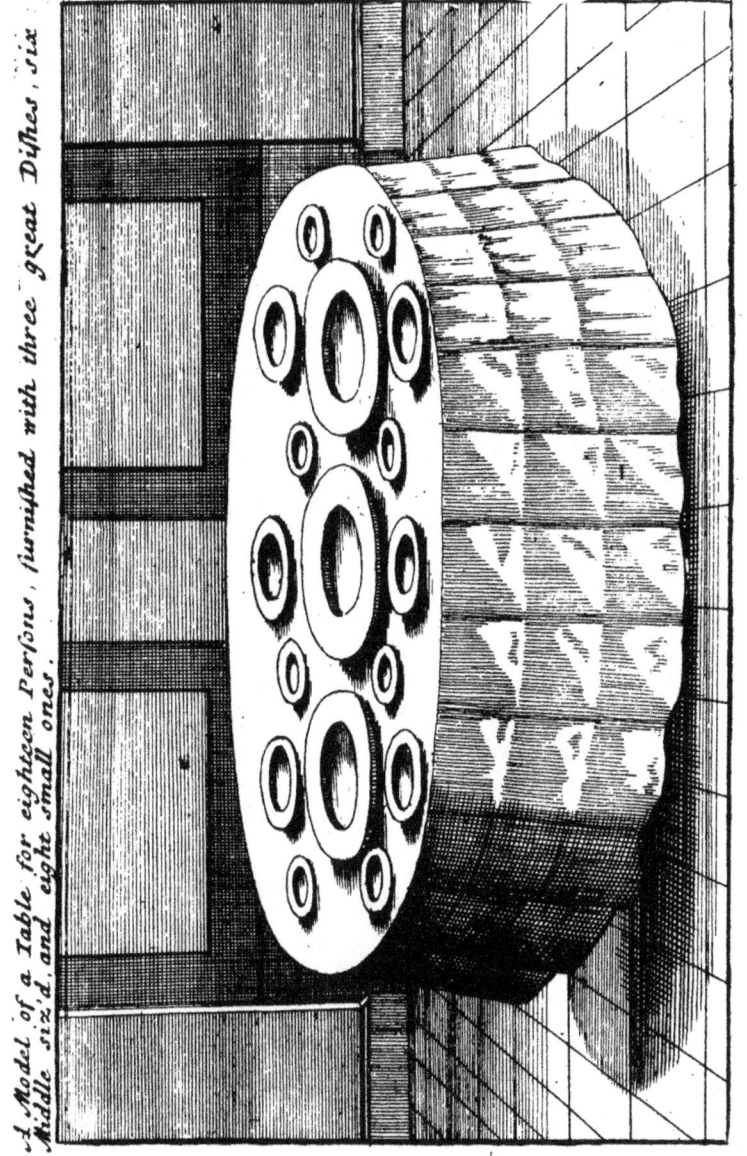

A Model of a Table for eighteen Persons, furnished with three great Dishes, six Middle siz'd, and eight small ones.

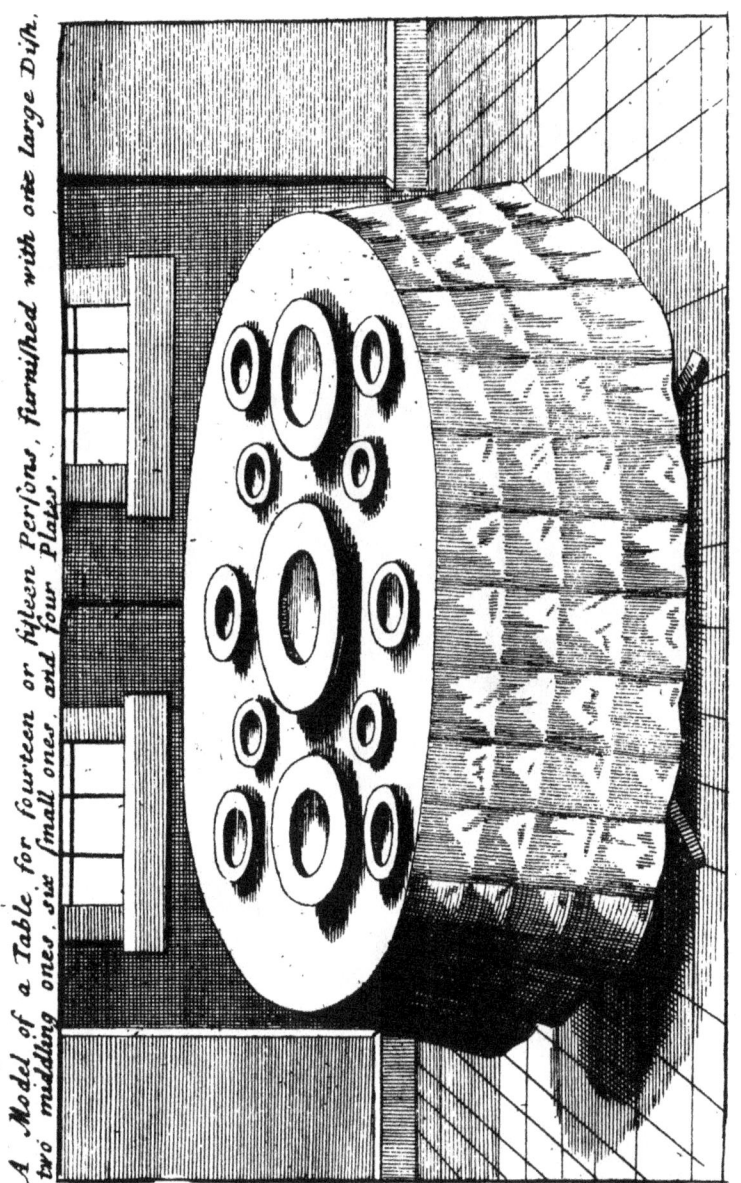

A Model of a Table for fourteen or fifteen Persons, furnished with one large Dish, two middling ones, six small ones, and four Plates.

A Model of a Table for twentyfive Persons, furnish'd with five large Dishes, ten Midling ones, and four small ones.

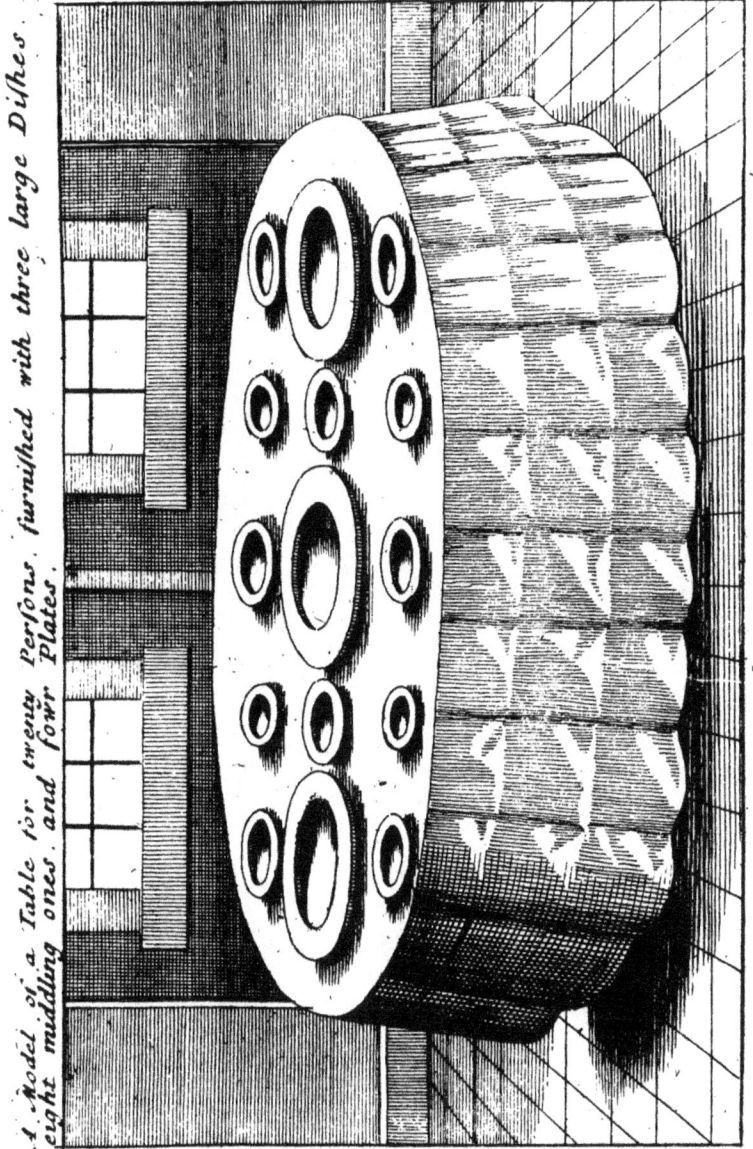

A Model of a Table for twenty Persons, furnished with three large Dishes, eight middling ones, and fowr Plates.

A Model of a Table for ten Persons, furnish'd with three large Dishes, and four small ones.

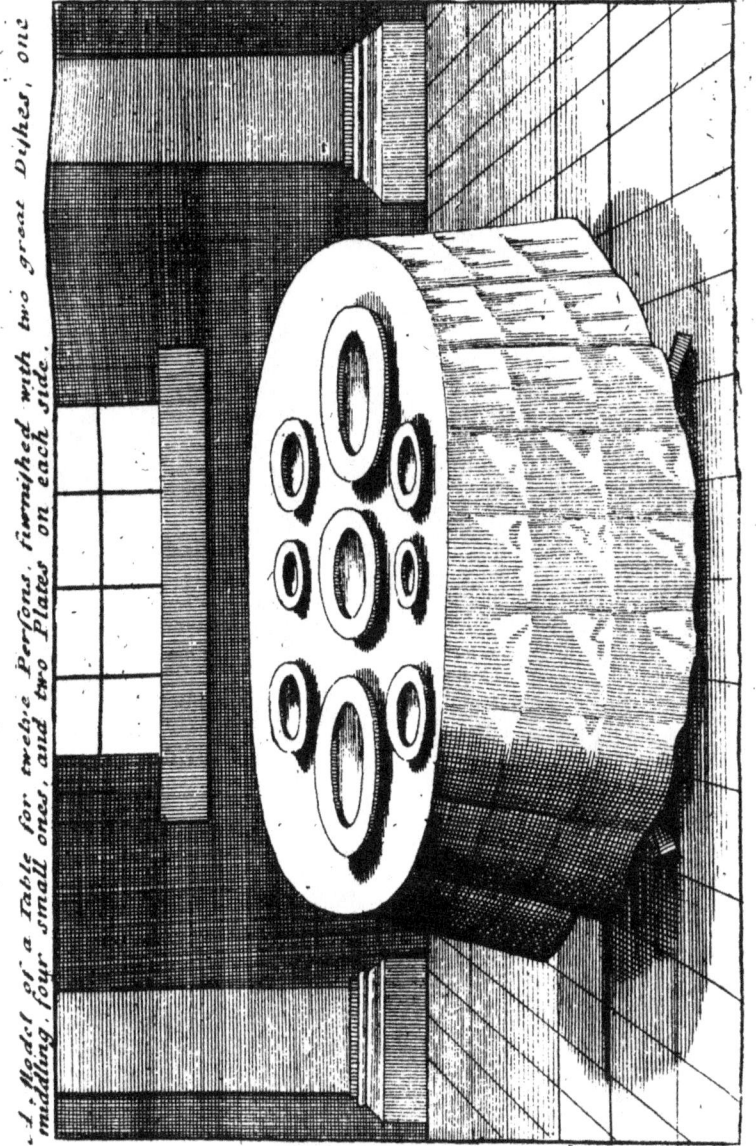

A Model of a Table for twelve Persons, furnished with two great Dishes, one middling, four small ones, and two Plates on each side.

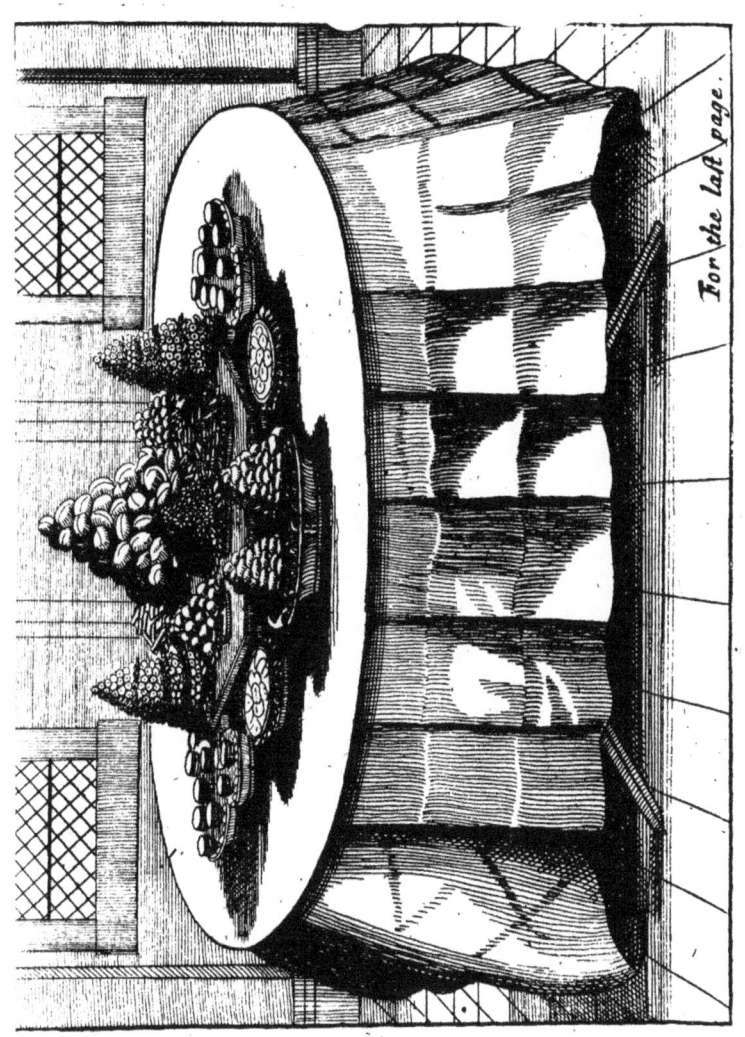

THE
Court and Country Cook:

DIRECTING

How to Order all manner of ENTERTAINMENTS and the beſt ſort of the moſt exquiſite *a-la-mode* RAGOO's.

The Entertainment which may be made in the Month of January.

SUppoſe a Table were to be furniſhed for twelve Perſons, one large Diſh in the middle, four leſſer Diſhes, and four Out-works may ſerve for each Courſe: For Example,

The Firſt Courſe.

Potages and Side-diſhes.

Two Potages, one middling Diſh of a *Bisk* of Pigeons, and the other of Capon with Roots.

Two other middling Diſhes for Side-diſhes; *viz.* one a Partridge-pye hot.

The other of a large fat Pullet and *Truffles* garniſh'd with *Fricandoe's*.

The great Diſh in the middle.

This ſhall conſiſt of two Pieces of roaſt Beef, garniſh'd with Cutlets of marinated Veal fried, with good Sauce.

For

For the Out-works.

A *Poupeton* of Pigeons.
A Dish of Quails broil'd upon the Coals.
One of farced Pullets, with Cullises or strained Liquor of Mushrooms.
One of Partridges, with Spanish Sauce.

The Second Course.

The Roast-meat.

This shall consist of two middling Dishes, *viz.*
One of a young Turkey garnish'd with Partridges, Chickens, Wood-cocks and *Mauviettes*.
And the other of a Quarter of Lamb garnish'd after the same manner.

For the Intermesses.

A Cream-tart for the great Dish in the middle, garnished with Puffs, *Feuillantins, Fleurons,* and Milk-*bignets* or Fritters.
The two other smaller Dishes, one of them of *Pain au Jambon*, garnish'd with small Toasts of Bread and Lemmon.
And the other of Gammon of Bacon and other Salt-meats.

The Out-works.

One of these shall consist of a *Blanc-manger*.
Another of the Livers of Capons.
The third of Asparagus in a Sallet.
And the fourth of *Truffles* in a *Court-bouillon*.

The Third Course.

This is to consist of Fruits and Confits, of which we shall say nothing in this place; that being the particular Business of another Officer and not of the Cook.

Such an Entertainment as this above-mentioned was made *Feb.* 15, 1691, by the Duke of *Chartres* for Mademoiselle his Sister.
Instead of what was served up for Roast-meat, two Dishes may be prepared; *viz.* one consisting of two fat and large young Hens, four Barn-door Pullets, and six wild Pigeons:
The other of Water-fowl, four Partridges, four Wood-cocks, and a douzen of Snipes. The

The Particulars hereafter specified may serve instead of the rest for the Side-dishes and Intermesses, as well as for the following Entertainments: See Page 7.

According to this first Entertainment you may easily regulate the Ordering and Disposition of the rest, which you would have made greater; by increasing the Number or Largeness of the Dishes in proportion to the Number of the Guests and Tables.

An Entertainment for the Months of February and March.

The First Course.

Side-dishes.

FOr the first Course, An hot Pye of young Rabbets and Partridges, in which may be put, during the time of serving, some good Cullise of Partridge or other Ragoo's.

A *Poupeton* farced with twenty or thirty young Pigeons, according to the number of Guests entertained; with all sorts of Garnitures.

A Dish of *Brusolles*, broiled upon the Coals, with a Cullise pour'd upon it.

A Dish of farced Sweet breads of Veal, broiled upon the Coals, with a Ragoo.

A *Marinade* of fryed Chickens.

A large fat Pullet roasted after the English Way, with a Ragoo put thereupon in serving it up.

A Dish of *Filets* cut in slices, with Gammon.

A Dish of *Croquets*.

One of *Filets* of a young fat Hen with Cucumbers.

One of farced *Fricandoe's* in a Ragoo.

The Second Course.

The Roast-meat.

Let there be three great Dishes of all sorts of wild Fowl that are in season, and four Sallets in the Corners; proportionably to the Courses that are served up, and the Guests that sit at Table.

For the Intermesses.

Twelve Dishes; *viz.* One of Gammon, garnish'd with dry'd Tongues, and *Bolonia*-sausages.

A Cream-pye garnish'd with little Tarts.
A *Blanc-manger* of Gellies of divers Colours.
A Dish of Asparagus in Cream.
One of *Morilles* in Cream.
One of Sweet-breads of Veal and Cocks-combs farced in a Ragoo.
One of marinated Sweet-breads of Veal fryed.
One of Capons-livers *à la Crêpine*, broil'd upon the Grid-iron.
One of the Kidneys of Capons.
One *Pain au Jambon*.
A Dish of *Truffles* in a *Court-bouillon*.
A Ragoo of the Sweet-breads of Veal, white Mushrooms and *Morilles*.

Monsieur *Langlois* caus'd such a Supper as this to be made, March 28, 1690, for the Duke of *Orleans*: There was for the Duke himself *Potage de Santé* prepared of a fat Pullet with Eggs in her, and of a Capon.

For this Entertainment they roasted fat and large Hens, Chickens and Partridges, that were used only in making of the farced Meats; particularly a Farce of *Croquets*: For this purpose, they took the Breasts and Legs of these Fowls, and left some *Filets* for the Side-dishes. This sort of farc'd Meat was made with parboil'd Bacon, Calves-udder boil'd, Sweet-breads of Veal parboil'd, *Truffles* and minc'd Mushrooms, some Marrow, Crums of Bread steeped in Milk, all sorts of fine Herbs, a little Cream-cheese, and some Milk-cream: The whole being well minced and seasoned, four or five Yolks of Eggs were put thereto, and the Whites of one or two: And this Farce was made use of for the *Fricandoe's*, *Croquets*, and *Filets Mignons*. The *Croquets* are made round, of the bigness of an Egg; they are to be breaded at the same time, and left in a Dish, to be fryed with Lard and served up hot.

The Carcasses of Fowls may serve to make different sorts of Cullises for the diversifying of the Ragoo's; Strainings may also be made of Bread, Partridge, young Hens, Pullets, *Essence de Jambon*, Beef and Veal-gravy. The Ragoo's of Side-dishes and Intermesses are dress'd apart into different Stew-pans with a Faggot of sweet Herbs always put thereto.

Those that have Cream put to them, ought to be toss'd up with good Butter, and a little Flower must be put to each Ragoo; which being ready, the Cream is to be poured on them, and

The Court and Country Cook.

in serving up the same they are thickned with some Yolks of Eggs.

You may hereafter observe the Method of managing the rest we have taken notice of, as well for Side-dishes as Intermesses, when we have run through the other Months of the Year, and seen what is proper, to be served up every Season, as we have already begun to do.

An Entertaiment for the same Month of March.

The First Course.

Potages.

A Potage of Capons, with Cullises of Lambs-livers, may be used.

One of Lambs-heads in green Pease-potage, garnish'd with their Feet.

And a large fat Pullet in a *Bisk*.

Great Side-dishes.

A great Piece of Beef.
A Breast of Veal farced in a Ragoo.
A Fricassy of Chickens, garnish'd with a *Marinade* of Chickens.

The small Side-dishes.

One of Cutlets of Mutton broiled upon a Grid-iron.
And the other of small *Bouillans* made of the Breasts of Capons.

The Second Course.

For the Roast.

A Dish of a roasted Capon, breaded and garnish'd with three Pigeons and three Chickens.

A Leg of Mutton, breaded and garnish'd with the same.

A Loin of Veal garnish'd with a *Marinade* of Veal round about.

A Dish of two roasted Ducks with Sauce.
One of two Rabbets.
And for the smaller Dishes, some large and fat Pullets breaded.

The Intermeſſes.

Shall be of a Ragoo of Artichokes.
A Diſh of *Truffles* and Capons-livers in a **Ragoo**.
A Cream-tart and a *Blanc-manger*.
A Diſh of breaded Muſhrooms baked.
One of new-laid Eggs, *à la Huguenotte*.
One of *Pain au Jambon*.
Apple-fritters.
And two Plates of Salt-meat.

This was the Duke of *Orleans*'s Dinner, *March* 26, 1690, being Eaſter-day.

For Supper.

Potages.

A *Potage de Santé* with a Capon.
A *Bisk* of Capons, or of Pigeons.
And a Potage of a young Hen with Eggs in her, nothing but good Gravy to be put into it.

The Side-diſhes.

The Sweet-breads of Veal larded and roaſted, with good Sauce.
Two large fat Pullets roaſted with a Ragoo underneath.
And a Diſh of ſtewed Pigeons.

The Roaſt.

A Loin of Veal garniſhed with three Pigeons and three Chickens, one half larded and the other barded.
A Leg of Mutton breaded and garniſh'd after the ſame manner.
A Diſh of two larded Rabbets.
And one of ſix roaſted Pigeons.

This is the ordinary Supper of the Duke of *Orleans*, all the difference is, that the Potages and Intermeſſes vary according to the Seaſon of the Year.

The Dutcheſs's Table is uſually ſerved with a large Potage, a great Diſh of Roaſt-meat, a Diſh of Intermeſſes, and two ſmall Diſhes at each Service.

A List of what may serve, during the Months of January, February *and* March, *besides the forementioned Dishes.*

Potages.

A Potage of Larks according to the English Mode.
Potage of Quails with a *Bouillon-brun.*
A Potage of boned Capon with Cardons and Cheese.
Potage of a Sucking-pig.
Potage of a Chine of Pork with strained Pease.
Potage of Pheasants with a *Pot-pourri,* or Hotch-potch.
Potage of Cheese, or *Jacobine.*
Potage of a Leg of Veal farced.
Potage of a young fat Hen, with *Milan-*cabbage.
Potage of young Rabbets according to the Italian Mode.
Potage of *Mauviettes* with a *Bouillon-brun.*
Potage of a fat Goose with Turneps.
Potage of Partridges with Mushrooms.
Potage of Partridges, *à la Reine* and *à la Royale,* (as they call it.)
Potage of young Pigeons crammed.
Potage of Turkey according to the German Mode.
Potage of farced Pullets.
Potage of Wood-pigeons with green Cole-worts.
Potage of Rice.
Potage of Teals with strained Turneps.

Side-dishes.

Lamb in a Ragoo.
Larks in a Ragoo, according to the English Mode.
A short Rib of Beef, after the English Manner.
Andouilles, or Chitterlings of Hoggs-guts.
Andouillets according to the Spanish Way.
Puddings.
A Sucking-pig *au Blanc.*
Legs of Mutton prepared divers ways.
A Shoulder of Mutton in a Ragoo.
A Leg of Veal stewed.
A Turkey broiled and served up cold.
An Hash of Partridge-breasts.
A Leveret or young Hare, according to the Swiss Mode.
A Partridge in a Ragoo.

Young Pigeons according to the Italian Mode.
A Turkey in a *Pot-pourri*.
Pullets according to the Spanish Way.
A *Pot-pourri* of Green-geese.
A Loin of Mutton according to the Swiss Mode.
Sausages.
Beef with Vinegar and Pepper.

They also make use of hot Pies of several sorts, which may be hereafter specified, when we have done with that which belongs to every Season, together with cold Pies and Tarts, which may serve for Intermesses; because they hold out almost the whole Year.

There are also several other sorts of Intermesses, of which a general Supplement may be made; tho' there are very many in the Entertainments that are set down for the ensuing Months.

As for Roft-meats, the following Fowls may be used:

Larks,	Wood-hens,
Wood-cocks,	Rabbets,
Snipes,	Leverets,
Bitterns,	Fat Geese,
Stock-doves,	*Mauviettes*,
Quails,	Plovers,
Ducks,	Turkies,
Fat Capons,	Capons or Wood-pigeons,
Barn-door Capons, or Pullets,	Young fat Hens,
Partridges,	Teals,
Wild Pigeons,	Lapwings.
Pheasants,	

These sorts of Meats are also in their Season for the Months of *October*, *November* and *December*, and some of the following Months, may be added; which will be remarked hereafter in due Place.

Enter-

The Court and Country Cook.

Entertainments for the Month of April.

The First Course.

Potages.

TWo sorts of Potages, *viz.* A *Bisk* of Pigeons, and a *Potage de Santé*, with a young fat Hen.

The Side-dishes.

A Quarter of Mutton farced.
A large fat Pullet in a Ragoo.
A Breast of Veal farced.
Pigeons with sweet Basil in their Bodies, together with a small *Farce*; and a large Piece of Beef in the middle.

The Second Course.

For the Roast.

A great Dish of Roast-meat, consisting of several Fowls, according to their Season, and two Sallets.

The Intermesses.

A Dish of *Pain au Jambon.*
Boil'd Cream.
A Ragoo of Sweet-breads of Veal and Capons-livers.
A Dish of Asparagus with Sauce of *Jus lié*, or thick Gravy.
And so there may be seven Dishes for each Course.

The Marquess *d'Arci*, formerly the French King's Ambassadour at *Turin*, and since Tutour to the Duke of *Chartres*, gave such an Entertainment at his House on the 10th Day of *April*, 1690.

Another

Another Dinner for the same time.

The First Course.

Potages.

TWo Potages, one of farced Pullets with Asparagus, and the other *Potage de Santé*, with a young fat Hen garnish'd with Roots.

For the Side-dishes.

A *Poupeton* farced, with six Pigeons in a Ragoo.
Pullets or Chickens with Gammon.
Calves-tongues farced and ragoo'd.
One or two young fat Hens in a Ragoo with *Truffles*.
A large Breast of Veal, garnished with farced Cutlets of Mutton.

The Second Course.

The Roast.

A great Dish of Roast-meat, consisting of divers Fowls and two Sallets.

The Intermesses.

The Sweet-breads of Veal in a Ragoo with Mushrooms and *Truffles*, besides good Cullises put into it.
Asparagus with Sauce of *Jus lié*.
A Marrow-pye.
A *Blanc-manger*.

The Out-works.

A Dish of the Bottoms of Artichokes with Cream.
One of Salt-meat in Slices.

This Dinner was prepared at the Marquess *d'Arci*'s, as also that which follows, for the Duke *de Chartres* and Mademoiselle his Sister, *April* 18, 1690.

Another Dinner for the Month of April.

The First Course.

Potages.

Two *Potages de Santé* with two young fat Hens, garnished with Asparagus-tops.
One of farc'd Pullets, garnish'd with farc'd Lettices.
A *Bisk* of Pigeons.
A Potage of Partridges, with Cullises *à la Reine*.

The Side-dishes of the Table.

For the grand Side-dish, you are to have a Quarter of Veal, garnish'd with fried Bread and Cutlets of fried Veal, larded with *Hatlets*, and a *Salpicon* put upon the Leg.
The others are a *Poupeton* farc'd with six young Pigeons.
A *Miroton*.
Sweet-breads of Veal, larded and farced in a Ragoo.
A Dish of *Filets* of large fat Hens with Oisters.
And a Rabbet-pye.

The Second Course.

For the Roast.

Two great Dishes of Roast-meat, and two little ones consisting of several Fowls, with two Sallets.

The Intermesses.

A Dish of Gammon, garnish'd with Sausages and dryed Tongues.
A Tart of Almond-paste farced with Marmelade of Apricocks.
A *Blanc-manger*.
A Dish of Asparagus, with ordinary Sauce.
One of *Morilles* in Cream.
One of *Mousserons*, or white Mushrooms in a Ragoo with the red.
One of Capons-livers in a Ragoo.

The great Entertainment for the Month of May.

The First Course.

Potages.

FOur *Bisks* of Pigeons.

Four Potages of farced Pullets, garnished with farced Lettices.

Three Potages of Geese with green Pease, garnish'd with Asparagus-tops.

Three young Turkies with white Succory.

Two *Oils* served up in *Cuvets*.

The Side-dishes of the Table.

Four great Side-dishes and twelve middling ones.

Two of two Rumps of Veal, *de riviere*, garnish'd with Cutlets and larded with *Hatlets*; the Veal being half larded, and a *Salpicon* pour'd upon the Leg.

Two Dishes of Roast-meat, one of Beef, the other of Mutton, garnish'd with fried Bread, and *Marinade* of Mutton-cutlets.

For the twelve lesser Dishes.

Two Pies of young Rabbets.

Two Pigeon-pies.

Two hot Pies of young Turkies.

Two Pieces of powder'd Beef, with a Hash of Gammon thereupon.

Two farced *Poupetons*,

Two *Mirotons*.

The Out-works.

Thirty two Dishes in number, *viz*.

Two of Pigeons with sweet Basil.

Two of Pullets with Gammon.

Two of roasted Partridges with Spanish Sauce.

Two of *Filets Mignons*, with a Ragoo apart.

Two *Filets* of Beef with Cucumbers.

Two Fricassies of Chickens with Cream.

Two of young Rabbets roasted, cut into two Parts, with Gammon-sauce.

Two of Mutton-*filets* in a Ragoo with *Morilles*.

Two

The Court and Country Cook.

Two of farced Pullets in a Ragoo.
Two of farced Pullets broiled on the Coals with a Ragoo.
Two of farc'd *Fricandoe's*.
Two of Sweet-breads of Veal and farced Gammon.
Two of farced Lettices, *à la Dame Simonne*.
Two of Sweet-breads of Veal larded on the Spit, and when roasted a good Ragoo put upon 'em.
Two of *Fricandoe's* without being farced.
Two of *Pains au Veau*.

The Second Course.

For the Roast.

Sixteen Dishes of Roast-meat, and as many Potages, consisting of all sorts of Poultry, wild Fowl, young Boars, sucking Pigs, &c.
Ten small Sallets.

The Intermesses.

Two great Gammon-pies.
Two others of young fat Hens and Mutton.
Ten lesser Dishes, viz.
Two of *Blanc-manger*.
Two of Salt-meats.
Two of Calves-ears farc'd.
Two of *Galantine*.
Two of Asparagus.

The Out-works.

Twenty two Out-works, which, with the ten Sallets, make up the same Number as in the first Course, *viz.*
Two of *Mine-droit*.
Two of Pigs-pettitoes, *à la Sainte Menehout*.
Two of *Hatlets* broiled upon a Grid-iron and breaded.
Two of the Bottoms of Artichokes with Gammon-sauce.
Two of *Pain au Jambon*.
Two of farced *Morilles* and *Mousserons* in a Ragoo.
Two of Cocks-combs farced and of Capons-livers in a Ragoo.
Two Pies of the Breasts of Capons.
Two of small Pease in Cream.
Two of *Rissoles*, made of the Breasts of Capons.
Two of boil'd Cream.

For

For a like Entertainment, Provision must be made the Evening before, and at Night three or four great Kettles are to be hang'd over the Fire with store of Meat therein, Faggots of fine Herbs and whole Onions: You must at the same time boil a great many Pullets and fat Hens, and roast some Partridges; which, with parboil'd Bacon and Fat, shall serve for the farced Meats that are to be made for the next Day's Entertainment; and the *Bouillons* will serve to make Beef and Veal-gravy, Soops, Cullises, and *Essence de Jambon*.

As for the Potages, the Gravies and strained Liquors are to be made apart, as also for the Side-dishes and Intermesses: You must moreover have good store of *Chibbols* and chopped Parsly, and several Bunches of fine Herbs to be put into the Ragoo's: Great quantities of Cullises of Partridges, Pigeons and Pullets are likewise to be made, all by themselves.

The Marquess *de Seignelay* made such a sort of Entertainment at *Seaux* for the *Dauphin*, the Duke and Dutchess of *Orleans*, the Duke of *Chartres* and Mademoiselle his Sister, and the whole Retinue of the Court, *May* 14, 1690.

The Kitchen-tackling used there, consisted in sixty small Hand-Stew-pans, twenty round ones, as well great as small, twenty Kettles or Pots of all sorts, thirty Spits; and, to prepare this Entertainment, thirty six Officers were employ'd; as well Master-Cooks as Assistants, *&c.*

Another Entertainment for the same Month of May.

The First Course.

Potages.

THree *Bisks* of Pigeons.
Three Potages of green Geese with Pease or Asparagus.
Three of farced Pullets with green Pease-soop.
Three *Julians* with young fat Hens.

The *Julians*, were garnish'd with Cucumbers; the Geese, with slices of young streaked Bacon; the Pease-potage, with farced Lettices and Asparagus-tops; and the *Bisks*, with Lemmon.

Side-

The Side-dishes of the Table.

Two Pigeon-pies.
Two Side-dishes of Beef somewhat corned.
Two of *Filets* of Beef with Cucumbers.
Two of the Fricassies of Chickens with Cream.
Two of young fat Pullets broiled upon the Coals.
Two *Mirotons*.

The Out-works.

Two of Pies according to the Spanish Mode.
Two of Cutlets of Veal broiled upon the Grid-iron.
Two of young Rabbets, *à la Saingaraz*.
Two of Pigeons with sweet Basil.
Two *Grenadins* of a large fat Pullet.

The Second Course.

For Roast-meat.

Two Dishes of young wild Boars.
  Eight lesser Dishes, viz.
Two with four young Turkies in each Dish.
Two of Chickens, garnish'd with young Pigeons.
Two of young Rabbets.
Two of Pheasants.
And eight small Sallets.

The Intermesses.

Two great Dishes of Gammon-pye.
Two dried Neats-tongues and Sausages.
  Twelve lesser Dishes, viz.
Two of common Pease with Cream.
Two of Artichokes *à l'Estoufade*.
Two of Mushrooms and Capons-livers.
Two of *Pain au Jambon*.
Two of Asparagus in Cream.
Two of the Sweet-breads of Veal and Cocks-combs.

The Out-works.

  Eight in number, viz.
Two of *Blanc-manger*.
Two of Fritters.

Two

Two of Calves-feet, *à la Sainte Menehout*.
Two Pies of the Breasts of Capons.
This Entertainment was made, *May* 18, 1690.

An Entertainment for the Month of June.

The First Course.

Potages.

A Potage of young wild Ducks or Chickens with Pease, garnished with Cucumbers.
A *Bisk* of Pigeons.
A Potage of Turneps with a Duck.
A Potage of Cole-worts with a Partridge.
A *Potage de Santé* with a Capon.
A Potage of a *Casserole* with Parmesan.
A Potage of young Stock-doves.
And another of Quails with Roots.

The Side-dishes of the Table.

The Leg of a Fawn with the Rump to it, half larded and half breaded, garnished with small Pies, and Sauce of Pepper and Vinegar.
A Piece of Beef somewhat corned and broil'd upon the Coals.
And for the great Side-dish, a Piece of roast Beef, garnish'd with a *Marinade* and Cutlets of fried Veal.
Having taken off the Potages, the following Dishes were serv'd up:

The Out-works.

Sheeps-trotters farced, after the same manner as the *Croquets*.
A *Filet* of a young fat Hen with Oisters.
Sheeps-tongues broiled, with a *Ramolade* for Sauce.
A Fricassy of Chickens with a Pike.
A Turkey-powt farced with fine Herbs.

The Second Course.

The Roast-meat

Consists of a great Dish of all sorts of wild Fowl, with four Sallets.

The Intermesses.

An Almond-pye.
A Dish of Artichokes, *à la Saingaraz*, garnish'd with fryed Artichokes.
A Ragoo of Capons-livers Mushrooms and Gammon.
Pease in Cream, garnish'd with Cheese-*Ramequins*.

The Out-works.

Four in number, viz.
One of Fritters made with Water.
One of *Rissoles*.
One of Mushrooms in Cream.
One of Eggs with the Juice of Oranges.

These are the ordinary Courses serv'd up at the French King's Table; and here follows the Model of an Entertainment made at Court for Monsieur *de Livri*, Principal Steward to his Majesty, *A. D.* 1690.

Another Entertainment for the Month of June.

A Table furnished for Twelve Persons.

The First Course.

A Great Potage, and six Side-dishes. The Potage is an *Oil* serv'd up in a *Cuvet* of Silver gilt, or another in a large Dish.

For the Side-dishes.

A Leveret-pye, hot.
A Side-dish of Pigeons, with Fennel.
A *Filet* of a young fat Hen, with Cucumbers.
A Side-dish of Veal-sweet-breads, *à la Dauphine*.
One of Loins of Mutton, *à la Sainte Menehout*.
One of farced *Fricandoe's*.
The Dishes garnish'd with fryed Bread, *Croquets*, *Marinades* and *Pain aux Perdrix*.

The Second Course.

The Roast.

Four Dishes of all sorts of Fowl roasted, according to the Season; and a Piece of Roast-beef between others, garnish'd with *Hatlets* and two Sallets.

The Intermesses.

Stewed Artichokes, garnish'd with fried Artichokes; for the great Dish.
An Almond-pye, garnish'd with Apple-fritters.
Pease in Cream, garnish'd with Cheese-*Ramequins*.
A Dish of Gammon.
And one of *Rissoles*.

Another Entertainment for the Month of June.

The First Course.

Potages.

Four in number, viz.
 A *Bisk* of Pigeons.
 A *Potage de Santé*, with a large fat Pullet.
 A Potage of farc'd Chickens, with green Pease-soop.
 A Potage of Quails, after the manner of an *Oil*.

Side-dishes.

A great Side-dish, of a Loin of Veal, half larded and a *Salpicon* thereupon; garnish'd with Cutlets of Marinated Veal.
 Two *middling Side-dishes*, viz.
One of a Rabbet-pye, and the other of farc'd Cabbage or Cole-worts, garnish'd with farc'd *Fricandoe's*.
 Two *small Side-dishes*, viz.
One a white Fricassy of Chickens, garnish'd with *Marinade*.
And the other of young Rabbets *à la Saingaraz*.

The Out-works.

A Dish of a young fat Pullet farced, in Cream.
One of Chickens *à la Polacre*, with a *Ramolade*.

One

One of *Pain de Perdrix*.
And one of a Loin of Mutton *a la Sainte Menehout*.
After having taken off the four Potages, four other Out-works were set on the Table, *viz.*
One of *Pain de Veau*.
One of Pigeons with sweet Basil in their Bodies.
One of *Hatlets*.
And a *Grenade*.
There were also two other Out-works, consisting of Sturgeons prepared, as for Flesh-days, two different ways, *viz.*
One after the manner of larded *Fricandoe's*.
And the other, *à la Sante Menehout* in thick Slices.

The Second Course.

The Roast-meats and Intermesses are of the Nature of the Preceding.

Such a sort of Entertainment was made *June* 20, 1690, in the Presence of the Cardinal *d' Estrées* and the Ambassadours, at the Table of the Grand Chamberlain and Purveyor to the French King.

As for the Potages served up in the Second Service, recourse may be had to those that have been already set down for the three first Months of the Year. Let us now observe what may be added, as well to the Side-dishes, as with respect to the Roast-meats.

A List of what may be served up, besides the abovementioned Dishes, during the Months of April, May *and* June.

Potage of Lamb, with Roman Lettice.
   Potage of Quails, with a natural *Blanc-manger*.
Potage of boned Capon, with Mushrooms.
Potage of Kids, with white Broth.
Potage of white Cabbage farced.
Potage of small Citrulls, farc'd after the Spanish Mode.
Potage of Artichoke-bottoms, Cucumbers and Lettice.
Potage of young Turkies, with farced *Morilles* and white Cabbage.
Potage of young Rabbets, with small Turneps.

Potage of green Geese, with Asparagus.
Potage of farced Bread with farced Lettice.
Potage of Partridges with brown Broth.
Potage of a farced Breast of Veal.
Potage of Chickens with farced Cucumbers.
Potage of Chickens in a Ragoo.
Potage of a *Poupeton* in form of a Triangle.
Potage of Calves-feet and Chaldrons.
Potage of Lambs-heads.
Potage of Calves-heads *à deux Faces.*
Potage after the Italian Mode.

Side-dishes.

Andouilles of Veal.
A Quarter of Mutton roasted.
Calve's-livers.
A Calve's Chaldron fried.
A Leg of Veal larded small, in a *Daube.*
Collops of Veal broiled, with Parsley-sauce.
Young Rabbets, with white and brown Sauce.
A Loin of Veal in a Ragoo.
Green Geese in a Ragoo.
Young Geese, in a *Daube.*
Calves-feet larded, with white Sauce.
Young Pigeons marinated, in a Fricassy.
A Breast of Veal marinated.
Boned Chickens.
Stew'd Chickens.
Chickens in a Fricassy, with Cream.
Young Turkies after the Swiss Mode, fried with Cucumbers.
Little Chickens with Cherry-sauce.
A *Poupeton* farced with young Pigeons.
A Cow's Udder, with sweet Sauce.

For the Roast.

This is the Season for Lambs, Kids, sucking Piggs, young Turkies a Year old, Pheasants, young Rabbets, *January*-Leverets, green Geese, young wild Boars, Partridges, young Pigeons, Chickens, and young Ring-doves, or Wood-pigeons.

A

A great Entertainment for the Months of July *and* August.

The First Course.

Potages.

Two *Bisks* of Pigeons.
Two *Julian*-potages with large fat Pullets.
Two of Quails with sweet Basil.
Two of Pease with a Duck.
Two Potages of farced Cucumbers with a Capon.
Two of *Oils*.
Two of *Casseroles*.
Two of Roots, with young Ring-doves.
Two of Turneps, with farced Chickens.
Two of Leaks, with Geese.
Two of Succory, with young Turkies.

The Side-dishes.

Two Pigeon-pies.
Two Rabbet-pies.
Two Legs of Mutton, *à la Royale*.
Two Side-dishes of Partridge fried on the Coals.
Two of young fat Hens, *à la Saingaraz*.
Two of large Pullets, farced in Cream.
Two *Mirotons*.
Two *Pains de Veau*.
Two *Terrines*.
Two Side-dishes of Ducks, with Oisters.
Two great Side-dishes of Roast-beef, garnish'd with Mutton-cutlets.
And two other of Veal *de Riviere*, garnish'd with Cutlets of fried Veal and a Hash upon the Leg.

The Out-works.

Two Dishes of *Croquets*.
Two of *Saucisses Franches*.
Two of *Saucisson Royal*.
Two of Veal after the Italian Mode.
Two of Pigeons with Fennel.
Two of farced Chickens broil'd on the Coals.

Two of Pigeons with sweet Basil.
Two of Chickens *à la Tartre*.
Two of young Pullets *à la Sainte Menehout*.
Two of *Bouillans*.
Two of *Marinades* of Chickens.
Two Courses of Pigeons, with white Sauce.
And two of *Pain de Perdrix*.

The Second Course.

Twenty two Dishes of Roast-meat, consisting of all sorts of large Pieces of Beef, Mutton and Veal, and of all sorts of Poultry, wild Fowl, young Boars, sucking Piggs, Pheasants, &c. with Sallets.

The Intermesses.

Twenty four in number, viz.
Two Dishes of Gammon-pies.
Two of Pheasants.
Two of Salt-meats, Tongues and Sausages.
Two Pies of Capons-breasts, garnish'd with little Tarts.
Two Pies made of crackling Crust filled with Marmelade of Apricocks.
Two *Blanc-mangers* garnish'd with several Gellies.
Two Dishes of Veal-sweet-breads *à la Dauphine*, garnish'd with fried Sweet-breads of the same.
Two of *Blanc-manger*-fritters, garnish'd with Water-fritters.
Two of Pigs-pettitoes, *à la Sainte-Menehout*.
Two of *Menus-droits*.
Two of *Hatlets*.
And two of *Galantine*.

The Out-works.

Two Dishes of *Pain au Jambon*.
Two of Mushrooms in Cream.
Two of Cocks-combs and *Morilles*.
Two of Artichoke-bottoms.
Two *Omelets*, and a Gammon-hash thereupon.
Two *Omelets* with Sugar.
Two of Apple-fritters,
Two of burnt Cream.
Two of *Rissoles*.

Two

The Court and Country Cook. 23

Two of Capons-livers.
And two of *Truffles* in a *Court-bouillon*.

An Entertainment of the like Nature was made by the Marquess *de Louvois*, Aug. 25, 1690, in his Castle at *Meudon*, for the Dauphin, the Duke and Dutchess of *Orleans*, the Duke of *Chartres* and his Sister, and the whole Retinue of the Court. There were three Tables furnished with the same Provisions; so that almost three Dishes of every Mess were reiterated.

Another Entertainment that may be made during the same Season, and in the following Months.

THree great Services of Pieces of Beef garnish'd with *Marinade*, either in a *Cuvet* or in a large Dish.
   Twelve other Dishes, viz.
Three of fat Pullets and young Turkies.
Three of Carbonado'd Mutton.
Three of Pies after the Spanish Mode.
Two of farced Lettice.
And one of Pigeons with Fennel.

The Out-works.

Four in number, viz.
Two of Veal-sweet-breads with white Sauce.
And two *Filets* with Cucumbers.

On another Day.

For the twelve Dishes,
Three of fat Chickens and young fat Pullets.
Three of Sausages and Partridges.
Three of Chicken-fricassies.
And three of Pies of Pheasants, Partridges and young Rabbets.

The Out-works.

Three Dishes of white Puddings, Sausages and *Andouilles*; and three others of Carbinadoes.

C 4   For

For Tables of leſs Strength.

A great Diſh of a Piece of Beef.

Two leſſer of Pieces of Beef likewiſe, but diverſified, after ſome of the manners elſewhere deſcribed.

A Pigeon-pye.

And a Fricaſſy of Chickens.

For the Out-works.

A *Filet*, with Cucumbers.
A Diſh of Carbonadoe's.
A *Filet* with white Sauce.
A Diſh of young Turkies, in a *Salmigund* or Hotch-potch.

At another time.

For the Grand Diſh, a Piece of Beef.

Two leſſer Diſhes, viz.

One of *Filets* with Cucumbers, garniſh'd with Carbonadoe's; and the other of fat Pullets entire, with *Truffles*.

For the Out-works.

Four Diſhes of Sauſages, Puddings and *Andouillets*.
A Fillet of Mutton, with *Truffles*.
And a Fricaſſy of Chickens with Pies.

For Suppers.

Three great Diſhes of Veal, garniſh'd with *Marinade* and Hatlets.

Twelve other Diſhes, viz.

Three of Pullets and young Turkies.
Two of Pigeons, with Fennel.
One of a Leg of Mutton, with Garlick.
Two of young Turkies, with Gammon.
One of Pigeons, with ſweet Baſil.
And three Haſhes of Partridges.

The Out-works.

Four in number, viz.

Two of *Filets* with Cucumbers, and two *Marinades* of Chickens.

For another Table of less Strength.

A Quarter of Veal garnish'd with *Marinade* for the great Dish.

Two other lesser Dishes, viz.

One of a young fat Hen with Gammon, and the other of a Leg of Mutton.

The Out-works.

A Dish of young Turkies, in a *Salmigund*, or Hotch-potch,
One of Sweet-breads *en rond.*
One of a Hash of Partridges,
And a *Filet* with white Sauce.

Another Table.

Three Quarters of Veal garnish'd with *Marinade*, for the great Side-dishes.

Twelve other Dishes, viz.

Three of fat Pullets, and young Turkies.
Three of *Filets* of a short Rib of Beef in the Gravy.
Three of young Turkies, with Gammon-sauce.
And three of *Salpicons.*

The Out-works.

Two Dishes of fried Sweet-breads of Veal, and two of large fat Pullets, with white Sauce.

Another Table,

Two Side-dishes, viz.

One of Calves-tongues, and the other of young Hens, with Gammon.

The Out-works.

A Dish of *Filets*, with Cucumbers.
One of a Fricassy of Chickens.
Another of a *Filet* in the Gravy.
And of one *Marinade* of Chickens.

The Order of all these first Courses is usually observ'd, during the same Season, in the Court of *France*, for the King's Table, and those of the Princes and the Comptroller of his Majesty's Houshold.

A

A List of what may be served up besides the abovementioned Messes during the Months of July, August *and* September.

Potages.

POtage of farced Quails.
——— of Capons with Mushrooms.
——— of Capon with *Prunes de Brignoles*.
——— of Turkey-powts, with Cucumbers.
——— of a Shoulder of Mutton with Turneps.
——— of young Pheasants with *Truffles*.
——— of Wood-hens with white Succory.
——— of a Leg of Veal farced and larded.
——— of Collops of Veal larded and broil'd.
——— of Thrushes, with brown Broth.
——— of a Knuckle of Veal *à l'Epigramme*.
——— of Melons with little Chickens.
——— of green Geese with Turneps.
——— of the Gibblets of young Geese.
——— of Partridges, in a *Capitolade*.
——— of young Partridges, with strained Broth.
——— of farced Chickens, with green Pease-soop.
——— of large Pullets, with Cabbage.
——— of a boned Turkey.
——— of Ring-doves, with Mushrooms.
——— of Veal-sweet-breads.
And *Potage de Santé*, with a Knuckle of Veal and Capon.

Side-dishes.

Beef *à la mode*.
A sucking Pig after the German Way.
A *Civet* of a Hare.
A Leg of Mutton after the Swiss Mode.
A Shoulder of Mutton, with Mushrooms.
Thrushes in a Ragoo.
A Breast of Mutton parboil'd, and afterwards fried.
Fresh Neats-tongues larded.
Calves-tongues, with sweet Sauce.
Young Rabbets in a *Casserole*.
A Loin of Veal hashed.
Green Geese quartered,

A

A Fricaſſy of young Pigeons.
Young Pigeons with Pepper and Vinegar.
A Breaſt of Veal ragoo'd.
A Turkey in a *Pot-pourri,* or ſort of Hotch-potch.
A boned Turkey.
A Fillet of Veal in a Ragoo.
A Loin of Mutton fried.
A Calve's Head fried.
A Calve's Udder, with ſweet Sauce.

Roaſt-meats.

Beccafigo's, young Quails, young Capons or fat Pullets, ſucking Pigs, Pheaſants and Pheaſant-powts, Thruſhes, Leverets, young wild Bores, *Mauviettes,* young Houſe-pigeons and Pullets of one Year.

Theſe ſorts of Meats are alſo proper for the enſuing Months; as likewiſe many of thoſe that have been ſet down for the Firſt and Second Seaſon, may be uſed at another time; if they are to be procured: Therefore we ought only to have regard to Convenience in this matter, and if that will allow it, to adhere in every thing to the Particulars of which the above-ſpecified Entertainments are compos'd, rather than to thoſe contained in the Liſts; which are more common Ragoo's, and leſs conformable to the new Mode.

An Entertainment that may be made in the Months of October, November *and* December.

The Firſt Courſe.

Potages and Side-diſhes.

A Great Diſh, four middling ones and four Out-works, *viz.*
  A *Bisk* of Pigeons.
 A Potage of Ducks, with a Culliſe of *Nantilles.*
  Three Side-diſhes, viz.
 One of a young fat Hen, *à la Saingaraz,* garniſh'd with Marinade.
 One of a Rabbet-pye.

And

And a short Rib of Beef, with the *Filet*, garnish'd with *Fricandoe's*.

The four small Dishes, or Out-works are,

One of Partridges, with Sauce, after the Spanish Way.
One of *Filets* larded and Roasted.
A Fricassy garnish'd with a Carbonadoe.
And a Dish of farced *Mauviettes* with Mustard.

The Second Course.

The Roast-meats and Intermesses.

Two middling Dishes of several sorts of Poultry and Wild Fowl, according to the Season.
A great Pye of crackling Crust garnish'd with little Tarts and Fritters.
A Dish of *Blanc-manger*.
And a Gammon-pye.

The four Out-works are,

A Dish of Cardoons, with Parmesan.
One of *Truffles* in a *Court-bouillon*.
One of Veal-sweet-breads and farced Cocks-combs.
One of *Hatlets* and four Sallets.

A Supper was served up in this manner at the Duke of *Chartres*'s Palace, *December* the 1st, 1690.

Another great Entertainment for the Month of December.

The First Course.

Potages.

TWo *Bisks* of Pigeons.
Two *Casseroles*, with Parmesan.
Two Potages of farced Chickens, with green Pease-soop.
Two of Ducks, with Turneps.

Two

Two of large fat Pullets, with Succory.
Two of farced Quails, with *Truffles*.
Two of *Cercelots*, or young Teals with sweet Basil.
And two of Partridges, with Cullises *à la Reyne*.

The Side-dishes.

Three great Dishes, viz.

A large Loin of Veal, garnish'd with *Marinade* and larded with *Hatlets*.

A Piece of Beef, with the *Filet* garnish'd with Cutlets.

A Piece of Roast-beef and another of Mutton, garnish'd with farced Cutlets.

Ten middling Dishes, viz.

Two of Slices of Beef roll'd and farc'd.
Two of farced Water-fowl, with Oisters.
Two of Pheasants minc'd in a Pye.
Two of fat Pullets, with *Truffles*.
And two of young Hens, with Cray-fish Cullises.

The Out-works.

Two Dishes of *Grenadins*, with large fat Pullets.
Two of Veal, *à la Bourgeoise*.
Two of Partridges, after the Spanish Mode.
Two of Pheasants, with Carp-sauce.
Two of Marinated Chickens.
Two of roasted Wood-cocks, with Wine.
Two of Quails broil'd on the Coals.
Two *Biberots* of Partridges.
Two *Mirotons* of Veal, with Asparagus.
Two Dishes of *Filets* of young fat Hens, with white Sauce.
Two of *Filets* of Beef, with Cucumbers.
Two of Pigeons with sweet Basil.
Two of Partridges, with Olives.
Two of *Saucisson Royal*.

The Second Course.

For the Roast-meat.

Sixteen Dishes of all sorts of Wild Fowl and other Poultry, particularly *Ortolans*, Pheasants, &c. with young wild Boars, and twelve small Sallets.

The Intermeſſes.

The three great Diſhes are to conſiſt of three Gammon-pies.
The middling Diſhes are ten in number, viz.

Two of *Blanc-manger.*
Two Pies made of Capons-breaſts.
Two of Cakes farc'd with Marmalade.
Two Pies of crackling Cruſt, garniſh'd with Marmalade.
And two *Omelets,* with Gammon.

The Out-works.

Two Diſhes of Apple-fritters.
Two of *Blanc-manger*-fritters.
Two of *Riſſoles.*
Two of Muſhrooms in Cream.
Two of *Pain au Jambon.*
Two of burnt Cream.
Two of *Truffles* in a *Court-bouillon.*
Two of Artichoke-bottoms.
Two of fried Artichokes.
Two of iced Artichokes.
Two of Aſparagus in a Sallet.
Two of *Menus-droits.*
And two of *Galantine.*

A Feaſt of the like Nature was prepared at the Duke of *Aumont*'s Palace, *December* 27, 1690. The Table was fix'd with Horſe-ſhooes; and foraſmuch as there were forty two *Covers* or *Services,* it was requiſite to reiterate three Diſhes of ſeveral Particulars; as well for the Side-diſhes, as for thoſe of the Roaſt-meats and Inter'meſſes.

If theſe Models are not ſufficient for a due Variety of Entertainments on different Days; or if they do not ſuit with the Convenience of Perſons and Places; a more proper Choice may be made out of the following Liſt.

A List of what may be served up, besides the abovementioned Dishes, during the Months of October, November *and* December.

POtages of Larks, with Hypocras.
——— of *Andouilles*, with Peafe.
——— of Lambs-heads.
——— of Ducks, with Cole-worts or Sprouts.
——— of Quails with Mushrooms.
——— of farced Mushrooms.
——— of Capons, with Colly-flowers.
——— of Capons, with Cardoons in white Broth.
——— of boned Capon, with Oisters.
——— of a farced Leg of Mutton, with Turneps.
——— of a farced Leg of Veal with white Sauce.
——— of a Leg of a Stag, or of a wild Boar.
——— of a fat Goose, with strained Peafe.
——— of Partridges, with *Milan*-cabbage.
——— of farced Partridges.
——— of large Pullets farced and boned.
——— of young Barn-door Chickens in a *Bisk* with *Truffles*.
——— of *Poupetons*.
——— of Teals, with Mushrooms.
——— of Teals, with Hypocras.
——— of *Vermecelli*, after the Italian Mode.
And *Potage de Santé*.

Side-dishes.

Puddings of Calves-livers.
A *Capitolade* of Partridges and Capon.
A Duck in a Ragoo.
A farced Duck, with sweet Sauce.
A fat Capon in a *Daube*.
A *Daube* of Veal, minc'd and larded.
Calves-livers in a *Marinade*.
Calves-livers larded and roasted.
Hoggs-livers in a Ragoo.
A *Gallimafry* of a Shoulder of Mutton.
A *Haricot* of a Breast of Mutton.
A Neat's Tongue larded.

Sheeps-

Sheeps-tongues broil'd.
A *Marinade* of Partridges.
A Partridge in a *Daube*.
A Piece of Beef well larded.
Sheeps-trotters, with white Sauce.
A Loin of Mutton à *la Croutade*.
A Fillet of Veal, with Oisters.
A Calve's Head in *Mine-droit*.

For the Roast-meats, *see* Page 15. because the same Provisions may also serve in this Season; as it has been already hinted. The Appurtenances of the Intermesses are much more general, as being in use throughout the greatest part of the whole Year: Therefore it may not be improper here to make a Collection of the different Messes, prepared for that purpose in the above-specified Entertainments for every Season; adding some others that may be substituted in their room, when Occasion serves, and accordingly as particular Exigencies may require.

A general Table of the Intermesses.

Almond-milk.
Apple-fritters.
Artichokes, with white Sauce.
Artichokes fried.
Artichokes iced.
Artichokes, *à la Saingaraz*.
Artichokes, with natural Butter.
Artichokes, *à l'Estoufade*.
Artichoke-bottoms put in Paste and fried.
Artichoke-bottoms, with Gammon-sauce.
Asparagus in Mutton-gravy.
Asparagus with natural Butter.
Asparagus in Cream.
Asparagus in a Sallet.
Beans in Cream with Bacon.
Beatils in a Ragoo.
Bignets, see Fritters.
Blanc-mangers of several sorts.

Calves-

Calves-kidneys, and others roasted.
Calves-ears farced.
Cardoons, with Parmesan.
Cheese-cakes.
Cocks-combs farced, and Capons-livers in a Ragoo.
Cocks-kidneys in a Ragoo.
Colly-flowers, with natural Butter and Mutton-gravy.
Creams of several sorts.
Cucumbers.
Echaudes or Simnels Iced.
Eggs and *Omelets* after several manners.
Fritters of *Blanc-manger*.
Fritters of Apples.
Fritters made with Water.
Galantines.
Gammon of Bacon in Slices and in a Hash.
Gruels.
Gammon-pies.
Heads of wild Boars.
Hatlets.
Hogs-ears *à la Barbe-Robert*.
Hogs-ears fried in Paste.
Hogs-tongues.
Jellies of several sorts.
Kidneys of Cocks in a Ragoo.
Kidneys of Calves roasted.
Livers of Capons *a la Crepine*.
Livers of Capons roasted.
Livers of Capons with Mushrooms.
Livers of Capons after other manners.
Livers of Rabbets in an *Omelet*.
Menus-droits.
Mousserons or white Mushrooms and *Morilles*, farc'd and fried.
Mushrooms in Cream.
Mushrooms fried.
Mushrooms in a Ragoo.
Mushrooms in a *Casserole*.
6. Neats-tongues dryed.
Omelets.
Pain au Jambon.

Pease,

Peafe, with Bacon and Cream.
Pigs-pettitoes, *à la Sainte Menehout*, and broil'd upon the Grid-iron.
Pyes of Pheafants, young fat Hens and feveral other forts, ferved up cold.
Poupelins.
Rabbets-livers in an *Omelet.*
Riffoles of Capons-breafts.
Salt-meats.
Simnels iced.
Tarts of feveral forts.
Trouts and other Fifhes, on Fifh-days.
Truffles in a *Court-bouillon.*
Truffles broil'd on the Coals.
Truffles in Mutton-gravy.
Veal-fweet-breads farc'd, *à la Dauphine.*
Veal-fweet-breads and Cocks-combs farc'd.
Venifon-pafties.
Water-*Bignets* or Fritters.

Not to tire the Reader with too many Tables or Lifts of the like Nature, relating to Pafties, Pies and Tarts as well hot as cold, as alfo to the different forts proper for fome Things expreffed in the the preceding Table; he is referr'd to the general *Index* or Table of the Meffes at the end of this Volume, where they are fet down at large; or elfe to every Letter in the Alphabetical Inftructions that treat of every Thing in particular; after having fpecify'd what relates to the Fifh-days.

Entertainments on Fifh-days throughout the whole Year.

IT were needlefs perhaps here to give a particular Account of the Services; becaufe it is an eafie thing to take meafures thereupon, from the Entertainments on Flefh-days that have been already defcrib'd. However, that nothing may feem to be wanting, we fhall reprefent fome Models; after having obferv'd what may be ufed, as well for the Potages and Side-difhes as for the Intermeffes; the fried Fifh that are in Seafon, fupplying the place of Roaft-meats. Let us then begin with the Potages.

The

The First Course.

Potages on Fish-days, for the Months of January, February *and* March.

POtages of Pike, with Turneps.
———— of farced Pike.
———— of Cardoons.
———— of *Milan*-cabbage.
———— of Cray-fish.
———— of Sturgeon.
———— of Smelts, with brown Broth.
———— of Oisters.
———— of *Julians*.
———— of the soft Roes of Fish.
———— of Lobsters with Pease.
———— of Sea-ducks.
———— of Onions with sweet Basil and otherwise.
———— of Parmesan.
———— of *Profitrolle*.
———— of fresh Salmon.
———— of farced Soles.
———— of Soles in *Filets* with white Sauce, with sweet Basil, with Lentils, and with Cucumbers.
———— of Soles, with Onions, in white Sauce.
———— of Turbot.
———— of farced Tench.
———— of Tortoise.

To these may be added Potages with Roots and Pulse, hereafter mentioned; more especially the *Oil* for Fish-days, and also certain Fish-potages that are set down for the ensuing Months.

Potages on Fish-days for the Months of April, May *and* June.

POtages of Asparagus.
——— of Mushrooms.
——— of white Cabbage, with Milk.
——— of farced Cucumbers.
——— of Rasberries.
——— of Froggs.
——— of Gudgeons.
——— of Lampreys.
——— of farced Lettice.
——— of fried Mackerel
——— of *Morilles*.
——— of young green Pease.

And *Potage de Santé* with Herbs, which is common for the following Months.

Potages on Fish-days for the Months of July, August *and* September.

POtages of Eels.
——— of Eel-powts, with brown Broth.
——— of farced Pike.
——— of farced Carps.
——— of white Cabbage.
——— of Citrulls, with Milk.
——— of Frogs, with brown Broth.
——— of Milk, with Pistacho's.
——— of Melons.
——— of Muscles.
——— of Muscadine-grapes.
——— of Perches with white Broth.
——— of Fish in a *Bisk*.
——— of Green Pease.
——— of Salmon with Mushrooms.

The Court and Country Cook.

Potages on Fish-days, for the Months of October, November *and* December.

POtages of Fish-*Andouillets*.
——— of Sandlings.
——— of Pike, with Cabbage.
——— of Cardoons.
——— of farced Mushrooms.
——— of Smelts with white Broth.
——— of a pickled Joll of Salmon.
——— of Marbled-Milk.
——— of poach'd Eggs, with Parmesan.
——— of Perches with brown Broth.
——— of young Pigeons.

There are also for all these Seasons, Potages of Rice, of *Vermicelli*, of Almond-milk and others.

Side-dishes of Fish for the whole Year.

A*Umar* in a Ragoo.
Bases.
Bouillans of Fish.
Breams in a Ragoo and roasted.
Burts.
Carps in a Ragoo and *à la Daube*.
Carps in *Filets* stewed, with *Sauffe-Robert*.
Carps farced in a Ragoo.
Carps in a *Demi-court-bouillon*.
Casseroles of Fish.
Cervelats of Fish.
Cod-fish fresh and otherwise.
Congers cut into Pieces and fried, with Anchovies.
Congers *Marinated*.
Cray-fish in a Ragoo, with white Sauce.
Dabs.
Daubes of Eels.
Eels roasted.

Eels

Eels broiled on the Grid-iron, with *Sauſſe-Robert*.
Eels, with white Sauce.
Eels fried.
Eels, with brown Sauce.
Filets of Carps, Soles, Perches, &c.
Flaïs in a *Caſſerole* and fried.
Flounders and Crabs.
Fricaſſies of Pikes, Quavivers and Soles.
Frogs fried.
Gold-fiſh in a Fricaſſy, in Pies, &c.
Gudgeons rolled in Paſte and ſtewed.
Haſhes of Carps, Cray-fiſh, Perches and Pikes.
Haricots of Fiſh.
Herrings, freſh and otherwiſe.
Kneelings.
Lampreys.
Lobſters in a Ragoo, Haſh, &c.
Mackerel.
Melwells.
Mirotons of Fiſh.
Mullets fried, with Anchove-ſauce and broil'd upon the Grid-iron.
Oiſters broiled, ragoo'd, fried or farced.
Pains of Fiſh.
Perches, with Anchove-ſauce.
Perches farced.
Perches, with white or green Sauce, or with Cucumbers,
St. *Peter*'s Fiſh, with *Truffles*, with white Sauce, with Artichokes, with Cucumbers, or with green Sauce.
Petits Patez or little Pies with white Sauce.
Plaice in a Ragoo.
Pies of Fiſh, ſerved up hot.
Pike with Pigeons-breaſts.
Pike farced.
Pike in a *Caſſerole*.
Pike in a Fricaſſy.
Pike farced, with Anchove-ſauce.
Pike fried in Paſte.
Pike cut in Pieces and put into a Ragoo.
Poupetons of Fiſh.
Pilchards.
Quavivers, or Sea-dragons in *Filets*, with Cucumbers, Capers, or *Mouſſerons*.

Quavivers, with Anchove-cullises.
Quavivers boned and stewed.
Quavivers in a Fricassy of Chickens with white Sauce.
Quavivers fried in a Ragoo.
Raies or Thorn-backs fried, with *Sausse-Robert*.
Roches in a *Casserole*.
Roches broiled upon the Grid-iron and breaded.
Roches farced or in a Pie.
Sandlings or Dabs and Eel-powts in a Ragoo, in *Casseroles*, or in *Filets*.
Sandlings with Cream, or Anchovies.
Salmon in a Ragoo, with Mushrooms.
Sardins.
Sausages of Fish.
Sea-ducks in a *Pot-pourri*.
Shads.
Shrimps fried.
Smelts with Anchovies and in a *Casserole*.
Soles broiled upon the Grid-iron, with Anchovies.
Soles marinated, farced, in a Ragoo, with white Sauce, or with fine Herbs.
Soles in *Filets*, with Lentils, with sweet Basil, Cucumbers, *Sausse-Robert*, or *Truffles*, after the Spanish Mode, with Cray-fish and with Capers, or Anchovie-cullises.
Soles *à la Sainte Menehout*.
Soles in a Fricassy of Chickens, or with burnt Butter.
Soles in *Pigeons*.
Soles with Laurel or Bay-leaves.
Stock-fish of several sorts.
Tenches farced, in a Ragoo, in a Fricassy, or in a *Casserole*.
Tortoises in a Ragoo, or in a *Marinade*.
Trouts in a Ragoo.
Tunnies marinated, broiled, put into a Pie or baked in a Pot.
Tunnies cut into Slices, with poor Man's Sauce.
Turbot with Oil, or with Anchovie-sauce.
Turbot in a Ragoo.
Whitings in a *Casserole*.

To these sorts of Fish may be added Dishes of Spinage, farced Cabbage, Pease, and other Herbs or Pulse, according to the Season.

The

The Second Course.

The abovementioned Fishes may be served up in a *Court-bouillon*, and fried, or broiled upon the Grid-iron, or Roasted: Among others, these that follow, *viz.*

Shads roasted, and in a *Court-bouillon*.

Sandlings, in a *Court-bouillon*.

Pike after the same manner; or else larded with Eels and roasted.

Carps in a *Court-bouillon*, broiled on the Grid-iron, or fried.

Sturgeon dress'd after the same manner.

Smelts fried.

Mackerel broiled.

Plaice fried.

Salmon, in a *Court-bouillon*.

Soles in a *Court-bouillon*.

Soles fried and broiled.

Tenches after the same manner.

Turbot in a *Court-bouillon*.

Quavivers broiled upon the Grid-iron, with Anchovie-sauce.

There are also several Pies and Pastry-works of Fish, which are to be set down elsewhere; and to these may be added divers Particulars belonging to the Intermesses on Flesh-days, such as Mushrooms, Artichokes, Asparagus, *Morilles*, Cucumbers, &c. Moreover out of *Lent*, the use of Eggs is considerable, with which a very great number of Dishes may be varied; and even during that Season, a good Choice may be made out of those that belong to the Entertainments with Roots, which shall be hereafter described.

We shall only here subjoyn the Fish-sallets that likewise constitute a part of this Service.

The Court and Country Cook.

A List of the Fiſh-ſallets.

Sallets of Sole-*filets*.
────── of freſh Turbot.
────── of freſh Sandlings.
────── of freſh Oiſters.
────── of *Filets* of Smelts.
────── of Salmon-trout.
────── of Ray or Thorn-back.
────── of Whiting-*filets*.
────── of Quaviver-*filets*.
────── of freſh Tunnies.
────── of Anchovies and Pilchards.
────── of freſh Salmon.
────── of Cray-fiſh.
────── of Lobſters and others.

A particular Account of the Root-ſallets is to be hereafter inſerted, and as for thoſe of Herbs during the Summer, nothing is more eaſie than the manner of making them; for then there is ſo great an Abundance of all ſorts of Garden-fruits, that they may be readily changed every Day, and ſeveral different ſorts may be uſed at the ſame time.

For ſeveral *Filets* of Fiſh 'tis requiſite to prepare a certain Sauce call'd *Ramolade*, which is made of chopped Parſley, Chibbols, Anchovies and Capers; the whole mixture being put into a Diſh, with a little Pepper, Salt, Nutmeg, Oil and Vinegar well temper'd together. After having dreſs'd the *Filets* in a proper Diſh, they are to be ſprinkled with this *Ramolade*, and Lemmon-juice is uſually added to ſome of the Diſhes; which are to be ſerved up cold.

If any Perſons are deſirous to have Models of Entertainments on Fiſh-days, they may here take a View of a very remarkable Ordinary as it is prepar'd in the Duke of *Chartres*'s Palace. Whenever it ſhall be requiſite to furniſh greater Tables, due meaſures may be taken for the management of them, from the Entertainments that have been ſpecify'd for Fleſh-days; and if more ſlender Proviſions are only required, 'twill be leſs difficult to retrench the number of the Diſhes, than to find means to match them and ſet them in good Order.

Mo-

The Court and Country Cook.

Models of Entertainments on Fish-days.

For a considerable Ordinary or Dinner.

Potages.

TWo middling Potages and four lesser.
The two middling ones consist of Cray-fish and farced Soles.
The four lesser are these, viz.
The first *Potage de Santé*, the second with Cabbage, the third with Pease, and the fourth with Onions.

The great Dish in the middle.

An Eel-pie.
Two Side-dishes, viz.
One of whole Perches, with white Sauce.
And the other of four Pikes.

The Out-works.

A Dish of Fricassied Oisters.
One of Spinage.
One of Soles in *Filets* with Cucumbers.
One of *Filets* of Perches, with white Sauce.
One of Quaviver-*Filets*, with Capers.
One a small Fricasy of Pike.
And the last of Eels broiled upon the Grid-iron, with *Sausse-Robert.*

The Roast.

Two middling Dishes, each consisting of two Pikes and eight Soles.
The great Dish of a Carp and six Pickerils round about it.
The rest of this Service consists of Particular Intermesses and *Filets* in a Sallet.

For the Supper.

Potages.

Two middling Potages ; *viz.* one of *Tortoises* and the other of farced Pike.
Two lesser ; one of Sole-*Filets* with sweet Basil and the other of Soles, with Lentils.

The

The Side-dishes of the Table.

For the great Dish in the middle, farced Mullets.
  Four Side-dishes, viz.
A Pike-pye.
A Dish of Gold-fish.
One of stewed Carps.
One of Bases.

Eight Out-works, viz.

A Hash of Carps.
One of Perches.
Tortoises.
Soles farced.
Sole-*Filets,* with *Sauſſe-Robert.*
Others with *Truffles,* and others with Cray-fish.

For the Roast.

Two middling Dishes of Sturgeon and Roches round about 'em.
  Two leſſer, each of five Soles.
Several Intermeſſes for the reſt of the Service.

The Second Table.

A great Dish in the middle, of Soles, with Anchovies.
  Four Side-dishes, viz.
A Pie.
A Fricaſſy of Pike.
Two Dishes of Gold-fish.
And two of Roaſt.

An Ordinary for another Day.

Potages.

TWo middling Potages and four leſſer.
  The two middling, are one of Perches with white Sauce, and the other of Lobſters.
  The four leſſer are a *Potage de Santé,* one of Onions with ſweet Baſil, one of *Profitrolles* and one of ſoft Roes.

The

The Side-dishes.

A great Dish of Roches.
Two middling ones, *viz.* the first of farced Perches and the other of whole Carps.

Eight Out-works, viz.

A *Poupeton* of Tunnies.
Filets of Perches, with green Sauce.
Farced Oisters.
A *Haricot*.
Filets of Soles, with *Truffles*.
Bouillans.
Soles broiled on the Grid-iron, with Anchovies.
And a Pie with white Sauce.

For the Roast.

Two middling Dishes; each of six Pikes and four Soles.
Two others lesser, of two Sandlings and four Soles round about.
The rest of the Service consists of divers Intermesses and *Filets* in a Sallet.

For the Supper.

Two middling Potages, *viz.* one of an *Oil* and the other of Muscles.
Two lesser; one of Sea-ducks with Lentils, and the other of Soles with Cucumbers.

Side-dishes.

A great Dish of Thorn-back.
Four others, *viz.* one of Roches, one of Quavivers in a Fricassy of Chickens, one a Pie, and one of *Grenots*.

The Out-works.

Soles *à la Sainte Menehout*.
Filets of Perches, with white Sauce.
Filets of Dabs, with Anchovies.
A Hash.
Tenches.
A farced Cabbage.
Quavivers, with *Mousserons*.
A *Casserole*.

For

For the Roast.

Two middling Dishes; each of seven Soles.
Two lesser, one of a Carp and the other of a Pike.

An Ordinary for another Day.

Potages.

TWo middling Potages; one of farced *Grenots* and the other of Pike, with Oisters.

Four lesser ones, *viz.* the first of Spinage, the second of Lentils, the third of farced Soles upon the Edges, and the fourth of Onions, with a Loaf in the middle.

The Side-dishes.

A Pike-pye, for the great Dish.
Two others; the first of broiled Tunnies and the second of Sandlings.

The Out-works.

A *Miroton.*
Sole-*Pains.*
Filets of Carps, with Cucumbers.
Filets of Soles, with Cullises of Capers.
Quavivers broil'd upon the Grid-iron.
Roches farced.

For the Roast.

Two middling Dishes; each of twelve Soles and two lesser; each of two Sandlings.

The Supper.

Potages.

Two middling Potages, *viz.* one a *Julian*, and the other of Sole-*filets.*
Two lesser; one with Parmesan, and the other of farced Crab-fish.

The

The Side-dishes.

The great Dish of Whitings in a *Casserole*.
Four middling Side-dishes, viz.
One of Mackerel.
One of fresh Cod-fish.
One of a *Poupeton* of Tortoises.
And one of Roches breaded and broil'd upon the Grid-iron.

Eight Out-works, viz.

A farced Loaf.
A *Gatoe* of Soles.
Quavivers, with Cucumbers and *Mousserons*.
Soles after the Spanish Way.
Lobsters in a Hash.
St. *Peter's* Fish, with white Sauce.

The Roast.

A large Dish of a Turbot and a Dab, garnish'd with Roches.

Two middling Dishes, *viz.* one of Shads and the other of fresh Salmon.

These Models are more than sufficient for the regulating of a considerable Ordinary. As for others that are less sumptuous it were requisite only to provide as many Out-works, as there are Potages; to the end that the former may be served up, when the others are taken away. In like manner the rest of the Messes may be proportioned for the second Course, every one accordingly as the Expences will admit of. Let us now take an Account of the Provisions of Roots.

Enter-

Entertainments with Roots.

The First Course.

Potages.

SIx in number, four middle ones and two lesser, *viz.*
A Potage of young Onions, with a Loaf in the middle.
One of Lentils with Oil, garnish'd with fried Bread.
One of Asparagus, with green Pease-soop.
And a Potage without Butter.
The two lesser Potages are, one of Almond-milk, garnish'd with crisp Almonds and the other of *Morilles*.
An *Oil* or Potage of Roots may also be served up and Sallets with Oil.

The Side-dishes.

A Dish of Lentils in a Ragoo, with fine Herbs.
One of Pease-soop, with fine Herbs.
One of French Beans.
One of Roots in a Ragoo.
One of Potatoes.
One of other different sorts of Herbs.
And four Dishes of Oisters.

The Second Course.

For the Roast.

Take several sorts of Roots, as Parsnips, Carrets, Turneps, Potatoes, Goats-bread, Parsley-roots, &c. Let them be well scrap'd and scalded: As soon as they are ready, take a Stew-pan, with a sufficient quantity of good Butter and Onions shred small. When the Butter turns somewhat reddish, throw in a handful of fine Flower, as also the Roots; which are to be fried and well seasoned. Afterwards the whole Mess is to be chopped upon a Table to make a *Farce*, mixt with a little Parsley and *Chibbol*, all sorts of fine Herbs, some Pieces of *Truffles* and Mushrooms, a Slice of Butter, a few Crums of Bread and Milk-cream. Thus this Farce is to be made delicious, not too fat and seasoned according to Art.

With

With the same Farce, all sorts of Fish may be represented upon Plates, at Pleasure, *viz.* Soles upon one, a Turbot upon another, Flounders upon a third; upon others, Roches, Quavivers, Mackerel, &c. A little Butter must be put into every Plate under the Farce that is thus formed in the Shape of Fish. Afterwards they are to be neatly breaded on the top and baked in an Oven. As for the Soles in particular, they may be made upon a Leaf of Patience or Monks-rhubarb, which very much resembles their Shape, and fried with a great deal of ease.

Carrets may likewise be taken, and more especially red Beets which being well scrap'd and boil'd according to Discretion, each Root a-part, are to be cut into large Slices; some in the Shape of Soles, others like Quavivers, and so of the rest: Then they are to be left in a Pickle, for a little while, till, with fine Flower, Salt and white Wine a proper Batter be made, like that of Apple-fritters, to cover the Roots, before they are fried with fresh Butter and Oil; every thing a-part. Thus they are to be fried as other *Marinades*; as well as Goats-bread and other Roots, of which one or two Dishes may be prepared for the Roast.

To diversifie them, 'tis requisite to have separate Ragoo's of several sorts; *viz.* some of minced Mushrooms, others of *Truffles*, others of Asparagus-tops and others of *Morilles*: As also a good *Sauſſe-Robert* a-part and white Sauce, without any Anchovies therein; which may serve chiefly for the Dishes that represent the shape of Fish and are made of a Farce. They are to be garnish'd with a little fried Bread, fried Parsley, pickled Roots fried in Paste, Artichoke-bottoms fried in Paste, and some Pieces of Cucumbers.

For the Intermeſſes.

A Dish of Asparagus in Cream.
A Tart of Almond-milk and Cream.
A Dish of burnt Cream.
One of *Morilles* in Cream.
One of Asparagus in a Sallet.
One of Jelly of Harts-horn.
A *Blanc-manger.*
Mushrooms breaded and baked.
Cabbage in a Sallet.
Spinage in Cream.

French

French Beans in the Cod preserv'd dry; some served up in a Sallet and others in Cream.
Pickled Artichokes, with white Sauce.
Dried *Truffles*, with Oil.
Apple-fritters.

This last Entertainment was prepared as a Dinner for the Duke of *Orleans*, on Good-friday, *Anno Dom.* 1690.

To that purpose, a sufficient quantity of Roots was provided the Day before, and three or four Tables were fill'd with them. They were pick'd, scrap'd and scalded according to the usual manner, as well for the Ragoo's and Side-dishes, as for the Roast; so that in the Morning, every thing was ready for the Farces.

A considerable quantity of Peas was likewise boil'd in the Evening, which serv'd to make a great deal of Onion-broth and to soak the Herbs and Roots for the *Oil*.

Altho' there needs no great variety of Messes on such Days, yet it will not be improper here to shew, how the preceding Particulars may be diversified or augmented; because they may serve upon other occasions during the whole Season of Lent.

For the Potages.

They may be made with,
Young Sprouts.
Ciboulets with Milk.
Mousserons and common Mushrooms.
Green Peas.
Truffles.
Turneps.
And Artichoke-bottoms.

For the Side-dishes and Intermesses.

Besides the ordinary Creams, Fritters, *Blanc-mangers* and Roots dipt in Butter and fried, which have been already describ'd, several Pies and Tarts may be made of some; particularly of Spinage, *Truffles*, *Morilles*, *Mousserons*, common Mushrooms, Plums, red Beets, &c. To these may be added Eggs and *Omelets*, disguised after divers manners; and for those that are eaten with Butter, several sorts of Roots may be dress'd with white or red Sauce: Thus a very great Entertainment may be easily prepar'd par'd upon any emergent occasion, and such Materials as are at hand, may be managed so as to give satisfaction, as far as the Abstinence of the Season will admit.

It remains only, that the particular Sallets be specified; because a greater quantity of them than ordinary, is requisite on that Day.

A List of the Sallets.

Artichokes,	Lettice,
Asparagus,	Mushrooms stewed,
Red Beets,	Olives,
Cardoons,	Oranges,
Celery,	Parsley of *Macedonia*,
Colly-flowers,	Pomegranates,
Cucumbers fried,	Potatoes,
Escreffionaire,	Purslain,
French Beans,	Young Sprouts,
Goats-bread,	Wild Succory,
Hops,	*Truffles.*
Lemmons,	

Let us now proceed to the main Point of the Business, and to the practical Part of this Work: Indeed the general *Ideas* that have been already given may be sufficient for Stewards, Purveyors and Caterers, who are thereby plainly instructed as to the particular Provisions to be bought, and in the Method of Ordering the Entertainments committed to their Charge. But some farther Directions are necessary for those that are Students in the Art of Cookery: 'Tis requisite to explain to them the Manner of Preparing every Mess, to the end that they may go on successfully in their Business without any difficulty; and this is what we undertake to do in the ensuing Treatise; without concealing any thing that is most *à-la-mode*, or most in use at the Court of *France*, and in the Houses of Persons of the greatest Quality: Such are the Entertainments that we have already produced for Models.

I N-

INSTRUCTIONS

IN

Form of a DICTIONARY,

DIRECTING

How to Drefs every particular Mefs, and how to Serve them up to Table, for the Side-difhes, Intermeffes and Roaft-meats, or otherwife, after the beft manner.

A.

ALMONDS.

Almonds ferve for feveral Ufes; particularly, to make Pafte, Potages, Almond-milk and Pies; and green Almonds are fometimes boil'd: All thefe Things are prepared according to the following Method.

Almond-pafte.

Take Almonds that are well fcalded and wafh'd in fair Water: Pound and moiften them with a little White of an Egg and Orange-flowers, whipt together; and, as you are working them, continue to moiften them by degrees, that they may not turn to Oil; they cannot be pounded too much: The Pafte thus prepar'd, is to be fpread upon a large Difh, and dried with fine Sugar, as if it were ordinary Pafte, till it becomes very pliable. This Pafte may ferve to make the Bottom or Under-cruft for Pies, and all forts of fmall Paftry-works to garnifh them; but 'tis requifite to let it lye by a little

little while, before you proceed to make use of it according to your Design.

The same may also be done after another manner, thus: When the Almonds are sufficiently pounded and moisten'd as before, take a Copper-Pan, such as Confectioners use, and put into it a greater quantity of Sugar than of Paste; which Sugar is to be clarified with the White of an Egg, and boil'd till it becomes feathered: Then put in your Paste, and with a *Spatula* work all well together. Set your Pan over the Furnace, and keep continually stirring it as much as is possible, until the Paste be loosen'd from the Pan. Afterwards it must be spread upon a Dish, with fine Sugar underneath, and rolled up in large Rolls, that it may lye by for some time, before it be us'd. It may be workt several ways, that is to say, squeez'd thro' a Syringe; and form'd into divers Figures. As for the Shreds or Remnants that are left, when dried, you need only put them into the Mortar, and pound them with a little White of an Egg, in order to soften them, and this will serve to make small *Petits Choux* or other fine Ornaments for the garnishing of the Dishes.

Almond-milk.

Almond-milk is us'd for the Intermesses, and made thus: Take Almonds, and having scalded them in order to Blanching, pound them in a Mortar, as before: Then take a little Milk, and be careful to strain all thro' a Sieve; which being done, take four Yolks of Eggs with the Whites, beaten together, and pour some Milk upon them, by degrees; adding also a little Salt and Nutmeg. In order to boil it, set a Kettle or Pot with Water upon the Furnace, and when it boils, put a Dish upon the Kettle, with a slice of very good Butter. Afterwards pour your Almond-milk into this Dish, and let it be continually stirr'd, till it becomes a Cream, which must be served up to Table hot without any Sugar.

Potage of Almond-milk.

Take a Pound or two of Almonds, according to the size of your Dish; and let them be scalded, and pounded all at once; moistening them with a little Water: When they are well pounded, set a Stew-pan on the Fire, with some luke-warm Water, and

and a very little Salt: Pour this Water into the Mortar, and strain all through a Sieve two or three several times. Then put this Milk into a clean Pot, with a lump of Sugar and a little piece of Cinnamon, and boil all together by degrees. To dress the Potage, cut the crummy part of a Loaf into Slices, and and put them in good order upon a Dish: When these Slices are toasted at the Fire, lay your Potage of the same Milk a soaking, and when 'tis ready to be serv'd up, moisten your Sippets with it, as much as is requisite.

Some boil about two Quarts of Water in a Pot, and put into it the Crum of two small Loaves, which they mingle together with the Almonds in a Mortar, and afterwards let it soak in a Pot, for the space of three or four Hours, with Sugar and Cinnamon, as before: Then they strain and dress it in the same manner.

This Potage may be garnish'd with March-pane or crisp Almonds; the latter of which may be made after this manner, if you'll take the pains to do it. Take Almonds that are well scalded and drain'd: Then Sugar them, and put them all at once into a Frying-pan that you have ready at hand, with good hot Oil: They must be continually stirred and turned, till they become of a Gold-colour: Then take them out speedily, and make four or five Heaps of them; because they are apt to stick together.

An Almond-Tourte or Pan-pie.

Take about two good Handfuls of sweet Almonds, and, as you are pounding them, sprinkle them with Orange-flower Water: Add thereto some candy'd Lemmon-peel, some Peel of green Lemmon and Sugar, and pound them all well together, with a very little fine Flower: Let the Whites of two Eggs be beaten up and pour'd therein, with three Yolks, and when the whole Farce is well mixt, let it be put into a little Dish. In the mean while, a sort of Paste is to be made with Flower, Butter, the Yolk of an Egg and a little Salt; but great care must be taken that this Paste be duly prepared. Then a piece for the Under-crust is to be rolled out and put into the Pie-pan, with a little Border round about it, made with the point of a Knife. When 'tis time to have the Pie bak'd, the prepared Farce is to be put into it, so as to fill up the whole Bottom-crust. Afterwards it must be iced with a little fine Sugar, and set into a Campain-Oven;

Oven; taking care of the Fire on the top, and continually supplying that underneath.

How to dress green Almonds.

When you have green Almonds, set a large Copper-Pan or Skillet upon the Fire, filled with Water and Ashes: Scum off the Coals that rise on the top, and when this Liquor has boil'd a great while, and you perceive by the Taste, that 'tis become sweet and slippery, as it were a perfect Lye, throw in your Almonds and let them have three or four Walms: Then take them out and put them into other fresh Water: Thus they are to be wash'd in four or five Waters, and afterwards a Pan is to be set on the Fire, with Water almost ready to boil. Put the Almonds into that Water, and to prevent their swimming on the top, thrust down into the Pan a Dish of almost the same breadth, yet so as to be conveniently let into it; by which means the Almonds will be hinder'd from becoming black. A good Fire must be continually kept underneath, and in case the Water inclines to boil, some other cold Water is to be pour'd in by degrees to give it a check. Thus your Almonds are to be dress'd with a moderate Heat; and to know whether they are sufficiently scalded, take a Pin and prick an Almond quite thro': If it stick to the Pin, 'tis a sign they are not yet well scalded; but if it be loose, it denotes that they are. Then, having taken them out, put them again into fair Water, and afterwards into good Syrup of clarified Sugar. In order to serve them up liquid, 'tis requisite that one half of your Sugar be in a Jelly; and to keep them dry, as soon as your Almonds are scalded in the aforesaid manner, take them out and let them be well drain'd: Boil your Sugar till it be greatly feather'd, and see that it be not thick, but of a fine gloss, to the end that the Almonds which are put therein, may appear very green. The same thing may be done with green Apricocks to preserve them liquid and dry.

ANCHOVIES.

Anchovie-cullises are frequently made, and put into several Ragoo's, as well for Flesh as Fish-days, so that it were needless here to give a particular account of them; since that is sufficiently done in the respective places where they are to be us'd. We shall only observe at present, that the Bones of the Anchovies,

vies, which have been already made use of, may be fried, after having put them into a Paste made of Flower and white Wine, with a little Pepper and Salt: So that you may either garnish another Dish with that Paste, or serve it up to Table for an *Out-work*, with Orange and fried Parsley.

ANDOUILLES.

Andouilles or Chitterlings, are used for Side-dishes more than for Intermesses; those of Hogs-guts are made after the following manner.

Andouilles de Cochon, or *Hogs-chitterlings*.

Take the great Gut of a Hog, and cut off the thick end of it, to be steep'd in Water for a Day or two: When that is done, let it be well wash'd and parboil'd in other Water, with a little Salt and some Slices of Onions and Lemmons. Slit this Gut, and put a little white Wine upon it, to take away the ill Savour. When it is parboil'd, put it into fresh Water, and having brought it to the Dresser, cut it according to the length you would have your *Andouilles* or Chitterlings to be of. Take some part of the Hog's Belly, pare off the Fat and cut that Meat into thick Slices of the same bigness with your Chitterlings: Thus you may make them, with half of one and half of the other; seasoning them as much as is needful. Afterwards take the Skirts from the inside of which the small Gut ought to be cut off, let them be well cleansed and scrap'd likewise for some time, to take away the ill taste. Then cut them of the same length with your Chitterlings, and having tied up the ends of every one, put them neatly into the Skirts, so as they may be cover'd and bound up therein. When your Chitterlings are made, put them into a Kettle of Water with Slices of Onion, an Onion stuck with Cloves, two Bay-leaves and a little Leaf-fat out of the Hog's Belly: Let them be gently boil'd and well scumm'd, pouring in, after the Scum is taken off, a Glass or two of white Wine: Let them cool in the same Liquor, and afterwards take them out, but be careful to avoid breaking them. They are usually broil'd upon a Grid-iron with Paper under them and serv'd up to Table all at once.

A Potage of *Andouilles* may likewise be serv'd up with strained Pease and good Broth, and to that end, each is to be made

E 4   apart;

The Court and Country Cook.

apart; that of the Chitterlings with a Faggot of Herbs and a Piece of green Lemmon: But you are to put into the Peaſe-ſoop, ſome fine Herbs chopt ſmall and toſs'd up in a Pan with Lard. The Chitterlings are cut into round Slices, to be laid upon your ſoaked Cruſts, with white Pepper, Mutton-gravy and Lemmon-juice, when ready to be ſerv'd up to Table, and are garniſh'd with fried Bread and Slices of Lemmon.

Andouilles de Veau, or Calves-chitterlings.

After having well waſh'd and prepar'd the larger Calves-guts, cut them according to the length you would have your Chitterlings to be of, and tye up one of the ends: Then take a ſufficient quantity of Bacon, Calves-udder, and Calves-chal-dron, all parboil'd, and cut them into ſmall pieces in form of a Die: Put them into a Stew-pan and ſeaſon them with Spice beaten ſmall, and a Bay-leaf. There muſt be alſo ſome Pepper and Salt, with a few minc'd Shalots, and you may add about a Gallon of good Milk-cream. Set the whole Mixture over the Furnace, and afterwards draw back the Pan; into which you are to put four or five Yolks of Eggs, and a few Crums of Bread: Thus all being well thicken'd, proceed to make your Chitterlings hot, with a Funnel, and tye up their ends. Afterwards let them be parboil'd in Water and dreſs'd in the ſame manner as the Hogs-chitterlings: They are like-wiſe to be boil'd and left to cool in their Liquor; then let them be broil'd upon a Grid-iron, with Paper, and ſerved up to Table. Theſe ſorts of Chitterlings may be made in Summer, when Pork is out of Seaſon; as alſo in thoſe Countries, where no Hogs are kill'd throughout the whole Year, as it happens at Paris.

ANDOUILLETS.

Veal-*Andouillets* are made of minc'd Veal, Bacon, fine Herbs and the Yolks of Eggs, with Pepper, Salt, Nutmeg and beaten Cinnamon, ſo as to give them a fine colour; and in ſerving them up, ſome beaten Yolks of Eggs are to be added, with Verjuice and Lemmon-juice. Theſe *Andouillets* are to be roaſt-ed on a Spit between Slices of Bacon, and baſted with their Dripping, with the Yolks of Eggs and Crums of Bread, ſome-times one and ſometimes another, to produce a fine Cruſt upon
them:

hem: When they are ready to be ferv'd up, add fome Mutton-gravy, or of another fort, with the Juice of a Lemmon and fried Parfley to garnifh them.

Andouillets are likewife made of Fifh, with the Flefh of Eels and Carps minc'd or pounded in a Mortar, and feafon'd according to the ufual manner: With part of this Flefh, a *Cervelas* is to be made in a Linnen-cloth, and boil'd with white Wine, Butter and a Faggot of fine Herbs; and *Andouillets* are made with the reft, which are likewife to be boil'd in Butter, with Broth and a handful of fine Herbs. Then tofs up fome Mufhrooms in a Pan, with Carp-roes and a little fine Flower, and after having caus'd them to boil a little while, with fome Fifh-broth and green Lemmon; put them to your *Andouillets*. Thus they may be ferv'd up for Side-difhes, or elfe in Potage; dreffing them on your foaked Crufts, garnifh'd with *Cervelas* in Slices and with fome Slices and Juice of Lemmon.

ARTICHOKES.

There are feveral Ways of dreffing Artichokes to be ferv'd up for Intermeffes, and amongft others thefe are the chief, *viz.*

Artichokes with white Sauce.

Let fome fmall Artichokes be boil'd in Water, with a little Salt. When they are fufficiently boil'd, put the Bottoms into a Pan, with Parfley feafon'd with Salt and white Pepper, and prepare a Sauce for them, with the Yolks of Eggs, and a little Vinegar and fome Broth.

Artichokes dreſs'd with natural Butter.

When your Artichokes are boil'd, as before, take off the Chokes, and make Sauce for them, with natural Butter, Vinegar, Salt and Nutmeg.

Fried Artichokes.

Take away the Chokes, cut them into Slices and let them boil three or four Walms: Let them be fteep'd in Vinegar, with Pepper, Salt and Chibbols. Then, having flower'd them, fry them in Lard or refined Butter, and ferve them up to Table with fried Parfley.

Arti-

Artichoke-bottoms fried in Paste.

The Artichokes being boil'd and freed from their Chokes, make a Paste, with Flower, Water, Pepper and Salt, and put them into it in order to be well fried: Let them also be serv'd up, with fried Parsley and a little Rose-Vinegar.

Other Ways of Dressing them.

Artichokes in Cream are likewise prepar'd after the same manner as Asparagus; others *à la Saingaraz* and with Gammon-sauce, on Flesh-days; for which see Gammon-essence under the Letter G. and young Rabbets *à la Saingaraz* under R. And lastly, others *à l'Estoufade* or stew'd and iced. Artichokes are of very great Use throughout the whole Year, for almost all sorts of Ragoo's Potages and Side-dishes; so that 'tis requisite to provide good store of them, observing the following Directions.

The manner of preserving Artichokes.

Take so much Water, according to the quantity of your Artichokes, as will be sufficient to cover them, and let them boil, with Salt proportionably; then take them off from the Fire, and let them lye by, to the end that the Dross of the Salt may sink to the Bottom. Afterwards pour the Liquor, into the Pot, wherein you would have your Artichokes put; which ought to be well turn'd and only scalded, to take off the Chokes and Scum. They are to be wash'd in two or three Waters, and afterwards put into a prepared Brine or Pickle; pouring Oil or good Butter thereon, to hinder the Air from penetrating them; you may, also if you please, add a little Vinegar. They must be carefully cover'd with Paper and a Board over it, that the least Air may not be let in. Thus they may be kept for a whole Year, but before they are us'd, the Salt must be taken away, by soaking them in fresh Water.

Artichokes may also be preserv'd dry; and to that purpose, when they are Scalded, and the Chokes taken off as before, you are to spread them upon Grates or Hurdles of wattled Oziers, in order to drain them; then they are to be dry'd in the Sun, or in an Oven moderately heated; till they become

as

as dry as Wood. Before they are us'd, they are to be fteept in Luke-warm Water during two Days; by which means they'll return to the same Condition as when they were fresh, and will relish much better than when prepared after the other manner. They are to be scalded in Water, with a little Verjuice Salt and new Butter, on Fish-days, and with good Beef-fat on Flesh-days.

Asparagus.

Asparagus is eaten several Ways, and Potages are made of it, with different sorts of Fowl, or with green Pease-soop; of which divers Examples have been already produced. 'Tis also usually serv'd up in Intermesses, Out-works and other Dishes; sometimes in a Sallet, sometimes in white or thick Gra- and sometimes in Cream.

Asparagus in Cream.

Let your Asparagus be cut into small Pieces, and scalded a little in boiling Water: Then let them be toss'd up in a Stew-pan with fresh Butter, or with Lard, if you have no very good Butter; taking care that the whole Mess be not too fat: Then put into it some Milk and Cream, and season it well; adding also a Faggot of fine Herbs. Before this Dish is serv'd up to Table, it would be requisite to beat up one or two Yolks of Eggs, with Milk-cream, in order to thicken your Asparagus.

The same thing may be done in dressing Artichoke-bottoms and green Pease, but for the latter some Sugar is to be used, with a little chopt Parsley, and then they may be order'd in the same manner.

Asparagus may also be serv'd up among green Pease, with a green Cullis of Pease-cods or somewhat else: Then put a Crust of Bread in the middle, and garnish your Dish round about, with *Pain de Jambon*.

Asparagus in Gravy.

Dress your Asparagus cut into Pieces, with Lard, Parsley, Chervil chopt small and a *Ciboulet*: Season them with Salt and Nutmeg, and let them soak in a Pot over a gentle Fire: Then take away the Fat, put therein some Mutton-gravy and Lemmon-juice, and serve it up, with short Sauce.

Asparagus with natural Butter.

Boil your Asparagus in Water, with a little Salt; prepare a Sauce with Butter, Salt, Vinegar and Nutmeg or white Pepper, continually stirring it; and pour it upon the Asparagus, when they are dress'd. There is nothing in this Article, that is not sufficiently known, as well as what relates to Asparagus in a Sallet. For the Potages, you may observe by means of the General Table, those that are hereafter mentioned and under the Article of *Tourtes* or Pan-pies, the manner of making one of Asparagus.

To preserve Asparagus.

Cut off the hard Stalks, and give them one seething with Salt and Butter: Throw them again into fresh Water, and let them be drain'd. When they are cold, put them into a Vessel, in which they may lie at their full length, with some Salt, whole Cloves, green Lemmon, and as much Water as Vinegar: Cover them with melted Butter, as 'tis usually done to Artichokes; putting a Linnen-cloth between, and keep them in a temperate Place. In order to make use of them, let them be steept and boil'd as the others.

B.

French BEANS *or* Kidney-beans.

The best Manner of Preserving and Dressing them.

FRench Beans may be preserved two several Ways, *viz.* either pickled with Vinegar, Water and Salt, as Cucumbers; or else dried, after they have been well pickt and scalded. They are usually dry'd in the Sun, and set in a Place that is not moist. To recover them, they are only to be steep'd in luke-warm Water for the space of two Days, and they'll resume almost the same Verdure that they had when first gather'd: Then let them be scalded and dress'd after the usual manner. As for those that are Marinated or Pickled; when they are sufficiently season'd in a Pot, with some Cloves and a little Pepper, they must be well cover'd, lest they should be

spoil'd

The Court and Country Cook.

spoil'd, and some melted Butter may be put upon them: As often as you have Occasion to use them, let them be soak'd in Water, as the others; to the end that all their Saltness may be taken away, and then they may serve either for Sallets or for Intermesses, after they have been scalded and put into Cream.

BEEF.

Forasmuch as Beef is a Thing no less common than necessary in Entertainments, 'tis requisite to devise several Ways of dressing it to the best Advantage, in order to make it delicious and graceful even on the most sumptuous Tables.

A short Rib of Beef, à la Godard.

Let the first short Rib of Beef, be Spitted and one half of it larded, with thick Slips of Bacon: When it is half roasted, take it off from the Spit, and put it into a Pot, after it has been well season'd, with good Gravy; a few *Truffles*, *Morilles*, common Mushrooms and Artichokes, only to give it a Relish: In the mean while prepare another Ragoo of *Truffles*, Mushrooms, *Morilles*, Artichoke-bottoms, Veal-sweet-breads, and Cocks-combs, all well thicken'd, which you are to put upon the short Rib; garnishing it with a *Marinade* of Chickens or marinated Cutlets.

A short Rib of Beef dress'd after the English Way.

Take a large short Rib of Beef, and let it lie two Days in Salt: Afterwards Spit it, and when 'tis well roasted, bread it and put a good Ragoo both on the top and underneath. Let this Dish be garnish'd with *Hatlets*, *Marinades* or roasted *Poupiets*.

A short Rib of Beef with Cucumbers.

Another middling Side-dish may consist of a short Rib of Beef, with a good Ragoo of Cucumbers, a few Shalots and fine Herbs chopt small; so as to give all a good Relish. It must be set out with marinated Veal-culets, fried Bread, or some other convenient Garniture.

A

A short Rib of Beef farced.

It may be farced with a *Salpicon*, of which see the manner under the letter S. Or else, when the short Rib is almost roasted, take some of the Flesh out of the middle, to be minced small with Bacon, Beef-sewet, fine Herbs, Spice and good Garnitures: Then farce your short Rib between the Skin and the Bone, and sow it up again neatly, lest the Meat should fall into the Dripping-pan, whilst you are making an end of roasting it. This Dish is to be garnish'd with *Fricandoe's* or Scotch Collops, in form of larded Cutlets, with fried Bread, and when serv'd up to Table, the Skins are to be taken off, to have the Liberty of eating the Meat with a Spoon.

A great Side-dish of a Buttock of Beef.

Take a Buttock of Beef, as large or small as you shall think fit; lard it with Gammon and other Bacon, that is well season'd with Pepper, Salt, Coriander-seed, Cinnamon, Cloves and grated Nutmeg; as also Parsley, Onions and small Shalots, all well mixt together. Stuff as much of these as you can into the Bacon, and lard your Meat both on the top and underneath. Season it again with all your Ingredients, and put it into a Stew-pan to be marinated a little while, with Onions, Parsley, Shalots, Garlick, sweet Basil, Thyme, Verjuice, Slices of Lemmon and a little Broth. It must be left therein two Hours, and boil'd in the Evening for the next Day: It must be put in a Napkin, with thin Slices of Bacon, and the Napkin is to be wrapt up close, so that no Fat may enter. In the mean while, you are to choose a Pot that is fit for it, and a Silver-Plate is to be laid on the Bottom, to keep the Napkin or Meat from being burnt. For the seasoning of it, you may put therein about two Pounds of Leaf-fat taken out of a Hog's Belly, or of fresh Beef-sewet, according to the bigness of the Piece of Beef; adding some Verjuice, white Wine, Ginger, Cinnamon, long Pepper, Slices of Lemmon, Nutmeg, Onion, Parsley Bay-leaves, as much Salt as is requisite, sweet Basil and Coriander whole, Fennel and Anis. Having put all into the Pot, cover it, and let your Piece of Beef be stew'd very gently: When 'tis sufficiently boil'd, let it cool in its own Fat; then make a great *Godivoe*, which is to be put into the Dish, in which the Piece

of

of Beef is to be drefs'd; cover it with the fame *Godivoe*, and fet it into the Oven for an Hour. In order to bring it to Table, a well feafoned Beef-cullis is to be prepar'd; then make a round Hole on the top of the *Godivoe*, to pour in your Cullis, fo as to penetrate into every part, and the Juice of a Lemmon thereupon. This fort of Beef may be ferv'd up cold in thin Slices inftead of Beef *à la Royale*.

A Side-difh of a Piece of Beef.

Take the hinder part of a Buttock, larded with thick Slips of Bacon, and having put it into a Pot or Kettle with two Pounds of Lard, fome good Slices of Bacon and the neceffary feafoning Ingredients, let it boil very gently, about two Hours: Take care that it be corned, and that no Air comes to it, when 'tis boiling. At leaft, you may put a little Brandy thereto, and garnifh it with *Marinade*.

Another Side-difh of a Piece of Beef.

Let a Buttock of Beef, moderately corned, be put into a Pot, with all forts of fine Spices and Onions. Having fill'd the Pot with Water, let it boil and be well fcumm'd: Then fome good Meat-gravy is to be put therein to enrich it. When 'tis boil'd and ready to be drefs'd in its Difh, you muft take away a little of the Fat from the top, and put upon it a Gammon-hafh, garnifh'd with a *Marinade* of larded Veal fried, and farc'd Cucumbers, according to the Method hereafter defcrib'd; or elfe with Artichoke-bottoms cut into two pieces, and Veal Sweet-breads, all fried and fteept in the fame manner as the Cucumbers.

A Side-difh of Beef-ftakes rolled.

Having cut fome good Slices or Stakes of Beef, beat them flat on the Dreffer, with a Cleaving-knife: For example, Take three or four large Slices, according to the fize of your Difh, and make a farced Meat of Capons-flefh, a piece of a Leg of Veal, Bacon, tried Sewet, boil'd Gammon, Parfley and Chibbols, with fome Veal-Sweet-breads, *Truffles* and Mufhrooms, all minc'd and well feafon'd with Spice and fine Herbs. To thefe are alfo to be added three or four Yolks of Eggs with a little Milk-cream,

cream, and when your Farce is well minc'd, lay it upon the Beef-ſtakes, which are to be neatly roll'd up, till they become very firm and compact, and of a convenient thickneſs. Thus they are to be ſtew'd over the Fire for a conſiderable time; then take them out of the Pot, drain off the Fat, cut them into two pieces, and dreſs them in a Diſh, on the ſame ſide that they were cut, which is uppermoſt. When they are ſet in order, ſome Ragoo or Cullis may be put upon them, and nothing elſe.

This Farce may ſerve for ſeveral ſorts of Fowl, when in great Entertainments there are many to be farced. It may alſo be uſed for ſcollop'd Veal, farced *Fricandoes* and other Things. Side-diſhes and Out-works of the like nature, are uſually made with Veal-ſtakes dreſs'd after the ſame manner.

A Side-diſh of a Piece of Beef, with Cucumbers.

Take a Piece of good tender Beef and roaſt it, barded or cover'd with thin Slices of Bacon, and wrapt up in Paper; but let it not be over-done: Then cut it into *Filets* or ſmall thin Slices, and put them into a Diſh. In the mean while, ſome Cucumbers are likewiſe to be cut into Slices, according to the quantity of the *Filets*; but they muſt be marinated: Squeeze them, and put them into a Stew-pan with ſome Lard to be well ſtew'd over the Furnace. Afterwards drain off all the Lard, throw in a little Flower and toſs them up again a little while: Laſtly, Soak them with good Gravy, proportionably to the quantity of your *Filets*. When they are ready, ſome good thickening Liquor muſt be put in, to make the Ingredients incorporate well together; a Spoonful of Gammon-eſſence, would be excellent for that purpoſe: Add to theſe, a little Verjuice or Vinegar, and let not your *Filets* boil any longer left they ſhould grow hard. They are to be ſerv'd up hot to Table, and garniſh'd with fried Bread, Marinades, or *Riſſoles*.

All other ſorts of *Filets*, with Cucumbers, may be made in the ſame manner.

Another Side-diſh of Beef-Filets.

Another Side-diſh may be prepar'd with Beef-*Filets* larded, and marinated with Vinegar, Salt, Pepper, Cloves, Thyme and Onions, which are to be roaſted by a gentle Fire: When they

The Court and Country Cook.

they are ready, put them into good Gravy with *Truffles*, and garnish them with marinated Chickens or Pigeons, or with *Fricandoes*.

Other Courses of Beef.

Some small pieces of Beef may be serv'd up for Out-works, which are to be a little corn'd and garnish'd with Parsly; but if it be a middling Side-dish, it may be garnish'd with what you shall think fit. They are also put into Gravy, when minc'd very small, with a Shalot, or a Clove of Garlick, and chopt Parsly.

A piece of Brisket-beef may be put into a Pot, and when parboil'd, larded with thick Slips of Bacon season'd with Salt, Pepper, beaten Cloves and Nutmeg; and the boiling of them may be finish'd in an Eatthen Pan, with thin Slices of Bacon at the Bottom, Pepper, Salt, a Bunch of Herbs, a little White-wine, green Lemmon, Bay-leaves and Broth. When 'tis boil'd, put thereto a Ragoo of Mushrooms, Oisters, Capers and stoned Olives, all well thicken'd; as also Lemmon-juice, when ready to be serv'd up to Table, and let it be garnish'd with Slices of the same.

For the Sauce with Vinegar and Pepper; take a Beef-stake, let it be well beaten, larded with thick Slips of Bacon, and boil'd in Water, with a Glass of White-wine; seasoning it high with Pepper, Salt, Cloves, Bay-leaves and a Faggot of Herbs. Let the Broth be well soaked, and when cold, the Stake being in the same Pot, it may be serv'd up with Lemmon-slices and a little Vinegar.

Beef-stakes may also be put into a Pie; to which purpose see that of a Fillet of Veal, under the Letter P, and observe the same Method; except that the Beef-stake Pie requires longer time in baking. But you must by no means forget to make a Hole therein, when put into the Oven, and to stop it up, when taken out.

Beef *à la Mode*, ought to be well beaten, larded with thick Slips of Bacon, and, if you please, stew'd in a Pan, before it be boil'd, with Pepper, Salt, Bay-leaves, green Lemmon, half a douzen of Mushrooms, a Glass of White-wine and two Glasses of Water: It may likewise be stew'd in its own Gravy, close cover'd over a gentle Fire. When 'tis boil'd, fry some Flower in a Pan, with Lard, which may be put thereto with Lemmon-juice.

The

66   *The Court and Country Cook.*

The Palate of an Ox is frequently us'd in *Mine-droit*, or *Menu-droits*, for which see the Letter M.

BISKETS.

The Manner of Making Savoy-*biskets.*

There are several sorts of Biskets very common, but for those that are call'd *Savoy*-biskets; take three or four new-laid Eggs, more or less according to the quantity of Biskets you intend to make: Then having provided a pair of Scales, put the Eggs into one, and some baked Flower into the other: Lift them up to render the Weight equal on both sides; for example, if four Eggs were put in, you are to take out one, and leave the three others: Weigh out as much fine Sugar pounded to Powder, as the weight of the Eggs amounts to, and take away the four Whites, to make as strong a Snow of them as possibly can be. Having minc'd some green Lemmon-peel, reduce it as it were to Powder, and mix it with the Flower that was weigh'd a little before: Beat them up a little, put some Sugar thereto, after having beaten them again, add some Yolks of Eggs, and whip all together for some time. Afterwards let the Biskets be made upon Paper, either in a round or long Form, at pleasure, and they may be neatly iced with Sugar beaten to Powder. They are to be bak'd in an Oven, taking care that it be not too hot, and as soon as they are done, cut them off from the Paper, with a thin Knife. They are us'd for Fruit or to garnish certain Pies.

Another sort of Biskets.

Take three or four Eggs, according to the quantity of Biskets you are desirous to make, and beat them up a little while; to which add as much rasped Sugar as you can take up between your Fingers at four or five times, with some Lemmon-peel, and mix all together, with four or five Spoonfuls of baked Flower. This Compound is to be laid upon Paper that has been strew'd thick with Sugar, and some Sugar being likewise strew'd on the top, set into the Oven, to be dried. When it is drawn out, cut the Biskets, all at once, with the Paper underneath, according to the bigness and shape, you would have them to be of, and with a Pen-knife cut off the Paper gently,

for

for fear of breaking any of them; which may be eafily done, becaufe they ought to be very dry. Thefe Biskets ferve, as the former, either for Fruit, or to garnifh Pies.

There are feveral other forts of Biskets, but befides that they fcarce differ in any thing, except the Name; it is the peculiar Province of the Confectioner: Therefore the inquifitive Readers are referr'd to the Inftructions that have been already publifh'd for the ufe of thofe Perfons.

BISKS.

Thefe forts of Potages are made with Quails, Capons and large fat Pullets, and moft commonly Pigeons; fo that we fhall firft fhew the manner of preparing the laft.

To make a Bisk of Pigeons.

Take Pigeons newly kill'd; fcald, pick and parboil them, and let them be ftew'd, in clear Broth, with feveral *Bards* or thin Slices of Bacon, an Onion ftuck with Cloves, and two Slices of Lemmon, all well fcumm'd. Set them on the Fire, only one Hour before they are us'd, according to their bignefs, and when they are drefs'd, lay them afide for a while. In order to make a proper Ragoo for them, 'tis requifite to take fome Veal-Sweetbreads cut into two parts, Mufhrooms cut into fmall pieces, *Truffles* in Slices, Artichoke-bottoms cut into four quarters, and one whole, to be put into the middle of the Potage. You muft carefully fry this Ragoo, with a little Lard, fine Flower, and an Onion ftuck with Cloves, and need not ftay till it grows brown. When 'tis thus drefs'd, put a little good Broth therein and ftew it, with a Slice of Lemmon. In the mean while, caufe to be boiled a-part in a little Pot, fome Cocks-combs well fcalded and pickt, with thin Slices of Bacon, Veal-fewet, fome clear Broth, a Slice of Lemmon and an Onion ftuck with three Cloves; but care muft be more efpecially taken, that the whole Mixture be well parboil'd: To which purpofe, ftrain a little Bread-crum, with only two Spoonfuls of good Broth thro' a Sieve. Your Pigeons, Cocks-combs and Ragoo being ready, make Sippets, with Crufts of Bread toafted at the Fire, and lay the Potage a foaking with good Broth: Then drefs the Pigeons therein, and the Artichoke-bottom in the middle; the Ragoo being put between the Pigeons, and the Cocks-combs

upon

upon their Stomacks: When the Fat is throughly taken away, pour in the reft of the Ragoo. At the fame time you are to provide a piece of Beef or Veal half roafted, which is to be cut in a Stew-pan or on a Difh, and to be fqueez'd hard, to get all the Gravy: It ought to be fet at a diftance from the Fire, to the end that it may become white; and when the Potage is drefs'd, fprinkle it with this Gravy, that it may be well marbled. It muft be garnifh'd with Lemmon, one half of which may be fqueez'd thereupon, and ferv'd up hot to Table.

Bisks of Quails and others.

Trufs your Quails neatly in the fame manner as Chickens, and drefs them with burnt Butter till they acquire a fine Colour: Then put them into a little Pot, with fome good Broth, Slices of Bacon, a Bunch of Herbs, Cloves, and other Things proper to feafon them; as alfo a piece of a beaten Beef-ftake, another of lean Bacon and fome green Lemmon, and let all boil over a gentle Fire. This Bisk muft be garnifh'd as the other, with Sweet-breads of Veal, Artichoke-bottoms, Mufhrooms, *Truffles*, *Fricandoes* and Cocks-combs, with the fineft of which you may make a Ring or Border round about the Difh; marbling the Potage with a Veal-cullis and Lemmon-juice, as it is a ferving up to Table.

The Bisks of Capons and fat Pullets are made after the fame manner as the preceeding, as well as thofe of young Barn-door Chickens.

As for Bisks of Fifh; chop fome Mufhrooms very fmall, and lay them upon the Crufts of Bread that are to be foaked with good Fifh-broth. The Ragoo may be made with Carp-roes, Pike-livers, the Tails and Claws of Cray-fifh, and Juice of Lemmon, garnifh'd with the fame.

BLANC-MANGERS.

Blanc-mangers are us'd in Intermeffes, or for middling Difhes or Out-works, and may be made thus: Take Calves-feet, and a Hen that is not very fat; let them be well boil'd without Salt and ftrain'd; taking care that it be not too ftrong nor too thin. If you have too great a quantity of Jelly, take out fome of it, putting fome Sugar, Cinnamon and Lemmon-peel to the reft, and let all boil a little while over the Fire, in a Stew-pan; after

ter having taken off the Fat. In the mean while, some sweet Almonds are to be provided, and if you please, seven or eight bitter ones among them, according to the quantity of your *Blanc-manger*: These are to be well pounded, and well moisten'd with Milk, that they may not turn to Oil. Then strain the *Blanc-manger*, that is not too hot, twice or thrice with the Almonds; wash the Sieves well, and strain them again once more, to the end that the Liquor may become very white. After having pour'd it into a Dish, ice it neatly, and pass over it two Sheets of white Paper, to take off the Fat. Let a little Orange-flower-water be put thereto, and when 'tis well congeal'd, serve it up cold to Table, garnishing it with Lemmon.

To make *Blanc-mangers* of divers Colours, see what is hereafter declar'd under the Article of *Jellies*.

A Blanc-manger *of Harts-horn.*

Take about a Pound of rasped Harts-horn, proportionably to the quantity you design to make, and let it boil for a considerable time; so that, dipping your Finger therein, you perceive that the Liquor is become as it were clammy; which is a sign that 'tis sufficiently boil'd. Strain this Jelly thro' a very fine Sieve, and pound the Almonds; moistening them with Milk and a little Cream. Then you must strain the same Jelly with these Almonds, three or four times, to render it very white, and put thereto a little Orange-flower-water.

If the Entertainment be made on Fish-days in Lent; for the Evening-course, the *Blanc-manger* must only be strain'd with pounded Almonds; squeezing a little Lemmon-juice therein, and no Milk is to be put into it. When 'tis ready it may be serv'd up in Ice.

BOAR'S HEAD, *see* HEADS.

BOUCONS.

To make *Boucons*, take a Fillet of Veal cut into small Stakes or Slices, that are somewhat long and thin, and beat them on a Table or Dresser: Then having prepar'd some small Slices of fat Bacon, with as many of raw Gammon, dispose them in Ranks a-cross your Veal-slices, that is to say, first one Slice of

F 3 Bacon,

Bacon, and then another of Gammon. Strew them with a little Parsley and Chibbols, and season them with Spice and fine Herbs. The Veal-stakes being thus cover'd with these Slices, are to be neatly roll'd up, as if they were *Filets Mignons* and broil'd upon the Coals. When they are dress'd, let the Fat be drain'd off, and serve them up hot, with a good Cullis, and a Ragoo of Mushrooms.

BOUILLANS

Are made thus: Take the Breasts of roasted Pullets or Capons, with a little Marrow, about the thickness of an Egg, some Calves-udder parboil'd, as much Bacon and a few fine Herbs, and put the whole Mixture well minc'd and season'd upon a Plate: Make some fine Paste and roll out two pieces, as thin as Paper: Wet one of them lightly with a little Water, and lay your farced Meat upon it in small heaps, at a convenient distance one from another: Cover them with the other piece of rolled Paste, and with the tips of your Fingers, close up every Parcel between the two Pastes; then with an Instrument proper for that purpose, cut them off one by one, and set the uppermost underneath; dressing them neatly, as if they were so many little Pies. Thus they are to be bak'd, and may be used for Out-works, or to garnish Side-dishes; but they must be serv'd up hot to Table.

BOUTON.

A Side-dish of a small Bouton.

Prepare a good well-season'd *Godivoe*, as for the *Poupeton*, according to the Method hereafter, described under the Letter G. Let it serve as it were for a Lay upon broad thin Slices of Bacon, that are capable of wrapping up your whole *Bouton*, and add thereto a good Ragoo of Mushrooms, Veal-Sweet-breads, Artichoke-bottoms, Cocks-combs, *Mousserons*, *Truffles* and Asparagus-tops dress'd with white Sauce. Then cover it again with another Lay of *Godivoe* and Bacon-slices, and let it be bak'd between two Fires, or dress'd otherwise. When 'tis ready to be serv'd up to Table, after the Fat is taken off, put some Lemmon-juice therein, garnish it with little farced Rolls, *Fricandoes* and *Marinades* intermixt.

The

The same thing may be done on Fish-days, making the *Godi-vœ* of the Flesh of Carps, Eels, Tenches and other sorts of Fish, well minc'd and season'd.

BRAISES.

We shall not here enlarge upon every Thing that may be bak'd or stew'd *à la Braise*, that is to say, between two Fires, *viz.* one on the top and the other underneath, which is a manner of Dressing that extremely heightens the Relish of Meat, and is very much in vogue. Some Examples of it have been already produc'd in the Article of *Beef*, and many others will be found hereafter, which shall be likewise explain'd in the respective Places to which the Things themselves belong, and if this be not always done, you need only consult the Articles that come near them, and have recourse for that purpose, to the Table of the principal Matters at the end of this Volume.

BROILING *upon a Grid-iron*, *see* GRILLADE.

BROTHS.

Altho' this Article might be referr'd to that of *Potages*, as properly belonging thereto; nevertheless we have judg'd it necessary to take notice of it in this place, to the end that the Reader may be freed from any Doubt that might arise concerning the different sorts of Broths which he has already observ'd or may meet with hereafter; or from the Pains he might otherwise take in searching for some Light in the matter elsewhere: Therefore we have here set down what is most remarkable, with respect to the Broths that are requisite, as well for the Potages, as for the Side-dishes.

Fat Broth.

Boil some part of a Buttock and Leg of Beef, with other Meats, and take out the Gravy and Broth; straining it thro' a Linnen-cloth: Let the same pieces be put a second time into the Pot, and having caus'd them to be well boil'd, take out the Broth again; keeping both these sorts hot a-part. The first will be of good use to be put to Capons, young Turkeys, Chickens, Quails, Veal and other farced Meats, that are to be serv'd up in white Potage. Capon or Veal-broth ought to be taken to soak young Pigeons for Bisks, and with the Broth of the Bisks, a Cullis may be made, for the Potages *à la Reine* and *à la Royale*. Lastly, The Broth of farced Meats will serve to make a Cullis for the same sorts of Meat, *viz.* young Turkeys and Pullets, Knuckles and Breasts of Veal, and other Joynts of Meat that ought to be farc'd and parboil'd.

The second sort of Broth taken out of the great Pot, is to be put into the brown Potages, particularly, those of Ducks, Teals, Rabbets, Ring-doves, Larks, Pheasants, Thrushes, Cabbage, Turneps and others; and the brown Ingredients which serve to thicken them, are to be mixt with the same Broth, without confounding that of one of these sorts, with the others. This Broth is also proper for the Side-dishes, and some of it may be used in boiling the Pickings of Mushrooms; of which the Pulp is to be taken out, to serve for that Cullis, for all the Potages, Side-dishes and Intermesses.

N. B. *The other sorts of Cullises are hereafter describ'd under the Letter* C, *and the Gravies under* G.

Morning-broth for Breakfast.

'Tis usually made with a piece of Buttock-beef, the scraggy end of a Neck of Mutton, a Neck of Veal and two Pullets. Take the Breasts of the Pullets when they are boil'd, pound them in a Mortar with a piece of Bread-crum, steept in some Broth; and all being well season'd, strain it thro' the Sieve, to be laid upon the Crusts soak'd in the same Broth that is then made.

The particular Broths for Potages *de Santé* and others are to be found in their proper Places, under the Letter P; only in favour of sick Persons, it may not be improper to subjoyn what may tend to their Advantage.

Jelly-broth for Consumptive Persons.

Put a Joynt of Mutton into an Earthen Pot, with a Capon, a Fillet of Veal and three Quarts of Water; which is to be boil'd over a gentle Fire, till one half be consum'd. Then squeez all together and strain the Liquor thro' a Linnen-cloth.

The Restaurative Broth is ranked among the Potages, under the Title of *Potage without Water.*

N. B.

N. B. *The following Liquors tho' not falling under the Order of the Alphabet ought to be inserted in this place,* viz.

Veal-liquor.

Having cut a Fillet of Veal into very thin Slices, let them boil in an Earthen Pot full of Water over a gentle Fire, for the space of an Hour; and then strain this Liquor thro' a Linnen-cloth, without squeezing the Meat.

Chicken or Pullet-liquor.

Put two or three Chickens or young Pullets into a Pot, with Water, and when they have boil'd two Hours over a gentle Fire, strain the Liquor thro' a Linnen-cloth; to which may be added Buglofs, Borage, Succory and other cooling Herbs, according to the Circumstances of the Patients and the Prescriptions of the Physicians.

Capon-liquor.

Let a Capon be set over a gentle Fire, in an Earthen Pot, with three Quarts of Water: When the Capon is boil'd, and one Pint of the Water wasted, take it out without squeezing.

Fish-broth.

This Broth is the chief Ingredient of all sorts of Fish-potages that can be prepar'd with the several Distinctions that are made for every one. To that purpose, cleanse Tenches, Eels, Pikes and Carps from their Slime, and cut off their Gills: Then put all into a great Kettle or Pot, with Water, Butter, Salt, a Faggot of fine Herbs and an Onion stuck with Cloves. When they have boil'd an Hour and half, strain the Broth thro' a Linnen-cloth, and pour some of it separately into three Pots: In one of them put the Pickings of Mushrooms, which afterwards are to be pass'd thro' the Sieve, with a Cullis, fried Flower and a piece of green Lemmon: This thickening Liquor may serve for the brown Potages, as also for the Side-dishes and Intermesses. In the second, may be put pounded Almonds, with the Yolks of hard Eggs, if the time will permit; and this is proper for white Potages, particularly those of *Profitrolles,* Smelts,

Smelts, Perches, Soles and other Fish dress'd in white Broth and for some Ragoo's of the like Nature. Lastly, in the third Pot, the Fish of all the Potages as well White as Brown, both for the Side-dishes and Intermesses may be boil'd together, and some Jelly may also be made of them.

Another sort of Fish-broth may likewise be prepared thus; Take a great Kettle or Pot, of a size proportionable to the quantity of Potage that is to be made. Hang it over the Fire, and put Water therein, with Parsly-roots, Parsneps, whole Onions, a handful of Parsly and Sorrel, all sorts of fine Herbs and good Butter, all well season'd. Add to these, the Bones and Carcasses of Fishes, whose Flesh has been taken to make Farces, and even the Entrails of those that have been farc'd, after having been well cleansed, and, if you please, some Cray-fish-tails pounded, with four or five Spoonfuls of Onion-juice. The whole Mess being well season'd and sufficiently boil'd, strain it thro' a Sieve, put it again into the Pot, and keep it hot, to lay the Soops a soaking, to prepare the Fish for the Potage, and for other Uses.

Broth on Fish-days, for the Potage with Herbs.

Let all sorts of good Herbs be put into a Pot, with two or three Crusts of Bread, season'd with Salt, Butter and a Bunch of fine Herbs: When they have boil'd an Hour and half, strain the Broth thro' a Linnen-cloth, or a Sieve. This will serve for the Potage *de Santé* without Herbs, and for many others; particularly for those of Lettice, Asparagus, Succory, Artichokes, Cardoons, &c.

A sort of Broth may likewise be made on Days of Abstinence, with Roots without Fish, and with clear Peas-soop; straining the whole Mess, as before.

BRUSOLES.

Take some Stakes, or Meat cut into Slices, beaten a little while with the back of a Knife, and put them into a Stew-pan, with several thin Slices of Bacon laid in order underneath: Strew them with Parsly, chopt Chibbols and Spices; continuing to make a Lay of the like sort of Seasoning, and another of Stakes, till at last you cover them well with broad Slices of Bacon, and set them between two Fires, on the top and underneath;

neath; after having caus'd the Pan to be close cover'd. When they are ready, a Cullis may be prepar'd with the Carcasses of Partridges: Then, having taken off all the Fat, put these Stakes into a Dish and pour the Cullis upon them: They are commonly call'd *Brusoles* or *Bursoles* in *French*, and are used for Side-dishes.

They may also be farc'd with a good *Godivoe*, minc'd and well pounded in a Mortar, with fine Herbs, Yolks of Eggs, Cream and the usual seasoning Ingredients; putting this farc'd Meat upon very large *Fricandoes* or *Scotch* Collops, that are to be wrapt up in broad Slices of Bacon and bak'd in a Pie-pan. As soon as they are ready, pour a Ragoo upon them, made of *Truffles*, *Mousserons* and a Veal-cullis to thicken them.

See under the Letter F. the Manner of Dressing farc'd *Fricandoes*, which have some relation to these *Brusoles*.

BURTS or *Bret-fish*.

In dressing Burts, you may endeavour to imitate the Method hereafter explain'd for Soles; for as to the Way of ordering them with natural Butter, or of making a Ragoo, by frying them in burnt Butter, after having cut off their Heads; 'tis so very common, that none can be ignorant of it.

Neither shall we insist on the Manner of stewing Bases, or other Appurtenances belonging to them; because 'tis only requisite to take Measures in those Cases, from other Things of the like Nature.

C.

CABBAGES and COLEWORTS.

AMong the Potages you may observe the Manner of those that are dress'd with Cabbages or Coleworts, for different sorts of Fowl, *viz.* Pigeons, Partridges, Wood-hens, Stock-doves, Pullets, Capons, Chicken, Ducks, &c. They may also be prepar'd with farc'd Cabbage, according to the following Directions; or else they may be serv'd up for Side-dishes, garnishing them with farc'd *Fricandoes*.

The

The Manner of Dressing a farc'd Cabbage for a Side-dish.

Take a good Cole-cabbage; cut off the Stalk, with a little of the Body, and let it be well scalded. Then take it out of the Water, spread it on the Dresser, so as the Leaves may lye together, and lay some farced Meat upon them, made of the Flesh of Fowls, a piece of a Leg of Veal, some parboil'd Bacon, Fat of boil'd Gammon, *Truffles* and Mushrooms chopt, Parsly, Chibbol and a Clove of Garlick; the whole Mixture being season'd with fine Herbs and Spice, with some Bread-crum, two whole Eggs, and two or three Yolks, all well minc'd. Your Cabbage being stuff'd with this Farce, let it be clos'd, neatly tied up and put into a Pot or Stew-pan. At the same time, take part of a Leg of Veal or of Beef cut into Stakes and well beaten; put them in order in a Pan, as it were to make Gravy: When they are colour'd, throw in as much Flower as you can take up between your Fingers, and let them be brought to a colour all together: Afterwards soak them with good Broth and season them with fine Herbs and Slices of Onion: When they are half boil'd, let the Cabbage, Stakes and Gravy be intermixt and all seathed up together, but be careful not to put too much Salt therein. All being thus made ready, dress them in a Dish without Broth, put a Ragoo upon them, as it may stand with your convenience, either *à la Saingaraz* or some other sort, and serve them up hot to Table.

A Cabbage may likewise be farced on Days of Abstinence, with some Flesh of Fish and other Things to garnish it, as if it were a Carp, Pike, or other Fish prepared to be farc'd.

How to make certain Ornaments call'd Petits-choux, *i. e.* Small Coleworts.

Take some Cheese that is very fat, such as the best sort of Cream-cheese, as much as you shall think fit: Let it be put into a Stew-pan, with two handfuls of Flower, proportionably to the quantity of Cheese, adding thereto some green Lemmon-peel minc'd, and some candy'd Lemmon-peel likewise cut very small: Then, taking a *Spatula* in your Hand, stir all together with a little Salt: When 'tis well mixt, put four or five Eggs therein, and make a sort of Paste or Batter like that of Fritters. Afterwards take some small Pie-pans, butter them on the inside, and
put

put a little of this Farce into every one of them: But before they are set into the Oven, they must be wash'd over with the Yolk of an Egg beaten up. As soon as they are bak'd, they may be ic'd over with fine Sugar, or a proper white Ice may be made for them, which is elsewhere described.

CAPONS.

It were needless here to make a Collection of the different sorts of Capon-potages; because they are particularly express'd in the General Table of the Messes. The Reader is also referr'd for the other Messes, that are made with Capons-breasts, such as *Tourtes* or Pan-pies, *Rissoles* and *Bouillans*, to the respective Letters of the Alphabet to which those Articles properly belong. And for roasted Capons, it may be observ'd with what Sauce they ought to be dress'd, under the Letter R; where every Thing is set down that relates to *The Roast*. Recourse may also be had, for those that are dress'd in a *Daube* to the Letter D; where Examples are to be found for other sorts of Fowl, which may be follow'd, without any difficulty, and so of the rest.

CAPONS-LIVERS, *see* LIVERS.

CARDOONS.

Pick your Cardoons very well, and leave nothing on them but what is good: Then, having cut them into pieces, let them be wash'd and scalded in Water, with a little Salt, Slices of Lemmon, Beef-sewet and *Bards*, or thin broad Slices of Bacon. On Fish-days, some Butter is usually put to them thicken'd with a little Flower. When they are scalded, let some good Gravy of a fine colour be prepared in a Stew-pan; drain the Cardoons and put them into that Gravy, with a Bunch of fine Herbs, some minced Beef-marrow and a little rasped Parmesan, and let them be stew'd in this manner, after they have been well season'd. Before they are set on the Table, a little Vinegar or Verjuice must be pour'd upon them, and care must be taken, that they do not turn black. They ought also to be well clear'd from the Fat, and so serv'd up hot for Intermesses, after having given them a colour with the red-hot Fire-shovel.

Cardoons are also broil'd in Broth and Gravy, with a thickening Liquor of a reddish colour: They are to be set in order in

a

a Dish or Plate, with a Crust of Bread underneath to make the *Dome* or Coronet. Strew them with rasped Cheese and a little grated Cinnamon, and bring them to a good colour.

CARPS.

A Side-dish of a Carp.

Leave the Carp with its Scales on, and make a Ragoo of *Mousserons*, or else of common Mushrooms, Fish-roes and Artichoke-bottoms: Then fry some Crusts of Bread, to be put into the Sauce as it is stewing, with Onions and Capers. When 'tis ready to be set on the Table and your Carp is taken up, without being broke, put the Ragoo upon it, and garnish it with fried Bread and Lemmon-juice.

Carp in a Daube.

Take a couple of Soles with a Pike; unbone them, and with their Flesh make farced Meat, chopping it small with a little Chibbol, beaten Spice, Pepper, Salt and Nutmeg. Then thicken this Farce with Yolks of Eggs, if the time will allow it, and you may try to do it with an *Andouillet* ready dress'd. Take one of the finest Carps you can get, stuff it with this Farce, season it with fine Herbs, and boil it with white Wine in an oval Stew-pan, over a gentle Fire. In the mean while, prepare a great Ragoo of *Mousserons, Morilles,* common Mushrooms, *Truffles,* Artichoke-bottoms and Cray-fish-tails strained. Keep your Ragoo a-part for a considerable time, and then pour it upon the Carp; which is to be dress'd upon an oval Dish, when ready to be set on the Table. It must be garnish'd with Cray-fish and Slices of Lemmon, and may serve for a great Side-dish.

Another Side-dish of Carps.

They are to be stuff'd with a well-season'd Farce soak'd in Cream, and then bak'd in an Oven: Garnish your Dish with Bread and Parsly fried, or with *Marinades.*

A Carp larded with Eel in a Ragoo.

When the Carp is fcal'd, lard it with thick Pieces of Eel and fry it in a Pan with burnt Butter. Then put it into a Diſh, with the ſame Butter, a little fried Flower and Muſhrooms; feaſoning it with Pepper, Salt, Nutmeg, Cloves, a Bay-leaf, a piece of green Lemmon, and a Glaſs of white Wine. As ſoon as it is dreſs'd, put thereto ſome freſh Oiſters and Capers, and let them ſoak together for a little while. This Diſh may be garniſh'd with Slices of Lemmon.

Farced Carps.

Let the Carps be fcal'd, and the Skin ſeparated from the Fleſh; leaving the Head and Tail: Make a Farce with the ſame Fleſh and that of an Eel, ſeaſon'd with fine Herbs, Pepper, Cloves, Nutmeg, Thyme, Muſhrooms and Butter. Farce your Skins likewiſe and ſow or tie them together: Then bake them in an Oven or otherwiſe, with burnt Butter, white Wine and Broth; pouring upon it ſome Butter well mixt with fried Flower and Parſly cut very ſmall. Let them be garniſh'd with Carp-roes, Muſhrooms, Capers and Slices of Lemmon.

Carp-Filets.

They may be mixt with Cucumbers and *Moufferons*, and 'tis only requiſite to follow the Directions ſet down for the Pike, under the Letter P, or thoſe for the Soles under S. The ſame thing ought to be obſerv'd with reſpect to the other ſorts of Fiſh, which we ſhall refer to their proper Places, to avoid needleſs Repetitions.

A Carp in a Demi-court-bouillon.

Cut a Carp into four quarters, leaving the Scales on, boil it with white Wine, or ſome other ſort of Wine, a little Verjuice and Vinegar, Pepper, Salt, Nutmeg, Cloves, Chibbols, Bay-leaves, burnt Butter and Orange-peel: Let the Broth be boil'd to a very ſmall quantity; add ſome Capers as it is a dreſſing, and Lemmon-ſlices to garniſh it.

Carps in a Court-bouillon.

Cut off the Gills and Entrails of your Carps and put them into a *Court-bouillon au bleu*, which is hereafter describ'd for the Pike under the Letter P: Then boil them in white Wine, with Verjuice, Vinegar, Onions, Bay-leaves, Cloves and Pepper, and serve it up to Table on a Napkin, with green Parsly and Slices of Lemmon, among the Intermesses.

Carps broil'd upon the Grid-iron.

Let your Carps be scal'd, and broil'd upon the Grid-iron, with Butter and Salt; whilst a Sauce is making for them, with burnt Butter, Capers, Anchovies, green Lemmon or Orange, and Vinegar, season'd with Pepper, Salt and Mustard. They may also be dress'd with white Sauce.

Potages of farced Carps and otherwise.

'Tis sufficient to have recourse to the preceding Article of *a farced Carp*, or to what is elsewhere specified concerning the Potage of a farced Pike. The latter may be garnish'd with Artichoke-bottoms, fried Oisters, Capers, Mushrooms in a Ragoo and in Slices, and Lemmon-juice.

Potage of *Profitrolles* is made with Carp-flesh minc'd, after the manner that shall be declar'd among the Potages for Fish-days.

For Carp-hashes, see the first Article of the Letter H, and look for Carp-pies, among those of Fish under P.

CASSEROLES.

Casseroles, take their Name from the Stew-pan in which they are dress'd, call'd *Casserole* by the *French*, and are generally used for Side-dishes and Potages: For the former, take a large Loaf wash'd over with Eggs, which must not be chipt on the upper side; bore a Hole therein underneath, and take away the Crum or Pith. Afterwards prepare a good Hash of roasted Chickens, fat Pullets, or some other sort of Roast-meat, and put this Meat well minc'd into a Stew-pan, with good Gravy, as if it were to make a Hash. When it is dress'd, put some of it with a Spoon into the Loaf, that was toasted at the Fire ; on the crummy side: After having thus pour'd in a little of this Hash, add some small Crusts of Bread, and proceed to fill up the Loaf alternately, with the Hash and small Pieces of Crust. Then take a Stew-pan that is no bigger than your Loaf; put a Sheet of Paper into it, or rather, some *Bards* or thin Slices of Bacon, and afterwards the Loaf on that side where it was farc'd; covering the bottom of it, with the same Loaf. Let it lye a soaking in this manner, with good Gravy; but it must not be too much press'd, nor too long steept, so that it may be kept altogether entire, and well cover'd. A little before 'tis serv'd up to Table, turn it out dextrously into a Dish, take away the Bacon-*Bards*, drain off the Fat, and cover your Loaf with a good Ragoo of Veal-sweet-breads, Artichoke-bottoms and *Truffles*; small tops of Asparagus being also spread round about the Dish, according to the Season.

A Casserole *with Cheese.*

The only difference is, that a little rasped Parmesan must be put into the farced Loaf, and when the same Loaf is dress'd in its Dish, it must also be strew'd with Parmesan. 'Tis usually brought to somewhat of a colour in the Oven, and the Ragoo put round about it. This is call'd a *Casserole* with Parmesan.

A Casserole *with Rice.*

Boil your Rice in a Pot, and make a Ragoo with *Morilles*, common Mushrooms, *Truffles*, Veal-sweet-breads, Cocks-combs and Artichoke-bottoms. If you please, the Combs and *Morilles* may be farc'd and dress'd a-part, and afterwards put into the Ragoo. Then make an Essence, with two or three Cloves of Garlick, sweet Basil, Cloves and Wine; let all boil together, strain the Liquor thro' a Sieve and pour it into the Ragoo. If you have a large fat Pullet, or any other tame or wild Fowl, to be serv'd up with your Soop, lay it in a convenient Dish, put the Ragoo to it, and cover it neatly with Rice; leaving a little Fat on the top, to render it smooth and cause it to come to a colour in the Oven; it must be serv'd up hot to Table. If there be no Fowl at hand, but only a good Loin of Mutton boil'd, put it in like manner into a Dish, when it is well dress'd, and cover it very thick with Rice: Then bread it, or rather

spread

spread on the top of it, some Fat, with Bacon and a few Chippings of Bread, to give it a colour.

See under the Letter S a Tail-piece of Salmon in a *Casserole*, and observe the same Method in ordering other sorts of Fish, that are to be dressed after the like manner.

CHEESE-CAKES.

To make Cheese-cakes, take some white Cheese that is very fat, and pound it well in a Mortar with a Lump of Butter as big as an Egg, and a little Pepper. When 'tis well pounded, put in a handful of Flower, a little Milk and two Eggs, and take care that this Mixture be not too thin. In the mean while, a fine Paste is to be made, and small pieces of it to be roll'd out, according to the bigness you would have the Cheese-cakes to be of. Put some of this Farce upon the pieces of Paste rolled out for the Under-crust; raise the sides with three Corners, as it were in form of a Priest's Cap, and pinch those Corners well with your Fingers, to the end that they may not fall or give way as they are baking: Then wash them over with an Egg well beaten, and set them into the Oven. They may be used in garnishing several Dishes.

CHICKENS.

We are now come to an Article that affords sufficient Materials for the making of a great number of different Side-dishes; let us then begin with the chief of them.

Chickens with Gammon.

Take Chickens, draw and truss them, but let them not be scalded: Cut some Slices of Bacon for every Chicken, beat them a little, and season them with chopt Parsly and Chibbols: Loosen the Skin over the Breast of your Chickens, to let in that Slice of Gammon, between the Skin and the Flesh, but more especially take care, that the latter be kept entire. Sindge them at the Fire, cover them with a good *Bard*, or thin Slice of Bacon, and let them be well roasted. When they are done enough, take off the *Bard*, pour some good Gammon-Sauce upon them, and serve them up hot to Table.

Chickens

Chickens farced with Oisters.

Take young Chickens, dress them as it were for roasting, and make a small Farce to stuff them with, between the Skin and the Flesh: To that purpose get some Oisters, a little Veal-sweet-bread, Mushrooms, *Truffles*, Parsly and Chibbols chopp'd, all well season'd and dextrously toss'd up in a Stew-pan, with a little Flower and strained Broth. The Chickens must be farc'd in the Body, well tied up at both ends, and roasted with a *Bard* on their Breasts. When they are ready, dress them in a Dish, pour a small Cullis of Mushrooms upon them, and serve them up hot to Table.

Chickens à la Mazarine.

Cut your Chickens, as if it were to make a white Fricassy, and set them a broiling upon the Coals; as the broil'd or fried Pigeons mentioned under the Letter P, with all sorts of fine Herbs: All being well dress'd, let them be neatly breaded and afterwards broil'd upon a Grid-iron. They may serve either for separate Dishes, or to garnish others, and are set hot upon the Table for a Side-dish; but they are not commonly fry'd, as Pigeons may be order'd. Many call these Chickens, Pigeons and other Fowls that are dress'd in this manner, *Pieces à la Sainte Menehout*. 'Tis requisite that the Bread, with which Chickens are breaded, be fine and white, to the end that it may take a good colour when they are broil'd.

A Side-dish of Chickens, with a Cullis of Cray-fish.

Take good fat Chickens, let them be well truss'd and roasted: If you are desirous to have them broil'd upon the Coals, they must be larded with thick Slips of Bacon and Gammon, accordingly as it shall be judg'd convenient. When they are dress'd either way, 'tis requisite to have a good Ragoo, made of all sorts of Garniture, and well season'd, *viz*. Veal-sweet-breads, *Truffles*, Asparagus-tops and Artichoke-bottoms, according to the Season. As soon as your Ragoo is made ready, the Chickens are to be put into it, which ought to have their Breasts somewhat beaten, to the end that they may imbibe the quintessence of the Sauce. Then take some Cray-fish, and let all their Legs

G 2   be

be well pounded, but neither their Thighs nor their Tails; because otherwise the Cullis would not be very red. Having pounded these in a Mortar, with a small Crust of Bread, soak them with some Gravy, or only the Legs, to the end that the Liquor may become more reddish. To thicken the Ragoo, prepare a Bread-cullis, and when all is dress'd, pour that of the Cray-fish into it: You may also add some Cray-fish-tails, and, if you please, an Anchovie. Take away the Fat from the whole Mess, and serve it up to Table.

Chickens à la Brochette.

Take Chickens, and cut them in the same manner as for a white Fricassy: Let some Lard be put into a Stew-pan, with a little Flower and afterwards the Chickens: When they are well season'd, soak them with good Gravy, and make an end of stewing them: Then prepare some Mushrooms and *Truffles*, as also a Glass of good *Champagne*-wine, a few Capers and minc'd Anchovies. If the Sauce be not sufficiently thicken'd, put a little good Cullis into it. The Chickens being thus well order'd and clear'd from the Fat, dress them neatly in a Dish, and pour the Sauce upon them. Let them be garnish'd with Cutlets, or any thing else, at pleasure, and serv'd up hot to Table.

Farced Chickens, with a Cullis of Mushrooms.

Take Chickens and truss them well, but do not parboil them. To make the Farce, take some raw Bacon, Marrow, Veal-sweet-breads, *Truffles*, Parsly, Chibbols, all sorts of fine Herbs, Capons-livers and Mushrooms, all chopt small, pounded together and well season'd. The same Farce may serve for Partridge-pies and all sorts of stuff'd Fowls, that are to be broil'd or roasted: Let the Sauce be thicken'd with two Yolks of Eggs. Roast your farc'd Chickens, well tied up and cover'd with Paper, and at last prepare your Mushroom-cullis, to which ought to be added a little Gammon, with some Capers, *Truffles* and Anchovies. Let the Chickens be dress'd in a Dish, with the Cullis pour'd upon them, and garnish'd with white Bread.

Chickens are likewise farced on their Breasts, after having taken out the Flesh, which is to be used for that purpose; but before they are serv'd up, they must be breaded, bak'd and brought to a fine Colour.

Chickens

Chickens à la Civette.

Take fat Chickens and trufs them well, in order to be roafted; parboil them, and cut off their Legs: Then let them be fteept in good Lard, about three or four Hours, with fome Slices of Chibbol, and feafon'd with all forts of beaten Spice and a little Salt: Afterwards they muft be roafted and bafted with the fame Lard. When they are dreffed, put to them a good Ragoo, or a Mufhrooms-cullis, or a Pepper and Vinegar-fauce, and let all be ferv'd up hot. The fame thing may be done for feveral forts of Fowl and even for fat Pullets à *la Sainte Menebout*.

Chickens drefs'd with Garlick.

Lard your Chickens with Bacon in Rows, and roaft them, after having firft ftuff'd them with fmall pieces of Garlick. Then make a good Pepper and Vinegar-fauce, or a Mufhroom-cullis, or a Ragoo of *Truffles*, putting a Clove of Garlick into it, and before the Difh is ferv'd up, fqueez the Juice of two Oranges into the fame Sauce.

Chickens in a Fricaffy.

Fricaffies of Chickens are made with white and red Sauce. For the latter, let the Limbs of the Chickens be flea'd, and fry'd with Lard. Then ftew them in a little Butter, Broth or Water, and a Glafs of white Wine, feafon'd with Pepper, Salt, Nutmeg, Chervil chopt very fmall and whole *Ciboulets*. Make a thick'ning Liquor, with fome of the fame in which the Chickens were drefs'd, with a little Flower; putting into it fome Veal-fweet-breads, Mufhrooms, Artichoke-bottoms and other Ingredients. Let them be garnifh'd with *Fricandoes* and roafted *Poupiets*, or Slices of Lemmon, and ferved up with Mutton-gravy and Lemmon-juice.

The Fricaffy of Pullets or Chickens with white Sauce is drefs'd with a good Thickening of three or four Yolks of Eggs, and Verjuice or Lemmon-juice. It may be garnifh'd with marinated Chickens and fried Bread and Parfly in the Intervals.

As for the Fricaffy of Chickens with Cream; when they are drefs'd as before, a little of the Fat is to be taken away, and Cream put to them, as they are ferving up to Table.

A

A Side-dish of Chickens à la Gibelote.

Take Chickens and cut them as if they were to be fricaffied: Then put them into a Stew-pan, and feafon them, in the fame manner as ftew'd Carps. Let Mufhrooms and other Garnitures be put to them, with a piece of Lemmon and fome Gravy in ferving them up to Table.

Another Side-dish.

Another Side-difh may be made of Chickens larded and roafted: When they are ready, put them into a Difh; cut their Joints and Legs, and pour upon them, a Ragoo of *Moufferons*, common Mufhrooms, Artichoke-bottoms, Veal-fweet-breads, Capons-livers and Capers.

Chickens drefs'd à la Braife or between two Fires.

Cut your Chickens thro' the Back to the Rump, and feafon them with Pepper, Salt, Chibbols, Parfly chopt very fmall and Coriander. Then let them be laid between thin Slices of Bacon, with their Breafts downwards, and heated, before they are fet between two Fires; one above and the other underneath. You may alfo add a little Gammon, a piece of Lemmon and a Faggot of fine Herbs: Chop the raw Gammon very fmall, ftrew it over your Chickens, and when they are ready, put their own Gravy upon them, as alfo fome Lemmon-juice at the very inftant of ferving them up. Thefe Chickens may alfo be farced, before they are drefs'd.

A Side-dish of boned Chickens.

Let the Chickens be farc'd with a good *Godivoe*, and drefs'd with red Sauce; whilft you are a preparing for them a Ragoo of Veal-fweet-breads, *Truffles*, Mufhrooms and Artichokes cut into fmall pieces: Let all be well feafon'd and fet out with *Marinades* or fome other proper Garniture, and Gravy put to them, as they are ferving up to Table.

Chicken-

Chicken-Filets, *for Out-works*.

They may be dress'd with white or red Sauce, and a Liquor to thicken them is to be made, of Bread-crum fried in Lard with fine Herbs, Broth and Lemmon-juice. Let all be strain'd thro' the Hair-sieve, with a little Gravy.

Chickens with Wood-cock *Sauce*.

They are to be dress'd with reddish-brown Sauce and a little Liquor to thicken them, or a Cullis of Wood-cocks: Then add an Anchovie chopt very small, with a *Rocambole*, or Clove of small Garlick, some Lemmon-juice and a little Wine. They are also us'd for Out-works and Side-dishes, as well as the following Messes.

Chickens in Gravy.

They are to be serv'd up without being either breaded or larded, only with a little fine Salt strew'd upon them; and may be garnish'd with small Crusts of Bread.

Chickens with Pike-sauce.

Let them be dress'd with brown Sauce, as in a Fricasly, and a chopt Anchovie put to them, with a Shalot, a few Capers, a little Vinegar, black Pepper, and Lemmon-juice, as they are serving up to Table.

Chickens, call'd Poulets-mignons.

After having farc'd your Chickens, lard them neatly, and cover them with a *Bard* or thin Slice of Bacon, and a Sheet of Paper. Then roast them on a Spit, and serve them up, with good Sauce.

Chickens dress'd after other manners.

Fat Chickens are likewise dress'd with *Truffles*; others *à la Tartre*, and others *à la Polacre*, with a *Ramolade*-sauce. Besides these, there are *Marinades* of Chickens; for which see the Let-

G 4   ter

ter M, and Chickens in *Civet* under C, as also Pies and Potages of Chickens, which are explain'd elsewhere under P, and Chicken-pies, with which we shall conclude this Article.

*A Chicken-*Tourte *or Pan-pie.*

Take Chickens and cut them as it were for a white Fricassy: Dress them with all sorts of good Garnitures, and make your Pie in the same manner as that of Pigeons, under the Letter P. Let a good Cullis be pour'd in, before it be serv'd up, and let it be well clear'd from the Fat.

When young Chickens are in season, let them is pickt and truss'd, as it were for boiling, but they must not be so much as parboil'd. Take away the Breast on the side of the Throat, as also all the Bones, if you please; but be careful nevertheless to keep the Skin entire: Take the Flesh with some pieces of Veal and chop them together, with a little Bacon, Marrow, *Truffles*, Mushrooms, Chibbols and Parsly; the whole Mixture being well season'd and bound with two Yolks of Eggs: Let this Farce be put into the Skin of the Chickens, that they may appear as it were quite whole, and let them be scalded a little in Water: Afterwards let them be laid in Paste, with all sorts of proper Garnitures. This Paste may be made very fine, with sweet Butter, Flower, Salt and two or three Yolks of Eggs. Some call this sort of Pie a *Tourte à la Parisienne*: As for the Cullis, it may be prepar'd according to your convenience. When the Pie is ready, take away the Fat carefully, and let it be serv'd up hot, garnish'd with its own Crust.

CHITTERLINGS, *see* Andouilles.

CIVETS.

Side-dishes of Chickens in Civet.

Let your Chickens be broil'd a little upon the Coals, and cut into Quarters: Then dress them with red Sauce, and put them into a little Pot with some Broth, or if that be wanting, with boiling Water. Pour in as they are boiling, a red thickning Liquor, a little Wine and a Clove of Garlick, or a Rocambole; also some Lemmon-juice, when they are serv'd up, and let them be garnish'd with *Marinade* and fried Parsly.

A *Hare*-Civet.

Take away the Legs and Shoulders entire, and cut the reft into pieces: Lard them with thick Slips of Bacon, fry them with Lard, and afterwards boil them with Broth and white Wine, a Bunch of fine Herbs, Pepper, Salt, Nutmeg, Bay-leaves and green Lemmon: Then fry the Liver, and, having pounded it, ftrain it thro' a Sieve, with fried Flower and a little of the fame Broth; putting into it fome Lemmon-juice and Slices of the fame.

A Civet *of a Hind, Stag or Roe-buck.*

Let the Hind or Stag be cut into pieces of the bignefs of a Hare's Shoulder, lard them with thick Slips of Bacon, fry them as it is expreſs'd in the preceding Article; and let them alfo boil after the fame manner. The Sauce is to be thicken'd with fried Flower and a little Vinegar.

COCKS-COMBS.

Befides the great ufe of Cocks-combs in the moft exquifite Ragoo's and Bisks, particular Courfes are made of them for the Intermeſſes; more efpecially farced Cocks-combs, either alone, or with Veal-fweet-breads, Capons-livers, *Morilles* and common Muſhrooms.

Farced Cocks-combs.

Take fome of the beft and largeft Cocks-combs, let them be parboil'd and afterwards open'd at the thick end, with the Point of a Knife: Then, having made a Farce with the Breaft of a Pullet or Capon, Beef-marrow, pounded Lard, Pepper, Salt, Nutmeg and the Yolk of an Egg; fry your Cocks-combs, and ftew them in a Diſh, with a little thick Broth and four or five Muſhrooms cut into Slices. To thefe add the Yolk of an Egg raw, and when the Diſh is ready to be ferv'd up, fome good Gravy and Lemmon-juice.

To preserve farced Cocks-combs.

Let them be well cleansed, put into a Pot with Lard, and kept upon the Fire a little while, without boiling: About half an Hour after, throw in a little fine Salt, an Onion stuck with Cloves, a Lemmon cut into Slices, some Pepper and a Glass of Vinegar: When the Lard begins to coagulate, take them out, pour in some melted Butter, and cover them with a Linnen-cloth, as it is usually done to other Things that are to be preserved.

COD-FISH.

It were needless to take any notice of the ordinary ways of dressing Cod-fish, either fresh or salted, as being sufficiently known, so that we shall here insist only on what may contribute to enrich them, and to heighten their Relish; such are the following Directions.

Fresh Cod in a Ragoo.

Scale your Cod, and boil it in Water, with Vinegar, green Lemmon, a Bay-leaf or two, Pepper and Salt: Prepare a Sauce for it, with burnt Butter, fried Flower, Oisters and Capers; adding thereto when serv'd up, some Lemmon-juice and black Pepper.

A Cods-tail in a Casserole.

Take a good Cod's Tail, and having scal'd it, loosen the Skin, so as it may fall off from the Flesh. Take away the *Filets*, and fill up the void space with a good Fish-farce, or with fine Herbs, Butter and Chippings of Bread. Afterwards put the Skin upon the Tail again, and having neatly breaded it, set it into the Oven, to give it a fine colour. Lastly, make a Ragoo for it with proper Garnitures, and serve it up to Table.

If you would have it fry'd, it must be scalded in hot Water, without boiling, to the end that it may remain altogether entire, and when 'tis drain'd, it must be flower'd and fry'd in refined Butter. Let it be serv'd up with Orange-juice and white Pepper. It may be garnish'd with some Pieces taken off from the Cod's Back put into Paste and fry'd; unless your

Ordi-

Ordinary be so mean, as not to afford a separate Dish of them.

COLLY-FLOWERS.

Colly-flowers are usually eaten with Butter, or Mutton-gravy. For the first Way, when they are well pickt, let them boil in Water, over a quick Fire, with Salt, Butter and Cloves: Then let them be well drain'd and put into a Dish, with Butter to keep them hot. When they are dress'd, make a thick Sauce for them, with Butter, Vinegar, Salt, Nutmeg, white Pepper and Slices of Lemmon.

For the other Way; when your Colly-flowers are boil'd as before; toss them up in a Pan, with Lard, Parsly, Chervil, Thyme a whole Chibbol and Salt, and let them soak together. When you would serve them up, put some Mutton-gravy into them, with a little Vinegar and white Pepper. Both these sorts of Dishes properly belong only to the Intermesses.

Colly-flowers are also eaten in a Sallet, and all that has been said on this Subject is so common, that it ought not be insisted upon; were it not that our Design leads us as well to instruct the meaner sort of People in what may be useful, as to shew what is usually practis'd in Noble-mens Kitchens.

COURT-BOUILLON.

Forasmuch as the *Court-bouillon* is common to many sorts of Fish, the Reader is referr'd to the Articles of *Pike* and *Carp*, directing what ought to be observ'd in that way of Dressing; to the end that unprofitable Repetitions of the same thing in several places may be avoided, as much as is possible.

CRAY-FISH.

Cray-fish may be dress'd after several manners, that is to say, they may be put into Ragoos, Hashes, Pies and Sallets; and Potages may be made of them, as well for Flesh-days as for those of Abstinence.

For a Ragoo; boil your Cray-fish in Wine, Vinegar and Salt: Then take the Tails, Claws and inside of the Body and toss them up in a Pan, with burnt Butter, fine Herbs chopt small, a piece of green Lemmon, Pepper, Salt, Nutmeg and a little

little fry'd Flower; adding some Mushroom-juice and Lemmon, when they are ready to be serv'd up to Table.

A Hash of Cray-fish is to be garnish'd with their Leggs marinated and fried, after having taken away the Flesh, and a Ring or Border may be made with them round about the Dish.

For a Cray-fish-*Tourte* or Pan-pie, see the Letter T, and Page 41, for a Sallet of the same Fish; for which, you may make the *Ramolade*-sauce there specified, after having boil'd them in Wine, with Vinegar, Pepper, Salt, Cloves, Bay-leaves and Chibbols: They are to be serv'd up entire with green Parsly.

Cray-fish may also be serv'd up in a Pan, with white Sauce, in the same manner as many other Things.

Cray-fish-Potage.

The Broth for this Potage, is that of Fish, which has been already describ'd. Having boil'd your Cray-fish according to the usual Method; take them out, and put all the Tails a-part into a Stew-pan, with *Truffles*, Mushrooms, Artichoke-bottoms and Asparagus-tops, such as are then in season: Dress this Ragoo with fresh Butter and a little fine Flower, and lay it a soaking, with good Fish-broth, or some other: Afterwards put your Roes into it, with a Faggot of fine Herbs, all well season'd, and let it boil over a gentle Fire.

To make the Cullis; all the Thighs and Legs of the Cray-fish must be pounded, and strain'd thro' a Sieve, with a little Broth and a small Crust of Bread: If you would have the Cullis redder, take only the Legs of your Cray-fish, and when all things are duely prepar'd, set them a-part. Some other Cray-fish are likewise to be provided; leaving their Tails and only taking the Shells and small Legs to thicken your Potage. Then take the Flesh of a good Carp, and make a well season'd Hash of it, which may serve for the same Potage. Let it soak with good Broth, and if you have a Loaf farc'd with the same Carp-Hash, and some small Garnitures, they may be opportunely put into the Potage; garnishing it with the Cray-fish, disposing of your Ragoo round about the Loaf, and soaking it all at once with the Cullis.

To garnish a Potage of the like nature; the Shells of the Cray-fish, may be stuff'd with a good Fish-farce, that is somewhat thick, and flower'd a little. When the Dish is ready to be set on the Table, they may be fry'd in fresh Butter, and serve
to

to garnish your Potage, as well as the above-mention'd Messes; more especially the Cray-fish-hash.

Thus all sorts of Cray-fish-potages for Flesh-days, that are found in this Book, may be easily prepar'd, by following what is even now express'd in this Article, for what relates to the Cullis, without making use of Gravy or Broth.

CREAMS.

There are several sorts of Creams; particularly of Almonds and Pistachoes, burnt Cream, crackling Cream, fried Cream, Cream after the Italian Mode and some others; of which in their Order.

Pistachoe-cream.

Take Pistachoes well scalded, and pound them in a Mortar, with some candy'd Lemmon-peel, and a little green Lemmon-peel: When they are well pounded, take as much Flower as you can get up between your Fingers at once or twice, with three or four Yolks of Eggs: Mix them together in a Stew-pan of the size of your Dish, and put some Sugar therein proportionably, afterwards pouring in some Milk by degrees, to the quantity of somewhat more than a Pint: Then take your pounded Pistachoes, and having temper'd them with the rest, strain all thro' a Sieve twice or thrice: Let it boil in the same manner as other sorts of Cream, and when it is ready, pour it into a Dish, to be kept cold for Intermesses. If you would have it serv'd up hot, you may, when 'tis cool'd, make a white Ice upon it, and set it into the Oven to be dried.

Almond-cream.

Almon'd-cream is made after the same manner as the former; but when it is to be prepar'd for Fish-days; on the Evening before the Collation, after having pounded the Almonds, strain them with Water thro' the Sieve, to make Almond-milk; to which purpose, a considerable quantity of Almonds is requisite. As soon as the Almond-milk is duely prepar'd, make your Creams, either of Pistachoes, Chocolate or others, with nothing but a little Flower, some Sugar and Orange-flower-water, without Eggs or Milk; only a little Salt and a great deal of Sugar.
When

When the whole Mixture is well boil'd, let it be serv'd up to Table, and if you design to make Pies of it, they are to be made with crackling Crust, hereafter describ'd, and garnish'd with *Savoy*-bisket, *Meringues*, or other Things of the like Nature.

Cream after the Italian Mode.

Take about a Pint of Milk, according to the bigness of your Dish, and boil it with some Sugar, a small Stick of Cinnamon, to give it a good Relish, and a little Salt: Then taking a large Silver-dish, with a Sieve, put four or five Yolks of new-laid Eggs into it, and strain the Milk and Eggs all at once, three or four times. Afterwards the Dish is to be set into a Campain or portable Oven, that is very straight, with Fire on the top and underneath, till the Cream be well coagulated and ready to be serv'd up hot. If some Milk-cream be put into all these sorts of Creams, it will render them much more delicious.

Pastry-cream.

If you would have a sufficient quantity for several Courses, it would be requisite to beat up the Whites and Yolks of a douzen Eggs, and having put to them, half a Pound of Flower, rather more than less, let all be well mixt together; to these another douzen of Eggs must be added and temper'd with the rest. At the same time, take about five Pints of Milk and put it into a Pan of a proportionable bigness, to be boil'd: When it begins to boil, turn the whole Mixture into it, and let it be continually stirr'd: Then having added a little Salt, about half a Pound of Butter, and a little white Pepper, let it be well boil'd, but take care that it do not stick to the bottom. Your Cream being thus thicken'd and duely prepar'd, pour it into another Pan and let it cool therein. When you have a mind to make Pies or Tarts of it, take as much as is requisite, according to the bigness you would have them to be of, and put it into another Pan: Let it be well mixt with the *Spatula*, and add thereto some Sugar, with Lemmon-peel cut small, both green and candy'd, a little Orange-flower-water, some Yolks of Eggs, and on Flesh-days, some Beef-marrow or fried Beef-sewet. The whole Mixture being well strain'd and clear'd, make your Pies of Puff-paste, with a little Border round about, and pour

in

in your Cream. When those Pies or Tarts are almost bak'd, they must be iced, and serv'd up for Intermesses. On Fish-days, melted Butter is generally us'd instead of Beef-marrow.

Burnt Cream.

Take four or five Yolks of Eggs, according to the bigness of your Dish or Plate; and beat them well in a Stew-pan, with as much Flower as you can take up between your Fingers; pouring in Milk by degrees to the quantity of about a Quart: Then put into it a small Stick of Cinnamon, with some green Lemmon-peel cut small and likewise some candy'd. Orange-peel may also be minc'd as that of Lemmon, and then 'tis call'd *Burnt Cream with Orange*. To render it more delicious, pounded Pistachoes or Almonds may be added, with a little Orange-flower-water. Then set your Cream upon the Furnace, and stir it continually, taking care that it do not stick to the bottom. When it is well boil'd, set a Dish or Plate upon a Furnace, and having pour'd the Cream into it, let it boil again, till you perceive it to stick to the side of the Dish: Then it being set aside, and well sugar'd on the top, besides the Sugar that is put into it; take the Fire-shovel heated red-hot, and at the same time, burn the Cream with it, to give it a fine Gold-colour. To garnish it make use of *Feuillantins* small *Fleurons* or *Meringues*, or other cut Pastry-works of crackling Crust. Ice your Cream if you please, or else let it be serv'd up otherwise, but always among the Intermesses.

Crackling Cream.

Take a Dish with four or five Yolks of Eggs, according to the quantity of Cream you would have prepared: Beat up these Yolks with a Spoon, and as you are working them, pour in some Milk by degrees, till the Dish be almost full: Then some rasped Sugar must be put into it with Lemmon-peel, and the Dish being set upon a Furnace, the Liquor is to be continually stirr'd about with a Spoon, till the Cream begins to be made. Afterwards having caus'd the Heat of the Furnace somewhat to abate, still keep stirring the Cream without intermission, and turn it upon the sides of the Dish, so as very little or none may remain in the bottom, and that a Border may be form'd round about: Care must be taken that it be not burnt to, but only continue sticking to the Dish. When it is ready, you may give it a fine colour, with the red-hot Fire-shovel, and with the Point of a Knife, loosen the whole Border, that it may remain entire: Let it be put again into the same Dish, and somewhat more dried in an Oven, so as very little be left in the Dish, and that it crackle in the Mouth. This sort of Cream is often serv'd up to the Duke of *Chartres*'s Table.

Virgin-cream.

Having taken five Whites of Eggs, let them be well whipt and put into a Pan, with Sugar, Milk and Orange-flower-water: Then set a Plate upon the Furnace, with a little Cinnamon, and pour in your Cream that is well beaten, and which, when made, may be brought to a colour by passing the red-hot Fire-shovel over it.

Fried Cream.

Take about a Quart of Milk, and let it boil upon the Fire, putting into it four beaten Yolks of Eggs with a little Flower: Stir all together over the Furnace, till the Cream be made, adding a little Salt, a small Lump of Butter and some minc'd Lemmon-peel: When your Cream is sufficiently boil'd, pour it into a flower'd Dish, so as it may spread it self, and that, when cool'd, it may become as it were a fried *Omelet* or Pan-cake: Cut it into pieces, of what thickness you shall think fit, and fry them with good Lard; taking care that they do not squirt in the Frying-pan. When they are colour'd, take them out, strew them with fine Sugar, and sprinkle them with Orange-flower-water: Dress them in a Dish, and having ic'd them (if you please) with the red-hot Fire-shovel, let them be serv'd up hot. Otherwise, when this sort of Cream is spread in a Dish upon the Dresser, you may put some Butter into a Frying-pan, and fry it in the same manner as an *Omelet*. As soon as it is colour'd on one side, turn it upon the Dish, and let it slip thence gently into the Frying-pan to give it the like colour on both sides. Then it may be sugar'd, ic'd and serv'd up hot among the Intermesses.

To render all sorts of Creams more delicious, instead of ordinary Flower, that of Rice may be us'd, which is much better for that purpose, and good Creams may be made even altho' no

Eggs

Eggs were put therein, *viz*. with Milk, if they are to be eaten with Butter, and with Almond-milk, if eaten only with Oil. A Quart of Milk muſt always be reduc'd to a Pint, in the boiling, to the end that the Flower may not be taſted.

Chocolate-cream.

Take a Quart of Milk with a quarter of a Pound of Sugar, and boil them together for a quarter of an Hour: Then put one beaten Yolk of an Egg into the Cream, and let it have three or four Walms: Take it off from the Fire, and mix it with ſome Chocolate, till the Cream has aſſum'd its colour. Afterwards you may give it three or four Walms more upon the Fire, and, having ſtrain'd it thro' a Sieve, dreſs it at pleaſure.

Sweet Cream.

Take three Quarts of Milk newly milk'd from the Cow, and let it boil; but when it riſes, take it off from the Fire, and let it lye by a little while. Then take off all the Cream that appears on the top, to be put into a Plate; ſet the Pan or Skillet again upon the Fire; and continue to do the ſame thing, till your Plate be full of ſuch Cream. Afterwards put ſome ſcented Waters into it, and forget not to ſugar it well, before it is ſerv'd up to Table.

White and light Cream.

Take three Gallons of Milk, with half a quarter of a Pound of Sugar, and let it boil half a quarter of an Hour: Then take it off from the Fire, and put in two Whites of Eggs well whipt, ſtirring all together without intermiſſion. Set your Milk or Cream upon the Fire again, and let it have four or five Walms, continually whipping it. Afterwards you may dreſs it as you pleaſe; ſprinkling it, as ſoon as it is cold, with Orange-flower-water, and ſtrewing it with fine Sugar. It may alſo be brought to a colour, with the red-hot Fire-ſhovel.

Cinnamon-cream is made after the ſame manner, as that of Chocolate.

As for the Sauces with Cream, ſee the Articles of Artichokes, Aſparagus, Muſhrooms, &c. as alſo the *Omelets*, with Cream of ſeveral ſorts, and other Meſſes mentioned in the General Table.

H

CREPINES.

Take some part of a Fillet of Veal, with a piece of Bacon, and let them be parboil'd together in a Pot: When they are cold, mince them with Leaf-fat out of a Hog's Belly, Chibbols, two or three Rocamboles and other seasoning Ingredients. Then beat them all in a Mortar, with a little Cream or Milk, and some Yolks of Eggs, and put this Farce into Veal-cauls after the manner of white Puddings. They are usually bak'd in a *Tourtiere* or Pie-pan, in an Oven moderately heated, and brought to a fine Colour; to be serv'd up for the Out-works of Side-dishes.

CROQUETS.

Croquets are a certain Compound made of a delicious Farce, some of the bigness of an Egg and others of a Walnut. The first sort may be us'd for Side-dishes, or at least for Out-works, and the others only for garnishing. To that purpose, take the Breasts of large fat Pullets, Chickens and Partridges, and mince this Meat with some Bacon, Calves-udder, Veal-sweet-breads, all parboil'd, *Truffles*, Mushrooms, Marrow, the crummy part of a Loaf, steept in Milk, and all sorts of fine Herbs, as also a little Cream-cheese, and as much Milk-cream, as shall be judg'd requisite: When the whole Mixture is well minc'd and season'd, let four or five Yolks of Eggs be put into it, and one or two Whites. With this Farce, the *Croquets* are to be form'd of a round Figure, then roll'd in a beaten Egg, breaded at the same time, and set by in a Dish, in order to be fried afterwards with sweet Lard, and serv'd up hot to Table. The same Farce may also serve to stuff *Fricandoes* or *Scotch*-Collops, and for the *Filets-Mignons* hereafter-mention'd.

As for the lesser *Croquets*, they may be made with the same Farce, or with any other that is somewhat delicious and thick, and are usually dipt into a certain Paste or Batter, like that of Apple-fritters, before they are fried: They may also be Flower'd or breaded, to garnish all sorts of Dishes, in which there are any Services of wild Fowl, and ought always to be serv'd up hot to Table.

Cu-

CUCUMBERS.

Cucumbers are usually farced to stuff great Joints of Beef, as it has been already obferv'd, and are also drefs'd after feveral other manners, particularly *à la Matelotte*, and in a Sallet: Potages are often garnifh'd with them; *Filets* of Cucumbers are fometimes prepar'd, and they are one of the principal Ingredients of the *Salpicon*. We have elfewhere explain'd what relates to the Cucumber-*Filets*, and the *Salpicon* fhall be defcrib'd in its proper Place. Therefore it will be fufficient here to give fome account of the farced Cucumbers and of thofe *à la Matelotte*; in regard that all the reft may be very eafily prepar'd; fuch as Potages, Sallets and Legs of Mutton with Cucumbers.

Farced Cucumbers.

Take Cucumbers, fuch as are not too thick, let them be clear par'd from their Seeds and kept whole. In the mean while, a Farce is to be prepar'd of all forts of Fowl, and if you pleafe, a piece of Veal, all well minc'd, with fome parboil'd Bacon, a little tried Fat, fome boil'd Gammon chopt, Mufhrooms, *Truffles* and all forts of fine Herbs; the whole Mixture being well minc'd and feafon'd. Then your Cucumbers, being fcalded a little while, are to be ftuff'd with this Farce, and boil'd in good Gravy or fat Broth, but not too much. Having taken them out, let them be cut into two pieces and fet by to cool, whilft a fort of Pafte or Batter is preparing, as it were for Apple-fritters: This Pafte is to be made of Flower mixt with white Wine or Beer, a little melted Lard and fome Salt. Afterwards certain fmall Skewers are to be neatly cut out, of the bignefs of a writing Pen, and the pieces of Cucumbers are to be pierc'd thro' with them, fo as all the ends may be on one fide, that they may be conveniently thruft into a piece of Beef. The Cucumbers are to be dipt in the faid Pafte, and brought to a fine Colour with melted Lard, and the piece of Beef being drefs'd with a Gammon-hafh, and the *Marinades* put upon it, is to be ftuff'd with thefe farced Cucumbers. If there be any Farce left, you may roll it up, with your Fingers dipt in Flower, and make round pieces of the thicknefs of an Egg, which are to be boil'd at the fame time with the Cucumbers; but very gently, that the

Farce may hold together: They must also be fried in the same manner.

Cucumbers dress'd à la Matelotte, or after the Sea-fashion.

They are to be farced as the former, and boil'd in good Gravy: Take care that the Fat be well taken away, and that too much Sauce be not put to them: Then thicken them with some good Cullis and pour in a little Vinegar, before they are serv'd up hot to Table: They ought to be all of a fine red Colour.

Farced Cucumbers are also put into a Ragoo and white Sauce.

To preserve Cucumbers.

Take the best sort of Cucumbers, that are not too ripe, and set them in good Order in a Pail, earthen Pan, or some other Vessel, in which is put an equal quantity of Water and Vinegar, with some Salt; so as they may be thoroughly steept: They must be well cover'd, and not touch'd for the space of a whole Month. Thus when Cucumbers are out of Season, these may be us'd, after they have been well par'd and soak'd. If you would garnish Potages with them, they must be scalded; also when they are us'd for *Filets*, as well on Days of Abstinence as on Flesh-days, they must be cut after the usual manner, and dress'd, as if they were fresh. Indeed they will be of great use throughout the whole Winter, and during the time of Lent. To those that are to be eaten in a Sallet, some Pepper is usually added, with some Handfuls of Salt, and they may be stuck with Cloves, at least one for every Cucumber. They are commonly call'd Girkins or pickled Cucumbers; and to this purpose, the lesser sort is to be chosen, such as grow in the latter Season. They are generally pickled with the Stalks or Leaves of Purslane, and more especially with Samphire, which serves instead of sweet Herbs for that sort of Sallet.

CULLI-

CULLISES.

A Cullis for different Potages on Flesh-days.

This sort of Cullis may serve for several small Potages on Flesh-days, particularly, of *Profiterolles*, Partridges, Quails, Larks, Wood-cocks and Teals; all which may be garnish'd with *Fricandoes* and Veal-sweet-breads. To make this Cullis, take a piece of Buttock-beef, and having caus'd it to be roasted very brown, let all the brownest part of it be pounded hot in a Mortar, with Crusts of Bread, the Carcasses of Partridges and of other Fowls that are at hand. The whole Mass being well pounded and soak'd with good Gravy, put it into a Stew-pan with Gravy and strong Broth, and season it with Pepper, Salt, Cloves, Thyme, sweet Basil and a piece of green Lemmon. Let it have four or five Walms, strain it thro' the Hair-sieve, and make use of it to be pour'd upon your Potages with Juice of Lemmon.

A Gammon-cullis.

Take one half Veal and the other Gammon, put it into a Stew-pan and order it, without Lard, as if it were for Veal-gravy: When it is sufficiently boil'd, add thereto some dry Crusts, Chibbol, Parsly, sweet Basil and Cloves, with the best sort of Broth: Let it be well season'd, strain'd thro' a Sieve and kept somewhat thick.

A Capon-cullis.

Take a roasted Capon, and pound it in a Mortar, as much as is possible: Then fry some Crusts of Bread in Lard, and when they are become very brown, put to them some Chibbol, Parsly, sweet Basil, and a few *Mousserons* well chopt: Mix these with the rest, and make an end of dressing them over the Furnace. Afterwards pour in as much of the best Broth, as you shall judge requisite, and strain it thro' the Hair-sieve.

A

A Partridge-cullis.

Take two roasted Partridges, and pound them well in a Mortar, with the *Bards* or thin Slices of Bacon with which they were dress'd: Then taking as many green *Truffles* as you can get up between your Fingers, with the like quantity of Mushrooms, fry them in Lard with fine Herbs, Chibbol, sweet Basil and Marjoram: Afterwards mix your pounded Meat together in the same Stew-pan, with two good Spoonfuls of Veal-gravy; let them soak over a gentle Fire, and strain them thro' the Sieve with Lemmon-juice.

A Cullis of Ducks.

Take a roasted Duck, and let it be well pounded in a Mortar: Then cause some Gammon to be fried brown in a Silver-dish, and put it into a Pot, with a Handful of Lentils to be stew'd all together; adding two or three Cloves, a Clove of Garlick, some Savoury and Chibbol: When they are all boil'd, pound them with the Duck-meat, and dress them in a Pan with Lard, as also afterwards with clear Broth, to the end that your Cullis may come to a lively fair colour: Lastly, let it be strain'd thro' the Hair-sieve with Lemmon-juice, and kept for use.

A Cullis of large Pigeons.

Let two or three large Pigeons be roasted, and pounded in a Mortar: Then mince three Anchovies, with as many Capers as can be taken up between your Fingers, a few *Truffles* and *Morilles*, two or three Rocamboles, some Parsly and Chibbols all chopt very small; mix them with the Pigeon-meat, and fry them in a Pan, with Lard: Let some of the best Gravy that you have be put thereto, strain it thro' a Sieve with the Juice of a Lemmon, and keep it as thick as you shall think fit.

A Cullis made with the Breast of a fat Pullet.

Take the Breast of a large fat Pullet, with a piece of Veal boil'd very white and pound them in a Mortar: Then provide a quarter of a Pound of sweet Almonds, which are likewise to be

The Court and Country Cook. 103

be pounded together, with the crummy part of a white Loaf foak'd in good Broth made of the Pullet's Bones, that was pounded before. The fame Broth may be us'd to lay the Meat and Almonds a foaking in a Stew-pan, giving them a Walm or two. In ftraining it thro' the Sieve, a little Milk or Cream may be put to it, to render it white, and care muft be taken, that it do not turn as it is heating.

A white Cullis for Fiſh-days.

Take as many Almonds, as you fhall judge requifite, and pound them in a Mortar: You are alfo to provide fome Bread-crum foak'd in Cream or Milk, and fome Fifh-*Filets*, drefs'd as white as is poffible. Add thereto fome frefh *Moufferons*, white *Truffles*, fweet Bafil and Chibbols, and take fome of the cleareft Broth you can get, to boil all for the fpace of one quarter of an Hour. Afterwards this Cullis is to be ftrain'd thro' the Hair-fieve and may ferve for all forts of Meffes that require white Broth.

Other Culliſes for Fiſh-days.

Some Onions and Carrets are to be fried as it were for a fort of Broth, and when they are turn'd brown, let a Handful of Par-fly be thrown in, with a little Thyme, fweet Bafil, Cloves, Crufts of Bread, Fifh-broth and a little Vinegar.

A Cullis of Roots.

Take Carrets, Parfly-roots, Parfneps and Onions cut into Slices, tofs them up all for a little while in a Stew-pan, and pound them in a Mortar, with a dozen and half of Almonds and a piece of Bread-crum foak'd in good Peas-foop: Let the whole Mix-ture be boil'd in a Pan, and well feafon'd as the others. Then ftrain it hot thro' the Sieve, and make ufe of it for all the Po-tages of white Onions, Leeks, Cardoons and Goats-bread that are fried, marinated, or put into Pafte; as alfo for the Potage of Skirrets.

A Cullis of Lentils.

Take fome Crufts of Bread, Carrets, Parfneps, Parfly-roots and Onions cut into Slices, fried in Oil or very hot Butter. If it be for

H 4   Flefh-

Flesh-days, you may put thereto some burnt Lard, and throw in your Pulse and Crums of Bread. Let all be fried brown, till that which sticks to the bottom of the Pan becomes very red: Then put some Lentils therein, with Broth, and let it be well season'd. When it has had four or five Walms, with a piece of Lemmon, let it be strain'd thro' a Sieve; so that it may serve for Lentil-potages, Crusts farced with the same, Crusts farced with Pike and Lentils, and several others; as Soles, Quavivers, Carps, &c. On Flesh-days 'twill also be of good use for Potages of Pigeons, Ducks, Partridges, &c.

There are also many other sorts of Cullises, that are made for different Things; as Cullises of Anchovies, Carps, *Truffles*, *Mousserons*, *Morilles*, common Mushrooms, Peas, Yolks of Eggs, and others that may be found by means of the General Table of the Messes, at the end of this Volume.

CUTLETS.

Farced Cutlets.

Take a Quarter of Mutton or Veal, and boil it in a Pot with good Broth: Then take it out and cut off all the Flesh, keeping the Bones of the *Cutlets* or small Ribs. This Flesh serves to make a Farce, with parboil'd Bacon, Calves-udder boil'd, a little Parsly and Chibbol, Mushrooms and *Truffles*, all chopt together, and pounded in a Mortar, with the necessary Spices and seasoning Ingredients; also the Crum of a Loaf soak'd in Milk or Gravy, and a little Milk-cream. Let the whole Farce be thicken'd with the Yolks of Eggs, so as it may not be too liquid. Then take *Bards* or broad Slices of Bacon according to the bigness of your Cutlets; put some of this Farce upon those *Bards*, with the Bones of the Cutlets, and do the same thing to every Cutlet which is to be made round, with a Knife steept in whipt Eggs, as if it were a real Cutlet. Afterwards they are to be wash'd over and breaded on the Top; and when put in good Order in a Baking-pan, they are to be set into the Oven, to give them a fine colour. These are call'd *Farced Cutlets, with Cream*, and may serve to garnish all sorts of Side-dishes and for Out-works.

Veal-Cutlets farced with nothing but Fennel are likewise in use, and some Gravy is to be put in the bottom of the Dish, as they are serving up to Table for Out-works.

Ano-

Another Side-dish of Cutlets.

Take the Cutlets of Veal or Mutton, that are very tender and well cut; lard them with thin Slips of young Bacon, as it were *Fricandoes*, and dress them in the same manner; seasoning them, as much as is needful. If these Cutlets serve for a separate Dish, all sorts of Garnitures ought to be put to them; but if they are to be us'd only for the garnishing of some other Side-dish, it would be only requisite to stew them in their own Gravy; because a particular Ragoo is to be pour'd upon the Mess in the middle of the Dish.

Cutlets in Haricot and otherwise.

Mutton-cutlets may be in *Haricot*, with stew'd Turneps, and a well-season'd Liquour to thicken them, as they are dressing: Some Chesnuts may be added, before they are prepar'd for Out-works. As soon as they are dress'd, they may also be steept in Lard, breaded and broil'd upon the Grid-iron; putting to them some good Gravy and Lemmon-juice, when ready to be served up. Otherwise they may be marinated, fried till they come to a fine colour and garnish'd with fried Parsly; or else a good Cullis and Gravy may be pour'd on them, with a piece of Lemmon and *Truffles*; so as they may be laid a soaking together for a while, and some Lemmon-juice squeez'd in, as they are serving up to Table.

D.

DABS or SANDLINGS.

A Side-dish of a marinated Dab.

LEt your Dab be cut thro' the Back, to the end that the *Marinade* may penetrate it, and when it is sufficiently pickled let it be well breaded with Bread-crum and season'd Chippings: Then let it be bak'd and garnish'd with *Petits-patez* or little Pies.

A Dab or Sandling in a Sallet.

Boil this Fish in a *Court-bouillon*, and when it is cold, cut it into *Filets*; with which, and some small Sallet-herbs, you are to dress a Plate; seasoning them, with Pepper, Salt, Vinegar and Oil: Or else you may make the *Ramolade*-sauce, mention'd Pag. 41. and serve them up for Intermesses.

Other manners of dressing Dabs.

If you have no other Dish with white Sauce, leave your Dab entire, and let it be serv'd up hot with white Sauce and Cream, for a Side-dish. Sometimes they are dress'd in *Filets*, with Anchovie-sauce, and in a *Court-bouillon*, to be serv'd up, when cold, upon a Napkin for Intermesses; and they may also be put into a Pie, as the Turbots, but they ought not to take up so long time in Baking.

DAUBES.

We have already explain'd the manner of preparing a Fish-*Daube*, under the Second Article of Carp, let us now shew how it ought to be order'd for Flesh.

A Daube of a Leg of Veal.

Having taken off the Skin from the Leg, let it be parboil'd, larded with small Slips of Bacon, and steept in white Wine, with Verjuice, a Faggot of fine Herbs, Pepper, Salt, a Bay-leaf or two and Cloves: Then let it be roasted, and basted with the same Wine, Verjuice and a little Broth. When it is ready, make Sauce for it, with the Dripping, a little fried Flower, Capers, Slices of Lemmon, Mushroom-juice and an Anchovie, and let your Leg of Veal soak therein for some time, before it is serv'd up to Table; which may be done for a Side-dish.

A Leg of Mutton may be dress'd in a *Daube* after the same manner.

Daubes

Daubes of green Geese and others.

Let your Geese be larded with middle-siz'd Slips of Bacon; seafon'd with Pepper, Salt, Cloves, Nutmeg, Bay-leaves, Chibbols and green Lemmon; and wrapt up in a Napkin: Then let them be boil'd in a Pot, with Broth and white Wine, and left till they are half cold, in their own Broth; in order to be serv'd up to Table upon a Napkin, with some Slices of Lemmon.

In like manner, you may dress Turkeys, fat Capons, Partridges and other sorts of Fowl.

DEER.

The Manner of Dressing it.

If you would have it roasted, let it be larded with thick Slips of Bacon, seafon'd with Pepper, Salt and beaten Cloves, and steept in Vinegar, with Bay-leaves and Salt: Then let it be roasted by a gentle Fire and well basted: When it is ready, put some Anchovies, Capers, Shalots cut small, and green Lemmon into the Sauce, which may be thicken'd with fried Flower. It may likewise be larded with small Slips of young Bacon, and put into a *Marinade*, with five or six Cloves of Garlick: Let it be roasted, cover'd with Paper, and eaten with Pepper and Vinegar.

The Fawn of a Deer may be dress'd after the same manner, except that the *Marinade* or Pickle for it, ought not to be so strong.

You may also prepare for a great Dish; the Leg of a Fawn, with the Rump, one half larded and the other breaded, garnish'd, with *Petits-patez* or little Pies, and having Vinegar and Pepper for Sauce; of which see an Example, Pag. 16. Or else being larded with thin Slips of Bacon, it may be eaten, with sweet-sour Sauce made of the Dripping, Sugar, Cinnamon, white Pepper, green Lemmon, a little Salt, fried Flower and a minc'd Shalot: Let all be boil'd over a gentle Fire, with Claret or Vinegar; let the Fawn be turn'd therein, from time to time, to take the whole relish; and let some Capers be added, as it is serving up to Table.

DUCKS.

Ducks.

Potages are sometimes made with Ducks; they are also roasted and serv'd up with Sauce, and dress'd after several other manners, of which these that follow, are most remarkable.

To dress Ducks with Oisters.

Take wild Ducks, let them be well truss'd; and make a Ragoo, with Veal-sweet-breads, *Truffles* and Oisters, seafon'd with fine Herbs, chopt Parsly and Chibbols: Care must be taken that this Ragoo be somewhat thick; but 'tis no matter whether it be red or not: When it is almost ready, the Ducks must be farced with it, well ty'd up, and roasted a little while. Afterwards a Mushroom-cullis, or Sauce after the *Spanish* Mode, such as is usually made for Partridges, may be pour'd upon them, and they are to be serv'd up hot, for a Side-dish, Other sorts of Water-fowl may be dress'd in the same manner.

Other Side-dishes of Ducks.

A Ragoo may be prepar'd for them, with Veal-sweet-breads, Artichoke-bottoms, *Truffles*, Mushrooms, a Clove of Garlick, a little Vinegar and a Bunch of fine Herbs; and they may be garnish'd with *Fricandoes*, and Lemmon-juice, before they are serv'd up to Table.

At another time, when your Ducks are roasted, cut them into *Filets*, and put them into a Ragoo of Cucumbers, with Rocamboles, Lemmon-juice and a little Vinegar; so as they may be serv'd up for Out-works.

Ducks may be also dress'd in a Ragoo; and Turneps boil'd with them, may serve for their Garniture.

Potages of Ducks.

Ducks may be us'd in Potages with Peas, a Cullis of Lentils, Cabbage, Turneps and other Roots: But forasmuch as this is common to them, with several other Messes, a particular Enumeration of which, would lead us too far and even to little purpose out of the Way; the Reader is referr'd to the respective Potages of those different sorts of Pulse under the Letter P. where

he

he may find general Instructions, as to what ought to be observ'd, with respect to all sorts of Wild-fowl and Poultry; for the avoiding of tedious Repetitions: So that this one Instance may be his future Direction, whenever any Matters shall occur of the like Nature.

See likewise under the Article of Pies, what relates to those of Ducks, as well hot as cold.

Sea-Ducks.

They may be put into a *Daube*, after the very same manner as green Geese or Ducks, and being well dress'd, may be serv'd up to Table, upon a white Napkin, garnish'd with Parsly and Slices of Lemmon.

A Side-dish may also be made of them, with Cucumbers, as well as many others, or else they may be dress'd after the following manners.

A Sea-duck in a Court-bouillon.

After having pickt and drawn your Sea-duck, let it be larded or stuff'd, with thick Slips of Eel-flesh, and boil'd four or five Hours over a gentle Fire, in Water, with Pepper, Salt, a Bunch of Herbs, a Bay-leaf or two, Cloves, a little white Wine and a Lump of Butter: Then prepare a Sauce for it, with natural Butter, fine Flower, white Pepper, Salt, green Lemmon and Vinegar, and let the bottom of the Dish, in which it is dress'd, be rubb'd with a Shalot.

A Sea-duck with Chocolate in a Ragoo.

Having pickt, cleans'd and drawn your Sea-duck, as before, let it be wash'd, broil'd a little while upon the Coals, and afterwards put into a Pot; seasoning it with Pepper, Salt, Bay-leaves and a Faggot of Herbs. Then a little Chocolate is to be made and added thereto; preparing at the same time a Ragoo with Capons-livers, *Morilles, Mousserons*, common Mushrooms, *Truffles* and a quarter of a hundred of Chesnuts. When the Sea-duck is ready dress'd in its proper Dish, pour your Ragoo upon it; garnish it with what you please, and let it be serv'd up to Table.

A Sea-duck in Haricot.

Let it be dress'd as before, and let a Ragoo of Turneps be made, which are to be fried somewhat brown: Then let all be soak'd with the Sauce of your Sea-duck, which, when ready must be cut into pieces and laid upon the Turneps. Lastly, let it be prepar'd and serv'd up to Table at a convenient time, garnish'd, as you shall think fit.

Sea-ducks in a Pot-pourri or Hotch-potch.

Lard your Sea-ducks with thick Slips of Eels-flesh, and toss them up in a Pan with burnt Butter: Then put them into a Pot or Earthen Pan, with a little of the same Butter, Flower and Water, season'd with Pepper, Salt, Nutmeg, Cloves, Mushrooms a Faggot of Herbs and green Lemmon: Let them boil over a gentle Fire, during four or five Hours, as it were in a *Court-bouillon*, and when you would have it serv'd up, add some Oisters, Capers and Lemmon-juice.

A roasted Sea-duck.

Let the Sea-duck be basted as it is roasting, with Butter and Salt, and then let a Sauce be made for it with the Liver; which is to be minc'd very small and put into the Dripping, with Pepper, Salt, Nutmeg, Mushrooms and Orange-juice.

A Sea-duck Pie.

Take Sea-ducks that are well pickt and truss'd, let them be beaten a little on the Breasts, broil'd on the Coals and tied up at the ends. Take the Liver, with some minc'd *Truffles*, Mushrooms, Parsly and Butter, a few Chibbols and Capers, with an Anchovie; all being well chopt, enrich'd and season'd: Then the Body of the Sea-duck is to be stuff'd with this Farce, and a little of the same kept, to be put underneath. In the mean while, roll out your Paste for the Under and Upper-crusts, and let the Pie be bak'd when fill'd with the Sea-ducks. If you would have it serv'd up hot, a good Ragoo must be made with Carps-roes, Cray-fish-tails, Mushrooms and *Truffles*, or one of Oisters; but if it be design'd for a cold standing Dish, you have

have no more to do, but to let it cool after it is bak'd, and to set it on the Table, as you shall find an occasion.

Potage of Sea-ducks.

As for the Potages of Sea-ducks; 'tis requisite that they be boil'd with good Fish-broth, and afterwards laid a soaking with the same. Then a good Fish-hash is to be prepar'd, to be pour'd upon the Sea-ducks, as soon as they are put into the Soop, which has been sufficiently soak'd. Let them be garnish'd with Sole-*Filets*, Whitings, Cray-fish, or other sorts of Fish; with a well season'd Ragoo, and a good Cullis of Cray-fish or Mushrooms. These are all to be serv'd up hot, and Potages may be made of Sea-ducks with Lentils.

E.

EARS.

Calves-ears farced.

Calves-ears farced are commonly us'd for Intermesses; to which purpose, some entire Ears are to be well scalded or par-boil'd a little: Then a good thick Farce being made, stuff the Insides of them, and sow them up neatly round about: They are to be boil'd, as Pigs-pettitoes, *à la Sainte Menehout*, and unsow'd, when ready, but so as the Farce may not fall out. Afterwards, roll them up in Eggs lightly whipt, bread them at the same time, fry them in Lard, as it were *Croquets*, and garnish them with fried Parsly.

Hogs-ears.

Hogs-ears may be dress'd with Herb-*Robert* Sauce, after they are cut into Slices, and fried in a Pan with a little Butter. You must also fry in the same Butter some Chibbols cut very small, season'd with Pepper, Salt, Nutmeg, Vinegar, Capers and a little Broth, and when you would have them serv'd up, add some Mustard: The same Slices may be put into Paste, fried and set on the Table with white Pepper and Lemmon-juice.

For a *Sousee* of Hogs-ears and Feet, see the last Article of the Letter S.

EELS.

Eels.

How to farce them.

The Bones of Eels may be farc'd in form of a white Pudding: To that purpose, a good *Godivoe* is to be made with the Flesh of the Eels, which you must pound in a Mortar, mixing with it some Cream, Bread-crum, two or three Rocamboles and half a Clove of Garlick: When the *Godivoe* is well season'd, farce your Bones neatly with it, bread them well with Bread-crum, and bake them in a Pie-pan, till they come to a fine colour.

Eels with white Sauce.

When the Eels are skinn'd, cut them into pieces, and let them be scalded in boiling Water: As soon as they are dried with a Napain, toss them up in a Pan, with natural Butter, and stew them with Pepper, Salt, Cloves, Nutmeg, a Bay-leaf and a piece of Lemmon; some add a Glass of white Wine to these Ingredients. In like manner dress some Artichoke-bottoms, Mushrooms and Asparagus-tops, with sweet Butter and fine Herbs, and make a white Sauce, with the Yolks of Eggs and Verjuice; accordingly, as the time will allow it, or when they are ready to be set on the Table: Let them be garnish'd with fried Bread and Slices of Lemmon, and serv'd up with the Juice of the same.

Eels with brown Sauce.

Let them be toss'd up in a Stew-pan with burnt Butter, fine Herbs chopt very small, Chibbols, Pepper, Salt, Cloves, Nutmeg and Capers; adding also a little Verjuice and white Wine, if you think fit, with fried Flower. Afterwards let all be stew'd together in a Dish or earthen Pan, and garnish'd with Lemmon, as they are serving up to the Table.

Fried Eels.

They must not be skinn'd, but the Bones being only taken away, let them be cut into pieces, and marinated with Vinegar, Pepper, Salt, Bay-leaves, Chibbols and Lemmon: Then they
are

are to be flower'd and fried in refined Butter. Before they are serv'd up, let a Sauce be made for them with Parsly, Rose-vinegar and white Pepper.

Eels broil'd upon the Grid-iron.

After having skinn'd your Eels and cut them into pieces, let them be marinated as before, and let a Sauce be prepar'd for them, with burnt Butter, Flower, Capers, Pepper, Salt, Nutmeg, Cloves, Vinegar and a little Broth. When the Eels are sufficiently broil'd upon the Grid-iron, let them be stew'd a little in that Sauce: They may also be dress'd with *Robert*-Sauce and sweet Sauce.

Eels in a Daube.

Let some of the Flesh of Eels and Tenches be minc'd, and season'd with, Pepper, Salt, Cloves and Nutmeg: Then let *Lardoons* be made of the other part of the Eels-flesh; of which one Lay is to be put upon the Skins, and another Lay of the minced Flesh, continuing so to do alternately. Then let all be wrapt up in a Linnen-cloth, and boil'd in the same manner as Fish-gammon, that is to say, in one half Water and the other red Wine; seasoning them with Cloves, a Bay-leaf or two and Pepper. When they are cool'd in their own Broth, let them be serv'd up in Slices for Intermesses, rather than Side-dishes.

Eel-potage.

When your Eels are skinn'd and cut into pieces, fry them in a Pan with burnt Butter, fine Herbs, Flower, and the proper seasoning Ingredients. Afterwards put them into a Pot with Fish-broth, the manner of preparing which is explain'd under the Letter B. As soon as the Crusts are soak'd, let your Potage be dress'd and serv'd up, with Capers and Lemmon-juice.

An Eel-pie and a Tourte or Pan-pie of the same.

An Eel-pie is generally serv'd up hot for a Side-dish: When the Eels are cut into pieces and their Skins pull'd off, let them be season'd after the usual manner, with Pepper, Salt, Cloves,
Nut-

Nutmeg, fine Herbs, Chibbols, Butter, Capers, Bay-leaves and Bread-chippings. The Pie muſt be made with fine Paſte either of an oval or round Figure: When it is half-bak'd, a Glaſs of white Wine may be pour'd into it, and ſome Lemmon-juice, when ready to be ſerv'd up to Table.

As for the *Tourte* or Pan-pie; the Eels may either be minc'd, after they have been skinn'd and the Bones taken out, or they may be cut into ſmall Slices; ſeaſoning them as before, with pieces of Muſhrooms, the Yolks of Eggs and Lemmon-juice as they are ſerving up, in order to make a white Sauce.

Eel-powts.

The Eel-powt is both a Lake and River-fiſh. They may be dreſs'd in Ragoo and *Caſſerole*; or they may be put into a Pie, and a Potage may be made of them, with brown Broth.

A Ragoo of Eel-powts.

Let the Eel-powts be cleans'd from their Slime, with hot Water, and afterwards flower'd, and fried: Then being put into a Diſh, with burnt Butter, Flower and diſſolv'd Anchovies, let all be ſtew'd together; ſeaſoning them with Salt, Nutmeg, a Chibbol and Orange-juice or Verjuice. Let them be garniſh'd with fried Parſly, and Slices of Lemmon, and ſerv'd up for Side-diſhes, as all other Fiſh-ragoo's.

Eel-powts in Caſſerole.

Cleanſe your Eel-powts from their Slime, laying the Livers a-part, and fry them in a Pan, with burnt Butter: Then put them into an earthen Pan, with the ſame Butter, a little Flower and white Wine; ſeaſoning them with Pepper, Salt, Nutmeg, a Faggot of fine Herbs, and a piece of green Lemmon. In the mean while, prepare a ſeparate Ragoo, with the ſame Sauce as that of the Eel-powts, as alſo with their Livers and ſome Muſhrooms, and garniſh your Diſh with it, adding the Juice of Lemmon; when ready to be ſerv'd up to Table.

Eel-powt Potage and Pie.

For the Potage, after having wash'd the Eel-powts, let them be fried whole in a Frying-pan, with burnt Butter and a little Flower: Then let them be stew'd in an earthen Pan, with Pepper, Salt, a Bunch of fine Herbs, some Fish-broth or Pease-soop, and a little white Wine. When they are ready, dress them upon your soaked Crusts, and garnish them with Mushrooms and Capers.

For the Pie, skin your Eel-powts, and make a fine Paste, to put them in, with their Livers and Roes, Mushrooms, Cray-fish-tails, Oisters and Artichoke-bottoms: Let them be season'd with Pepper, Salt, Nutmeg, fine Herbs and Chibbols; adding some Lemmon-juice, when they are brought to Table.

EGGS.

There is not any one Particular throughout the whole Practice of Cookery that affords greater Variety of Dishes, than Eggs, which are us'd even on Flesh-days, and serve altogether for the Out-works of Intermesses: the principal ways of dressing them, are as follows *viz.*

Eggs with Orange-juice.

Let some Eggs be whipt, according to the bigness of the Dish you would have prepar'd, at the same time squeezing in the Juice of an Orange and taking care that none of the Kernels or Seeds fall into it. When they are all well beaten and season'd with a little Salt, take a Stew-pan, and put a slice of Butter therein, if it be a Fish-day, or a little Gravy on a Flesh-day: Pour in your Eggs, and keep continually stirring them, as if it were Cream; lest they stick to the bottom: As soon as they are ready, turn them into a Plate or Dish, garnish them if you think fit, with fried Eggs, and let them be serv'd up hot to Table.

Farced Eggs.

Take two or three Cabbage-lettices, scald them, with Sorrel, Parsly, Chervil and a Mushroom, and let all be chopt very small, with some Yolks of hard Eggs, season'd with Salt, and

Nutmeg: Then stew them with Butter, adding also some natural Cream, when they are sufficiently stew'd; and covering the bottom of the Dish with them. Let the Sides be garnish'd with fine Herbs and the Whites of the Eggs stuff'd with another Farce, giving them a Colour with a red-hot Fire-shovel.

Farced Eggs may also be fried, after having dipt them into a clear Paste or Batter, and serv'd up with fried Parsly.

Eggs with Tripe.

Let the Whites of Eggs only be cut into long or round Slices, and toss'd up in Butter with Parsly and Chibbol chopt very small: Then thicken them a little, season them with Salt and Nutmeg; adding also some Cream; and let the Yolks be fried to garnish your Dish.

Petits Oeufs or small Eggs.

Take a Gallon of new Milk, and heat it till almost ready to boil, with a little Salt and pounded Sugar, a piece of Cinnamon, a Slice of Lemmon, and some Orange-flower-water: Break four or five new laid Eggs, take away the Whites of some of them, and beat them up with your Milk or Cream scalding hot: Then heat a Plate upon a Chafing-dish, and when it is very hot, pour in some of your prepar'd Mess, after having strain'd it thro' a Sieve. Let it run about, so as the Plate may be cover'd all over, and let it be brought to a Colour with the red-hot Fire-shovel. Afterwards beat your Yolks without Whites, and a little Flower to thicken them, with the rest of the Milk: Set the Plate again upon the Fire to be heated, so as the Eggs may become, as it were a Cream, and put the Yolks into it: Lastly, let the whole Mess be strew'd on the Top with Sugar, adding the Juice of a Lemmon and some Orange-flower-water, as it is serving up to Table.

Eggs after the German Mode.

Break some Eggs into a dish, as it were *au Miroir*, and put a little Peas-soop therein: Mix two or three Yolks with a little Milk, and strain them thro' a Sieve: Then take away the Broth in which the Eggs were dress'd, put the Yolks upon them, with some scraped Cheese and give them a good Colour.

Eggs

Eggs after the Burgundian Way.

Take a piece of red Beet, that has not an earthy or unsavoury taste, and pound it well with a Slice of Lemmon, a few Macaroons, Sugar and beaten Cinnamon: Then taking four or five Eggs, without the Sperm, mix all together very well, and strain them thro' the Hair-sieve, with a little Milk and Salt. Afterwards they may be dress'd in the same manner as Eggs with Milk, and brought to a fine colour.

Eggs fried in Hogs-ears.

The Yolks must not be us'd in this Fricassy, which is to be garnish'd with Mustard, if you please, and Lemmon-juice, when serv'd up to Table.

Eggs with Bread.

Let some Bread-crum be well soak'd in Milk during two or three Hours, and afterwards strain'd thro' a Sieve, or fine Cullander; putting thereto a little Salt, Sugar, candy'd Lemmon-peel cut very small, grated Orange-peel and Orange-flower-water. Then rub the inside of a Silver-dish with Butter somewhat heated, pour in your Eggs, keeping a Fire on the top and underneath, that they may take a fine colour, and let them be orderly serv'd up to Table.

Eggs after the Swiss Way.

Having dress'd your Eggs as it were *au Miroir*, bread them with Crum: Then let them be cover'd with a Pike-hash and some scrap'd Cheese, and brought to a fine colour.

Eggs with Gravy or à la Huguenotte.

Let some Mutton-gravy or any other sort be put into a hollow Dish, and when 'tis hot; break your Eggs into it either *au Miroir* or mingled together: Season them with Salt, Nutmeg and Lemmon-juice, and pass the red-hot Fire-shovel over them, to give them a good colour.

Eggs

Eggs after the Portuguese Way.

Let some Sugar be dissolv'd, with Orange-flower-water, the Juice of two Lemmons and a little Salt. Then set it upon the Fire with your Yolks and stirr all with a Silver-spoon. When the Eggs slip from the sides of the Dish, they are sufficiently boil'd, and may be left to cool. Afterwards let them be dress'd in form of a Pyramid and garnish'd with Lemmon-peel and Marchpane.

They may also be serv'd up hot in a Dish, after they are ic'd over with Sugar, and colour'd with the red-hot Fire-shovel.

At another time, they may be mix'd in a Mortar with some Gooseberry-jelly or Beet-juice boil'd in Sugar, and then squeez'd thro' a Syringe, or a Hair-sieve, to be serv'd up dry in a green or red Rock.

Eggs with Pistachoes.

Pound your Pistachoes with a piece of candy'd Lemmon-peel; boil a sufficient quantity of Sugar with Lemmon-juice, and when the Syrop is half made, put the Pistachoes into it, with the Yolks of Eggs: Let them be stirr'd as before, till they leave sticking to the Skillet, and serv'd up with sweet Water.

Eggs with Orange-flower-water.

Let Sugar and Orange-flower-water be put into a Dish or Skillet, with some natural Cream, candy'd Lemmon-peel grated, and a little Salt. Then pour in eight or ten Yolks and stir them about after the manner of mingled Eggs.

Eggs in Filets.

Prepare a Syrop of refin'd Sugar and white Wine, and when it is above half done, beat your Eggs therein: Then taking them up with a Skimmer, to the end that the *Filets* may be well made, let them be dried at the Fire, and serv'd up with Musk or some other Perfume.

Eggs after the Italian Mode.

Let a Syrup be prepar'd with Sugar and a little Water: When it is above half made, take the Yolks of Eggs in a Silver-spoon, one after another, and hold them in this Syrop to be poach'd. Thus you may dress as many as you shall think fit, continually keeping your Sugar very hot, and they may be serv'd up to Table garnish'd and cover'd with Pistachoes, Slices of Lemmon-peel, and Orange-flowers boil'd in the rest of the Syrop, with Lemmon-juice sprinkled upon them.

Eggs with Rose-water.

Having temper'd your Yolks with Rose-water, Lemmon-peel, Macaroons, Salt and beaten Cinnamon; let them boil in a Pan over a gentle Fire, with refined Butter: When they are ready, ice them over with Sugar and Rose-water or Orange-flower-water, and put to them some Lemmon-juice, with Pomegranate-kernels, as they are serving up to Table.

Eggs with Sorrel-juice.

As your Eggs are poaching in boiling Water, pound some Sorrel, and put the Juice of it into a Dish, with Butter, two or three raw Eggs, Salt and Nutmeg: Let this thick Sauce be pour'd upon the Eggs, when served up to Table.

Eggs with Verjuice.

Beat up your Eggs with good Verjuice and season them with Salt and Nutmeg: Then let them be poach'd with a little Butter, and garnish'd with fried Bread or fried Paste.

Eggs with Cream.

When your Eggs are poach'd whole with Butter in a Stew-pan, take them out, and dress them upon a Plate: Then put to them some natural Cream, with a little Salt and Sugar, and serve them up hot with Pomegranate-kernels or other sorts of Garniture.

An Egg-sallet.

'Tis usually made with Anchovies, Capers, Fennel, Lettice, red Beets, Purslain and Chervil; either of all these Herbs, or of every one of them in particular, and ought to be well seafon'd.

There are also many other sorts of Eggs, which it will be sufficient here only to mention, *viz.*

Eggs with young Chibbols and other fine Herbs.
——— poach'd with *Robert*-Sauce.
——— with Milk.
——— dress'd *au Miroir*.
——— dress'd whole with green Sauce.
——— in a Hash, poach'd with fine Herbs and garnish'd with small round Pellets of fried Eggs.
——— with rasped Cheese.
——— Eggs put into a Paste and fried.
——— fried in a Pan with burnt Butter.
——— poach'd in Water, with thick Butter.
——— poach'd with Sugar.
——— with Anchovies.
——— with Sorrel, *&c.*

Counterfeit or artificial Eggs.

Artificial Eggs of several sorts may be made use of during the time of Lent, and more especially on Good-friday: To that purpose, take two Quarts of Milk, and let it boil in an earthen Pot or a Silver-pan; continually stirring it with a wooden Ladle, till it be reduc'd to a Pint: Then pour one third part of it into a Dish, by it self, and set it on the Fire again, with some Rice-cream and a little Saffron: When it is thicken'd and become somewhat firm, you may make with it, as it were Yolks of Eggs, which are always to be kept Luke-warm. With the rest of the Milk fill up some Egg-shells that you have open'd, after having wash'd and topt them, and in order to serve them up to Table, put your artificial Yolks into those Shells, as also on the top, a little Almond-cream, or raw Milk-cream and Orange-flower-water. These are usually serv'd up, on a ruffled Napkin and call'd *Artificial soft Eggs*.

As

As for the other sorts, you are to mix at first with your Milk some fine Flower or Starch, and make as it were a kind of Pastry-cream, without Eggs, season'd with Salt: When it is boil'd, take some part of it to make the Yolks; adding some Saffron, and put these Yolks into certain half Egg-shells wash'd and steept in Water or white Wine: Afterwards fill up other whole Shells with the rest of the Cream, which being cold, these Whites and Yolks may be taken out of their respective Shells, to make such sorts of artificial Eggs, as you shall think fit. As for example:

For *farced Eggs*, after having taken away the Shell, cut the Whites into two equal parts, and hollow each of them with a Silver-spoon, in order to be stuff'd with the above-mention'd Farce. Then let them be dress'd in the same manner and garnish'd with artificial Yolks, that have been flower'd and fried for that purpose.

For *Eggs with Tripe*; after having cut and made them hollow, as before, stuff them with Yolks and cut them again into Quarters; then let them be flower'd and well fried. Having dress'd them upon a Plate, let a Sauce be prepar'd for them, with burnt Butter, fine Herbs, Mushrooms boil'd and chopt, Pepper, Salt, Nutmeg and Rose-vinegar: They may be garnish'd with Bread, Parsly and Mushrooms fried.

For *Eggs with Milk*; take boil'd Milk, and Almond-cream, and temper them with Marmelade of Apricocks: Let all these be put with Butter into a Plate over a gentle Fire and afterwards the Compound of Eggs: Then cover them with a Tin or Copper-lid with Fire upon it, to give them a colour like that of a Custard, and let them be serv'd up with Orange-flowers and Sugar.

Artificial Eggs *au Miroir* are made after this manner: Fill the bottom of a Plate with your Cream, and let it boil with Butter, cover'd with a Lid having Fire upon it. As soon as you perceive it to grow firm, take away the Fire; make ten or twelve hollow places, with a Spoon, and fill them up with artificial Yolks: Afterwards prepare a Sauce, with thick Butter, fine Herbs chopt very small, Pepper, Salt, Nutmeg and a little Vinegar, or otherwise, and when you would have the Dish serv'd up to Table, pour it in hot upon the Eggs. The same thing may be done with several other sorts.

F.

F.

FARCES.

The number of Farces is very great; so that it would be difficult to give a particular account of them after a better manner, than in speaking of every Thing in which they are us'd. For example, Directions have been already given how to make those of *Croquets*, Veal and Mutton-cutlets, *&c.* And so of the rest: Therefore the Reader is referr'd to every one of these Articles, to observe the nature of every Farce, and we shall here only explain that of Fish.

To make a good Fish-farce.

Take Carps, Pikes and other Fishes that are at Hand, and let all be well minc'd upon the Dresser. Let an *Omelet* be likewise prepar'd, that is not fried too much, with Mushrooms, *Truffles*, Parsly and Chibbols cut small, and let all be put upon the Farce, when it is well order'd and season'd: To these may be added the Crum of a Loaf soak'd in Milk, with Butter and Yolks of Eggs, and in a Word, care must be taken that the Farce be well thicken'd. It may serve to farce Soles and Carps, as also Cabbage; to make small *Andouillets*, *Croquets*, and every Thing else that you shall judge expedient, as it were on Flesh-days.

FAWN, see *Deer*.

FEET.

A Side-dish of Lambs-feet.

The Lambs-feet must be well scalded, boil'd and farc'd, after having taken away the Bone in the middle: Then they must be dipt in a beaten Egg, well breaded and fried in the same manner as *Croquets*. This Dish is to be garnish'd with fried Parsly.

They may also be us'd for Out-works, or to garnish a Side-dish of a Lambs-head, with white Sauce; as if they were Pigeons with white Sauce: Lastly, they may be of further use to garnish the Potage of Lambs-heads, and ought to be serv'd up hot to Table.

For Hogs-feet in a *Soufce*, see the Letter S.

-Pigs-feet, see *Pigs-pettitoes.*

FILETS.

We have already explain'd what relates to the Manner of Dressing a *Filet* of Beef with Cucumbers, and we have observ'd in that Place, that the same thing may be done with all other sorts of *Filets:* Let us now give some Account of the *Filets Mignons* that are serv'd up both for Side-dishes and Outworks.

To make Filets Mignons.

Take good *Filets* of Beef, Veal or Mutton, cut them into large Slices, and beat them well upon a Table or Dresser: Then a Farce is to be made of the same Ingredients as those of the *Pain au Veau,* except that it must be thicken'd with Yolks of Eggs; consisting particularly, of Bacon, part of a Fillet of Veal, a little Gammon-fat boil'd, and some Flesh of Fowl, with Parsly, Chibbols, *Truffles* and Mushrooms; as also some Bread soak'd in Broth or Milk, and a little Milk-cream. Your Farce being thus prepar'd, spread it upon the *Filets,* according to the quantity that you would have, and roll them up very firm. Afterwards, having provided a Stew-pan that is not too large, let several thin Slices of Bacon be laid in order on the bottom of it, with some Slices of Veal well beaten, as also your farced *Filets* well season'd with all sorts of fine Herbs, and some Slices of Chibbol and Lemmon: Cover them on the top as well as at bottom, and set the Pan between two Fires; but such as are not too vehement, to the end that they may boil gently. When they are ready, let them be taken out, clear'd well from the Fat, and serv'd up hot, with a good Cullis, according to discretion, and some Lemmon-juice: A small Ragoo of *Truffles* may also be added, if you think fit. If any other Side-dish of farc'd Fowl be requir'd, you may make use of the same Farce, and bake them likewise between two Fires with your *Filets*; but to distinguish them, when they are all ready, different Ragoo's or Cullises ought to be made for them: Then they are to be well

drain'd

drain'd from the Fat; and every Thing a-part ferv'd up to Table.

Filets *of a fat Pullet, with Cream.*

Take the *Filets* of large fat Pullets roafted, and cut them into pieces: Then put into a Stew-pan a little Lard and Parfly, and, having tofs'd it up with a little Flower, add Artichoke-bottoms cut into quarters, Mufhrooms and Slices of *Truffles*, a Faggot of fine Herbs, and a little clear Broth, all well feafon'd. When they are fufficiently ftew'd, put your *Filets* to them, and a little before they are ferv'd up, pour in a little Milk-cream; taking care to keep them hot. To thicken them, let one or two Eggs be beaten with Cream, and having brought it to a due confiftence, let all be fet on the Table at once, as well for Side-difhes as Intermeffes.

The *Filets* of a fat Pullet are likewife drefs'd with white Sauce, Oifters and Cucumbers; the *Filets* of Mutton with *Truffles*; others in Slices, with Gammon; and fo of feveral others that may be found by means of the General Table.

As for the *Filets* of Fifh that may be ferv'd up in a Sallet during the time of Lent, fee Page 41.

FRICANDOES.

Ficandoes or Scotch Collops ferve not only to garnifh very fumptuous Side-difhes; but alfo to make particular Difhes: When they are us'd for garnifhing, 'tis requifite only to lard them; but when farced for a feparate Difh, they are to be prepar'd in this manner:

To make farc'd Fricandoes *or Scotch Collops.*

Cut a Leg of Veal into fomewhat thin Collops, and having larded them fet them in order upon a Table or Dreffer, with the Bacon underneath: Then put on the middle of every one, a little of fome good Farce, and ftroak the Sides of it with your Fingers dipt in a beaten Egg, to the end that the *Fricandoe* or Collop when put thereupon, may ftick to it and be as it were incorporated with it; but care muft be taken that the Bacon appear on all fides. Having put thefe *Fricandoes* in due order into a Stew-pan, let them be well cover'd and fet over a Fire that

is

is not too quick; neither must there be any on the top. They are to be brought to a colour on both Sides, then taken out and drain'd a little from the Fat, to the end that they may be render'd somewhat brown, with a little Flower: Afterwards you must soak them in good Gravy that is not black, and put them again into the Stew-pan to be thoroughly dress'd. If they are design'd only for Garniture, they may be left in this manner; but if you would have a particular Dish made of them, it would be requisite to add some *Truffles*, Mushrooms and Veal-sweet-breads, with a good Bread-cullis, and to take care that all be well clear'd from the Fat. When they are ready, sprinkle them with a little Verjuice; dress them in a Dish, pouring your Ragoo on the top, and let them be serv'd up hot. Some call this sort of *Fricandoes*, by the Denomination of *Scollop'd Veal*.

The manner of preparing *Fricandoes* to make a *Grenade*, will be explain'd hereafter under the Letter G.

F R I T T E R S.

Fritters are made several Ways, that is to say, with Apples, *Blanc-mangers*, Milk, or Water; and all these sorts are us'd for Intermesses.

Intermesses of Water-fritters.

Let some Water and a little Salt be put into a Stew-pan, with green and candy'd Lemmon-peel minc'd very small: Let it boil over a Furnace, and having put therein two good Handfuls of Flower, with a little Butter, stir it about, as much as is possible, till it be loosen'd from the Pan: Then, drawing it aside, put in the Yolks of two Eggs and mix them well together; continuing to put in two Eggs at once successively, to the number of ten or twelve, till your Paste or Batter become very rich. Afterwards, having flower'd the Dresser-board, dip your Fingers likewise into Flower, and draw out your Paste into pieces: When they have lain by a little while, they are to be roll'd out, and cut into small round pieces, so as not to stick one to another, and when ready, they may be fried in good Lard: Having taken them out of the Frying-pan, strew some Sugar upon them, sprinkling also a little Orange-flower-water, and let them be speedily serv'd up for Out-works. They may likewise be us'd for the garnishing of Cream-tarts.

Inter-

Intermesses of Blanc-manger-fritters.

Take Rice, wash it in five or six Waters and dry it well at the Fire: Then pound it in a Mortar, and sift this Flower thro' a Sieve to render it very fine. It would be requisite to use a good half ounce of it, according to the bigness of your Dishes. Having put this Flower into a Stew-pan, dilute it well with Milk, afterwards pour in a Quart of Milk, and set all over the Furnace; but care must be taken to stir it continually. You must also put thereto the Breast of a roasted fat Pullet minc'd small and make your Paste as if it were for Pastry-cream; neither would it be improper to add a little Sugar, some candy'd Lemmon-peel and green Lemmon-peel grated, as it is boiling. In the mean while, the Dresser-board is to be flower'd, and the Paste being laid upon it, must be roll'd out with a Rolling-pin: Then having cut it into small pieces like those of the Water-fritters, flower your Hand, make them up neatly, and fry them in good Lard, as before. As soon as they are ready to be serv'd up to Table, strew them with Sugar, and sprinkle them with Orange-flower-water. If they are to serve for a particular Dish, let them be garnish'd with Water-fritters or others.

Milk-fritters.

They are made after the same manner as the Water-fritters, but a less quantity of Flower must be us'd, to the end that the Paste may be somewhat finer; and if it be not sufficiently fine, some more Yolks of Eggs may be put into the Stew-pan. Then let the Batter be turn'd into a Plate and well spread over the bottom of it. Afterwards having provided some melted Lard in a Frying-pan and a Spoon, you may make the Fritters with the end of it, which is to be dipt from time to time, in the Lard, to keep the Batter from sticking to it. The Frying-pan must be gently mov'd without intermission, and the Fritters, when well colour'd must be taken out, in order to be sugar'd hot, and sprinkled with Orange-flower-water. Afterwards being sugar'd again a little, they may be ic'd over, if you please, with the red-hot Fire-shovel, and serv'd up hot to Table.

Other

Other sorts of Fritters.

Fritters may also be made with Apples, Apricocks preserv'd dry, Plums, Cherries in Ears, smooth Pistachoes, red Gooseberries preserv'd, Pomegranate-kernels and Parmesan; some of them requiring a thin Paste or Batter, and others thicker. But forasmuch as this is rather the Business of a Confectioner than a Cook, we shall take no farther notice of these Matters in this Place.

FRUIT.

How to make Pastes of several sorts of Fruit.

As for white Gooseberries, they must not be too ripe, but for other sorts of Fruit, 'tis no great matter. Take these Fruits, every one of them a-part, let them be well pickt, and put into a Copper-pan, with a little Water; but if you would have a Jelly made of them, the Liquor of every particular Fruit must be drawn off separately: When they are scalded in that little Water, pour all into a Sieve, in order to be well drain'd, and this Liquor will serve to make your Jelly. As soon as the several sorts of Fruit are sufficiently drain'd in this manner, take a *Spatula* and squeez every one of them separately thro' a Sieve into different Silver-dishes; so as it may become, as it were a kind of Marmelade: Set one of these Dishes upon the Furnace, and dry up this Paste neatly with the *Spatula* till no moisture be left. The same thing may be done with every sort of Paste, and they may be left to cool in their proper Dishes. In the mean while, you are to provide a large Copper-pan and put into it seven or eight Pounds of Sugar, according to the quantity of your Paste: Pour in some Water, with the White of an Egg whipt, and let it be scumm'd as soon as it boils; for after three or four Walms, a thick Scum will arise, which must be carefully taken off, to the end that your Syrop may become very clear. Then let it boil till it be greatly feather'd, and having set the Dishes of Marmelade in order, pour some of this Syrop into them, according to the quantity of your Pastes; so as every Thing may be well temper'd a-part. Afterwards you are to take some Slates with several little Tin-moulds made in the Shape of a Heart, Square, Flower-de-luce, or the like, and of some other Figures:

Set

Set these Moulds in order upon the Slates, and by means of a Spoon, fill them up with your Paste or Marmelade; taking care not to confound them one with another: Lastly, let these Slates be put into a Stove, with a little Fire underneath, and shut up close, to the end that the Paste may be well ic'd over. When they are so order'd, and become firm, the Moulds may be taken away, and they will serve for a considerable time, provided that sufficient care be taken of them in the Stove.

For the Jelly of these Fruits, take the Liquor that is drain'd from them, that of every sort a-part, and let it boil with Sugar well clarify'd and boil'd till it become pearled. As it is boiling, take off the Scum from time to time, with Paper; and when your Jelly is made, fill up several Pots with it, which are to to be set by to cool. When the Jelly is cold, cover them with Paper, and tye up the Pots all at once, writing on the top of every one, the Name of the Jelly contain'd therein, according to the variety of Fruits, from which the several Liquors were extracted.

G.

GALANTINE.

THe Nature of an Intermess of *Galantine* shall be hereafter explain'd in the Article of Sucking-Pigs, under the Letter P. and there also shall be shew'd the Manner of Garnishing it and Serving it up to Table: We shall only intimate here, that it may also be garnish'd with its Skin well breaded and brought to a fine colour, by means of the red-hot Fire-shovel; for the rest, the Reader is referr'd to the Place even now mentioned.

GALLIMAWFRY.

'Tis no new thing nor very difficult to dress a Shoulder of Mutton, or some other Joynt in a Gallimawfry: However in regard that it may serve to diversifie the Messes in those Ordinaries, where there is greater store of Butchers-meat than Fowl; it may not be improper here to shew the manner of preparing it, which is as follows, *viz.*

Let the Skin of a Shoulder of Mutton be slipt off, yet so as it may continue sticking to the Knuckle; mince the Flesh small, and put it into a Frying-pan, with Lard, fine Herbs, whole Chibbols,

bols, Pepper, Salt, Nutmeg, Mushrooms, green Lemmon and some Broth, to be fried or stew'd all together: Then dress it under the Skin, which may be breaded and colour'd; adding some Lemmon-juice and good Gravy, when the Dish is ready to be serv'd up to Table.

GAMMON.

Take small Slices of raw Gammon; let them be well beaten and toss'd up in a Stew-pan, with a little Lard: Then set them over a Chafing-dish, and by the means of a Spoon, bring them to a brown colour, with a little Flower. As soon as they are colour'd put to them good Gravy, a Bunch of Chibbols and fine Herbs, a few Cloves, a Clove of Garlick, some Slices of Lemmon, a Handful of chopt Mushrooms, *Truffles* likewise minc'd, some Crusts of Bread and a little Vinegar: When they are all sufficiently boil'd, strain them thro' a Sieve and put this Liquor or Gravy into a convenient Place, without suffering it to boil any longer. It will be of use for the dressing of all sorts of Dishes in which Gammon is us'd.

A Gammon-pie.

Having provided a good Gammon, take off the Skin or Sward with the bad Fat, and cut off the Hock and the Bone in the middle. Then covering it with *Bards* or thin Slices of Bacon and Beef-stakes, also Spice, fine Herbs, pieces of Onion and a Bay-leaf, set it between two Fires in a Pot, with the Lid close stopt, so that no steam may evaporate: Stew it thus during twelve or Sixteen Hours; taking care that the Fire be not too quick, and let it cool in the same Pot: In the mean while, prepare a thick Paste, with a little Butter, an Egg, Flower and Water, and taking the Dish in which you would have it serv'd up, make a large Border round about it with the same Paste: This Border ought to be thick, having a Foot to bear some Weight, because there is no Bottom-crust, and may be wrought on the out-side with little Flower-de-luces and other fine Pastry-works: Set it into the Oven, and when it is bak'd, take out your Gammon, pouring off all the Fat that lies round about, and put it into a Dish, with its own Gravy. You may also make use of the same Stakes or Slices of Beef, to fill up the Intervals, and some Fat, and compleat the filling them, as if it were done in the Pie. 'Tis also requisite to add a little chopt Parsly, to strew it with Bread-chippings, and to give it a colour with the red-hot Fire-shovel, in order to be serv'd up cold to Table.

Another Intermeß of Gammon-pie.

Take away the Skin with the bad Fat of your Gammon, cut off the thin End or Hock, as before: Then, having prepar'd a thick brown Paste, with Rye-flower and Water, make your Pie of a round Figure and a considerable heighth; putting on the bottom a sufficient quantity of Bacon minc'd and pounded: Then having well fix'd the Gammon therein, put some Bay-leaves, four or five Slices of Lemmon and several other *Bards* or thin Slices of Bacon on the top: Afterwards cover it with a Lid, and when the Pie is quite finish'd, wash it over with the Yolk of an Egg: Let it stand in the Oven during six Hours and set it by cold, before it is brought to Table.

Gammon in a Ragoo, with Hypocras.

Take raw Slices of Gammon, and fry them in a Pan; making a Sauce with Sugar, Cinnamon, a pounded Macaroon, red Wine and a little white Pepper beaten. Then put your Slices into this Sauce, and sprinkle them with Orange-juice, when ready to be serv'd up to Table.

Gammon is dress'd otherwise among the Salt-meats, with Sausages and dried Tongues.

For a Gammon-*Omelet* recourse may be had hereafter to the Letter O. and for Pigeons with Gammon, to the Letter P. in like manner as Chickens with Gammon and the Gammon-cullis are already set down under C.

Fish-gammon.

Take the Flesh of Tenches, Eels and fresh Salmon, and the Roes of Carps, which are to be minc'd and pounded in a Mortar, with Pepper, Salt, Nutmeg and Butter. Mix all these sorts of Flesh well together, and make of them as it were a kind of Gammon, upon the Skins of Carps: Then wrap up the whole Farce in a new Linnen-cloth, which is to be sow'd up very close, and let it boil in one half Water and the other Wine; seson'd with Cloves, a Bay-leaf and Pepper. Let it cool in its own

own Broth, and serve it up with Bay-leaves, fine Herbs chopt very small, and Slices of Lemmon. It may also be cut into Slices, as the real Gammon.

A Leg or shoulder of Mutton may be imitated after the same manner, as also Chickens and Pigeons; or else with a sort of Fish-farce before describ'd in the first Article of the Letter F.

GODIVOE's.

We have already taken notice of several sorts of *Godivoe's* for different Messes; so that it may be sufficient here only to shew the manner of making the *Godivoe* of a *Poupeton*, which may serve for many other Things of the like nature.

To make the Godivoe of a Poupeton.

Take part of a Leg of Veal; with some parboil'd Bacon and other Fat, all well minc'd: Then adding to these, some chopt *Truffles* and Mushrooms, Chibbols, Parsly, the Crum of a Loaf soak'd in good Gravy, four whole Eggs and two Yolks; make the *Poupeton*, as it were a Pie, in the Stew-pan with *Bards* or thin Slices of Bacon underneath. You must also have at Hand, some Pigeons well dress'd, with all sorts of fine Herbs and good Garnitures, and some very small Slices of Gammon; all well season'd: Let your Pigeons be put into the *Poupeton*; and make an end of covering them with the Farce. To keep it from breaking, you may beat up an Egg, and lay it on neatly with your Hand: Then let the *Bards* or Bacon-slices, that are round about be turn'd upon it, and let it be bak'd between two gentle Fires, *viz.* on the top and underneath. This is commonly call'd a *Poupeton* farc'd with young Pigeons, and serves for a Side-dish. Quails may also be farced with it, or other Fowls of the same nature.

GOOSE-GIBBLETS.

There has been occasion to make mention of a Potage of Goose-gibblets Pag. 26. in order to prepare which, let your Gibblets boil in good Broth season'd with a Bunch of fine Herbs and Salt: Then cut them into pieces and fry them in Lard, with Parsly, Chervil and a little white Pepper: Lastly, having stew'd all with Yolks of Eggs, a little Verjuice and the Juice of a Lemmon

mon, dress your Potage upon the soaked Crusts. The same thing may be also done with the *Beatils* or Tid-bits of other sorts of Fowl.

A Gibblet-pie.

Gibblet-*Tourtes* or Pan-pies may be likewise made in this manner: Let your Gibblets be cut into pieces, scalded and well cleans'd: Then make your Pie with a fine Paste, both for the Under and Upper-Crust; seasoning it with Pepper, Salt, Cloves, fine Herbs, Chibbol and Nutmeg, and adding some pounded Lard, Artichoke-bottoms *Morilles*, and common Mushrooms: Let it be bak'd about two Hours, and serv'd up with a little white Sauce.

GRAVY.

Veal-gravy.

Cut a Fillet of Veal into three parts, put it into an earthen Pot, and stop it up so close with its Lid and some Paste, that no Air may come to it: Let it stand over a gentle Fire about two Hours, and your Gravy will be made; to be us'd for those Messes, into which, according to our Directions, some of it is requisite to be put, to render them more succulent and to heighten their Relish,

The same thing may be done, in preparing the Gravy of Mutton or Beef; or else recourse may be had to what has been laid down in the first Article of Cullises.

Partridge and Capon-gravy.

Let both be roasted, and when they are ready, let them be squeez'd separately to get their Gravy. The same thing may be put in practice for Veal-gravy and others.

Fish-gravy.

Take Tenches and Carps, cleanse the former from their Mud, cut them quite thro' the Back, and scale the Carps: Having taken away the Gills from both, put them into a Silver-dish, with a little Butter: Let them be brought to a brown colour, like a

piece

piece of Beef, and when they are dress'd, put to them a little Flower, which is also to be made brown with the rest, and afterwards some Broth, according to the quantity of Gravy that you would have made: Strain all thro' a Linnen-cloath and let it be very well squeez'd. Lastly, season this Liquor or Gravy, with a Bunch of Herbs, Salt and a green Lemmon stuck with Cloves, to be us'd, as well for Potages, as for Side-dishes and Intermesses of Fish.

GRENADE.

To make a *Grenade*, 'tis requisite to have a sufficient quantity of *Fricandoe's*, or *Scotch*-Collops larded with small Slips of Bacon, and a round Stew-pan, that is not of too large a size. Then put some thin Slices of Bacon on the bottom, and set your *Fricandoe's* in Order, with the Bacon on the outside; so as they may meet in a Point in the middle, and touch one another. To keep this Order from being confounded in the dressing of the Meats, they must be bound together, with the White of a beaten Egg; into which you may dip your Fingers, to moisten them on the Sides, which ought to be thinner than the rest. Into the hollow place made by this means, and also round about, you are to put a little of the Farce of *Mirotons*, or of some other *Godivoe*; reserving the middle for six Pigeons dress'd in a Ragoo, with Veal-sweet-breads, *Truffles*, Mushrooms and small Slices of Gammon, all well seaon'd: The Ragoo is likewise to be pour'd into it, as if it were a *Poupeton*. Then cover the rest of the Farce on the top, ordering it with your Fingers dipt in a beaten Egg, and join the *Fricandoe's* quite opposite thereto: Some *Bards* or thin Slices of Bacon are likewise to be laid on the top, and the whole Mess is to be bak'd *à la Braise* or between two Fires, to give it a fine colour. In order to serve it up hot, it must be turn'd upside down, and when the Fat is all taken away, the Point of the *Fricandoe's* or Collops must be open'd like that of a *Grenade* or Pomegranate; from whence this sort of Mess takes its Name.

K 3

A GRENADIN,

Of fat Pullets, Chickens, Pigeons, Partridges and all sorts of Fowl.

Let a well-season'd *Godivoe* be prepar'd, after the same manner as before for the *Poupeton*; remembring to thicken it with Yolks of Eggs and Bread-crum soak'd in good Gravy, or in a little Milk-cream: Then take a Baking-pan, according to the bigness of your Dish, and put into it some *Bards* or very thin Slices of Bacon: Let your *Godivoe* be laid upon these *Bards*, and with your Fingers dipt in a beaten Egg, make a Hole proportionably to the size of your Dish or Plate; raising up the sides to the heighth of three Inches, and so as they may be somewhat firm. Take your fat Pullets or other Fowls as they are raw, cut them into pieces, and let them be well beaten: Then fry them in a Pan, with Lard, Parsly, Chibbol and a little Flower, and afterwards put to them a little Gravy; seasoning them well, and adding *Truffles* cut into Slices, Mushrooms and Veal-sweet-breads. When they are almost ready, so that little Sauce is left, set the Fowls in order in your *Grenadin*, and let it be neatly breaded on the top, to give it a good colour in the Oven. As soon as it is drawn, drain it well from the Fat, cut off the *Bards* round about, and turn it into your Dish or Plate. A Mushroom-cullis may also be pour'd upon it, in order to serve it up hot to the Table for a Side-dish.

A GRILLADE, or
Dish of Meat broil'd upon the Grid-iron.

When any Turkeys, or other sorts of Fowl are left cold, a Side-dish may be made of them in this manner: Take their Wings, Legs and Rumps, and broil them upon the Grid-iron, with Pepper and Salt. Then fry some Flower in Lard, with Oisters, Anchovies, Capers, Nutmeg, a Bay-leaf and a piece of green Lemmon, also a little Vinegar and Broth, and let them all be well soak'd together.

GRU-

GRUEL.
An Intermeß of Gruel or Milk-potage.

Let some fine Oat-meal be put into a little Pot, full of Milk, with a Stick of Cinnamon, a piece of green Lemmon-peel, a little Salt, Coriander-seed and a few Cloves: Let it boil till it becomes a fine Cream; then strain it thro' the Hair-sieve, and having pour'd it into a *Cuvet*, Bason, or Dish, put a little Sugar therein: Afterwards bring it to a Furnace, the Fire of which is not too quick; because it ought not to boil any longer: Stir it about gently, from time to time, and when the Sugar is melted, set it upon the hot Embers; covering it close, till a kind of thick Cream over-spread the top: Then take it off, and let it be serv'd up hot in the same Dish.

H.

HASHES.

A Hash of Partridges.

TO make a Hash of Partridges, the same Method is to be observ'd, as in preparing an ordinary Mutton-hash; only you may add some Gammon, and temper it with good Gravy; garnishing your Dish with small Crusts of fried Bread, and sprinkling it with Lemmon-juice, when ready to be serv'd up to Table.

A Carp-hash.

For a Carp-hash, a few Capers are to be put into it, with Mushrooms, *Truffles* and other proper Garnitures, after all has been well minc'd and seafon'd.

There are also some other sorts of Hashes, which may be found by means of the General Table, in the several Places to which they properly belong, and where they are treated of in particular.

HARICOTS.

The manner of dreſſing an *Haricot* of Mutton, has been already explain'd in the laſt Article of *Cutlets* under the Letter C; and for Fiſh-*Haricots*, they may be prepar'd as a Pike in *Haricot*, under P.

HATLETS.

A Diſh of *Hatlets* is proper for the Intermeſſes, and may be thus made, *viz.* Let ſome Veal-ſweet-breads be parboil'd and cut into ſmall Pieces, with Capons-livers and young ſtreaked Bacon likewiſe parboil'd: Then let all be well ſeaſon'd and fry'd with a little Parſly, Chibbol and fine Flower. When they are almoſt ready, ſo that only a little thick Sauce is left, you are to make ſmall *Hatlets*, and ſpit the pieces of Livers, Sweet-breads and Bacon upon them, according to the bigneſs you would have them to be of. Afterwards, having dipt them in the Sauce and well breaded them, they may be broil'd upon a Grid-iron or fried.

Hatlets are alſo often us'd for the garniſhing of Diſhes of Roaſt-meat.

HEADS.

An Intermeſs of a Boar's Head.

Let a Boar's Head be well ſindg'd at a clear Fire, and rubb'd with a piece of Brick to take off all the Hair; let it alſo be ſcrap'd with a Knife and well cleans'd: After having boned it, cutting out the two Jaw-bones and the Snout; ſlit it underneath, ſo as it may ſtick to its Skin on the top, and take away the Brain and Tongue: Then take up ſome Salt with the Point of your Knife, and cauſe it to penetrate thro' all the Parts of the Fleſh: Afterwards let the whole Head be ſet together again, and well tied up, wrapping it in a Napkin. In the mean while, a great Kettle, almoſt full of Water, is to be hang'd over the Fire, and the Head put into it, with all ſorts of fine Herbs, ſome Leaf-fat out of a Hog's Belly, two Bay-leaves, Coriander and Anis-ſeed, Cloves and Nutmeg beaten, and ſome Salt, if it has not been ſufficiently corned before; adding alſo ſome Onion and Roſemary. When it is half boil'd, pour in a Quart

of

of good Wine, and let it continue boiling for the space of twelve Hours; the Tongue may also be boil'd in the same Liquor. If time will permit, the Head may be salted before it is dress'd, and left for a while in its Brine. When it is ready, let it cool in its own Liquor; then having taken it out, let it be neatly put into a Dish and served up to Table cold; either whole or in Slices.

Fish-heads.

The Head of a Pike may be dress'd in a *Court-bouillon*, as it appears in the Second Article of Pike under the Letter P, and may also be serv'd up in Potage, as well as others; more especially that of Salmon, for which see *Joll*.

Lambs-heads in Potage, or for a Side-dish.

Take the Heads, Feet and Livers of Lambs, with young Bacon, and having well scalded them, let them boil all together in some Broth in a great Pot: As soon as they are boil'd and well season'd, lay your Potage a soaking with good Broth and Gravy, and set the Lambs-heads in Order in the middle: Then having breaded the Brains, fry them, 'till they become as it were *Croquets*, and put them again into their Place; garnishing your Potage, with the Livers, Feet and Bacon: To these is to be added a White Cullis, made with a piece of Bread-crum steept in good Broth, a Douzen and half of sweet Almonds, and three Yolks of hard Eggs, all pounded in a Mortar, strain'd thro' a Sieve, well soak'd and season'd; with the Juice of a Lemmon, when ready to be serv'd up to Table.

A green Cullis may also be prepar'd with Chibbol-tops, Spinage and Crusts of Bread, which are likewise to be soak'd in a Stew-pan, with good Broth, well season'd with Cloves, Thyme and Gravy: Pound your Chibbol-tops and Spinage in a Mortar; and having strain'd the rest thro' a Sieve, put them into the Potage; strewing it with Asparagus-tops, and sprinkling it with the Juice of a Lemmon.

Instead of this Cullis, a good sort of green Pease-soop may be pour'd upon the Potage of Lambs-heads; otherwise to diversifie them, a Cullis may be made of the Livers, to be garnish'd with the Feet and young Bacon. At another time, they may be cover'd with green Pease, and a Cullis of the same, according

'ding to the Seaſon. And at another time, the Lambs-heads may be carefully ſcalded in Water that is not too hot; then all the Bones muſt be cut out with the Tongue, taking care that the Skin remain quite entire: Theſe Heads are to be ſtuff'd with ſome good Farce, and neatly tied up, in order to be dreſs'd: Then they are to be put into the Potage, and garniſh'd as before; or elſe with Lambs-lungs marinated and fried in Paſte.

A ſmall Side-diſh of Lambs-heads may be prepar'd with a good Ragoo pour'd upon it; as alſo a kind of Lamb-potage, with Roman Lettice farced; garniſhing the ſaid Potage with the Stalks of the Lettice fried in a Pan with Lard and Flower, and afterwards laid a ſoaking in a Pot with good Broth, which muſt be thicken'd before it is dreſs'd, with Yolks of Eggs ſtrain'd thro' the Hair-ſieve.

HIND.

To know the manner of dreſſing a Hind, 'tis only requiſite to have recourſe to the Article of a *Stag*; as being of the ſame Nature, except that the former is ſofter and more inſipid. Therefore it ought to be ſteept in a Marinade of the ſame, after it has been larded, with ſmall Slips of Bacon: It muſt be well baſted as it is roaſting; and when it is ready, Capers and fried Flower are to be put into the Dripping, with a little green Lemmon; it muſt alſo be ſoak'd in its Sauce.

When your Hind is larded, marinated and roaſted, cover'd with Paper; a ſweet Sauce may likewiſe be prepared for it, with Vinegar, Pepper, Sugar, Cinnamon and a whole Shalot.

For a Hind-*Cives*, ſee the Letter C.

I.

JELLIES.

THe manner of making a Jelly of Fruits has been already expreſs'd under the Letter F, and in the Article of *Blancmanger* may be found the Jelly which is requiſite for that purpoſe, as alſo that of Harts-horn, for Fiſh-days; ſo that we ſhall only here produce a ſort of Jelly proper for ſick Perſons; which nevertheleſs will be of a much better Reliſh to thoſe that are in Health, when ſerv'd up among the Intermeſſes as the reſt.

To

To make an excellent Jelly.

Take Calves-feet, according to the quantity of Jelly that you would have made, with a good Cock, and having well wash'd all, put them into a Kettle or Pot, filling it with a proportionable quantity of Water. Let them boil together, and be more especially careful to look after the scumming of the Pot. When these Meats are almost reduc'd to Rags, 'tis a sign that the Jelly is sufficiently boil'd, but care must be taken that it be not too strong. Then having provided a good Stew-pan, strain the Jelly thro' a Sieve, that is to say, nothing but the pure Broth; clear it well from the Fat, with two or three Feathers; and put some Sugar into it proportionably; with a Stick of Cinnamon, two or three Cloves and the Peel of two or three Lemmons, the Juice of which must be kept. Let your Jelly boil thus a little while, and in the mean time, make some Snow with four or six Whites of Eggs: Squeez the Juice of your Lemmons into it, and pour all into the Jelly; stirring them together, a little while over the Furnace: Then leaving them till the Liquor rises, and is ready to run over the Pan; pour it out into the Straining-bag, and strain it two or three times, till you perceive it to be clear. Whilst the Jelly is boiling with the Meats, some think fit to pour in a little white Wine. In order to serve this Jelly up to Table, it must be put into a very cold Place, to the end that it may be well coagulated in the Dishes.

How to colour Jellies.

These Colours being well order'd, may produce very agreeable Effects in a *Blanc-manger*, or any other Mess of the like nature. For Example, the Jelly may be left in its natural Colour, or made white with Almonds pounded and strain'd after the usual manner: For yellow, some Yolks of Eggs may be put into it; for Grey, a little Cochineel; for Red, some Juice of red Beet or Turnsole of *Portugal*; for Purple, some purple Turnsole, or Powder of Violets; and for Green, some Juice of Beet-leaves, which is to be boil'd in a Dish to take away its Crudity.

JOLL.

JOLL.

A Joll of Salmon.

Let your Joll be ſcal'd, larded with Slips of Eels-fleſh and ſeaſon'd with Pepper: Then fry it with burnt Butter and afterwards ſtew it in an Earthen Pan, with clear Peaſe-ſoop, fine Herbs and green Lemmon: Add to theſe, ſome Capers, Muſhrooms and Oiſters, fry'd with burnt Butter and a little Flower; and dreſs all artificially in the Potage, with Lemmon-juice, as they are ſerving up to Table.

JULIAN.

The *Julian* is a very conſiderable Potage, and may be made in this manner: Having roaſted a Leg of Mutton, let the Fat and Skin be taken away, and let it be put into a Kettle or Pot, of a ſufficient bigneſs to hold ſome Broth for the Potage. Then add a good piece of Beef; another of a Fillet of Veal; a fat Capon; Carrets, Turneps and Parſneps, two of each; Parſly-roots, Celery and an Onion ſtuck with Cloves; and let all boil together a long while, to the end that your Broth may be ſufficiently enrich'd. In the mean time, another Pot muſt be provided, and therein three or four Bundles of Aſparagus, as much Sorrel as may be cut with a Knife at two ſtrokes and ſome Chervil. Let them be well boil'd with ſome Broth taken out of the great Pot, and when the Cruſts are ſoak'd, let the Aſparagus and Sorrel be laid in order upon them, but nothing round about.

Julian-Potages are alſo made of a Breaſt of Veal, Capons, fat Pullets, Pigeons and other ſorts of Meat: When they are well prepar'd and ſcalded, let them be put into a Pot with good Broth and a Bunch of fine Herbs; afterwards adding the above-mentioned Roots and Pulſe; which may alſo ſerve to garniſh the Potage, with Heaps of Aſparagus chopt into pieces, and nothing elſe, but what is green, ſuch as green Peaſe, &c.

K

K.

KIDS.

Kids may be dress'd after the same manner as Lamb, either in Potage, or for Side-dishes; so that it is only requisite to peruse what is hereafter set down in that Article; and for roasted Kids, to turn to the Letter R.

L.

LAMB.

IT were needless to take notice, That Quarters, or whole Sides of Lamb, often serve for the great Roast, when it is in season; and more especially, for the meaner sort of Ordinaries. And in regard, that there is nothing either difficult or unknown relating to this Article, we shall here only shew the manner of making a Ragoo of Lamb; at the same time, referring the Reader, for Lambs-heads, to the third Article of *Heads*, and, for Lambs-feet, to the Letter F.

Lamb in a Ragoo.

A Ragoo of Lamb may be prepar'd thus: Cut it into four quarters, and, after having larded it with middle-siz'd Slips of Bacon, and given it somewhat of a colour, let it be boil'd in an Earthen Pot or Stew-pan, with Broth, Pepper, Salt, Cloves, Mushrooms, and a Faggot of fine Herbs. When it is ready, let a Sauce be made for it, of Oisters fried with a little Flower, two Anchovies, and Lemmon-juice, when ready to be serv'd up to Table, and let it be garnish'd with fried Mushrooms.

LAMPREYS.

Lampreys may be dress'd two several ways, *viz.* Take some of their Blood and let it be kept a-part: Then cleanse them from their Slime with hot Water and cut them into pieces; which are to be stew'd in an Earthen Pot, with burnt Butter, white Wine, Pepper, Salt, Nutmeg, a Bunch of Herbs and a Bay-leaf. Afterwards let their Blood be put to them, with a little

fried

fried Flower and Capers, and let them be garnish'd with Slices of Lemmon.

To dress them with sweet Sauce; when they are clear'd from their Slime, let them be stew'd in red Wine, with burnt Butter, Cinnamon, Sugar, Pepper, Salt and a piece of green Lemmon; adding some Lemmon-juice, when they are set upon the Table.

If it be requir'd to make a Potage of Lampreys, cut them into pieces, after having taken away their Slime, and fry them in burnt Butter, with Salt, Flower, fine Herbs chopt small, Mushrooms, strained Pease-soop, and a piece of green Lemmon. Then let them be dress'd upon the soak'd Crusts, and sprinkled with Lemmon-juice, as they are serving up to Table.

For Pies of Lampreys, see the Letter P.

LARKS.

Larks may be put into a Ragoo for Side-dishes, as also into a standing Pie, to be serv'd up hot, and into a *Tourte* or Pan-pie; for the two latter, it would be requisite only to observe the Directions given for the dressing of other sorts of Fowl of the like nature, and among others, for young Pigeons; except that Larks are not farced as larger Birds. Only their Ghizzards are usually taken out, and set in order on the bottom of the Pie, which is also to be fill'd with Mushrooms, Capons-livers, *Truffles*, pounded Lard and other seasoning Ingredients. When the Pie is ready to be serv'd up, some good Gravy of Veal or Mutton must be put into it, with the Juice of a Lemmon; and some Capers must be reserv'd for the Pan-pie.

As for the Ragoo; after having drawn your Larks, fry them in Lard with a little Flower, and afterwards stew them in an Earthen Pan, in Broth, with white Wine, Dates cut into pieces, candy'd Lemmon-peel, Pistachoes, Cinnamon, Pepper, Salt and Prunelloes; adding Lemmon-juice when ready to be brought to Table. They may be garnish'd with the same Things, and serv'd up with short Sauce.

It will not be worth the while to observe, that fat Larks are sometimes roasted; it being a very common Dish.

For Potages of Larks, see the Letter P.

LEGS.

LEGS.

Altho' there is nothing more common than a Leg of Mutton or Veal, yet they may be dress'd after several manners, so as to give good satisfaction, and even to grace the most sumptuous Tables.

Legs of Mutton.

A Side-dish of a farced Leg of Mutton.

As soon as your Leg of Mutton is dress'd, take away all the Meat, so as nothing may remain but the Bones sticking together: Then clear this Meat from the Fat, and mince it with parboil'd Bacon, a little Sewet, or Marrow, some fine Herbs, Chibbol, Parsly, a little piece of Calves-udder, the Crum of a Loaf soak'd in good Broth, two whole Eggs and two separate Yolks. Thus, all being well minc'd and seasoned, let the Bone be laid in the Dish, that is to be serv'd up, so as the small end of the Leg may appear; one half of this *Godivoe* being put round about. Afterwards, having made a hollow place of the shape of the Leg, and having dipt your Fingers in a beaten Egg, that nothing may stick to them, fill up that place with a Ragoo of all sorts of Garnitures, well boil'd, strain'd and season'd; as also, the rest of the vacancy with the Farce, which may supply the place of a real Leg. Then having breaded the whole Mess, set it into the Oven, to give it a colour, and afterwards, when drawn, take away the Fat, that lyes round about the Dish. Lastly, pour in a small quantity of a well-season'd Cullis, thro' a little hole on the top, and cover it again, to be serv'd up hot to Table.

Another way of dressing a Leg of Mutton.

Another middling Side-dish may be made of a large farced Leg of Mutton with Cream. Having boned it, take the Flesh, with a piece of Veal, another of Bacon, some Leaf-fat out of a Hog's Belly and Beef-sewet, and let all be well minc'd together; adding a little Chibbol and Parsly chopt, with two or three Rocamboles, a little sweet Basil and Thyme, all well season'd, with Pepper, Salt, Spice and a few Coriander-seeds.

Then

Then mingle and beat the whole Mass in a Mortar, with Cream, Yolks of Eggs and Bread-crum; stuff the Bone with this Farce in the Shape of a Leg; wash it over with the White of an Egg, covering the top with Bread-crum; and give it its due Form, if you please, with the Back of a Knife. Let it be bak'd in a Silver-dish or in a Baking-pan, with *Bards* or thin Slices of Bacon laid underneath; but your Farce must be made very strong, lest it should break, or fall in the Oven. The Dish may be garnish'd with *Petits-patez* or little Pies, farced Veal-cutlets, marinated Chickens, or any other proper Garniture; taking care, that all be well dress'd and brought to a fine colour.

A middling Side-dish may also be made of a Leg of Mutton farc'd in its Skin, and dress'd in a Ragoo with Artichoke-bottoms, Veal-sweet-breads, *Truffles*, Mushrooms, Capons-livers and Asparagus-tops, all well season'd. It ought to be garnish'd with little Rolls of Fennel and farced *Poupiets*, and sprinkled with Lemmon-juice, when serv'd up to Table.

A Leg of Mutton dress'd à la Royale.

Having taken away the Fat from a good Leg of Mutton, with the Flesh round about the small End, let it be beaten and larded with thick Slips of Bacon; a piece of Buttock-beef or of Veal may also be larded with it at the same time. Let all be well season'd, let the Leg and the other Meat be flower'd, and let them be brought to a colour with some melted Lard: Then being put into a Pot with all sorts of fine Herbs, an Onion stuck with Cloves, some good Broth, or Water; let them be close cover'd, and boil'd for a considerable time. In the mean while, a proper Ragoo is to be made, with Mushrooms, *Truffles*, Artichoke-bottoms, Asparagus-tops, Veal-sweet-breads; all well prepar'd, and enrich'd with a good Cullis. Afterwards having taken your Leg out of the Pot, dress it in a Dish, and cut your pieces of Beef or Veal, very neatly into Slices, to make a Border round about; so as the Bacon may appear on the Slices. Lastly, the Ragoo must be pour'd upon it scalding-hot; but if you would have the Leg take its whole relish, when it is almost ready, let it be stew'd a little while in the said Ragoo, and serv'd up in the same manner. It may also be garnish'd with larded *Fricandoe's* or Scotch-Collops and *Marinade*.

Ano-

Another Side-dish of a Leg of Mutton.

Take a Leg of Mutton, and having cut off the Fat, as before, let it be well larded and seafon'd; it may alfo be larded with raw Gammon. Then provide a Pot with fome *Bards* or thin Slices of Bacon, and Stakes of Beef or Veal and fet them in order therein, as it were for baking or ftewing between two Fires: Let the Leg be put into this Pot, and let a Fire be kindled both underneath and on the top; fo as to bring it to a fine colour. Afterwards take out the *Bards* and the other Meat, and drain them a little from the Fat, but let the Leg of Mutton be ftill left for fome time; whilft you put as much Flower as may be taken up between your Fingers, round about the Pot, and caufe it to take a colour with the Leg: As foon as it is colour'd, put the Meat in again, that was taken out, with good Gravy and a little Water, keep the Pot clofe cover'd, and make an end of boiling all together. As for the Sauce, it ought to be fomewhat thick; otherwife a Cullis muft be pour'd into it, made of the Meat which lay round about the Leg, pounded, and ftrain'd with good Gravy. To thefe may be added all forts of Garniture, particularly, Afparagus, *Morilles*, and common Mufhrooms, and let all boil together, as alfo fome *Truffles*, Cockscombs and Veal-fweet-breads, if they may be conveniently procur'd. When every thing is ready, drefs the Leg after the ufual manner, let the Ragoo be well clear'd from the Fat, and put a little Verjuice into it. The Difh may be garnifh'd with farced Cutlets of Mutton or Veal, as is before fpecified.

A Leg of Mutton drefs'd with Succory and Cucumbers.

Let a Leg of Mutton be roafted, taking care that it be not done too much, whilft a Ragoo is preparing with Succory, that is fcalded a little and cut into pieces. Take fome Lard, make it fomewhat brown, with Flower and good Gravy, and let all be well feafon'd; adding a Faggot of fine Herbs and a few drops of Vinegar: Then let your Succory be boil'd, fo as not to turn black, but that it may have a fomewhat ftrong Savour, and let it be put under the Leg. The fame Thing may be done with Cucumbers, but they muft be marinated, cut into fmall Slices, and afterwards drefs'd in the fame manner. If you would not have the Leg ferv'd up whole, it may be cut into thin Slices, and

L put

put into the same Ragoo; taking care that they do not boil together, and that the Sauce be not either too thick or too thin. Let all be well clear'd from the Fat and brought hot to Table.

A roasted Leg of Mutton may also be serv'd up with *Robert*-Sauce, Capers and Anchovies, either for Out-works, or even for a Side-dish, when set out with proper Garnitures, and a Shoulder of Mutton may be dress'd after all the manners that have been before-describ'd for a Leg.

Legs of Veal.

Having already shewn how a Leg of Veal may be dress'd in a *Daube*, under the Letter D; we shall here explain some other Preperations that may be made with that Joint of Meat, *viz.*

A farced Leg of Veal.

The Farce must be made of the same Flesh, with Sewer, Bacon, fine Herbs, Chibbols, Pepper, Salt, Nutmeg, Yolks of raw Eggs and Mushrooms, and when 'tis sow'd up, let it boil in good Broth. Thus a Side-dish may be made of it, or it may be serv'd up in Potage; adding a Cullis of poach'd Yolks of Eggs and Almonds, strain'd thro' a Sieve, with the same Broth. When the Dish is ready to be serv'd up, let some Lemmon-juice and good Gravy be put therein; garnishing it with Mushrooms farced and ragoo'd, or any Thing else that you have at Hand; as Cutlets, Veal-sweet-breads, &c.

A Leg of Veal à l' Estoufade, or stew'd in a Pan.

Let your Leg of Veal be larded with thick Slips of Bacon, and fried a while in a Frying-pan: Then stew it in an earthen Pan, with Mushrooms, a Spoonful of Broth and a Glass of white Wine; seasoning it with Pepper, Salt, a Faggot of fine Herbs, Cloves and Nutmeg. When it is ready, let some Flower be fry'd to thicken the Sauce, and garnish it with fry'd Bread, Veal-sweet-breads and Lemmon-juice, as it is serving up to Table.

LEMMONS.

To preserve Lemmon-peel dry.

Take Lemmons, and let them be well turn'd with clean Hands, to the end that your Fruit may be always kept white: Then cut them into quarters taking away all the inner Rind, and order them so as their Pulp may be very thin: Let them be steept in fair Water, and afterwards scalded in hot Water; but care must be taken, that they be not done either too much or too little: Throw them again into fresh Water, and having prepar'd some Syrop with clarified Sugar, let them boil a little therein: Let them lye by a while, and then let them be laid upon a Grate or Hurdle, to dry up their moisture. In the mean time, having boil'd up your Sugar, till it become a little feather'd, put the Lemmon-peels into it with a Table-fork, but be careful that the Liquor be not too thick. When they are sufficiently boil'd, take them out, leave them again on the Grate to be dried, and let them be well ic'd. There are several other Ways of preserving Lemmon-peels, which we shall pass by at present; as being the Business of a Confectioner, rather than of a Cook.

LENTILS.

A Cullis of Lentils has been already describ'd under the Letter C, and for Lentil-potage, it may readily be found among the other Potages under P.

LETTICE.

To farce Lettice à la Dame Simonne.

Let headed or Cabbage-lettice, be only heated a little in scalding Water, and well drain'd: Then taking the Flesh of roasted Capons and Chickens, mince it with some pieces of boil'd Gammon, Mushrooms and fine Herbs: Let all be well season'd, and put into a Stew-pan, with two Handfuls of Bread-crum, and four or five Eggs, according to the nature of the Farce. The Lettice, when stuff'd with it in the middle, must be well tied or sow'd up, and boil'd in good Broth: In the mean while, a good White Sauce being duely prepar'd, with several Yolks of Eggs,

L 2

so as it may not turn, take your Lettice and after having thoroughly drain'd and untied them, put them into this Sauce, to be kept hot. They are usually serv'd up for Out-works and sometimes among the Side-dishes.

The Soops of farced Fowls are also garnish'd with the same sort of Lettice; and the Lettice, on Fish-days, are commonly stuff'd with a good Fish-farce, or with Herbs and Eggs.

LEVERETS.

Leverets or young Hares larded.

Let one Shoulder with one Leg of your Leverets be larded, and the others left in their natural condition. Then having roasted them; let them be serv'd up, with Sweet Sauce, or else with Vinegar and Pepper, and garnish'd with *Marinade*.

A Leveret dress'd after the Swifs Mode.

Having cut a Leveret into quarters, and larded them with thick Slips of Bacon, let them boil in some Broth, season'd with Pepper, Salt, Cloves and a little Wine. Then fry the Liver and the Blood with some Flower, and mingle all together; adding a little Vinegar, stoned Olives, Capers and Lemmon-slices for their Garniture.

Leveret-potage, after the Italian manner.

Let the Leveret be cut into quarters; larded with thick Slips of Bacon, and fried in Lard: Then let them be stew'd in good Broth, such as is describ'd in the Article of Broth, with Dates, Currans, Lemmon-peel, Cinnamon, Salt and a little white Wine: Lastly, let the whole Mess be dress'd upon the soaked Crusts, and serv'd up to Table, with Lemmon-juice, garnish'd with Pomegranate-slices or Kernels.

For Leveret-pies, see the Letter P. among the other sorts of Pies.

LIQUORS, see *Broth*.

LIVERS.

An Intermefs of Capons-livers drefs'd in a Veal-caul.

Take the largeft and leaneft Capons-livers and having minc'd them, with some parboil'd Bacon, a little Sewet and Marrow, *Truffles*, Mushrooms, and Veal-sweet-breads; also a little Parfly, Chibbol and boil'd Gammon, let the whole Farce be bound with the Yolk of an Egg. Then cut a Veal-caul into pieces, according to the thicknefs of your Livers, fo as they may be conveniently roll'd up in them; and let fome of the Farce be put upon the Caul, then a Liver upon that, and afterwards the Farce again thereupon, and take care that all be well wrapt up in the Caul. Thefe Livers fo drefs'd are to be laid upon a Sheet of Paper in order to be broil'd upon the Grid-iron, with a little Lard; or elfe in a Baking-pan and fet into an Oven. When they are ready, let them be taken out, thoroughly drain'd from the Fat, and drefs'd in a Difh, with a little hot Broth pour'd upon them: Afterwards feafon them with Pepper and Salt, and having fqueez'd in the Juice of an Orange, ferve them up hot to Table.

An Intermeß of Capons-livers and Mushrooms.

After having well cleans'd your Livers from the Gall, take a Baking-pan, lay fome *Bards* or thin Slices of Bacon on the Bottom of it, and the Livers upon them: Let them be feafon'd and cover'd with other *Bards* on the top, and then fet into the Oven; taking care that they be not too much dry'd. Let fome Mushrooms well pickt and wash'd be put into a Difh, with a little Bacon and Verjuice, having before caus'd their moifture to be dry'd up, by fetting them on the Fire, and let fome Slices of Gammon be fried a-part, with a little Lard and Flower, and a Bunch of fine Herbs: Afterwards pour in fome good Veal-gravy, that is not Salt, and ftew it with the Mushrooms and Livers well drain'd, in the fame Sauce. Laftly let it be incorporated with fome good thickening Liquor, if there be occafion, and when the Fat is taken away, add a little Vinegar, and let it be ferv'd up hot to Table. The Difh may be garnifh'd with what you pleafe, provided it be fomething that is proper for Intermeffes.

Capons-livers dreſs'd otherwiſe for Intermeſſes.

Having provided ſome good Capons-livers with a Baking-pan; for every Liver prepare a thin Slice of Bacon, and ſet them in order ſeparately in the Pan, laying the Livers upon them, when well ſeaſon'd: Let them alſo be cover'd with another Slice of Bacon, and dextrouſly breaded, to the end that they may be well bak'd and brought to a fine colour: When they are drawn out of the Oven, let them be ſufficiently drain'd, and neatly laid in a Diſh: Laſtly ſome good Gravy may be added with the Juice of an Orange, and ſo let it be immediately brought hot to Table.

Capons-livers with Gammon.

Let ſome Gammon be cut very ſmall, and fry'd brown, with your Livers, alſo a young Chibbol and a little Parſly well chopt: When they are ſeaſon'd as much as requiſite, let them boil over a gentle Fire, with a piece of Lemmon, and ſerve them up with good Gravy for Out-works and Intermeſſes.

Capons-livers dreſs'd between two Fires.

Having ſtrew'd your Livers with Pepper and fine Salt, cover them with a thin Slice of Bacon and a piece of Paper, which muſt be wet a little on the top, to keep them from burning: Then tye up the Livers and putting them between two Fires, let them be ſtew'd by degrees, and ſerv'd up to Table, with Gravy.

Another Intermeſs of Capons-livers.

When the Livers are well clear'd from the Gall, and ſcalded a little, put them into fair Water afterwards with the ſame Water into a Diſh, and let them be well ſeaſon'd. Then chopping a few Muſhrooms, *Truffles*, Parſly and Chibbol, let all boil together. As for the Livers, they are to be wrapt up in thin Slices of Bacon, as before, and ſet into an Oven, till they come to a fine colour; but if it be not ſufficiently done, it may be brought to perfection, with the red-hot Fire-ſhovel. When it is ready to be ſerv'd up, drain the Fat well off, ſet the Livers in order in a Diſh, and pour a little Gravy upon them, with the Juice of one or two Oranges.

LOAVES,

LOAVES, *see* PAINS.

LOBSTERS.

It were needless to insist on the manner of making a Lobster-hash, as being common with that of other Hashes of the like nature: In order to dress them in a Sallet, it would be requisite only to observe what has been laid down Pag. 41. concerning the other Fish-sallets; adding to the Sauce of this sort, the inside of the Lobster's Body. They are also prepar'd in a Ragoo, and in Potages, taking away the Shells, after they are boil'd; neither is there any difficulty in this Matter, provided the Directions be follow'd, that are given elsewhere in several Places, for the ordering of other sorts of Fish.

M.

MACKAREL.

WHen the Mackarel are gutted, slit or cut them a little along the Back, and cause them to take Salt, with Oil, Pepper, fine Salt and Fennel. They may be also wrapt up in the same green Fennel, in order to be roasted; whilst a Sauce is preparing for them, with burnt Butter, fine Herbs chopt small, Nutmeg, Salt, Fennel, scalded Gooseberries in their Season, Capers and a little Vinegar. Then they are to be serv'd up to Table, and garnish'd with Slices of Lemmon.

They may also be dress'd in Potage, when they have been well fry'd before in refined Butter, and afterwards laid a soaking in a Stew-pan, with good Fish-broth or Herbs: Let them be garnish'd with a Ragoo of Mushrooms, Capers, Gravy and Slices of Lemmon.

MARINADES.

Several Things are put into a *Marinade* or Pickle, either for the garnishing of other Messes, or to make a particular Dish. Fricassies of Chickens are usually garnish'd with other marinated Chickens; a *Marinade* of Veal serves to garnish farced Breasts of Veal, or roasted Loins of Veal, and so of the rest;

as Pigeons, Partridges and others, with which separate Services may be prepar'd for Side-dishes. Let us here give some Account of what is most observable under this Article.

A Marinade of *Chickens*.

Let your Chickens be cut into quarters, and marinated, with Lemmon-juice and Verjuice, or with Vinegar, Pepper, Salt, Cloves, Chibbols and a Bay-leaf or two. Leave them in this *Marinade* for the space of three Hours, and having made a sort of clear Paste or Batter, with Flower, white Wine and the Yolks of Eggs, dip your Chickens into it: Then fry them in Lard, and let them be serv'd up in form of a Pyramid, with fry'd Parsly and Slices of Lemmon, if you design to make a particular Dish of them.

A Marinade of *Pigeons*.

Pigeons ought to be marinated in Lemmon-juice, and Verjuice, as before, with the other Ingredients; after having slit them on the Back, or cut them into quarters, to the end that the *Marinade* may penetrate into the Flesh. Thus they are to be left three or four Hours in Pickle and afterwards dipt into Paste, or flower'd when all over Wet; in order to be gently fried. They may be serv'd up with fried Parsly strew'd upon them, and round about the Dish, adding a little Rose-vinegar and white Pepper.

A Marinade of *Partridges*.

Let the Partridges be cut into two pieces and steept in a *Marinade*, as the preceding Particulars: They must also be fry'd after the same manner, and serv'd up to Table with Garlick-vinegar and white Pepper.

A Marinade of *Veal*.

This sort of *Marinade* is likewise prepar'd in order to garnish other Dishes, cutting the Veal into Slices, as it were for *Fricandoes* or Scotch Collops, and so of the other Things that are to be marinated. For marinated Mutton-cutlets, see the last Article of *Cutlets* under the Letter C.

A

A Marinade *of Fish.*

Some forts of Fish are ufually put into a *Marinade* and Tortoifes among others. As foon as they are drefs'd, let them be fteept in Vinegar, with Pepper, Salt and Chibbols: Then let them be flower'd, fry'd in refined Butter, and ferv'd up with fry'd Parfly, white Pepper and Orange-juice.

Another fort of *Marinade* for Fish, may be made, after they have been fried, in this manner: Let fome Slices of Lemmon or Orange be put into the Frying-pan with Bay-leaves, refined Butter, Chibbols, Pepper, Salt, Nutmeg and Vinegar, and let this Sauce be pour'd upon the Fish; fuch as Soles, Congers, Pilchards, Tunnies cut into round Slices, &c. Other forts of Fish-*Marinades* may alfo be found in the Article of Potages, which are fet down in the General Table of the Meffes.

MAUVIETTES.

Befides that for roafted *Mauviettes*, recourfe may be had to the Article *of Roaft-meats*; under the Letter R; a Side-difh may be prepar'd of farced *Mauviettes* with Muftard, as appears from the Example Pag. 28. and a Potage of *Mauviettes*, with brown Broth.

MENUS-DROITS *or* MINE-DROIT.

Difhes, or Out-works of *Menus-droits* are made for Intermeffes, of different Things, and among others, of an Ox-palate, cut into thin Slices: After having fry'd them in Lard with Parfly, fmall Chervil, Thyme, a whole Chibbol, Pepper, Salt, Broth and white Wine; they are to be laid a foaking in a Pot or Difh, and the Sauce is to be thicken'd with Bread-chippings; adding Mutton-gravy and Lemmon-juice, when ferv'd up to Table.

The *Menus-droits* of a Stag and others are drefs'd after the fame manner.

MERINGUES.

Meringues properly belong only to the Confectioner's Art; but forafmuch as Cooks fometimes have occafion to ufe them, for the garnifhing of feveral Things; it may not be improper here to fhew the manner of making them. To

To that purpose, take three or four new-laid Eggs, according to the quantity of *Meringues* requir'd to be made; reserve the Whites, and whip them till they form a rocky Snow. Then you are to put to them a little green Lemmon grated, with three or four spoonfuls of fine Sugar pass'd thro' the Sieve, and let all be whipt together; a little prepar'd Amber may also be added: Afterwards take some white Paper, and with a Spoon make your *Meringues* of a round or oval Figure, accordingly as you shall think fit, about the thickness of a Walnut; leaving some Distance between every one of them: In the mean while, let some powder'd Sugar be put into the end of a Napkin, and strew the *Meringues* with it. On the same Table, where they are dress'd, may be laid the cover of a Campain-oven, that has not been put into the Fire, but only has had some Fire upon it, and the *Meringues* may be cover'd with it, to give them a kind of Ash-colour; but no Fire must be put underneath: When they are bak'd and well ic'd, let them be taken off from the Paper. You may also put in a little Fruit, as a Rasberry, Strawberry or Cherry, according to the Season, and joyn other *Meringues* to them, to make Twins.

Pistachoe-Meringues.

Take a handful or two of Pistachoes, and let them be well scalded: After having whipt the Whites of Eggs, as for the preceding *Meringues*, and having beaten all together, with fine Sugar; put in the Pistachoes, the Water being well drain'd from them, and with a little Spoon, make the *Meringues* of what thickness you please; icing them in the same manner. If you are not desirous to have them ic'd, their natural colour will be as white as Paper. These *Meringues* may serve to garnish all sorts of Pan-pies for Intermesses, and chiefly those of Marchpane.

MILK-POTAGE, *see* GRUEL.

MIROTONS.

A *Miroton* is usually serv'd up for a Side-dish, and may be made several ways; among others thus: Take a good Fillet of Veal, and cut it into several very thin Slices, which are to be beaten on the Dresser with a Cleaver: Another Fillet of Veal must

The Court and Country Cook. 155

must also be provided, which is to be minc'd with parboil'd Bacon, some Sewet, a little Marrow, Mushrooms, *Truffles* and fine Herbs, all well seafon'd: To these add two or three Yolks of Eggs, and, as soon as the Farce is made, take a round Stew-pan, that is not too large: Lay some *Bards* or thin Slices of Bacon in good order on the bottom, then the Veal-stakes that were beaten, and at last the Farce, which must be cover'd on the top, with the rest of the Slices, and all must be well stopt up. Afterwards let the Bacon-*Bards* be turn'd, and, having well cover'd the whole Mess, let it be bak'd or stew'd *à la Braise,* that is to say, between two gentle Fires, one on the top and the other underneath: When it is ready, let it be well clear'd from the Fat, and laid upside-down in a Dish; adding, if you please, a little Cullis, before it is serv'd up hot to Table.

Mirotons *dress'd after another manner.*

Some Cooks prepare a well thicken'd *Godivoe* of the same nature as that for a *Poupeton,* and afterwards make a Border of it, round about the Dish, made of the Whites of Eggs, as it were for Milk-potage: Then they wash it over with beaten Eggs; and, having neatly breaded it, bring it to a colour in the Oven; taking away all the Fat when it is dress'd. In the mean while, an Earthen Pan must be fill'd with a Breast of Mutton, cut into pieces, the scraggy end of a Neck of Mutton, young streaked Bacon, Pigeons and Quails, as occasion may serve. All these being well bak'd or stew'd in the Pan, as it were *à la Braise,* between two Fires; prepare some strained green Pease, or Asparagus-tops, according to the Season; take your Meats out of the Pan; let the Liquor be well drain'd from them; and put them into a Dish, with the Pease on the top: To these may be added some Lettice, scalded and boil'd in the same Sauce, and then let all be serv'd up hot to Table. Instead of the Earthen Pan, when the Border is only left, all sorts of good Ragoo's are to be pour'd in the middle. A Mutton-hash may also be put to them, with Mutton-gravy and Lemmon-juice, when ready to be set on the Table.

To make another Miroton.

Take *Truffles,* Mushrooms and boil'd Gammon, and let all be well minc'd together: Then let them be put into a Stew-
pan,

pan, with two or three Anchovies, according to the bigness of your *Miroton*; let a handful of Capers be well chopt and thrown into the same *Miroton*: As soon as you perceive it to be almost ready, put your Hash into a Stew-pan, with a little Parsly, Chibbol and Lard, all well dress'd; soak it with some Gravy; pour in a little Cullis; and let it boil; taking care that it be not too thick. Afterwards, having provided some tender and lean Beef, cut it into small Slices, somewhat larger than if it were for a *Filet*, with Cucumbers, and put them into the Ragoo: Stir it very little, and let it not boil too much. Before it is serv'd up, let some Lemmon-juice be squeez'd in, and let the Dish be artificially dress'd.

To make a Miroton for Fish-days.

Take four or six Whitings, according to the bigness of your Dish, and let them be scrap'd and well wash'd; they must also be slit all along before, but care must be taken that their Backs be not spoil'd. Take away the Bones, cut off the Heads, and spread them upon a Table or Dresser. Then, having made a good Fish-farce, according to the above-specified Directions, put some of it upon every Whiting; and roll them up, as it were, *Filets-mignons*. Afterwards, taking a Stew-pan, or a round Earthen Pan, without a Handle, make an *Omelet* or Pancake with a little Flower, which being entire, may cover the whole bottom of the Pan, and let your farced Fish be laid upon it; a little Butter being first put under the said Pancake. When the Fish is thus set in order with some *Truffles* and Mushrooms well season'd, another Pancake must be made, to be laid on the top, so as it may in like manner take up the whole compass of the Pan. Let the Stew-pan be well cover'd, to the end that the Fish may be stew'd by degrees, between two gentle Fires, on the top and underneath; and take care that nothing stick to the bottom. The whole Mess being thus made ready, let the Butter be drain'd off, and the *Miroton* turn'd upside-down into a Plate or Dish: Then, cutting a small round piece out of the middle, as if it were a *Poupeton*, pour in a small Mushroom-cullis, and cover it again with the same piece. Lastly, when the Fat is thoroughly taken away, rub the side of the Dish with a Shalot, and serve it up hot to Table.

A Farce may also be prepar'd in the same manner as for the *Poupeton* hereafter describ'd, and a Ring or Border may be

made

made with it round about the Dish; which is to be bak'd in an Oven and fill'd with a good Ragoo of *Mousserons*, *Morilles*, common Mushrooms, *Truffles* and Anchovies, all well chopt together, as also all sorts of Fish-*Filets* and Capers; making a tray of Ragoo and another of *Filets*, till the whole Space be fill'd up. Then let it be set a soaking over a gentle Fire, and serv'd up, with the Ragoo-sauce and Lemmon-juice.

MORILLES.

Forasmuch as it will be requisite in the following Article of Mushrooms, to shew how they may be preserv'd, and in regard that the Directions there laid down, may also serve for *Morilles* and *Mousserons*, as differing from them only in *specie*; it may be sufficient here only to take notice of the particular Dishes that may be made of them for Out-works or Inter-messes.

Morilles *in a Ragoo*.

Morilles may be fry'd brown with Butter or Lard, after they have been cut long-ways and well wash'd. Then it will be requisite to put to them some Salt, Parsly and Chervil chopt very small, Chibbol, Nutmeg and a little Broth, and to lay them a soaking in a little Pot or Stew-pan: Let them be serv'd up to Table with short Sauce and Lemmon-juice.

They may be also put into Cream and otherwise dress'd, as well as common Mushrooms.

Fried Morilles.

Let your *Morilles* be cut long-ways, as before, and boil'd in a little good Broth, over a gentle Fire. When the Broth is somewhat wasted, let them be flower'd and fry'd in Lard. In the mean time, having prepar'd a Sauce, with the rest of the Broth, season'd with Salt and Nutmeg, pour it under your *Morilles*, with Mutton-gravy and Lemmon-juice.

Farced *Morilles* are also used in Potage, and *Tourtes* or Pan-pies may be made of them, which shall be hereafter specify'd among those of common Mushrooms.

MOUS-

MOUSSERONS.

Mousserons *in a Ragoo*.

After having well cleans'd your *Mousserons*, let them be wash'd a little, and shak'd in a Linnen-cloath: Then stew them in a Dish or Stew-pan, with Butter or Lard, a Bunch of Herbs, Salt and Nutmeg, and thicken the Sauce with Yolks of Eggs and Flower or Bread-chippings: When it is ready to be serv'd up, squeez in some Lemmon-juice and garnish it with Slices of the same.

MULLETS.

Let your Mullets be broil'd upon a Grid-iron, after they are scal'd, cut and rubb'd with Butter; whilst a Sauce is preparing for them with burnt Butter, fry'd Flower, Capers, Lemmon-slices, a Faggot of Herbs, Pepper, Salt, Nutmeg and Verjuice, or Orange-juice.

They may be also fried in refined Butter, and then put into a Dish, with Anchovies, Capers, Orange-juice, Nutmeg, and a little of the same Butter in which they were dress'd; having before rubb'd the Dish, with a Shalot, or a Clove of Garlick.

Lastly, Mullets may be put into a *Tourte* or Pan-pie, and more especially into a standing Pie, as well as many other sorts of Fish.

MUSCLES.

Muscles are generally put into a Ragoo, either with white or brown Sauce, and a very considerable Potage may be made of them: The Ragoo with white Sauce is prepar'd in this manner, *viz*.

Let the Muscles be taken out of their Shells, and fried in natural Butter, with Thyme and other fine Herbs chopt very small: Afterwards season them with Pepper, Salt and Nutmeg, and when their Liquor is consum'd, put in Yolks of Eggs with Verjuice or Lemmon-juice; garnishing the Dish, with the Shells and fry'd Bread.

The Ragoo with brown Sauce is made after the same manner; except that no Eggs are to be put into it, but only a little fry'd Flower.

Muscle-

Muscle-potage.

Take good Muscles; let them be well cleans'd and wash'd in four or five Waters: Then put them into a Pot with Water, which may serve for the Broth, if there be not other good Fish-broth at Hand: Add to your Muscles, a little Parsly, sweet Butter, and an Onion stuck with Cloves, and scald them till the Shells open, which signifies, that they are sufficiently done; but let the Liquor or Broth be pour'd into another Pot a-part: Take the Muscles out of their Shells and only leave a few to garnish your Potage; whilst the Flesh of the others is put into a little Pot or Stew-pan. Afterwards you must throw in some Mushrooms cut into pieces, *Truffles* in Slices, and Carp-roes, with a whole Artichoke-bottom, if you have no mind to farce a Loaf with a Carp-hash; that is to say, the Artichoke bottom must be reserved entire to be laid in the middle of the Potage, and three or four other Artichoke-bottoms are to be cut into Quarters: Having toss'd up this whole Ragoo in a Stew-pan, with good Butter and a little Flower, let it be soak'd in the Muscle-broth, and boil'd a little while: Let a Faggot of fine Herbs be added, with a Slice or two of Lemmon; all being stew'd by degrees and well season'd. Then lay your Potage and Crusts of Bread a soaking with the same Muscle-broth, which must not be too fat: Garnish your Dish with the Muscles, that were laid by in their Shells, and if you have a farced Loaf, leave some also to serve for Garniture round about it. When the Potage is thus throughly soak'd, and the Ragoo pour'd thereupon, a white Cullis must be prepar'd with Almonds, Bread-crum, and six or eight Yolks of Eggs, all strain'd thro' the Hair-sieve, with a little of the same Muscle-broth; taking care that it do not turn, nor be too much season'd with with Salt: Lastly, having sprinkled your Potage, with this white Cullis, let it be serv'd up hot to Table.

MUSHROOMS.

Mushrooms are of great use in Ragoo's; separate Dishes and Potages are also made of them for Intermesses; so that it is absolutely necessary to be always provided with good Store of them for that purpose, and they well deserve a particular Description in this Place.

Fried

Fried Mushrooms.

Having tofs'd up your Mushrooms in a Stew-pan, with a little Broth, to take away their bitterness, ftrew them with fine Salt, a little Pepper and Flower, and fry them in Lard. They may be ferv'd up to Table, with Beef-ftakes, Parfly and Lemmon-juice, for Intermeffes; or elfe they may be ufed for the garnifhing of fome other Difh.

Mushrooms in a Ragoo.

Let the Mushrooms be cut into Slices, and fried in Lard or Butter, feafoning them, with Salt, Nutmeg and a Bunch of Herbs: The Sauce may be thicken'd with a little Flower, Yolks of Eggs and Lemmon-juice.

Mushrooms drefs'd in Cream and otherwife.

Having cut your Mushrooms into pieces, and fry'd them in Butter over a quick Fire, let them be feafon'd with Salt, Nutmeg and a Faggot of Herbs. When they are ready, and very little Sauce is left, pour fome natural Cream upon them, and let them be ferv'd up to Table.

They may alfo be put into a Baking-pan, with Lard or Butter, Parfly and Thyme chopt very fmall and whole Chibbols; after they have been feafon'd with Pepper, Salt and Nutmeg: Thus they may be bak'd in the Oven as it were a Pan-pie, till they become very brown; let them alfo be well breaded; in order to be ferv'd up with Slices and Juice of Lemmon, and garnifh'd with Parfly.

Potage of farced Mushrooms.

Let a Farce be made with Veal, Beef-marrow and Lard; feafon'd with Pepper, Salt, Nutmeg and the Crum of a Loaf foak'd in Broth or in Yolks of Eggs. Stuff your Mushrooms with this Farce, and bake or ftew them in an Earthen Pan, with Salt, a Bunch of Herbs and fome Broth: When they are ready, let them be drefs'd upon the foaked Crufts, and garnifh'd with Chickens-livers in a Ragoo, fried Mushrooms and Lemmon-juice, as they are ferving up to Table.

They

They may alfo be garnifh'd with Veal-fweet-breads, larded *Fricandoe's*, Cocks-combs and *Truffles*, and a *Profitrolle*-loaf may be fet in the middle, farced with Mufhrooms, Artichoke-bottoms, and Veal-fweet-breads, all cut into pieces in form of a Die, and drefs'd in a Ragoo. A white or brown Cullis may be prepar'd for both, but the latter is moft proper. The Beef and Veal, of which you would have the Cullis or Gravy to be made, muft be pounded in a Mortar, with Crufts of Bread, and ftrain'd thro' the Hair-fieve, with fome Broth, and then it may be us'd for the Ragoo.

Other Potages are made of Mufhrooms, with different forts of Fowls, as Capons, Quails, &c. And on Days of Abftinence, your Mufhrooms may be farced to that purpofe, with the Flefh of Fifh, as for other Difhes.

To extract the Juice of Mufhrooms.

After having well cleans'd the Mufhrooms, let them be put into a Difh with a piece of Lard, or Butter, if it be a Fifh-day; and let them be brought to a brown colour over the Fire, till they ftick to the bottom of the Difh : Then throw in a little Flower, and let that alfo be made brown with the Mufhrooms: Afterwards let fome good Broth be added, and let them be taken off from the Fire; putting that Gravy into a Pot a-part, feafon'd with a piece of Lemmon and Salt. The Mufhrooms may ferve, either whole or chopt fmall, for Potages, Side-difhes, or Intermeffes.

To Preferve Mufhrooms.

Let your Mufhrooms, as foon as they are well pickt and wafh'd be tofs'd up a little in a Stew-pan, with good Butter, and feafon'd with all forts of Spice. Then put them into a Pot with a little Brine and Vinegar, as alfo, a great deal of Butter on the top and let them be well cover'd : Before they are us'd, they muft be thoroughly clear'd from the Salt, and then they will be ferviceable upon all manner of Occafions.

A Powder may alfo be made of them, when they are very dry, and the fame thing may be done for the *Moufferons* or white Mufhrooms. To preferve the latter entire, let them be dry'd in an Oven, as Artichokes, after they have been fcalded in Water: When they are dry, put them into a Place where there is no

M   Moi-

Moisture, and when you would make use of them, let them be steept in Luke-warm Water.

MUTTON.

Among the several Messes that may be prepar'd with Mutton, we have already explain'd the different Manners of Dressing Legs for Side-dishes; and we have also observ'd what relates to Cutlets and *Filets* of Mutton under the Letters C and F. In like manner, in the Second Article of *Mirotons*, mention is made of an Earthen Pan fill'd with a Breast of Mutton, the scraggy end of a Neck of Mutton and some other sorts of Meat; so that it remains only here, to take notice of some other Joynts of Mutton that are proper for Side-dishes.

A great Side-dish of Mutton.

Take a Crupper of very tender Mutton, let the first Skin be dextrously loosen'd on the top to the small end, and left hanging: Then having prepar'd some thin Slices of Gammon, season'd with Parsly, Chibbol, and black Pepper, let them be laid upon the Joint of Mutton, with some *Bards* or thin Slices of fat Bacon, and let the Skin be turn'd over them: Afterwards let it be tied up and roasted on a Spit, cover'd with Paper: When it is ready, let it be neatly breaded, and garnish'd with Mutton-cutlets: Lastly, having pour'd an exquisite Ragoo thereupon, let it be serv'd up hot to Table.

The same thing may be done with a Quarter of Mutton or of Lamb.

Another Side-dish of a Quarter of Mutton.

Let it be farced on the Leg, with a *Salpicon*, or with a Hash of the same Meat that was taken out of it, according to the Method before observ'd in ordering a short Rib of Beef in the Article of Beef, or for a *Salpicon* hereafter explain'd under the Letter S. Then let your Quarter of Mutton be breaded, and set into an Oven to be brought to a good colour: Let it also be garnish'd with fry'd Bread, marinated Cutlets and fried Parsly, and marbled with Lemmon-juice and its own Gravy.

Carbonado'd Mutton.

Let a Joint of Mutton cut into Carbonadoe's be fry'd in a Pan with Lard, before it is stew'd in Broth, with Pepper, Salt, Cloves a Bunch of Herbs, Chesnuts and Mushrooms; whilst some Flower is frying to thicken the Sauce: Then let the Dish be garnish'd with Mushrooms and fried Bread, and serv'd up, with Capers and Lemmon-juice.

A Breast of Mutton.

In order to dress a Breast of Mutton for an Out-work, let it be stuff'd with Parsly and roasted: Then let it be season'd with Bread, white Pepper and Salt; adding the Juice of an Orange and good Gravy, when ready to be serv'd up to Table.

At another time, after the Breast has been boil'd in a Pot, let it be dipt into a clear Paste or Batter, and fry'd in Lard: Then adding some Verjuice with the Grapes entire, and white Pepper, it may be serv'd up to Table.

For Mutton-cutlets, See the Article of *Cutlets* under the Letter C.

A Loin of Mutton à la Sainte Menehout.

To dress a Loin of Mutton in this manner, such a Kettle or Pot must be provided, as is convenient for that purpose; covering the Bottom of it with good *Bards* or thin Slices of Bacon, Veal-stakes, and Slices of Onion. Then let the Loin of Mutton be laid upon them, which likewise must be cover'd with other Slices of Veal and Bacon; all well season'd with fine Herbs and Spice. Afterwards set your Pot into an Oven, or between two Fires, and let all be well bak'd, but not over-done. When they are drawn, or taken out, they must be well breaded and broil'd upon a Grid-iron; whilst a Sauce call'd *Ramolade* is preparing, with Anchovies, Capers cut small, Parsly and Chibbols chopped a-part: Having stew'd these in good Gravy with a little Oil, a Clove of Garlick and other seasoning Ingredients, pour them upon the Loin, in order to be dress'd in a Dish, and serv'd up hot to Table. This Sauce may serve for several sorts of cold Fowl, which are to be breaded and broil'd, and also for many other necessary uses.

A Loin of Mutton dreſs'd after other manners.

A Loin of Mutton may be larded with thick Slips of Bacon, and boil'd in a Pot a-part, with Water and a little white Wine, well ſeaſon'd with Pepper, Salt, Bay-leaves, Cloves, a Bunch of Herbs, and a Slice of Lemmon. In the mean while, let ſome Capers and Anchovies be fried in Lard and a little Sauce in which the Loin was dreſs'd, and let it be pour'd upon it when ready to be ſerv'd up to Table, with Lemmon-juice, or a little Garlick-vinegar.

At another time, when the Loin of Mutton is boil'd, take off the Skin, and ſteep the Fleſh in a ſort of Batter made with Flower, Yolks of Eggs, Pepper, Salt and Broth, in order to be well fried in a Pan. It may be ſerv'd up, with white Pepper, Verjuice with the Grapes, and fried Parſly.

Otherwiſe, after having taken off the Skin, let your Loin be baſted with Lard; breaded three ſeveral times, to produce a fine Cruſt upon it in the Oven; and ic'd, by rubbing it with the White of an Egg.

N.

NEATS-TONGUES.

Neats-tongues bak'd between two Fires.

HAving cut off the Roots of your Neats-tongues, broil them a little on the Coals, to the end that the Skin may more eaſily be peel'd off, and lard them with thick Slips of Bacon and raw Gammon; all well ſeaſon'd. Let ſome *Bards,* or thin Slices of Bacon be laid in order on the bottom of a Pot, with Beef-ſtakes beaten, and the Tongues upon them, with Slices of Onions, and all ſorts of fine Herbs and Spices, ſeaſoning them alſo with Pepper and Salt: Then having cover'd the Tongues, with other Beef-ſtakes and Bacon-*Bards,* in the ſame manner as they were put underneath, ſo as they may be well wrapt up on all ſides; ſet the Pot between two Fires, that is to ſay, one on the top, and the other underneath. Let it continue therein for the ſpace of eight or ten Hours, till the Meats are well bak'd, or ſtew'd, and in the mean time, prepare a good Cullis of Muſhrooms, or ſome other choice Ragoo, with all ſorts of Garnitures,

nitures, *viz.* Mushrooms, *Truffles*, Veal-sweet-breads, &c. When the Tongues are taken out, let them be drain'd, thoroughly clear'd from the Fat, and dress'd in a Dish; turning the Ragoo upon them. The Juice of a Lemmon may be squeez'd into the Cullis, and if you would have the Dish garnish'd, one of the Tongues must be cut into Slices, or else you may garnish it with *Fricandoes* or Scotch Collops. The same thing may be done in dressing Calves-tongues; but if it be requir'd to farce them without larding, you may make use of the same Ragoo; taking care nevertheless, that both the Neats-tongues and Calves-tongues be always serv'd up hot to Table.

Dried Neats-tongues.

Dried Neats-tongues are usually salted after the same manner as dried Hogs-tongues hereafter specify'd, except scalding. However they must be steept in Water, the thick End or Root being cut off, and salted after they have been well wip'd: They must be left three or four Days in the Brine or Pickle, and when they are taken out, if you have any petty Salt-meats to be prepar'd, this Pickle may serve for that purpose; whether it be a wild Boar, Hog or Fawn; so that within the space of five or six Days, some of these Salt-meats may be dress'd, and serv'd up for Out-works, or Side-dishes with good Peas soop. As for the Neats-tongues, they must be tied at the small end or tip, and hang'd up in the Chimney to be smoak'd and well dried: They may be kept, as long as you please, and dress'd in the same manner as Hogs-tongues.

A Side-dish of Neats-tongues.

Let your Tongues be boil'd in fair Water with a little Salt, and a Faggot of fine Herbs: Then cut the end next the Root, peel off the Skin, and Lard them with somewhat long Slips of Bacon. Afterwards they must be roasted, but not too much, and as they are serving up, you may pour upon them a good Ragoo, according to the season, or a rich Cullis, or a *Ramolade*-sauce: The same thing is to be done with Calves-tongues, as well as for the following Dish.

Another Side-dish of Neats-tongues.

After having order'd your Tongues, for the peeling off their Skins, as before, and having larded them a-cross with thick Slips of Bacon, let them be well bak'd *à la Braise*, or between two Fires: As they are dressing in the Dish, slit them all along, so as the Bacon may appear, and make a Ragoo, or a Cullis to be pour'd upon them. Let them be well clear'd from the Fat and serv'd up hot to Table.

O.

OILS.

THe *Oil* is a very considerable Potage, which may be serv'd up as well on Days of Abstinence, as on Flesh-days.

An Oil *for Flesh-days.*

Take all sorts of good Meats, *viz.* Part of a Buttock of Beef, a Fillet of Veal, a piece of a Leg of Mutton, Ducks, Partridges, Pigeons, Chickens, Quails, a piece of raw Gammon, Sausages and a Cervelas, all roasted or fried brown: Let them be put into a Pot, every Thing according to the time that is requisite for boiling it, and let a thickening Liquor be made of the brown Sauce to be mingled together. As soon as the scum is taken off, season your Meats, with Pepper, Salt, Cloves, Nutmeg, Coriander-seed and Ginger, all well pounded, with Thyme and sweet Basil, and wrapt up in a Linnen-cloth. Afterwards add all sorts of Roots and Herbs well scalded, accordingly as you shall think fit, such as Carrets Turneps, Parsnips, Cabbage, Parsly-roots, Onions, Leeks and other Herbs in Bunches. In the mean while, you are to provide *Cuvets*, Silver-pots and other Vessels proper for that purpose, and when your Potage is sufficiently boil'd, let some Crusts be broken into pieces, and laid a soaking in the same Broth, after it has been clear'd from the Fat, and well season'd. Before it is serv'd up, pour in a great deal more Broth, still continuing to take away the Fat; dress your Fowls and other Meats, and garnish them with the Roots, if you have only one great Dish: Otherwise they may be serv'd up without Roots; putting the *Cuvets* on a Silver-dish, with a Silver-ladle in it, with which every one of the Guests may take out some Soop, when the *Oil* is set on the Table.

See among the Potages, another sort of *Oil* with young Ringdoves and other Fowl.

An

An Oil for Fish-days.

Take some good Broth, Peas-soop, or half Fish-broth; let all the above-mentioned Roots be put into it, and boil'd as much as is requisite: Then dress your Oil, with a *Profitrolle*-loaf in the middle, and garnish it with Roots.

An *Oil* or Potage of Roots and several sorts of Pulse with *Oil*, may likewise be prepar'd for Good-Friday, as it has been observ'd Pag. 47.

OISTERS.

To dress Oisters.

Let your Oisters be put into a Stew-pan, with a little Water and Verjuice, and let them have one Walm or Seething: Then take them out, and reserve the Liquor that is in the Shells, to be put into the Ragoo's, when ready to be serv'd up to Table.

Thus a Side-dish may be made of Chickens farced with Oisters, as it appears in the Second Article of Chickens, under the Letter C. We have also elsewhere explain'd the manner of dressing a Duck with Oisters under the Letter D, and that of preparing a Pike with other sorts of Fish with Oisters shall be shewn in its due Place under P.

Oisters in a Daube.

Open your Oisters, and season them with fine Herbs, *viz.* Parsly, Chibbol, Thyme and sweet Basil, putting a very little of each into every Oister; as also, some Pepper and a little white Wine: Then cover them again with their Shells, lay them upon a Grid-iron, and pass the red-hot Fire-shovel over them from time to time: When they are ready, they may be dress'd, and serv'd up uncover'd.

Farced Oisters.

Having open'd your Oisters, let them be scalded and afterwards minc'd small, with Parsly, Chibbols, Thyme, Pepper, Salt, Anchovies and good Butter. Let the Crum of a Loaf be soak'd in the Sauce, with Nutmeg and other Spice, and two or three

M 4

three Yolks of Eggs, and let all be pounded together. Then let the Oister-shells be farced, and having breaded, or wash'd them over, let them be put into an Oven upon a Grid-iron. They may be brought to Table, either dry or with Lemmon-juice.

Oisters marinated and fried.

After the Oisters have been marinated in Lemmon-juice, they may be put into Fritters, and fried till they come to a fine Colour.

OLIVES.

Side-dishes may be made of large fat Pullets, Wood-cocks, Partridges, and other sorts of wild Fowl with Olives; all which are dress'd after the same manner: So that explaining one, a sufficient light will be given as to what relates to the others.

A Side-dish of fat Pullets, with Olives.

Take large fat Pullets that are very tender; let them be well truss'd and roasted with a good Slice of Bacon upon their Breast: In the mean while, prepare a Ragoo, with Chibbols and Parsly chopt, and fried with a little Lard and Flower. Then put into it two Spoonfuls of Gravy, a Glass of *Champagne*-Wine, minc'd Capers, an Anchovie, bruised Olives, a little Oil of Olives and a Bunch of fine Herbs: To thicken the Sauce, add a good Cullis, and let all be well season'd, and thoroughly clear'd from the Fat: Then take the roasted Pullets, cut off their Legs at the Joints, and tie up their Wings, Legs and Breast: Let them also be bruised a little, and afterwards put into the Sauce. A little before they are serv'd up hot to Table, they must be dress'd in a Dish, pouring in the Ragoo, and squeezing upon them the Juice of an Orange.

OMELETS.

An Omelet with Sugar.

Having whipt as many Eggs as you shall think fit, put to them a little Milk-cream and Salt, with some Lemmon-peel cut very small: Let all be well beaten together, and make your

your *Omelet*. Before it is put into the Dish it must be sugar'd in the Frying-pan, and turn'd as it is frying on the side that is colour'd; the Plate upon which it is to be laid must likewise be turn'd downwards: Then strew it with Sugar and some candy'd Lemmon-peel minc'd, and Ice it all at once with the red-hot Fire-shovel; in order to be serv'd up hot to Table.

Omelets *of green Beans and other Things, with Cream.*

Let your Beans be shell'd, slipt out of their Skins, and fried in good Butter, with a little Parsly and Chibbol: Then, having pour'd in a little Milk-cream, let them be well season'd, and soak'd over a gentle Fire. Let an *Omelet* be made with new-laid Eggs and Cream, and let some Salt be put into it according to discretion. When it is ready, dress it on a Dish, bind the Beans with one or two Yolks of Eggs, turn them upon the *Omelet*; so as they may stick to the side of it, and bring it hot to Table.

Omelets of the like nature may be made with *Moufferons, Morilles*, common Mushrooms, green Pease, Asparagus-tops and Artichoke-bottoms, white and black *Truffles*, Spinage, Sorrel, &c. all with Cream; but 'tis requisite that they be cut into small pieces.

A very great quantity of *Omelets* may be thus disguised, and these little Cream-sauces may serve to fill up your Plates or Dishes, garnishing them with small Garnitures; such as fried Artichokes, Bread-tostes, Puffs, *Fleurons, Feuillantins*, Artichoke-bottoms fried in Paste, and others of the like nature that shall be judg'd requisite; and taking care that all be serv'd up hot to Table.

*To make a Gammon-*Omelet.

Having prepar'd a Hash of good boil'd Gammon, with a little raw Gammon; let your *Omelet* be made and dress'd in a Dish, ordering it with this Gammon-hash according to the preceding Method. The same thing may be done with boil'd Neats-tongues.

Another farced Omelet.

Take the Breast of a roasted Chicken or other Fowl, cut it into little pieces in the form of a Die, as also some boil'd Gammon and Mushrooms likewise in little square pieces, with Capons-livers, *Truffles*, and other sorts of Garniture, all well dress'd in a Ragoo. In the mean time, let the *Omelet* be made, but before it is dress'd in the Dish, let some Crum or Crust of Bread be put therein, and let your Ragoo be turn'd into the same Frying-pan. When it is ready, let it be moisten'd with a little Gravy and serv'd up hot to Table. Thus *Omelets* may be farc'd with all sorts of Ragoo's, so that it were needless to insist on them any longer, particularly, with Calves-kidneys boil'd, Veal-sweet-breads, Livers of Rabbets, or Leverets, those of Capons, &c. as well as on Fish-days, with a Fish-farce, Carp-roes and a good Herb-farce.

P.

PAINS.

THere are several Side-dishes call'd *Pains*, *i. e.* Loaves, as being made of Bread stuff'd with different sorts of Farces; such are the *Pains* of Gammon, Partridge, Veal, and the Spanish *Pain*: Let us give some Account of these in their order.

To make a Gammon-Pain.

Let some Slices of Gammon be dress'd in the same manner as for Gammon-essence, already described in the first Article of *Gammon*, under the Letter G; except that you must not put any Mushrooms to them, nor strain them thro' a Sieve. If your Slices, when dress'd, are not sufficiently thicken'd, a little Bread-cullis may be added to bring them to a due Consistence: Then, having provided a Potage-loaf, cut it thro' the middle, so as both the upper and under Crusts may remain entire; take away the Crum from the inside, and let the rest of the Loaf be toasted and brought to a colour at the Fire, or in an Oven, till it become brown. When it is ready, joyn the two Crusts together, in a little Dish, after having soak'd them a little in the Sauce; and put your Ragoo into it with the Sauce. It may be gar-

The Court and Country Cook. 171

garnish'd with Capons-livers dress'd in a Veal-caul, and serv'd up among the Intermesses.

A Side-dish of Partridge-Pains.

Take roasted Partridges, with the Flesh of a Capon or Pullet, parboil'd Bacon, tried Sewet, *Morilles* and common Mushrooms chopped, also *Truffles,* Artichoke-bottoms, fine Herbs, and a Clove of Garlick, all well season'd and cut small; and, to bind them, add the Crum of a Loaf soak'd in good Gravy and some Yolks of Eggs: Then let your *Pains* be made upon Paper, of a round Figure, and of the thickness of an Egg, at a convenient distance one from another. The Point of your Knife must be dipt in a beaten Egg, in order to shape them, and bread them neatly. They may also serve to garnish other Side-dishes of a larger size, and of more considerable Meats.

To make a Veal-Pain.

Having cut a Fillet of Veal into thin Slices, beat them with the Back of a Knife, and take as great a quantity of them, as will be requisite, proportionably to the bigness of your Dish. Then let another Fillet of Veal be well minc'd, with parboil'd Bacon, dress'd Gammon, tried Sewet, all sorts of fine Herbs, the Breast of a Capon and Partridge, a few *Truffles, Mousserons,* and common Mushrooms chopped, all well season'd with all sorts of fine Spice, and mixt with a little Milk-cream. Afterwards let some *Bards* or thin Slices of Bacon be laid in order in a round Stew-pan, as also one half of the beaten Veal-stakes, and then the Farce; continuing to cover it on the top, in the same manner as underneath; so as the whole Farce may be enclos'd on all sides: Lastly, let it be well cover'd and bak'd *à la Braise,* between two Fires. A little piece of Garlick may be put into the Farce, which must be brought hot to Table, after it has been well clear'd from the Fat, and neatly dress'd in a Dish.

This Veal-*Pain* may also be serv'd up with green Pease and Asparagus, when they are in season.

T

To make a Spanish Pain.

Take the Breasts of roasted Partridges, mince them small, with a Handful of scalded Pistachoes and a little beaten Coriander-seed, and let all be well pounded in a Mortar; adding three or four Yolks of Eggs, according to the bigness of your Dish, a little Lemmon-peel and some good Veal-gravy. Let the whole Mixture be well temper'd in a Mortar, and strain'd thro' the Sieve, as if it were Cream made after the Italian Mode: Then let the Dish be set into the Oven, and let all be turn'd into it, keeping a Fire on the top and underneath, till it be thoroughly coagulated. But it must be set on the Table by a neat-handed Servitor, lest it should be broken, as it is serving up.

Another Side-dish of a farced Pain.

Another Side-dish may be made of a *Pain* or Loaf farced with Veal-sweet-breads, Artichoke-bottoms, *Truffles* and Gammon dress'd in a Ragoo, with a white thickening Liquor of roasted Veal and Lemmon-juice: Let your Loaf be well soak'd for a quarter of an Hour in good Broth, and serv'd up with Mutton-gravy, a little thickening Liquor and Lemmon-juice.

You may hereafter observe among the Potages, the manner of preparing *Profitrolle*-loaves, and several sorts of farced Crusts, as well for Flesh-days, as those of Abstinence; of which also may be made as many Side-dishes, for the meaner sort of Ordinaries.

PAN-PIES, *see* TOURTES.

PARTRIDGES.

Having a little before explain'd the manner of making Partridge-*Pains*, as also Partridge-Hashes in the first Article of *Hashes*, under the Letter H; we shall here produce some other Side-dishes of the same sort of Fowl.

Partridges, with Spanish Sauce.

After having roasted some Partridges; let one of them be well pounded in a Mortar, and soak'd in good Gravy: The Livers

The Court and Country Cook. 173

vers of the Partridges muſt likewiſe be pounded with ſome pieces of *Truffles*, and let all be well moiſten'd with Gravy, ſo as the Cullis may become ſomewhat thick; ſetting it aſide for a while in a Diſh. Then pour two Glaſſes of *Burgundy*-wine into a Stew-pan, with a Clove or two of Garlick, two or three Slices of Onion, a few Cloves, and two Glaſſes of the Sauce; ſo that only one may be left; but if the Diſh be large, the Quantity of the Wine and Cullis may be augmented. When your Sauce is ready, ſtrain it thro' a Sieve into a Stew-pan, pour the Cullis upon it, and let all be well ſeaſon'd: To theſe add a little Gammon-eſſence, and let all boil together for ſome time. Laſtly, cut your Partridges into pieces, put them into the Sauce, and let them be kept hot; ſqueezing in the Juice of two or three Oranges, before it is ſerv'd up to Table.

A Partridge-Biberot.

Take the Breaſts of roaſted Partridges, and if they are not ſufficient, ſome of fat Pullets likewiſe roaſted, and let them be minc'd upon a Dreſſer that is well flower'd: Let the Carcaſſes be pounded in a Mortar, and ſtew'd in a Pan with good Gravy: Then, having ſtrain'd them thro' a Sieve, put them into a little Pot, with your *Biberot* or minc'd Meat: Let it boil over a gentle Fire, taking care that it do not ſtick to the bottom, and adding a Spoonful of Gammon-eſſence; but it muſt be ſo order'd, as not to be too thin or too fat. When it is ready, it may be diſpoſed of in a Plate or two, and ſerv'd up hot to Table. Some are content to make uſe of it in this manner; and others, after having dreſs'd the whole Meſs in a Plate or Diſh, ſtrew it with Bread-chippings grated very fine, and give it a colour with the red-hot Fire-ſhovel. When ſo order'd it may be eaten with a Fork, and otherwiſe with a Spoon.

Partridge-Filets, *with Gammon*.

When your Partridges are roaſted, let them be cut into *Filets*, and ſtew'd with Gammon, an Anchovie, Capers, Chibbol and Parſly chopt very ſmall. Thus they are to be ſerv'd up among the Out-works, and may alſo be dreſs'd with Woodcock or Pike-ſauce.

Ano-

Another Way of dressing Partridges.

Partridges may likewise be bak'd between two Fires, or roasted in *Sur-tout*, according to the Method hereafter laid down for Pigeons; or else dress'd with Olives, as it has been already observ'd under the Article of *Olives*.

For Partridge-pies, see the first Article of Pies, as also Partridge-potages under that of Potages; or rather, look for them in the General Table of the Messes.

Pastes.

It would be needless here to insist on the different sorts of Pastes, which are usually made; that is to say, some thin as it were Batter, and others of a more firm Consistence; the latter to be us'd for Pies and Pan-pies, and the other for Fritters, or to cover several Things in order to be fried. It may well be presum'd, that the Reader is sufficiently instructed in this Matter, and some particular kinds of Pastes have been already produc'd, as those of Almonds and Fruit, under those Articles; so that we shall only add one or two that are no less curious and remarkable.

Paste for crackling Crust.

Take Sugar beaten to Powder, with as much fine Flower, Whites of Eggs, according to the quantity of your Paste, and a little Orange-flower-water. Then having caus'd the Paste to be well made upon the Dresser-board, so as it be not too soft, roll out a piece for the Bottom-crust, as thin as Paper, if it be possible, and flower it continually underneath, working it in with your Hands: And indeed, it will be ready almost to spread of it self, after it has been beaten a little with the Rolling-pin. Then rub a Plate or Baking-pan with a little Butter, put your piece of Paste into it, and pare it round about; afterwards it must be prickt with the Point of a Knife, that it may not puff in the Oven. When it is sufficiently bak'd, let it be dress'd on a Dish or Plate, laying thereon, before it is serv'd up, some Marmalade, with Apricocks, Peaches, Plums, and other sorts of preserv'd Fruit.

With

With this Paste, you may roll out several very thin pieces, which may be neatly cut and dried in an Oven; always remembring to butter the Plate or Pie-pan, left they should stick to it. Afterwards they may be ic'd, if you shall think fit, and laid upon the *Tourtes* or Pan-pies, which are to be set out with *Savoy-*Biskets, or other small Garnitures.

Syringed Paste.

Take Almond-paste, prepared according to the Method describ'd in the first Article of Almonds, pound it in a Mortar, with a little natural Cream boil'd, and having pass'd it thro' the Syringe, let it be fried in a Pan, adding some musked Sugar and sweet Water, when ready to be serv'd up to Table. This Paste may be prepar'd after many other manners, at pleasure, as has been before observ'd in the same place.

PASTIES.

Pasties made of Stags-flesh or other sorts of Venison.

Having caus'd your Venison to be mortified, or marinated, let it be larded with thick Slips of Bacon, and season'd with Pepper, Salt, Nutmeg and Cloves, all well beaten together. Then let a brown Paste be made with Rie-flower; as being more proper to preserve Meats, and more portable, adding some Salt and a little Butter. After having dress'd the Pasty with pounded Lard, *Bards* or thin Slices of Bacon, Bay-leaves, and the above-mention'd seasoning Ingredients, let it be wash'd over with the Whites of Eggs, and bak'd for the space of three or four Hours. A Hole must be made in the middle, left it should burst, or the Liquor should run out; but it may be stopt up when taken out of the Oven, and the Pasty set upon a Hurdle or Pie-plate. It may be serv'd up to Table either entire, or cut into slices.

A Pasty may be made after the same manner, with the Flesh of a wild Boar, or Roe-buck; but it is not necessary to bake it so long, or to season it so high.

PERCHES.

A Side-dish may be made of Perches in a Sauce of *Mouffotons,* fried in natural Butter with Cream: They may also be
serv'd

serv'd up in *Filets*, with Cucumbers, as well as Soles, hereafter mentioned; cutting them into pieces, after they have been scal'd, and boil'd in Broth. Lastly, Perches may be dress'd with green Sauce, or otherwise thus:

Perches in Filets, *with white Sauce.*

Let Mushrooms be toss'd up in a Pan, with natural Butter, and afterwards boil'd in a little Cream, without any thing to thicken them: Then let your Perch-*Filets*, ready cut, be put to them, and thicken'd with three Yolks of Eggs, chopt Parsly, grated Nutmeg, and the Juice of a Lemmon: Let all be stirr'd together very gently, for fear of breaking the *Filets*, and dress'd with Slices of Lemmon, or some other sort of Garniture.

PETITS OEUFS, *see* EGGS.

PETITS PATES, *see* PIES.

PHEASANTS.

Two particular Side-dishes may be made with Pheasants, *viz.* one a hot Pie and the other with Carp-sauce.

A Side-dish of Pheasants, with Carp-sauce.

Let your Pheasants be well truss'd, barded with a good Slice of Bacon, and roasted, taking care that they be not dry'd. To prepare the Sauce, let some tender Veal-stakes be laid in order on the bottom of a Stew-pan, as if it were to make Gravy, with several Slices of Gammon and Onions, Parsly-roots and a Faggot of fine Herbs. In the mean while, having gutted a Carp, wash it only in one Water, without scaling it, cut it into pieces, in the same manner as for stewing, and put it into the same Pan: Then set it over the Furnace to give it a fine Colour, as is usually done in making Gravy, and soak it with good Veal-gravy and a Quart of *Champagne*-wine; adding a Clove of Garlick, some chopt Mushrooms, *Truffles,* and small Crusts of Bread. Let the whole Mess be boil'd, taking care that it be not too much salted; strain it well thro' the Hair-sieve, and order the Sauce so as it may be somewhat thick. Otherwise, some Partridge-cullis may be added, and put with it into a Stew-pan.

Afterwards having tied up the Pheasants let them be laid in this Sauce, and kept hot, till it be requisite to serve them up to Table: Then dress them in a Dish, and pour the Sauce upon them. They may be garnish'd with Partridge-*Pains*, which have been already describ'd in the second Article of *Pains*.

A Side-dish of a hot Pheasant-pie.

Take the Flesh of a Pheasant, with that of a large fat Pullet and a tender piece of a Leg of Veal, and let all be well minc'd together, with Parsly, Chibbol, *Moufferons*, common Mushrooms, Veal-sweet-breads, boil'd Gammon and raw Bacon: Then having season'd them with fine Herbs, Spice, Pepper and Salt, make a good *Godivoe* of them, as also, a somewhat strong Paste, and let your Pie be rais'd either with double, or single Crusts, accordingly as you shall think fit. As soon as it is bak'd, take away the Fat, pour in a Mushroom-cullis, and serve it up hot to Table.

PICKLES, *see* MARINADES.

PIES.

Pies are brought to Table, either hot or cold; that is to say, the former for Side-dishes, and the other for Intermesses.

A hot Pie of Partridges, Wood-cocks, &c.

Take two Partridges and as many Wood-cocks, and let them be well drawn, reserving the Livers: Let them also be neatly truss'd, and beaten on the Breast, with a Rolling-pin: Then having larded them with thick Slips of Bacon and Gammon, season them with Pepper and Salt, and slit them thro' the Back. In the mean time, let a Farce be made of a tender piece of Veal, as thick as an Egg, with raw Bacon, a little Marrow, Parsly and fine Herbs, a few *Truffles* and Mushrooms chopped, and a little Veal-sewet: When the whole Farce is thus duely prepar'd, let it be bound with the Yolk of an Egg, and let the four Fowls be stufft with it on the Back. It will also be requisite to mince and pound some Bacon, with the two Partridge-livers, and to season all with beaten Spice. Afterwards having made some Paste, with an Egg, fresh Butter, Flower and a little Salt, roll out

N two

two pieces of it; lay one of them on butter'd Paper, and let some Lard pounded in a Mortar be neatly spread upon it. Let your Partridges and Wood-cocks be seafon'd, and set in order round about, after all their Bones have been broken; adding some *Truffles* and Mushrooms, with a Bay-leaf, and covering all with *Bards*, or thin Slices of Bacon: After having laid on your other piece of Paste for the Lid, close up the Sides round about, wash over the whole Pie, and set it into the Oven; taking care of the Fire. When it is bak'd, let the Paper be taken away from underneath; preparing at the same time a good Cullis of Partridges, Veal-sweet-breads, Mushrooms and *Truffles*: Then cutting off the Lid of the Pie, remove all the Bacon-*Bards*, clear it well from the Fat, and squeez in the Juice of a Lemmon. Let the whole Cullis be likewise pour'd into the Pie very hot, and having cover'd it again with the Lid, let it be immediately serv'd up to Table for a Side-dish.

Hot Pies of Chickens, Pigeons, Larks, Quails, Thrushes and others of the like nature, are usually made after the same manner, and we have already shewn in the preceding Article, how to prepare a hot Pheasant-pie, which is a kind of *Godivoe*.

A Pie of large Pigeons, or young Turkeys.

Having provided large Pigeons, let them be drawn, truss'd and beaten on the Breast, to Break the Bones: Then let them be larded with thick Slips of Bacon, and well seafon'd. Take the Livers, with raw Bacon, Parsly, Chibbol, fine Herbs, all well chopt and seafon'd; as also, some *Truffles*, Mushrooms and Marrow, and pound all together in the Mortar: Stuff the Bodies of your Pigeons, or young Turkeys with this Farce, and reserve a little of it to be put underneath. In the mean while, the Pie being made of good Paste, some of the Farce must be put on the Bottom, and afterwards the Pigeons in due order, and well seafon'd; adding also a Bay-leaf: Then all must be cover'd with thin Slices of Bacon, and with a Lid on the top. When the Pie is bak'd, let it be clear'd from the Fat, and at the same time, let a good Ragoo be pour'd into it, ready prepar'd with Veal-sweet-breads, Mushrooms, Cocks-combs, &c. accordingly as occasion may serve, or the Season will admit. But let it be set on the Table hot among the Side-dishes.

A

A Chicken-pie, with Cream.

As soon as the Pie is made, let your Chickens be put into it in Quarters, season'd with Pepper, Salt, Nutmeg, Cinnamon, melted or pounded Lard and fine Herbs; and let it be cover'd with a Lid of the same Paste. When it is bak'd, pour in some Cream, and let it stand a little while longer in the Oven: Lastly, add some Mushroom-juice, and serve it up hot to Table.

A Pie of a boned Capon.

The Capon is to be stuff'd with a Farce made of its own Flesh, part of a Fillet of Veal, Beef-marrow, or Sewet and Bacon; seafon'd with Pepper, Salt, Nutmeg, Cloves, Veal-sweet-breads, *Truffles*, Mushrooms and fine Herbs: Then it must be cover'd with *Bards*, or thin Slices of Bacon, and put into a Pie made of fine Paste, which is to be wash'd over, and bak'd about two Hours. Some Lemmon-juice must also be squeez'd upon it, when ready to be brought to Table.

A Duck-pie.

After having beaten the Breasts of the Ducks, let them be larded with middle-siz'd Slips of Bacon, and dress'd as the above-mentioned sorts of Fowl; covering them with Mushrooms, Capons-livers, *Truffles*, and the necessary seasoning Ingredients. When the Pie has been bak'd during two Hours, let some Juice of Shalots or of Garlick, with that of Orange be put therein, as it is serving up to Table.

A Pie after the German Mode.

Take Lamb cut into Quarters, which is to be larded with middle-siz'd Slips of Bacon, and put into a Pie made of indifferent fine Paste; season'd with Pepper, Salt, Nutmeg, Cloves, a Bay-leaf or two, pounded Lard, fine Herbs and Chibbol: Let it be cover'd with a Lid of the same Paste, and bak'd three Hours. Lastly, let some Oisters be fried in Lard, with Flower, Capers, stoned Olives, Mushrooms, Mutton-gravy and Lemmon-juice, and let all be turn'd into the Pie with the Oister-liquor.

A Godivoe-Pie.

Let a good *Godivoe* be prepar'd, with a Fillet of Veal, some Marrow or Beef-sewet, and a little Lard; season'd with Pepper, Salt, Cloves, Nutmeg, fine Herbs and Chibbols; and let your Pie be made of fine Paste, of the height of three or four Inches, and of a round or oval Figure, accordingly as you shall think fit; garnishing it with *Morilles*, common Mushrooms, Veal-sweet-breads, Artichoke-bottoms and *Andouillets*, round about the opening in the middle, and pouring in a white Sauce, when ready to be brought to Table.

The Plate-pies, of a round Figure, are made in the same manner, when they are entirely cover'd, and a little Coronet is usually set on the middle. They are to be wash'd over, and scarce require an Hour for Baking.

A Pie made of a Fillet of Veal.

The Fillet is to be cut into pieces larded with thick Slips of Bacon: Afterwards, being dress'd in a good *Godivoe*, it must be fill'd with Asparagus-tops, Mushrooms, Veal-sweet-breads and Artichoke-bottoms: When it is ready to be serv'd up, it would be requisite to pour into it a little thickening Liquor, with some Lemmon-juice, and to garnish it with its own Crust, as well as the other sorts of Pies.

A Blood-pie for a Side-dish.

On those Days that young Turkeys, fat Pullets and other sorts of Fowl are kill'd, some of their Blood may be preserv'd, to the quantity only of a large Glass full. It must be put into an Earthen Pan, with some *Filets* of a Hare and of Veal: Let these *Filets* be larded with Gammon and thick Slips of Bacon, and steept in the Blood; seasoning them a little. To make the *Godivoe*, you are to provide some Flesh of Chickens and Partridges, a good piece of a Leg of Veal, some Bacon, Marrow and a little Sewet; with Parsly, Chibbol, a Clove of Garlick and *Truffles*, all well season'd, enrich'd and chopt small: Let the Blood be put into this Farce and temper'd with it. In the mean time, let two sorts of Paste be prepar'd, *viz.* one ordinary, of a greater quantity, and the other less, consisting of Eggs,

But-

Butter, Flower and Salt, all well workt, without any Water. Thus two large pieces are to be roll'd out of the common Paste, and two lesser ones of the finer sort: Let the great piece for the Bottom-crust be put upon Paper, and the lesser on the top of it: Take one half of your *Godivoe*, and spread it neatly upon those two pieces of Paste; then set your *Filets* in order, and the rest of the Farce upon them; covering all with *Bards* or thin Slices of Bacon, and afterwards with a small piece of the fine Paste; wetting the greater round about: At last, the other large piece being put on the top, to compleat the Lid or upper Crust; the whole Pie is to be wash'd over with an Egg, and bak'd in the Evening, for the space of eight or ten Hours: For it must be left all Night till the same Hour next Morning, taking care that the Oven be not over-heated. It must be serv'd up hot to Table, after having pour'd a Partridge-cullis into it, and both the Meat and Crust ought to be eaten with a Fork.

A Chibbol-pie.

For the Farce, or *Godivoe*, 'tis requisite to provide a piece of Beef, or of very tender Veal, with Beef-sewet, raw and tried, Parsly and a great deal of young Chibbol: Let it be chopt together, sufficiently enrich'd, and well season'd with all sorts of beaten Spice; adding a little Beef-marrow, Bread-crum steept in Gravy, some pieces of *Truffles* and Mushrooms cut small: Then let two pieces of good Paste be roll'd out, *viz.* one for the Lid very thin, and the other for the Bottom-crust somewhat thicker; let the Pie be rais'd upon Paper, three or four Inches high; and let the Farce be put into it, all well season'd and dispos'd of in good order: Lastly, let it be cover'd with Bacon-*Bards* and Slices of Lemmon, and when the Lid is laid on over all, let it be set into the Oven. As soon as it is drawn, a good white Cullis, or one of Partridges, may be pour'd into it, in order to be set hot on the Table.

A Pie after the English Way.

Take the Flesh of a Hare, and of a tender Leg of Veal, according to the size of your Pie: Let all be chopt upon the Dresser, with good raw Bacon, Marrow, a little Veal-sewet, candy'd Lemmon-peel, Sugar, beaten Cinnamon, and Coriander-seed; all well order'd and season'd with all sorts of sweet Spices, and

and bound with four or five Yolks of Eggs. In the mean while, a Paste being duly prepar'd, raise it of a convenient height, put your Farce into it, with some Slices of Lemmon and Bacon-*Bards*, and cover it with a Lid. When the Pie is bak'd, let a Sauce be made for it, of two good Glasses of Vinegar, with a little Sugar, some Cloves and a Stick of Cinnamon: Let all boil together, till the Sauce be almost ready, and if the Pie be large, a proportionable quantity will be requisite: Afterwards, the Pie being open'd, clear it thoroughly from the Fat, and pour in the Sauce. It may, if you please, be adorned with fine cut Pastry-works, and ought to be serv'd up hot for a Side-dish.

A Fish-pie.

For a Fish-pie to be serv'd up on Days of Abstinence, let a *Godivoe* be made in the same manner as the Fish-farce describ'd in the Article of *Farce*; except the Yolks of Eggs and the *Omelet*, which may be omitted: For the rest, the Mushrooms and *Truffles* must be chopt, as before, and this *Godivoe* may serve as it were instead of a *Godivoe*-pie on Flesh-days. After having made the Paste and rais'd the Pie, one half of this *Godivoe* is to be put into it, as also at the same time, all sorts of Garniture for Fish-days; such as *Truffles*, Mushrooms, *Andouillets*, Artichoke-bottoms, and raw Fish-*Filets* cut into small pieces: Then having put the rest of the *Godivoe* well season'd on the top, let your Pie be cover'd and bak'd: Lastly, you may prepare for it a white Sauce or Cullis of Mushrooms, or some other sort of Ragoo; but more especially take care, that it be serv'd up hot to Table.

The General Table at the end of this Volume, shews some other particular Fish-pies, that are occasionally describ'd upon account of the same Fishes: Those that remain are as follows, *viz.*

A Carp-pie.

The Carp must be scal'd and larded with Eels-flesh, season'd with good Butter, Pepper, Salt, Cloves, Nutmeg, a Bay-leaf and Oisters: Then the Pie being made of fine Paste, according to the length of the Carp, must be cover'd, and set into an Oven moderately heated; so as half a Glass of white Wine may be pour'd in, when it is half bak'd. The

The Carp may also be farc'd, according to the Method explain'd in the fifth Article *of Carps*, with Roes of the same, Oisters, Mushrooms and Artichoke-bottoms; in order to be serv'd up, with Lemmon-juice: Or else it may be cut into *Filets*, of the same nature as those for the above-mentioned Pies, as well as the following sorts of Fish and others.

A Turbot-pie.

A Turbot may be bak'd in a round or oval Dish, or in a standing Pie, after the usual manner: When it is well scal'd and wash'd, let the Tail be cut off, with the end of the Head and the Gills: Season your Pie with Pepper, Salt, Cloves, Nutmeg, young Chibbols, fine Herbs, *Morilles*, or common Mushrooms and sweet Butter, and cover it with a Lid. As soon as it is half bak'd, pour in a Glass of white Wine, and serve it up with Lemmon-juice or Verjuice with the entire Grapes.

A Roach-pie.

A Roach-pie may be made, as that of a Tunny, and set out with the same sort of Garniture; only adding some Cray-fish-claws, if you have any at hand: When it is half bak'd, let the Livers be first fried in a Pan with burnt Butter, then pounded in a Mortar, and strain'd thro' the Hair-sieve, with half a Glass of white Wine: Let all be put into the Pie, with some Lemmon-juice, when ready to be brought to Table.

A Trout-pie.

The Trout being well scal'd and cut, may be larded with Eels-flesh, and afterwards put into a Pie, made in the usual manner; season'd with Pepper, Salt, Cloves, Nutmeg, a Bay-leaf, Butter and fine Herbs, and enrich'd with Mushrooms, Artichoke-bottoms, Capers, Oisters and Fish-roes; squeezing in some Lemmon-juice before it is serv'd up to Table.

A Sole-pie.

When your Soles are scal'd and wash'd, let them be put into a Pie made of Paste, and season'd with Pepper, Salt, Nutmeg, fine Herbs chopt very small, Chibbols, *Truffles*, *Morilles* or *Mouserons*, *ferons*, common Mushrooms, fresh Oisters, and a great deal of Butter: As soon as it is bak'd, let it be serv'd up with Lemmon-juice.

A Tunny-pie.

Let the Tunny be cut into round Slices, and dress'd, as it is usually done, with Oisters, Artichoke-bottoms, and other seasoning Ingredients; as also, one or two Slices of green Lemmon: Let it be bak'd in an Oven moderately heated, and put in some Lemmon-juice, or a little Vinegar, as it is serving up to Table.

A Lamprey-pie after the English manner.

Let your Lampreys be well cleans'd from their Slime, reserving their Blood, and afterwards put into a Pie of fine Paste, season'd with Pepper, Salt, beaten Cinnamon, Sugar, candy'd Lemmon-peel, Dates and Currans: When it is half bak'd in an Oven moderately heated, pour in the Blood, and half a Glass of white Wine; adding also some Lemmon-juice, before you serve it up to Table.

Petits Patez, *or little Pies of Fish.*

Take the Flesh of Carps, Eels and Tenches; let all be half stew'd in a Pan with Mushrooms, and afterwards chopt small, with Parsly, Chibbol, Thyme, Pepper, Salt, Cloves and Nutmeg: Then put in as great a quantity of Butter as of Meat, and let your Pies be made of Puff-paste.

Petits Patez *after the Spanish way.*

With this Article we shall conclude what relates to hot Pies for Side-dishes, as well on Flesh-days, as those of Abstinence. To make this sort of Pies, take only a Slice of Bacon, a little piece of Veal and the Breast of a Chicken: Let all be parboil'd in a Pot, minc'd very small, and season'd with beaten Spice: They must also be pounded in a Mortar, adding a little Garlick and Rocambole; whilst your *Petits Patez*, or little Pies are made with fine Paste; which will serve for garnishing other Dishes, or instead of an Out-work.

Cold

Cold Pies for Intermesses.

Having already given Directions for making a Gammon-pie in the third Article *of Gammon*, let us now take a View of some other sorts of Pies that are likewise serv'd up among the Intermesses, *viz.*

Pies of Beef-stakes and other sorts of Butchers-meat.

Take some Buttock-beef cut out into Stakes; let them be well beaten, larded with thick Slips of Bacon and seasoned as before: Let them also be dress'd and bak'd in the same manner.

According to the bigness, you would have your Pie to be of, a Leg of Mutton may likewise be added; or else a particular Pie may be made of it: To that purpose, having taken away the Skin and Fat from the Leg, let it be boned, well beaten and larded with middle-siz'd Slips of Bacon; seasoning it at the same time, with fine Herbs, Parsly, Chibbol and Spice. In the mean while, let a piece of ordinary Paste for a strong Undercrust, be roll'd out and laid upon thick Paper well butter'd; and let the Joynt of Mutton be dress'd upon the same Paste, with thin Slices of Bacon, Bay-leaves and the necessary seasoning Ingredients: Then cover your Pie with a Lid, and having shap'd it neatly, let it be bak'd as the former, about three Hours. When it is drawn out of the Oven, let a Clove of Garlick, or a Shalot bruised be put in thro' the Breathing-hole, and let it lye by, in order to be serv'd up cold to Table.

To make a Pie of a Fillet of Veal, it must be larded in like manner, after it has been marinated for a while, with well seasoned Vinegar; and for the rest, you need only observe the Directions even now laid down for the Mutton-pie.

A Hare or Leveret-pie.

If you would have your Hares and Leverets entire, with the Bones, let them be larded with middle-siz'd Slips of Bacon, and season'd with Pepper, Salt, Nutmeg, Cloves and a Bay-leaf: Neither must you be sparing of your pounded Lard or Bacon-*Bards*, in making the Pie, either of course or fine Paste. When it is bak'd, let it be set a-side in a dry place and stopt up close.

If the Hares or Leverets are to be boned, endeavours must be us'd to keep the Flesh, as entire, as is possible, and they must be larded with thick Slips of Bacon: Then having season'd them, they may be put into a Pie and bak'd as the others.

A Pullet-pie and others.

Having neatly truss'd your large fat Pullets, and broken their Bones, let them be larded with thick Slips of Bacon; also season'd with fine Herbs, Parsly, Chibbol and Spice: Then let them be laid in order in a Pie made of ordinary Paste, with fresh Butter, *Bards*, or thin Slices of Bacon, a Bay-leaf or two, and other seasoning Ingredients: Lastly, let the Pies when well order'd, be bak'd during two or three Hours according to the Heat of the Oven.

PIGEONS.

Pies of young Turkeys, Ducks, Partridges, Pheasants, Woodcocks, large Rabbets, young Rabbets, green Geese, Teals and others are usually made after the same manner.

Pigeons afford a great Variety of Ragoo's and some of them have been already produced; particularly, a *Bisk* of Pigeons, in the first Article of *Bisks*; a *Godivoe* farced with young Pigeons, in that of *Godivoe*; and a Pie of large Pigeons, a little before, in the second Article of Pies: There still remain many other sorts, so that it would be expedient here, to give some account of them in their Order.

To dress Pigeons, with sweet Basil.

Let your Pigeons be well scalded, and slit a little on the Back, to let in a small Farce, made of raw Bacon well minc'd, with Parsly, sweet Basil and Chibbol, all well season'd. Then having stew'd them in a Pot, with some Broth, an Onion stuck with Cloves, a little Verjuice and Salt, let them be roll'd in beaten Eggs, and at the same time wrapt up in Bread-crum, to the end that they may be well breaded. Every one of the Pigeons being thus order'd a-part, they must be fried in hot Lard, till they come to a fine colour, and afterwards fried again all at once with Parsly; which is to garnish them when they are ready to be serv'd up among the Side-dishes.

A

A Side-dish of Pigeons, with Fennel.

Having provided Pigeons of the best sort, let them be well truss'd and only sindg'd at the Fire: Then taking the Livers, with some Lard, Chibbol, Parsly, and a little green Fennel; let all be chopt and well season'd, in order to stuff the Bodies of the Pigeons. Afterwards let them be roasted, and let a good Ragoo be turn'd upon them, when ready to be brought to Table.

A Side-dish of Pigeons bak'd between two Fires.

Take large Pigeons, that are well truss'd; and, if you please, prepare a somewhat thick Farce to stuff their Bodies. Then let them be bak'd, or stew'd between two Fires, as many other Things are usually dress'd: Afterwards they must be laid in order in a Dish; and well clear'd from the Fat; pouring upon them at the same time, a Ragoo of *Truffles*, and Veal-sweetbreads.

Pigeons stewed in Compote.

The Pigeons must first be larded with thick Slips of Bacon, and fried for some time in melted Lard: Then they are to be stew'd in Broth, with a Glass of white Wine, Pepper, Salt, Nutmeg, green Lemmon, Cloves, Mushrooms and *Truffles*; whilst a white or brown Cullis is preparing, as it were for a Fricasly of Pigeons cut into pieces: The Dish may be garnish'd with little Rolls cut into halves, or any thing else at pleasure, and some Lemmon-juice must be squeez'd in, as it is serving up to Table.

A Side-dish of Pigeons, with Gammon.

This Dish is usually prepar'd after the same manner, as that of Chickens, with Gammon, already specified in the first Article of Chickens, under the Letter C. If the Pigeons are very large, they must be larded with thick Slips of Bacon and others of Gammon, and bak'd between two Fires: Then let them be put into a Gammon-ragoo, prepared for that purpose, and let all be well clear'd from the Fat; sprinkling them with a little Verjuice, or Vinegar: Take care that they be not too high season'd with Salt and let them be brought hot to Table.

Ano-

Another Side-dish of Pigeons, with Truffles.

Another Side-dish may be made of larded or farced Pigeons, in a Ragoo, with *Truffles* and Radishes, or dress'd in a well seson'd Ragoo of a fine colour, with Artichoke-bottoms and Asparagus-tops. They may be garnish'd with Veal-sweet-breads in white Sauce, and fried Parsly; adding some Lemmon-juice, before they are serv'd up to Table.

A Side-dish of Pigeons broil'd or fried, à la Sainte Menehout.

Take large Pigeons, that are well truss'd; let them be cut into two parts and broil'd upon the Coals: Then let them be neatly breaded, taking care that they be not spoil'd. If you would have them fried; before they are breaded, they must be roll'd in beaten Eggs, to the end that the Bread may more easily stick to them. When they are dress'd either way, they may serve for garnishing; but if a separate Dish be made of them, a *Ramolade*-sauce must be put underneath, ready prepared, with Anchovies, Parsly, chopt Capers, a little Chibbol, Vinegar and Gravy, and then all may be set hot on the Table.

All other sorts of Fowl, may be dress'd in the same manner: Pigeons may also be larded, if you shall think fit, with thick Slips of Bacon and Gammon, to heigthen their Savour, and some call Fowls so dress'd *Pieces à la Sainte Menehout.*

Moreover Pigeons, after they have been well season'd, may be stew'd in a *Court-bouillon,* that is duly order'd and made very Savoury: Then they must be well breaded, so as no part of the Meat may be any longer seen, and brought to a colour, with the red-hot Fire-shovel.

Pigeons in Sur-tout, roasted, and bak'd between two Fires.

Having caus'd large Pigeons to be well order'd and truss'd; let a Farce be made of raw Bacon, boil'd Gammon and Veal-sweet-breads, with *Truffles* and Mushrooms, chopt with the Livers, also Parsly, Chibbol and a Clove of Garlick; all cut small, well season'd, and bound with one or two Yolks of Eggs. Let the Pigeons be stuff'd with this Farce between the Skin and the Flesh, as also in the Body, and afterwards well tied up; providing at the same time a large *Fricandoe*, or *Scotch* Collop larded, ed, for every Pigeon, which is to be laid upon the Breaſt. Then all the Pigeons being neatly tied and ſpitted, are to be cover'd with Paper, and roaſted in this manner; whilſt a good Ragoo is preparing for them. Before they are ſerv'd up, 'twill be requiſite to dreſs them in a Diſh, taking away the Collops, and pouring on them the Ragoo or Cullis, of whatſoever Nature it be; provided it be well boil'd and ſeaſon'd. Laſtly, let the Collops be laid again upon the Breaſts of all the Pigeons, and let them be brought hot to Table.

The ſame thing may be done for Pigeons in *Sur-tout* bak'd between two Fires: All the difference between them, and other ſorts of Fowl dreſs'd in this manner, is, That no Bacon-*Bards*, nor Meat are to be put upon the Collops, to the end that they may take a fine colour. As ſoon as the Pigeons are ready, let the Fat be taken away, and a Ragoo prepar'd with *Truffles*, accordingly, as occaſion may require.

Other Side-diſhes of the like nature, may be made of Partridges, Wood-cocks and other ſorts of Fowl, and to diverſifie them, a Ragoo may be dreſs'd with Oiſters, or *à la Saingaraz*, or a Partridge-cullis, according to the Expences allotted to be laid out: But all muſt be well clear'd from the Fat, and ſerv'd up hot to Table.

A *Pigeon*-Tourte, or *Pan-pie*.

After having provided good tame Pigeons, let them be well ſcalded and truſs'd: Then taking melted Lard, Marrow, Veal-ſweet-breads cut into halves, Artichoke-bottoms in quarters, and a whole one to be ſet in the middle, with Capons-livers, Cocks-combs well pickt, Muſhrooms cut into ſmall ſquare pieces, and *Truffles* in Slices; let all be well ſtew'd in a Pan, with a little Flower, and well ſeaſon'd. In the mean while, let your Paſte be made (according to the bigneſs of the Pie-pan) of an Egg, Butter, Salt and Water; as alſo, a piece of Puff-paſte: Let a good piece of the former be roll'd out for the Bottom-Cruſt, which is to be put into a Pie-pan of a ſize proportionable to that of your Diſh: Then having pour'd in ſome melted Lard, that is moderately hot, let the Pigeons be well moiſten'd and laid in order, with the Artichoke-bottom in the middle, the Slices of *Truffles*, Muſhrooms and Veal-ſweet-breads in the Intervals. Afterwards let the reſt of the Sauce be infus'd, and taking another piece of Paſte, that was roll'd out of a round Figure,

gure, let it be clapp'd with your Hand, spreading it upon the dresser-board; to the end, that the Puff-paste may be put upon it, and that the Lid may be neatly spread on the top: But too great a quantity of Puff-paste must not be made, that the other Piece may be thicker. Having thus cover'd your Pie with this Lid, make a neat Border or Side-crust round about, and when 'tis ready to be serv'd up, remove the Bacon-*Bards*, drain off the Fat, and pour in a Cullis of Pigeons-carcasses, or some other white thickening Sauce.

Other ways of dressing Pigeons.

Pigeons may be otherwise dress'd *au Pere Douillet*; and to that purpose; after they have been well order'd, let them be stew'd in a little Pot, well seasoned and enrich'd, with Salt, Cloves, Thyme, Onion, and a little white Wine. They may be garnish'd with Parsly and Lemmon-slices; squeezing in some of the Juice, when ready to be brought to Table.

At another time, your Pigeons, after they have been roasted, barded and brought to a fine colour, may be serv'd up in Veal-gravy, without any other Garniture, or with white Sauce; or lastly, in a *Marinade*, as it appears from the second Article of *Marinades*.

PIGS.

A Side-dish of a young sucking Pig.

After a young sucking Pig has been well scalded and drawn; let the Liver be minc'd a-part, with parboil'd Bacon, *Truffles*, Mushrooms, an Anchovie, half a Clove of Garlick, a few fine Herbs and a little Sage. The whole Farce being thus dress'd in a Stew-pan and well season'd, stuff the Body of your Pig with the same, tye it up neatly, and let it be roasted; basting it with good Oil of Olives. It must be serv'd up hot to Table, and may be garnish'd with fried Bread.

To scald a sucking Pig well, it must be rubb'd with Rosin, and put into Water moderately heated.

A sucking Pig dress'd after the German Fashion.

The Pig must be first cut into quarters, and fried in a Pan with Lard: Then let it be stew'd in Broth, with a little white
Wine,

Wine, a Faggot of Herbs, Pepper, Salt and Nutmeg. Afterwards having toss'd up in a Stew-pan with Lard, some Oisters and Flower, a piece of Lemmon, Capers and stoned Olives, let them be added to the rest, with Slices and Juice of Lemmon, as they are serving up to Table.

For a sucking Pig roasted, see the Letter R.

An Intermeß of a sucking Pig in Galantine.

After having caus'd your Pig to be well scalded and drawn, cut off the Head and the four Legs: Then let the Skin be slipt off, beginning at the Belly; but care must be taken that it be not cut, especially on the Back: Let this Skin be neatly spread upon the Dresser, whilst a Farce is preparing, with the Flesh of the Pig, a piece of very tender Veal, a little raw Gammon, and Bacon; also, a little Parsly, chopt Chibbol, and all sorts of fine Herbs, except Rosemary and Sage. In the mean while, a Strong Liquor is to be made, with a Quart of Water, two Bay-leaves, some Thyme, sweet Basil, Savoury, three Cloves of Garlick, and two or three Shalots; this Liquor when half boil'd away, will serve to moisten your Farce. Let some Pistachoes and Almonds be also scalded, according to discretion, and let six Eggs be harden'd to get their Yolks: Afterwards let some of your Bacon and Gammon be cut into thick Slices, taking only the lean part of the Gammon: When they are all well season'd, let a Slice of Gammon, another of Bacon; as also, a Lay of Almonds, another of Pistachoes, and a third of hard Yolks be set in order. Besides, you must put into the Farce, some *Truffles* and Mushrooms cut small, with a little Milk-cream, and soak them in your strong Liquor, adding afterwards the Yolk of one Egg. The Bacon and other Things being thus order'd, this Farce is to be spread over them, beginning at one of the ends of the Skin, and then roll'd up; drawing the two Swards on both Sides close together, so as the Farce may not fall out: When it is well roll'd up of a convenient length, let it be tied, or sow'd up on all Sides, and put into a Napkin; which must be bound at both end Ends and in the middle, to keep it very firm and compact. At last, it must be bak'd in a Stew-pan between two Fires, *viz.* one upon the Lid and the other underneath, for the space of ten or twelve Hours, with some Slices of Bacon and Beef-stakes, both on the Bottom and Top of the Pan: Let your farced Pig cool in the same Pan, and as soon as it is

taken

taken out of the Napkin, let it be untied, and cut into Slices, which are to be laid in a Dish, upon a clean Napkin, and so serv'd up cold, with Slices of Lemmon and Flowers.

A Pig dress'd au Pere Douillet.

When the Pig is well scalded in Water, and order'd as before, it must be larded with middle-siz'd Slips of Bacon, and season'd high, with Pepper, Salt, Cloves, Nutmeg, Bay-leaves, young Chibbols and green Lemmon: Then let it be wrapt up in a Linnen-cloth, and boil'd in a Pot, with Broth and a little white Wine. Afterwards it may be set by, till it be half cool'd, and so serv'd up for a Side-dish.

Pigs-pettitoes à la Sainte Menehout.

Take Pettitoes that are well dress'd, cut them into halves, and let every Pettitoe be tied up together: Then having provided a Pot, put into it a Lay of *Bards*, or thin Slices of Bacon; another of Pettitoes and fine Herbs, and a third of Pettitoes and *Bards*; and so on, till all your Pettitoes are disposed of; as also, afterwards a Glass of Spirit of Wine, and a Quart of white Wine, with Anis, Coriander, a Bay-leaf or two, and a little Quick-silver: Let all be cover'd with Bacon-*Bards*, and let the Edges of the Pot be lin'd with strong Paper; so as the Lid may be exactly fitted, and kept close stopt. Then let the Pot be set between two Fires, which must not be too quick, that the Pettitoes may be leisurely stew'd, during ten or twelve Hours, more or less. When they are taken out and cool'd, they are to be neatly breaded, and broil'd upon the Grid-iron, in order to be serv'd up hot among the Intermesses. They may be dress'd with less charge, only with Water and white Wine mingled together; seasoning them well, and putting in some Leaf-fat out of a Hog's Belly; as it may also be done, in the other Way of dressing them.

The Denomination of *à la Sainte Menehout* is likewise attributed to Pigeons, Chickens, or other sorts of Fowl, dress'd in that manner, which some call *à la Mazarine*, and which has been elsewhere explain'd in the third Article of Chickens, under the Letter C.

PIKES.

PIKES.

Pike with Oisters.

Let the Pike be cut into pieces and put into a Stew-pan, with white Wine, Parsly, Chibbol, Mushrooms, chopt *Truffles*, Pepper, Salt and good Butter. In the mean while, let your Oisters be scalded a little in Water, with a few Drops of Verjuice, and thrown in among the rest, with their Liquor, when the Pike is ready to be serv'd up to Table: Afterwards let all be dress'd in a Dish, and garnish'd with what you shall think fit.

The same thing may be done for other sorts of Fish that are dress'd with Oisters.

A Side-dish of a large Pike.

After having cut your Pike into four Quarters, let the Head be dress'd in a *Court-bouillon*; one of the middle-pieces with white Sauce; the other in a Hash, or in a Ragoo, and the Tail-piece fried with Caper-sauce. The Hash is to be garnish'd with small Crusts of fried Bread, and all dress'd in a large Dish. To these may be added a small Ragoo of Pike-livers, Roes and Capers; garnishing the Dish with Flowers, or green Herbs.

A Pike with Sauce, after the German Way.

When the Pike is well cleans'd and gutted, let it be cut into two parts and boil'd in Water, but not outright: Having taken it out, let it be scal'd till it become very white, and put into a Stew-pan, with white Wine, chopt Capers, Anchovies, Thyme, fine Herbs and Mushrooms cut small, as also *Truffles*, and *Morilles*: Then let all boil together gently, lest the Fish should break, and throw in a Lump of good Butter, to thicken the Sauce, with a little Parmesan. When it is ready, you may dress your Dish, and garnish it with what you please.

Pike-Filets fried and otherwise.

As soon as your Pike is gutted and scal'd, cut it into pieces, and make *Filets* of it, which are to be marinated for some time: Then let them be fried, after having dipt them into a thin Paste

O or

or Batter, or otherwife, and let them be ferv'd up to Table, garnifh'd with Parfly and Slices of Lemmon.

Pike-*Filets* may alfo be put into white Sauce, which is a kind of thickening Liquor proper for that fort of Fifh, made of a little Bread-crum pounded and ftrain'd thro' the Sieve, after having boil'd two or three Walms in a Stew-pan, with a little Broth, or Fifh-cullis. Let your *Filets* be foak'd in this Sauce, that is well feafon'd, and if you pleafe, fome *Truffles* may be added, with *Moufferons* and common Mufhrooms, as alfo fome Lemmon-juice, as they are ferving up to Table.

Laftly, they may be drefs'd with Cucumbers, as many other Things, and fprinkled likewife with Lemmon-juice.

A Pike-pie.

The Pike may be cut into *Filets* or fmall pieces of the length of your Finger, which are to be fcalded, well feafon'd, and tofs'd up in a Stew-pan with fweet Butter, Mufhrooms, *Truffles*, Afparagus-tops and Carp-roes, alfo a piece of Lemmon thrown in as they are Stewing. Then a fmall *Godivoe* is to be made of the Flefh of Carps or Eels, feafon'd, according to the ufual manner, and bound with Bread-crum foak'd in Broth. The bottom of your Pie muft be fill'd with this Farce, and a thickening Liquor with Lemmon-juice muft be pour'd in, before it is brought to Table.

A Pie may likewife be made of a boned Pike, and farced in the mannner hereafter exprefs'd in the eighth Article. The Pafte for this Pie out to be fine, and it muft be fhap'd according to the fize of your Pike. Both thefe forts of Pies muft be bak'd in an Oven moderately heated, and ferv'd up hot for Side-difhes.

A Pike in Haricot *with Turneps.*

Let the Pike be cut into fmall pieces about the length of half your Finger, and then fcalded: When they are drain'd, let them be fried brown, and one half of the Turneps likewife fried brown. Afterwards they muft be ftew'd together, over a gentle Fire; adding a good thickening Liquor and Lemmon-juice, when they are ferv'd up to Table.

Pike

Pike in a Court-bouillon or au Bleu.

The Pike being cut into quarters, and put into a Dish, let Vinegar and Salt be pour'd upon it boiling hot. Then having caus'd white Wine, Verjuice, Pepper, Salt, Cloves, Nutmeg, a Bay-leaf, or two, Onions and green Lemmon, or Orange, to boil together, over a quick Fire; let your Pike be put in, and afterwards serv'd up dry among the Intermesses.

Farced Pike.

Let the Pikes be scal'd, and let the Bones be taken out at the Back, yet so as the Heads and Tails may be left sticking; whilst a Farce is preparing with some of the same Flesh and that of Eels, seasond with Pepper, Salt, Nutmeg, Cloves, Chibbol, Butter, Mushrooms and fine Herbs. Let the Skins be stuff'd with this Farce and sow'd up, in order to be stew'd in a Dish, with burnt Butter, fried Flower, white Wine, Verjuice, a little Broth and a piece of green Lemmon. Then a Ragoo of Oisters, Carp-roes and Mushrooms is to be added; garnishing the Dish, with fried Bread, Lemmon-slices and Capers.

Pike in Casserole.

Scale your Pikes, Lard them with Eel-flesh, and let them be stew'd with burnt Butter, white Wine, Verjuice, Pepper, Salt, Nutmeg, Cloves, a Bunch of Herbs, Bay-leaves and green Lemmon. In the mean while, let a Ragoo be made for them, with Mushrooms, Oisters, Capers, fried Flower and some of the same Sauce in which they were stew'd. They may be garnish'd with Lemmon-slices, Carp-roes and fried Mushrooms.

Pikes fried with Anchovie-sauce.

Let the Pikes be cut open in the Belly, and marinated in Vinegar, with Pepper, Salt, Chibbols and Bay-leaves; let them also be flower'd before they are fried. For the Sauce, let Anchovies be dissolv'd in burnt Butter, and having strain'd them thro' the Sieve, add some Juice of Orange, Capers and white Pepper. The Dish is to be garnish'd with fried Parsly and Slices of Lemmon, before it is brought to Table.

Roasted

Roasted Pike.

The Pike must be scal'd, cut lightly and larded with middle-siz'd Slips of Eels-flesh, season'd with Pepper, Salt, Nutmeg, Chibbols and fine Herbs: It must be Spitted at its whole length, and basted with Butter, white Wine, Vinegar and green Lemmon. Then having dissolv'd Anchovies in the Sauce, strain them thro' the Hair-sieve, with a little fried Flower, and add some Oisters mortified in the Sauce, with Capers and white Pepper. The Dish may be garnish'd with fried Mushrooms, Carp-roes and Lemmon-slices.

Pike on Flesh-days, for an Intermess.

After having scal'd your Pike, and drawn out the Guts at the upper part of the Belly, it must be scalded in luke-warm Water, and larded with thin Slips of Bacon: Then it must be roasted on a Spit, and basted as before; the same sort of Sauce being also prepared for it. The Dish is to be garnish'd with larded Veal-sweet-breads, farced Mushrooms and Lemmon-slices.

It may also be dress'd according to the Directions laid down in the first Article of *Trouts* under the Letter T.

Pike-potage.

This sort of Potage may be made with Oisters, Turneps, or Cabbage; cutting the Pike into several pieces, which are to be first fried in a Pan with Butter, and afterwards stew'd in an earthen Pot, with some Fish-broth, or strained Pease-soop, season'd with Pepper, Salt, and a Bunch of Herbs: Then having added Oisters, the Potage is to be laid a soaking with the Broth, in which the Fish was stew'd; the Pike must be dress'd in the same Potage, as also the Oisters; and the whole Mess must be garnish'd with Bread and Mushrooms fried, squeezing in some Lemmon-juice, as it is serving up to Table.

When Turneps are us'd, they must be fried with burnt Butter, and Flower and then stew'd with Pepper and Salt. Afterwards they are to be laid in good order upon the soaked Crusts, with the Pike.

The same thing may be done with the Cabbage, after it has been scalded and chopt small, and as for the Pike, it may be larded with Eels-flesh.

A

A Potage may alfo be made of farced Pike, and to that purpofe, it would only be requifite, to look a little backwards upon the Inftructions contain'd in the preceding Article of *farced Pike* Pag. 195. and for the Potage of Pike-*Filets* and Crufts farced with Pike, fee the following Articles of Potages.

PLAICE.

After having roafted and flafh'd your Plaice on the Back, in form of a Crofs, cutting off the Nofe and Tail, they are to be put into a Stew-pan, with white Wine, Fifh-roes, *Morilles*, common Mufhrooms, *Truffles*, Parfly, Chibbol, Thyme, and a Slice of good Butter, all well thicken'd; but care muft be taken to ftir them gently leaft they fhould break. When they are ready, let them be neatly drefs'd and made very white; pouring fome good Sauce upon them, and garnifhing them with any thing that is at Hand.

As for thofe that are fried, they muft be firft ftrew'd with Salt and Flower, and when drefs'd, they may be ferv'd up, with Salt and Orange-juice.

POTAGES.

Altho' mention has been already made of feveral Potages, as well for Flefh-days, as thofe of Abftinence; particularly, the *Bisk*, *Cafferole*, *Oil* and *Julian*, as alfo Potage of Lambs-heads, Pike, Cray-fifh, Sea-ducks, Mufcles and fome others, according to the refpective Meffes that were treated of: Neverthelefs this Subject is very copious, and capable of furnifhing matter for a large Article. A general Account has likewife been given of the peculiar Broths, that ought to conftitute the Body of all thofe Potages, and of all others, as alfo of the Cullifes that are ufually made: Let us now proceed to a more particular Enumeration of them; beginning with the Potages of Pulfe, that may be proper for feveral forts of Fowls, to avoid the unprofitable Repetition of the fame Thing, for every one of them.

POTAGES FOR FLESH-DAYS.

Potage with Peafe.

Take green Peafe, and having fhell'd them, let the Peafe be fet by a-part, which will ferve to make green Peafe-foop. To that purpofe, taking the Cods with the Peafe, let them be fcalded a little, with the green top of a Chibbol and a little Parfly, and drain'd from their Liquor: Then they muft be pounded with a little Bread-crum foak'd in good Broth, and well ftrain'd thro' a Sieve; fo as your Soop may be fomewhat thick. Afterwards your Peafe muft be put into a Stew-pan, with a little Lard; having before fried in it, a little chopt Parfly and Savoury: Let all be ftew'd together, and moiften'd with good Broth; adding a Faggot of fine Herbs: When the whole Mefs is put into a Pot, and almoft ready, the Soop may be pour'd in, and fome Cabbage-lettice, cut into fmall Slices, may alfo be ftew'd before the green Peafe are put in, all being well feafon'd. Let your Potage be laid a foaking with good clear Broth, and having pour'd in a little Peafe-foop, let your Fowls be laid in order upon the Potage. They may be garnifh'd either with farced, or unfarced Lettice, or with Cucumbers, or elfe with lean Bacon, accordingly as you fhall think fit. Laftly, let your Potage be foak'd with the Soop and green Peafe, and let all be ferv'd up at once.

Many Potages of the like nature are ufually made with green Peafe in their Seafon, particularly for Lambs-heads, Ducks, green Geefe, farced Chickens, young Turkeys and others, which ought to be boil'd feparately in a Pot, with good Broth. They are to be garnifh'd with Afparagus-tops, farced Lettice, or Cucumbers. When green Peafe are out of Seafon, the Soop may be made with old ones; and this fort is more efpecially proper for Ducks, *Andouilles*, &c.

'Tis an eafie Matter to take Meafures in reference to this Article, for Peafe-potage on Fifh-days; for then the Peafe are to be ftew'd with natural Butter, and the Crufts laid a foaking, with good Herb-broth, according to the Directions laid down in the laft Article of *Broths*, under the Letter B.

For the Fowls that are farced, the Method is explain'd in the refpective Articles, where mention is made of thofe Fowls; and for the reft, fee what is obferv'd in the following Potages.

Potage,

Potage, with Turneps.

After having well ſcrap'd your Turneps, cut them into round pieces, or long-ways, and fry them with Lard and a little Flower: You may make uſe of the ſame Lard, in which your Fowls were fried brown, whether they were Ducks, Teals, green Geeſe, or others; at leaſt if you would not have them roaſted a little on the Spit. So that either Way, all may be put into a Pot together, with good Broth, ſeaſon'd with Pepper, Salt, and a Faggot of Herbs; adding a brown thickening Liquor, as they are ſtewing: Thus, having laid your Potage a ſoaking with the ſame Broth, let the Fowls and Turneps be neatly dreſs'd, and garniſh'd, ſometimes with fried Bread, and ſometimes with Sauſages, *Andouillets*, or young Bacon boil'd together: Afterwards let ſome Lemmon-juice and good Gravy be put to them, before they are ſerv'd up to Table. Some cauſe the Turneps to be boil'd ſeparately.

Large Geeſe, green Geeſe, Ducks and other Fowls of the like nature, that are uſually dreſs'd with Turneps, ought to be larded with thick Slips of Bacon, before they are fried; and the lighter Fowls may be farced, more eſpecially Chickens.

The Houghs of a Stag, and of a wild Boar, may alſo be ſerv'd up in the ſame ſort of Potage.

A Potage with Turneps may likewiſe be prepar'd for a Shoulder of Mutton; which being well mortified, you are to lard with thick Slips of Bacon, and cauſe it to be half roaſted; as well as for a farced Leg of Mutton, which muſt be fried as the above-mentioned Fowls.

Cabbage-potage.

Take large Pigeons, Partridges and other ſorts of Fowl well truſs'd; lard them with three or four Rows of Bacon, and let them be roaſted only till they come to a colour: In the mean time, having provided Cabbages that are well headed, let them be cut into quarters and ſcalded: Then they muſt be drain'd and put into a Pot, as alſo the Fowls, with young Bacon parboil'd, a little ſweet Baſil, an Onion ſtuck with Cloves, and one or two Cloves of Garlick: They muſt alſo be ſeaſon'd, pouring in ſome good Gravy and Broth, and afterwards all boil'd together. When they are half boil'd, a brown thickening Liquor must be prepar'd with Lard and Flower, as if it were to make a good *Robert*-Sauce. As soon as the Flower has taken colour, moisten your thickening Ingredients with good Gravy, or with the same Cabbage-broth, and when it is ready, turn all upon the Cabbage. Let your Potage be laid a soaking with good Gravy and the Cabbage-broth, when you perceive them to be savoury, and that they are well boil'd. Afterwards let the Fowls be laid in order upon the Potage; let a fine Border be made round about the Dish, or in the Intervals, with young streaked Bacon cut into Slices, let all be soak'd with good Broth, and serv'd up hot to Table.

As for *Milan*-Cabbages and others, after having scalded them, they may be chopt small and fried, before they are put into a Pot, in the above-mentioned manner; except some of the Insides, which are to be preserv'd for garnishing. See also what has been already deliver'd upon this Subject in the first Article of Cabbage, under the Letter C.

Root-potages.

After having made good Broth, pour it into a Pot, and put in at the same time a fat Capon, with Parsly-roots, Parsnips, and small Chibbols, entire. Then, all being boil'd together, let your Potage be laid a soaking, with the Capon on the top; garnishing it with Parsnips and young Chibbols, and soaking it with good Veal-gravy, before it is serv'd up to Table.

Potages may also be made of Quails, young Ring-doves, fat Pullets and others, with Roots, after the same manner.

Potages, with Lentils.

Having provided Partridges, Pigeons, Ducks, or other Fowls; let them be larded with several Rows of Bacon and spitted: When they are half roasted, let them be put into a Pot and boil'd with good Broth, a Faggot of fine Herbs, and other seasoning Ingredients. Then taking some Lentils ready boil'd, pound them with Onions, Carrets and Parsly-roots, and strain them thro' the Hair-sieve, in order to make the Cullis. In the mean while, having caus'd other Lentils to be stew'd in a Pan, with a little Parsly, Chibbol and Savoury chopt small, pour in some of the Broth, in which your Fowls were boil'd, as also the Cullis, and let all be put into a Pot, till you have laid them

a

a ſoaking and dreſs'd your Potage. 'Twill be requiſite to provide ſome young ſtreaked Bacon, Cervelas, or Sauſages for the Garniture; and, if the Expences are not grudged, a Border may be made round about the Diſh, with Cocks-combs and Veal-ſweet-breads in a Ragoo; all well dreſs'd and clear'd from the Fat. The Potage may alſo be enrich'd with a Beef-cullis, Partridge-carcaſſes, Cruſts of Bread, and a piece of green Lemmon, all pounded in a Mortar, ſtrain'd thro' a Sieve, and well ſeaſon'd. See the Lentil-cullis, in the laſt Article of *Culliſes*, under the Letter C.

Another ſort of Lentil-potage is ſometimes made, and garniſh'd with a farced Loaf in the middle, as well on Fleſh-days, as thoſe of Abſtinence: For the latter, it may be ſerv'd up with Oil, and more eſpecially for the Entertainments with Roots, or on other Days of Lent, when a particular Plate, or Diſh may be made of them, dreſs'd in a Ragoo, with fine Herbs.

Potage of young Ring-doves, in form of an Oil.

After having neatly truſs'd your Ring-doves, let them be ſcalded in Water, and put into a Pot with good Gravy; throwing in at the ſame time, a Bunch of Leeks cut into pieces, another of Celery, a third of Turneps, a fourth of other ſorts of Roots, a few Chibbols, and a Faggot of fine Herbs. All being well boil'd, you muſt lay your Potage a ſoaking with the ſame Broth; ſetting the Ring-doves in order in it, and garniſhing the whole Diſh with your Roots: Let them alſo be ſoak'd with good ſavoury Gravy, and ſerv'd up hot to Table. The Garnitures ought only to take up the ſides of the Diſh, ſo as the Soop may be left free: And the ſame thing may be done for Quails, and all other ſorts of Fowl.

At another time, young Ring-doves may be dreſs'd in Potage, with Cabbage, Muſhrooms, or otherwiſe at pleaſure.

Potage à la Reyne, *with Partridges, Quails, or other ſorts of Fowl.*

Let freſh Partridges, after they have been ſcalded and well truſs'd, be boil'd in good Broth, with a good Faggot of fine Herbs, ſome thin ſlices of Bacon and pieces of Lemmon; whilſt a Cullis is making of the Breaſt of a roaſted fat Pullet, or Capon; minc'd and pounded in a Mortar, with the Crum of a

Loaf

Loaf soak'd in Broth, and strain'd thro' the Hair-sieve. Let this Cullis be put into a little Pot, well cover'd; and let your Potage, that ought to be made of Bread-crusts, be laid a soaking with strained Broth. Afterwards set your Fowls in the same Potage, sprinkle all with good Gravy, and before they are served up, squeez the Juice of a Lemmon into the Cullis: A farced Loaf must also be put in the middle of the Potage, with the Fowls round about; the Cullis must be pour'd upon them; and a Border is to be made about the Dish, with farced Cocks-combs, Sweet-breads of Veal larded and roasted, other Slices of Veal-sweet-breads in a Ragoo, and Artichoke-bottoms: Lastly, the Breasts of the Partridges, or other Fowls, must be cover'd with Slices of black *Truffles*, and all dispos'd of in good order. As for the farced Loaf, it must be stuff'd with a good Hash of a roasted Fowl, pieces of *Truffles* and Mushrooms, and small Asparagus-tops, according to the Season.

A lesser quantity of Potage, may be made of a single Partridge, without a farced Loaf, observing all the rest of the Circumstances, as much as Convenience, or the allotted Expences will admit of.

A Potage of farced Partridges, may be also prepar'd; which ought to be garnish'd with larded *Fricandoes* dress'd in a Ragoo, also Veal-sweet-breads, Mushrooms, Artichoke-bottoms, Cocks-combs, and *Truffles*; adding the Juice of a Lemmon, when brought to Table.

Another white Potage à la Reyne.

This sort of Potage does not require any Fowl; only the Breast of a Capon, and a piece of a Neck of Veal, some Almonds, two or three Yolks of hard Eggs, and the Crum of a Loaf steept in good Broth. All these Ingredients are to be pounded in a Mortar, and afterwards laid a soaking in a Sauce-pan, with good Gravy and Broth, till they have acquir'd an exquisite Relish: Then they must be strain'd thro' a Sieve, and spread over the Potage, when it is sufficiently soak'd; which may also be marbled with well season'd Gravy.

Potages of farced Quails and young Partridges.

Having caus'd your Quails to be farced, with Capons-breasts, Beef-marrow, Pepper, Salt, Nutmeg, and the Yolks of raw

Eggs,

Eggs, let them be stew'd in good Broth, with a Bunch of Herbs, as in the preceding Potage. For the Cullis, strain thro' the Sieve, two Bottoms of boil'd Artichokes, and six Yolks of Eggs, with the same Quail-broth, and let them be gently stew'd over the hot Embers. Then dress your Quails upon the soaked Crusts, and garnish them with small Artichoke-bottoms; pouring in the Cullis, with Mushroom-juice and Mutton-gravy, as they are serving up to Table. A Ragoo of Turkeys may also be made, for that purpose, or else the Quails may be stuff'd with Sweet Basil.

As for large Partridges and young Partridges, that are farced, after they have been boil'd in good Broth, a white Cullis may be prepar'd for them, with Almonds and green Lemmon. They may be garnish'd with Cocks-combs and Mushrooms, adding some Mutton-gravy and Lemmon-juice, when ready to be brought to Table.

Potage, without Water.

Take a good piece of Beef, another of Mutton, part of a Fillet of Veal, a Capon, four Pigeons and two Partridges; all the Fowls being well truss'd, and the Butchers-meat sufficiently beaten. Then put them into a Pot that is well tinn'd over, with Slices of Onions, Parsnips and Parsly-roots, and season them with all sorts of fine Herbs and a little Salt. In the mean while, having provided some Paste and strong Paper, let the Edges of your Pot be stopt up close; so as all the Steam may be kept in, and that the least Air may not either be let in or out. Afterwards let this Pot be set into another of a larger size, the void space being fill'd with hot Water and stuff'd with Hay, to the end that the lesser Pot may remain steady in its proper place, without moving on either side: Thus the Water in the greater Pot must be kept continually boiling, and close stopt up, for the space of five or six Hours. When that time is expir'd, it must be uncover'd, so as all the Gravy of the Meat may be pour'd off, and well clear'd from the Fat: Let the Fowls that were stew'd, be minc'd, in order to farce a Loaf, with good Garnitures; then let the Soop, as well as the Loaf, be soak'd with the same Gravy; and let a Ragoo be made of all sorts of Garnitures, fried in Lard, to be pour'd thereupon. Lastly, let the whole Mess be neatly dress'd, and garnish'd with farced Cocks-combs, Veal-sweet-breads, or something else of the like nature, in order to be serv'd up to Table. *Po-*

Potage de Santé.

After having caus'd some good Broth of Buttock-beef, a Knuckle of Veal and Mutton, to be put into a Pot, with Capons, fat Pullets, or other Fowls proper for the Potage *de Santé*, and having made the same Broth very savoury; let the Crusts be soak'd with it, whilst some fine Herbs are boiling in another Pot, such as Sorrel, Purslain, Chervil, &c. all cut very small. These Herbs may serve to garnish your Potage and Fowls; or they may be strain'd, so as nothing be put into the Dish, but the Broth and good Gravy, when served up to Table.

Another sort of Potage *de Santé*, is made quite clear, of a Chicken or Pullet, and a piece of a Fillet of Veal, without any Garniture; only it may be brought to a colour, by passing the red-hot Fire-shovel over it.

Potage of farced Chickens.

The Chickens must be farced with a good *Godivoe*, between the Skin and the Flesh; the Breasts may be also taken away. When they are well order'd and scalded, they must be put into a Pot, with good Broth, and may be garnish'd with Veal-sweet-breads and Cocks-combs, as a *Bisk*, or with Pulse; a Cullis and some Gravy being added, before they are set on the Table.

See hereafter, different sorts of farced Chickens.

Potage of Barn-door-chickens.

After they have been farced with a delicious *Godivoe*, soak'd in Cream, let them be well boil'd in a Pot, and garnish'd with fried Paste or Pulse; squeezing in some Lemmon-juice, before they are brought to Table.

Potage of farced Chickens, with Onions.

Let a white Cullis be made of Capons-breasts, or of Veal, and three or four Yolks of hard Eggs, all well pounded in a Mortar, with some Bread-crum soak'd in good Broth: After this Mixture has been season'd, let it have five or six Seethings in a Stew-pan. Then, having strain'd it thro' the Hair-sieve, squeez in the Juice of a Lemmon, and sprinkle all your Potage with it, when ready to be serv'd up to Table. The

The Potage of Pigeons with a white Cullis, garnish'd with white Onions, or Cardoons, is usually prepar'd after the same manner.

Potage of farced Chickens, garnish'd with Chesnuts.

Let your Chickens be boil'd in the ordinary Pot, and the Chesnuts in a little Pot a-part (after their second Skin has been peel'd off) with savoury Broth; but so as they be not broken. With these a Border is to be made round about the Dish and the Chickens, which are to be sprinkled with a good Cullis, as they lye a soaking, and with Lemmon-juice, as they are serving up to Table.

Another Potage of farced Chickens.

A Potage of Chickens is also sometimes made, with a green Cullis, Asparagus, and a Border of young streaked Bacon.

A Potage of Chickens and other sorts of Fowl, with Cucumbers.

Let your Chickens, Pullets, or Capons, be boil'd, in well-seson'd Broth, according to the usual manner. As for the Cucumbers; after having taken out the Seeds and scalded them in Water, let them be stuff'd with a good Farce, and stew'd in Broth, with Salt and a Bunch of Herbs: In the mean while, let some Yolks of poach'd Eggs be strain'd thro' the Hair-sieve, with Beef-juice and good Broth, and let them be boil'd and soak'd a-part. Then dress your Potage with the Crusts, the Chickens in the middle, the farced Cucumbers for Garnitures, and the Cullis pour'd upon all, with Lemmon-juice. The same thing ought to be observ'd in dressing Turkey-powts, and other Fowls of the like nature.

Other Potages may be prepar'd with Cucumbers, without farcing, only frying them in Lard, and dressing them, as before.

Potage, with Crusts farced with Partridge-breasts.

As soon as the Partridges are roasted, take their Breasts and cut them into small pieces, in form of a Die, and some Artichokechoke-bottoms in like manner: Let these be stew'd together, and made very savoury, in order to farce your Crusts; and let a Cullis be made of a piece of Beef roasted brown, which you must pound in a Mortar, with the Partridge-carcasses, and let all boil in a Sauce-pan; seasoning them as much as is requisite. Afterwards they are to be strain'd thro' the Sieve, with good Gravy and a piece of Lemmon, and the Crusts are to be soak'd with them. Lastly, let a small Mutton-hash be made, which is to be strew'd on the top, whilst a Border of Crusts is set round about the Dish.

Another Potage is sometimes made of Crusts farced with Lentils, with a Cullis of the same; as for Pigeons, and other sorts of Fowl, before-mention'd in the fifth Article, and 'tis an easie thing to order others, conformably to the Model of the former, according to the Variety of Meats that are to be dress'd; or else the Loaf may be stuff'd with a good Ragoo.

Another Potage, with Crusts farced with Gammon.

The Crusts are to be farced with Gammon, Veal-sweet-breads, Capons-breasts, *Moufferons* and Artichoke-bottoms, all cut into little square pieces, and stew'd in a Ragoo with a Veal-cullis: Let these Crusts be enclos'd in others, and neatly tied up, that they may not be broken, as they are soaking. When they are ready, let them be dress'd in the Potage, and garnish'd in a Dish, sprinkling them with the Juice of a Lemmon.

Potage of Profitrolle.

Having provided a little round Loaf, of the same sort as those for Soop, with Crusts; let it be farc'd, and soak'd with Veal-gravy and good Broth: Let it also be dress'd upon the other soaked Crusts, with a little of a Partridge or Capon-hash. Then having prepar'd a Cullis, with the Meats of which the Gravy was made, and having strain'd it, let it be pour'd upon the Potage. When you would have it serv'd up, a fine Artichoke-bottom may be laid upon the Loaf, with some Mushrooms on the inside, and it may be garnish'd with *Fricandoe's*, or Veal-sweet-breads.

A Potage of Profitrolle, *garnish'd with* Poupiets.

Let the *Poupiets*, the manner of ordering which you'll find in its proper place, be put into a Dish or Sauce-pan; and let a Cullis be made of a piece of roasted Veal, pounded in a Mortar, well season'd and strain'd thro' the Hair-sieve, for the soaking of your *Poupiets*. Then a Ragoo is to be made of Veal-sweet-breads, Cocks-combs, *Truffles, Morilles, Mousserons,* common Mushrooms and Artichoke-bottoms, all dress'd with white Sauce, and well season'd; with which the Potage is to be garnish'd, the *Profitrolle*-loaf being laid in the middle, and the Juice of a Lemmon squeez'd in, as it is serving up to Table.

Another Potage of Profitrolle.

This Potage is to be set out with six small Loaves and one great one in the middle, that is to say, three farced with Gammon; three others with Capons; and the large one, with a Hash of Gammon and Capon; as also, Veal-sweet-breads, *Truffles, Mousserons,* common Mushrooms, and Artichoke-bottoms cut into pieces in form of a die. The whole Mess is to be garnish'd with larded *Fricandoes,* or Scotch Collops fried brown, a Border of Cocks-combs, and a Ragoo of *Mousserons,* or common Mushrooms, with Artichoke-bottoms and Asparagus-tops, all dress'd with white Sauce; squeezing in the Juice of a Lemmon, when ready to be brought to Table.

See afterwards the Potages of *Profitrolles* for Fish-days.

Potage of a Capon, or of a Fat Pullet, with Rice.

Let the Rice be boil'd in good Broth, and then serve to garnish your Capon or fat Pullet; upon the soaked Crusts. Afterwards you must strew some rasped Parmesan and grated Cinnamon on the top, and give it a colour, with the red-hot Fire-shovel. The Side of the Dish may be garnish'd with Bread-crusts made very brown with Lard, in order to be serv'd up with Mutton-gravy and Lemmon-juice.

The Potage of *Vermicelli* is made after the same manner.

Potage

Potage of Teals and other Fowls, with Mushrooms.

Lard your Teals with middle-siz'd Slips of Bacon, and after having fried them in Lard, let them be stew'd in good Broth, according to the usual manner, with Salt, and a Bunch of Herbs: In the mean time, let some Mushrooms and Flower be toss'd up in the same Lard, and put to the Teals, when they are half-stew'd. Lastly, let them be neatly dress'd, and serv'd up in Slices, with Mutton-gravy and Lemmon-juice.

The Mushroom-potages have been already explain'd in the fourth Article of Mushrooms.

Potage, with Truffles.

The *Truffles* must be boil'd in good Broth and Gravy in a little Pot, with a Faggot of Herbs and a thickening Liquor, that is well enrich'd. When the Potage is sufficiently soak'd, and the *Truffles* dress'd, they must be laid in order therein, adding some Lemmon-juice, when the Dish is serv'd up to Table: A *Profitrolle*-loaf may also be set in the middle.

For the Potages of young Pheasants, Quails and other sorts of Fowl, which you would have dress'd with *Truffles*, let them be put into a Pot in the usual manner, and well season'd. But your *Truffles* must be cut into little pieces and not into Slices, and after having fried them in a little Lard, they must be stewed, as before. To make the Potage brown, let a good Cullis of Beef or Mutton be pour'd in, and some Lemmon-juice, before the Dish is brought to Table.

Potage, with Truffles and Mousserons.

Let a Cullis of Veal or Capons-breasts be well season'd, and let a Loaf farced with every thing that you shall think fit, be set in the middle of the Potage. Then dress your *Truffles* and *Mousserons* in a good Ragoo, and garnish the Potage with them; squeezing in the Juice of a Lemmon, when ready to be set on the Table.

Potages of farced Pigeons, with a brown Cullis.

Let Onions be fried brown to make the Border; whilst a Cullis is preparing with a piece of Beef roasted very brown, and pounded in the Mortar with Crusts of Bread: Then let all be stew'd in a Sauce-pan and well season'd, and afterwards strain'd thro' a Hair-sieve, with the Juice of a Lemmon, to soak the Potage, when ready to be serv'd up. It ought also to be enrich'd with Mushrooms, Artichoke-bottoms, and other sorts of Garnitures.

Potage of Pigeons, with Radishes.

Having larded your Pigeons, with thick Slips of Bacon, and having fried them till they come to a fine brown colour, let them be gently stew'd in good Broth, with a Bunch of Herbs: Let a thickening Liquor be also prepar'd with fine Herbs and pour'd upon them. When the Crusts are soak'd in good Broth, garnish your Potage with the Radishes that are very white and neatly dress'd; one part of them being cut into little square pieces, and the other remaining entire.

A Potage of farced Pigeons, likewise fried brown, may be made after the same manner; so as a thickening Liquor may be added as they are stewing, and the Dish garnish'd in the same manner, with Radishes.

Potage of Pigeons, with a white Cullis.

This Potage may be garnish'd with *Poupiets*, and the Limbs of Barn-door-chickens marinated and fried. A white Cullis is to be pour'd upon the Pigeons, and a Loaf set in the middle; or else a Border may be made of Asparagus, with a *Profitrolle*-loaf, squeezing some Lemmon-juice upon it, when served up to Table.

See the white Potage of Pigeons with Onions, before described in the fourteenth Article.

Parmesan-potage.

This Potage may be garnish'd with little *Profitrolle*-loaves, very neatly chipt, which are to be soak'd in melted Lard, and
after-

afterwards strew'd with rasped Parmesan, to be brought to a colour in the Oven. When the Potage is laid a soaking in a Dish, a Lay must be made of Parmesan, another of some good Meat-hash, and a third of Cinnamon: This is to be done twice, and all may be colour'd by means of the red-hot Fire-shovel. Then let your Potage be garnish'd on the Sides, with Crusts of Bread made very brown, the Middle with your Loaves, and the Intervals with Veal-sweet-breads, larded *Fricandoes*, *Truffles* and Cocks-combs; squeezing in the Juice of a Lemmon, when serv'd up to Table.

For another Parmesan-potage, let the Flesh of a Chicken be minc'd very small, which must be strew'd upon the Crusts, and afterwards some rasped Parmesan on the top. A Loaf may be laid in the middle, and the whole Mess may be set out with Artichoke-bottoms, and other usual Garnitures; or else it may be left without garnishing, only giving it a fine colour with the red-hot Fire-shovel.

For a *Casserole*, with Parmesan, see the second Article of *Casserole*, under the Letter C.

Potage of Quails, with a Blanc-manger.

Having stew'd your Quails in good Broth, with Salt and a Bunch of Herbs, pound some Almonds, which are to be strain'd thro' a Sieve into the same Broth, and let them boil, with a little Cinnamon and Sugar: Then cover the Bottom of your Dish of Potage, with Macaroons, Biskets and March-panes, and when the Quails are dress'd, pour the white Broth upon them; garnishing all with Slices of Lemmon, as also with the Juice and Kernels of Pomegranate, when ready to be serv'd up to Table.

The other Potages of Quails shall be hereafter explain'd, either in particular in the Article of Quails, under the Letter Q, or elsewhere, with respect to other Fowls.

Potage of Partridges, with brown Broth.

Lard your Partridges with middle-siz'd Slips of Bacon, fry them in Lard with a little Flower, and afterwards put all into a Pot, with good Broth, a Faggot of Herbs, and as much Salt as is needful. In the mean while, the Cullis is to be made of a piece of roasted Beef, stew'd in the same Partridge-broth, and kept hot: Then let some boil'd Artichoke-bottoms be cut into

pieces

pieces and thrown into the Cullis, with Slices of Lemmon and Cocks-combs ftew'd, and put into a Ragoo. When the Potage is fufficiently foak'd, drefs your Partridges and Garnitures, pour the Cullis upon them, with fome Slices and Juice of Lemmon, as they are ferving up to Table.

A Potage may alfo be made with Cray-fish, obferving the Directions given for the making of that fort of Potage on Fish-days, in the fecond Article of Cray-fish. It may be garnish'd with Veal-fweet-breads, Capons-livers, *Fricandoes*, Partridge-*Pains*, and other Things that are at hand.

See above, the Partridge-potages that are made with Cabbage, Lentils, and other forts of Pulfe.

Potage of a Breaſt of Veal and Capon, with a Loaf in the Middle.

The Loaf muſt be farc'd with the Breafts of Capons and Partridges and fome Mutton minc'd together, as alfo Artichoke-bottoms and Veal-fweet-breads cut into little fquare pieces, *Truffles*, Cocks-combs and Mushrooms in a Ragoo, and a Veal-cullis. This Loaf ought to be open on the Top, fo as the Ragoo may be feen, and marbled with Veal-gravy and Lemmon-juice. After having drefs'd the Potage, it muſt be garnish'd round about the Veal-fweet-breads and Cocks-combs, all ftew'd with white Sauce, adding fome Lemmon-juice when ferv'd up to Table.

Potage of young Turkeys, with Succory.

Take young Turkeys, large fat Pullets, Chickens and other Fowls, and boil them in a Pot after the ufual manner, with Broth, Salt and a Bunch of Herbs: Let your Succory be fcalded in Water, and boil'd with the reſt: Then let the Potage be drefs'd and laid a foaking, garniſhing it with Succory, and ferving it up, with natural Broth, Mutton-gravy and Mushrooms.

Potage of fat Pullets.

Let a large fat Pullet be cut into pieces, and marinated in Lemmon-juice or Verjuice, with the other feafoning Ingredients: Then let a Paſte be made with Verjuice to fry them in, till they come to a fine colour, in order to garniſh the Potage

round

round about another fat Pullet, that has been well boil'd in good Broth. In the mean while, prepare a Cullis with the Bones of the marinated Pullet, Crusts of Bread and good Broth, and sprinkle your Potage with it, as it lies a soaking, as also with the Juice of a Lemmon, before it is brought to Table.

Potage after the Italian Mode.

This Potage is a kind of *Oil* dress'd in a large Dish, after having made a Partition in it, in form of a Cross, with Paste baked in the Oven. In one of the Squares, a *Bisk* is to be put; in the second a Potage, of young Chickens; in the third, a Potage à *la Reyne*, with a *Profitrolle*-loaf; and in the fourth, a Potage of farced Partridges; all in their peculiar Broths, and with different Garnitures, as rich as they possibly can be.

Potage of farced green Geese.

Let a Farce be made with the Livers and Hearts of Geese, fine Herbs, and an Omelet of four Eggs, which are to be pounded together in a Mortar, and well season'd, in order to stuff your Geese between the Skin and the Flesh. Then boil them in good Broth, and prepare some green Pease-soop to be pour'd upon the Potage. For want of new Pease, old ones may be taken, to make the green Cullis; and the whole Mess may be garnish'd with farced Lettice.

White Potage.

The Potage à *la Reyne*, described in the seventh Article, may be so call'd, as well as these that follow.

Having caus'd the Breasts of Chickens or Capons to be minc'd very small, strew them upon your soaked Potage; marbling it with very brown Veal-gravy, and squeezing in some Lemmon-juice, when serv'd up to Table.

Otherwise pound the Flesh of a Pullet or some Capons-breasts in a Mortar, with a piece of very white Bread-crum, strain all thro' the Hair-sieve, and when the Crusts are soak'd, pour this Cullis upon them, without any Garniture.

Po-

Potage of boned Capons, with Oisters.

After having taken out the Bones of your Capons, reserving the Skins entire, stuff the Skins with the same Flesh, Beef-sewet or Marrow, pounded Lard, fine Herbs, Pepper, Salt, Nutmeg and Yolks of Eggs, and let them boil in good Broth: Afterwards fry Oisters, Mushrooms and Flower in a Pan, and put all to the Capons, when they are almost ready: Let them be dress'd and orderly serv'd up, with Lemmon-juice and Mushrooms.

For the other Potages that are made of Fish on Flesh-days, see here after that of Soles.

POTAGES FOR FISH-DAYS.

Potage de Santé.

Let Purslain, Lettice, Sorrel, Beets and other good Herbs, be cut and stew'd a little with Butter in an earthen Pot, to take away their Crudity: Then put some boiling Water to them, with Salt, a Bunch of fine Herbs, and a Loaf, or Crust which is to be set in the middle of the Potage. The Herbs may be strain'd, if you shall think fit; or they may be serv'd up to Table and garnish'd, with young Lettice, Mushroom-juice, and a Spoonful of Pease-soop.

The Potage without Butter, and the *Julian*, come so near to this, that it would be needless to give a particular Description of them.

Potage of Mousserons and Morilles, with Cream.

The *Mousserons* and *Morilles* must be stew'd, or fried in good Butter with fine Herbs, after the same manner as in Oil, for other sorts of Potages. When the Crusts are sufficiently soak'd, the Cream must be put with the *Mousserons* into the Stew-pan in which they are dress'd, with a Faggot of Herbs, and all must be well thicken'd. At the same time, the Potage is to be dress'd, with a *Profitrolle*-loaf in the middle, and Lemmon-juice, before it is served up. The side of the Dish may be set out with *Mousserons* fried in Fritters, or some other convenient Garnitures.

P 3   Po-

Potage of Onions, with a white Cullis.

This Potage may be drefs'd, if you pleafe, with a Loaf in the middle; whilft a Cullis is preparing, with white Almonds, Parfly-roots and Bread-crum foak'd in Peafe-foop, all ftrain'd thro' a Hair-five. The fame Cullis is proper not only for the Onions; but alfo for Cardoons, Goats-bread, Skirrets, &c.

Another Potage may be made of Onions, cut into fquare pieces, and fried brown; to be garnifh'd with other Onions cut into round pieces, and fried as Fritters, or elfe whole: As alfo a Potage of Onions, with fweet Bafil.

Potage, with Hops.

The Hops are to be well fcalded, tied up in Bunches, and ftew'd in good Peafe-foop, or in fome other fort of Broth proper for Fifh-days: Then the Potage may be garnifh'd, with a Loaf in the middle.

Potage of Purflain.

The Purflain, if it be fmall, muft be laid at its whole length into a little Pot, and boil'd in Broth, or Peafe-foop, with an Onion ftuck with Cloves, a Carret, a few Parfnips, and a thickening Liquor: When it is ready, and the Crufts are well foaked, the Potage may be garnifh'd in the ufual manner.

Potage, with young Sprouts.

Let fome Sprouts be well pickt and thrown into fair Water: Then after they have been fcalded, let them be put into a Pot, pouring in a fmall Cullis, as for the Purflain; and let them be garnifh'd with other Sprouts.

Potage of Radifhes.

After they have been well fcrap'd, leave a fmall Bunch of the Greens at the end: Then let them be fcalded and boil'd in good Broth, with fome thickening Liquor. This Potage muft be drefs'd after the fame manner as that of Purflain.

Potage, with Cucumbers.

Let your Cucumbers be scalded, and stew'd in good Pease-soop, with an Onion stuck with Cloves, and some Roots of Herbs chopt small: Then a thickening Liquor must be made, as for other Potages, on Flesh-days, and the Dish set out with Cucumbers and Capers. They may also be farced with Herbs, or Fish, and garnish'd with Asparagus-tops, according to the Season.

Asparagus-potage.

For want of Pease, pounded Asparagus may be strain'd thro' the Hair-sieve, with Herb-broth, to make the green Cullis; whilst other Asparagus are fried in Butter, with fine Herbs, and afterwards laid a soaking, season'd with Salt and Nutmeg. The Potage must be cover'd, with the Cullis pour'd into it, and you may add some natural Cream, or Yolks of Eggs, if the time will allow it.

Potage, of farced Lettice.

Observe the preceding Directions for farced Lettice, laid down in that Article, under the Letter L; except, that they ought now to be stuff'd with a good Fish-farce, such as is before described in the Article of *Farces*; and, if the Entertainment be provided for Days of greater Abstinence, or if Fish be wanting, let them be stuff'd with a good Farce of fine Herbs, season'd with Pepper, Salt, Nutmeg and Yolks of Eggs, or Cream. For the rest, they must be boil'd in strained Pease-soop, or Herb-broth, and dress'd upon the Crusts, soak'd, with the same Broth; adding a white Cullis and Mushroom-juice, when ready to be serv'd up. The whole Mess may be set out with fried Bread, or some other convenient Garniture.

Marbled Potage.

This is a Potage of Almond-milk, to which are added, Yolks of Eggs, Sugar, Cinnamon and a little Salt. It must be dress'd upon Bread, or Biskets, and marbled with the Juice, or Jelly of Currans, Beet-juice boil'd with Sugar and Orange-flowers. The Dish is to be garnish'd with Pomegranate-kernels and small Sugar-plums,

Potage, with Fennel.

Let Fennel be chopt very small, and put into a little Pot; observing, for the rest, the same Directions as for the following Potage.

Potage, with Spinage.

Take only the Heart or soundest part of the Spinage, which must be chopt small and stew'd in a little Pot with Pease-soop, a Carret, an Onion stuck with Cloves, and the other seasoning Ingredients. As the Crusts are soaking, scrape in some Parmesan, and dress your Potage; garnishing it with sticks of Cinnamon, round about, and one in the middle; or else with Onions, or fried Bread.

Potage of Vine-buds.

Cut off the largest Leaves of your Buds, and take care that none of the Wood be left: Then having scalded 'em in boiling Water and tied them up in Bunches, let them be stew'd in a little Pot, with a Carret, a Parsnip, Parsly-roots, an Onion stuck with Cloves, a few Turneps cut into quarters, and a Clove of Garlick. Add to these as they are dressing, a little thickening Liquor, and garnish your Potage, with other Buds and a Loaf in the middle.

Green Pease-potage.

See the Pease-potage for Flesh-days, and observe the same Method; except, that your Pease must now be dress'd with sweet Butter, and serv'd up in good Broth. For simple Pease-soop, the Dish may be set out with Cucumbers, Artichoke-bottoms, Asparagus-tops, and other things of the like nature.

Cabbage-potage.

See likewise the Cabbage-potage for Flesh-days, in the third Article, where the manner of preparing it is fully explain'd; retrenching the Lard, and making use only of Butter and Broth that is proper for Fish-days, or strained Pease-soop. This Po-

tage

tage muft be garnifh'd with the infide of fome Cabbage, Artichoke-bottoms and fried Bread.

Potage of Citrulls, with Milk.

Cut your Citrulls into very fmall fquare pieces; and fry them in natural Butter, with Salt, Parfly, Chervil and fine Herbs. Then let them be put into an Earthen Pot, with boiling Milk, and drefs them upon the foak'd Crufts. Garnifh the Difh with with fried Bread, and ftrew it with white Pepper, as it is ferving up to Table.

Melon-potage.

Let the Melons be cut as the Citruls, and fried likewife with Butter: Then let them be ftewed, feafon'd with Pepper, Salt and a Bunch of Herbs, and ftrain'd thro' the Hair-fieve, with the fame Broth; with which the Crufts are alfo to be foak'd. Afterwards having drefs'd the Potage, ferve it up, garnifh'd with fried Melons and Pomegranate-kernels.

Potage, with Mufcadine-grapes.

Let good Almond-milk be prepar'd, according to the Method laid down in the fecond Article of *Almonds,* under the Letter A. and when you have a mind to drefs your Soop, let fome Mufcadine-grapes be put into it, after they have been ftoned. Inftead of Crufts, or other pieces of Bread, let the Potage be drefs'd with Macaroons, or Biskets, and garnifh'd with Mufcadine-grapes, preferv'd with Sugar; marbling it with the Juice of a Lemmon and that of Currans, when ferv'd up to Table.

Potage of Artichoke-cardoons.

The Cardoons muft be cut very fhort, fcalded and boil'd in Water, with Butter, Salt, and a Cruft of Bread: Then they are to be put into melted Butter; whilft the Potage is foaking with good Herb-broth: Let the Cruft of a fmall Loaf be laid entire in the middle; let the Cardoons be drefs'd in form of a *Dome* or Coronet, upon the Bread; and let fome fcraped Parmefan be added. You may alfo prepare a white Cullis, ftrewing

the

the whole Mess again with scrap'd Cheese, and garnishing it with Capers and Lemmon-slices.

Potage of white Cabbage and young Chibbols, with Milk.

After the Cabbage has been scalded in Water, let it be chopt and fried in natural Butter: Then let it be put into hot Milk, season'd with Pepper, Salt and a Faggot of fine Herbs, and dress'd upon Slices of Bread.

The same thing is to be done with young Chibbols cut very small.

Potage of Artichoke-bottoms.

Cut your Bottoms into halves, and fry them in burnt Butter, with Flower, or in natural Butter; reserving one entire, for the middle of the Potage: Then put them into an earthen Pot, with clear Pease-soop, Salt and fine Herbs, and when they are ready, dress them upon the soaked Crusts; in order to be serv'd up, with Capers and Mushroom-juice.

These Potages are more than sufficient, as to what relates to Herbs and Pulse; either for Good Friday, or for the other Fish-days throughout the whole Year: Let us now proceed to the Fish-potages, of which we have not as yet given a particular Account.

FISH-POTAGES.

Sturgeon-potage.

When the Sturgeon is well cleans'd, let it be stew'd for a while in Water, with Butter, Salt and a Bunch of fine Herbs: As soon as it is half done, take away this Liquor or Broth, and put the Fish again into a Stew-pan, or earthen Pan, with white Wine, Pepper, Salt, beaten Cloves, Verjuice, Onions, and a Bay-leaf or two, with which you must make an end of boiling it: In the mean while, fry some Mushrooms and Flower in Butter, which are to be put into the first Broth for your Potage, with a Spoonful of Pease-soop. Then let the Crusts of Bread be soak'd with it, in a round or Oval Dish, and the Sturgeon dress'd therein, after having been well drain'd. You may garnish the whole Mess, with Oisters, Mushrooms and Capers; adding some Juice and Slices of Lemmon, when ready to be serv'd up to Table.

Tur-

Turbot-potage.

Let the Turbot be scal'd, wrapt up in a Linnen-cloth and boil'd in one half white Wine and the other Water, with Verjuice, Pepper, Salt, Nutmeg, Cloves and Bay-leaves: Then let the Crusts be soak'd in good Fish-broth, and when the Turbot is drain'd, let it be dress'd and garnish'd, with Mushrooms, upon the Body of the Fish; but the sides of the Dish must be set out, with farced Mushrooms, Roes, Oisters, Capers and Slices of Lemmon, with Juice of the same.

Potage of fresh Salmon.

The Salmon must be scal'd, cut into pieces, and parboil'd as the Sturgeon, to get the Broth: Afterwards it must be season'd with Salt, fine Herbs chopt small, and strained Pease-soop; and whilst the Crusts are soaking, your Salmon when well season'd, must be boil'd outright over a gentle Fire. When 'tis requisite to serve it up, let it be dress'd, and garnish'd with farced Mushrooms, Carp-roes, stew'd Mushrooms, Capers, the Juice and Slices of Lemmon and Mushroom-juice.

Sole-potage for Fish-days.

To prepare a Potage of Soles, having provided some of the best sort, that are very fresh, let them be scrap'd and well wash'd: If they are small, take two of them to be farced, but if large, only one, to be set in the middle of your Potage. The Sole that you would have farced, must be neatly taken by the Head, and squeez'd on the top, to get out the Bone entire. Then taking a little of this Flesh and of that of a Carp, to make a Farce of it, with Chibbol, Parsly and Bread-crum, set it together again in the same manner as when it was whole. It must be farc'd all at once, and other Soles must be fried, in order to get the *Filets* for the garnishing of the Potage. In the mean while, a good Ragoo ought to be made, in the same manner as for the Cray-fish-potage, and also a Cullis of the like nature. Afterwards let the Potage be laid a soaking with good Fish-broth, whilst the farced Sole is frying, which must be laid in the Potage, when it is sufficiently soak'd, and ready to be serv'd up. Lastly, let the *Filets* of the other fried Soles be garnish'd with

Carp-

Carp-roes and Artichoke-bottoms; let the Ragoo be pour'd round about, and let the Sole remain uncover'd, so as it may appear of a fine colour, when the whole Mess is brought hot to Table.

If it be not the time of Lent, an *Omelet* may be made to be mingled with the Farce, and instead of frying the Soles, they may also be put into a Baking-pan rubb'd with Butter: They must be breaded to give them a colour, and bak'd in an Oven moderately heated.

A Potage may likewise be made only of Sole-*Filets*, with a Loaf in the middle, garnish'd with Onions fried brown; also a Potage of Sole-*Filets*, with sweet Basil.

Potage of Soles on Flesh-days.

The Broth and Gravy are the same as for other Potages that are proper for Flesh-days. For the rest, having provided Soles, take the raw *Filets* of some of them, and stuff them neatly with larded Veal-sweet-breads, which may serve for the Garniture of your Potage: For the farced Sole in the middle of the Potage; let it be scrap'd, and a Hole made in the Head, to get out the Bone, so as the Skin may remain altogether entire: Take some of the Flesh of the same Sole, with a little parboil'd Bacon, a few pieces of Veal-sweet-breads, *Truffles* and Mushrooms, all well minc'd, and to make the Farce more delicious, 'twould be requisite to put into it some Bread-crum soak'd in a little Milk; binding it with two Yolks of Eggs, and adding a little chopt Parsly and Chibbol. Then the Sole must be stuff'd with this Farce, and when ready to be serv'd up, it must be flower'd and fried in Lard, till it come to a fine colour. With the rest of the Farce, some small *Andouillets* are to be made and fried, flowering and breading them, after they have been dipt in beaten Eggs, to the end that the Bread may stick to them. As for the *Filets*; when they are larded with the Veal-sweet-breads, they must be flower'd a little, and fried in the same Lard. The Potage being well soak'd, let it be garnish'd with these *Filets*, as also with Veal-sweet-breads and *Andouillets*; let the Sole be set in the middle of the Potage, with a Ragoo of Lamb-sweet-breads and *Truffles*, according to the Season; let all be well garnish'd; let the Potage-loaf be soak'd in good Gravy; and let the whole Mess be serv'd up hot to Table.

At another time, the Sole in the middle may be larded, and

to

to that purpose, after it has been scrap'd, wash'd and well wip'd, the red-hot Fire-shovel must be lightly pass'd over the Back, to the end that the Larding-pin may have a freer Passage: Then it may be fried as the other Sole; it may also be put into a Baking-pan with Bacon underneath, and be brought to a colour upon the Spit, or in the Oven.

For Side-dishes, they may be made of Soles, with the abovemention'd Ragoo; garnishing them with *Filets, Andouillets* and other Things, all brought hot to Table.

Potage of Tortoises on Fish-days.

Having cut off the Heads and Legs of your Tortoises, the Day before, steep them in Water, to take away the Blood, and then let them be well boil'd in a little Pot of a proportionable size, in Water, with a little Salt and Parsly, fresh Butter, a Chibbol stuck with Cloves, and a few fine Herbs. If you would have the Broth of a more exquisite relish, add the Bones of Carps or other Fish, the Flesh of which was taken to make Farces. Then take out the Tortoises, and strain the Broth, which will serve both for the Potage and for the Ragoo: The Shell on the top of the Tortoises must be taken away, as also the Skin, reserving the Flesh, which must not be too much boil'd: But you must be sure to clear it from the Gall, and keep the Shell to make a thin Paste or Batter for the frying of it, as if it were marinated Meat in Paste; this will serve to be put in the middle of the Potage. Having likewise taken some of the Flesh of the Tortoise, stew it in a Sauce-pan with a little Butter, Chibbol and Parsly, and moisten the Ragoo with the same Broth. Afterwards turn in the Roes, *Truffles*, Mushrooms and other Garnitures, if you have any, with a little Cullis of Cray-fish, or some other sort of Fish, and let your Crusts be well soak'd: Let some fried Fish-*Filets* be also ready at hand, as being very proper to garnish the Potage: Moreover, it will be requisite to provide a small white Cullis of Pikes-flesh, to sprinkle the Potage, that it may be marbled with the Ragoo; and also, some Cray-fish Cullis. At last, you may dress your Potage with the Ragoo pour'd on the top, the *Filets* round about marbled with both the Cullises, and the Shell that was fried, in the middle.

Potage of Tortoises, on Flesh-days.

For this Potage, the Tortoises muſt be order'd as before, to get their Fleſh, which is to be fried in Lard with fine Herbs; whilſt a Cullis is preparing, with a piece of Veal roaſted very brown, which is to be pounded in a Mortar, with the Breaſt of a Capon or Pullet, five or ſix Almonds, and a piece of Bread-crum ſoak'd in good Broth: Let all be boil'd in a Stew-pan well ſeaſon'd, and afterwards ſtrain'd thro' the Hair-ſieve, with a piece of green Lemmon. This Cullis will ſerve to enrich the Potage as it lies a ſoaking: Then you may garniſh the ſides of the Diſh, with Veal-ſweet-breads cut into pieces, Artichoke-bottoms, and larded *Poupiets* fried brown a-part; and the Middle with the Shells fried till they come to a fine colour; ſqueezing in ſome Lemmon-juice, when ſerv'd up to Table.

A Potage, with Cruſts farced with Quavivers and Perches, with a white Cullis.

Let your Quavivers, or Perches be boil'd in Water with Salt, and having taken away the Skin, let the Fleſh be minc'd very ſmall: Then let a Cullis be made with ſome of the ſame Fleſh, and a douzen of Almonds; pounding them with three or four Yolks of Eggs, if the time will permit. Laſtly, let the Haſh be dreſs'd with good Butter and fine Herbs, and make uſe of it to ſtrew upon the ſoaked Cruſts; adding ſome Lemmon-juice, before it is brought to Table.

Potage, with Cruſts farced with Soles.

The Haſh muſt be made as before, after having fried the Soles, with Lentils dreſs'd in the Cullis; or elſe a green Cullis may be prepar'd with Aſparagus-tops.

Potage, with Cruſts farced with Pike.

This Potage muſt be order'd as the former, with a green Cullis and Aſparagus-tops, in their Seaſon, or elſe with a white Cullis.

Perch-potage, with a white Cullis.

After having well wash'd the Perches, let them be boil'd in Water, with Pepper, Salt, Cloves, an Onion and Thyme, and afterwards neatly pickt: But one of them must be taken to make a Cullis, with a few pounded Almonds and some Yolks of Eggs, according to the Season: Let all be pounded together in a Mortar, well season'd and strain'd thro' the Hair-sieve. Then some Carp-hash must be put upon the Crusts, with the Cullis, and the whole Mess must be garnish'd with fried Bread.

Frog-potage.

Let the Legs of your Frogs be cut off, and the Thigh-bones broken, after the Flesh has been taken away; reserving the thickest to be fried: These being marinated with Verjuice, Pepper and Salt, and dipt into a thin Paste or Batter, must be fried till they come to a fine colour, to make a Border round about the Potage. The rest are to be dress'd in a Ragoo, with Roes, Mushrooms and other Garnitures, all dress'd with a white Sauce. Lastly, the Potage must be garnish'd, after it has been well soak'd, pouring a Cullis upon it, and squeezing in the Juice of a Lemmon.

Potage, with a Profitrolle-loaf.

Having prepar'd a Carp-hash dress'd in Broth, with Butter, fine Herbs and a piece of green Lemmon, let it be stew'd and season'd till it has acquir'd a good relish. Then cut some Pike, or Quavivers into Collops, which are to be marinated in Verjuice, with Pepper, Salt and Onion; and, when flower'd, must be fried till they come to a fine colour; these will serve to garnish the Potage. Afterwards turn your Hash upon the soaked Bread, set the *Profitrolle*-loaf in the middle, and squeez in some Lemmon-juice, as the Dish is serving up to Table.

Tortoise-potage, with a Profitrolle-loaf.

This Potage may be garnish'd with Cray-fish, and fried Shells in the Intervals. Let a brown Cullis be made, as for Cray-fish, and let the Tortoises be cut into *Fricandoes* or Collops, as
it

it were Chickens; with a white Cullis, and a piece of green Lemmon. As the Crufts are foaking, let fome Fifh-hafh be laid upon them, and Roes fried brown, with fine Herbs. Afterwards your Tortoifes may be drefs'd, with a Loaf in the middle, and Lemmon-juice.

Potage à la Royale.

Take Eels-flefh, with the like quantity of Mufhrooms, which are to be fried in natural Butter, chopt all together, and put into a Pot, with good Fifh-broth, feafoned with Salt and a Faggot of Herbs. In the mean time, the Crufts being foaked with the fame Fifh-broth, cover them with your minc'd Meat, and garnifh them with Carp-roes, Pike-livers, and farced Mufhrooms; adding fome Slices and Juice of Lemmon, with the Juice of Mufhrooms and Capers, when ferved up to Table.

Oifter-potage.

It would be requifite to fry the Oifters in burnt Butter, and to referve their Liquor, as it has been elfewhere obferv'd: At the fame time, you muft alfo fry with your Oifters, fome Mufhrooms cut into pieces, and a little Flower, and afterwards let all boil in ftrained Peafe-foop, with Salt and a piece of green Lemmon: Then the Bread being foak'd in good Fifh-broth, and the Oifters and Mufhrooms drefs'd, they may be garnifh'd with Capers and Lemmon-flices, and fo ferv'd up, after having pour'd the Oifter-liquor into the Potage, with the Juices of Mufhrooms and Lemmons.

Potage of farced Tenches, with brown Broth.

The Tenches muft be firft cleans'd from their Slime in hot Water, and their Skins entirely taken away, as the fame thing may be done with Soles: Then prepare a Farce with the Flefh, alfo Mufhrooms, fine Herbs, Yolks of Eggs, Salt and Nutmeg, and having ftuff'd them with it, as if they were whole; let them boil in ftrained Peafe-foop, or in fome other Broth, with Butter. In the mean while, let Mufhrooms be fried in Butter, with Flower, and ftew'd in other Broth, or Liquor, feafon'd with Salt, Cloves, and a Bunch of Herbs. This Broth will ferve to foak the Crufts, upon which the Tenches are to be drefs'd; garnifhing

ing the Dish with Mushrooms, Capers, Carp-roes; as also with Lemmon-juice and Slices of the same, as it is serving up to Table.

Farced Crabs, and other Fish of the like nature, may also be dress'd in the same sort of Potage.

A POT-POURRI, or Hotch-potch.

This Way of dressing is proper for several sorts of Meat, particularly, Ducks, young Turkeys, Leverets, &c. They must first be larded with thick Slips of Bacon, and fried in Lard to give them a colour: Afterwards, they are to be boil'd or stew'd in Broth, with white Wine, a Faggot of Herbs, Pepper and Salt: When they are half done, let some Mushrooms be fried in the same Lard, with a little Flower, and let all be mingled together, with Gravy, or an Artichoke-cullis, *Andouillets*, Veal-sweet-breads, Oisters (if you shall think fit) and Cucumbers marinated, according to the Season. This Hotch-potch, when neatly dress'd with Mutton-gravy and Lemmon-juice, must be serv'd up hot to Table for a Side-dish.

POUPETONS.

In giving Directions for making the *Godivoe* of a *Poupeton* in the Article of *Godivoe*, under the Letter G, we have also explain'd, what is most remarkable, with respect to all the rest; particularly, for a *Poupeton* farced with young Pigeons and other sorts of Fowl: So that it only remains here to shew the manner of diversifying them, when green Pease are in season.

A Poupeton, *with green Pease.*

The *Poupeton* being made after the usual manner, let two or three Handfuls of strained Pease be thrown into it, before it is cover'd with its Farce, and let all be enclos'd with the *Godivoe*. Then it must be bak'd *à la Braise*, that is to say, between two Fires, one on the top and the other underneath, and afterwards put into a Dish. Some Spoonfuls of Pease may also be added, before it is brought hot to Table.

A

A Poupeton *for Fish-days*.

Take the Flesh of Carps and Pike, and let a well season'd *Godivoe* be made of it, with Bread-crum or Flower; all being well chopt together: To these you may add an Egg or two, if it be not in Lent; shaping your *Poupeton*, as the former, and laying some Sole-*Filets*, or others in the middle, which are to be dress'd with sweet Butter and all sorts of good Garnitures. A fine Artichoke-bottom must likewise be set in the middle, after the Ragoo and Fish-*Filets*, and the *Poupeton* is to be quite fill'd up with the Ragoo-sauce. Afterwards, let all be cover'd with your *Godivoe* or Farce, and bak'd or stew'd between two gentle Fires. When it is ready, it must be turn'd into a Dish upside downwards, and serv'd up with Lemmon-juice.

POUPIETS.

To make *Poupiets* it will be requisite to provide some *Bards*, or thin Slices of Bacon that are somewhat long, but not too broad, according to the thickness you would have the *Poupiets* to be of, with as many Veal-stakes; which, when well beaten, must be laid upon every *Bard*. In the mean while, having prepar'd a good Farce season'd with a Clove of Garlick and other Ingredients, let as much of it as you shall think fit, be put upon the Stakes or Slices, and then let them be close roll'd up. Afterwards they must be pierc'd with a small Iron-Spit, and roasted wrapt up in Paper. When they are almost ready, the Paper is to be taken away, in order to bread them, and give them a fine colour. These *Poupiets* may serve either for a particular Dish, or for Out-works, or only to garnish other Messes. They are also sometimes dress'd in a Ragoo, as *Fricandoes*, with a piece of Lemmon, as they are stewing, and some Juice of the same, as they are serving up to Table.

Larded Poupiets.

Larded *Poupiets* are likewise prepar'd upon occasion, and fried brown, with pieces of *Truffles*, *Morilles*, and good Gravy, or a little Cullis to enrich them; squeezing in some Lemmon-juice, when ready to be brought to Table.

PUDDINGS.

There are two sorts of Hogs-puddings, *viz.* white and black, and both are usually serv'd up among the Side-dishes: The former is most delicious, and may be made thus.

To make white Puddings.

Having roasted a young Turkey, and also a Capon (if a great quantity of Pudding be required) take the Breasts of those Fowls, and let them be well minc'd: Then cut some Leaf-fat taken out of a Hog's Belly, very small, and put all into a Stew-pan, with a litle chopt Onion, that was fried in it before, and a few fine Herbs of all sorts, except Parsly: Season these Ingredients with the ordinary Spices, and pour in as much Milk, as you shall judge needfull: Let them also boil together, for a while, and then having drawn back the Stew-pan, add two or three Whites of Eggs whipt, taking care that the Farce be not too liquid. Afterwards, the Puddings may be made with the prepared Guts, and as they are filling, they must be prickt a little, to let out the Wind: They must also be scalded in a little Water and Milk, with some Slices of Onion, and when taken out, left to cool upon a clean Napkin. In order to serve them up, they must be broil'd upon Paper, over a gentle Fire, lest they should break; putting to them a little Lard or other Fat; and, when ready, they must be brought hot to Table.

To make black Puddings.

Let some Hogs-blood that is not coagulated be put into a Stew-pan, with a little Milk, and a Spooful of fat Broth, to render it more delicious, and let some Leaf-fat out of the Hog's Belly be cut into small pieces, and mingled with chopt Parsly, Chibbol, and all sorts of fine Herbs, which are to be fried in some of the same Fat: Then let them all be turn'd into the same Sauce-pan, and season'd with beaten Spices. In the mean time, a Pot or Kettle is to be hang'd over the Fire, with boiling Water, and the Stew-pan containing the Blood must be set in it, to be kept hot; stirring it neverthelefs, continually, to hinder it from sticking to the bottom. As soon as you percieve all to have acquir'd a good Relish, the Puddings may be made

of

of what thickness, or length, you shall think fit, and scalded in Water; but as they are scalding, let them be prickt with a Pin: If nothing comes out but Fat, 'tis a Sign that they are sufficiently parboil'd; so that they may be neatly taken out, and when cold, they must be broil'd upon a Grid-iron, as occasion requires, in order to be serv'd up hot, as before.

Other sorts of Puddings.

Puddings may be also made of the Livers of Capons and Calves: For the former, let a quarter of a Pound of Hogs-leaf-fat be chopt small, with a Pound of the Livers, and as much of the Flesh of Capons, and let all be well season'd with fine Herbs, Chibbols, Pepper, Salt, Nutmeg, beaten Cloves, Cinnamon, six Yolks of raw Eggs, and two Quarts of Cream. Then fill up the Guts of a Hog, Sheep, or Lamb, and boil your Puddings in Milk, with Salt, green Lemmon and Bay-leaves: They must be broil'd in the same manner as the former, and serv'd up with Orange-juice. For the other sort of Pudding, you are to mince a Calves-liver, and pound it in a Mortar, with Hogs-fat, to the quantity of one third part; which must likewise be cut into small square pieces: Let this Mixture be season'd, as before, and stuff'd into Hogs or Calves-guts. These Puddings must be scalded in white Wine, with Salt and a few Bay-leaves, over a gentle Fire, and left to cool in their own Liquor, to be broil'd and order'd as the others.

PULLETS.

We have already produc'd a Side-dish of fat Pullets dress'd with Olives, which may also be made in like manner, with other sorts of Fowls, and shall here subjoyn some other particular Dishes of Pullets, no less remarkable and delicious.

Large fat Pullets dress'd after the English Way.

A Farce is to be first prepar'd, with Bacon, Calves-udder, Veal-sweet-breads, and a little Marrow; as also, *Truffles*, Mushrooms, Artichoke-bottoms, Capers, and a little Garlick; all scalded, minc'd and well season'd. The Pullets, being stuff'd in the Body with this Farce, and well tied up, with a good Slice of Bacon on their Breasts, must be roasted, wrapt up in Paper: Then

they

they may be dress'd with a little Sauce, made of *Truffles*, Mushrooms, Anchovies, a few Capers and Veal-gravy; all chopt small, stew'd and well soak'd. A little Cullis must also be added, and the Juice of an Orange squeez'd in, when the Dish is ready to be serv'd up to Table.

Fat Pullets farced upon the Bones, with Cream.

After having roasted large fat Pullets, let the Flesh of their Breasts be well minc'd, with boil'd Bacon, a piece of dress'd Gammon, a few Mushrooms, *Truffles*, Chibbols, Parsly, and the Crum of a Loaf steept in Cream, after it has been soak'd a little at the Fire; to all these, when chopt very small, some Yolks of Eggs are also to be added. Afterwards, having stuff'd your Pullets upon the Bones with this Farce, set them in order in a Dish or Baking-pan, and bread them neatly on the top: Then let some whipt Whites of Eggs be put to them, and let them be brought to a colour in the Oven. If you have some of this Farce to spare, and if any Legs or Wings of Pullets, or Chickens are at hand, they may be stuff'd with it, and these will serve to garnish your Dish. A small Ragoo (if you please) may also be made for the Pullets, of Mushrooms, and Capons-livers dress'd in Cream, to be put underneath.

Fat Pullets dress'd à la Sainte Menehout.

Let your Pullets be truss'd for boiling, and slit in the hinder part: Then spread them upon the Table, or Dresser; break their Bones, and take away those of the Legs: Then they must be stew'd in a Sauce-pan, with a great deal of good Lard, a little Parsly, Chibbol, and other seasoning Ingredients. Afterwards, leaving them in the same Pan, let them be cover'd with some *Bards*, or thin Slices of Bacon, and set between two Fires, *viz.* one on the Lid, and the other underneath; taking care that they be not too quick. Some Slices of Onions must also be put to them; and, as soon as they are ready, they may be neatly breaded, put into an Oven for a while, to give them a colour, and serv'd up hot, with a *Ramolade*-Sauce underneath; if you shall think fit.

Ano-

Another Side-dish of fat Pullets in Filets.

Having caus'd large fat Pullets to be roasted, let the *Filets* and all the Flesh be neatly taken away: Then let those *Filets* be clear'd from the Fat, and laid in the bottom of a Dish; whilst the following Sauce is preparing for them: Let some Parsly be chopt, with a little Chibbol, Capers and Garlick; and let all, when well season'd, be put into a Stew-pan, with a little Oil and Vinegar: They must be well temper'd together, squeezing in the Juice of a Lemmon; but the Sauce must not be set upon the Fire. When it is ready, it may be pour'd into the Dish, that contains the Pullet-*Filets*, which are to be serv'd up cold to Table.

A fat Pullet accompanied with a delicious Farce.

Take a large fat Pullet or Capon, or some other Fowl of the like nature, as a Pheasant or Wood-cock: Slit it along the Back, and cut out all the Bones that you can come at in the inside. Then let a Farce be made of delicious Meats, *viz.* the Flesh of young Pigeons, small Chickens, Snipes, *Mauviettes*, &c. and a little well season'd Ragoo incorporated with it. The Pullets, when stuff'd with this Farce, must be neatly sow'd up again, and leasurely stew'd between two gentle Fires, in a Pot that is well stopt, with thin Slices of Bacon, Beef-stakes, a piece of green Lemmon, a Bunch of Herbs, and all sorts of Spice. When it is ready, it must be dress'd upon the Back, and put into a Ragoo of Mushrooms, Veal-sweet-breads, *Truffles* and Artichoke-bottoms, all well season'd. The Dish may be set out, with marinated Pigeons, or some other convenient Garnitures.

Large fat Pullets dress'd with Gammon-sauce, or otherwise.

When your Pullets are roasted, let a Gammon-sauce be made for them, with Capers and a thickening Liquor; adding some Lemmon-juice, before they are set on the Table. At another time, they may be dress'd in a Ragoo with *Truffles*, or *à la Saingaraz*, or with a Cray-fish Cullis, or else they may be bak'd, or stew'd between two Fires, as many other Things.

Q.

Q.

QUAILS.

Quails may be bak'd *à la Braise*, that is to say, between two Fires, and dress'd in a Ragoo. Otherwise they may be serv'd up in a hot Pie, such as that of Partridges, describ'd in the first Article of *Pies* under the Letter P. They may also be order'd several Ways in a Potage, and a *Bisk* of Quails has been elsewhere explain'd in the Article of *Bisks*: Let us now produce some other Methods of dressing this sort of Fowls.

A Side-dish of Quails dress'd à la Braise *and in a Ragoo.*

For Quails bak'd or stew'd *à la Braise*, or between two Fires, 'tis requisite only to follow the Directions specified in the third Article of *Pigeons*, and to prepare a Ragoo for them, of Lambs-sweet-breads dress'd in white Sauce, with Mushrooms, *Truffles* and Cocks-combs. The Quails being put into this Ragoo, a little before they are serv'd up, the Yolk of an Egg, or two, and some Milk-cream, may be temper'd with it.

The other sort of Ragoo is made, by slitting the Quails into halves, without separating them, and frying them in Lard, season'd with a Faggot of Herbs, Pepper, Salt, Nutmeg, three or four Mushrooms and a little Flower; adding some Mutton-gravy and Lemmon-juice, at the Instant of serving them up to Table.

Quail-potages.

If you would have your Quails stuff'd, a Farce may be made for that purpose, with Capons-breasts and Beef-marrow; season'd with a little Pepper, Salt, Nutmeg, and the Yolks of raw Eggs. Let them boil in an Earthen Pot or otherwise, with a Bunch of Herbs and good Broth, such as is describ'd in the first Article of Broth: Then strain two boil'd Artichoke-bottoms thro' the Hair-sieve, with six Yolks of Eggs and some of the Quail-broth, and let all be stew'd upon the hot Embers. When the Crusts are sufficiently soak'd, dress your Quails, and pour the Cullis upon them; they may also be farc'd with *Truffles*. The Dish must be garnish'd with Artichoke-bottoms, Mutton-gravy and Mushroom-juice.

Ano-

Another sort of Quail-potage is made with a brown Cullis, without farcing, only stewing them in a proper Broth with a piece of Veal, and preparing the Cullis, with a piece of a Beef-*Filet* pounded with Bread-chippings. This Potage is to be garnish'd with Mushrooms and *Truffles*, and some Lemmon-juice must be squeez'd in, when brought to Table.

A Potage of Quails may likewise be serv'd up with Roots and *à la Reine*, as it appears from the seventh and eighth Articles of Potages and elsewhere: Also a Quail-potage in form of an *Oil*, another sort with sweet Basil, as that of Pigeons; others with Mushrooms and otherwise: So that due measures may be taken, upon occasion, from the like *Species*, which may be easily found by means of the General Table.

QUAVIVERS.

Quavivers may be fried, and put into a Ragoo made of *Morilles*, *Mousserons*, common Mushrooms and Artichoke-bottoms, and garnish'd with what you shall think fit. They may also be broil'd upon the Grid-iron, and dress'd with a Sauce of Capers and Anchovies.

As for Quavivers in *Filets*, with Cucumbers and *Mousserons*, let them be boil'd in a *Court-bouillon*, and cut as the Perches and Soles that are so dress'd, according to the Instructions given in the third Article of *Soles*. See also that of *Perches*, for Quaviver-*Filets*, with white Sauce, which are prepar'd after the same manner, and may be otherwise serv'd up, with Capers.

Quavivers are likewise put into a Fricassy of Chickens, or a Hash may be made of them, with chopt Anchovies and whole Capers, all well season'd, garnish'd with Crusts of fried Bread, and sprinkled with Lemmon-juice, as they are serving up to Table.

R.

RABBETS.

RAbbets may be put into a standing Pie, in order to be serv'd up cold among the Intermesses, as it has been already intimated in the last Article of Pies; or a hot Pie may be made of them for a Side-dish, in this manner.

A Rabbet-pie to be served up hot.

Let the Rabbets be larded, and put into a Pie made of beaten Paste, season'd with Pepper, Salt, Nutmeg, Cloves, pounded Lard, a Bay-leaf or two, and a Shalot. After having wash'd the Pie over, let it be bak'd for the space of two Hours, and let some Orange or Lemmon-juice be squeez'd in, when brought to Table.

Rabbets and young Rabbets in Casserole.

Cut your Rabbets into quarters, lard them with thick Slips of Bacon; and, after they have been fried, stew them in an earthen Pan with Broth, a Glass of white Wine, a Bunch of Herbs, Pepper, Salt, fried Flower and Orange.

Rabbets dress'd with white and brown Sauce.

After having cut the Rabbets into quarters, slit their Heads, and fried them in Lard, as before; let them be stew'd in an earthen Pot, with Broth, white Wine, Pepper, Salt, Nutmeg and green Lemmon. Let a little fried Flower be put to those that are to be dress'd with brown Sauce; and for the others, let white Sauce be made, with the Yolks of Eggs, as upon other occasions.

Rabbets in a Tourte, or Pan-pie, and otherwise.

Large fat Rabbets and young Rabbets may likewise be put into a *Tourte*, or Pan-pie; cutting them into pieces, which are to be fried in Lard, with a little Flower, fine Herbs, young Chibbols, Pepper, Salt, Nutmeg, and a little Broth. When they are cold, let your Pie be made of them, with fine Paste; adding some *Morilles*, *Truffles* and pounded Lard, and covering all with a Lid of the same Paste: Let it be bak'd an Hour and half; and, when it is half done, pour in the Sauce in which the Rabbets were dress'd, as also, some Orange-juice, as it is serving up to Table.

At another time, when the Rabbets are roasted, they may be cut into halves, and dress'd with a good Gammon-sauce.

Young

Young Rabbets dress'd à la Saingaraz.

The Rabbets being neatly larded and roasted, some beaten Slices of Gammon are to be fried in Lard, with a little Flower, a Faggot of fine Herbs, and some good Gravy that is not Salt: A few Drops of Vinegar are also to be added, and the Sauce may be thicken'd with a little Bread-cullis. Then let the Rabbets be cut into quarters, and dress'd in a Dish or Plate; pouring the Sauce upon them, with Slices of Gammon, in order to be serv'd up hot, after they have been well clear'd from the Fat.

Large fat Pullets may be likewise dress'd, *à la Saingaraz*; as also, Chickens and Pigeons, except that they must not be cut into quarters.

RAMEQUINS.

To make Cheese-*Ramequins*; a Farce is to be prepar'd of the same sort as that before describ'd for Cheese-cakes, only adding a little pounded Parsly, and, if you please, some Yest to render them lighter. Then let some Bread-crum be cut into small square pieces, with the point of a Knife; and let a little of this Farce be put upon every one of those Slices: But it would be requisite to dip your Knife into a whipt Egg, to hinder the Farce from sticking to it; so as the *Ramequins* may be made of a round or square Figure: They are to be bak'd in a Pie-pan, with a little Butter underneath; and care must be taken, that they be not too much colour'd. These *Ramequins* will serve to garnish Pease in Cream, or any thing else that you shall think fit, and may even be set among the Out-works of Intermesses.

A piece of refined Cheese may also be taken, with a Lump of Butter, as much Flower as you can get up between your Fingers at twice, three Yolks of Eggs, a little Pepper and Lemmon-juice. When the whole Mixture or Farce is well pounded together, let it be spread upon a Plate, and bak'd under the Lid of a Pie-pan, with Fire on the top; taking care that it do not burn.

RISSOLES.

Rissoles are proper for the Intermesses, and, to render them more delicious, ought to be made with Capons-breasts. As for the

the rest, they may be season'd and order'd almost after the same manner as the *Bouillans*, specified under the Letter B; but they must be well fried and brought to a fine colour.

They may also be made on Days of Abstinence, of a delicious Fish-farce, and even of *Mousserons* and Spinage, for the Entertainments with Roots. As for the *Mousserons*, they must be dress'd before, with Butter, fine Herbs, Spice, the Juice of a Lemmon, and a little fried Flower: And the Spinage being boil'd, must be chopt small, and season'd with Salt, Sugar, Cinnamon and Lemmon-peel pounded or rasped. These *Rissoles* must be bak'd in an Oven, and serv'd up with Sugar and sweet Water.

ROACHES.

A Side-dish of marinated Roaches.

The Roaches, being first marinated in Oil, with Wine, Lemmon-juice, and the usual seasoning Ingredients, let them be well breaded, and gently bak'd in an Oven, till they come to a fine colour: Afterwards they must be neatly dress'd in a Dish, and garnish'd with fried Bread and Parsly.

Roaches dress'd in a Ragoo, and several other Ways.

Another Ragoo may be made of Roaches, broiling them upon the Grid-iron, after they have been soak'd in Butter; whilst the Livers are fried with a little Butter, in order to be pounded, and strain'd thro' the Hair-sieve. Let this Cullis be pour'd upon the Roaches, when season'd with white Pepper, Salt, and Orange or Lemmon-juice; rubbing the Dish or Plate, before it is dress'd, with a Shalot or Clove of Garlick.

Roaches may also be farced, as well as many other sorts of Fish; otherwise they may be dress'd in *Casserole*, or put into a Pie; for which last, see the fifteenth Article of Pies.

ROAST-MEATS.

Altho' there seems to be little or no difficulty, as to what relates to the Roast-meats; nevertheless it would be expedient to give some account of them; that is to say, not to shew the Degree of Heat, or the Time that is requisite for the roasting of every
parti-

particular Joint of Meat, or Fowl; because those Circumstances may be sufficiently discern'd by the Eye, and may be regulated according to the Thickness, or Nature of the Meats: But only to explain the Manner of Dressing, or Preparing them before they are spitted, and the Sauces which are most proper for them. For example:

Large Quails and young Quails must be drawn and eaten barded, with Pepper; or they may be larded, and serv'd up with Orange.

Pheasants and Pheasant-powts ought to be well pickt and drawn: They are usually larded with thin Slips of Bacon, and eaten with Verjuice, Pepper and Salt, or with Orange.

Large fat Partridges and young Partridges are serv'd up in the same manner, as well as Wood-hens.

Wood-cocks and Snipes must not be drawn, but only larded with very small Slips of Bacon: As they are roasting, a Sauce is to be prepar'd for them, with Orange, white Pepper, Salt, and a young Chibbol.

Plovers are dress'd and eaten, after the same manner.

Turkeys and Turkey-powts must be basted, as they are roasting, with a little Vinegar, Salt, Chibbols, and white Pepper.

Ring-doves, or Wood-pigeons, and young Fowls of that sort, may be serv'd up with Verjuice and the entire Grapes, or Orange, or else in Rose-vinegar, with white Pepper and Salt.

Turtle-doves are usually order'd in the same manner: They must be drawn and larded with thin Slips of Bacon, as the former; as well as *Bisets*, which are a kind of Stock-doves, or Wood-pigeons.

Ducks, Teals, and other sorts of Water-fowl, ought to be drawn and spitted without larding. When they are half-roasted, they may be basted with Lard; and eaten all over bloody, with white Pepper, Salt and Orange-juice, or a natural Pepper and Vinegar-sauce. As for Barn-door Ducks, they may be larded with some Rows of Bacon, and roasted somewhat longer than the others.

Geese, both wild and tame, must be drawn, but not larded; if they are fat: They are to be basted with Lard, and eaten with Pepper and Vinegar, or with Salt and Orange.

Let green Geese be drawn and barded; whilst a Farce is preparing for them, with the Livers, Bacon, chopt Herbs, young Chibbols, Pepper, Salt and Nutmeg; to which may be added,

Mut-

Mutton-gravy and Lemmon-juice, when ready to be serv'd up to Table: Or else they may be eaten with Verjuice and the entire Grapes, or with Vinegar, Pepper and Salt.

Thrushes must be basted, and stew'd with Bread and Salt, in order to be eaten, with Verjuice, Pepper, and a little Orange-juice; after having rubb'd the Dish, with a Shalot.

Larks are serv'd up in the same manner, except that a little Sage may be put into the Sauce.

Fat Capons ought to be drawn and barded; putting into the Body, an Onion stuck with Cloves, with Salt and white Pepper: When they are ready, take off the *Bards*, or Slices of Bacon, bread them, and let them be eaten with Cresses scalded in Vinegar, with Salt; or else with Orange and Salt, or with Oisters stew'd in the Dripping. As for the other Capons, they may be larded with small Slips of Bacon, and serv'd up after the same manner as the others, as well as large fat Pullets.

Ortolans must be drawn, and roasted on a small Spit, and basted with a little Lard: Then they may be cover'd or strew'd with Bread and Salt, and eaten with Salt and Orange.

Mauviettes ought not to be drawn, but larded with thin Slips of Bacon; leaving the Feet. Then having made a Sauce of the Dripping, with Verjuice and Grapes, white Pepper and Salt, let them be eaten with Salt and Orange.

Beccafigo's require only to be well pickt, after having cut off their Heads and Feet: Then they are to be roasted on a little Spit, and strew'd with grated Bread and Salt; in order to be eaten with Orange, or with Verjuice with the Grapes entire and white Pepper.

Hares and Leverets ought to be imbru'd with their own Blood, and larded with thin Slips of Bacon: They are usually eaten with Pepper and Vinegar, or with sweet Sauce made of Sugar, Cinnamon, Pepper, Wine and Vinegar.

Large Rabbets and young ones are eaten with Water, white Pepper and Salt, or with Orange.

Lamb and Kid must be parboil'd in Water, or broil'd a little upon the Coals, and larded with thin Slips of Bacon. Then they may be eaten, with green Sauce, or with Orange, white Pepper and Salt, or with Rose-vinegar.

A sucking Pig ought to be well scalded in Water, taking out the Entrails, and putting into the Belly some Pepper, Salt, Chibbols and a Lump of pounded Lard: When it is almost roasted, let it be sindg'd and basted with Water and Salt. It may be eaten with white Pepper, Salt and Orange.

A

A young Wild Boar may be larded with thin Slips of Bacon, without cutting off the Head or Feet, and when well roasted, may be eaten with Pepper and Vinegar, or with Orange, Salt and Pepper.

An old Wild Boar must be dress'd after the same manner, and serv'd up with Pepper and Vinegar, or *Robert*-Sauce.

A Roe-buck must likewise be larded with small Slips of Bacon, and as it is roasting, a Sauce must be prepar'd for it, with Onions fried in Lard, and afterwards strain'd thro' the Hair-sieve, with Vinegar, a little Broth, white Pepper and Salt; or it may be dress'd with sweet Sauce.

A Joint of a Stag or Hind ought to be larded with thin Slips of Bacon, and eaten with Pepper and Vinegar.

Fallow Deer and Fawns must be larded in the same manner, as they are roasting, basted with a Liquor made of Vinegar, green Lemmon, a Bunch of Herbs, Pepper and Salt. They are also eaten with Pepper and Vinegar.

Other Sauces proper for the Roast-meats.

Sauce made of Duck-gravy.
Wood-cock Sauce.
Sauce of Gravy of a Leg of Mutton, with a Shalot.
Sauce of Veal-gravy, with Orange.
Sauce of Veal-gravy, with a Shalot.
Sauce of chopt *Truffles* and fine Herbs.
Sauce of raw Gammon and Oisters.
Sauce of Onion and Veal-gravy.
Sauce of a Partridge-cullis and Capers.
Sauce of Anchovies and Shalots.
Sauce of Oil and Mustard, after the Spanish Way.
Sauce of young Chibbols, fried brown.
Sauce of Verjuice with the entire Grapes and Veal-gravy.
Sauce of fresh *Mousserons* chopt.
Poor Man's Sauce, with Garlick.
Poor Man's Sauce, with Oil.
Sauce of Gravy of a short Rib of Beef, with Garlick.
Sauce of Fennel and green Gooseberries.
Sauce of green Oisters and minc'd Gammon.
Ring-dove Sauce, with Pomegranate.
Sauce with Capons-livers.
Sauce of green Corn.
Sauce of new Verjuice, with a Shalot.

The Court and Country Cook. 239

Many other sorts of Sauces may be found in their proper places, by the means of the General Table of the Messes, at the end of this Volume.

ROE-BUCKS.

To dress a Roe-buck.

When it is larded with thin Slips of Bacon and roasted, it may be eaten with natural sweet Sauce; or with Sweet-sour Sauce; or with a natural Pepper and Vinegar-sauce: Or else the Spleen of the Roe-buck may be fried in Lard, with an Onion; afterwards pounded in a Mortar, and strain'd thro' the Hair-sieve, with Mutton-gravy, the Juice of a Lemmon and Mushrooms, and white Pepper.

Other Ways of dressing a Roe-buck.

Let the Flesh of your Roe-buck be larded with thick Slips of Bacon, and fried for some time in Lard. Then Stew it in a Sauce-pan, with Beef-broth or Water, season'd, with Pepper, Salt, Bay-leaves, Nutmeg, and a Faggot of Herbs; adding also a Glass of white Wine, and a piece of green Lemmon. Let the Sauce be thicken'd with fried Flower, and serv'd up with Lemmon-juice and Capers.

This sort of Meat, after it has been larded with thick Slips of Bacon, and dress'd as before, may be left to cool in its own Broth, and brought to Table, upon a Napkin, with Slices of Lemmon, and Cresses boil'd in Vinegar and Salt.

ROULADES.

Take part of a Fillet of Veal with Beef-sewer, and mince them very small as it were a *Godivoe*, adding two Eggs with the Whites and some Salt: Then having prepar'd a piece of a Leg of Mutton, or of Veal, or a Veal-caul, strew it with Parsly, and put seven or eight Slices of Lemmon in the Intervals: You must also provide a Calve's Tongue, or a Sheep's Tongue boil'd, to be cut into small thin Slices, with little *Bards* of Bacon. Let your *Godivoe* be spread over all, with Parsly, Pepper and Salt on the top; and let all be roll'd up together and bound, in order to be stew'd as it were in a good *Court-bouillon*, with one piece,

or

or several Slices of Bacon. Let the whole Mess be serv'd among the Out-works or for a Side-dish, after having garnish'd it, with whatsoever you shall judge requisite.

See also the Article of *Beef-stakes roll'd up*, under the Letter B. and that of *Poupiets*, under P.

S.

SALMON.

Several Ways of dressing Salmon.

FResh Salmon may be put into a Ragoo, made brown, as it were *Fricandoes*, with Veal-sweet-breads, *Truffles* and Mushrooms; adding good Broth or Beef-gravy, as it is stewing, and some Lemmon-juice, before it is serv'd up to Table. The following Directions for the Trout may also be observ'd; or else your Salmon, larded with middle-siz'd Slips of Bacon and well seasion'd, may be roasted by a gentle Fire, basting it with white Wine and Verjuice, and putting a Faggot of fine Herbs with a piece of green Lemmon into the Sauce. You must also temper with the Dripping, some Oisters, boiled Mushrooms, Capers, fried Flower and the Liver of the Salmon, adding some white Pepper and Lemmon-juice, when the Dish is ready to be serv'd up, among the Intermesses.

A Tail-piece of Salmon in Casserole.

See the Instructions before given for the dressing of a Codfish-tail in the second Article of *Cod-fish*, under the Letter C. and having farc'd your Tail-piece of Salmon in the same manner, let it be breaded, and bak'd in an Oven, with white Wine, Salt, Chibbol, Thyme, a Bay-leaf or two, and Lemmon-peel. When it is ready, pour a Ragoo upon it, and garnish it with what you please.

Salmon in a Ragoo.

Take a Joll or any other piece of Salmon, and having cut it into Slices, let it be bak'd in a cover'd Dish set into the Oven, with a little Wine, Verjuice, Pepper, Salt, Cloves, a Bunch of fine Herbs, Nutmeg, Bay-leaves, green Lemmon and a little

Fish-

Fish-broth. In the mean time, having prepar'd a good Ragoo of Oisters, Capers, fried Flower, Mushrooms, and the Liver of the Salmon, turn all upon it, and let it be serv'd up, with Lemmon-juice.

Salmon dreſs'd with ſweet Sauce.

Having cut your Salmon into Slices and flower'd them, let them be fried in refined Butter: Then, soaking them a little while in a sweet Sauce made of red Wine, Sugar, Pepper, Salt, Cloves, Cinnamon, and green Lemmon, let them be serv'd up, with such Garniture as you shall think fit.

For the Salmon-sallet, see Pag. 41. and for a Salmon-pie, the Letter P.

SALPICON.

The *Salpicon* is a Ragoo usually made for large Joints of Beef, Veal, or Mutton, which are to be serv'd up roasted, for the principal Side-dishes. To that purpose, having provided Cucumbers, boil'd Gammon, Capons-livers, the *Filets* of a fat Pullet, *Truffles*, Mushrooms, and Artichoke-bottoms, let all be cut into small square pieces: But the Cucumbers, being taken a-part, must be fried in Lard, and well clear'd from the Fat, throwing in a little Flower: Afterwards, having fried them again a little while, they must be put to the rest of the above-mention'd Ingredients, with good Gravy; and all must be boil'd or stew'd together. If you have any Gammon-essence, put in one Spoonful of it; and, to thicken the Sauce, prepare a good Cullis, to be sprinkled at last with a little Vinegar: In the mean while, a Hole being made in a short Rib of Beef, or in the Leg of a Quarter of Veal, all that Meat must be taken away, which will serve for other Farces, and the Ragoo even now describ'd, must be substituted in its room.

A *Salpicon* may also be serv'd up separately for a Side dish.

SANDLINGS, *see* DABS.

SAUSAGES.

To make Sausages, let some Pork and Leaf-fat out of the Hog's Belly be chopt small, well season'd, and mixt with a little Parsly, other fine Herbs and a Shalot. If you would have them

them more delicious than ordinary; it will be requisite also to mince the Breasts of Capons, or fat Pullets, with a little raw Gammon and Anis, in the same manner as for white Hogs-puddings. When the whole Mixture is well order'd and seafon'd, adding a little Gammon-essence, it may be bound with the Yolk of an Egg. Afterwards, having provided Sheeps-guts that are well cleans'd, according to the thickness that you would have your Sausages to be of, they may be made of a convenient length, and broil'd upon Paper, or fried; in order to be serv'd up to Table.

The same Compound or Farce may also be wrapt up in a Veal-caul and dress'd as Capons-livers in a Caul; for which see the Article of *Livers* under the Letter L.

Veal-sausages are made in the same manner, after having minc'd part of a Fillet of Veal, with half as much Bacon, seafon'd with Pepper, Salt, Nutmeg and fine Herbs chopt very small. They may also be broil'd upon the Grid-iron, with thick Paper underneath, and serv'd up with Mustard, as the former, among the Side-dishes.

Royal Saucissons, *or thick Sausages.*

Having provided some Flesh of Partridges and of a fat Pullet or Capon, a little Gammon and other Bacon, and a piece of a Leg of Veal, all raw, with Parsly and Chibbols, let them be well chopt with Mushrooms and *Truffles*, and season'd with Pepper, Salt, beaten Spice, and a Clove of Garlick; adding also two whole Eggs, three or four Yolks and a little Milk-cream. Then roll up this Farce into thick pieces, according to the quantity that you have of it, and to the end that it may be dress'd, without breaking, let it be wrapt up in very thin Slices cut out of a Fillet of Veal, and beaten flat upon the Dresser, for that purpose; so as the Sausages may be made at least as thick as a Man's Arm, and of a convenient length. When they are thus order'd, they must be put into an oval Stew-pan, with a great many *Bards* or thin Slices of Bacon at the bottom, and stopt up close; covering them with Beef-stakes, and other Bacon-*Bards*. Afterwards, the Pan must be set between two Fires, taking care that they be not too quick, and the Sausages must be bak'd or stew'd in this manner about eight or ten Hours. As soon as they are ready, let them be remov'd from the Fire, and left to cool in the same Pan: Then they must be carefully taken out so as

none

none be broken, and all the Meat round about muſt be taken away, with the Fat: At laſt you may cut the Sauſages into Slices with a ſharp Knife, and ſet them in good order in a Diſh or Plate, to be ſerv'd up cold to Table. If there be occaſion to make a *Galantine* at the ſame time, with the Royal Sauſages, it may be dreſs'd in the ſame Stew-pan.

SEA-DRAGONS, *ſee* QUAVIVERS.

SHADS.

Broiled Shads.

When they are well ſcal'd and cut, rub them with Butter and Salt, or elſe cauſe them to take Salt in a Baking-pan, with Oil: Then they muſt be broil'd upon the Grid-iron, over a gentle Fire, and brought to a fine colour. They may be ſerv'd up, with Sorrel and Cream; adding alſo ſome Parſly, Chervil, Chibbol, Pepper, Salt, Nutmeg and ſweet Butter. They may alſo be dreſs'd in a Ragoo of Muſhrooms, or in a brown Sauce, with Capers.

Shads in a Court-bouillon.

After having ſcal'd and cut your Shads, let them boil in white Wine, with Vinegar, Pepper, Salt, Cloves, Bay-leaves, Onions and green Lemmon, and let them be ſerv'd up to Table upon a Napkin.

SIMNELS.

Iced Simnels.

Iced Simnels, may ſerve either for Intermeſſes, or to garniſh other Diſhes, and are prepar'd after the following manner. Having provided Simnels made of Water, according to the ſize of your Diſh, cut them into halves, as it were an Orange, leaving the Cruſt on the top and underneath; and ſoak them in Milk, with Sugar, proportionably to the quantity of Simnels. Then let them be cover'd and laid under hot Embers, to be kept warm for the ſpace of about four or five Hours; but they muſt not be boil'd, leſt they turn to Pap. Afterwards, having taken them out, let them be well drain'd and fried in freſh Lard. As

R 2   ſoon

244 *The Court and Country Cook.*

soon as they are colour'd, let them be ftrew'd with fine Sugar and iced over: At laft, after they have been turn'd and iced on the other Side, they may be brought hot to Table.

SMELTS.

We fhall not here infift on the manner of Dreffing Smelt-potages, with white and brown Broth, or of Filets of the fame Fifh, in regard that it is only requifite to obferve the Directions already laid down for other forts of Fifh. But it may not be improper to give fome account of the Side-difhes that are ufually made of Smelts.

Several Ways of dreffing Smelts.

Smelts may be fried and ferv'd up in a Sauce made of diffolv'd Anchovies, burnt Butter, Orange-juice and white Pepper.

At another time, They may be ftew'd in a Sauce-pan, with Butter, a little white Wine, Nutmeg, fried Flower and a piece of green Lemmon; adding fome Capers and Lemmon-juice, when ferv'd up to Table.

Smelts may be alfo boil'd in a *Court-bouillon*, with white Wine, green Lemmon, Pepper, Salt and a Bay-leaf or two, and brought to Table, upon a Napkin, with Parfly and Slices of Lemmon, to be eaten with white Pepper and Vinegar; or elfe they may be drefs'd with the *Ramolade*-fauce defcribed Pag. 41.

SNIPES.

Snipes may be ferv'd up in a Ragoo, as well as roafted; to which purpofe, they muft be flit into halves, without taking away any of their Entrails: Then let them be fried in Lard, and feafon'd with white Pepper, Salt, a Chibbol, and a little Juice of Mufhrooms and Lemmon. The Difh may be garnifh'd with Slices of Lemmon.

SOLES.

Soles drefs'd after the Spanifh Way.

Let the Soles be fried, and afterwards cut into *Filets*; whilft a Sauce is preparing for them, with good *Champagne*-wine, two
Cloves

Cloves of Garlick, Pepper, Salt, Thyme and a Bay-leaf. Then soak them by degrees in this Sauce, and garnish them, with what you shall judge most requisite.

A Side-dish of fried Soles.

Open the Back of your Soles, on both sides, and take away the Bone, till the white Flesh appears. When they are fried, let them be garnish'd with the Flesh of other Soles, and let a white Sauce be made with an Anchovie and Capers, or *Robert*-Sauce; or else a Ragoo of Mushrooms with Pike-livers, Artichoke-bottoms chopp'd very small and Carp-roes, squeezing in some Lemmon-juice, before the Dish is set on the Table.

Sole-Filets *with Cucumbers.*

Having cut fried Soles into *Filets*, let them be mingled with Cucumbers dress'd in the following manner: Let marinated Cucumbers cut into Slices, be fried and soak'd with Gravy or Broth; in which they must be afterwards stew'd and well season'd, taking care that they do not stick. The *Filets* being put to them, may be serv'd up a little after, and garnish'd with what you please.

Soles farced with fine Herbs, and dress'd otherwise.

Let your Soles cool, after they have been fried, and let a Farce be made of fine Herbs, *viz.* Parsly, Chibbol, Thyme, Savoury, and sweet Basil, all chopt together, with Pepper, Salt, Cloves and Nutmeg: Then dress all these with a good Lump of Butter, and farce the Soles, taking out the Bones of every one, at the top of the Back: Afterwards, soak them in melted Butter, and having breaded them, let them be broil'd upon the Grid-iron and brought to a fine colour, with the red-hot Fire-shovel. They may be serv'd up, with Lemmons cut into halves.

Other Soles are farced with Bread-crum, Anchovies, Parsly, Chibbols and sweet Butter, all well chopp'd, kneaded and season'd: When they are thus stuff'd, let them be steept in Oil, breaded and dress'd as Pigs-pettitoes, *à la Sainte Menehout*. A little brown Sauce must be prepar'd for them, and some Lemmon-juice added, as they are serving up to Table.

R 3 Other

Other Ways of farcing Soles for Potage may be seen in the 65th Article of *Potages*, under the Letter P. and as many Side-dishes may be made of them; enriching them with Mushrooms, Oisters, Cray-fish and Capers, adding Lemmon-juice, when serv'd up to Table.

In any season out of Lent, three or four Eggs may be mingled with the Farce, which is to be made of the Flesh of boned Soles, when they are half-fried, with fine Herbs and Bread-crum soak'd in Milk. Having stuff'd the Bones of your Soles with this Farce, bake them in an Oven, till they come to a fine colour, and set out the Dish with Lemmon, or some other proper Garniture.

Sole-Filets, *with a Lentil-cullis*.

After the Soles have been fried and cut into *Filets*, they must be put into a good Ragoo of Lentils, such as is produc'd in the fifth Article of Potages, and gently boil'd a little while over the Fire. When the *Filets* are ready to be serv'd up, let them be dress'd in the Ragoo, or Cullis, and garnish'd with what you please, for a Side-dish.

Quavivers, Dabs and Perches may also be dress'd in the same manner, but the latter must be handled more gently.

Other Ways of dressing Soles.

Sole-*Filets* are likewise serv'd up in a Cullis of Capers, others with *Truffles*, and others with *Robert*-Sauce, with sweet Basil, or with Cray-fish: A *Pain*, or farced Loaf and *Gatoes*, may also be made of Soles, or they may be dress'd in a *Court-bouillon*, or in a *Marinade*, as it has been observ'd in the last Article of *Marinades*. As for those that are fried, they may be eaten with Salt and Orange-juice.

Souces.

To make an Intermess of *Soufce*, let Hogs-ears and Feet be boil'd after the usual manner, and left to cool in their own Liquor; Then let them be cut into very small thin Slices, and let all the Bones be taken away; whilst some of the best sort of Vinegar is put into a Stew-pan, with Sugar, proportionably to the quantity of Meat: Let the Vinegar and Sugar be boil'd, with a Stick of Cinnamon, three or four Cloves, a little Pepper and Salt, and two or three Slices of Lemmon: Let all be ſtrain'd thro' the Hair-ſieve, and when the Meat is cut into *Menus-droits*, let all boil together, till the Sauce becomes thick, as if it were for *Menus-droits* with Muſtard. Afterwards, having remov'd the Stew-pan from the Fire, and having provided certain little ſquare Boxes, of what ſize you ſhall think fit, all the Fat being alſo taken off with a Spoon, let the whole Meſs be turn'd into them, with ſmall *Lardoons*, or Slices of Bacon, of the ſame length as the Boxes. When they are fill'd, let them not be cover'd, till all be well coagulated. Afterwards, cover them with Paper, and the Lids of the ſame Boxes. This Compound, or Jelly, may be kept during four or five Months, but the newer it is the better. It is uſually ſerv'd up in thin Slices, and laid in good order, on a Diſh or Plate, with a clean Napkin underneath.

S T A G.

A Joint of Stag may be dreſs'd ſeveral Ways; that is to ſay, it may be larded with thick Slips of Bacon, and ſeaſon'd with Pepper, Salt, Nutmeg, and beaten Cloves: Otherwiſe, having larded it with ſmall Slips of Bacon, let it be ſteept in white Wine and Verjuice, with Salt, a Faggot of Herbs, a piece of green Lemmon, and three or four Bay-leaves, and roaſted at a gentle Fire; baſting it with its *Marinade*, or Pickle. When it is ready, let it be dreſs'd in the Dripping, with fried Flower to thicken the Sauce; adding Capers, Vinegar, or Lemmon-juice, and white Pepper, when ſerv'd up to Table.

Another Way of dreſſing Stags-fleſh.

Let the Loin or Shoulder of a Stag be larded with very thin Slips of Bacon, and cover'd with Paper. As it is roaſting, let a Sauce be prepar'd for it, with Vinegar, Pepper, Salt, Nutmeg, fried Flower, Slices of Lemmon and Shalots.

Another Way.

After your Joint of Stag has been well roaſted, it may be eaten with a ſweet Sauce, made in this manner: Take a Glaſs of Vinegar, with Sugar, a little Salt, three or four whole
Cloves,

Cloves, Cinnamon and a little Lemmon; and, when these Ingredients are boil'd together, put in a little fried Flower, white Pepper and Orange-juice.

Stag in a Ragoo.

Having larded a piece of Stags-flesh with thick Slips of Bacon, season'd with Pepper and Salt, let it be fried in Lard: Then let it boil for the space of three or four Hours in an earthen Pan, with Broth or Water, and two Glasses of white Wine, season'd with Salt, Nutmeg, a Bunch of Herbs, three or four Bay-leaves, and a piece of green Lemmon. When it is ready, let the Sauce be thicken'd with fried Flower, and add Capers and Lemmon-juice as it is serving up to Table.

Pasties are also made of Stags-flesh, which may be found in the Article of *Pasties*, under the Letter P.

STOCK-FISH, *see* COD-FISH.

STURGEON.

A Side-dish of Sturgeon for Flesh-days.

Sturgeon for Flesh-days may be dress'd after different Manners; that is to say, either in form of larded *Fricandoes* or Collops; or in thick Slices, *à la Sainte Menehout*. For the latter, let the Slices of Sturgeon be gently stew'd in Milk and white Wine, well season'd, with a Bay-leaf and a little melted Lard: Then let them be breaded, and broil'd upon a Grid-iron; pouring a Sauce underneath, in the same manner, as for Loins of Mutton, in order to be serv'd up hot to Table.

For Collops of the same Sturgeon, after they have been cut and larded, they must be flower'd a little, and brought to a colour with Lard: Then they are to be boil'd in a Sauce-pan, with good Gravy, fine Herbs, Slices of Lemmon, *Truffles*, Mushrooms, Veal-sweet-breads, and a well-season'd Cullis. Afterwards, the Fat being thoroughly drain'd from them, they may be sprinkled with a little Verjuice, and serv'd up hot, as well as the other sort, among the Side-dishes and Out-works.

Ano-

Another Way of dressing Sturgeon.

Sturgeon may also be dress'd in *Haricot*, with Turneps; to which purpose, it must be boil'd in Water, with Pepper, Salt, Thyme, Onions and Cloves. If you have any Broth at hand, some of it may be pour'd in, and then your Sturgeon must be fried brown in Lard: Afterwards, it must be clear'd from the Fat, and put into a prepared Cullis, with the Turneps, and a little Gammon cut into Slices, or chopt small. It may be serv'd up, with Lemmon-juice, and set out with *Marinade*, or some other Garniture.

Sturgeon for Fish-days.

Let your Sturgeon be boil'd in a good *Court-bouillon*, and dress'd in a well-seafon'd Ragoo of Mushrooms, &c.

A *Haricot* may also be made of Sturgeon, with Turneps, as on Flesh-days, cutting it into pieces of the length of your Finger, in order to be boil'd in Water and Salt, and afterwards fried brown. Then the Fat being drain'd off, it must be put into a Cullis of the same, and mingled with the Turneps, after they have been scalded and well seafon'd.

T.

TARTS.

Tarts made of Cherries and other sorts of Fruit.

TAke preserv'd Cherries, and let a piece of well-made Paste, half puff'd be roll'd out very thin for an Under-crust, to be spread over the bottom of the Pie-pan: Then lay your Cherries in order, and roll out some Slips of Paste, which cannot be made too small. With these, fine Ornaments may be made for your Tart, in form of a Star, a Basket, a Royal Banner, and several others, at pleasure: Thus, having shap'd all with the Point of a Knife, the Tart must be bak'd, and afterwards ic'd with fine Sugar, passing the red-hot Fire-shovel over it. It may be garnish'd with *Feuillantins*, or small *Fleurons* of all sorts of Fruit. Tarts may also be made of other Fruits, and even of Cream, after the same manner: When Apricocks, Verjuice,

juice, &c. are in season, they are natural; and at other times, Marmelade may be us'd. However, the Tarts may be always render'd more delicious, by making the Crust, with Almond-paste, or crackling Crust, such as is describ'd in the first Article of Pastes.

A Peach-tart.

Let ripe Peaches be ston'd, well pounded in a Mortar, and left in Heaps: In the mean while, having put some Sugar, with candy'd Lemmon-peel cut small, into a Dish, let a fine Paste be made somewhat stiff, with a little Butter, Flower, Salt, Water, and the Yolk of an Egg. Then roll out a round piece, very thin, for the Bottom-crust, according to the size of your Dish, and make a little Border of the same Paste, for the Side-crust, about two Inches high: Afterwards, the Peaches being put into it in good order, the Pie may be set into the Oven, and brought to a fine colour, with the red-hot Fire-shovel, after having strew'd it with Sugar. This is commonly call'd *a broiled Tart* by the French, and ought to be serv'd up hot to Table.

Tarts of the like nature, may be prepar'd with Apples and other sorts of Fruit; and, if you'll give your self the trouble, they may be made of Paste proper for crackling Crust, neatly cut, dried in an Oven, and afterwards iced over with the Yolk of an Egg, fine Sugar and a little preserv'd Lemmon-peel, well temper'd together. Having thus order'd your Paste for the Lid, causing it to be ic'd in the Oven, till it become very white; it must be laid upon the Tart that is dress'd in the Dish, a little before it is serv'd up, and may be garnish'd with *Meringues*.

A sweet-sour Tart.

Take a Glass of Verjuice, or Lemmon-juice, with a quarter of a Pound of Sugar, and when half is boil'd away, add some Cream, with six Yolks of Eggs, a little Butter, Orange-flowers, candy'd Lemmon-peel grated, and beaten Cinnamon: Let all be put into a Tart made of fine Paste, and bak'd without a Lid.

Other sorts of Tarts.

A kind of *Marmelade* or Cream, may be made of Apples, Beets, Melons, and other sorts of Fruit; boiling them in white Wine, and

and afterwards pounding them with Sugar, Cinnamon, Orange-flowers and Lemmon-peel: Then they muſt be ſtrain'd thro' the Hair-ſieve, and put into a Tart made of very thin Cruſt, with a little Butter, in order to be ſerv'd up with musked Sugar and Orange-flowers.

Tarts may alſo be made of all the different ſorts of artificial Creams ſpecify'd under that Article.

TENCHES.

Tenches may be cut into pieces, and a white or brown Fricaſſy may be made of them, with *Mouſſerons* or common Muſhrooms, *Truffles*, Artichoke-bottoms and fine Herbs; adding a thickening Liquor, as for Chickens, and an Anchovie chopt very ſmall, as alſo ſome Lemmon-juice, before it is ſerv'd up to Table, ſet out with *Marinade*.

A Haſh may be alſo made of Tenches, garniſh'd with the Heads marinated and fried: Or elſe they may be dreſs'd in *Caſſerole*, frying them, in burnt Butter, after they have been cut, and ſtewing them in white Wine, with the ſame Butter, Verjuice, a Faggot of Herbs, Pepper, Salt, Nutmeg, a Bay-leaf or two, and a little Flower. When they are ready, let Oiſters be put into the Sauce, with Capers, ſome Juice of Muſhrooms and Lemmon, and let all be garniſh'd with fried Bread.

Moreover, Tenches may be farc'd, as Carps, or dreſs'd in a Ragoo, cutting them into pieces, to be fried in refined Butter, in which an Anchovie is to be afterwards diſſolv'd; adding Orange-juice, Pepper, Salt, Nutmeg and Capers: Then the Diſh may be ſerv'd up with fried Parſly and Slices of Lemmon.

As for thoſe Tenches that are ſet a-part for frying, they muſt be ſlit on the Back, and ſtrew'd with Salt and Flower. When they are ſufficiently fried, let them be ſerv'd up to Table with Orange-juice.

TERRINE.

A *Terrine* is a very conſiderable Side-diſh, and may be thus prepar'd: Take ſix Quails, four young Pigeons, two Chickens, and a Breaſt of Mutton cut into pieces; and let all be bak'd or ſtew'd in an earthen Pan, call'd *Terrine* in French, between two gentle Fires, with Bacon-*Bards* at the bottom to keep them from burning, or young ſtreaked Bacon cut into pieces: Then let

let the Fat be drain'd off, and some good Veal-gravy put in its place, with boil'd Lettice, a little green Peafe-foop, and green Peafe or Afparagus-tops: Let all be ftew'd again together for fome time, and thoroughly clear'd from the Fat, before they are ferv'd up to Table.

N. B. Somewhat has been already deliver'd on this Subject, in the fecond Article of *Mirotons*, under the Letter M.

THRUSHES.

Amongft other Difhes, Thrufhes may be put into a Pie, to be ferv'd up hot, or into a Rágoo; frying them, for the latter, in Lard, with a little Flower, a Faggot of fine Herbs, Pepper, Salt, Nutmeg, a little white Wine and Capers; fqueezing in fome Lemmon-juice, as they are ferving up to Table.

For Potage made of Thrufhes, let them likewife be fried in Lard, after they have been drawn, and then boil'd with brown Broth proper for that purpofe, as it has been already hinted, in the firft Article of *Broth*, under the Letter B. The Livers being alfo fried in the fame Lard, muft be afterwards pounded, and ftrain'd thro' the Hair-fieve, with the fame Broth, in order to be put upon the Thrufhes, or into the Potage; which are to be drefs'd and garnifh'd with Mufhrooms.

TONGUES.

Having already explain'd divers Services of Neats-tongues, under the Letter N. let us now give fome Account of the other forts.

Calves-tongues.

To prepare farced Calves-tongues.

Let a Hole be made in the Tongues at the Root, with a little Knife; taking care that they be not cut in any part: Then thruft in your Finger quite thro', as if it were a Gut; fo as a Ragoo may be put into it, made of Veal-fweet-breads, Mufhrooms, *Truffles*, Parfly and Chibbol; all well feafon'd, and fried with a little Lard and Flower, that is not made brown. The Tongues, being farced with this Ragoo, muft be tied up very clofe at the Hole, and thrown into hot Water, to the end that the

the firſt Skin may be peel'd off. Afterwards, they muſt be broil'd upon the Coals, or ſtew'd between two Fires, and when the Fat is thoroughly drain'd from them, they may be dreſs'd in a Diſh, with a good Ragoo, garniſh'd with *Fricandoes*, that are well larded but not farc'd.

Another Way of dreſſing Calves-tongues.

Two other Side-diſhes may be made of Calves-tongues; that is to ſay, they may be dreſs'd in the ſame manner as the Neats-tongues, ſpecified in the third and fourth Articles; or elſe they may be roaſted after having been half done, and ſerv'd up with ſweet Sauce.

Hogs-tongues.

To dreſs dried Hogs-tongues.

Take what quantity you pleaſe of Hog's-tongues, and ſcald them, only to get off the firſt Skin; but the Water muſt not be too hot: Then wipe them with a Cloath, and cut off a little of the thick End or Root. To ſalt your Tongues, take green Juniper-berries, and dry them in an Oven, with two Bay-leaves, a little Coriander, Thyme, ſweet Baſil, and all ſorts of fine Herbs, except Roſemary, Sage, Parſly and Chibbol: All theſe Herbs being well dried, muſt be pounded in a Mortar, and ſtrain'd thro' a Sieve. Afterwards, having provided ſome pounded Salt and Salt-petre, mingle them together with the reſt, and let your Tongues be put into a Pail or Pot, laying them in order, one by one, as they are ſeparately ſalted; every Row of them being ſeaſon'd with all theſe Ingredients. They muſt be preſs'd cloſe together; and, when they are all ſalted, let a Slate be laid over them, and a great Stone on the top, leaving them thus cloſe ſtopt for ſix or ſeven Days. Then take them out, drain them a little; and, having cut ſome Hogs-skirts, according to the length of the Tongues, let every one be put into its Caſe, made of thoſe Skirts, tying up both ends. When your Tongues are thus order'd, let them be faſten'd at the ſmall end or tip, to a Pole laid a-croſs the Chimny, at a convenient diſtance, ſo as they may not touch one another, and that they may be well ſmoak'd, for the ſpace of fifteen or twenty Days, till they become dry. Thus they may be preſerv'd,

if

if well order'd, throughout the whole Year; but in their best condition, they must be eaten at the end of six Months: To that purpose, they may be boil'd in Water, with a little red Wine, a few Slices of Chibbol and Cloves. When they are ready, they may be cut into Slices or left entire, at pleasure, and serv'd up cold among the Intermesses.

Sheeps-tongues.

Several Ways of dressing Sheeps-tongues.

Sheeps-tongues may be serv'd up with sweet Sauce, in which, after they have been flower'd and fried till they come to a fine colour, they may be soak'd by degrees, with *Truffles* and *Mousferons*.

Sheeps-tongues may also be broil'd upon the Grid-iron, with Salt and Bread-crum, in order to be stew'd in a Sauce, made of Verjuice, Broth, Mushrooms, Pepper, Salt, fried Flower, Nutmeg and green Lemmon; or else a *Ramolade*-Sauce may be prepar'd for them, according to the Directions laid down, Pag. 41.

Dried Sheeps-tongues may be order'd after the same manner as dried Calves-tongues above specified.

TORTOISES.

Tortoises may be put into a Fricassy of Chickens; and to that purpose, having cut off their Heads, Feet and Tails, let them boil in a Pot, with Pepper, Salt, Onion, Cloves, Thyme and Bay-leaves. Afterwards, having cut them into pieces, taking care of the Gall, toss them up in a Stew-pan, with fine Herbs, Chibbols, Pepper, Salt, Artichoke-bottoms, *Morilles, Mousferons,* common Mushrooms and *Truffles*. If you would have them brown, let them be soak'd with Onion-juice, or else with good Fish-broth and a little fried Flower. To dress Tortoises in a white Fricassy, the Sauce must be thicken'd, with Yolks of Eggs, adding some Verjuice and Lemmon-juice when serv'd up to Table. The Dish may be garnish'd with Roes, Lemmon-slices and Oisters, either fried or raw, according to the nature of the Fricassy.

A *Poupeton* may also be made of Tortoises, or else they may be steept for some time, in Vinegar, Pepper, Salt and Chibbols: Afterwards they must be flower'd and fry'd, in order to be serv'd up with fry'd Parsly, Oranges and white Pepper. TOSTS.

Tosts.

Tosts may be serv'd up both on Flesh-days and those of Abstinence, and are very frequently us'd. For Flesh-days, boil'd Veal-kidneys chopt very small, with Chervil, Salt, Sugar, Cinnamon, and the Yolk of an Egg, may be laid upon the Tosts of Bread, and strew'd with other Bread, or else neatly ic'd over.

For Wood-cock Tosts, let the Flesh and Entrails of the Woodcocks be likewise cut small, except the Ghizzard, and seafon'd with white Pepper, Salt and melted Lard. All being well mingled together, the Tosts may be made, and bak'd in a Pie-pan over a gentle Fire. They ought to be serv'd up without Sugar, only with Mutton-gravy and Orange-juice, or with a Shalot.

Tosts of the like nature may also be made, with Capons-livers fried in pounded Lard, three or four Mushrooms, fine Herbs and the usual seasoning Ingredients.

For Fish-days, the Tosts are generally prepar'd with Butter, Oil of Olives or Hypocras; which manner of dressing is so easie and so well known, that it does not deserve to be any longer insisted upon.

Tourtes, or Pan-pies.

There are two sorts of *Tourtes* or Pies made in a *Tourtiere*, or Baking-pan, as well as of standing Pies both for Flesh-days and those of Abstinence; that is to say, one sort for Side-dishes and the other for Intermesses. Some of the first Service have been already describ'd, particularly *Tourtes* or Pan-pies of Chickens and Pigeons in their respective Articles: And as for the Intermesses, we have also produc'd Almond-pan-pies, Tarts of Cream, and of Fruit-Marmelades, and even some Fish-pan-pies; let us now proceed to explain the most considerable of those that remain.

A *Quail*-Tourte or Pan-pie.

After having well cleans'd and truss'd your Quails, let them be put into a Pan-pie made of beaten Paste, as the former, seafon'd with Pepper, Salt, Nutmeg and a Bunch of Herbs. This Pie must also be fill'd with Veal-sweet-breads, Mushrooms,

Truffles

Truffles cut into pieces, pounded or melted Lard underneath the Quails and Beef-fewet: Then it may be cover'd with a Lid, and bak'd during two Hours. Let some Lemmon-juice be squeez'd in, as it is serving up hot to Table for a Side-dish.

A Tourte *or Pan-pie, after the Spanish Way for a Side-dish.*

Take Quails, Pigeons, *Mauviettes*, or *Ortolans*; that is to say, any one of these sorts, provided they be all small and tender Fowls: For example, if they are Pigeons, after they have been well truss'd, a Farce must be made of a little Marrow, Mushrooms, *Truffles*, a little piece of parboil'd Bacon, all well season'd with Spice and fine Herbs of all sorts. Let your Pigeons be only slit on the Back to let in this Farce, and if they are somewhat tough, they may be scalded a little before they are stuff'd. In the mean time, let some Veal-sweet-breads, Mushrooms, Cockscombs and Artichoke-bottoms cut into Quarters be well season'd and stew'd a-part; whilst the Paste is making, with Water, Flower, the Yolk of an Egg, a little Salt and Butter, but it must not be too stiff: Having set it by a little, let it be beaten with the Rolling-pin, and divided into eight pieces, according to the bigness of your Baking-pan. Of these eight pieces of Paste, take four to serve for the Bottom-crusts; roll out every piece almost as thin as Paper; rub the inside of the Pie-pan with Butter or Lard, and having put one piece of Paste therein, wash it over with melted Lard, to the end, that another may be laid upon it, and so of the rest. Then the Pigeons or other small Fowls, may be set in order, with the Ragoo, and cover'd with *Bards* or thin Slices of Bacon. Afterwards, taking the four pieces of Paste that were left for the Lid, order them in the same manner, as those for the Bottom-crusts, that is to say, let them be wash'd with Lard, before they are laid one upon another. The Pie being thus cover'd must be wash'd over again on the top, and set into the Oven, taking care that it be not of too brown a colour: When it is bak'd, dress it in a Dish or Plate, take off the Lid and *Bards*, pour in a good white Cullis, or one of Mushrooms, according to the nature of the Fowls, and let all be serv'd up hot to Table.

A Tourte or Pan-pie of a Capon's Breast for an Intermeß.

Take the Breast of a Capon or Pullet, and pound it in a Mortar with a little grated Lemmon-peel, a March-pane, three or four Yolks of Eggs, Orange-flower-water, and a little beaten Cinnamon; all well thicken'd. Let this Mixture be spread upon a piece of beaten Paste roll'd out for the Bottom-crust, and let the Pie be bak'd without the Lid. Then ice it over with fine Sugar, and having caus'd the Cover of a Pie-pan to be heated very hot, let it be laid upon the Pie, to give it a colour; adding a little sweet Water and Lemmon-juice, when ready to be brought to Table.

Another Pan-pie made of a Capon's Breast.

Let the Breast of a raw Capon, be minc'd, with as much Marrow or Beef-sewet: Then let your Pie be made of beaten Paste, and the intervals stuff'd with Mushrooms, *Truffles*, Cocks-combs, Veal-sweet-breads, a little pounded Lard, Pepper, Salt and Nutmeg: Let it be cover'd with a Lid of the same Paste, wash'd over, and bak'd for the space of an Hour and half: Lastly, let some Pistachoes, with Mutton-gravy and Lemmon-juice be put into it at the instant of serving it up, and let it be set out with little Tarts, or some other sort of Garniture.

A Pan-pie of Capons-livers.

Let the Livers be scalded in Water, and afterwards laid in Order in a Pie-pan upon fine Paste, with chopt Mushrooms, fine Herbs, Chibbol and pounded Lard, seafon'd with Pepper, Salt, Nutmeg, Cloves and a piece of green Lemmon: Then covering the Pie with a Lid of the same Paste, let it be wash'd over, and bak'd a full Hour. In the mean while, taking one of the Livers that were reserv'd, fry it with a little Lard and Flower; let it also be pounded and strain'd thro' the Hair-sieve, with Mutton-gravy and Lemmon-juice, after having rubb'd the bottom of the Dish with a Shalot. Lastly, let all be put into the Pie, as it is serving up hot to Table.

Gammon-Tourtes, or Pan-pies.

A piece of good Gammon may be cut into small Slices, and laid in order in the Pie-pan upon a piece of fine Paste, with Herbs chopt small, Pepper, Cinnamon, Nutmeg, fresh Butter and a Bay-leaf: It must be cover'd, and wash'd over as the former, and only set into the Oven for half an Hour. When it is bak'd, let some Mutton-gravy be put into it, with Lemmon-juice and a Shalot.

The Gammon may be minc'd, if you shall think fit, to make a Pie of the like nature; adding Sugar, Cinnamon, white Pepper, candy'd Lemmon-peel and a little pounded Lard. When it is dress'd and bak'd as before, let Lemmon-juice and Sugar be put into it, in order to be set on the Table.

A Pan-pie of Sheeps-tongues.

Sheeps-tongues cut into Slices may be put into a Pie-pan, with candy'd Lemmon-peel, Currans, Dates, Pepper, Salt, Sugar, Cinnamon, two pounded Macaroons, some melted Lard, and a piece of green Lemmon. Then let your Pie be cover'd with a Lid, wash'd over, and bak'd for an Hour; putting into it some Lemmon-juice, Sugar and sweet Water, when serv'd up to Table.

A Pan-pie of a Neats-tongue.

Having cut a salted Neats-tongue into very thin Slices, as the former, let it be laid upon a piece of Paste in a Pie-pan, seafon'd with Cinnamon, Pepper, Sugar and melted Lard. Then cover it with a Lid of the same Paste, and when it is half bak'd, that is to say, about half an Hour after it was set into the Oven, pour in half a Glass of good Wine. Afterwards, let it be bak'd outright, and as it is serving up, put some Sugar into it, with Lemmon-juice and Pomegranate-kernels.

A Tourte, or Pan-pie of Veal-sweet-breads.

After having scalded the Sweet-breads in very hot Water, let them be put into a fine Paste, with small Mushrooms, *Truffles*, Pepper, Salt, Nutmeg, green Lemmon and pounded Lard. Then cover-

covering the Pie with a Lid of the same Paste; wash it over, and set it into the Oven for an Hour. When it is bak'd, pour in some Veal or Mutton-gravy, adding Pistachoes and Lemmon-juice, a little before it is brought to Table.

A Pan-pie of Beatils.

The *Beatils* being well cleans'd in hot Water may be put into a Pie-pan, with Mushrooms, *Truffles*, Veal-sweet-breads, Artichoke-bottoms and Beef-marrow; all well seafon'd, with Pepper, Salt, Nutmeg, a Faggot of Herbs, and pounded or melted Lard: Let it be cover'd with a Lid, and wash'd over as the others, and after it has been bak'd about two Hours in an Oven moderately heated, let some Mutton-gravy be pour'd into it, with Lemmon-juice, in order to be serv'd up to Table.

A Pan-pie of Veal-kidneys.

This *Tourte* or Pan-pie may be made two several Ways: For the first, let your Veal-kidneys be chopt small, with a little Lard, seasoned with Pepper, Salt, Nutmeg, Cinnamon, Chibbols, fine Herbs, Mushrooms and Veal-sweet-breads. The Pie being thus made of beaten Paste, must be cover'd, and bak'd as before, during a full Hour.

For the other Way; let your Kidneys be boil'd, minc'd, and put in like manner between two pieces of fine Paste, with Sugar, Cinnamon, Lemmon-peel, Dates, a little Butter, two Macaroons, and the other necessary seasoning Ingredients. Three quarters of an Hour are sufficient for the baking of this sort of Pie, into which you must put some Lemmon-juice, Sugar and Orange-flower-water, when ready to be serv'd up to Table.

Tourtes, or Pan-pies made of Butter, Lard and Marrow.

For the Butter Pan-pie, take very fresh Butter, to the quantity of eight Ounces, according to the bigness of your Pie, let it be refin'd and well clear'd from the Scum; adding a little chopt Marrow, if the Entertainment be prepar'd for a Flesh-day, otherwise, it must not be us'd. The Butter, being thus refin'd, must be taken off from the Fire, and set by for some time. Then, breaking three new laid Eggs, take the Whites, and make some Snow; into which you are to put fine Sugar, four Yolks of Eggs, candy'd Lemmon-peel cut very small, green Lemmon-peel grated, and a little Orange-flower-water, all proportionably beaten: Pour the Butter into the same Farce, and let all be well whipt together. In the mean while, having provided a fine Paste, let a piece of it be roll'd out very thin, to be laid on the Pie-pan that is butter'd a little, and let the sides of the Pie be shap'd with the Point of a Knife. Afterwards, the Farce being put into it, it must be bak'd with a little Fire on the top, only in the middle of the Pie-pan, lest it should take too brown a colour. To know when these sorts of Pies are sufficiently bak'd, 'tis requisite to observe, whether they are ready to slip off from the Baking-pans; and before they are serv'd up, they must be strew'd with fine Sugar, and ic'd over with the red-hot Fire-shovel. They may be garnish'd with *Rissoles*, Apple-fritters, or any thing else of the like nature.

The Lard Pan-pie is prepar'd after the same manner, only making use of tried Lard instead of Butter; but care must be taken, that it have not the least ill taste, and that the Eggs be always newly laid: If the Pies are large, a greater quantity of Eggs will be requisite.

As for the Marrow-pie, it may likewise be made as the former; that is to say, when the Marrow is refined or well melted, the Eggs are to be beaten in the same manner, and the Lemmon-peels, with the other Ingredients must be added. Others pound the Marrow, Sugar, and Lemmon-peel all together, with a little Flower and Orange-flower-water. Afterwards, they whip the Whites of the Eggs, with three or four Yolks, and mingle them with the rest in the Mortar. However, a fine Paste ought to be made as for the other Pies, and 'tis no great matter how different the Ways of making them may be, provided they tend to the producing of the same good Effect.

A sugar'd Pan-pie for an Intermeß.

Take five or six Biskets, March-panes or Macaroons, with Sugar, and four or five Yolks of Eggs; pound them in a Mortar, with a little Orange-flower-water; and let the whole Mass be laid upon Puff-paste. Then let the Pie be bak'd with a gentle Fire; and Iced over, till it comes to a fine colour.

An

An Artichoke-Tourte, or Pan-pie.

When the Artichoke-bottoms are well boil'd, and become very white, they may be put into a Pie, with fine Herbs, Chibbols chopt small, Pepper, Salt, Nutmeg and Butter. Cover your Pie with a Lid, and put into it a white Sauce, with a little Vinegar, when ready to be serv'd up to Table.

Otherwise, the Artichoke-bottoms may be pounded and strain'd thro' the Hair-sieve, with melted Butter or Lard, to make as it were a kind of Cream; adding two raw Yolks of Eggs, with Salt and Nutmeg: Let all be put into a very fine thin Paste, and when bak'd, serv'd up with Mutton-gravy and Lemmon-juice.

A pounded Macaroon may also be put into the Artichoke-cream, with Sugar, Cinnamon, candy'd Lemmon-peel, a little Milk-cream and Salt. This Pie may be made without a Lid, but before it is brought to Table, it must be ic'd over with Sugar, and Orange-flower-water.

An Asparagus-pan-pie.

Let the tender part of the Asparagus be cut, and the Tops reserv'd for garnishing. Afterwards, they must be scalded in Water, and dress'd in a Pie, with melted Lard, Marrow, or Butter, fine Herbs, Chibbols, Pepper, Salt and Nutmeg. This Pie ought to be cover'd with a Lid, and when bak'd, some Cream may be put into it, or Mutton-gravy, and the Yolk of an Egg.

A Spinage-pan-pie.

Take Spinage-leaves, and scald them in Water, or else stew them in an earthen Pot, with half a Glass of white Wine, to take away their Crudity. As soon as the Wine is consum'd, let the Spinage be drain'd, and chopt very small, season'd with a little Salt, Cinnamon, Sugar, Lemmon-peel, two Macaroons and sweet Butter. Then let them be put into fine Paste, and cover'd with Slips of cut Pastry-work; adding some Sugar and Orange-flower, as it is serving up to Table.

A

A Truffle-*pan-pie*.

Having cut the *Truffles* into Slices, and caus'd the Skin to be well peel'd off, they may be laid in order on a piece of fine Paste roll'd out for the Bottom-crust: Then let a little Flower be fried in Butter, with fine Herbs chopt small, and a whole Chibbol, and let all be put into the Pie; seasoned with Pepper, Salt and Nutmeg. This sort of Pies is not usually cover'd, but must be serv'd up with Lemmon-juice.

A Tourte *or Pan-pie made of* Mousserons, Morilles *and common Mushrooms*.

Let your Mushrooms be cut into Slices and laid upon a piece of fine Paste in the bottom of a Pie-pan, with fine Herbs, Chibbols, Salt, Nutmeg, fried Flower and Butter. Then cover your Pie with a Lid, wash it over, and when bak'd, serve it up, with Mutton-gravy and Lemmon-juice, after having taken away the Chibbols: A thickening Liquor may also be added with burnt Butter.

The Pan-pies of *Morilles* and *Mousserons* are usually made after the same manner.

An Egg-*pan-pie*.

Take the Yolks of Eggs, a Lump of Sugar, a little Butter and Orange-flower-water; make as it were a kind of Cream; and put it into a piece of very thin fine Paste rais'd with a little Border for the Side-crust: Then having grated some Lemmon-peel upon it, let it be bak'd and ic'd over, when ready to be brought to Table.

A Pan-*pie, with Sorrel-juice*.

After having pounded the Sorrel, to get the Juice, let it be put into a Dish, with Sugar, Cinnamon, Macaroons, a Lump of Butter, three Yolks of Eggs, candy'd Lemmon-peel grated and Orange-flowers: Then let all be boil'd together, as it were Cream, and afterwards laid upon a piece of very fine Paste in the bottom of a Baking-pan. When the Pie is bak'd, it may be serv'd up, with Sugar.

Pan-pies of divers Colours.

Another Pan-pie may be made of a kind of green Cream; mingling some Beet-juice with Pistachoes and Almonds, as they are straining thro' the Hair-sieve: For all the other sorts of Colours, see what has been deliver'd on that Subject, for Jellies and *Blanc-mangers*, in the second Article of *Jellies* under the Letter I.

Other sorts of Tourtes, or Pan-pies.

Many other sorts of Pan-pies may also be prepar'd, to be serv'd up, as the former, among the Intermesses, as well for Flesh-days, as those of Abstinence; particularly, Pies made of the Pulp of Oranges cut into Slices and laid upon fine Paste, with Sugar, a pounded Macaroon, Cinnamon and Pistachoes. The same thing may be done with green Lemmons; only some candy'd Lemmon-peel grated must be us'd instead of Pistachoes. Both these sorts of Pies are to be serv'd up, with Musked Sugar. Others may likewise be made of Pomegranate-kernels, candy'd Lemmon-peels, preserv'd Plums, cut Pistachoes, &c. For Almond-pies, it would be only requisite to follow the Directions, as well for the most proper Pastes to be used for that purpose, as the rest of the Managery, which have been laid down in the first and fourth Articles of *Almonds*, under the Letter A.

It may not be improper here to subjoin some other Pan-pies made of Fish, that are generally provided for Side-dishes, on Fish-days, *viz*.

A Cray-fish-Tourte, or Pan-pie.

Let the Cray-fish be stew'd in a Glass of white Wine, after they have been well wash'd; reserving the Claws and Tails: Let all the rest be pounded in a Mortar, to be strain'd thro' the Hair-sieve, with a little Broth, and melted Butter: Then the whole Mixture may be put into a Pan-pie, with Pepper, Salt, Nutmeg, young Chibbols and Mushrooms cut into pieces, and when the Pie is cover'd with a Lid, it must be wash'd over, in order to be bak'd, and serv'd up with Lemmon-juice.

Otherwise, the Flesh of the Cray-fish may be minc'd and put into

into a Pie, with Carps-roes, Pikes-livers, *Morilles*, common Mushrooms, Truffles, Butter and the other seasoning Ingredients, in order to be serv'd up with Lemmon or Orange-juice.

A Pan-pie made of Carps-roes and Tongues.

The Tongues and Roes of the Carps must be laid in order upon a piece of fine Paste, in the bottom of the Pan; seafon'd with Pepper, Salt, Nutmeg, fine Herbs, Chibbols, *Morilles*, common Mushrooms, *Truffles* and sweet Butter. Then, all being cover'd with a Lid of the same Paste, let the Pie be bak'd with a gentle Fire, and serv'd up with Lemmon-juice.

Pan-pies made of Pikes-livers.

These are to be seafon'd as the former, except that burnt Butter must be us'd, and a dissolved Anchovie put into them, with Capers and Lemmon-juice, before they are brought to Table.

A Salmon-pan-pie.

After having stew'd the Salmon for a while in Claret, it must be cut into Slices or *Filets*, and dress'd in the Pie, with candy'd Lemmon-peel, Dates, Sugar, Cinnamon, a little Pepper, Salt and Butter: When the Pie is half bak'd, pour in the Wine in which the Salmon was stew'd; let it also be ic'd over, and serv'd up, with Lemmon-juice.

Otherwise, the Salmon may be chopt small, with Mushrooms, fine Herbs, Chibbols, Artichoke-bottoms, Pepper, Salt and Nutmeg, and serv'd up in the same manner.

A Tourte, *or Pan-pie made of Smelts, Pike, Soles, and other sorts of Fish.*

Let your Fish be cut into *Filets*, with chopt *Morilles*, common Mushrooms and *Truffles*, to be laid on the bottom of the Pie; seafon'd with Pepper, Salt, Nutmeg, fine Herbs, Chibbols and pieces of Mushrooms: Or else the Bones and Heads of the Fish may be taken away and fried, to serve for Garniture. But the Pies must always be set on the Table, with Orange or Lemmon-juice.

An Oister-pan-pie.

This Pie is usually made after the same manner, only it will be requisite to add a little Bread-chippings, with Capers and a Slice of green Lemmon, as also the Liquor of the Oisters, before it is serv'd up to Table.

A Muscle-pan-pie.

The Muscles, being well cleans'd and wash'd, must be fried in a Pan, and clear'd from their Shells, in order to be dress'd in a Pie, with Mushrooms cut into pieces, *Morilles*, Pepper, Salt, Nutmeg, Thyme and Butter. When the Pie is half bak'd, the Muscle-liquor must be put into it, with Bread-chippings, as also Lemmon-juice, at the instant of serving it up to Table.

A Pan-pie of farced Tench.

When your Tenches are well cleans'd from their Slime, slit them on the Back, and take away the Flesh, so as the Head and Tail may stick to the Skin: Then mince this Flesh with Mushrooms, Carps-roes, fine Herbs, Pepper, Salt, Nutmeg and beaten Cloves; and, having stuff'd the Bones of the Fish with the same Farce, dress them in a Pie, with Oisters, Mushrooms, Carps-roes, Pikes-livers and Butter; adding half a Glass of white Wine, when the Pie is half-bak'd, and some Lemmon-juice, as it is serving up to Table.

Other Tourtes, or Pan-pies made of Fish, &c.

Tourtes, or Pan-pies, are likewise made of Perches, Tortoises, and many other Fishes; for which due Measures may be easily taken from the former, or from the particular Instructions given in their proper places, for the dressing of those sorts of Fish. To these may be added Pan-pies of *Beatils*, and others of Pigeons dress'd with a good Fish-farce, prepar'd with the Flesh of Eels, Pikes and Carps, with pounded Roes: To that purpose, the Rumps of those Pigeons must be made hollow, and a piece of a Pike's Liver, or some other stuff'd into it: Then they are to be stew'd a little in melted Butter, and put into a Pie, with artificial Cocks-combs and Veal-sweet-breads, made of the same Compound or Farce, and scalded separately in a Ladle. This Pie must be season'd with Pepper, Salt, Nutmeg, Mushrooms, Fish-roes, *Morilles* and sweet Butter; adding a little white Wine at last, and Lemmon-juice when serv'd up to Table.

Trotters.

A Side-dish of Sheeps-trotters farced.

Let the Trotters be well scalded, and afterwards stew'd in good Broth, with a little Parsly and Chibbol; taking care that they be not over-done. As soon as they are taken out, let the Feet be cut off, leaving the Legs; the Bones of which must be taken away, and the Skins spread upon the Table or Dresser, in order to be stuff'd with a little of the Farce of *Croquets*, or some other, and roll'd up one by one: Then, after having laid them in a Dish, and sprinkled them with a little melted Fat, they must be neatly breaded on the top, and brought to a Colour in the Oven. When they are colour'd, let the Fat be drain'd from them, and let the side of the Dish be rubb'd with a Shalot; pouring a little Ragoo upon them, or a Mushroom-cullis, before they are serv'd up hot to Table.

Another Way of dressing Sheeps-trotters.

Sheeps-trotters may also be dress'd with white Sauce, frying them in Lard, with fine Herbs, young Chibbols, Pepper, Salt and Nutmeg: The Sauce must be thicken'd with Yolks of Eggs and Rose-vinegar; garnishing the Dish with the Trotter-bones fried in Paste and Parsly.

Trouts.

A Side-dish of broil'd Trouts.

The Trouts may be either breaded, or left in their natural condition; for the latter, a Ragoo may be prepar'd, with *Mousserons*, *Truffles*, Fish-roes, and Pikes-livers fried brown, also an Anchovie, fine Herbs, and a few Capers. Let the Trouts be laid a soaking for some time in this Sauce, and afterwards serv'd up, with Lemmon-juice.

For

For the others, that you would have breaded, they ought to be steept in a good *Marinade*, for the space of a full Hour, after having cut them into pieces, to the end that they may take the whole relish: Then they may be broil'd over a gentle Fire, and sprinkled with Lemmon-juice, whilst the Dish is garnish'd with *Petits-patez*, *i. e.* little Pies made of Fish, or with Marinade

An Intermeß of Trouts on Flesh-days.

Having provided two or three good Trouts, let them be neatly gutted at the Gills, scrap'd and well wipt: Then, laying them on the Dresser, let the red-hot Fire-shovel be gently pass'd over them, yet so as not to touch them, and let it be re-iterated from time to time: When they are sufficiently harden'd by this means, they may be larded with small Slips of Bacon in rows. Afterwards, some good *Bards*, or thin Slices of Bacon being laid in the bottom of an oval Stew-pan, the larded Trouts must be set in order upon them; kindling a little Fire underneath, and putting some live Coals on the top of the Cover, to give the fish a fine colour: They must also be stirr'd at several times, lest they should stick to the bottom. When they are well colour'd, take away all the Bacon, soak your Trouts in good Gravy, with a little *Champagne*-wine, and an Onion stuck with Cloves, and let all be gently stew'd together, and well season'd in the same Pan. As soon as they are almost done enough, and little Sauce is left, let some *Truffles*, Mushrooms and all sorts of Garniture, according to the Season, be put into a little Gammon-essence, in order to make a well-season'd and somewhat thick Ragoo. Then dress your Trouts in a large Dish, either of an Oval or round Figure, and pour the Ragoo round about, after the Fat has been thoroughly drain'd off. The Dish may be garnish'd, if you please, with Artichoke-bottoms, *Andouillets*, or small Trout-collops well larded and order'd as those of Soles.

As for the large Sea-fish, they must be larded with thick Slips of Bacon, and when well tied up, they may be boil'd in a good court-*bouillon*, proper for Flesh-days, that is well season'd, and enrich'd with all sorts of exquisite Ingredients; adding a little champaigne-wine. When the Fish are ready, let them be dress'd in Oval Dishes, and let a Ragoo be turn'd upon them, made of all sorts of Garnitures. Some fresh Oisters may also be added, with their Liquor, or else a Carp-sauce, or one of Gammon-essence, may

may be prepar'd for that purpose; taking care that all be well clear'd from the Fat, and serv'd up hot to Table.

TRUFFLES.

The Way of dressing *Truffles* most in vogue, is that of a *Court-bouillon*, so as they may be stew'd in white Wine or Claret, and season'd with Pepper, Salt and Bay-leaves.

They may also be broil'd upon the Coals, slitting them in half to put in some white Pepper and Salt, and closing them up again, in order to be wrapt up in wet Paper and laid over a Fire that is not too quick: Then they may be serv'd up to Table, on a folded Napkin.

Or else, after having cleans'd your *Truffles*, cut them into Slices, and fry them in Lard or Butter, with Flower. Then they must be stew'd in a little Broth, with fine Herbs, Pepper, Salt and Nutmeg, and laid a soaking in a Dish, till there be little Sauce left; to be serv'd up, with Mutton-gravy and Lemmon-juice.

Otherwise, several Ragoo's may be made of *Truffles* and Capons-livers, as also *Tourtes* or Pan-pies; as it has been before observ'd: And in the Entertainments with Roots or Collations during the time of Lent, they may be eaten dry, with Oil, but they must be always set on the Table among the Intermesses.

TUNNIES.

Tunnies may be dress'd in Slices or *Filets*, with Poor Man's Sauce, and in a Sallet, with the *Ramolade* describ'd Pag. 41. They may also be fried in round Slices, and serv'd up in a kind of Fish-*Marinade*, such as is specified in the last Article of *Marinades*. Or else, they may be broil'd upon a Grid-iron, after having rubb'd and strew'd them with Pepper, Salt and Butter, to be eaten with Orange and burnt Butter. Otherwise, a *Poupeton* may be made of them; or they may be bak'd in a Pot-pie, putting the Flesh chopt small into a Pot, or earthen Pan, with burnt Butter and white Wine; also a piece of green Lemmon, Pepper, Salt, Mushrooms, or Chesnuts and Capers: The Dish may be garnish'd with Bread and Oisters fried, and Slices of Lemmon. For the other Tunny-pies, see the eighteenth Article of *Pies*, under the Letter P.

TURBOT.

A Side-dish of Turbot, in a Court-bouillon.

Let a well season'd *Court-bouillon* be prepar'd, with Vinegar, Verjuice, white Wine, Pepper, Salt, Cloves, Thyme, Onions, Lemmon and a Bay-leaf or two; let a little Water be also added, and at last some Milk, to render it very white: Then the Turbot must be leasurely stew'd in it, over a gentle Fire, and garnish'd with Parsly, Lemmon-slices laid upon it, and Violets in their Season.

A Turbot serv'd up among the Intermesses on Flesh-days.

Having scal'd and wash'd your Turbot, put it into a large Dish, with *Bards* or thin Slices of Bacon, seasoned with melted Lard, white Wine, Verjuice, a Faggot of Herbs, Bay-leaves, Pepper, Salt, Nutmeg, whole Cloves and green Lemmon: Then let it be cover'd with other *Bards*, and bak'd in a Pot between two Fires, or in an Oven: In order to serve it up to Table, take away the Bacon-*Bards*, dress your Turbot in a Dish, pouring upon it a good Ragoo of Mushrooms, made of the Sauce, and garnish it with Slices of Lemmon.

TURKEYS.

Among the several Ways of dressing Turkeys, either roasted or in a Ragoo, the two following are, without doubt, the most modern, and consequently deserve to be first taken notice of: One of these, is a Side-dish of Turkeys farced with fine Herbs, and the other a Side-dish of the same, dress'd with Onion-essence. Turkeys are also stew'd in a *Salmigund* or Hotch-potch, and with Gammon-sauce, as some other Messes specified in the General Table.

Turkeys farced with fine Herbs.

Let the Turkeys be truss'd for roasting, but not parboil'd: The Skin on their Breast must also be loosen'd, to the end that they may be conveniently stuff'd with a Farce made of raw Bacon,

con, Parsly, Chibbol, and most sorts of fine Herbs, all chopt small, pounded a little in a Mortar and well season'd: The Turkeys being thus farced between the Skin and the Flesh, as also a little in the Body, must be well spitted and roasted. Afterwards, they are to be dress'd in a Dish, pouring upon them a good Ragoo, of all sorts of Garnitures, and serv'd up hot to Table. The same thing may be done with Chickens, Pigeons and other sorts of Fowl, and to diversifie them on several Days, they may be bak'd or stew'd in a Pot between two Fires, after they have been stuff'd, as before. When they are ready, let them be well drain'd, and serv'd up with a good Ragoo of *Truffles*, and Veal-sweet-breads; all well dress'd, clear'd from the Fat, and garnish'd with small *Croquets*.

A Side-dish of Turkeys, with Onion-essence.

The Onions must be cut into Slices and fried in a Stew-pan, with Lard: Then the Fat being drain'd a little from them, they must be toss'd up again, with as much Flower as can be got up between your Fingers; adding some good Gravy, Cloves, and the other necessary seasoning Ingredients. When all have been stew'd together a little while, let them be strain'd thro' the Hair-sieve, and afterwards put into the Stew-pan a third time, with a few drops of Verjuice and a little Bread-cullis. In the mean while, the Turkeys having their Wings, Breast and Legs well tied up, ought to be roasted, and dress'd in a Dish; pouring the Sauce upon them, before they are serv'd up after the usual manner.

Other Side-dishes of Turkeys.

Sometimes young Turkeys, one of them larded, and the other only barded, or cover'd with thin Slices of Bacon, without being breaded, are roasted and serv'd up in Gravy.

At another time, your Turkeys being barded and roasted, take away their Legs, Wings and Breasts, and cut them into *Filets*, to be put into a Ragoo of Cucumbers fried brown, with a brown thickening Liquor, and a piece of Lemmon, as they are dressing.

V.

V.

VEAL.

IN several places of this Book, we have taken occasion to shew, how Veal may be dress'd in order to make a great number of Messes and Dishes for every Service; particularly, Veal-stakes for Side-dishes, Veal-cutlets, Pies made of a Fillet of Veal, &c. not to mention, a very great number of other Dishes that are made of Veal, or at least, in which Veal is us'd: So that it remains only to produce some other manners of dressing this sort of Meat, for separate Dishes.

A Side-dish of Veal, after the Italian Way.

Having provided some Slices or Stakes of Veal that are very tender, and cut them as it were to make *Fricandoes* or Scotch-collops; let them be beaten a little with the Cleaving-knife. Then let some good *Bards*, or thin Slices of Bacon be laid on the bottom of a Stew-pan; let the Veal-stakes be likewise laid in good order upon them; and let all be well season'd. The quantity of these Stakes must be adjusted, according to the bigness of your Dish or Plate; which being cover'd on the top, with other Bacon-*Bards*, the Pan must be set *à la Braise*, or between two Fires. When all have been sufficiently bak'd in this manner, take out all the *Bards* and the Meat a-part, and drain off the Fat; only leaving as much as will serve to make some brown Sauce, with a little Flower, in the same Stew-pan, but not too much: Afterwards, soaking it with good Gravy, put your Veal-stakes again into the Pan, and make an end of dressing them; with Veal-sweet-breads, *Truffles* cut into Slices, Mushrooms, boil'd Cocks-combs, two Slices of Lemmon, a Faggot of fine Herbs, a few drops of Verjuice, a bit of Shalot, and a little Bread-cullis to thicken the Sauce: But all must be well clear'd from the Fat, and brought hot to Table.

To dress Veal à la Bourgeoise.

Let some Veal-stakes be cut somewhat thick, and larded with a small wooden Larding-pin; the *Lardoons* being season'd a little, with Parsly, Chibbols, beaten Spices, Pepper and Salt:
Then

Then let several small *Bards* of Bacon be put into a Stew-pan, and let the Veal-stakes be laid in order upon them. The Fire ought to be very gentle at first, to the end that the Meat may sweat, and may be brought to a Colour on both Sides, by putting in a little Flower: When it is sufficiently colour'd, let it lye a soaking, with good clear Broth and boil gently. Afterwards, the Sauce must be thicken'd a little, and clear'd from the Fat, sprinkling it with a little Vinegar or Verjuice; so as the whole Mess may be conveniently dress'd in a Dish and serv'd up hot to Table.

A Loin of Veal in a Ragoo.

Lard your Loin with thick Slips of Bacon, season it with Pepper, Salt and Nutmeg, and when it is almost roasted, put it into a Stew-pan close cover'd, with Broth, a Glass of white Wine, some of the Dripping, fried Flower, a Bunch of Herbs, Mushrooms, and a piece of green Lemmon: Lastly, let all be serv'd up with short Sauce, after having taken away some of the Fat, and let the Dish be set out with larded Veal-sweet-breads, Cutlets, or other sorts of Garniture.

Other Ways of dressing a Quarter and Loin of Veal.

A Quarter of Veal may be larded with small Slips of Bacon, except the thick end; which is to be well breaded and season'd. It must be garnish'd with *Rissoles* and Capons-breasts, and some Veal-gravy must be pour'd upon it, when ready to be set on the Table.

It may also be marinated in an oval Stew-pan, and well order'd with the usual seasoning Ingredients: When it is roasted, take the Kidney to make farced Tosts to garnish the whole Quarter, or else an *Omelet*, and let the Dish be set out with *Marinades*, either of Cutlets or Chickens, or with farced Cutlets and fried Parsly.

Another middling Side-dish may be made of half a Loin of Veal, boil'd in a *Court-bouillon* that is well season'd and enrich'd; wrapping it up in a Napkin, lest it should break. It must be garnish'd with fried Bread, Parsly and Lemmon-slices.

A

A great Side-dish of a Quarter, or Crupper of Veal farced upon the Leg.

For the Ragoo that is proper for the stuffing of this Joint of Meat, see the Article of *Salpicon*, where it is explain'd at large; or else make a well season'd Hash of the Flesh that is taken out of the Leg, and cover it again neatly with the Skin. Then let that part, which is not larded, be breaded with Bread-crum; garnishing the Dish with Cutlets either farced or unfarced; or with *Rissoles* and Crusts of fried Bread, all brought to a fine colour: A Quarter of Veal may also be larded with *Hatlets*.

Several Ways of dressing a Breast of Veal.

A Side-dish may be made of a farced Breast of Veal, garnish'd with roasted *Poupiets* in the form of Quails, and a good Ragoo pour'd on the top: This Joint must be first roasted brown, and afterwards stew'd in a Pot. A piece of a Beef-stake must also be added, as it is dressing, to enrich it, and a brown thickening Liquor with Gravy, when ready to be serv'd up to Table. As for the Farce, it must be made of other Veal, with Beef-sewet or Marrow, Bacon, fine Herbs, Mushrooms and Veal-sweet-breads, and season'd with Pepper, Salt and Nutmeg. A Breast of Veal may also be boil'd in an earthen Pan, or in a Stew-pan, with Broth and a Glass of white Wine. Then some Mushrooms are to be fried in the same Lard, in which the Meat was dress'd; with a little Flower, and all must be mingled together.

Another Side-dish may be made of a Breast of Veal in a *Tourte* or Pan-pie, with a well season'd *Godivoe*, and good Garnitures; as for other Pies; adding a proper thickening Liquor and some Lemmon-juice, before it is brought to Table: Lastly, another Dish may be prepar'd of a farced or unfarced Breast of Veal, roasted and put into a Ragoo, with Lemmon-juice, when serv'd up; garnishing it with Veal-sweet-breads, Cocks-combs and Mushrooms fried: Or else the Breast of Veal being first parboil'd, may be marinated in Vinegar, with Pepper, Salt and Bay-leaves: Afterwards it may be flower'd and well fried, in order to be serv'd up with fried Parsly, and the rest of the Sauce.

T   VEAL.

VEAL-SWEET-BREADS.

Besides the Place that Veal-sweet-breads have in all the best sorts of Ragoo's, as it plainly appears in very many Particulars; several separate Dishes may be made of them, or Out-works, both for Side-dishes and Intermesses, of which the following, is one of the most considerable.

Veal-sweet-breads farced à la Dauphine.

Let some good Veal-sweet-breads be scalded a little, and larded with boil'd Gammon: In the mean while, having prepar'd a delicious and somewhat thick Farce, make a Hole with the point of a Knife on the Side of your Sweet-breads; but so as it may not pass quite thro': Then they must be neatly stuff'd in that Hole and bak'd in a Pot, or Pan between two gentle Fires; whilst a good Ragoo is making for them, of *Mousserons*, common Mushrooms, *Truffles* and Artichoke-bottoms: All being well dress'd some Cocks-combs stuff'd with the same Farce must be added and a little Chicken-cullis, to the end that the Sauce may not turn black: Then having thoroughly clear'd the Sweet-breads from the Fat, let them be put into the Ragoo and stew'd a little: Afterwards the whole Mess must be dress'd in a Dish, squeezing in the Juice of an Orange, and set hot on the Table.

Other Ways of dressing Veal-sweet-breads.

Otherwise the Veal-sweet-breads, being larded with thin Slips of Bacon and roasted, may be order'd with a good Ragoo, or Sauce pour'd upon them: Or else, after having been marinated, cut into Slices and flower'd, they may be fried, in order to be serv'd up, with fried Parsly and Lemmon-juice: Or lastly, different Ragoo's may be made of them, *viz.* sometimes with a white Sauce; sometimes with *Morilles*, and common Mushrooms; and sometimes with *Truffles*; but they must be always set among the Intermesses.

VENISON, *see* Deer, Hinds, Roe-bucks, Stags, wild Boars, &c.

VENISON-PASTIES, *see* PASTIES.

W.

W.

WHITINGS.

Whitings may be dress'd in *Casserole*, after the same manner as many other sorts of Fish: They may also be fried, and serv'd up with Orange-juice and white Pepper; to which purpose, they must be slit on the Back, and strew'd with Pepper and Salt: They must also be steept in Vinegar, flower'd and dipt in a thin Paste or Batter, before they are put into the Frying-pan. Otherwise Whitings may be farced; as it appears in the Article of a *Miroton* for Fish-days, and their *Filets* may not only be serv'd up in a Sallet, as it has been observ'd Pag. 41. but also in several sorts of Ragoo's and even in a Standing-pie, in a *Tourte*, or Pan-pie and in Potage; for which see the respective Articles whereto they belong, as those of Pikes, Soles, &c.

WOOD-COCKS.

How to make a Side-dish of Wood-cocks, with Wine, &c.

Take Wood-cocks and cut them into Quarters, as it were Chickens for a white Fricasy; as also some *Truffles*, cut into Slices, with Veal-sweet-breads, *Mousserons* and common Mushrooms; all which are to be fried together, and soak'd with good Gravy: Afterwards, two Glasses of white or red Wine may be pour'd in, and when the whole Mess is well stew'd and season'd; a Wood-cock-cullis, to thicken the Sauce, or some other good Cullis, accordingly as it may stand with your Convenience. A Spoonful of Gammon-essence may also be added, and all must be thoroughly clear'd from the Fat. Then lay your Wood-cocks in order in a Dish, turn the Ragoo upon them, and squeez in the Juice of a Lemmon, before they are brought hot to Table.

To make a Salmigund *or Hotch-potch of Wood-cocks, with Wine.*

When the Wood-cocks are half roasted, let them be cut into pieces, and put into a Stew-pan with Wine, proportionably to their quantity: Let some chopt Mushrooms and *Truffles* be also thrown

thrown in, with a few Anchovies and Capers and let all be well stew'd together. Then the Sauce being thicken'd with a good Cullis, the Wood-cocks must be dress'd and kept hot, without boiling: Afterwards, having drain'd off all the Fat, and squeez'd in the Juice of an Orange, they may be serv'd up hot to Table.

A Side-dish may be also made of Wood-cocks in *Sur-tout*; for which see the eighth Article of *Pigeons* dress'd in that manner, under the Letter P; and for a hot Pie of Wood-cocks and Partridges, recourse may be had to the first Article of *Pies*.

The End of the Court and Country Cook.

NEW

NEW INSTRUCTIONS FOR Confectioners;

DIRECTING

How to Preserve all sorts of Fruits, as well dry, as liquid; also how to make divers Sugar-works, and other fine Pieces of Curiosity belonging to the Confectionary Art.

CHAP. I.

Of the different Ways of Boiling Sugar; of the Choice of it, and of the Manner of Clarifying it.

FOrasmuch as the Ground-work of the Confectioner's Art, depends upon the different Ways of Boiling Sugar, it is requisite in the first place, to give a particular Account of them; to the end that the Reader may more readily apprehend the meaning of several Terms hereafter us'd to express them, and that unprofitable Repetitions may be avoided; which would inevitably happen if they were explain'd in every distinct Article, as the variety of Matter would require. These Boilings then, are perform'd by degrees, and bear the following Denominations; that is to say, Sugar
may

may be boil'd till it becomes *Smooth, Pearled, Blown, Feather'd, Crack'd* and *Caramel:* These Degrees are also distinguish'd with respect to their proper Qualifications; as the lesser and the greater Smooth, the lesser and the greater Pearled, Feathered a little, and a great deal; and so of the rest.

The Boiling of Sugar call'd Smooth.

As soon as your Sugar is clarified, and set again on the Fire in order to be boil'd, you may know when it has attain'd to its smooth Quality, by dipping the Tip of your Fore-finger into it; afterwards applying it to your Thumb, and opening them a little, a small Thread or String sticks to both, which immediately breaks and remains in a Drop upon the Finger: When this String is almost imperceptible, the Sugar is only boil'd till it becomes a little smooth, and when it extends it self farther before it breaks, 'tis a sign that the Sugar is very smooth. To avoid scalding your self, in making this Experiment; as it may happen, if your Finger were directly dipt into the Sugar, you need only take out the Skimmer, which ought always to be kept in the Copper-pan to stir the Sugar from time to time, and to cause it to boil equally: Then holding it a little while on the top, after having shaken it, touching the Pan, with the Handle of the Skimmer, receive the Sugar that still runs from it, and only pass the tip of your Finger upon the edge of the said Skimmer, which is sufficient to know, whether the Sugar is become smooth, or not, by observing the former Directions.

The Pearled Boiling.

After having boil'd your Sugar, a little longer, re-iterate the same Experiment, and if in separating your Fingers, as before, the String continues sticking to both, the Sugar is Pearled. The greater Pearled Boiling is when the String continues in like manner, altho' the Fingers were stretch'd out farther, by entirely spreading the Hand. This sort of Boiling may also be known by a kind of round Pearls that arise on the top of the Liquor.

The

The Blown Boiling.

When your Sugar has boil'd a few more Walms, hold the Skimmer in your Hand, and having shaken it a little, as before, beating the side of the Pan, blow thro' the Holes of it, from one side to the other; and if certain Sparks as it were, or small Bubbles fly out, the Sugar is come to the degree of Boiling, call'd *Blown*.

The Feathered Boiling.

When after some other Seethings, you blow thro' the Skimmer, or shake the *Spatula* with a Back-stroke, till thicker and larger Bubbles rise up on high, then the Sugar is become Feathered: And when after frequent Tryals, you perceive these Bubbles to be thicker, and in greater quantity, so that several of them stick together, and form as it were a flying Flake; then the Sugar is greatly Feathered.

The Crack'd Boiling.

To know when the Sugar has attain'd to this degree, a Pot or Pan, must be provided, with cold Water: Then dip the tip of your Finger into that Water, and having dextrously run it into the boiling Sugar, dip it again immediately into the Water, at least if you would avoid scalding your self: Thus keeping your Finger in the Water, rub off the Sugar, with the other two; and if it breaks afterwards, making a kind of crackling Noise, it is come to the point of Boiling, call'd *Crack'd*.

The Caramel Boiling.

If in the condition, to which the Sugar is reduc'd in the former Boiling, it be put between the Teeth, it would stick to them as it were Glue or Pitch; but when it is boil'd to *Caramel*, it breaks and cracks, without sticking in the least. Therefore care must be taken to observe every Moment, when it has attain'd to this last degree of Boiling; putting the preceding Directions into Practice, to know, when it is Crack'd, and afterwards biting the Sugar so order'd with your Teeth, to try whether it will stick to them: As soon as you perceive, that it does

T 4   not

not stick, but on the contrary, cracks and breaks clever, take it off immediately from the Fire; otherwise it would burn, and be no longer good for any manner of use, because it will always taste burnt: Whereas with respect to the other well-condition'd Boilings, if after having preserv'd any Sweet-meats, some Sugar be still left, that is Crack'd, for example, or greatly Feathered, and that is of no further use in that condition, it would be only requisite to put as much Water to it, as is needful to boil it over again, and then it may be brought to whatsoever degree you shall think fit, and even intermix'd with any other sort of Sugar, or Syrup.

This last *Caramel*-boiling is proper for Barley-sugar, and for certain small Sugar-works call'd by that Name, which shall be hereafter explain'd: The Pearled Boiling is generally us'd for all sorts of Confits, that are to be kept for a considerable time: Some cause their Sugar to be boil'd to a higher degree, but it is soon undone and reduc'd to the Pearled Quality, by the Moisture and Coldness of the Fruits, that are thrown into it. The Use of the other Ways of Boiling shall be shewn in treating of the several sorts of Sweet-meats, for which they are requisite.

It is also necessary to understand, That sometimes Fruit may be preserv'd with thin Sugar, that is to say, when two Ladles full of clarified Sugar are put to one of Water, four to two, six to three, and so on proportionably to the quantity of the Fruit, that ought to be well soak'd in it: To that purpose, the Sugar and Water must be heated together somewhat more than lukewarm, to be poured upon them.

The choice of Sugar.

For the best manner of Preserving Fruits, a Confectioner ought to make choice of the finest and whitest Loaf-sugar, that can be procur'd; such as is hard and ringing, nevertheless light and sweet, without the least sharpness. If there be occasion to use Powder-sugar, the whitest and cleanest must likewise be chosen: However both these sorts ought to be clarified; so that there will be much less Work to do than otherwise, if the Loaf-sugar or Powder-sugar were not well-conditioned.

How

How to clarifie Sugar.

The Confectioner's Work begins with the clarifying of Sugar; to which purpose; an earthen Pan must be provided with Water, into which an Egg is to be broken with the Shell, or more, according to the quantity of Sugar: Then let all be whipt together with Birchen Rods or a Whisk, and pour'd upon the Sugar that is to be melted: Afterwards, having set it over the Fire, stirr it continually and take off the Scum carefully when it boils: As often as the Sugar rises, a little cold Water must be pour'd in, to hinder it from running over and to raise the Scum; adding also the Froth of the White of an Egg, whipt a-part. When after having well scumm'd the Liquor, there is only left a small whitish Froth, and not black and foul, as before; and when you perceive the Sugar to be altogether clear upon the Skimmer, in laying it upon the Surface, it must be remov'd from the Fire, and being pass'd thro' the Straining-bag it will be perfectly clarified.

When a considerable quantity of Sugar is clarified at once, and consequently a great deal of Scum rises, which is always accompanied with a little Sugar; this Scum being temper'd with Water, may be boil'd in the same Pan, into which it was put, and afterwards all strain'd thro' the Bag.

Private Persons, who in preserving Fruits, use only four or five Pounds of Sugar at once, to avoid this trouble, and yet not lose any Sugar, may clarifie it in the following manner. Let the Sugar be melted with Water, and set over the Fire, with the White of a whipt Egg. As soon as it boils and swells up ready to run over, a little cold Water must be pour'd in to give it a Check: But when it rises a second time, let it be remov'd from the Fire, and set by about a quarter of an Hour, during which space, it will sink, and a black Scum will only settle on the top, which is to be gently taken off with the Skimmer: Afterwards, strain it thro' the Bag and it will be sufficiently clarified. Indeed Sugar so order'd is not so clear nor so white as the former, nevertheless it will serve to make all sorts of good Comfits.

The Water that is proper for the boiling of Sugar, ought to be taken out of a Spring or River, and very clear; altho' for many other Things Well-water may also be us'd: The lesser quantity of Water is put to the Sugar, which is to be melted and clarified, so much the less time is requisite for the performing of
the

the neceſſary Boilings; whereas the contrary happens, when there is a great deal of Water, becauſe it muſt all evaporate. As to this particular, no ſcruple ought to be made, concerning a Maxim deliver'd in ſome Books, *viz.* That in cauſing Sugar to be boil'd a-part without the Fruit, its beſt Spirits exhale with the Water, and it becomes only capable of Preſerving the upper Part of the Fruits, as being made greaſie and thick by the Boiling; whereas (in their Opinion) the Fruits are more eaſily penetrated, when both are boil'd together in the Beginning: For this Aſſertion is contrary, not only to the general Practice of Confectioners, but alſo to Experience and Truth; ſince the Fruits always appear to have as much Sugar in the Inſide, as on the Surface, provided they be well order'd, which may be done by working and boiling them, ſeveral Days, in the manner hereafter deſcrib'd. For altho' generally ſpeaking, the Preſerving of Fruit may be finiſh'd in one Day; yet it is expedient that divers be taken up in carrying on the Work, if you would have them kept for any conſiderable time, and order'd as they ought to be.

The common People only judge the Sugar to be ſufficiently boil'd, when the Drops that are put upon a Plate grow thick, as it were a Jelly and ceaſe to run, any longer; Indeed this Way of boiling is proper for certain Jellies of Fruit, and for *Compotes*; but no great Progreſs would be made in the Art of Preſerving, if nothing elſe were known: So that it is abſolutely neceſſary to underſtand all the different Degrees of boiling above-ſpecified, and the diſtinction is only made by thoſe Tryals, at leaſt without a long Practice; and even the moſt skilful Confectioners know nothing otherwiſe, after the Feathered Boiling.

Chap. II.

Of the Utenſils and Inſtruments neceſſary for a Confectioner, and of their Uſe.

THe underſtanding of this Article ought alſo to be preſuppos'd, without which what is hereafter laid down, cannot be well apprehended; as neither is it poſſible to put thoſe Directions

rections into Practice, if the greater part of these Utensils be wanting. Therefore it is requisite to provide Pans, with their Skimmers, and *Spatula's*, one or two Furnaces, Sieves, Grates, a Stove, a Campain-oven, a Cistern, several Mortars, a Marble-stone, and a Syringe; not to mention the Trunks, Boxes, Pots, Glasses, and some other little Knacks, that are very common.

The Pans ought to be of several Sizes, some flat and others hollow, for different Uses. The flat Pans are for those Fruits that ought to be soak'd in their Syrup, without laying them in heaps one upon another; and the hollow ones, are us'd when any Thing is to be preserv'd dry, by boiling and working the Sugar; as for Oranges, Lemmons and Conserves. All these Pans are usually made of red Copper, as also the Skimmers and *Spatula's*, and there are a few Houses of Persons of Quality, where they are wanting; otherwise such Pans may be us'd as are at hand, and the ordinary hollow ones may serve well enough, for all sorts of Operations.

Upon this occasion, it may not be improper to undeceive those, who upon the Asseveration of some Writers, might be induc'd to believe, That the Copper causes an ill Taste in preserved Fruts, when they are set by in a Pan, from the Fire; for as yet it could never be perceiv'd, altho' it is very customary to leave them therein indifferently during several Days: Indeed care ought to be taken to keep them clean, and not to follow the Example of some Slovenly Work-men who when they intermix some old Syrups, let in the green Rust that sticks on the sides of the Pan, with a great deal of other Filth; which does not hinder them from proceeding in their Work, and disposing of all Promiscuously with a great deal of Assurance.

It is expedient, that all the Pans be stampt according to the Standard, or have the mark of their Weight engrav'd upon them, in order to know the quantity of Sugar that has been boil'd in them, when they are put into one Scale, and the Fruits, which are to be preserv'd into the other, with the Tare of what the Pan weighs; to regulate and proportion the Weight of both, conformably to the Directions hereafter given.

The management of a Furnace is sufficiently known, only those of Confectioners ought to be somewhat larger than the common ones, to the end that the Fire spreading itself in a greater extent round about the Pan, the Sugar and Fruits which are to be preserv'd may boil more equally on all sides.

Upon

Upon any emergent Occasion, almost all the Operations may be perform'd over the ordinary Kitchen-furnaces, if they may be freely us'd without any disturbance.

The Sieves are also a sort of Instruments the use of which is not unknown: They serve to make an end of drying the Pastes of Fruits, when they are turn'd; to strain Jellies and Syrups; to drain Fruits, that have been laid in Water, and for several other good purposes. A finer Sieve call'd a *Drum* must likewise be provided, to sift powder'd Sugar, that is us'd in divers Works.

To these must be added a kind of Cullander to drain the Fruits, either after they have been scalded in Water, or when they are taken out of the Sugar. This Instrument, for want of which an ordinary Cullander may be us'd, is a Piece of Copper or Tin somewhat hollow, bor'd thro' with many Holes, and flexible, so as the Fruits may be easily slipt into it at pleasure. When Fruits taken out of the Sugar are to be drain'd; it is requisite to set this Cullander over a Pan to receive the Sugar that drops from it.

The same thing may be done with the Grates, which are made of several Circles of Wires set very close together in form of Cross-bars; upon which those Comfits are chiefly laid, that are to be preserv'd dry, whilst the Sugar is preparing to ice them over.

The Stove is a little Closet, well stopt up on all sides, where there are several Stories, or Rows of Shelves, one above another, made of the same sort of Wires, to hold the Sweet-meats that are to be dried, and which are usually laid upon Slates, pieces of Tin, smooth Boards, or Sieves; having first caus'd the Syrup out of which they were taken, to be drain'd off. Then a Pan, or large Chafing-dish, with Fire, is to be set on the bottom, and sometimes two, if there are many Things to be dried, or if the Business requires dispatch. Thus the Stove must be shut up close, and in the Evening, or the next Morning, the Sweet-meats contain'd in it, either Pastes or Fruits, must be turn'd, to cause them to dry equally: The latter are to be strew'd with Sugar, except some sorts, as green Apricocks and green Almonds; but the Pastes must not be turn'd again, till they become firm, some of which are also strew'd with Sugar on one side: Then they may be gently remov'd from the Slates, with a Knife and laid upon others, or upon Sieves, as it has been already hinted: Afterwards they must be

put

put again into the Stove, changing the Stories, if it be judg'd expedient, and renewing the Fire: So that the Art of Preserving cannot be put into Practice, without one of these Stoves, or some other Machine of the like nature; for in drying Sweetmeats at the Fire, they would not receive the heat equally on all sides, and the Fruits would be shrivell'd up: It would also be too tedious to dry them in the Sun; because they would give, and grow soft during the coolness of the Night, and at other times, when depriv'd of the Raies of that great Luminary.

The Campain-oven is a portable Oven made of red Copper, three or four Inches high, of a convenient length, and raised a little upon Feet, so that a Fire may be kindled underneath, as occasion requires: The Cover or Lid of it ought to have Ledges, to hold Fire likewise, when it is necessary to put some on the top, or on both sides: This Cover must be taken off from time to time, to see whether that which is contain'd in the Oven be sufficiently bak'd or brought to a good Colour. For want of such an Instrument, the Kitchen-oven of Masons-work, or some other may be us'd, accordingly as a convenient opportunity may be found; or else a Silver-dish and certain large Baking-pans that are order'd almost in the same manner.

The Cistern is another kind of portable Instrument, in form of a Box, into which *Blanc-mangers*, Jellies, Creams, and more especially Liquors are put, in order to be iced. The Construction and Use of it shall be hereafter explain'd, in treating of those respective Articles.

Besides the Stone-mortar, in which Sugar, Almonds and other necessary Ingredients are pounded, another little one of Brass or some other Metal must be also provided for the beating of Cinnamon, Cocheneal, Cloves, Amber and other Things that ought to be reduc'd to a finer Powder.

The Marble-stone, which is much of the same nature as that us'd by Painters for the grinding of their Colours, serves only to prepare the Barley-sugar, that is rubb'd with Oil of Olives.

The little Trunks, Boxes, Pots and Glasses, are different Vessels proper to hold dry or wet Sweet-meats, and such may be us'd as are at hand.

A Confectioner ought also to be furnish'd with a Strainingbag, to clarifie his Sugar, and to strain other Liquors; a Rolling-pin to roll out pieces of Paste for crackling Crusts and March-panes; divers Tin-moulds to shape them, and to dress the

the Pastes of Fruits; a Syringe made on purpose for other sorts of March-pane and Biskets; certain wooden Stamps, to make an Impression upon the *Pastils*; and several other little Knacks, by the means of which he may set off his Work to the best advantage.

C H A P. III.

Of the Confectioner's Employment throughout the whole Year, according to the Seasons of the Flowers and Fruits.

After the Instructions contain'd in the fore-going Chapter, it is expedient, before we proceed to the main Body of the Work, to expose to publick View, every Thing that may be preserv'd, as well Fruits and Flowers as other sorts of Works; to the end that the Confectioners and other Officers may have a general Idea of what they are to perform, and at the same time, of what may be serviceable in every particular Season.

January and *February.*

During these two Months *Sevil*-Oranges, those of the Port, and others, are usually preserv'd Whole, in Quarters, or in Sticks: Pastes, Conserves and Marmelades, are also made of them; and their Peels are candy'd either in *Zests*, or in Faggots.

Lemmons, *Cedres*, and yellow Citrons, are preserv'd after the same manner; and if the Provisions that were made of other sorts of preserved Fruits are now consum'd, that Defect may be reciprocally supply'd by these; the pleasant Variety of which will be very grateful, and give a great deal of satisfaction.

March and *April.*

These are the two first Months of the Year that afford Matter for new Comfits, that is to say, Violets, which are the first Flowers of a fragrant smell that the Earth brings forth, after

it

it has been deliver'd from the Tyranny of the sharp Winter.

With these Flowers, Conserves and Pastes are made, as also Syrup of Violets, the gross Substance of which may be kept in Marmelade; to make dry Pastes, at other times: For want of these, when it is requisite to prepare any Thing, that has the taste and smell of a Violet, Indigo and Powder of Orrice are generally us'd; particularly for *Pastils* and Mosses, which are Sugar-works that may be made in any Season.

May.

In this Month green Goose-berries first appear, of which *Compotes* and Jellies are made: They are also preserv'd liquid for the rest of the Year, either for Tarts, or to be serv'd up again in *Compote,* upon certain Occasions.

Green Apricocks come about the same time; affording Matter likewise for *Compotes,* Pastes and Marmelades: But they are chiefly preserv'd dry, and kept for a considerable time.

Green Almonds, which belong to the same Season, may be order'd after as many different manners, *viz.* for *Compotes,* Pastes and Marmelades, as well as preserv'd dry or liquid, in order to be us'd upon any emergent Occasion.

Straw-berries begin likewise to appear, which may be serv'd up, not only in their natural Condition, but also in *Compotes,* to diversifie the former Banquets.

June.

This Month affords good store of Rasberries, Cherries and Currans: *Compotes,* Conserves and Pastes are frequently made of the first of these Fruits; and 'tis now a proper time to begin to Preserve them dry and liquid.

Cherries, as soon as any ripe ones can be procur'd, are likewise put into *Compotes,* half Sugar and Conserves: They may be iced over with Powder-sugar, and as this Fruit comes to a fuller growth, or when better sorts of them may be gather'd, they are preserv'd in Ears, in Bunches and after other manners: Cakes or Pastes are then prepar'd with Cherries, as also Marmelade, and at last they are preserv'd liquid, in order to be kept for a considerable time: A Jelly may be also made of them, and the Juice extracted from those that are boil'd for Pastes, and of others out of which the Stones were taken, to be preserv'd, ferv'd, may be us'd to very good purpose, in that Jelly, and for the Liquor call'd *Ratafiaz*, as well as the Syrup of those that are dried.

As for Currans; Pastes, Conserves and *Compotes*, are first made of them, besides those that are iced; others are preserv'd in Bunches and liquid; and afterwards Marmelade is made of them, with Jellies of several sorts. Moreover, Syrups and Liquors are prepar'd with all these sorts of Fruit.

This is also a proper time for the Preserving of Orange-flowers dry, and for the making of Conserves, Pastes and Marmelade of them; which may be serviceable during the rest of the Year; because now there is the greatest plenty of these Flowers.

Conserves and Syrup of Roses are likewise made; so that this is one of the Months, in which the most Pains is to be taken, and that affords the greatest Variety of Fruits and Flowers at once.

July.

The Fruits of the former Month still take up the greater part of this, and the Preserving of them is continu'd, after the above-mentioned Ways. This is the chief time for wet and dry Cherries, as also for the Jellies and Marmelades of Currans and Rasberries.

In the beginning of the Month, white Walnuts are preserv'd, either liquid or dry, to be kept during the whole Year, and a little afterwards ripe Apricocks, of which *Compotes* and Pastes are first made: Others are par'd in order to be preserv'd with half Sugar, or in Ears, and Marmelade is made of them, which is us'd in many Things, out of the Season, particularly, for drying the Paste; for Apricock-pastils; or the Royal March-pane. At the same time, the Syrup and *Ratafiaz* of Apricocks are usually prepar'd.

Pears now begin to provide Employment for the Confectioner, and to afford an agreeable Variety: So that *Compotes* may be made of them, and Muscadine-pears may be iced, to the number of six or seven in Clusters, as they are; whilst the *Blanquets* are preserv'd, and some few other sorts dried.

There are also Plums and Grapes in the end of the Month, and altho' the latter are fine enough then to appear in their natural Colour; yet they are sometimes iced with powder'd Sugar. The same thing is done with Plums; besides that Pastes

are

are already made of them, and they may be put into *Compotes*, or into half-Sugar, to be dried.

August.

Much more Pains may be taken in this Month, in ordering these latter Fruits, because they are succeffively renew'd, by other kinds that are more proper for Preserving. Thus Orange-plums and Amber-plums, those of *Ifle-verd* and others are preserv'd dry to be kept: Pastes and Marmelades are made of them, and they are still iced, and put into *Compotes*.

The same thing is done with the Pears in their Season, more especially the *Rouffelet*, or Ruffetin, and some others, that are of an exquisite taste.

There are also certain Plums, proper for drying, in order to make Prunes, as occasion serves.

Figs are preserv'd and dried in the same Month, and they may be iced with Powder-sugar, as well as Grapes: Syrup of Mulberries is likewise prepar'd, and some think fit to preserve them: Apples are put into *Compotes*, and preserv'd after some other manners.

About the end of the Month, Girkins or small Cucumbers, Samphire, Purflain and other Herbs are pickled with Vinegar and Salt, for the Winter-fallets.

September.

Plums continue still, for a confiderable time, and Apples and Pears much longer: So that new *Compotes*, Pastes and Marmelades may be made of them, and the best ought to be chosen for that purpose; such as the *Bon-chretien*, the *Bergamot*, and the Summer-*Certoe*, among the Pears: This last is also preserv'd dry.

Peaches, which continue for a long while, likewife furnish Matter for Pastes, *Compotes* and Marmelade, and they may be order'd so as to make dry Sweet-meats.

Moreover, Bell-grapes are then preserv'd liquid, and Pastes, Jellies and *Compotes* are made of them. Muscadine-grapes are order'd in the same manner, and serve to make a very delicious sort of *Ratafiaz*.

Barberries, which are generally ripe at the same time, are proper for Conferves.

October.

In this Month and the following, you have other sorts of Apples and Pears, for all the above-mentioned Uses, and also for Jellies, if you shall think fit to prepare them.

But this is the chief time, for making the Pastes, Jellies and Marmelade of Quinces, as also Comfits with *Must* or sweet Wine and others, which nevertheless only fall under the management of the Country People.

The Officers and Butlers are otherwise employ'd in this Season, that is to say, in gathering the Fruits, that ought to be in their Custody, which requires a more than ordinary Skill and Precaution.

November and December.

Forasmuch as the Fruits of the Earth now cease, recourse must be had to the Provisions that have been made during the preceding Months; as well with respect to dry and wet Sweetmeats, as to Jellies and Marmelades, which may be dried, in order to make Pastes that are wanting: A greater quantity of roasted Apples and Pears are likewise prepar'd, from time to time, with some *Compotes* of Chesnuts, which may also be iced and dried.

Lastly, The assistance of Oranges and Lemmons, which are brought over at this time, is considerable, more especially *China-Oranges*; but the others are not preserv'd till the following Months.

During the whole Year.

Besides all these sorts of Sweet-meats, that depend on the Season of every particular kind of Fruit, there are divers Sugar-works and others, that may be prepar'd throughout all the Year: Such are several sorts of Almonds, Biskets, March-panes, *Meringues*, and Pastils; as also, the *Caramel*, *Sultans*, Mosses, candy'd Comfits, and some others, which with the raw Fruits, serve at all times, for the better filling up of a Desert, more especially in Winter, and upon other Occasions, when preserved Fruits are wanting.

Besides

New Instructions for Confectioners.

Besides these Employments, the Confectioners and other Officers, ought to be diligent in keeping their Sweet-meats in good order; and to that purpose, it is requisite from time to time, to inspect those that are liquid, to see whether they are not grown sour or musty, and to remedy such Accidents; as also to change the Papers of those that are in the Boxes; and to take care that they be not laid up in any Place that is too moist; observing many other Precautions which their own Discretion, may sufficiently suggest to them.

Those Officers that are entrusted with the management of the raw Fruits, ought in like manner to apply themselves to that purpose; and thus there is no time, but what may be taken up, in some of these Employments; if to them be added, what is requisite for the preparing of the Sallets, dressing of Deserts, and performing the other Duties incumbent on such Officers, especially in Noble-mens Houses.

In the Confectioner's Apartment, instead of some part of the latter Functions, they may be employ'd to very good purpose, in the making of Sugar-plums; but it would be needless to shew the manner of carrying on that Work; because it depends upon an habitual Practice, that is not exercised in an Office, nor in the Houses of private Persons, where this Book may give sufficient Drections for managing all the other Concerns: Therefore, the Utensils proper for that Business, are not explain'd among the others in the fore-going Chapter: So that all this Tackle is left to those who are Confectioners by Trade; and if any Persons are desirous to be of that Number, the Apprenticeship that ought to be serv'd, well supply the defect of our Silence as to these Matters.

Let us now proceed to shew the best Method of managing all the rest, and begin with the Fruits, that are to be preserv'd dry or liquid, almost according to the natural Order of their Seasons: Afterwards, the same Order shall be observ'd in treating of the *Compotes*, Marmelades and Pastes, which we have thought fit to describe all together under their respective Articles. Lastly, a particular Account shall be given of the Sugar-works and others, that may be made in any Season of the Year; comprehending in general, every Thing that relates to the Art of preserving of Sweet-meats with Sugar; and even discovering the choicest Secrets of the Confectioner's Trade: As it appears from the Contents of the Chapters, and the general Table of the principal Matters.

CHAP.

Chap. IV.
Of green Apricocks.

THe first Fruits that present themselves to be preserv'd, after green Goose-berries, which do not properly belong to this Place, are green Apricocks: To that purpose, they are usually taken, before their Stones begin to grow hard, and they are preserv'd with their Skin; as also others pared, which appear much more fine and clear. Both these Ways may be perform'd according to the following Method.

How to prepare and boil green Apricocks.

Those Apricocks that are design'd to be preserv'd with their Skin, ought first to be well clear'd from the soft Hair, or Down with which they are cover'd, and this may be done by the means of a good Lye, in which they are to to be scalded after the same manner as green Almonds. To that purpose, let some Water with new Ashes be pour'd into a large Pan, and set over the Fire, scumming off all the Coals that rise on the top: When this Lye has boil'd for some time, and you perceive by the Taste, that it is become sweet and oily, remove it from the Fire, and having set it by for a while, take all the clear Liquor: Then set it over the Fire again, and as soon as it begins to boil, put three or four Apricocks into it, observing whether they be well cleans'd, by that means: If the Experiment succeeds, the rest may be thrown in, but care must be taken to keep them from boiling, by stirring them about continually with the Handle of the Skimmer. The Apricocks being thus sufficiently scalded, must be taken out, toss'd a little in a Cloth, and wash'd in fair Water: Afterwards, you must run them thro' the middle with a Knitting-needle, and throw them as they are so order'd, into other fresh Water: To cause them to recover their green Colour, the Water is to be chang'd again, and they must be boil'd over a quick Fire; taking out some of them from time to time, and pricking them with a Pin: If they stick to the Pin, 'tis a sign that they are not done enough; but as soon as they slip off from it, they must be taken away and carefully cool'd, by steeping them in cold Water.

Ano-

New Instructions for Confectioners. 17

Another Way of preparing green Apricocks.

Having provided green Apricocks, before their Stones are grown hard, let two Handfuls of Salt, more or less, according to the quantity of your Apricocks, be pounded in a Mortar to a very fine Powder: Then let the Apricocks be put into a Napkin, with the Salt, and let all be well stirr'd about, from one end to the other; sprinkling them with a little Vinegar. As soon as you perceive, that they are clear'd from the Moss or Down, rub them a little with your Hands to get off the Salt; wash them in fair Water, and scald them immediately. As soon as they are scalded (which may be known, by pricking them with a Pin, or when they easily receive an impression from the Finger) let them be thrown into fresh Water. In the mean while, take as much clarified Sugar, as will be requisite, and set it in a Pan over the Fire: When the Sugar begins to boil, put in your Apricocks, after having drain'd them from the Water, and stew them over a gentle Fire, till they begin to grow green: When they are well impregnated with the Sugar, let them be laid on a Grate, to be dryed, and afterwards set in order upon Slates; strewing them lightly with powder'd Sugar, put into a Napkin: Then being dried for some time in the Stove, they must be taken off from the Slates, and put into Sieves to be more thoroughly dried: At last, they are to be laid up dry in Boxes, and kept for Use. This sort of Fruit is very good, when Preserv'd.

To preserve green Apricocks.

These Apricocks must be first order'd with thin Sugar, that is to say, for every two Ladlesful of clarified Sugar, one of Water is to be allow'd, and all made luke-warm together. Having put your Apricocks well drain'd, into an earthen Pan, pour this Syrup upon them, and let them be soak'd in it till the next Day: Then setting all over the Fire, in a Copper-pan, cause them to Simper, stirring them about gently from time to time. Afterwards, they must be turn'd again into the earthen, Pan, or even left in the Copper-pan, and may be so order'd at any other time. The next day, let the Apricocks be drain'd on a Cullander, and give the Syrup seven or eight Boilings; adding a little more Sugar; then throw in your Fruit, and let all

simper

simper together. The same thing is to be re-iterated for four or five Days; giving your Syrup fifteen, sixteen, or twenty several Boilings; and always augmenting it with a little Sugar, by reason of its diminution, and to the end that the Fruit may be equally soak'd therein: Afterwards, the Apricocks must be put into the Syrup, and made to simper at every time. To bring them to perfection, boil your Syrup till it becomes pearled, adding also some other Sugar likewise Pearled, and having turn'd in the Fruit, let all have a cover'd Boiling: Then remove the Pan from the Fire, and take off the Scum: As soon as the Apricocks are cool'd, let them be drain'd in a Cullander and laid upon Slates or Boards, in order to be dried in the Stove. The next Morning, they may be turn'd, if it be requisite, and in the Evening, shut up in Boxes, or little Trunks, with Paper between every Row.

If you would have green Apricocks preserv'd liquid, put them into a Pot, with their Syrup, when the whole Work is finish'd; and they may be dried at any time, as occasion requires. To that purpose, you need only heat Water over the Fire, and set your Pot of Apricocks into it, as it were in *Balneo Mariæ*, to the end that, by the heat of the Water, which is to boil, the Syrup may become liquid again, as if it were newly made, and by that means, the Apricocks may be taken out to be dried in the Stove, as before, after they have been drain'd. But this is usually done at once, because they are apt to grow greasy, and on the contrary, they keep very well dry.

Green Apricocks peeled.

These Apricocks after they have been neatly peel'd, must be likewise pierc'd thro' the middle and thrown into fair Water: They ought also to boil in other Water, but when they rise on the top, they must be thrust down, and left to cool in their own Liquor. Afterwards, being set on the Fire again, to recover their green Colour, they must be boil'd till they slip off from the Pin, and put into Sugar in the same manner as the former, as well to be kept dry as liquid.

For the *Compotes*, Pastes and Marmelades of green Apricocks, See those Articles, which are hereafter describ'd together, for every kind of Fruit.

C H A P.

CHAP. V.
Of ripe Apricocks.

ALtho' there is a confiderable fpace of Time, between the Seafons in which green and ripe Apricocks are preferv'd; neverthelefs, we fhall here continue the defcription of them to follow the Order of the Matter; having already accounted for what relates to the Lift of the Fruits according to their Seafons, in the third Chapter; to which the Reader is referr'd.

Pared Apricocks.

After having neatly par'd and fton'd the Apricocks, flitting them on one Side, they are to be fcalded in Water, almoft boiling hot: As the Apricocks rife on the top, take them up with the Skimmer, and put them into fair Water to cool; if they are fomewhat foft: If they are otherwife, flip them into the Pan, again, continuing fo to do, till the end; except, when the Water being ready to boil, cafts them altogether on the top; then let them all be taken out and cool'd. Afterwards, you are to pick out thofe that are fofteft, thofe that are indifferent foft, and thofe that are leaft fo: The firft fort muft be immediately put into Sugar, that has had three or four Boilings; the Second into Sugar, as it comes from the Straining-bag; and for the hardeft, the Sugar muft be boil'd again for a while, fetting it over the Fire, and adding a little Water. When the Apricocks are all equally entire and foft, they muft be put into clarified Sugar, and boil'd, till no Scum or Froth arifes any longer, which muft be always carefully taken off. The Apricocks being thus left in the Sugar, till the next Day, are to be drain'd; whilft the Syrup is boil'd till it has attain'd to its fmooth Quality, augmenting it with Sugar: Then turn the Apricocks into the Pan, and having given them a Boiling, let them be fet by. On the Day following, let them be drain'd, and let the Syrup be boil'd till it becomes Pearled: Afterwards, let them be flipt into the Pan again, adding fome Sugar likewife Pearled, and having given them a cover'd Boiling, let them be fet into the Stove, till the next Morning; when they are to be taken out, and put into Pots, in order to be dried, or to be eaten in the fame condition, at pleafure. To

To dry your Apricocks at all times, set a Copper-pan, with Water over the Fire, and the Pot or earthen Pan containing the Fruit, in the middle of the same Pan, which ought, upon that account, to be of a proportionable size: Let the Water boil about half an Hour; by which means, the Apricocks will be heated, and you'll have the liberty to take them out, to be drain'd. Then they may be dress'd upon the Slates or Boards, in order to be set into the Stove, after they have been strew'd with Sugar.

N.B. Forget not, in peeling or turning your Apricocks at first, to put them into fair Water.

Apricocks preserv'd in Half-Sugar.

Let four Pounds of Sugar be made Feathered; let four Pounds of Apricocks be put into it; and let all be boil'd a little, to cause them to cast their Juice: Then, having set them by to cool, bring them to the Fire again, and let them boil, till no Scum appear any longer: Having remov'd the Pan, let them be left in the Syrup, till the next Day; when they may be drain'd in a Cullander; whilst the Syrup is boil'd, till it become Pearled; at which instant it must be pour'd into an earthen Pan, and the Apricocks must be slipt into it: Afterwards, they must be scumm'd and set into the Stove, to be thoroughly soak'd: On the Day following, they are to be drain'd and dress'd upon the Slates, in order to be dried in the Stove, strew'd with Sugar. Otherwise, they may be kept liquid, till another time, and afterwards dried as the former.

Apricocks in Ears.

Apricocks that have been order'd according to either of these Ways, may be dress'd in Ears; and to that purpose, it is only requisite, to turn one of the Halves, without loosening it altogether from the other; or to joyn the two Halves together, so as they may mutually touch one another at both ends, one on one side and the other on the other.

'Tis observable, That ripe Apricocks are apt to grow greasie, as well as the green ones; so that they cannot be kept long liquid; because there is no way to prevent this Inconveniency: Then they require a great deal more pains in drying, and are less agreeable to the Palate. Therefore in regard that they keep

best

beft dry, it is moft expedient to order them fo at firft; or elfe
the Confectioner or Officer will be oblig'd to alter their Pro-
perty, making ufe of them for March-panes, or other forts of
Works.

For the *Compotes*, Marmelades and Paftes of Apricocks, fee
the particular Chapters, to which thefe Articles belong, as well
as for thofe of all the other forts of Fruits, which fhall not be
mention'd any longer for the future; in regard, that recourfe
may be had to the Table or *Index* of the principal Matters,
precifely fhewing the Page where thofe Matters are handled at
large.

CHAP. VI.

Of Green Almonds.

GReen Almonds follow the green Apricocks, as well with
refpect to the Seafon, as to the manner of Preferving:
However, we fhall here explain the feveral Ways of ordering
them, at large; becaufe there are certain particular Circum-
ftances to be obferved, that were not mention'd in the preceding
Articles.

How to cleanfe, and boil green Almonds.

Let Water, with new Afhes be fet over the Fire in a Pan,
and let the Coals that rife on the top be fcumm'd off; when,
after having boil'd for fome time, you perceive it to be fweet
and flippery, as a good Lye ought to be, remove the Pan, and
fet it by for a while, in order to get the clear Liquor. Then
bring it to the Fire again, and when the Lye begins to boil,
throw in three or four Almonds; obferving, whether the Flocks
or Husks that cover them, be well clear'd: If not, it is a fign,
that the Lye is not good, and fome other muft be made, or that
muft be recruited with new Afhes; otherwife the Almonds
would only open and flit, and not be cleans'd. On the contrary, if the Husks flip off well, the reft of the Almonds may be
turn'd into this Lye, but you muft hinder their boiling, by continually ftirring them about, with the Handle of the Skimmer.

As

As soon as it appears, that the Husks are easily rubb'd off, take them out, and shake them a little in a Cloth, holding it at both ends: Afterwards, one of the ends of the Cloth being open'd, let your Almonds fall into a Pan full of fair Water. Thus having caus'd them to be well wash'd, pierce them thro' the middle, with a Knitting-needle, or some other Instrument of the like nature; and as they are done, throw them into other fresh Water.

This Way of preparing and cleansing Almonds, is more certain, than to give them some Boilings in the Lye, before they are taken out, or to put them into it with the Ashes; for it is to be feared, lest that should cause them to open, if care be not taken to prevent such Accidents. The same Inconveniency often happens, if according to any Method that is observ'd, all the Fruit should be imprudently thrown into this Lye, without making the above-mentioned Tryal, at the hazard of two or three Almonds, to know, whether it be not too hot, or whether it be in its due Condition.

To bring the Almonds again to their green Colour, it is requisite, that the fair Water be chang'd, and that they be boil'd in it, over a quick Fire: They may also be scalded or stew'd by degrees, without boiling; to which purpose, having put the Almonds into a Pan with Water, a Dish of almost the same breadth is to be thrust down into it, which may hinder them from rising on the top, and consequently from turning black, and when the Liquor is ready to boil, some cold Water must be pour'd in by degrees. In following either of these Ways, it may be known, that the Almonds are sufficiently prepar'd, when they slip off from the Pin; at which instant, they ought to be remov'd from the Fire, and set by to cool.

To put Almonds into Sugar.

As to this particular, it is only requisite, to observe the Directions already given for Apricocks. Thus for every two Ladlesful of clarified Sugar, take one of Water, till you have a sufficient quantity for the soaking of your Almonds, or somewhat more; because it will afterwards serve to augment the Syrup in other Boilings or for some other Uses. Let the Sugar and Water be heated as hot, as you can well endure to hold your Finger in it, and pour it upon the Almonds in an earthen Pan, leaving them thus till the next Day; when all must be put into a Copper-pan set over the Fire, and heated, till almost ready to boil:

New Instructions for Confectioners. 23

boil: Then they are to be turn'd again into the earthen Pans, or left in the Copper-pan, and the next Day, the Almonds must be drain'd in a Cullander; giving the Syrup seven or eight Boilings, and augmenting its quantity, with a little Sugar: Some time after, throw in your Fruit, and let all simper together. The same thing is to be done for four or five Days successively, causing the Syrup to have some other Boilings; which must be still encreas'd with Sugar, every time, to the end, that the Fruit may always be equally soak'd. When you would have the Work finish'd, let the Syrup be boil'd, till it has attain'd to its Pearled Quality; adding, if it be requisite, some other Sugar Pearled in like manner: So as the Fruit may be conveniently slipt into the Pan, and have a cover'd Boiling. Afterwards, having remov'd it from the Fire, take off the Scum, on the top; and, as soon as the Almonds are cool'd, lay them a draining in a Cullander; in order to be dress'd upon Slates or Boards, and dried in the Stove. These Almonds are not usually strew'd with Sugar, no more than green Apricocks, because they appear finer in their natural Colour, and are very easily dried. However, the Day following, they must be turn'd on the other side, if it be needful, and put into Boxes, when you perceive them to be very firm and dry.

Green Almonds may also be preserved liquid, as well as Apricocks, either to be eaten in that manner, or to be dried, as occasion requires, and to that purpose recourse may be had to the Directions before laid down, *Pag.* 17 and 18. for green Apricocks.

CHAP. VII.
Several other Ways of Preserving Almonds.

BEsides new raw Almonds that are serv'd up to Table, when ripe, there are several Ways of Drying them, which may be very serviceable at those times, when there is no great variety of Fruits or Sweet-meats.

Almonds order'd à la Siamoise.

Having dried and brought Almonds to a reddish Colour in the Oven, let them be thrown into Sugar, boil'd till it becomes
Pearled;

Pearled; ſtirring them about well in the Pan, without ſetting it over the Fire: Then they muſt be laid in order upon a Grate, and put into the Stove, if you would have them ſerv'd up after that manner. Otherwiſe, being taken out of the Pan, they may be roll'd one by one, in powder'd Sugar or *Sedan-Nomparel* and continually ſtirr'd about, to the end that they may be cover'd, on all ſides, with the Sugar or with the *Nomparel*. Afterwards they muſt be taken out, and ſet into the Stove upon Papers.

Blown Almonds.

After having ſcalded and blanch'd your Almonds, let them be ſtirr'd about in the White of an Egg: Then let them be put into powder'd Sugar, and well roll'd in it. Having thus ic'd them over once, if you perceive that they are not done enough, dip them again into the White of an Egg, and afterwards into powder'd Sugar: At laſt, they may be laid upon a Sheet of Paper, and bak'd in an Oven, with a gentle Fire.

Iced Almonds.

Take blanched Almonds, and put them into an Ice that is ready prepared, with the White of an Egg, powder'd Sugar, Orange or Lemmon-flowers and *Sevil*-orange: Let them be well roll'd in this Compound, ſo as to be neatly iced, and afterwards dreſs'd on a Sheet of Paper, in order to be bak'd in the Campain-oven, with a gentle Fire, as well underneath, as on the top.

Several ſorts of criſp Almonds.

Criſp Almonds of a gray Colour.

Let a Pound of Loaf or Powder-ſugar be melted, with a little Water, and let a Pound of Almonds be boil'd in it, till they crackle: Then remove the Pan from the Fire, and ſtir all about inceſſantly with the *Spatula*. If any Sugar be left, it muſt be heated again over the Fire, to the end that it may entirely ſtick to the Almonds; continuing to ſtir them, without intermiſſion, till the Work be finiſh'd. Thus the Almonds will become criſp, and of a gray Colour.

Red

Red crisp Almonds.

To give your Almonds a red Colour; cause three quarters of a Pound of Sugar to be dissolv'd with a little Water, throw in the Almonds, and boil them as before, till they crackle; taking care to stir them from time to time, that they may not stick to the Pan. Then remove them from the Fire, and keep stirring them continually, till they have taken up all the Sugar, without setting them any longer over the Fire. Afterwards, having sifted them, the Sugar that runs thro' the Sieve, must be put again into the same Pan, with another quarter of a Pound of Sugar, and a little Water, to dissolve the whole Mass. The Sugar being boil'd till it become crack'd, add as much prepared Cocheneal, as will be requisite to give it a fine Colour, and let it boil again over the Fire, to cause it to return to its crack'd Quality; by reason that the Cocheneal brings it down from that degree of boiling. At that very instant toss in your Almonds, and at the same time take them off from the Fire; stirring them, without intermission, as at first, till they become dry.

If you are minded to make a greater quantity of this sort of crisp Almonds at once; it will only be requisite to augment that of the Sugar proportionably, that is to say, allowing a Pound of one, for every Pound of the other.

As for the prepared Cocheneal; it is only the Liquor in which that Grain has been boil'd, with Allum and Cream of Tartar. It is generally us'd for every thing that is to be brought to a fine red Colour, particularly *Blanc-mangers*, Creams, Jellies, Marmelades, Pastes, &c.

White crisp Almonds.

Crisp Almonds are also made white; to which purpose, after having scalded and blanch'd them, they must be thrown into sugar boil'd till it become crack'd: Then let all have a Walm or two together, and for the rest, let the Almonds be order'd in the same manner as before; that is to say, stirr'd and turn'd continually, to the end that the Sugar may stick close to them, on all sides.

If you have at hand a Pearling-pot proper for Sugar-plums, or any other Vessel of the like nature, some boil'd sugar, that
is

is Pearled, may alſo be pour'd into it, and dropt by degrees upon the Almonds; cauſing the Pot to be held by a Servant, till they are thoroughly ſoak'd and cover'd over with it.

Criſp Almonds of a Gold-colour.

There is another Way of Preparing criſp Almonds uſually practis'd by Cooks, which may be perform'd thus: When the Almonds are blanch'd, drain'd and roll'd in powder'd Sugar, let them be thrown into a Frying-pan, in which Oil has been heated: After having fried them in this manner, ſtirring them about, till they have acquir'd a fine Gold-colour, they muſt be ſpeedily taken out with the Skimmer, in order to be dreſs'd in different Heaps. Some call theſe *Fried* Languedoc-*almonds*, and they are us'd for the Garniſhing of Potages of Almond-milk, or other Meſſes of the like nature.

Piſtachoes in Sur-tout.

Take what quantity you pleaſe of Piſtachoes, clear them from their Shells, and cauſe them to be made criſp, which may be done thus: When the Sugar is boil'd till it become Feathered, throw in your Piſtachoes, and when they have continu'd a little while on the Fire, take them off, ſtirring them well with the *Spatula*, till they are all cover'd, but they muſt not be ſet again over the Fire. Afterwards, having beat up the White of an Egg with a Spoon, add a little Orange-flower-water, and dip the Piſtachoes into it: Then let them be taken out, and roll'd in Powder-ſugar, that is very dry. At laſt, being laid in order upon white Paper, they muſt be gently bak'd in a Campain-oven, with a little Fire underneath, and more on the top: As ſoon as they are ſufficiently bak'd, and brought to a good Colour, they may be taken out of the Oven, and dried in the Stove.

CHAP.

CHAP. VIII.
Of Preserv'd Cherries, as well dry as liquid.

CHerries are the first red Fruits that present themselves to be preserv'd, at least those that appear early. These forward ones are usually put into Sugar with their Stones; because they are as yet attain'd to little maturity, and serve only as a Novelty: But it will be no difficult matter to take measures in ordering all sorts of Cherries, according to the following Directions.

Cherries in Ears.

Take fair Cherries, that are stoned, put them into Blown Sugar, and give them fifteen cover'd Boilings: Then having set them by, till the next Day, let them be drain'd in a Cullander, and let your Syrup boil till it be Pearled: Afterwards, throw in your Fruit, and let them have seven or eight cover'd Boilings; taking care that they be well scumm'd, even after the Pan is remov'd from the Fire. When the Cherries are cool'd, take them out of their Syrup, to be dried in the Stove upon Slates, and strew'd with Sugar. They are call'd *Cherries in Ears*, by reason of the manner of dressing them; which is to open and spread them, joyning two together, so as their Skins may remain on the out-side and the Pulp on the inside: Then another Cherry of the same nature is to be added on each side, the Pulp of which is laid upon the Skin of the others.

Cherries preserv'd in half Loaf-sugar.

After having stoned your Cherries, give them five or six Boilings in Pearled Sugar, and then take off the Pan from the Fire. On the next Day, they are to be drain'd, whilst the Syrup is boil'd Smooth, and put into it: Then they ought to have twenty Boilings, as also to be well Scumm'd and to lye in the Stove, during the whole Night. Afterwards, they must be drain'd in a Cullander, and dress'd upon the Slates, to be dried in the same Stove. One Pound and half of Sugar is sufficient at first for six Pounds of Fruit.

Cher-

Cherries in half Powder-sugar.

Having provided four Pounds of stoned Cherries, with one Pound of Powder-sugar, let all boil together over the Fire; taking care to stirr the Fruit continually, till they have imbib'd the Sugar; which may be known, by touching them, when they are very soft and tender. Then being set by till the next Day, they may be drain'd; whilst the Syrup is boil'd smooth: Let the Cherries be thrown into it, and give them fifteen or twenty Boilings, always taking care, that they be well scumm'd: Afterwards, they must be remov'd from the Fire, and laid in earthen Pans, to continue in the Stove all Night: On the next Day, they are to be drain'd, dress'd upon Sieves, and set into the Stove again, after they have been strew'd with fine Sugar.

Cherries preserv'd liquid.

Let Sugar be boil'd till it be Blown, and let the Cherries be slipt into it, having cut off part of the Stalks. They ought to have ten or twelve cover'd Boilings, before they are set by till the next Day: Then they must be drain'd, and put into the Sugar again, when boil'd, till it become Pearled, augmenting it with some other Sugar likewise Pearled: At last, you may add some Syrup of Currans of the same Quality, to give them a finer Colour, and put them into Pots, to be kept for Use.

Another Way.

The Cherries may be order'd as the former, or as those that are preserv'd dry, except that a greater quantity of Sugar is to be added, and in finishing the Work, they must have some cover'd Boilings, after having brought the Sugar to the greater Pearled Quality. When they are cool'd, they may be put into Pots, and if you would have them tinctur'd with Straw-berries, some of that Fruit must be put amongst your Cherries, as they are preserving.

Cherries

Cherries preferv'd dry, with Straw-berries.

You are to provide Cherries preferv'd dry, out of which the Stones have been already taken; fubftituting in their room, as many Straw-berries likewife preferv'd dry: Then let all be dried in the Stove, after they have been ftrew'd with Sugar, as well in the dreffing, as the turning of them.

Cherries in Bunches.

Take fair Cherries, that are of an equal bignefs, and tye them up, with Thread, into little Bunches: Then put them into Blown Sugar of the fame Weight, and give them about twenty Boilings. Afterwards, let them be taken off from the Fire, and fcumm'd, and as foon as they are cool'd, put them into the Stove as they lye in their Pan, till the next Day; when they may be conveniently dried upon Slates.

Cherries booted, à la Royale.

Let *Kentifh* Cherries, with fhort Stalks, or others of the like nature, be thrown into Sugar, boil'd till it become Pearled. Some only caufe it to fimper, ftirring the Fiuit from time to time, and the next Day, having caus'd the Syrup to be Pearled, put the Cherries therein, adding other Sugar likewife Pearled. Before they are fet into the Stove, other Cherries preferv'd in Ears are alfo provided, which muft be laid upon them crofs-wife, to the number, of three, four, or fix, and afterwards fet into the Stove. Thefe are commonly called *Booted Cherries*. The Cherries that are left with the Stalks, may alfo be order'd altogether after the fame manner, as the others preferved in Ears, and the fame Method may be follow'd for the reft.

Cherries preferv'd liquid, after the manner of the City of Tours.

Having provided five Pounds of Cherries, with three Pounds of Feathered Sugar, throw your Fruit into it, give them fifteen Boilings, and afterwards add two other Pounds of Sugar likewife Feathered. The whole Work ought to be finifh'd at once, without removing the Pan from the Fire, caufing the Fruit to

X   be

be boil'd in the Syrup, till it has attain'd to its Pearled Quality. Cherries are preserv'd after this manner, to very good purpose, as also Straw-berries. If you would impregnate the latter, with the Syrup of the Cherries, it must not boil with the Fruit; neither the one, nor the other; but this Syrup must be pour'd upon them, when they are quite done, and taken away from the Fire.

Currans may also be order'd after the same manner.

To make a Cake, or Paste of Cherries.

After having ston'd your Cherries, let them boil in a Pan, till you perceive, that they have cast their Juice: Then set them in order in a Sieve, and let them be well drain'd: Afterwards, you must pound them in a Mortar, and set them on the Fire again, to be thoroughly dried. In the mean time, having boil'd the Sugar, till it be Crack'd, pour it upon this dried Cherry-paste, allowing a Pound of Sugar for every Pound of Paste: Let all be well temper'd together so as they may simper a little over the Fire; and let them be continually stirr'd. A little while after, they may be dress'd upon the Slates, with a Spoon, and set into the Stove. If you are of opinion, that the Paste has not as yet acquir'd a good Colour, a few Currans may be intermixt with it, as it is drying; having first caus'd those Currans to cast their Juice, and then strain'd them thro' a Sieve.

Other Ways of Preserving and Ordering Cherries.

For *Compotes*, Conserves and Marmelades of Cherries, recourse may be had to those Articles, relating to all sorts of Fruits, which are hereafter explain'd.

As for Cherry-water, we shall only here observe, That all the Juice of Cherries extracted, either in making Cakes, Marmelades, Conserves, or other Sweet-meats, may serve for the preparing of *Ratafiaz*, so that nothing will be lost, or thrown away as useless.

The Syrup of Cherries, that have been preserv'd dry, may also supply the place of Sugar; at least, if you have no mind to keep it, for the diversifying of March-panes or other Comfits of the like Nature; or to make use of it, in the preserving of other sorts of Fruit. It may likewise be us'd to very good purpose, in preparing the Jelly of Cherries; as to which Particular, it will only be requisite to observe the Directions hereafter laid down,

down, for the different Jellies of Fruits, particularly for the quaking Jelly of Currans.

As for Cherries that are serv'd up to Table in their natural Condition, there is a particular Way of embellishing them, hereafter explain'd in the 30th Chapter, under the Article of *Caramel*.

C H A P. IX.
Of Strawberries and Rasberries.

STrawberries and Rasberries are very serviceable in Entertainments, and, when full ripe, afford Delight to three Senses, *viz.* those of Seeing, Smelling and Tasting: They have a vinous Taste, and serve to corroborate the Heart, Stomack and Brain, after the same manner as vinous Liquors. These good Qualities cause them to be so much esteem'd in their natural Condition, that they are seldom preserv'd, more especially Strawberries: They are usually eaten, soak'd in Water or Wine, and strew'd with Sugar: However they may be iced, as Cherries, Currans and Rasberries; and these last may be preserv'd as well dry as liquid.

Rasberries preserv'd dry.

Having provided Rasberries that are not too ripe, let them be pick'd and put into Sugar that has attain'd to its Blown Quality; giving them a cover'd Boiling: Afterwards, being taken off from the Fire, they must be scumm'd, and slipt into an earthen Pan, to continue in the Stove during twenty four Hours. As great a quantity of Sugar is requisite as of Fruit, for example, about four Pounds of each. When they are cool'd, drain them from their Syrup, and dress them as other Sweet-meats, in order to be strew'd with Sugar, and dried in the Stove after the usual manner.

X 2   *Ras-*

Rasberries preserv'd liquid.

Take four Pounds of good Rasberries, and put them, when pick'd, into three Pounds of Pearled Sugar. Then give them a small Boiling lightly cover'd, and stir them from time to time: Afterwards, let them be cool'd, drain'd and dry'd as Cherries, but not to so great a degree, because they have not so much Moisture: The quantity of Pearled Sugar ought also to be augmented, to the end that it may be sufficient for the soaking of the Fruit: But if the Rasberries are somewhat greenish or tart, they must not be put at first into Sugar so boil'd, because they would grow hard; so that it is expedient to make a due choice of them. Rasberries with thick Grains are not so fit for preserving, as being full of Juice, which soon turns to Marmelade: Those that have small Grains, are most proper for that purpose, in regard that their Substance is more firm and compact: Rasberries that grow in moist Places, are not so good as those brought forth in a dry Soil; neither is so much Sugar requisite for the ordering of the latter sort; by reason that Fruits growing in marshy Grounds always dissolve in Sugar.

Other Ways of using Strawberries and Rasberries.

For *Compotes* of these sorts of Fruit, see the Directions hereafter given under that Article: Marmelades, Jellies and Pastes are likewise made of them, which shall be explain'd among those of other Fruits.

CHAP. X.
Of Gooseberries and Currans.

GOoseberries and Currans are usually preserv'd at the same time with Cherries and Strawberries, and green Gooseberries are the first of all the Sweet-meats made in the Spring. Among the different kinds of Currans, the common, which ripens soonest, is the most proper for Preserving, as having more Substance, and being most agreeable, as well to healthy Persons,

sons, as to those that are sick, by reason of their grateful Tartness. The larger *Dutch* Currans are likewise preferrable on that account to the ordinary ones, which are very sweet, and better eaten raw, than when preserv'd, as being too full of Juice. These Currans are generally serv'd up to Table in iced Bunches, and if design'd for Preserving, ought to be taken early, before they are grown ripe. The same thing is done in ordering the white *Dutch* Currans, which are likewise preserv'd in single Stalks, in Bunches, or in Jelly, as well as the common white Currans.

Green Gooseberries preserv'd liquid.

The Gooseberries must be slit on one side with a Pen-knife, and all the small Grains that are on the Inside must be taken out: Then they are to be put into very clear Water, and set over the Fire, which is to be kept moderate. As soon as they rise on the top of the Water, they are to be remov'd, and set by in the same Liquor: When they are cool'd, let them be put into other fresh Water, over a gentle Fire, till they recover their green Colour, and become very soft. Afterwards, having cool'd them again in fair Water, let them be well drain'd, and put into Sugar, pass'd thro' the Straining-bag: At the same time, give them fourteen or fifteen Boilings, to the end that they may thoroughly imbibe the Sugar, and leave them till the next Day: Then, being drain'd, let them be slipt into the Syrup boil'd till it become Pearled, and let them have four or five cover'd Boilings. At last, they may be put into Pots, and us'd as occasion shall require.

Jelly of green Gooseberries.

Your Gooseberries being prepar'd as before, boil an equal Quantity of Sugar, till it be Pearled: Throw in the Fruit, and let all boil together; taking off the Scum, till they return to the Pearled Condition. Then removing them from the Fire, strain them thro' a Sieve into a Copper-pan, and at the same time, put the Jelly so receiv'd into Pots in the same manner, as other Jellies of that sort of Fruit.

Red Currans preserv'd Liquid.

The Currans being pick'd, ought to be put into Pearled Sugar, and to have a light cover'd Boiling; Then they must be scumm'd, and brought to perfection the next Day; to which purpose they are to be strain'd thro' a Sieve, whilst the Syrup is boil'd to a Degree between Smooth and Pearled. Afterwards, let the Fruit be slipt in, and let as much other Pearled Sugar be added as is sufficient for the well soaking of them. They ought also to have several cover'd Boilings, between Smooth and Pearled, taking off the Scum, even after they have been remov'd from the Fire, and stirring them, from time to time, till they are cool'd a little, lest they should turn to a Jelly. Lastly, they must be put into Pots and cover'd for some Days.

Currans preserv'd in Bunches.

Take four Pounds of Currans tied up in Bunches, and boil your Sugar till it becomes Feathered: Then set them in Order in the Sugar, and let them have several cover'd Boilings: They must be speedily scumm'd, and not suffer'd to boil long; that is to say, only two or three seethings: Afterwards, let them be scummed again, and set into the Stove in the Copper-pan. On the next Day, they may be cool'd and drain'd, dressing them in Bunches of a convenient thickness, in order to be well strew'd and dried in the Stove.

Jelly of Currans.

Take six Pounds of Currans, and cause the like quantity of Sugar to be brought to its Crack'd Quality: Throw in your Currans, and let the Syrup boil to a Degree between Smooth and Pearled, and till the Scum ceases to rise any longer: Then let them be laid in a fine Sieve, without pressing them too much, and only left in it, to be thoroughly drain'd. Afterwards, having given the Jelly, a Boiling, let it be scumm'd, and put into several Pots. When it is pour'd into the Pots, another thin Scum will arise which must be taken off, to render the Liquor clear, and two or three Day after, it may be cover'd with Paper cut round, to be kept for Use.

A Jelly of the like nature may be made of Pomegranates,
as

as also of Barberries, or elſe another ſort of Curran-jelly, after the following manner.

Quaking Jelly of Currans.

Having provided ſix Pounds and a half of Currans, let as much Juice be ſqueez'd out of them, as is poſſible, and let the Sugar be order'd, as before: Then ſtrain your Curran-juice thro' a fine Sieve, and pour it into the Sugar: Let all be lightly boil'd together to a Degree between Smooth and Pearled, and afterwards let the Jelly be conveniently diſpoſed of in Pots.

Jelly of Currans tinctur'd with Raſberries.

If you are deſirous, that the Curran-jelly have a Tincture of Raſberries, a Handful or two of Raſberries may be added, according to the quantity of your Jelly: And to make it chiefly of Raſberries, it will be requiſite only to take four Pounds of Raſberries, two of Currans and five of Sugar, and to order all, after the ſame manner, as for the former Jelly of Currans.

Jelly of Currans, according to the Way of the City of Tours.

Having provided three Pounds of Currans, with two Pounds and a half of Sugar, boil'd till it be crack'd, throw in your Fruit, and give them ſeven or eight Boilings, till they return to the Pearled Quality; cauſing the Scum to be carefully taken off: Then let them be ſtrain'd thro' a Sieve, and pour'd into Pots, at the ſame time.

In ordering theſe ſorts of Jellies, whoſoever deſigns to play the good Husband, may take the Fruit or groſs Subſtance, remaining on the Sieve, and boil it over again, with a little Water: Afterwards, it muſt be ſtrongly ſqueez'd thro' the Hair-ſieve, and by that means a great deal more good Jelly will be extracted: But this is only requiſite to be done, when a great quantity of the groſs Subſtance is left; otherwiſe it would not quit coſt, by reaſon that the Profit will not countervail the Trouble.

For the *Compotes*, Conſerves, Marmelades and Paſtes of Currans, recourſe may be had to thoſe Articles hereafter deſcribed in particular.

CHAP.

Chap. XI.
Of Walnuts.

IN the Interval, or rather during the Season of red Fruits, and the first that succeed them, Walnuts are usually preserv'd, when they are come to their full Growth, nevertheless before the Wood is form'd; which happens in the beginning of *July*, and a little after the Festival of *St. John* Baptist.

White Walnuts.

The Walnuts must be neatly par'd, till the White appears, and thrown into fair Water: Afterwards, they must be boil'd for some time in the same Water, whilst some other Water is set over another Furnace, into which the Walnuts are to be put, as soon as it begins to boil. It may be perceiv'd, whether they be done enough, by pricking them with a Pin, after the same manner, as green Almonds and green Apricocks; so that when they slip off from it, they ought to be remov'd from the Fire. To render them White, it is requisite at first, to throw in a Handful of beaten Allum, and to give them one Boiling more: Then they must be immediately cool'd, by turning them into fresh Water, in order to be put into thin Sugar, that is to say, allowing one Ladle-full of Water, for every two of Sugar.

Some time after, having drain'd your Walnuts, slip them into earthen Pans, and having caus'd the Sugar and Water to be heated together, pour it upon them. On the next Day, let the Syrup be clear'd from the Pans, without removing the Walnuts; because they must not be set over the Fire, at all: Let this Syrup have five or six Boilings, augmenting it a little with Sugar, and let it be pour'd upon the Walnuts: On the next Day, it ought to have fifteen Boilings; on the third Day, it must be boil'd, till it become somewhat Smooth; as also on the following Days successively, till it be very Smooth, between Smooth and Pearled, and at last entirely Pearled; encreasing the quantity of Sugar, at every time, to the end that the Walnuts may be always equally soak'd in the Syrup. To bring the whole Work to perfection, let them continue in the Stove during the Night, and afterwards let them be put into Pots. By this means
the

New Instructions for Confectioners, 37

the Walnuts will become very white, provided, that good fine Sugar be us'd in the Operation, and they may be dried in the Stove, at pleasure, as other sorts of Fruit. For Walnuts preserv'd liquid, if some Syrup of Apricocks be added they'll keep much better.

If you have a mind to stuff them with Lemmon-peel after the manner of *Roan-*walnuts, it may be done, before they are put into the Stove, to be dried : To that purpose, the necessary Opening may be made with the point of a Knife, either quite through, or on the top of the Walnut, and then the Lemmon-peel, issuing forth from thence, will appear, as if it were the real Stalk. Some Amber may also be added, which will give it a Perfume very grateful both to the Taste and Smell.

Chap. XII.

Of Plums.

AMong the different kinds of Plums, the most proper for Preserving, are the *Perdrigons*, or Orange-plums, Amber-plums, those of *Isle-verte* and some others, that have not only an exquisite and very sweet Taste, but also a Pulp that is of a more firm and durable Substance.

To Preserve white Orange-plums.

These sorts of Plums must have three or four Pricks with a Pin, near the Stalk, and some others in several other Places, to the end that they may not afterwards be apt to tear, and that the Sugar may more easily penetrate their Body. As they are done, they must be thrown into Water, whilst some other Water is boil'd, into which they are to be slipt. When they begin to rise, they may be remov'd from the Fire, and set by to cool: Then let them be set again over a gentle Fire, to be brought to their former green Colour, and let them be cover'd; taking care that they do not boil, lest they should turn to Marmelade. As soon as you perceive them to be very green, and somewhat soft, let them be cool'd in fresh Water and drain'd, in order to be put into thin Sugar; allowing, as it has been already hinted,

two

two Ladles full of Sugar, for one of Water, till the Fruit, being laid in earthen Pans, is well soak'd, without rising on the top. On the next Day, they are to be slipt into a Copper-pan, to simper over the Fire, stirring them gently from time to time, to hinder them from boiling; and, on the third Day, they may be drain'd on a Cullander or Sieve: Then slip them into the Syrup, that has had seven or eight Boilings, cause them to simper for a while, and let all by, till the next Day; when the Syrup is to have fifteen or sixteen Boilings, augmented with Sugar, or Syrup of Apricocks, which is better for that purpose, as preventing them from candying; so that the Plums may be always equally soak'd. On the Day following, let the Syrup be boil'd Smooth, and on the next, between Smooth and Pearled, and having slipt in the Fruit, let it simper every time, before it is taken off from the Fire. Lastly, Having boil'd your Syrup till it be Pearled, and slipt in the Plums, give them seven or eight cover'd Boilings, taking off the Scum, and dress them, when you shall think fit, in order to be dried in the Stove.

The Orange-plums must be chosen, before they are altogether ripe, as well as the most part of other sorts of Fruits. The other kinds of Plums, that are of kin to these, are usually preserv'd after the same manner, and, among others, those of *Isle-verte* and the Muscle-plums.

Amber-plums.

Let your Amber-plums be prickt with a Pin, in several Places, and boil'd in the same Water into which they were thrown: As soon as they rise on the Surface of the Water, remove them from the Fire to be speedily cool'd in fresh Water: Then let them be drain'd, and soak'd in clarified Sugar, which is to be heated, and pour'd upon the Fruit lying in the earthen Pans: On the next Day, drain them again, and let the Syrup be boil'd a little Smooth: On the second Day, the Syrup must be likewise boil'd till it become very Smooth, and on the third, till it be Pearled; when the Plums are to have seven or eight Boilings. As often as they are thus set over the Fire, they must be augmented with Sugar, which has attain'd to the same Degree of Boiling, to the end that the Fruit may be always equally soak'd, in the earthen or Copper-pans, in which they are left, after they have simper'd for some time. When you have a mind to finish the Work, let them lye in the Stove during the whole Night,

so

so as they may be conveniently drain'd and dress'd the next Morning, in order to be dried in the same Stove, after the usual manner.

Red-Plums.

Having provided these sorts of Plums, such as red Orange-plums, Bell-plums, Imperial, or Apricock-plums, or others of the like nature, let them be slit as it were Apricocks, and stoned. If you have four Pounds of Fruit, take the same quantity of Sugar, pass'd thro' the Straining-bag; put all together into a Copper-pan over the Fire, and keep continually stirring them, lest the Skins of the Plums should break, if they should happen to boil: After having caus'd them to simper, for a while, set them by to cool: Then drain them on a Cullander or Sieve, whilst the Syrup is boil'd Smooth; slip your Fruit into the same Syrup; and give them seven or eight cover'd Boilings; carefully taking off the Scum, as well as when the Pan is remov'd from the Fire. Afterwards the Plums, being put into earthen Pans, must continue in the Stove all Night; so that the next Morning they may be drain'd as soon as they are cold, and dress'd, to be dried in the Stove upon Slates, or Sieves.

Plums preserv'd with half Sugar and otherwise.

Take four Pounds of Fruit, with the like quantity of Pearled Sugar; give them one little Boiling, and set them by till they have cast their Juice. Then let them be set again upon the Fire, and boil'd to the Pearled Quality: Afterwards, they must lie in earthen Pans, till the next Day; when they may be drain'd, and dress'd as the others, for drying in the Stove: All sorts of good Plums may be preserv'd after the same manner; and they may also be par'd, after having scalded them in Water: For the rest, the above-specified Directions may be observ'd in every Particular; only they must be strew'd with Sugar, before they are dried in the Stove.

Moreover, there are *Compotes*, Pastes and Marmelades of Plums, which are explain'd among the others, under those Articles.

CHAP.

CHAP. XIII.
Of Pears preserv'd dry and liquid.

THere is a much greater variety of kinds of this Fruit; yet very few of them are commonly preserv'd, *viz.* the great Muscadine, the *Muscadil*, or lesser Muscadine, the *Blanquet*, the *Certoe*, the Orange-pear, and more especially the *Rousselet* or Russetin. The most part of the others, are either too soft, or too hard for that purpose; and if they are not eaten raw, Pastes, Marmelades and *Compotes* are only made of them; all which are hereafter describ'd under their respective Articles.

Rousselets, or *Russetins*.

Let these Pears be prickt round about the top, with a Bodkin, and set over the Fire; taking care that the Water do not boil, and pouring in fresh, from time to time, when it is ready to bubble up: As soon as the Pears are become somewhat soft, let them be cool'd, par'd, and put into other fair Water: Afterwards, being drain'd, they must be slipt into Sugar, newly pass'd through the Straining-bag, and ought to have between forty and fifty Boilings: On the next Day, they are to be drain'd again, whilst the Syrup is boil'd Smooth, in the which you are to slip the Fruit, and to give them one or two Boilings: On the third Day, let the Syrup be boil'd to a Degree between Smooth and Pearled; and, on the fourth, till it be thoroughly Pearled, for the finishing of the whole Work; so, as the Pears may have ten or twelve cover'd Boilings. When they are cool'd, they may be put into Pots, and kept to be dried, as occasion shall require, which may be done in the same manner that has been before explain'd for Apricocks. To that purpose, some Water being boil'd in a Pan, the Pot must be set into it, and by the means of this kind of *Balneum Mariæ*, or vaporous Bath, the Syrup will be melted, so that the Fruits may be readily taken out and drain'd, in order to be dried in the Stove, upon Slates or Boards, after they have been strew'd with Sugar. They are also dried at first, and keep very well when so order'd; but care must be taken to turn and change them often, and at last to lock them up in Boxes, with Paper between every Row.

Blan-

Blanquets.

Forasmuch as this sort of Fruit is sooner ripe than the Russetin, and very much esteem'd; some of them are early preserv'd for a Rarity, and immediately dried. To that purpose, they are usually prepar'd in the same manner; that is to say, they are scalded after having been prick'd on the top; taking care that they do not boil: As soon as the Pears are made very soft, only by means of a gentle heat, they must be cool'd and par'd, throwing them, as they are done, into fresh Water: Afterwards, they are to be put into Sugar newly clarified, and finish'd in the same manner as the Russetins. Both these sorts must be strew'd with fine Sugar, in an Handkerchief, when they are set into the Stove, or turn'd; in which Particular, 'twill only be expedient to follow the Instructions already given, for other sorts of Fruits, as Apricocks, Plums, &c.

Large *Muscadines*, *Orange-pears*, Certoes, *and others*.

All these kinds of Pears and others, that are design'd to be preserv'd entire, may be scalded and boil'd in Water and Sugar, as the Russetin; so that it would only be an unprofitable Repetition, to insist any longer on them.

The musked Bergamot.

This sort of Pear is likewise excellent, when preserv'd, being a small dry Pear, very much musked. 'Tis also call'd the Dovepear, the Sicilian Pear, or the little Autumn-muscadine. To order it to the best advantage, see what has been already laid down for the former, more especially for the Russetin, and take Measures, altogether according to that Method, which is as general as certain, for all these kinds of Summer-pears.

Pears preserv'd in Quarters and otherwise.

Besides the above-mentioned Pears, which may be preserv'd whole and dry; there are others larger, that can only be so order'd in Quarters, as to be kept liquid: To that end, some Confectioners slit them into Halves, before they are scalded in Water; but it is more expedient to leave them entire, and not to pare them till afterwards, because otherwise they would
be

be apt to grow black, being also more liable to be fill'd with Water, and to turn to Marmelade. For the rest, it is only requisite to follow the preceding Directions, relating to the other sorts of Pears.

If you are desirous to preserve Pears of a somewhat large size, altogether entire, it would be expedient to scoop out their Core, with some of the Pulp in the middle, as it were that of an Orange: They are brought to perfection, by causing them to be boil'd in Sugar, at several times, and may also be dried.

To these Ways of preserving Pears, may be added the Marmelades, Pastes and more especially the *Compotes* of them, that are kept even till the Season of new Fruit, and which shall be hereafter describ'd under those Articles.

C H A P. XIV.
Of Peaches and Figs.

THese two sorts of Fruit are so highly esteem'd in their natural Condition, that they are very seldom preserv'd: As for the latter, this Care is left to the *Genoeses*, and to the Inhabitants of *Provence*, in *France*, in which Countries, they are more common, and even of a more exquisite and sweet Taste, by reason of the heat of those Climates; so that most People content themselves generally to make use of such as are brought from thence. However, we shall not forbear here to subjoyn, what is most observable in the ordering of both, when they are design'd to be preserv'd.

Green Peaches.

When Peaches are yet green and small, they may be preserv'd as green Apricocks before specified in the fourth Chapter; preparing them after the same manner, to get off the Flocks or Down, and to bring them again to a green Colour, before they are put into Sugar. But if they are larger, and the Stone is already form'd, they must be par'd and slit, to take it away. Then they are to be scalded in Water, till they become very soft. As soon as they are cool'd and drain'd, let

them

them be made green again in other Water, set over a gentle Fire, and put into thin Sugar; allowing for every two Ladles full of clarified Sugar, one of Water; which being heated, the Peaches must be slipt in, and have some Boilings; carefully taking off the Scum. On the Day following, the Syrup being boil'd somewhat Smooth, and the Fruit being turn'd into it, cause all to simper together for a while, and leave them till the third Day; when the Syrup is to be boil'd very Smooth, augmenting its quantity with Sugar, whilst you slip in the Peaches, and give them a Boiling. Lastly, the whole Work may be finish'd, as soon as you perceive, that they have thoroughly imbib'd the Sugar; to which purpose, let the Syrup be boil'd, till it become Pearled; encreasing it with Sugar of the same Quality, and having slipt in the Fruit, let them have a cover'd Boiling. Afterwards, removing the Pan from the Fire, clear all from the Scum, and in regard, that the Peaches have a somewhat cold and waterish Pulp, let them lye, during that Night in the Stove, to dry up all their moisture: On the next Day, you may dress them on Slates, glazed Tiles, or any thing else of the like nature, to be dried in the Stove, strew'd with Sugar. Or else, they may be disposed of in Pots or Glasses, to be dried upon any emergent Occasion, according to the Instructions given, Pag. 17. Peaches that are preserv'd, before the Stone or Kernel is form'd, must be put into Sugar, no otherwise than green Apricocks, or green Almonds, and the same Precautions are to be us'd, for which see Pag. 16. *Compotes,* Marmelades and Pastes may be also made of them, as well as of the following sorts, as it shall be observ'd in its proper Place.

Ripe Peaches.

Altho' mention is made of ripe Peaches, yet when they are to be preserv'd, it is not expedient to stay, till they are absolutely so; but they must be taken, when they are half turn'd, by reason of their soft and clammy Pulp. They ought to be neatly par'd, as also slit, to get out the Stones, and scalded in Water: As they rise on the top of it, they must be taken out with the Skimmer, and turn'd into other Water to cool. Then, being drain'd, they are to be put into Sugar, as it runs from the Straining-bag; and boil'd till the Scum ceases to rise, which must be carefully taken off from time to time. Having left them in this condition, till the next Day, let them be drain'd, whilst the Syrup is is boil'd Smooth, augmenting it with Sugar. Afterwards flip in your Fruits, give them a Boiling, and take them off from the Fire. On the third Day, being drain'd again, as before, and the Syrup boil'd till Pearled; let the Peaches be likewise flipt into it, adding some Pearled Sugar. After they have had a cover'd Boiling, let them continue in the Stove all Night, in order to be dress'd upon the Slates, or Boards, and dried; strewing them with Sugar, on every side, as often as they are turn'd; unless you would have them kept liquid for some time.

Peaches may also be preserv'd in half Sugar, as Apricocks, specified Pag. 20. and dress'd either way, in Ears, as that sort of Fruit; by turning one of the Halves, as they stick together; or by laying two, one upon another, so as they may be mutually conjoyn'd; when they are small.

Nectarins.

Nectarins may be preserv'd, after the same manner as Peaches, following the Method already express'd for the putting them into Sugar, and white Nectarins are more especially proper, for this Sort of Sweet-meats.

Dried Figs.

Let the Figs be prick'd near the Stalk, with the point of a Knife, before they are scalded, which may be done by throwing them into boiling Water, over the Fire, and a little while after, setting them by to cool. Some defer the pricking of them to that time, and bring them again to the Fire, without suffering the Water to boil; so as when they are become soft, and rise on the top, they may be remov'd, and set a-part to cool. Afterwards, their green Colour must be recover'd, by scalding them once more in Water, over the Fire: Then being taken out, and drain'd, they may be preserv'd with half Sugar, or at most, clarified, as it runs from the Straining-bag; accordingly, as the Figs are either green, or somewhat ripe; which ought to simper in this Sugar, and to lye by during the whole Night: On the next Morning, the Syrup must be boil'd Smooth; on the third Day, between Smooth and Pearled, and at last, quite Pearled, adding every time, as much Sugar as is needful: At those several times, the Fruit must also be slipt into the Syrup that has attain'd to such different Degrees of Boiling, and ought

to

to simper for a while. Whenever you have a mind to dispatch the Work, let the Figs have some cover'd Boilings, in order to be thoroughly scumm'd, and laid up in Pots, or Glasses; unless you would have them dried all at once: To that purpose, the Fruits must be dress'd upon Slates, after they have been well drain'd, and set into the Stove; strewing them with fine Sugar, put into a Kandkerchief, for that purpose.

'Tis requisite to choose such Figs, as are only half ripe, or even somewhat green, provided they be of a sufficient thickness. The *Genoa*-Fig, call'd *Aubicon* by the *French*, or the Feaver-fig, is the best for this Use; and in regard that these Figs are of a dark Violet-colour, if they were already turn'd, when design'd to be preserv'd, they must not be brought to a green Colour, nor any other sorts of the like nature.

CHAP. XV.

Of Apples.

THis Fruit is of no great Use in the Business of Preserving, and not very delicious, when so order'd; at least with respect to the drying of them *in Specie*: For as for Pastes, Marmelades, and more especially *Compotes* of Apples, great quantities of them are usually made, even till the new Fruits appear. However, some may be preserv'd, after the two following Ways, when other sorts of Fruit are wanting.

Green Apples.

Any kind of Apples may be chosen that are sweet and very small; which are to be par'd, leaving the Stalks, and slit a little, to the end, that the Sugar may be more thoroughly imbib'd. Having thrown them into Water, to be cleans'd and scalded, they must be cool'd and afterwards brought again to a green Colour, in the same, or other fresh Water: As soon as they are become very soft, let them be cool'd again, drain'd, and put into Sugar newly clarified, giving them some Boilings: On the next Day, the Syrup must be boil'd Smooth, at another time, between Smooth and Pearled, and at last very much

Pearled;

Pearled; flipping in the Fruit, that all may fimper together, and be fet by, till the next Morning: At this laft time, the Apples ought to have a cover'd Boiling, before they are remov'd from the Fire, to be cool'd and drain'd; if it be requir'd to dry them: But they are moft proper for liquid Sweet-meats; fo that they may be immediately difpofed of in Pots, or Glaffes, and kept to be us'd as occafion may ferve.

John-*apples and Pippins preferv'd in Quarters.*

The former retain a very delightful red Colour, and the others may pafs for Apricocks, if fome Syrup of Apricocks be pour'd upon them, as they are finifhing. Both thefe forts of Apples, after they have been par'd, are to be cut into two Parts, fo as the Cores may be taken out of each Half; or elfe, the paring and cutting of them may be deferr'd, till they have been fcalded in Water, to render them foft. Afterwards, being cool'd and drain'd, they muft be put into Sugar, newly pafs'd thro' the Straining-bag, in order, to have thirty Boilings. On the next Day, they are to be ftrain'd again, and the Syrup boil'd, till it has attain'd to its Smooth Quality: Then flip in the Fruits, and let them have one or two Boilings: On the third Day, let the Syrup be boil'd to a Degree, between Smooth and Pearled; and, on the fourth, till it be quite Pearled; caufing the Apples to have ten, or twelve cover'd Boilings. As foon as they are cool'd, they may be dried, as all other forts of Fruit, fetting them by to drain, for a while, dreffing them upon the Slates, and ftrewing them with fine Sugar, put into a Handkerchief: Otherwife, they may be kept liquid, and when, at another time, you are minded to dry them, boil fome Sugar, till it be Pearled, and give them a few Boilings therein: By this means they'll become more fair, in drying, as well as all other forts of Fruit, fo order'd; becaufe it always happens, that their Moifture, caufes the Sugar to give, a little, in procefs of time, which hinders them from being eafily dried.

CHAP.

C H A P. XVI.

Of Bell-grapes and Muscadine-grapes.

Altho' these two kinds of Grapes are very different, yet they are no less esteem'd, amidst the great variety of Sweetmeats. The Bell-grape, well known at *Paris* by the Name of *Verjus*, is distinguish'd into three sorts, *viz.* the White, the Red, and the Black. For want of these, the *Pergoleise*, or *Italian* Grapes may be us'd, which are somewhat long and clear. The best Muscadine-grapes for Preserving, are the long, or *Passe-musqué*, and the white Muscadine of *Frontignan*.

Bell-grapes preserv'd liquid.

Having caus'd some Water to simper over the Fire, throw in your Grapes, and set them by, as soon as it rises, in order to be cool'd, and afterwards brought again to a green Colour in the same, or other fresh Water: Whilst the Fruit is draining, boil the Sugar, till it be Pearled, and slip in the Grapes, till all begin to simper: At that instant, let them be remov'd and left in the Pan, till the next Day; when they are to be set over the Fire again, and gently stirr'd, till ready to boil: On the third Day, having drain'd them, on a Cullander, and caus'd the Syrup to be somewhat Pearled, let the Grapes be slipt into it, and let all simper together a little while. On the fourth Day, the Fruit must be drain'd again in the same manner, whilst the Syrup is brought to its Pearled Quality; then, the Grapes being turn'd into it, ought to have seven or eight Boilings. At last, being taken off from the Fire, to cool, they may be put into Glasses, or Pots, and us'd as occasion requires.

It would be expedient, to make choice of these Grapes, before they begin to grow ripe, and only to take the fairest, which are to be stoned, and slit on one side.

Bell-grapes preserved dry.

They ought to be prepar'd, and put into Sugar, after the same manner, as the liquid Grapes, only the Sugar may be made somewhat more Pearled, for the last time of Boiling, before

fore the Work is brought to perfection; to the end, that they may more easily be dried, after having caus'd them to be cool'd and drain'd, as the Cherries in Ears, described Pag. 27. They may also be dress'd in like manner, except that the Grapes must be clos'd again, and their Stalks left entire. But you must not forget, either Way, to ftrew them lightly with Sugar, as they are set in the Stove and turn'd.

Bell-grapes are most commonly preserv'd liquid, either entire, or after the Stones have been taken out. They are also preserv'd pared, and it is requisite only to observe, what has been before deliver'd, with respect to those that are otherwise order'd.

The Paftes and *Compotes* of Bell-grapes, are hereafter specified, under those Articles.

Jelly of Bell-grapes.

When the Grapes are prepar'd as before, let them be thrown into Pearled Sugar, and boil'd till it returns to the fame Quality: Then let all be pour'd into a Sieve, and let the Liquor that paffes thro', without squeezing, or at least after a very little preffing, be conveniently difposed of in Pots or Glaffes. To this purpose, it is requisite, to produce as many Pounds of Sugar, as of Fruit.

Some make a Jelly of Bell-grapes, by squeezing them, after they have been fcalded in Water, without opening them, and afterwards adding a Decoction of Apples: But the former Way is much better, and the Jelly fo order'd will keep longer.

Muscadine-grapes preserv'd liquid.

You are to choose such Muscadine-grapes, as are only half ripe, or even somewhat greenish and tart, and to pare them, if you shall think fit; picking out the Stones, after they have been flit on one fide; or else they may be left entire: They may also be fcalded in Water, over the Fire; but they may be very well preferv'd, without this particular Circumstance: To that end, let the Sugar be boil'd Smooth, and, having thrown in the Fruit, let all fimper a little while, leaving them in the fame condition, till the next Day. If you perceive, that they have fufficiently imbib'd the Sugar, compleat the Work, by caufing the Syrup to be Pearled, and flip in the Grapes, in order to

have

have some cover'd Boilings; taking off the Scum from time to time. Then they must be neatly put into Glasses, or Pots, and cover'd as soon as they are cool'd. Otherwise, the Muscadines may have three Boilings, before they are brought to Perfection, the second of which, is to be between Smooth and Pearled, but in the last, the Sugar must be always Pearled. If it be melted at first with the Juice of other Muscadine-grapes squeez'd for that purpose, the Perfume will be more fragrant and grateful to the Palate.

Muscadine-grapes preserv'd dry.

Let the Sugar be boil'd till it become Feathered, and let the Grapes be thrown into it, after having remov'd the Pan. Then set it over the Fire again, and give the Fruit a cover'd Boiling; taking off the Scum; as in the preceding Article. Afterwards, the Syrup being only brought again to its Pearled Quality, it must be taken away, and set by to cool; so as the Grapes may be conveniently drain'd and dress'd, in order to be dried in the Stove.

Muscadine-grapes so order'd, may be taken more ripe, than for liquid Sweet-meats, and those that are thoroughly ripe, may be iced: *Compotes* and Pastes may be also made of them, which shall be hereafter explain'd under their respective Articles.

CHAP. XVII.
Of Quinces and Marmelade made of them.

QUinces, when preserv'd, are one of the domestick Sweet-meats most in vogue, as well upon account of their grateful Taste, as by reason of their Usefulness for certain Indispositions of the Body: So that the Way of Preserving them in Quarters, Marmelade or Jelly, is generally well known; nevertheless, we shall here give a particular Description of them, to the end, that it may be done after the best and surest manner,

Quinces

Quinces preserved liquid.

Having chosen the ripest, yellowest and soundest Quinces, let them be prick'd, and scalded in Water, over the Fire: They must also be par'd and cut into Quarters, taking out the Cores: Some order them thus, before they are scalded; but it is more expedient, not to do it till afterwards, as well as with respect to the other sorts of Fruit; because otherwise, being too much fill'd with Water, they would become soft and spungy, and more apt to turn to Marmelade. However, care must be taken to put the Quinces into fair Water, as they are par'd, whilst a Decoction is made of the Parings, Cores, and some Parts of other Quinces. This Liquor being strain'd, will serve for the stewing of those that are design'd to be preserv'd, till they become very soft; otherwise they may be scalded after the usual manner. Then they must be remov'd from the Fire, in order to be cool'd and drain'd: In the mean while, some clarified Sugar is to be heated somewhat more than luke-warm, and pour'd upon the Quinces in an earthen or Copper-pan: On the same Day, or the next, the Syrup being only made Smooth, the Fruit must be slipt into it, and very gently boil'd, carefully taking off the Scum. It is supposed, that they may be brought to a redder Colour, by covering them, but this may be done by the means of prepared Cochineel, or even of Wine, which will make them red enough, if it be requisite. After the Quinces have had thirty or forty Boilings, so as the Syrup may return at least to its Smooth Quality, they must be taken off, and set by till the next Day: Then, having boil'd the Syrup between Smooth and Pearled, slip in the Fruit, and give them some Boilings, before they are remov'd from the Fire. To finish the Work, the Syrup being Pearled, and the Quinces turn'd into it, let them have a cover'd Boiling, and let the Syrup be brought again to its Pearled Quality: At last, when it begins to sink, all must be taken out, and put into Pots or Glasses, to be kept for Use.

The Quinces may also be dress'd separately in Boxes, and cool'd in that manner; whilst the Syrup is set again over the Fire, till it become Pearled, in order to be pour'd upon the Fruit, so as they may be cover'd with a fine Jelly: Then the prepar'd Cochineel may be added, or else, during the last of the former Boilings, when they are potted, without any other Management.

Marme-

Marmelade of Quinces, according to the Mode of the City of Orleans.

Take the best sort of Quinces, and cut them into Pieces, which are to be par'd and clear'd from the Cores and Kernels: At the same time, having provided two Pounds of Sugar, boil'd till it is become Crack'd, throw in about six Pounds of Fruit and let all boil together, to a Pap. Afterwards, they must be turn'd into a new Cloth, to be well strain'd, and the Liquor which passes thro', will serve for the Marmelade: To that purpose, let this strained Liquor, be pour'd into other Pearled Sugar, to the quantity of four Pounds, and as soon as the whole Mess returns to the same Degree of Boiling, let it be carefully Scummed. Then you may remove it from the Fire, taking off the Scum again, if there be occasion, and pour it into Boxes, Pots or Glasses, which must be left in the Air, for some Days, before they are cover'd.

Other sorts of Marmelade of Quinces.

Having cut the Quinces into Quarters, without Paring them, or taking away the Kernels, let them boil in Water, till they dissolve, and turn to Marmelade: Then let all be strain'd thro' a Linnen-cloath, or else thro' the Straining-bag, without squeezing, and let the Liquor be set by; whilst as much Sugar is boil'd, till it become Crack'd; into which it must be pour'd, with a little white Wine, or Claret, according to the Colour, that you would have given to the Marmelade. Some Sticks of Cinnamon beaten a little, may also be added, with Nutmeg, Cloves and Mace: Let all boil together gently, and take care to clear off the Scum; stirring them from time to time, with the *Spatula*, or with a Spoon. As soon as the Marmelade returns to its Pearled Quality, or is boil'd to the consistence of a fine Jelly, which falls in great Drops, when taken up with the Spoon; take it off from the Fire, and pour it into a Sieve set over a Pan, or else strain it thro' a Linnen-cloath, in order to be put into Pots or Glasses, as before: The Marmelade may also be pour'd into leaden Moulds, and when it is cool'd, they may be put into hot Water, as it were in *Balneo Mariæ*, or a vaporous Bath, so as the Pieces of Marmelade may be easily loosen'd and let fall one upon another in the Boxes.

If

If you have a mind to give a finer Tincture to the red Marmelade, it may be done by the means of prepar'd Cocheneal, that is to say, such as has been boil'd in Water, with Allum and Cream of Tarter; and then all may be strain'd, to be us'd, as occasion requires.

Marmelade is also made, into which may be put a lesser quantity of Sugar than of Fruit, or of their Decoction; and this is all the difference, between these two Ways of preparing it.

CHAP. XVIII.
Of Oranges and their Flowers.

WE are now come to the Winter-fruits, and these are not of the least consequence; on the contrary, they hold one of the principal Ranks, among those that are proper for sweet-Meats. But it will be requisite at first, to give some Account of the Orange-flowers, which are chiefly preserved during the Summer, and then to procede in shewing the manner of preserving the Oranges themselves, according to their several kinds, *viz.* those of *China*, *Sevil*, the Port and others; which are either sweet or sour, or else both sweet and sour together.

To preserve Orange-flowers.

The Orange-flowers must be thrown into Water and Salt, and left in that Pickle during five Days: Then they are to be scalded in two Waters, over the Fire, with a little Lemmon-juice, as the Orange-flower-buds hereafter described; in order to be put into Sugar, newly pass'd thro' the Straining-bag, and already heated: On the next Day, let the Sugar be boil'd, a little Smooth, and pour'd upon the Flowers; for they ought not to be set on the Fire, any longer. On the third Day, boil your Sugar quite Smooth, and pour it likewise upon the Flowers: Afterwards, having set all by to cool, let the Flowers be drain'd, and dried with Powder-sugar; laying them in order, upon Sieves. On the Day following, they must be turn'd on the other side, and strew'd likewise with Sugar put into a Handkerchief.

Orange-

Orange-flower-Buds.

Let them be thrown into Water and Salt, as before, and continue therein, during eight Days: Then let them be drain'd, and prick'd in two places, with a Pin; that is to say, on the Bottom, and thro' the Middle, to the end that they may more easily imbibe the Sugar: In the mean while, some Spring-water is to be set over the Fire, and when it boils, the Flowers are to be put into it, with a little Lemmon-juice. When they are half done, some Water must be set over another Furnace, and the Buds laid a draining, which are to be thrown into it, as soon as it begins to boil: Afterwards, they must be drain'd again, and order'd with Sugar, as the former Orange-flowers; that is to say, they must be first put into clarified Sugar, and then scalded, three several times, without setting them over the Fire; only pouring off the Sugar, from the earthen Pans, that contain the Buds; giving it the proper Boilings, above express'd, and at last turning it upon the same Buds. Then it being set by to cool, they may be drain'd and dried with Powder-sugar.

As for the Conserves, Marmelades, Pastes and Pastils made of Orange-flowers, recourse may be had to those different Articles hereafter specified, in their Order.

Sevil-*Oranges preserv'd in Quarters, or in Sticks.*

The Oranges are first to be Turn'd or else Zested, after the same manner, as Lemmons which shall be explain'd Pag. 57. except that the Surface of the Orange-peel, must only be par'd off very lightly. The Oranges being thus prepar'd, may be cut either into Quarters, or into Sticks, accordingly, as you shall think fit; but the Skin on the inside and the Juice must be taken away. In the mean while, some Water is to be set over the Fire, and the Oranges are to be thrown in, as soon as it begins to boil: It may be perceiv'd, that they are done enough, by their slipping off from the Pin, and then they may be cool'd, putting them into fresh Water; as also afterwards, into clarified Sugar: At the same time, they ought to have seven, or eight cover'd Boilings, and to be set by to cool. However, they must be boil'd over the Fire again, till the Syrup becomes almost Smooth, and drain'd the next Day, to be put into Pots, whilst your Syrup is made Pearled; which being pour'd upon the Oranges, they

may

54   *New Instructions for Confectioners.*

may be kept thus, till you shall judge it expedient to dry them; observing the Directions hereafter laid down for Lemmons, Pag. 57 & 58.

Sevil-*Oranges preserved entire.*

As the Oranges are Turn'd or Zested they must be thrown into fair Water, and afterwards scalded over the Fire, till they become very soft, and slip off from the Pin: Then they must be cool'd, and scoop'd with a little Spoon, made for that purpose, at a little Hole bor'd in the middle, where the Stalk grew. They are usually put into Sugar, and dried after the same manner, as the Quinces and Sticks of Oranges, even now described.

China-*Oranges preserved whole, or in Quarters.*

China-Oranges are preserv'd whole, as the former; except, that Part of them may be left without scooping, as being very delicious when done altogether entire, by reason of their sweetness: So that it is sufficient only to make a Hole on the top, as well to take away the inner Skin, as to the end that the Sugar may penetrate into the inside.

As for those that are preserv'd in Quarters, every Orange must be cut into three Parts, and the same Instructions must be follow'd, that were given a little before, for *Sevil*-Oranges.

Oranges of the Port.

This kind of Oranges, that are of a sweet-sour Taste, may likewise be preserv'd in Quarters, or in Sticks; in performing which Work, there is nothing else to be observ'd, but what has been already express'd for the other sorts of Oranges.

Sour Oranges.

These are likewise preserv'd both in Quarters and in Sticks; but it is observable, That after having scalded them, they ought to be steept for one or two Days in certain Pails or other Vessels fill'd with Water, which is to be chang'd from time to time, to the end that their Bitterness may be taken away, as it may be perceiv'd by the green Tincture, which they give the Water.

For

For the rest, it is expedient only to observe, what has been already deliver'd, with respect to the other sorts of Oranges. These last are chosen either from among the *Bigarrades*, or the *Sevil*-Oranges, which are of that Nature.

Faggots of Oranges.

The Orange-peels, that are turn'd or par'd very thin are often preserv'd, more especially those of sweet Oranges, drawing them out, to as great a length, as is possible, and these are commonly call'd Faggots. To that purpose, they are to be scalded in Water, over the Fire, till they become very soft, and put into Sugar newly clarified; giving them twenty Boilings: Then they are to be remov'd, and set by; but the next Day the Syrup must be made Smooth and the Orange-parings slipt into it, that they may have two or three Boilings. On the third Day, let them be drain'd, whilst the Sugar is brought to its Pearled Quality, and let them have a cover'd Boiling, in order to be taken off, and distributed into Pots, unless you are minded to dry them at the same time. This may be done, by causing other Sugar to be made white, rubbing it on one side of the Pan with the Skimmer, and boiling it till it be Feather'd. Then the Faggots are to be slipt into it and dress'd in Rocks. Otherwise, having caus'd the Sugar to be Blown, throw in your Orange-Parings, give them a cover'd Boiling, and set them by, in order to be laid upon a Grate, or Hurdle, and dried in the Stove; which may be done in a short time, but the other Way is more preferrable.

Thus both yellow and white Faggots are made after the same manner: The former are those Parings which are made of the first Peel of the Orange; and the others are taken off afterwards, by turning them a second time.

Zests of Sevil-Oranges.

They are order'd altogether after the same manner, as those of Lemmons, for which Directions shall be given hereafter: So that recourse may be had to them, and it would be needless to anticipate the Matter in this Place.

Orange-flips.

Small Slips may likewise be made of the same Oranges, and to that end, the same Method may be follow'd, which shall be anon explain'd for Lemmon-flips, of which a greater quantity is usually preserv'd.

Certain Slips of sour Oranges are generally put into a kind of Sugar-plums, call'd *Orangeaz*, which are very grateful to the Taste, when order'd with good Sugar. The same sort of Sugar plums, are also made with Lemmon-flips.

C H A P. XIX.

Of Lemmons.

Lemmons may be preserv'd after different manners; and are of several sorts. Certain green ones are sometimes brought over entire, which pass for *Indian* Lemmons: The ripe ones that come to our Hands, are frequently preserv'd whole, in Sticks, Slips Zests, and otherwise; not to make mention of the Pasts, Marmelade and Conserves that are made of this Fruit. Let us begin with the first sort, altho' we have no longer an opportunity to preserve such in these Parts.

To preserve green Indian Lemmons.

These small Lemmons are to be lightly slit on one side, to the end, that the inside may be as much soak'd in the Sugar, as the other Parts: Then let them be thrown into Water over the Fire, but prevented from boiling, by pouring in fresh Water from time to time to cause it to sink. As soon as the Lemmons rise on the top, let them be taken off, and set by to cool: Afterwards their green Colour must be recover'd, by setting them over the Fire again in the same or other Water, which ought to boil by degrees, till the Lemmons become very soft, and slip off from the Pin. Then being taken out and cool'd again, nothing will remain to be done, only to put them into Sugar, after the same manner, as the following sorts of Lemmons.

White Lemmons preserv'd in Sticks.

These Lemmons must be Zested or else Turn'd, according as your Intention is, either to preserve them in Zests or Chips, or to make Faggots. To Turn, in this Sense, is a Term of Art, signifying to pare off the superficial Rind or Peel, on the outside, very thin and narrow, with a little Knife; turning it round about the Lemmon or Orange, so as it may be extended to the length of several Fathoms: To Zest, is to cut the Peel, from top to bottom, into small Slips, as thin, as it can possibly be done. The Lemmons thus order'd, are to be first cut into Quarters, and then into Sticks; dividing those Quarters into two or three Parts, according to their Thickness. Afterwards, they must be thrown into Water boiling over the Fire, and scalded with their Juice and innermost Skin, which keeps them whiter, and could not be got off from the Pulp, without difficulty, unless they were thus heated over the Fire: Care must also be taken to throw them into fair Water, as they are Turn'd, or Zested; otherwise they would soon grow black.

When you perceive, That the Lemmon-pulp is become very soft, let it be cool'd, and afterwards put into Sugar, newly pass'd thro' the Straining-bag: Then give it seven or eight Boilings, and pour all into earthen Pans. On the next Day, let the Syrup be pour'd off, without taking away the Fruit, and let it have twenty or thirty Boilings, having augmented it with a little Sugar. Some time after, the Lemmons are to be put into it, and so on the following Days successively, as the Syrup is boil'd, first a little Smooth, then altogether Smooth, at another time, between Smooth and Pearled, and at last thoroughly Pearled; always adding some other Sugar, as often as the Pan is set over the Fire.

As soon as the last Boiling is perform'd, for bringing the Fruit to perfection, they may be drain'd and disposed of in Pots or other Vessels, if they are design'd for keeping. The Lemmons may also be dried at the same time, or any other, at pleasure; and for that purpose, it is only requisite to cool them, which may be done more speedily, upon any urgent Occasion, by setting the bottom of the Pan into cold Water. In the mean while, let some Sugar be made Feathered; and, having drain'd the Fruit, slip them into it, in order to have a cover'd Boiling. Then take all off from the Fire, and as soon as as the Boiling entirely ceafes, begin to work and make you Sugar white, in a Corner, by rubbing it with the Back of Spoon, or Skimmer, againſt the Side of the Pan. Afterwards the Lemmons muſt be boil'd in this clarified Sugar, and ſet draining, upon Grates: Thus they'll become dry in a few Hours and at any other time, when you would have them dried, yo need only put the ſame thing into practice.

Lemmons preſerv'd in Zeſts, or Chips.

As the Lemmons are Zeſting, in the above-mention'd manner, let the *Zeſts* be thrown into fair Water on one ſide, and the Quarters, on the other, to prevent them from turning Black Afterwards, let the Water be heated, and the *Zeſts* put into it to be ſcalded, till they become very ſoft: Then, having turn'd them into freſh Water, they muſt be cool'd, and order'd with thin Sugar; putting one Ladle full of Water into a Pan for every two of clarified Sugar; thus all muſt be heated over the Fire, as long as you can well endure to hold your Finger in the Liquor. In the mean while, the Lemmon-chips being drain'd, and ſlipt into an earthen Pan, the Sugar is to be pour'd upon them, and they ought to be ſoak'd in it, ſomewhat longer than ordinary. They may be left in this condition, till the next Day, when they are to be drain'd in a Cullander, whilſt the Syrup is boil'd, till it become a little Smooth: Some time after this Syrup muſt be pour'd again upon the *Zeſts*; as alſo, on the third Day, after having brought it to its Pearled Quality, and augmented it with a little Sugar. On the fourth Day, the Lemmon-chips are to be drain'd again, and dried in the Sieve, upon Hurdles, or upon the Grate, with a Pan underneath, to receive the Syrup that diſtills from thence. They ought alſo to be turn'd from time to time, till they become very dry, and at laſt ſhut up in Boxes, to be kept for Uſe.

Lemmons preſerv'd in ſmall Slips.

Having Zeſted your Lemmons, cut your Pulp into Slips, which are to be ſlit again in their thickneſs, to render them very thin, and by that means certain ſmall Slips will be made, of the length of *Lardoons*, or Slices of Bacon, that are proper for Larding. Theſe Lemmon-ſlips, are to be ſcalded, at firſt, in Water over the Fire, till they become very ſoft. Then let ſome

clari-

New Instructions for Confectioners. 59

clarified Sugar, newly pass'd thro' the Straining-bag, be likewise set over the Fire, and, when it is ready to boil, throw in your Slips, in order to have twenty Boilings: They may also be put into the Sugar all at once, without staying till it is hot. On the next Day, having boil'd the Sugar Smooth, and slipt them into it, let them have seven, or eight Boilings. On the third Day, or the Evening before, if they were made ready in the Morning, you may bring your Sugar to its Pearled Quality, and give the Lemmon-slips a cover'd Boiling. Afterwards, they are to be put into Pots or other Vessels, according to the quantity, and dried, as occasion serves; which is to be done after the following manner:

Let your Lemmon-slips be well drain'd from their Syrup, and put into Feather'd Sugar; giving them a cover'd Boiling, and stirring them from time to time. After this cover'd Boiling, remove the Pan from the Fire, and, as soon as you can endure to touch the Handles, begin to work the Sugar, and make it white, in a Corner, as before; by rubbing and beating it by degrees, with the back of the Ladle or Skimmer, against the side of the Pan: Then, taking up the Slips, with two Forks, let them be turn'd and soak'd in this Sugar, till they are well ic'd over. Lastly, they must be laid a draining upon Hurdles, and dress'd in Rocks; by which means they will be speedily dried, and brought to perfection. However, if the Business does not require Dispatch, or if you have no mind to ice them in this manner; some Sugar may be boil'd till it has attain'd to its Blown Quality, and the Lemmon-slips may be put into it: Then, having given them a cover'd Boiling, let them be taken out, and dress'd a little while after, upon a Grate, or Hurdle, to be set into the Stove: But care must be taken to turn them on all sides, so as they may be thoroughly dried, and at last laid up in Boxes, to be us'd as occasion shall require.

If the Lemmon-slips should happen to puff, or turn sour in the Vessels, in which they are kept, they must be set over the Fire, with a little Water to cause them to give, and then boil'd, till a thick and black Scum rises on the top, which must be taken off. When they have recover'd their former Degree of Boiling, which is Pearled, their sourness will be entirely taken away, and they may be disposed of at pleasure. To that purpose, some cause the Syrup to be first set over the Fire, which being scumm'd, they turn in the Slips, to give them a Boiling; but this Matter is altogether indifferent. The Management of

others

others is yet more inconsiderable, who, for fear of too much diminishing the quantity of their Sugar, defer the scumming of it till it settles when taken off from the Fire, and till the grossest Substance of the Scum is only left: For by that means, they run the hazard of being put to the trouble, to renew the same Work, within a very short time, and the same thing may be affirm'd, with respect to other sorts of Sweet-meats, that are to be clear'd from their sourness.

Faggots of Lemmon.

As to this Particular, it is only requisite to follow the Instructions given for the Ordering of Orange-faggots, Pag. 55. so that the Reader is referr'd to that Article; because few Lemmons are preserv'd after this manner, and a much greater quantity of Oranges, more especially the sweet ones.

Lemmons preserv'd entire.

Having Zested, or else Turn'd your Lemmons, according to the Method explain'd in the second Article; throw them, as they are done, into fair Water, with some Juice of other Lemmons, to prevent them from turning Black. Let them also be scalded over the Fire, in Water, with Lemmon-juice likewise, till they become soft and tender, and slip off from the Pin. Then, being cool'd in cold Water, they must be scoop'd with a little Spoon, made for that purpose, at a little Hole bor'd on the top. As soon as they are well scoop'd and cleans'd, they are to be put into Sugar, pass'd thro' the Straining-bag, and the whole Work is to be finish'd after the same manner, as Lemmons in Sticks. They may also be prepar'd for Drying thus: Let the Sugar be brought to its Feathered Quality, and made white in a Corner, according to the Directions elsewhere laid down. Then, having slipt in the Lemmons, let them be drain'd upon Hurdles, with the Hole underneath, after they have been taken out, with a Spoon and Fork.

For Marmelade, and Pastes of Lemmon, see those Articles hereafter specified.

CHAP.

C H A P. XX.
Of Cedres, Limes, and yellow Citrons.

THese three sorts of Fruit have so near a relation, one to another, that there is no difference in the preserving of them, and very little, with respect to the common Lemmons: However, we shall here subjoin the particular Ways of ordering them to the best advantage.

Green Cedres preserv'd in Sticks or Quarters.

In these Parts, only ripe *Cedres* are us'd, such as are brought over from beyond Sea; but in the Countries, where they grow, as in *Provence*, and on the Coasts of *Genoa* and *Nice*, great quantities of them are preserv'd Green, after having taken out the Juice, to make the Liquor call'd *Cedrax*. To that purpose, they are usually cut into Quarters, to be reduc'd afterwards to Sticks, of any size that shall be thought fit: They may also be cut according to their Thickness, and thro' the middle, by reason of the extreme largeness of this Fruit; by which means there will be two sorts, *viz.* one entirely Green, and the other White. They are generally preserv'd liquid, and transported in that condition; so that there is no more to be done, but to dry them, as Occasion serves, which may be perform'd in this manner: At first they must be drain'd from their former Syrup, and put into Feathered Sugar, in order to have a cover'd Boiling: As soon as they are somewhat cool'd, and you can endure to touch the Handles of the Pan, the Sugar may be work'd and made white, by beating and rubbing it by degrees against the side of the Pan: Afterwards, your *Cedres* must be laid in the same Sugar and turn'd: Then they are to be taken out, and drain'd upon a Cullander, or Hurdle, so as their Pulp may lie downwards; by which means they will be finely ic'd over, and dried in a short time, without the help of a Stove.

To preserve ripe Cedres and Limes or Pomecitrons.

They are usually cut, altogether as the green *Cedres*, or according to the following Method for Citrons; to which Article recourse may also be had, for the Way of ordering and putting them into Sugar; because it is absolutely the same, without any difference. The same thing may likewise be done, with respect to Limes, or great Lemmons, of which a kind of Syrup is also made, as well as Limonade.

Citrons.

Yellow Citrons are preserv'd either in Sticks, or in Slices, and sometimes without taking away the inner Skin and Juice: As for those that are order'd after this last manner, it is only requisite to cut them into round Slices, of a convenient thickness, and afterwards to divide those Slices into two parts. But the other Way is most usual, and to that purpose, after the Citrons have been Turn'd, or Zested, they are to be cut thro' the middle, and each half is to be divided into four Quarters: However, nothing but the Pulp ought to be taken, of which lesser Slices or Sticks are made, which may be cut again, according to their thickness, and preserv'd conformably to the following Directions.

To preserve the Pulp of yellow Citrons.

Having cut the Citrons, as before, let them be thrown into boiling Water, and to facilitate the scalding of them, add an Handful of beaten Allum. As soon as you perceive the Fruit to be soft, let them be cool'd, and put into Sugar newly clarified: Afterwards let all have seven or eight Boilings, in order to be set by in earthen Pans till the next Day; when the Syrup being taken out, and boil'd somewhat smooth, must be augmented with other Sugar, and pour'd upon the Citrons. On the third Day, let the Syrup be made very Smooth, and likewise pour'd upon the Fruit. To make them ready for the Repository, they are to be drain'd, and set in order in Pots, or other Vessels; whilst the Syrup is brought to its Pearled Quality, to be pour'd upon them. When you would have your Citrons dried, you need only observe, what has been before laid down, for the ordering of *Cedres*.

Zests

Zests *of Citrons,* &c.

The *Zests,* or Chips of yellow Citrons, *Cedres* and Limes, are preserv'd altogether after the same manner, as those of ordinary Lemmons; for which see Pag. 57.

CHAP. XXI.
Of Compotes *for the whole Year.*

WE have hitherto treated only of Fruits, as they are preserv'd in their natural Condition; either dry, or liquid; but now it is requisite to give some Account of the other sorts of Sweet-meats that may be made of them; observing likewise the Order and Season of every one of them, as before; of these, the most common are the *Compotes*: Neither is it difficult to prepare them duly, when the Method of Preserving all kinds of Fruit is well known; because, before they are entirely brought to perfection, they come to the Degree, which is sufficient for *Compotes*. However, we shall not forbear here to express the best Manner of Ordering them, to the end, that the Reader may have greater Advantage in this Particular; and so much the rather, in regard, that, these sorts of Sweet-meats being design'd to be immediately eaten, or at least, in a short space of time; it is not necessary, to take so many Precautions, nor to observe so many nice Circumstances, as in the Managing of Fruits, that are to be thoroughly preserv'd.

Compotes *of green Apricocks.*

Having par'd your Apricocks, or put them into a Lie, such as is describ'd Pag. 16. let them be cool'd and pierc'd thro' the middle; throwing them into other fresh Water: They must also be brought again to their green Colour, changing the Water once more, in which they are to be boil'd, till they slip off from the Pin. As soon as they are cool'd and drain'd, they must be put into thin Sugar, allowing one Ladle full of Water for every two of Sugar, and causing both to be made Luke-warm;

Z 2 by

by which means they'll soon throw out all their Moisture, and imbibe the Sugar. They may be left in this condition till Night, or the next Morning, according to the time, when they were put in, or as there may be occasion for the *Compote:* Then bring all to the Fire, and give them thirty or forty Boilings, till the Apricocks are become soft, and have thoroughly imbib'd the Sugar. Afterwards, they must be set by to cool; but if you have only two or three *Compotes* of Fruit, and too much Syrup is still left, you may give it some Boilings a-part, and then pour it upon the Apricocks, dress'd in *China*-dishes or Bowls provided for that purpose.

But it is expedient to prepare a much greater quantity, at once, to serve from time to time, during the Season: Besides, that what is left, may always be brought to perfection, by causing the other Boilings to attain to higher Degrees, which are necessary for the keeping of the Apricocks, as well liquid, as dry.

Another Compote *of green Apricocks.*

If you have a mind to make a *Compote* of green Apricocks, out of Season, it may be easily done, provided, there be some liquid ones at hand: For you need only take such a quantity of Fruit as is requisite, with part of the Syrup; setting the latter over the Fire in a Copper-pan, with a little Water to cause it to give. Then let it have some Boilings, and pour it upon your Apricocks, in order to be serv'd up, either hot, or cold, accordingly as it shall be judg'd expedient.

Altho' dried Apricocks were only left in the Repository, nevertheless a very good *Compote* may be made of them; by putting them into a Pan, with some Syrup of other green Apricocks, or other Syrup of the like Nature, and causing them to give, as before. Then after a few Boilings, you have no more to do, but to dress your *Compote* and serve it up to Table.

Compotes *of green Almonds.*

Having put Almonds into a Lie prepared according to the Directions in Pag. 16. let them be brought again to their Colour, and boil'd. Then they are to be put into Sugar, observing what has been even now deliver'd with respect to *Compotes* of green Apricocks, made ready at all times: So that the like may

be

New Instructions for Confectioners. 65

be prepared, with green Almonds, either in Season, or otherwise, when preserv'd wet, or dry.

Compotes *of green Gooseberries.*

Slit your Gooseberries on the side, and pick out the small Grains that are enclos'd therein: Then let them be scalded in Water, over the Fire, and taken off, as soon as they rise on the top of the Water; setting them by, to cool: Afterwards, they must be brought again to their Colour, and heated in other fresh Water, till they become very soft and tender: At that instant, they may be remov'd from the Fire, in order to be cool'd, drain'd, and put into Sugar newly clarified; but they must only be soak'd in it, and the same thing is to be observ'd, with respect to other sorts of Fruit. Some time after, give them fourteen or fifteen Boilings, and if you percieve, that they have thoroughly imbib'd the Sugar, you may reserve them, for the making of *Compotes,* at any time, till the Season is pass'd: So that the rest of the Work may be finish'd, by giving them the Boiling, that is peculiar to this sort of Fruit, and specified in its proper Place, Pag. 33.

When these Boilings are perform'd, only for *Compotes,* if too much Syrup be left, it must be boil'd several other times, after having taken out the Gooseberries, upon which it is to be pour'd, at last. At another time, if you are desirous to make a *Compote* of green Gooseberries, out of hand, take those that lie by liquid, and cause them to give, with a little Water: Then let them have a Boiling, with the Gooseberries, and dress them, upon your *China*-dishes.

Compotes *of Cherries.*

Having provided Cherries, and cut off part of their Stalks, take a quarter, or half a Pound of Sugar, which will be sufficient, if you design only to make one or two *Compotes*: Let it be melted, with a very little Water; because the Cherries will yield a great deal of Juice, and let all boil together; carefully taking off the Scum, till the Cherries become soft, and have thoroughly imbib'd the Sugar. If too much Syrup be left, give it some other Boilings, and afterwards pour it upon your Fruit.

Upon any emergent Occasion, even out of the Season, a *Compote* may be made of dried Cherries, or others; following

the

the Instructions that have been given for the preceding Fruits.

Compotes of *Rasberries*.

Having caus'd some Sugar to be brought to its Pearled Quality, let your Rasberries be thrown into it: Then give them a cover'd Boiling, and the Business will be effected.

Compotes of *Strawberries*.

These *Compotes* are usually made after the same manner, but if the Strawberries are somewhat over-ripe, the Sugar must be boil'd to a little higher Degree.

Compotes of *Currans*.

Take Sugar newly pass'd tho' the Straining-bag, and boil it till it is Blown: Then throw in your Currans, give them a Boiling, and remove them from the Fire. If you percieve, that they have thoroughly imbib'd the Sugar, they may be dress'd upon *China*-dishes, and serv'd up to Table: Otherwise, let them be brought to the Fire again, and have another Boiling.

Compotes of *ripe Apricocks*.

When ripe Apricocks first begin to be in Season, they may be us'd without paring; but afterwards they must be Turn'd and Ston'd, in order to be scalded over the Fire, as those that are design'd for Preserving: As soon as they rise on the top, and become soft, they must be taken off, and set by to cool: Then let them be put into Sugar, as it runs from the Straining-bag, and boil'd till the Scum ceases to rise any longer; which is a sign, that the Apricocks have cast all their Juice, and sufficiently imbib'd the Sugar. But if they do not appear to be boil'd enough, you may give them a few more Boilings, as also the Syrup, in case, too great a quantity of it be left, so as it may be conveniently pour'd upon the Fruit.

Another Way of making Compotes of *ripe Apricocks*.

Compotes of Apricocks are likewise made without scalding; so as to render them more delicious, and that they may retain a

greater

greater relish of the Fruit: Having par'd and ston'd them, you need only put them all at once into clarified Sugar; or if that be wanting, into Sugar melted with Water, that is to say, a Quarter of a Pound, or somewhat more, for every *Compote*. Thus they are to boil, till they become very soft; to which purpose, a sufficient quantity of Water must be put to them, altho' they also yield some Juice. When the Scum ceases to rise, and the Apricocks have imbib'd the Sugar, take them off from the Fire, and observe, whether it be not expedient to boil your Syrup, a little longer, that it may be sufficiently consum'd, and only so much left, as is requisite for the soaking of your Fruit.

Compotes *of Plums.*

Let your Amber-plums, Orange-plums, or others, be prick'd with a Pin, and thrown into Water: Then scald them over the Fire, in the same, or other Water, and take them off, as soon as they rise on the top, causing them to be speedily cool'd: Then let them be brought again to their Colour, and made soft, according to their kind, and conformably to the Method explain'd in the Article of *Plums.* Afterwards, they are to be put into thin Sugar well heated; allowing one Ladle full of Water, to two of Sugar. They are to be left in this condition till the next Day, or only till the Evening, if Occasion require it; and then they must be put again into a Copper-pan, in order to have as many Boilings, as shall be judg'd expedient, till the Sugar be thoroughly imbib'd. At that instant, it may be perceiv'd, that the Scum does not rise any longer, and that the Plums are become soft and tender. A great quantity may be thus prepar'd at once, and kept for a considerable time.

Another sort of Compote *of Plums.*

Compotes may also be made of Plums, without scalding; either leaving the Stones, or taking them away. Having put them into thin Sugar, let all simper together, and after they have been set by for some time, let them be brought to the Fire again, to boil, till no Scum is left, and till they have thoroughly imbib'd the Sugar: Or else, those Directions may be follow'd, that are specified in the last Article of Apricock-*Compotes.*

Compotes of *Summer-pears*.

These sorts of Pears are to be scalded over the Fire, till they become somewhat soft, and prick'd on the top, with a Bodkin, even to the Core: Afterwards being cool'd, they must be par'd; and thrown into fresh Water, in order to be put into clarified Sugar; adding a little Water, to boil it. If the Pears are large, they may be cut into Halves or Quarters; so as they may simper in the Sugar, and cast their Juice. Then let them boil, till the Scum ceases to rise, and your *Compote* will be made. If too great a quantity of Syrup be left, let it be consum'd a little by boiling, and pour'd upon the Fruit. *Compotes* may be made after the same manner, of *Blanquets*, Russetins, Muscadines, and other sorts of Pears.

The clarifying of the Sugar may also be dispens'd with, only throwing a Lump of Sugar of a convenient Thickness, into the Water, in which they are to be boil'd; and taking care that the whole be well Scumm'd: A good quarter of a Pound of Sugar may be sufficient for a *Compote* of the like Nature.

Compotes *of other sorts of Pears*.

Winter-Pears may also be put into *Compotes*, in the same manner, particularly the *Bon-chretiens*, those of St. *Francis* and others. They must be first prick'd to the Core, with a Bodkin, and scalded in Water: Then they are to be cool'd, par'd and divided into Quarters, throwing them again into fresh Water: Afterwards, they must be put into one half Sugar and the other Water, and boil'd, till they have thrown out all their Scum; which is to be carefully taken off, with the Skimmer. Let the Pan be remov'd from time to time, and set aside, as soon as the Pears have thoroughly imbib'd the Sugar, and are become soft; otherwise they would turn to Marmelade. Then let the Pears be dress'd upon *China*-dishes, and having given the Syrup, some other Boilings, if it be requisite, pour it upon your Fruit, and squeez in the Juice of a Lemmon, or Orange: The same thing may also be done in the preceding *Compotes*.

Com-

Compotes of Pears made in a Bell.

There are certain Pears, as the *Certoe*, the Pound-pear and some others, of which another sort of *Compote* may be made, by causing them to be stew'd in a Bell, thus: Having par'd and cut your Pears into Quarters, put them into an earthen Vessel, or one of Copper, made for that purpose; in form of a Bell, with Water, Sugar, Cinnamon and Cloves: A quarter of a Pound of Sugar, or somewhat more, will be sufficient for a Pound of Fruit, and only so much Water, as may serve to soak them: Let them be stew'd over a gentle Fire, and when they are half done, let half a Glass of red Wine be added: But the Pot must be kept close stopt, and the Fruit stirr'd from time to time, lest they should stick to the Bottom. Afterwards, the *Compote* is to be dress'd, and the Syrup pour'd upon it, if there be no more than is needful; otherwise it must be consum'd by degrees, because too great a quantity of it ought not to be left.

Compotes of roasted Pears.

Compotes may likewise be made of roasted Pears: When they are sufficiently done, and par'd as neatly as is possible, let them be slit and the Cores taken out: Then they are to be put into a Pan, with Sugar and a little Water, which is to be boil'd and and consum'd, till the Pears become very red, and till very little Syrup be left; but they ought to be often stirr'd, to hinder them from burning, and sticking to the Bottom. Afterwards, having dress'd them for your *Compote*, you may squeez in the Juice of an Orange, or Lemmon, which will wonderfully heighten their Relish.

Pears may be also put into a Silver-dish or Plate, and bak'd in an Oven, or otherwise, with Powder-sugar, after they have been first scalded in Water, in order to be par'd; or else they may be par'd, without scalding: Then let them be dress'd, strew'd again with Sugar; and brought to a Colour, with the red-hot Fire-shovel; adding the Juice of an Orange, when ready to be serv'd up to Table.

See hereafter the *Compotes* of Peaches, among which mention is made, of another manner of diversifying these *Compotes*, accordingly as occasion may require.

Compotes *of Apples.*

Pare your Apples, cut them into Halves, or Quarters, take out the Cores, and, as they are done, throw them into fair Water: Then put a good Quarter of a Pound of Sugar, if it be only for one *Compote*, or a greater quantity, proportionably for several *Compotes*, into a Quart of Water, or more, and let all boil with the Apples. As soon as they are become very soft, and have thoroughly imbib'd the Sugar, take them out, and lay them in order upon your *China*-dishes; whilst the rest of the Syrup is boil'd and consum'd, till it turn to a Jelly, which happens, when it falls from the Spoon, in thick drops, and does not run in Threads. Then pour it upon your Fruit, and, if you please, squeez in the Juice of an Orange, or Lemmon.

Other *Ways of preparing* Compotes *of Apples.*

Let a Decoction be made of the Parings and Cores, with some other Apples, which being strain'd will serve for the Boiling of your *Compote*, in the same manner as before. Or else, when the Apples are stew'd, and a great quantity of Syrup is still left, let the same Parings and Cores be boil'd in it, and let the Syrup be pass'd thro' a Sieve, before it be pour'd upon the Fruit.

Compotes of roasted Apples may also be made, observing the Directions already laid down for Pears: But you must remember, to cause your Fruit to be stew'd over a good Fire, and to turn them, from time to time, with the Ladle.

A Compote *of Apples* à la Dauphine.

Having cut your Apples into eight Quarters, every one of which is to be made round, in form of little Balls, as it were Plums; let them boil in a Decoction, of all the Parings, and some other Apples, with the necessary quantity of Sugar, as for other *Compotes*. At last, a little Cochineal is to be added, to give them a red Colour, and the Syrup must not be so much wasted; unless you would have the *Compotes* ic'd over, to diversifie them.

Com-

Compotes *of farced Apples.*

Take about a quarter of a Pound of the dried Pulp of Oranges and Lemmons, and pound it in a Morter: Then let some Apples be chopt small, and mingled with Marmelade of Apricocks, or some other sort that is at Hand: Afterwards, having bor'd the Apples thro' from top to bottom, without paring them, let the Hole, which ought to be wide enough to receive your Thumb, be fill'd with the said Marmelade, let all be gently bak'd, upon a Silver-plate, in the Oven; or else Fire may be put round about the said Plate, and when the Apples are done enough, they may be soak'd in a little Syrup, as the others.

Compotes *of Peaches.*

When the Peaches are full ripe, they can only be roasted; because this sort of Fruit is too soft. Therefore they must be neatly par'd ston'd and laid in Quarters, upon a Silver-dish, or Plate, with Sugar, and, if you think fit, with candy'd Lemmon-peel chopt small: Then, being bak'd in an Oven, let them be dress'd, if they are to be serv'd up with any Thing else, and let the red-hot Fire-shovel be pass'd over them, to give them a fine Colour, after they have been strew'd with Sugar.

This *Compote*, and others of the like nature, may be put into a *Tourte*, or Pan-pie, and to that end, a Border of Paste, and even the whole Furniture that is usually provided for other Pan-pies, must be laid in the Dish, in which the Peaches are to be roasted, and the Fruit must be set in order therein. In the mean while, another Piece of Paste for Crackling Crust, being roll'd out, may be cut into slips, and separately bak'd in an Oven; in order to be ic'd over with the White of an Egg, and Powder-sugar, well temper'd together. This ic'd Crust must also be dried in the Oven, till it become very white, and laid upon the Pie, a little before it is serv'd up to Table.

Other Compotes *of Peaches.*

Compotes may be made of Peaches that are less ripe, according to the Instructions before given for those of Apricocks, Pag. 62. and others may likewise be prepar'd, upon occasion, of green Peaches, in their Season, or such as have been already preserv'd;

in

in the ordering of which, it is only requisite to observe the Method laid down for *Compotes* of green Apricocks.

Compotes *of Bell-grapes.*

The Bell-grapes must be first scalded in Water, and brought again to their Colour, as those that are design'd for preserving liquid, or otherwise: To that purpose, let your Water simper over the Fire, throw the Fruit into it, and, as soon as they begin to rise, set all by to cool: Then cause them to become green again, in the same, or other Water, and when they are very soft, let them be laid a draining; whilst some Sugar is boil'd Smooth, or only simpers a little. Afterwards, having remov'd the Pan aside, till the Evening, or the next Day, accordingly as you have time, and, having set it again over the Fire, give the Fruit ten, or twelve Boilings, and your *Compote* will be brought to perfection.

Thus, if you think fit, a sufficient quantity for several Services, may be prepar'd, and kept for a considerable time. If you have a mind to make a *Compote* of Bell-grapes, out of the Season, you need only take some of those that have been already preserv'd liquid, and cause the Syrup to give a little: Then let it have a Boiling, slip in the Grapes, and dress all upon your *China*-dishes.

Compotes *of Quinces.*

Let the Quinces be cut into Quarters, proportionably to their Thickness, without absolutely loosening them, one from another; so as they may stick together, as if the Fruit were still entire: Or else, they may be only pierc'd to the Core, with a Bodkin, and scalded in Water, till they become soft: At that instant, let them be remov'd from the Fire, to be cool'd and par'd, taking away the Kernels, and throwing them as they are done, into other fresh Water: Then, putting them, as the Pears, into one half Sugar, and the other Water, let all simper together, and set them by for a while, accordingly as the time will permit. Afterwards, being set over the Fire again, they must be boil'd, and scumm'd, till they have thoroughly imbib'd the Sugar, in order to be dress'd for your *Compote*, with the Syrup, when only so much is left, as will be requisite for the soaking of them. Lastly, let the Juice of an Orange, or Lemmon be squeez'd upon all, and let them be serv'd up hot to Table.

Other Ways of making Compotes of Quinces.

The Quinces may be wrapp'd up in wet Paper, and roasted by degrees under hot Embers: Then they are to be cut into Quarters, taking away the Cores, par'd, and put into a Copper-pan, with Sugar and a little Water; causing them thoroughly to imbibe it. When the Syrup is sufficiently consum'd, they may be dress'd, and serv'd up hot; in the same manner, as the former.

Or else, when your Quinces are roasted, pare them, and cut that part which is most done, into Slices: Then putting them into a Dish, or Plate, with Powder-sugar, and a little sweet Water, let them be cover'd, and laid upon the hot Embers; by which means they'll be well soak'd, by degrees, and a Syrup will be made of an exquisite Taste.

Compotes of Chesnuts.

Having roasted and peel'd your Chesnuts, let them be beaten flat, and put into a Dish; pouring upon them some Syrup of Fruits, or a Decoction of Apples, boil'd with Sugar, till it become Smooth: Then cover the Chesnuts, and lay them a soaking, over a gentle Fire; adding other Syrup, from time to time, as the former is consum'd. They ought to be serv'd up hot, to Table; and to that end, the *China*-ware must be set in order upon a Dish, so as the Fruit may be turn'd upon them. Then moisten all, with Syrup, if it be requisite, and squeez upon them the Juice of a Lemmon, or Orange.

Compotes of *Lemmons,* or *Oranges.*

Let your Oranges, or Lemmons be Turn'd, or else Zested, and scalded in Water, over the Fire: Then, having set them by, to cool, cut them into Slices, or Sticks, or into round Slices, cross-wise, and take out the Kernels; throwing the Fruits, as they are done, into fair Water. Afterwards, having made a Decoction of Apples, with Sugar, let it be reduc'd almost to a Jelly, and let the Oranges, or Lemmons be slipt into it: Otherwise, let them be put into Sugar, newly pass'd thro' the Straining-bag, and have eight, or ten Boilings: Then they may be set by, for some time, and finish'd at pleasure, by giving them

twen-

twenty other Boilings, in order to dress the *Compote*, and serve it up to Table.

Chap. XXII.

Of the Conserves of Flowers and Fruits.

THis Article is as remarkable as the preceding, and of no less importance, in the Art of Preserving; more especially, for the preparing and dressing of a Desert, or Banquet of Sweet-meats.

Conserves of Orange-flowers.

Take about three Pounds of Sugar, and boil it, till it becomes Feathered: Then, having pick'd a Handful of Orange-flowers, let them be chopt, and thrown into the Sugar, when the Boiling ceases: But care must be taken to temper and mingle them well with the Sugar, to the end, that they may be impregnated with it, on all sides. Afterwards, you are to work the Sugar, quite round about the Pan, till a small Ice be made on the top, and then speedily pour off your Conserve, into Paper-moulds, or others: When it is cold, that is to say, about two Hours after, it must be taken out of the said Moulds, and kept for Use. To serve it up to Table, it may be cut after what manner you please, either into Lozenges, or otherwise; to which purpose, it is only requisite to mark it with the point of a Knife, and it will easily break. If you have a mind to dress it in an oval, or round Form, it may be done with a Spoon, when the Conserve is newly made, and so of the rest.

Conserve of Cherries.

Let the Cherries be ston'd, scalded over the Fire, and well dried: Then boil the Sugar till it be Blown, and throw in the thick Substance of the Cherries; tempering it well with the Sugar, to the end that all may be thoroughly intermixed: Afterwards work the Sugar round about the Pan, till it makes a small Ice on the top, and then pour your Conserve into Moulds. This Me-

Method is to be obferv'd, when Cherries firft appear, but when they are in their full Seafon, you muft caufe them to caft their Juice, and afterwards lay them upon a Sieve: As foon as they are drain'd, they muft be pounded in a Mortar, and fet over the Fire again, to be well dried: Some time after, their thick Subftance muft be put into Blown Sugar, as before, and order'd, after the fame manner.

Conferve of Currans.

Having pick'd your Currans, and put them into a Copper-pan, over the Fire, to caufe them to caft their Juice, let them be well drain'd on a Sieve: Then ftrain them, and let that which runs thro' the Sieve be fet again over the Fire, to be dried. In the mean while, let the Sugar boil, till it has attain'd to its Crack'd Quality, and throw in as much of the thick Subftance of your Fruit, as will be fufficient to give the Conferve a good Colour and Tafte; tempering all well with the Sugar. Afterwards, let the Sugar be work'd and made white, round about the Pan, as upon other Occafions, and when you perceive a thin Ice, on the top, take off the Pan and drefs your Conferve in the Moulds.

Conferve of Rafberies.

This fort of Conferve is ufually made as the former, only it muft be mix'd with a few Rasberries to give it a Smell and Tincture, as if it were made altogether of that Fruit: To that purpofe, a Handful of Rasberries may be added, with their Grains, but thefe Grains are fomewhat troublefome to the Teeth, and may fpoil your Conferve, when you are about to cut it.

Conferve of Smallage.

Let the greeneft Leaves of Smallage, or Celery be fcalded over the Fire, and give them three or four Boilings: Then let them be well drain'd, pounded in a Morter, and ftrain'd thro' the Sieve; whilft fome Sugar is boil'd, till it be a little Feathered: As foon as the Boiling ceafes, throw in what was ftrain'd, and temper it well with the Sugar, which muft be work'd as before, and when an Ice appears on the top, the Conferve may be pour'd into the Moulds.

White

White Conserve.

For want of Orange-flowers, some Marmelade made of them may be us'd; if you have any at Hand; Otherwise, take a little Marmelade of Lemmons, with Orange-flower-water, or the Juice of a Lemmon, if you are minded to diversifie the Conserves. In the mean time, the Sugar being boil'd, till it become Feathered, temper your Marmelade with it, and for the rest, observe the Instructions given for the preceding Conserves.

Conserve of Violets.

Conserve of Violets is made in the same manner, as that of Orange-flowers; only the Violet-flowers must be pounded in a Mortar, after they have been pick'd, and you are to put into the Sugar, what is requisite to give your Conserve, the Colour and Taste of Violets. It may also be made, with Marmelade of Violets, if any of the gross Substance taken from your Syrup of Violets, be left; incorporating it with Pearled Sugar: For by that means, it will keep, as long as you shall think fit, and Pastes may likewise be made of the same Substance, mingling it with Marmelade of Lemmons, which easily imbibes its Tincture.

Other sorts of Conserves.

Many other Conserves may be made, in taking measures from the former; particularly of Barberries and Pomegranates, by observing the Directions before laid down for those of Currans; of Roses and Jessemin, imitating the Conserves of Violets, or Orange-flowers; and so of others, which may be prepar'd, according to Discretion.

CHAP. XXIII.
Of Marmelades.

AN Account might be given of what relates to this Article, in treating of every kind of Fruit in particular; but forasmuch as several sorts of Marmelade may be made at once, it was judg'd more expedient, to comprife all in one Chapter, fo as recourfe may be more conveniently had thereto. Thefe Marmelades are of great Ufe, in an Office, for the making of Pan-pies, or Tarts; or elfe, by the Mixture and Diftribution of their Colours, the Coats of Arms of feveral Families may be reprefented; as alfo, Flower-de-luces, Croffes and many other Devices. When you would have more than one fort of them made in one Day, and with the fame Stock of Sugar; all thefe Fruits muft be firft pick'd, fcalded in Water, or boil'd over the Fire, according to their Qualities; then ftrain'd thro' Sieves, and dried in different Copper-pans, or Silver-difhes: In the mean while, Sugar is to be boil'd, proportionably to the Quantity of Paftes; which are to be put in, when it has attain'd to the degrees of Boiling hereafter exprefs'd. To that purpofe, it is expedient to begin with thofe Paftes, or Marmelades that require a lefs ftrong Sugar, and whilft they are foaking and fimpering over another Furnace, the Sugar may be brought to that degree of Boiling, which is neceffary for the others; which afterwards are to be order'd in the fame manner.

Marmelade of green Apricocks.

Let the Apricocks be put into a Lie, fuch as is defcrib'd Pag. 16. and cool'd in frefh Water, to take off the Skin: Then they muft be well boil'd, till they become very foft, and being drained, pafs'd thro' a Sieve, into a Pan. Afterwards, this Pafte muft be dried over the Fire, carefully ftirring and turning it, on all fides, with the *Spatula*, fo as no Moifture may be left, and till it begins to ftick to the Pan. In the mean while, let fome Sugar be boil'd, till it become Crack'd, which is to be temper'd with the Marmelade, after having weigh'd out as much as is needful, that is to fay, a Pound of one, for every Pound of the other: When this is done, it remains only, to caufe all to fimper together, for a while, and to put your Marmelade into Pots, or Glaffes, or elfe to procede to the drying of it.

Marmelade of Cherries.

The Cherries muft be firft fton'd, and fet over the Fire in a Copper-pan to caufe them to caft their Juice: Afterwards they are to be drain'd, bruis'd and pafs'd thro' a Sieve, and the Marmelade must be put again into the Pan, to be dried, over the Fire, as before. Then let some Sugar be boil'd, till it be greatly Feathered; allowing one Pound of it, for every Pound of Fruit, or Paste: Let all be well intermix'd together, in order to simper for some time, and at last let the Marmelade be put into Pots, or Glasses strew'd with Sugar: They ought not to be left long upon the Fire, lest they should become too black, and for that reason, they must be set over one that is quick, in order to be thoroughly dried.

Marmelade of Currans.

Having provided Currans, and stripp'd them off from the Bunches, soak them in boiling Water, till they break: Then removing them from the Fire, let them be drain'd upon a Sieve, and as soon as they are cold, pass'd thro' the same Sieve, by reason of the Grains; some time after, they must be dried over the Fire, according to the usual Method, whilst the Sugar is brought to its Crack'd Quality, allowing a Pound of it for every Pound of Fruit. Lastly, let it all be well temper'd together, and having caus'd them to simper a little, let them be strew'd with Sugar, in order to be conveniently dispos'd of in Pots or Glasses, as before.

Marmelade of Bell-grapes is made after the same manner.

Marmelade of Rasberries.

The Body of this Marmelade is usually made of very ripe Currans, to which is added a Handful of Rasberries, to make it appear as if it consisted altogether of the latter. For the rest, it is only requisite to observe, what has been even now deliver'd, with respect to the preceding Marmelade.

Marmelade of ripe Apricocks.

Take five Pounds of very ripe Apricocks, boil them in two Pounds of Pearled Sugar, till they have thrown out all their Scum, and then remove them from the Fire. When they are cold, set them again over the Fire, to be broken and dried, till they do not run any longer. In the mean time, three Pounds and half of Sugar, being made Crack'd, let it be incorporated with the Paste; let all simper together for a while, and let the Marmelade, strew'd with fine Sugar, be dispos'd of in Pots, or Glasses, as the others:

Mar-

Marmelade of Plums.

If they are such Plums, as slip off from their Stones, let those Stones be taken away: Otherwise, let them be scalded in Water, till they become very soft; let them also be drain'd and well squeez'd thro' the Sieve: Then dry your Marmelade over the Fire, and let it be incorporated, with the same Weight of Crack'd Sugar: Lastly, having caus'd it to simper, for some time, let it be put into Pots, or Glasses, and strew'd with Sugar.

Mirabolan Plums, as well red, as black, are very proper for this sort of Sweet-meats.

Marmelade of Pears.

Let your Pears be scalded in Water over the Fire, and when they are become very tender, let them be taken out and drain'd: Then strain all thro' a Sieve, and let your Sugar boil, till it be very much Feathered; allowing three quarters of a Pound of it for every Pound of Fruit: Lastly, having temper'd it with the Paste, which ought to be well dried, and having caus'd them to simper for a while, pour the Marmelade into Pots or Glasses strew'd with Sugar.

Marmelade of Apples.

Marmelade of Apples is made altogether according to the Method even now explain'd; as well for the manner of ordering the Fruit, as with respect to the Quantity, and the Degree of boiling the Sugar, which is necessary, for that purpose.

Marmelade of Sevil-Oranges.

Having cut your Oranges into Quarters, without Turning or Zesting them, take away the Juice and the tops, where there is a tough Skin, which cannot easily be soften'd: In the mean time, let some Water be set over the Fire, and when it is ready to boil, throw in your Orange-peels which must boil, till they become very soft, and yield to the touch of your Finger: Then they are to be cool'd in fresh Water, drain'd, and strongly squeez'd thro' a Linnen-cloath: This Pulp must also be pound-

A a 2   ed

ed in a Mortar, and pass'd thro' the Sieve; whilst some Sugar is boil'd till it be Feathered, which is to be mingled with the Marmelade in the Copper-pan, into which it was put, to be heated again a little, to the End that the moistness may evaporate. The usual quantity of Sugar is requisite, as well that it may slip off, from the bottom of the Pan, as that, what is taken up with the *Spatula* may be entirely separated from the rest, without running. At last, set your Marmelade upon the Fire again, to simper, and let it be pour'd hot into Pots or other Vessels.

Marmelade of Lemmons.

The Lemmons being Zested, cut into quarters, and clear'd from their Juice, must be thrown into Water, as they are done, to hinder them from turning black: Then having caus'd other Water to boil over the Fire, let them be put into it, and when they have had four or five Boilings, squeez in the Juice of a Lemmon, as also that of another, some time after. As soon as your Lemmon-pulp is become very soft, it must be cool'd, drain'd and squeez'd in a Linnen-cloath, before it is pounded in the Mortar, and pass'd thro' the Sieve. Lastly, your Marmelade must be set over the Fire again, a little while, as the former, and the Sugar is to be order'd, after the same manner.

Marmelade of Orange-flowers.

Take only the Leaves of your Orange-flowers, without the Yellow; or Stalks, and as they are pick'd, throw them into fair Water, into which the Juice of a Lemmon has been squeez'd: Then scald them over the Fire, as it has been shewn, in the preceding Articles, till they become very soft; adding likewise, the Juice of another Lemmon. Afterwards, being well press'd in a Linnen-cloath, or else with your Hands, they must be pounded in a Mortar, and strain'd thro' a Sieve, if it be requisite. As for the Sugar, it must be made greatly Feathered, and incorporated with the Marmelade, till it slips off from the bottom and sides of the Pan. Lastly, having caus'd all to simper, a little, the Marmelade may be pour'd into Pots, and kept for use; if you are not desirous, to have it immediately dried.

This is the best Way of preparing the Marmelade of pure Orange-flowers; otherwise, to save some Charges, it may be

min-

New Instructions for Confectioners. 81

mingled, as Occasion requires, with a little Marmelade of Lemmons, which is equally white and of the same Taste: Insomuch, that some Confectioners cause it to pass for the true Marmelade of Orange-flowers; contenting themseves only to throw in a Handful of Flowers, when it is made, to give it a little Smell, or Tincture of them.

Observations upon the several sorts of Marmelade.

The manner of drying all these different sorts of Marmelades shall be explain'd in the following Article of Pastes: Those of green Apricocks, and green Almonds are apt to grow greasy, and will not keep very long; so that it is requisite either to dry them immediately, or in less space of time, than three Months; otherwise they cannot be well dried. The Marmelades of Orange-flowers and Lemmons, generally candy within a little while, altho' they are duely prepar'd, but that is no great dammage. Whenever you would have them dried, let all the Candy be put with a little Water into a Copper-pan, over the Fire, and let it be brought again, to the necessary Degree of Boiling, with other Sugar, as much as is needful for the drying of your Paste; so as all may be mingled with the said Paste, according to the Method, hereafter specified.

CHAP. XXIV.
Of the Pastes of Fruits.

IF is only requisite to have recourse to the particular Marmelades, of every sort of Fruit, described in the fore-going Chapter, to know how to make as many Pastes; in regard that it is almost the same thing, and the whole Work is brought to Perfection by drying those Marmelades. To that purpose, when the Business requires dispatch, the Sugar must boil, till it be crack'd, or at least, greatly Feathered; to be incorporated with the dried Fruit. Afterwards, the Marmelade being made according to Art; may be taken up with a Spoon, and dress'd upon Slates, or in Moulds, in order to be dried in the Stove, with a good Fire. In the Evening, or the next Day, they

A a 3   must

must be turn'd on the other side, and laid again upon the same Slates, or upon Sieves: As soon as these Pastes are become very firm and compact, they are to be lock'd up in Boxes, and may be us'd, as Occasion requires.

At other times, when you would have any Paste dryed, let as much Marmelade, as you shall think fit, be put into a Copper-pan, and having caus'd some Sugar to be brought to its Feathered Quality, pour it in; tempering it well till it slips off from the bottom of the Pan; after the same manner, as in the making of Marmelade. Then let all simper together, for a while, and let the Paste be immediately dress'd upon Slates, or in Tin-moulds, made in form of a Heart, Square, Flower-de-luce, &c. which are usually set into the Stove, to be dried as before. These are the general Directions that may be given, for the ordering of such Fruit-pastes as are made of Marmelades; allowing two Pounds of Sugar, for every Pound of Fruit. But for other Pastes, that are made on purpose, an equal quantity of each will be sufficient, and the Sugar must be boil'd till it has attain'd to its Crack'd Quality.

Pastes of green Apricocks.

Let your green Apricocks be prepar'd, and made into a Paste according to the Method laid down for the Marmelade of the same Pag. 77. Then your Sugar being boil'd till it become Crack'd, must be incorporated with the Paste; allowing a Pound of one, for the like quantity of the other. Afterwards, let all simper together, and at the same time dress your Paste, as before; in regard that it will not keep long, by reason of it aptness to grow greasy.

The Pastes of green Almonds, if any are made, may be prepared after the same manner.

Cherry-pastes.

The Cherry-cakes described under the Article of that Fruit, Pag. 30. may be now us'd to very good purpose, but when they are out of Season, some Marmelade of Cherries is to be taken; which, being cool'd and boil'd again in new Sugar, that is Feathered, as it has been already hinted, may be order'd with a Spoon, and set into the Stove to be dried. When this Paste is turn'd on the other side, it must be lightly strew'd with Sugar put,

New Instructions for Confectioners. 83

put into a Handkerchief, and it will appear finer, being dress'd the first side uppermost, to be serv'd up to Table.

Pastes of Currans.

Let your Currans be set over the Fire, to cause them to cast their Juice, and laid upon a Sieve, when cool'd: Let them also be strain'd thro' the same Sieve, and dried over the Fire, whilst an equal quantity of Sugar, that is to say, a Pound for every Pound of Fruit, is brought to its Crack'd Quality, which is to be incorporated with it, in the same manner, as for making Marmelade of Currans, explain'd Pag. 78. Thus the Paste may be dress'd, after having caus'd it to simper for a while, if you have a mind to dry it at the same time: Otherwise, let this Marmelade be boil'd over again in other Crack'd or Feathered Sugar; observing, for the rest, what has been already deliver'd, upon the like Occasion, concerning Fruit-pastes, in general.

Rasberry-paste.

The Body of this sort of Paste is usually made in the same manner, as for the Marmelade; that is to say, with Currans, and a few Handfuls of Rasberries, and the whole Work is finish'd, as the former: Both these sorts are also to be strew'd with Sugar, as the Cherry-paste, as they are turning to be dried on the other side, and ought to be serv'd up to Table with the first side uppermost.

Pastes of ripe Apricocks.

Apricock-paste is usually made, as the Marmelade of the same, specified Pag. 78. or else the Apricocks may only be scalded at first, as the rest of the Fruits, without Sugar. If your Apricocks are not thoroughly ripe, they must be bruis'd, as much as is possible, and even pounded in a Mortar. Afterwards, the Sugar must be boil'd, till it become Crack'd; that is to say, a Pound for every Pound of Fruit, and temper'd with the Paste that has been well dried over the Fire. Then, having caus'd it to simper, dress it as the others, in order to be dried in the Stove. This Paste is not so grateful to the Palate, when kept for a considerable time; because it is apt to grow greasy, as that of green Apricocks.

A a 4   Plum-

Plum-paste.

This Paste may be made of dried Marmelade of Plums; putting to it, some new Feathered Sugar, as it has been intimated, in the beginning: Or else having prepar'd your Fruit, that is to say, strain'd and dried it, cause it to be incorporated with Crack'd Sugar. Afterwards, let all simper together, and let the Pastes be dress'd after the usual manner.

Pastes of Apples and Pears.

Scald these Fruits in Water, as the former, and when they are become soft, let them be drain'd, pass'd thro' a Sieve, and dried over the Fire; stirring them with a *Spatula*, both on the bottom and round about, lest they should burn. When the Paste slips off from the bottom and sides of the Pan, remove it from the Fire, and cause some Sugar to be greatly Feathered, or Crack'd; which must be well temper'd with it; allowing a Pound of Fruit, for the like quantity of Sugar. Afterwards, set your Paste again over the Fire, to simper, and dress it, as the others, with a Spoon, either upon Slates, or in Moulds, putting them into the Stove, at the same time, to be dried.

Pastes of roasted Apples and Pears.

These sorts of Pastes may be made at all times, and more especially during the Winter-season: To that purpose, your Apples, or Pears being well roasted, take that Part of them which is reddish and most done, and strain it thro' a Sieve: Then let as many Pounds of Sugar, as of Fruit, be brought to the crack'd degree of Boiling, and let the Work be finish'd, after the same manner, as for all other sorts of Pastes.

Peach-paste.

When the Peaches are somewhat ripe, they may be order'd, according to either of those Ways, express'd for ripe Apricocks, Pag. 83. And as for the Paste of green Peaches, it is only requisite to follow the Directions given, for green Apricocks, Pag. 82.

Quince-paste.

Take the yellowest and soundest Quinces that can be procur'd, pare them, and cut out the Cores, if you shall think fit, or else let all be left; contenting your self, only to cut the Quinces into quarters: Then, having caus'd some Water to boil over the Fire, throw in your Fruit, and let them be boil'd, till they become very soft, in order to be drain'd upon a Hurdle or Grate, and pass'd thro' the Hair-sieve. Afterwards, the Paste must be set over the Fire again, to be dried, and temper'd with Crack'd Sugar, to the quantity of somewhat more than a Pound, for every Pound of Fruit. Lastly, you must cause your Paste, to simper, for a while, and to be dress'd, as the others.

Orange-paste.

This Paste is usually made as Orange-Marmelade, according to the Method explain'd under that Article, Pag. 79, and 80. or else of the Marmelade it self, as it has been already declar'd, in treating of the Fruit-pastes, in general; that is to say, it must be incorporated with new Sugar, brought to its Feathered Quality, till it slips off from the bottom of the Pan: Then, having caus'd it to simper, dress it after the usual manner, to be dried in the Stove. Thus Orange-pastes may be prepar'd at all times, provided there be a constant Supply of the Marmelade; which will keep very well for that purpose, and for the making of Conserves.

Lemmon-paste.

For this Article, recourse may also be had to the Lemmon-Marmelade, described Pag. 80. if you have none ready made in the Repository: But if there be any left, you need only renew it, with Feathered Sugar, as in the preceding Article, and having caus'd your Marmelade, or Paste to simper, a little while, dress it with a Spoon, upon the Slates, or in Moulds, so as it may conveniently be dried in the Stove.

Pastes

Pastes of Orange-flowers.

Take pure Marmelade of Orange-flowers, or the other sort specified, Pag. 80, and 81. accordingly as Occasion may serve; and for the rest, follow the same Method that is us'd in ordering the former sorts of Paste. For want of Marmelade, take Orange-flowers, which are to be prepar'd, as for the same Marmelade, and mingle them with any other Marmelade, that you shall judge to be most proper for that purpose, as in the following Article.

Violet-paste.

After having made Syrup of Violets, take the gross Substance that is left, and mingle it with the same quantity of Pearled Sugar: So that whenever you are minded to dry the Paste, it will only be requisite to incorporate it, with as much Marmelade of Lemmons, or of Apples, as is needful; adding some Feathered Sugar, and causing all to be well intermix'd: Then let your Paste simper for some while, and dress it after the usual manner, to be dried in the Stove.

If you have no thick Substance of Violets, the Flowers may be us'd in their Season; which are to be pick'd and pounded in a Stone-mortar, in order to be mingled with either of the above-mention'd Marmelades, and as much Feathered Sugar, as is requisite; till the Paste slips off from the bottom and sides of the Pan: Then having caus'd all to simper, let it be dress'd and dried in the Stove as before. When these Violet-pastes are turn'd to be dried on the other side, they must be lightly strew'd with Sugar put into a Handkerchief, and by that Means a greater Lustre will be added to the Colour, on the first side, being that which is uppermost, when they are serv'd up to Table; as it has been already intimated, in treating of the Pastes, of Cherries, Rasberries and Currans.

Bell-grape-paste.

Having pick'd your Grapes off from the Bunches, throw them into hot Water, and let them boil till they break: Then let them be drain'd upon a Sieve or Cullander, and squeez'd hard, all at once, to separate the Grains and Skin. In the mean while,
some

some green Apples are to be scalded, and the Pastes of both put into a Copper-pan, to be brought again to their Colour, over the Fire, and dried all together; continually stirring and turning them, till they begin to slip off from the sides of the Pan: Then let them be incorporated with an equal quantity of Feathered Sugar, and dress'd upon Slates with a Spoon, to be dried in the Stove, with a good Charcoal-fire: As these Pastes are turn'd on the other side, strew them with Sugar as the former, and take care, that they be well harden'd.

Another Way of making Pastes of Bell-grapes.

Take good Bell-grapes, and having caus'd them to cast their Juice in a Copper-pan over the Fire, after the same manner, as Currans; let them be drain'd upon a Sieve, and when cold, pass'd through the straining Sieve. Then they are to be dried over the Fire, and continually stirr'd on all Sides, with the *Spatula*; whilst your Sugar is boil'd till it become Crack'd; allowing a Pound, for every Pound of Fruit, in order to be incorporated with the Paste; which ought to be dress'd upon Slates, as the others, and dried in the Stove. On the next Morning, or Evening, turn your Pastes, so as they may be dried in Sieves, on the other side, and shut them up in Boxes, with Paper, between every Row.

Pastes of Muscadine-grapes.

Pastes of Muscadine-grapes, are usually made in the same manner as these last, or else as those of Currans; so that, it were altogether needless to insist on them, any longer in this Place.

C H A P. XXV.
Of the Jellies of Fruits.

Although it is a customary Practice, only to make Jellies of certain peculiar Fruits; nevertheless they may be also prepar'd, with the most part of the others. To that purpose, measures may be taken, from those that have been before occasionally de-

describ'd, in treating of the Fruits, of which they are generally made, *viz.* the Jellies of green Goosberries, white and red Currans, Bell-grapes, *&c.* But for the more clear understanding of the whole Matter, it will be expedient, here to give a particular Account of these Jellies, beginning with that of Cherries:

Jelly of Cherries.

Take the best sort of Cherries, that are very ripe, and extract their Juice by pressing them through a white Linnen-cloth, or something else of the like nature; whilst the same Weight of Sugar, or somewhat less, is boil'd till it be crack'd: Then pour in your Cherry-juice, after it has been strain'd to render it more clear, and let all continue boiling; so as the Scum may be carefully taken off, till the Syrup is brought again to a degree between Smooth and Pearled: At that very Instant, the Jelly will be made, which may also be perceiv'd, when some of it taken up in a Spoon, or Ladle, falls in thick Drops; or else, by putting some of the Drops upon a Plate, from whence they'll rise up, when cold. Afterwards, the Jelly may be pour'd into Pots or Glasses, taking off the thin Scum that rises on the top; but these Vessels ought to be left three Days, without covering; which must be done at last, with round pieces of Paper.

The Juice extracted from Cherries, over the Fire, in order to make Pastes and Marmelades, may likewise serve for this sort of Jelly; if you have no mind to make use of it for *Ratafiat*: And in regard, that this Juice would be only of a somewhat pale red Colour, it is expedient, to mingle it with a little of that of Currans; or else, the Colour may be heighten'd with some prepar'd Cochineal; although it may also be of Use, in its natural Condition, when red Colours, more, or less deep, are to be represented in a Pan-pie, or any other Device, of the like nature.

Jellies of Gooseberries and Currans.

The particular Way of making a Jelly of green Gooseberries has been already explain'd, Pag. 33. as also several Methods of preparing those of Currans, Pag. 34, 35.

Ra-

New Instructions for Confectioners. 89

Rasberry-jelly.

Some mention has likewise been made of the manner of ordering this kind of Jelly, Pag. 35. under the Article of *Curran-jelly, with a Tincture of Rasberries*: To that purpose, it is requisite to provide four Pounds of Rasberries, with two of Currans, and five of Sugar; which being brought to its Crack'd Quality, the Fruits must be thrown in, and boil'd together, till the Scum ceases to rise, and the Syrup has attain'd to a degree of Boiling, between Smooth and Pearled: Then let all be pour'd into a Sieve set over a Copper-pan, and a very fine Jelly, will pass through, even without squeezing the Fruit, if you shall think fit: At last, having given it another Boiling, take off the Scum, and dispose of it in Pots, or other Vessels, after the usual manner.

Jelly of Apples and other sorts of Fruit.

Cut your Apples into pieces, and set them over the Fire, in a Copper-pan, with Water, to make a strong Decoction; causing them to boil, till they turn, as it were to Marmelade. Then having strain'd the Liquor through a Linnen-cloth, or a fine Sieve; for every Quart of this Liquor, take three quarters of a Pound of crack'd Sugar, in which all must be lightly boil'd to a degree between Smooth and Pearled; carefully taking off the Scum. If it be requir'd to give the Jelly a red Colour, it must be cover'd, as it is boiling; at the same time, adding some red Wine, or prepared Cochineal: But if you would have the Jelly left white, as that of Pippins; nothing is to be put therein, neither ought it to be cover'd at all.

A Jelly may also be made of Pears, and other sorts of Fruit, accordingly as it shall be judg'd expedient, by using the same Method.

Jelly of Bell-grapes.

Several Ways of preparing this Jelly, have been already explain'd at large, Pag. 48.

Quince-

Quince-jelly.

Quince-jelly is usually order'd after the same manner, as in the making of Marmelade of Quinces; for which, recourse may be had to the 49, and following Pages: or else, observe what has been even now deliver'd, with respect to the Jelly of Apples; it being only requisite, to boil the Quinces a little longer, to get a good Decoction of them.

Other sorts of Jellies.

Another kind of Jelly, or rather thick Confection, is sometimes made in the Country, only with the Juice of Fruits, without Sugar; Boiling and Scumming it till it comes to the Consistence of a Jelly: But in regard that this Way is not extraordinary, nor conformable to the Rules of Art, it does not deserve any farther Consideration.

CHAP. XXVI.

Of Biskets.

Biskets are generally made in all Seasons, and constitute part of the Entertainment throughout the whole Year. The best sort of them, are these that follow, *viz.*

Almond-biskets.

Having provided a Pound of sweet Almonds, with a quarter of a Pound of bitter ones, let them be blanch'd and pounded in a Mortar; tempering all from time to time, with the White of an Egg, to hinder them from turning to Oil: When they are well pounded, so that no Clods, or Lumps are left; take out the Paste, and put it into one Scale of a Ballance, with the same Weight of Powder-sugar into the other, as also some Whites of Eggs: Then knead and mingle all well together in a Copper-pan, with the *Spatula*, or with your Hand, if it be necessary, as when a greater quantity of it is to be made; proportionably augmenting

the

the Ingredients: Afterwards, take up some of your Paste in a a Spoon, with which you are to scrape the Sides of the Pan, drawing it towards your Body, with the Edge downwards, so as only to get an entire Spoonful; which will be sufficient to make three or four of these Biskets of the breadth of a Shilling, or Copper Half-penny: To that end, take part of this Paste, with the tip of your Finger, and having turn'd it upon the edges of the Spoon, to make it of a round Figure; as it is spread along your Finger, let it fall upon a sheet of Paper, provided for that purpose, ordering the rest of the Paste, after the same manner.

To manage the Business with greater Neatness, some of this Paste may be taken up, with the blade of a Table-knife, and without touching it with the Fingers, the Biskets may be dress'd with another Knife; taking as much Paste, as is requisite for every one, from the first, on which it was spread: When the sheet of Paper is fill'd with them, at the distance of about a Finger's breadth, one from another, set them into a Campain-oven, with Fire only at the top, at first, and as soon as the Biskets begin to rise, and are sufficiently brought to a Colour, let some Fire be likewise put underneath, to make an end of Baking them. Afterwards, another sheet of Paper, that has been dress'd in the mean time, may be laid in the Oven, and so on, till the whole Mass of Paste is us'd. These Biskets may serve for the garnishing of Dishes, to dress Pyramids upon *China*-dishes, and for other Uses.

Another Way of making Almond-biskets.

Take about a quarter of a Pound of bitter Almonds with the like quantity of sweet ones, and having scalded them in boiling Water, let them be blanch'd, without throwing them into fresh Water: Then let them be pounded in a Mortar, without one drop of any Liquor; so that 'tis no great matter, whether they turn to Oil or not: In the mean while, having beaten up four or five Whites of Eggs at most with a Spoon, in an earthen Pan, put in it your Almond-paste, and temper it well with a Spoon. Afterwards, adding a Pound and two Ounces of Powder-sugar, and mingling all well together with the *Spatula*, let the Paste be dress'd upon white Paper, with two Knives; spreading it upon one, and shaping the Biskets with the other, of the thickness of the tip of your Finger. At last, they are to be set into the O-

ven,

ven, with a gentle Fire, in the beginning, but when they rise, it must be made somewhat quicker. As soon as they are bak'd, and have acquir'd a good Colour, they may be taken out of the Oven, but must not be cut off from the Paper till they are cold, in order to be kept dry in the Stove.

Chocolate-biskets.

Scrape some Chocolate upon the white of an Egg, but not too much; because it is only requisite to give it the Taste and Colour of the Chocolate. Then take Powder-sugar, and mingle it well with the rest of the Ingredients, till they become a pliable Paste: Afterwards dress your Biskets, upon sheets of Paper, in any Figure, that you shall think fit, and set them into the Oven, to be bak'd with a gentle Fire, as well on the top, as underneath.

Orange and Lemmon-biskets.

These sorts of Biskets are made after the same manner, only instead of Chocolate, some grated Orange or Lemmon-peel is to be us'd, with a little Marmelade, if there is any at hand. Other Biskets of the like Nature may also be prepar'd with Orange-flowers, and those of Jessamine, pounding them well, before they are intermix'd with the other Ingredients.

Another Way of making Orange-biskets.

Let some old Orange-paste, with some dried Pulp of Oranges and Lemmons, be well pounded in a Mortar, and let the Whites of four Eggs be whipt, as it were, for the making of *Savoy*-biskets: Then slip in the four Yolks, which are also to be well whipt together, and add three good Handfuls of Powder-sugar; stirring the whole Mass with a Spoon: Afterwards throwing in a Handful of Flower, stir all again, with the Marmelade, already pounded in a Mortar, to the quantity of about a Pound; and let all be well beaten with the Spoon. In the mean time, certain Moulds being made of white Paper, an Inch thick, the Confection is to be laid on them, and set into the Oven, without Icing; but a quick Fire ought to be made, both on the top, and underneath. As soon as the Biskets are bak'd, they must be turn'd upside down, and the Paper is to be gently taken a-

way

way from the bottom, so as they may be conveniently cut into square Pieces, as stuff'd March pane, and set by to cool. Some time after, they may be ic'd on one side, with Orange-flower-water, and on the other, if it be thought fit, with another Colour, and at last the Ice must be bak'd, with the Lid of the Campain-oven.

Savoy, *or French Biskets.*

Take three or four New-laid Eggs, or more, according to the quantity of Biskets that you would have made, and having provided a pair of Scales, put your Eggs into one of them, as also, some bak'd Flower into the other; so as there may be an equal Weight of both. Thus for Example, If four Eggs were put in, one is to be taken out, and the three others left. In the mean while, some Powder-sugar is to be provided of the same Weight as the Eggs, the Whites of which are to be taken, to make the strongest Snow that possibly can be, by whipping them well with a Whisk: To this is to be added, at first, some candy'd Lemmon-peel, grated, or beaten as it were to Powder, and then the Flower that was weigh'd before. All being thus mingled together, let the Sugar be put in, and after having beaten the whole Mass again a little while, add the Yolks of the Eggs; so as the Paste may be well temper'd. The Biskets may be made upon Paper, with a Spoon, of a round, or oval Figure, and neatly ic'd with Powder-sugar, after having wash'd them over with the Whites of Eggs. Afterwards, you are to blow off the Sugar that lies upon the Paper, and cause the Biskets to be bak'd in an Oven, that is not over-heated; giving them an agreeable Colour, on the top. When they are done enough, they must be cut off from the Paper, with a very thin Knife, and may serve to set off Fruit, or for the garnishing of Pies, or Tarts.

Some do not allow so many Whites of Eggs, and of six that have been weigh'd, only take two, to make the rocky Snow; but this is an indifferent Matter. The Lemmon-peel may likewise be dispensed with; as also, the baking of the Flower, and yet the Biskets will prove good: However, for six Eggs, it is requisite to use Sugar, to the weight of four.

Another Way of making French Biskets.

Let the Whites and Yolks of eight Eggs be set by separately, and let the former be well whipt, till they rise up to a Snow: Then let the Yolks of nine Eggs be slipt in, and let all be whipt again; adding a Pound of Powder-sugar, and beating them well with the *Spatula*: Let three quarters of a Pound of Flower be also weigh'd out, and put to the Mass, continuing to beat it with the *Spatula*; a little grated Lemmon-peel may likewise be added, if you please, to heighten the Relish. In the mean while, certain Tin-moulds being provided, are to be wash'd over, a little, on the inside, with fresh Butter melted, or else the Moulds may be made with Cards, which must not be butter'd: But the Paper on which the Biskets are laid, must be rubb'd with the same Paste, to the end that the Moulds may stick to it. If you have a mind to make small Biskets of this sort, they may be dress'd with a Spoon, upon white Paper, of the bigness of a Half-crown Piece, and ic'd with Powder-sugar, which is to be strew'd upon them, and blown off a little, lest too much of it, should be left on the top. Afterwards, they are to be set into a Baker's Oven, moderately heated, and to that end, a tryal may be made with a single Bisket: But care ought to be taken, that they do not languish in the Oven, and as soon as they are drawn, the Moulds must be taken away; or the sheet of Paper, if the Biskets are small, which may be done, by slipping a Knife underneath; for if they were cold, they could not be any longer cut off, without breaking the Ice.

Lisbon-*biskets*.

Take three or four Eggs, according to the quantity of Biskets design'd to be made, and beat the Whites a little with the Yolks; adding as much Powder-sugar, as can well be taken up between your Fingers, at four or five times, with Lemmon-peel, and four or five Spoonfuls of bak'd Flower. When this Confection is well temper'd together, let it be turn'd upon a sheet of Paper strew'd with Sugar, and after having likewise strew'd the Paste on the top, with the same Sugar, let it be bak'd in an Oven, moderately heated. As soon as the Biskets are taken out, they must be cut all at once, with the Paper underneath, according to the Size and Figure, that you would have

have them to be of, and then the Paper may be gently cut off, with a Pen-knife, for fear of breaking any part of them, which is soon done, because they ought to be very dry.

Light Ic'd-biskets.

Having provided three quarters of a Pound of bitter Almonds, with one quarter of a Pound of sweet Ones, let them be scalded, blanch'd and pounded in a Mortar, as much as is possible; adding two Whites of Eggs, at several times. Then let all be insensibly mingled, with four Pounds of Powder-sugar, and well beat together, till the Paste becomes very pliable. Afterwards, this Paste must be squeez'd through a Syringe, one Roll after another, and the Biskets are to be made of it, cutting that which passes through, and is received upon a sheet of Paper, according to any length that you shall think fit; either into large, or small Pieces. These Papers of Biskets are to be laid upon a Board, and the Oven-lid with Fire on the top, to give them a Colour, on that side: As soon as you perceive them to be done enough, and that they are considerably puff'd up, take away the Fire, and having gently slip'd them off from the Paper, cause them to be ic'd on that side, which lay undermost. This Ice is usually made, with the White of an Egg and Sugar, well temper'd and beaten together, till it turns almost to a kind of Pap: Then it may be spread upon the Biskets with a Knife, and dried with a gentle Fire, till it is thoroughly coagulated. These sorts of Biskets may also be cover'd with an Ice, made of sweet Water, or some other Water and Sugar beaten and temper'd together, as the former.

Common Biskets.

Break six or eight Eggs, and having slipt the Whites and Yolks into an earthen Pan, or Bason; beat them well for some time, with the *Spatula*: Then adding a Pound of Powder-sugar, with as much Flower, let all be well mingled together, and dress your Paste in Paper-cases, or Tin-moulds, in any Form or Figure, that you shall judge most expedient. Afterwards, let the Biskets be Ic'd, strewing them with fine Sugar, put into an Handkerchief, and set into an Oven moderately heated, till they rise, and come to a good Colour: When they are sufficiently bak'd, take them up, with the point of a Knife,

B b 2 and

and make an end of drying them in the Stove, or some other Place, convenient for that purpose.

Biskets for Lent.

This sort of Bisket is made with Gum-dragant, steept in the same manner as shall be hereafter explain'd for Pastils, Pag. 104. Having caus'd the Gum-water to be well stirr'd about, add some Powder-sugar, continuing to whip all together, as it is strewing in, till the Liquor becomes as thick as Pap. If you are minded to mix Marmelade, with this Paste, as in making the *Biscotins*; by that means it will be render'd so much the richer, and have a greater Consistence, whereas, otherwise it is only a Compound of Sugar and Wind. They may also be made, as the light Biskets above specified; only retrenching the Whites of Eggs, in the place of which the Gum is to be substituted, and a somewhat less quantity of Almonds is to be us'd in preparing the Paste. These Biskets may be dress'd how you please, and bak'd as the former.

Crackling-biskets.

The same sort of Paste is to be us'd, as for the *Savoy*-biskets, being brought to a due Consistence, with four Eggs, and augmented with three or four Handfuls of Powder-sugar: Then having caus'd all to be well temper'd with a Spoon, let them be dress'd, as the Biskets of bitter Almonds, and bak'd in the Campain-oven, with more Fire on the top, than underneath. When they are taken out, the sheet of Paper must be turn'd upside down, and laid under a wet Napkin, to the end that the Biskets may be clear'd from it; for if the Paper be not wet, it cannot possibly be done, by any other means. Afterwards, the Biskets are likewise to be laid upside down upon other white Paper, and set into the Stove; but they must not be dress'd on the Dishes, before they are ready to be serv'd up to Table; because they are too apt to give, and contract Moistness.

Biscotins.

Take three Whites of Eggs, four Spoonfuls of Powder-sugar, and one of any kind of Marmelade particularly, of Oranges, Lemmons, Apricocks, &c. The rest of the Confection is to be be made of fine Flower, which you are to knead all together, till the Paste becomes very pliable, and then make your *Biscotins* of different Figures, *viz.* some round, others long, others in form of Love-knots, Ciphers, and other pretty Devices: They ought to be bak'd with a gentle Fire, and taken out of the Oven, as soon as you perceive them to have acquir'd a somewhat brown russet Colour: To clear them from the Paper, wet the sheet on the back-side with Water, and the Business will be easily effected, but it must be done immediately after they are drawn.

Another sort of Biscotin.

Having caus'd half a Pound of Sugar to boil in a little Copper-pan, or Skillet, till it become Feathered, remove it from the Fire, and throw in three quarters of a Pound of Flower, except one Handful, which is to be reserv'd, to work it upon the Table: Then stir all about with the *Spatula*, and when the Paste is well temper'd, take it out of the Pan, in order to be laid upon a very clean Table, or Dresser-board, strew'd before with a little Sugar: The Paste must also be strew'd, both on the top, and underneath, with prepared Musk and Powder-sugar, and continually work'd, whilst it is hot: At the same time, it must be roll'd out, and cut into Pieces, to make certain little Balls, of the thickness of a Man's Thumb; which must be speedily done, in regard that when the Paste is cold, it will no longer take effect. These Balls are to be bak'd in an Oven, without Paper, but afterwards some must be put underneath, when they are ready to be set into the Stove.

CHAP. XXVII.

Of March-panes.

MAarch-panes consist of a sort of Paste made of Almonds and Sugar, and are in Use, as well as Biskets, during the whole Course of the Year: Only they may be diversified in the several Seasons, with different Marmelades, according to the variety of Fruits; as it will more plainly appear, from the following Instructions.

Com-

Common March-panes.

The Almonds are to be first scalded in hot Water, and toss'd into other cold Water, as they are done: Then being wip'd, and drain'd, they must be pounded in a Marble-Mortar, and moisten'd from time to time, with the White of an Egg, to hinder them from turning to Oil. In the mean while, let half as much clarified Sugar, as Paste, boil, till it become Feather'd, and let the Almonds be thrown in by Handfuls, or else the Sugar may be pour'd upon them, in another Vessel: Afterwards, let all be well incorporated together, with the *Spatula*; carefully stirring the Paste to the bottom, and round about, lest it should stick to the Pan, even tho' it were remov'd from the Fire. You may know when this Paste is done enough, by passing the Back of your Hand over it, till nothing sticks thereto; at which instant, it must be laid upon Powder-sugar, and set by to cool: To work it, you are to roll out several Pieces, of a convenient Thickness, out of which your March-panes must be cut, with certain Moulds; gently slipping them off, with the tip of your Finger, upon Sheets of Paper; in order to be bak'd in the Oven, so as the Fire may heat them at first, only on one side: Afterwards, the other side is to be Ic'd over, and bak'd in like manner: Thus the March-panes are usually made of a round, long, or oval Figure; curled or jagged, in the Shape of a Heart, &c. The Paste may also be roll'd out, or squeez'd thro' a Syringe; so that the March-panes, will have as many particular Names, altho' they differ only in Shape, and in the manner of Icing them; as it may hereafter, be more clearly observ'd.

Another sort of Paste for March-panes.

After having blanch'd, cool'd and drain'd your Almonds, as before, let them be pounded in a Mortar, and moisten'd with the White of an Egg, and a little Orange-flower-water beaten together. As soon as they are thoroughly pounded, so that there does not remain the least Clod, or Lump, an equal quantity of Sugar must be brought to its feather'd Quality: Then throwing in your Almonds, temper all together, with the *Spatula*, and set the Paste over the Fire again, to be dried; continually stirring it, till it becomes pliable, and slips off from the bottom

tom of the Pan: Afterwards, it muſt be laid in a Baſon, with Powder-ſugar underneath, and made up into a thick Roll, to be ſet by, for a little while, as the former; in order to be ſhap'd and dreſs'd, in the ſame manner.

This laſt ſort of Paſte is more crackling and more grateful to the Palate than the former, and in that reſpect, it may be plainly diſtinguiſh'd from the common March-panes.

Another ſort of March-pane.

The Almonds are to be pounded, as before, and moiſten'd with the White of an Egg and Orange-flower-water, or ſome other ſort: The only difference is, that this Paſte muſt be drawn out, and dried in a Baſon, with Powder-ſugar, till it becomes very pliable, as it were ordinary Paſte; ſo that after it has been ſet by, for ſome while, ſeveral Rolls may be made, of any thickneſs, which ſhall be judg'd expedient; out of which the March-panes are to be cut, and ſhap'd, according to Diſcretion.

Royal March-pane.

The Paſte of this March-pane is the ſame with that of the preceeding, a Piece of which is to be roll'd out upon the Table, or Dreſſer, a Finger's breadth thick, and divided into as many Parts, as are requiſite to make ſeveral Wreaths, or Rings round about your Finger, cloſing the two ends, ſo as they may ſlip out, or be ſeparated again: Theſe Rings are to be dipt into the White of an Egg, with which a Spoonful of Marmelade of Apricocks has been intermix'd, and afterwards roll'd in Powder-ſugar: But you muſt not forget to blow upon them, as they are taking out, ſo that too much Sugar may not be left, and to lay them on Paper, in order to be bak'd in the Campain-oven, with Fire underneath, and on the top, becauſe at that Inſtant, they are ic'd on both ſides: Then a ſort of Puff will riſe in the middle, as it were in form of a Coronet, producing a very agreeable Effect; to render which more certain, as the March-panes are dreſſing, you may put upon the void ſpace of theſe Rings, a little round Pellet of the ſome Paſte, or a ſmall grain of Fruit, ſuch as a Cherry, Rasberry, Piſtachoe, or any Thing of the like Nature.

Orange-

Orange-flower March-pane.

The Almonds being pounded and moisten'd with the White of an Egg, are to be well temper'd with Feathered Sugar, adding a Spoonful of Orange-flower-marmelade; or you may content your self only to mingle it with the Ice, with which they are cover'd, to be diversified: For the rest, the same Method is to be observ'd, as in preparing the common March-panes. Thus for Instance, Half a Pound of Sugar may be sufficient for a Pound of Almond-paste, and the Paste must always be set by, for some time, before it is us'd. For want of the Marmelade of Orange-flowers, sprinkle your Almonds as they are blanch'd, with a little Water of the same Flowers, and pound in a Mortar, some Orange-pulp that is preserv'd Liquid; in order to be mix'd with the Almonds, or to constitute the Body of your Ice: But the Paste ought to be dried at the Fire, by reason of the Orange-flower-water.

Lemmon March-pane.

Instead of what has been even now deliver'd in the last Article, these March-panes are to be diversified with Lemmon-marmelade, or with the Pulp of preserved Lemmons pounded in a Mortar: or else a little grated Lemmon-peel may only be intermix'd, either with the pounded Almonds, before they are put into the Sugar, or with the Ice. But this Peel ought to be grated very fine, and well beaten with the White of the Egg and the Sugar.

March-panes, with a Tincture of Rasberries, or other sorts of Fruits.

During the Season of Fruits, more especially the red, your March-panes may be diversified, several other Ways; by tempering some of them, with the Juice of Rasberries, and others with those of Currans, Strawberries, Cherries, &c. But observe by the way, That if those Juices are us'd, for the soaking of your Almonds, when they are pounded with the White of an Egg, the Paste ought to be well dried at the Fire, or else it must be done with Powder-sugar, as in the third Article.

Iced

Iced March-panes.

When any sorts of March-pane, that is to say, the round, long, oval, or curled, are sufficiently bak'd and colour'd, on one side, they are to be gently cut off from the Paper, with a Knife, and ic'd on the other side, that lay undermost; according to either of the following Methods.

Having provided a sufficient quantity of sweet Water, either of Orange-flowers, or some other sort; or else the above-mention'd Juices and Marmelades, according to the Quality, which you are minded to confer on your March-panes; intermix them by degrees with fine Powder-sugar, and temper all well together, till they come to the consistence of Pap: Then taking up some of this Ice, with a Knife, spread it neatly upon the March-panes, and set them again in order, upon Paper, with the Oven-lid, and a little Fire on the top, to cause the Ice to coagulate. Afterwards, they may be lock'd up in Boxes, and kept for Use.

The other sort of Ice is made only with the White of an Egg and Powder-sugar, or mingled with some kind of Marmelade; compleating and using it, as the former. At another time, both these sorts of Ice may be prepar'd at once, to diversifie part of the March-panes; when different Figures are made of the same Paste, to the end that they may be more easily distinguished one from another.

Stuff'd March-pane.

Having made the same sort of Paste as that of Royal March-pane, work it well upon a Table, or Dresser, with Powder-sugar, and roll out a Piece, as thin as is possible, strewing some Sugar underneath, to hinder the Paste from sticking to the Board: Then having divided it into two Parts, and cut it a little round about, spread any sort of Marmelade at pleasure, upon one of them, of the thickness of a Half-crown, and cover it with the other: Afterwards, you are to cut the Paste into great, or small Pieces, according to Discretion, and lay them in order upon White Paper, to be bak'd on one side, with the Oven-lid: As soon as they have taken Colour, set them by to cool, and ice them over on the other side, with the White of an Egg, beaten up with Powder-sugar; or else with Orange-flower-water, temper'd per'd in like manner with the same Sugar: Some time after, they are to be laid upon Paper again, and the baking of them finish'd upon the Table, with the Oven-lid, as before. Certain little Pies, or Tarts may also be made with the same Paste; to which purpose, taking a Piece as thick as a Walnut, shape it with your Thumb and Fore-finger, the tip of which may just enter into it, and work it very thin: These little Pies are to be laid upon Paper, and gently bak'd in the Oven, with a little Fire, in the beginning, on the top, and underneath, till they come to a Colour; and then fill'd with a preserv'd Cherry, Rasberry, or Grape, or any kind of Marmelade: They may also be ic'd, if you please, and the Ice is to be bak'd with the Oven-lid; but they must only be fill'd, as Occasion requires.

Chap. XXVIII.

Of Meringues and Macaroons.

This small Sugar-work is of great Use, and very easily prepar'd: It is also very convenient in an Office, in regard that it may be made in a trice; after the following Manner.

Meringues in Pairs.

Take three or four new-laid Eggs, according to the quantity of Meringues, that you would have made, and set a-part the Whites, to be whipt, till they make a rocky Snow. Then let a little grated Lemmon-peel be put into it, and three or four Spoonfuls of Powder-sugar: A little Amber may also be added; and the whole Mass must be whipt together, till it become very Liquid. Afterwards, you may make your Meringues upon a Sheet of white Paper, with a Spoon, of a round or oval Figure, and of the thickness of a Walnut; leaving some distance between every one of them: At the same time, they are to be strew'd with fine Sugar put into a Handkerchief, and cover'd with the Oven-lid, with Fire on the top; without removing them from the Table: Whereupon they'll immediately rise and take Colour, leaving a void space in the middle; which

which may be fill'd up, with a grain of preserv'd Fruit, according to the Season, such as a Rasberry, Cherry, Strawberry, &c. At last, every one of them is to be cover'd with another *Meringue,* enclosing the whole Substance, and these are call'd Twin-*Meringues.*

Dry Meringues.

Having caus'd the Whites of four new-laid Eggs to be whipt, as before, till they rise up to a Snow, let four Spoonfuls of very dry Powder-sugar, be put into it, and well temper'd with a Spoon: Then let all be set over a gentle Fire, to be dried a little at two several times, and add some Pistachoes, that are pounded and dried a little in the Stove. Afterwards, they are to be dress'd as the others, and bak'd in the Oven somewhat leisurely, with a little Fire underneath, and more on the top: When they are sufficiently done, and very dry, let them be taken out, and cut off with a Knife: Lastly, as soon as they are somewhat cold, let them be laid upon Paper, and set into the Stove to be kept dry.

*Pistachoe-*Meringues.

Take a Handful, or two of Pistachoes, and blanch them in scalding Water: Afterwards, having whipt the Whites of Eggs, as for the other sorts of *Meringues,* and having beat them together with the Powder-sugar, put in the Pistachoes, well drain'd from the Water, and make the *Meringues,* with a Spoon, of what thickness you shall think fit, icing them over in the same manner: If you have no mind to ice them, their natural Colour will be as white as Paper; but a Pistachoe must be allow'd for every one of the *Meringues* which will serve for the garnishing of Pies made of Crackling Crust, and also to Dress Pyramids upon the *China-*dishes, for the Desert.

Macaroons.

Macaroons are a particular Confection of sweet Almonds, Sugar, and the White of an Egg, and to make them it is requisite to provide a Pound of Almonds; which are to be scalded, blanch'd, and thrown into fair Water: Afterwards, they must be drain'd, wip'd and pounded in a Mortar; moistening ftening them at the same time, with a little Orange-flower-water, or the White of an Egg, left they should turn to Oil. Then taking the same quantity of Powder-sugar, with three or four other Whites of Eggs, beat all well together, and dress your Macaroons upon Paper, with a Spoon, in order to be bak'd with a gentle Fire: When they are half done, they may be ic'd over at Pleasure, as the March-panes; or they may be bak'd outright, without Icing, as the *Savoy*-biskets, or those of bitter Almonds, which they very much resemble in their Nature and Quality.

CHAP. XXIX.
Of Pastils.

PAstils are also a kind of Sugar-paste, of which there are several sorts, usually dress'd upon *China*-dishes, to set off a Desert, or Banquet of Sweet-meats.

Cinnamon-pastils.

Let some Gum-dragant be dissolv'd in Water, pour'd into a Pot, or earthen Pan; that is to say, one Ounce of it will be sufficient for four Pounds of Sugar. At the end of two or three Days, when the Gum is well steept and stirr'd about with a Spoon, it must be strain'd thro' a clean Linnen-cloth, to separate all the Dross from it. Then this Gum-water being put into a Mortar, with one or two Whites of Eggs, all must be well incorporated with some Cinnamon beaten very small, and pass'd thro' a fine Sieve. Afterwards, some Powder-sugar must likewise be sifted thro' a fine Sieve, and mingled with the rest, by little and little; continuing to temper all together, till the Paste become very pliable: At that Instant, the Pastils may be made of a round, or long Figure, or of any Shape whatsoever; and if you have any Seals, or Ciphers at Hand, an Impression may be made with them, upon the Pastils; which afterwards are to be dried in the Stove.

White-

New Instructions for Confectioners. 105

White Paſtils.

The Gum is to be firſt ſteept in a little Water, with the Juice of three or four Lemmons, and the *Zeſts*, or Chips that were made of them. At the end of two or three Days, when you perceive the Gum to be well diſſolv'd, ſtrain it thro' a clean Linnen-cloth, as before, and pour it into the Mortar, with double refin'd Powder-ſugar, ſifted thro' the Drum or fine Sieve: After having thrown in the firſt Handful of Sugar, let the whole Maſs be well work'd and beaten, and add another Handful; continuing to beat and temper your Compound on all ſides, as it is augmenting with Sugar, till you have a very white and pliable Paſte; with which the Paſtils are to be made, according to the former Method, and dried in the Stove.

Orange-flower Paſtils.

Theſe ſorts of Paſtils are uſually prepar'd after the ſame manner; only ſome Leaves of Orange-flowers, and Water of the ſame, are to be intermix'd with the Lemmon-juice, in which the Gum is ſteept.

Apricock-paſtils.

Inſtead of Gum-dragant take Gum-*Arabick*, which is diſſolv'd a great deal ſooner, and having caus'd it to be ſteept and ſtrain'd thro' a Linnen-cloth, pour it into a Mortar, with Syrup of Apricocks: Then let all be well temper'd together, and augmented with Sugar, at ſeveral times, till the Paſte becomes pliable, in order to make round Paſtils, which are dried in the Stove, to be made white, if you ſhall think fit, in the wide Pan, after the ſame manner as Sugar-plums.

Violet-paſtils, and other ſorts.

The ſame ſort of Gum-*Arabick* is to be uſed for theſe Paſtils; becauſe they are uſually made white in the Sugar-plum Pan, as well as the following Clove-paſtils. To give them the Colour and Smell of Violets; ſome Indigo and Orrice is to be ſteept in Water, and mingled with the Gum, when it is diſſolv'd and pour'd into the Mortar: Afterwards, you are to add ſome fine

Pow-

Powder-sugar, continuing to work and temper the whole Mass, till it turns to a pliable Paste: Then round Pastils may be made of it; or if design'd for fine Sugar-plums, they may be shap'd in form of Hearts, Diamonds, Clubbs and Spades by the means of a Tin-mould, in which these Figures are express'd, and at last these Pastils are to be made white, after they have been thoroughly dried in the Stove.

Clove-pastils.

Having caus'd your Cloves to be well pounded and sifted thro' the Drum, or fine Sieve, mingle them in the Mortar, with the steept Gum-*Arabick*; adding as much Sugar as is requisite to make a pliable Paste: Then roll out a slip of this Paste, to be cut into little Pieces, in the shape of Cloves, which are to be made white in the Sugar-plum Pan: Otherwise, gray Pastils may be made of them, as those of Cinnamon.

CHAP. XXX.

Of the Caramel Sugar-work, and Candy'd Comfits.

THese two sorts of Sugar-works are very curious, and may be made upon several Occasions for the embellishing of a Desert, according to the following Instructions.

Candy'd Cinnamon.

Cut your Cinnamon in form of small larding slips of Bacon, as also of the same bigness, and put them into thin Sugar, over the Fire, so as they may boil only in a little Syrup: Then removing the Pan, let them imbibe the Sugar, during five or six Hours, and let them lye a draining upon a Hurdle, or Grate in the Stove. As soon as they are half dry, they must be gently taken off, and laid upon a Sieve in the same Stove, to make an end of drying them. Afterwards, they are to be set in order in Tin-moulds, upon little Grates made for that purpose, and let into the Moulds; so as three Rows may be plac'd one above another, separated with those little Grates; but a piece

of

of Lead, or somewhat else of the like nature must be laid on the uppermost Grate, to keep all close stopt: In the mean while, having caus'd a sufficient quantity of Sugar to boil till it is Blown, pour it into your Mould, so as some of it may lie upon the last Grate, and pass thro' several parts of the Mould; which is to be set into the Stove the next Evening, with a good cover'd Fire, and to continue therein all Night: In the Morning, observe, whether the Cinnamon be well coagulated, and make a little Hole, at one Corner of the Mould, so as the Sugar may be drain'd thro' it: Then set the Mould again into the Stove, upside down, with a Plate underneath, and when it is sufficiently drain'd, take out your Cinnamon-sticks, which must be gently loosen'd, by little and little, and laid upon a Sieve, to be throughly dried in the Stove.

Candy'd Fennel.

Take Fennel run up to Seed, as soon as it comes from the Flower, and having caus'd it to be well dried on a Board, cut it into halves, or quarters, according to the thickness of the Stalk: Then let it be scalded and put into thin Sugar, ordering it, for the rest of the Work, in the same manner as the Cinnamon. The same thing may be done in the candying of pickt Cherries, and old Paste, particularly those of Quinces, either red or white, and of roasted Pears, as also Orange or Lemmon-chips, Bell-grapes, *Biscotins*, and Pastils: But it is requisite, that all be well dried before, in the Stove, to serve as a proper Garniture for all sorts of Fruit.

Sugar-candy.

The preceding Methods are only an Imitation of that of preparing Sugar-candy, the Virtue of which is so well known, in the Curing of Defluxions and other Indispositions of the Breast: For it is made in like manner, by causing Sugar to boil to the Degree, call'd, *Blown*, and puting it into an earthen Pot, wherein certain small Sticks are laid in order; round about which, the Sugar coagulates, when set into the Stove, with a Fire, as before. Some Confectioners, after having taken away the first Crust, set the rest again into the Stove, till another is form'd, and so proceed, till the whole Work is finish'd; more especially if the Sugar be boil'd over again, to cause it to return to its

Blown

Blown Quality: Others, having laid these little Sticks in Order, side-wise, cross-wise, or upright, pour in the Sugar, and leave all for the space of fifteen Days, in the Stove, or some other warm Place: Afterwards, having pour'd in hot Water, at several times, they leave them again, for a whole Day, and breaking the Pot, the next Morning, find the Sugar-candy round about the Sticks; of which there are two sorts, *viz.* White and Red: The former being the best, is usually prepar'd with Sugar brought from the *Canaries,* and the other, with that of St. *Thomas*'s Island.

To make the Caramel *Sugar-work.*

One of the chief Uses of the Sugar-work, call'd, *Caramel,* is to make a kind of Cap or Net, to cover a Service of Cheese-curds: To that purpose, the Sugar must be brought to the *Caramel,* or last Degree of Boiling, whilst a Plate, or *China*-dish is provided of a convenient size; upon which, several sorts of small preserv'd Fruits are to be set in order, at a certain distance, one from another; such as Cherries, Rasberries, Apricocks, green Almonds, Orange and Lemmon-slips, or other Things of the like Nature; artificially intermixing their different Colours, to render all more pleasant to the Sight, by the means of that agreeable Variety. The Fruits being thus dispos'd of, on the bottom and sides of the *China*-dish, a Pearling-pot is to be us'd, or else a Tin-mould in Form of a Funnel; but the Hole of it ought to be very small; otherwise, a kind of Pin, or Stopple must be put into it, which may be slipt up and down, to cause the Sugar to run thicker, or finer, accordingly as it shall be judg'd most expedient: Then pour the *Caramel*-sugar into this Mould, and sprinkle your Fruits; turning it about, from one to another, till you have fill'd up the whole Compass of the *China*-dish, or Plate. As the Sugar thickens, and is dried in an instant, sticking to the Fruits, as it falls, a kind of curious Filigreen, or Net-work will be form'd, very proper, for the covering and adorning of the *China*-dishes; which will pleasantly deceive the sight of the Guests that have a mind to take up some of the Fruit, with a Fork: Besides that the broken Sugar falling among the Cheese-curds and Sweet-meats, will cause the whole Mess to be eaten together, with a great deal of satisfaction.

Thus

Thus Pyramids of raw Fruit, particularly, of Cherries, Strawberries, Plums, &c. may be diversified, and when they are dress'd, some *Caramel*-sugar is to be pour'd upon them, in like manner; beginning at the bottom, and continuing to turn it about to the uppermost Point: By which means the Fruit will be entirely hid, so as some part of their Colour may only be discern'd, making a very fine shew, under this Sugar-work.

CHAP. XXXI.
Of Mosses and Sultanes.

Mousselines or Mosses were in great repute, some Years ago, and may still, be us'd to very good purpose, as well as another sort of Sugar-work, call'd, *Sultanes*. They are also convenient to fill up a large Desert; for want of Fruits preserved dry, or other kinds of Sweet-meats.

Moss of several Colours.

To make white Moss, let some Gum-dragant be steept in fair Water, with Lemmon-juice, and afterwards strain'd thro' a Linnen-cloth: Then take as little of it as you please, to work up a white Paste, with double refin'd Sugar pouder'd and pass'd thro' a Sieve; tempering and beating all well together, in a Mortar, till the Paste become pliable.

For red Moss, let some of the same sort of Gum be put into the Mortar, with prepar'd Cochineal, to give it a red Colour. Afterwards, add Sugar, as before, causing all to be well mingled, and work'd together, till your Paste be made no less pliable.

At another time, let the Gum be intermix'd with Indigo and Orris, if you are minded to have it of a Blew, or Violet-colour: Then being put into a Mortar, with fine Powder-sugar, all must be thoroughly temper'd together, to make a Paste of the same nature as the others.

A yellow Paste may likewise be made with Gum-booge or with Saffron, and a green Paste, with the Juice of Beat-leaves, which must be scalded a little over the Fire to take away their Crudity.   C c   If

If you have a mind to make marbled Mofs of all thefe Paftes, take a piece of every one of them, and lay them one after another, upon a Sieve; fo that as they are fqueez'd thro' with a Spoon, certain little Rocks are form'd, which will be marbled, and of thofe different Colours.

If it be requifite, to make fome of every fort of Pafte a-part, and of the fame Colour, they muft be feparately ftrain'd, in like manner, and thefe different Rocks are to be drefs'd in form of Pyramids upon *China*-difhes, for the Defert. They are dried in a very fhort fpace of time, without putting them into the Stove, or ufing any other means for that purpofe.

Sultanes.

Take the Whites and Yolks of four Eggs, with an equal Weight of Powder-fugar, and as much fine Flower, as will counterpoife the Weight of two Eggs: Let all be well temper'd together, and if you would have a grain of Musk added, it muft be pounded with a little other Sugar, and mingled with the reft: Afterwards, the *Sultanes* are to be drefs'd with a Spoon upon Papers, and ftrew'd on the top, with fine Sugar: But a convenient diftance muft be left between every one of them; becaufe they are apt to fpread very wide, and then they may be fet into the Oven, with Fire on the top and underneath: As foon as they are fufficiently bak'd, and well colour'd, they are to be clear'd from the Papers; wetting them gently on the back-fide, and bringing them to the Fire, by which means they may be eafily flipt off. Laftly, the *Sultanes* are to be roll'd up in form of Wafers, fo as the Ice may remain on the out-fide, and drefs'd upright upon *China*-difhes or Plates; or elfe they may ferve for the garnifhing of fome Pie, or other fort of Service.

CHAP. XXXII.

Of certain natural and artificial Flowers.

BEfides Orange-flowers, the particular Way of preferving which, has been already explain'd, Pag. 52. Some other forts

forts may also be prepar'd, for Curiosity; which will produce a very agreeable Effect: Indeed, those Confectioners, who follow their Trade, have no regard to these little Knacks, because they are unwilling to bestow their time and pains about them; but they may be made in an Office, where the Officers sometimes have more leisure, and may lay hold of an opportunity to shew their utmost Skill.

Tuberosa-flowers.

Take Flowers that are not blown, and lay them a soaking in Water and Salt, as the Orange-flowers, to take away a certain Bitterness that is natural to them: At the end of two Days, they are to be scalded in Water, over the Fire, with the Juice of a Lemmon, then drain'd and thrown into clarified Sugar made luke-warm. To that purpose, a flat Copper-pan ought to be provided, or an earthen Pan of the like Form, to keep them from being squeez'd. On the next Day, let the Sugar boil, till it become somewhat Smooth, and pour it upon your Flowers: On the third Day, having caus'd the Sugar to be thoroughly brought to its smooth Quality, or between smooth and Pearled, turn it in like manner upon the Flowers, and set them by to cool: Then let them be drain'd upon Hurdles, or Grates, and dried upon Sieves, strew'd with Sugar, in order to be set into the Stove.

Another Way of preserving Tuberosa-flowers.

After having order'd the Flowers, as before, or even without using that Method, let them be put into the Copper, or earthen Pan; whilst some Sugar is boil'd till it become very much Pearled, or Blown: Afterwards, let this Sugar be pour'd upon the Flowers, so as they may be sufficiently soak'd therein, and let all be left in the Stove, till the next Day: Then they are to be drain'd upon Hurdles, or Sieves, and thoroughly dried.

Orange-flowers may also be prepar'd, after the same manner, altho' that which has been elsewere describ'd, is more certain, when they are to be kept for a considerable time.

Violet-flowers and other sorts.

Take the finest double Violet-buds, with part of their Stalks, and

and put them into a flat earthen, or Copper-pan, as before: Then having caus'd some boil'd Sugar to be Blown, pour it upon the Flowers, so as they may be well soak'd in it, and finish the whole Work, according to the Method, laid down in the last Article.

The Flowers of Spanish Broom, may also be preserv'd after the same manner, and many other sorts, at pleasure. Some of them may likewise be ic'd over, with Powder-sugar, after they have been dipt into the White of an Egg and Orange-flower Water, in order to be dried at the Fire. In drying these Flowers, they may be dress'd in Bunches upon small Twigs disposed of to that purpose, and they may be put to the same Use, as the Artificial Flowers hereafter specified; or else they may serve single, for the garnishing of some other Dish.

Counterfeit, or Artificial Flowers.

It is requisite at first to make Pastes of divers Colours, according to the Instructions already given in the Article of *Mosses*; that is to say, with Gum-dragant thoroughly steept, and mingled with Powder-sugar, which is to be well temper'd and beaten in the Mortar, till the Paste become pliable: For the Red, some prepared Cochineel may be added; for the Blew Indigo and Orris; for the Yellow Gum-booge; and for the Green, Beet-juice, which ought to be first stew'd over the Fire in a Pan or Silver-dish. The Pastes being thus order'd and roll'd out into very thin Pieces, may be shap'd in the Form of several sorts of Flowers, as Tulips, Wind-flowers, Roses, &c. by the means of certain Tin-moulds; or else they may be cut out, with the point of a Knife, according to Paper-models: Then the Flowers must be finish'd all at once, and dried upon Egg-shells turn'd upside-down, or otherwise: As for the lesser sort, particularly the Wind-flowers, they may be stuck upon Thimbles, or something else, of the like nature, that may facilitate the forming of their Shape. In the mean while, different sorts of Leaves are to be cut out of the green Paste, to which you may likewise give several Figures, to be intermix'd among your Flowers, the Stalks of which are to be made with small Slips of Lemmon-peel. For the Wind-flower, a Rasberry preserv'd dry, is to be us'd, after it has been dipt into Indigo and Orris; because the top or Bud of those Flowers, represented by this Fruit, is generally of that Colour. For Tulips, some small

points

New Instructions for Confectioners. 113

points of Lemmon-flips may be put in the middle; for Roses, a little Bud of Lemmon or Orange-chips; and so for the other kinds of Flowers: In all these Particulars, their natural Figure and Colour may be very well imitated, with a little Precaution, and by that Means you may have the Satisfaction, of pleasantly imposing upon the Credulity of some Persons, when they see such variety of Flowers in the midst of Winter. The tops of the Pyramids of dryed Fruit, may be garnish'd with these artificial Flowers, or else a separate Nosegay may be made of them for the middle of your Desert, or they may be laid in order in a Basket, or kind of Cup, prepar'd with fine Pastry-work of crackling Crust, neatly cut and dried for that purpose: If they are tied up in a Bunch, a Foot or Stock may be made of March-pane, roll'd out and wreathed, after the same manner, as Nosegays are usually bound with Wire, or Thread; and the Branches of this Stock are to support on the top, a kind of winding Wreath, neatly shap'd or cut, into which your Leaves and Flowers are to be put; artificially intermixing them, according to their various Colours: So that for the bringing of the whole Business to perfection, 'twill be requisite to bestow some time, with a particular Application of Mind.

All these sorts of Works may also be made with the Paste that is proper for *Biscotins*, and which has been already describ'd, Pag. 96 and 97.

Of Fennel.

Forasmuch as Fennel, or Anis may have a place among the above-specified Confections, it will not be improper, here to subjoyn the manner of ordering them to the best Advantage; besides the Use that may be made of the Stalks alone, for the dressing of Flowers that are preserved dry; more especially those of Spanish *Jessamin*.

Fennel may be serv'd up to Table iced, after it has been soak'd in Orange-flower Water and the White of an Egg, and then roll'd in Powder-sugar; causing it to be dried in the Sun, or at the Fire, upon Paper. If it be judg'd expedient to give it divers Colours, an Ice may be made with Pomegranate-juice, or Cocheneal, and the White of an Egg beaten together, for the red Colour; or with Indigo and Orrice-powder, for Blew, and so of the rest.

As for the Anis, it is to be steept in like manner, and dried n the Stove, upon Sieves or Grates: It may alſo be cover'd, as thick as you pleaſe, with that Ice, by ſoaking it ſeveral times in the ſame.

Moreover, when any Oranges, or Lemmons are preſerv'd dry, the Fennel may be thrown into the Sugar, as ſoon as it is made white on the ſides of the Pan; or elſe it may be candy'd, according to the Method elſewhere explain'd under the Article of *Candy'd Confections*.

Chap. XXXIII.

Of Pies made of Crackling-cruſt and Puff-paſte.

THis Article having ſo near a Relation to the Art of preſerving Sweet-meats, ought not to be omitted here; and indeed, 'it is not ſufficient to know how to make theſe ſorts of Paſte, but 'tis alſo requiſite to be well vers'd in the Method of ordering and diſpoſing them for a Deſert, and upon all other Occaſions. Now it cannot be denied, that Pan-pies hold a conſiderable rank among theſe Particulars; more eſpecially thoſe made of Crackling-cruſt, which are at preſent, very often prepar'd, even for the moſt curious Palates, and ſerv'd up, to the moſt ſumptuous Tables, both at Court and elſewhere.

Paſte for Crackling-cruſt.

Having provided about two Handfuls of Almonds, which are ſufficient for one Pan-pye, let them be ſcalded, blanch'd, and thrown into freſh Water: Then they are to be wip'd, and pounded in a Mortar, moiſtening them from time to time, with a little White of an Egg and Orange-flower Water, beaten together, to prevent them from turning to Oil. 'Tis very material, that they be well pounded, and they may alſo be ſqueez'd through a Sieve, to take away all the Clods, or Lumps. The Almond-paſte being thus prepar'd, muſt be ſpread on a Baſon, or Diſh, and dried with Powder-ſugar, as an ordinary ſort of Paſte, till it become very pliable. Afterwards, having ſet it by for ſome time, you are to roll out a Piece for the under-cruſt, to be dried in the Oven upon the Pie-pan; whilſt other ſmall

Pa-

New Instructions for Confectioners. 115

Paſtry-works are making, with what was par'd off, ſuch as *Petits Choux*, Ciphers, Knots and other Devices, that may ſerve for the garniſhing of your Pie.

Cracling-cruſt made after another manner.

After the Almonds have been thoroughly pounded and moiſten'd, as before, let as much Sugar as Paſte, at leaſt, be put into a Copper-pan, and boil'd till it become Feathered: Then throwing in your Almonds, let all be well temper'd and mingled together with the *Spatula*, and having ſet them over the Fire again, keep continually ſtirring the whole Maſs, till your Paſte ſlips of from the bottom and ſides of the Pan. Afterwards, it muſt be laid in a Diſh, ſtrew'd with Powder-ſugar on the top, and ſet by, for a while, as the former, in order to make a Pye of it, after the ſame manner.

In preparing the Paſte conformably to either of theſe Methods, the Pie will certainly become crackling and delicious to the higheſt Degree: But if you are minded to avoid the trouble, and perhaps the charge of Almonds, very good Pies may alſo be made according to the following Inſtructions.

Another Way.

Take one, or two Whites of Eggs, with three or four Spoonfuls of fine Sugar, and as much Flower, if you would only make one Pan-pye: The Sugar being firſt temper'd with the Whites of the Eggs, and then the Flower, knead all together, till your Paſte become pliable, and roll out a very thin Piece; ſtrewing it with fine Sugar: Afterwards, having put it into the Pie-pan, let the Sides be neatly pinch'd, at certain Intervals, and prickt with the point of a Knife, to hinder them from puffing: In the mean while, the remaining part of the Paſte is to be roll'd out into Slips of the thickneſs of a Lace, to compleat the inſide of the Pie; which may be made in form of a Sun, Star, *Malta*-croſs, Flower-de-luce, Coat of Arms, or the like. At laſt, it muſt be gently bak'd in the Oven, and when ready to be brought to Table, the void Spaces are to be fill'd up, with ſeveral ſorts of Marmelades, or Jellies, according to the Colours, that ſhall be judg'd moſt expedient: The ſame thing ought alſo to be obſerv'd, with reſpect to Pies made of the preceding Paſtes. To the latter, may be added a little Orange-

Cc 4   flower

flower Water, or some other sweet Water, and if it be requisite to prepare a greater quantity of either sort of Paste, another Piece, of an equal thinness, may be roll'd out for the Lid; which must be cut round, and dried in the Oven, upon a Pie-pan, or Plate, in order to cover the Pie, after it has been ic'd over, if you have no mind to leave it in its natural Colour.

Wafers.

Let as much Flower, as you please, be mingled, with new Cream in the Evening; taking care that it do not sour: On the next Day, when they are well temper'd and clear'd from the Lumps, add a somewhat greater quantity of Powder-sugar than that of the Flower, and intermix all with a Spoon: Then pour in more Cream, with a little Orange-flower Water, till the whole Mess becomes almost as thin as Milk, and stirr all well together. In the mean while, the Wafer-iron is to be heated, and rubb'd on both sides, from time to time, with fresh Butter, put into one corner of a Napkin: Then let your prepared Cream, or Batter be turn'd upon the Iron, but it must not exceed a Spoonful and half for every Wafer; which will be render'd so much the more delicious, if the Iron be press'd a little. Afterwards, the Wafer-iron is to be laid upon the Furnace, so that when the Wafer is bak'd on one side, it may be turn'd on the other: To know whether the Wafer be done enough, let your Iron be gently open'd a little and observe whether it be come to a good Colour: At that very instant, take off your Wafer from the Iron, with a Knife; rolling it a little round the same: Lastly, let the Wafers be spread hot upon a Wooden Roller, made for that purpose, to give them their due Shape, and set them into the Stove, as they are finish'd, to the end that they may be kept very dry.

Rock-cream.

Let a Quart of sweet Cream, more or less, according to the quantity that you would have made, be put into an earthen Pan, with Powder-sugar, according to Discretion, and as much Culverized Gum-dragant: as you can take up between two Fingers: Then having caus'd all to be well whipt together, it will rise, as high as you shall think fit, and continue two Days in the same Condition: A little Orange-flower Water may also be added as the Cream is Whipping. Boil'd

Boil'd Cream.

Having boil'd a Quart of Milk, with what quantity of Sugar you please, when it begins to rise, slip in six Yolks of Eggs well beaten, and a little fresh Butter: Then keep continually stirring all together, till your Cream is brought to a due Consistence, and dress it in *China*-dishes, or Cups.

Puff-paste.

Let some Paste be made after the usual manner, with Flower, Water, Salt, and if you please, the yolk of an Egg: As soon as it is well kneaded, and made very pliable; roll it out upon the Dresser-board, of a convenient length and thickness: Then cover it with as much good Butter, and having turn'd one of the ends upon the other, so as all the Butter may be enclos'd on the inside; roll it again, continuing to do the same thing five or six times. Two Pounds and half of good fresh Butter, ought to be allow'd for every three Pounds of Flower.

This sort of Paste is proper for other Pan-pies that are brought to Table without a Desert, in which it is not customary to serve up any thing that is prepar'd with Butter. However, *Feuillantins* and *Mazarines*, which are certain small Tarts of the breadth of the Palm of a Man's Hand, may be made of it, being usually fill'd with Sweet-meats, to garnish some other Pie of a larger size, set among the Intermesses; but if these little Tarts are design'd for the Desert, they may be made of Crackling-crust, as before.

CHAP. XXXLV.

Of Chesnuts and Mulberries; with some particular Observations upon several other sorts of Fruit.

IT remains only to give some Account of Chesnuts and Mulberries, in regard that no notice has been taken of them among the other sorts of Fruit, and we shall afterwards add certain New and particular Remarks upon the Way of preserving

some

some of them; so that it is presum'd, That nothing will then be wanting that relates to the whole Art and Mystery of Confectioners.

To preserve Chesnuts.

Having chosen the best sort of large Chesnuts, let them be scalded in Water, and neatly peel'd with a little Knife, proper for that purpose, paring off the two Skins, and taking care that they do not break: Afterwards, some clarified Sugar made lukewarm being pour'd upon them, in a Copper-pan, they are to be left for a while, in order to have ten, or twelve Boilings the same Day: But it is not requisite, to soak them entirely in the Sugar, or to give them a cover'd Boiling, because by that means they would be all broken into pieces. On the next Day, boil your Sugar till it be greatly Feathered, and almost ready to be blown, and slip in the Chesnuts: This strong Boiling of the Sugar, causes them absolutely to cast their Juice, and then it returns to its Pearled Quality, which is the usual Degree for Sweetmeats: The Chesnuts ought not to be set over the Fire any longer, lest they should grow Black; but to dry them, they are to be drain'd from their Syrup, and turn'd into Feathered Sugar: Then having caus'd the Boiling to be cover'd, take them off from the Fire, and set them by for some time: As soon as they are cool'd a little, let the Sugar be made white by rubbing it with the Ladle, or Skimmer against one of the Sides of the Pan, and put your Chesnuts into it, with a Spoon and Fork, as dextrously as is possible, for fear of breaking them. Afterwards, being dress'd upon Hurdles, or Grates, in the same manner as Lemmons, they will be soon dried, and finely Ic'd over.

If you have any other Sweet-meats to be dried at the same time, such as Oranges, or Lemmons, it is expedient to begin with them; more especially the latter, which ought to be very White; because the Chesnuts extremely blacken the Sugar; so that it is no longer fit for any other Use, but only to serve for Compotes.

Of Mulberries, as well dry as liquid.

For the former, take such Mulberries as are not too ripe, but rather somewhat greenish and tart: In the mean while, having caus'd sugar to be Blown, throw in your Mulberries, and give them

them a cover'd Boiling: Then remove the Pan from the Fire, take off the Scum, and leave all in the Stove till the next Day: And it ought to be obferv'd, that as much Sugar is requifite as Fruit, and that it may be alfo melted with the Juice of Mulberries to clarifie it. As foon as they are taken out of the Stove, and cool'd, let them be drain'd from their Syrup, and drefs'd upon Slates, in order to be dry'd in the Stove, ftrew'd with Sugar, as the other forts of Fruit; laftly they muft be turn'd again upon Sieves, and when thoroughly dry, lock'd up in Boxes to be ufed as occafion requires.

For liquid Mulberries, let the Sugar be boil'd till it be a little Pearled, allowing three Pounds of it, for four Pounds of Fruit, and let them have a light cover'd Boiling in the fame Sugar; gently ftirring the Pan by means of the Handles: Then take it off from the Fire, and having fet it by, till the next Day, drain off the Syrup, in order to be brought to its Pearled Quality: Afterwards flip in your Fruit, adding a little more Pearled Sugar, if it be needful, and difpofe of them in Pots, as foon as they are fufficiently cool'd.

Mulberries may alfo be preferv'd wet after the following manner: Take five Pounds of Fruit, with three Pounds of Sugar boil'd till it become Feathered; into which you are to flip them, giving them at the fame time, twelve, or fifteen Boilings: Then they are to be augmented, all at once, with two, or three other Pounds of Sugar, likewife Feathered, and brought to Perfection, without removing them from the Fire, only caufing the Syrop to return to its Pearled Quality.

Additional Obfervations upon green Figs.

Befides the Inftructions elfewhere given, Pag. 44. for the preferving of green Figgs, it may be obferv'd here, That before they are fcalded, the cutting of them is fometimes difpenfed with, only pricking them along their whole length, from one end to the other: Then fet them over the Fire in a Copperpan, with Water, and give them ten, or, twelve Boilings: Afterwards, being cool'd in the fame Liquor, and turn'd into frefh Water; they are to be brought to the Fire again, with a Glafs of Verjuice, and boil'd, till they become very green and foft: At that inftant removing them from the Fire, let them be cool'd, drain'd and put into earthen Pans: In the mean while, fome clarified Sugar, that is to fay two Ladles full of it

for

for one of Water, is to be heated, and pour'd upon the Figgs, so as they may be well soak'd therein. On the next Day, drain off the Syrup, give it two, or three Boilings, and turn it upon your Fruit: Some time after, the whole Work may be finished, almost in the same manner as is express'd Pag. 45 by causing the Syrup to be boiled one Day, a little smooth, at another time very Smooth, then to a degree between Smooth and Pearled, and at last, entirely Pearled: And the Figgs must be set over the Fire, from one Day to another, alternately, only to simper, and at the other times, it will be sufficient only to pour the Sugar upon them: However the last time, your Fruit ought to have seven, or eight cover'd Boilings, and then being set by for a little while in their Syrup, they may be either immediately dried, or laid up in Pots, till a more convenient Opportunity, shall offer itself for that purpose.

Additional Remarks upon Bell-grapes.

It has been already observ'd Pag. 48 That pared Bell-grapes are usually preserv'd after the same manner, as those that are left in their natural Condition: But it ought to be understood only with respect to the Sugar; because they are not to be scalded, in water as the latter, nor soak'd to bring them again to their Colour, as being riper; otherwise the Skin would not be so easily par'd off. If it be perceiv'd, that the Pearled Boiling is not strong enough, the first time that such juicy Fruits are put into Sugar, it may be boil'd till it become greatly Feathered, allowing the same quantity of it, as of the Grapes; which ought to have four, or five Boilings, at once, before the Pan is remov'd from the Fire: For the rest, the whole Work may be finish'd, altogether according to the Directions before laid down, for unpared Bell-grapes; unless, instead of leaving them to simper a little, every time that they are set over the Fire, after having brought the Sugar, to the necessary Degree of Boiling; you have a mind to give them several Boilings together, as at the first.

For Pastes made of Bell-grapes, as they are scalding over the Fire, in their own Liquor, according to the Instructions given in the second Article of *Bell-grape-pastes*, Pag. 86. remember to take off the Scum as soon as it boils, and when your Paste lies a drying at the Fire, after having squeez'd it through the Sieve, add, if you please, a little Powder-sugar: Neither must
you

New Instructions for Confectioners. 121

you forget, to cause the same Paste to simper for a while, when incorporated with the Blown Sugar, before it is dress'd upon the Slates; it being more especially requisite to observe this particular Circumstance, in the preparing of all sorts of Pastes.

Additional Observations upon Quinces.

Forasmuch as the Method of preserving Quinces explain'd Pag. 50. may seem somewhat tedious, we shall now try another that is easier, and of greater dispatch, being also at least, of equal efficacy and certainty.

Having caus'd your Quinces to be cut into pieces, clear'd from the Cores and par'd, let all boil together in a sufficient quantity of Water; and when they are become very soft, remove the Pan from the Fire: Then taking up the Pieces that are to be preserv'd, with the Skimmer, put them into fresh Water, to cool; set the rest over the Fire again, and give them twenty other Boilings: Afterwards, this Decoction being strain'd thro' the Straining-bag, or thro' a doubled Napkin, take two Ladles full of it, with one of clarified Sugar, proportionably to the quantity of your Fruit, and turn all into a Copper-pan, with the Quinces; in order to boil over a gentle Fire: Let some Sugar be also added; accordingly as the first Syrup consumes away, without pouring in any more Decoction, and let the whole Mess be well boiled, till the Syrup becomes Pearled: Then let it be cool'd, and dress your Quinces in Boxes, Pots, or Glasses; pouring the Syrup upon them, which will be very fine, and of a lively red Colour, if the Pan were cover'd in the Boiling.

Additional Remarks upon Oranges.

When mention was made of *China*-oranges, Pag. 54 it ought only to be understood of the large and sweet ones, as it may be easily discern'd. The lesser Sort of *China*-oranges are not to be clear'd from their Juice, but being lightly Zested, or par'd, to take away the Yellow, they must only be prick'd, with a Knife, making a little slit on the top, and thrown into fair Water: Then they are to be scalded and boil'd in fresh water, till they slip off from the Pan, adding a Handful of pounded Allum, in order to have twenty other Boilings; which Method may also be observ'd in the preparing of other sorts of Oranges. Afterwards, they must be cool'd, and put into clarified Sugar, newly ly pass'd thro' the straining-bag, with a very little Water; because a great deal of Juice will be extracted from them: For that very reason, it is requisite to boil them at the same time, till the Sugar be somewhat smooth; which nevertheless will be altogether undone, the next Day: Then let it be brought again to its smooth Quality, augmenting it with other Sugar, and having slipt in the Oranges give them fifteen, or twenty Boilings. On the Day following, let them be drain'd again, whilst the Syrup is made Pearled; in which they are to have ten, or twelve cover'd Boilings: A little while after, they are to be cool'd and drain'd, and disposed of in Pots or Glasses, and the Syrup being boil'd till it become greatly Pearled, must be pour'd upon them in the usual manner: But you must not forget to augment it with as much Sugar as is needful, to the end that the Fruit may be sufficiently soak'd therein. The particular way of drying these Oranges, is the same with that which is proper for other Fruits of the like nature, and it has already been describ'd at large, more especially, in the Article of Lemmons.

Barley-Sugar.

Having caus'd Barley to be well boil'd in Water, strain it thro' the Hair-sieve, and let this Decoction be put into clarified Sugar, brought to the *Caramel*, or last Degree of Boiling: Then remove the Pan from the Fire, till the Boiling settles, and pour your Barley-sugar upon a Marble-stone rubb'd with Oil of Olives, taking care to hinder it from running down. If the Marble be wanting, a Silver-dish, or one of some other sort of Metal, may be us'd, for the same purpose: So that as the Sugar cools, and begins to grow hard, it must be cut into pieces, and roll'd out of what length you please, in order to be kept for Use.

C H A P. XXXV.

Of the Accidents that may happen to Sweet-meats, and of proper Means for the remedying of them.

IT may be perhaps be affirm'd, That all sorts of Sweet-meats, well made according to Art, are not apt to decay, or to be
spoil'd,

spoil'd, and that this Defect proceeds from the Unskilfulness of those Persons who are employ'd in the preparing of them; nevertheless it may so happen sometimes, notwithstanding the utmost Precautions that have been taken to prevent such Inconveniencies. So that altho' we have laid down the most certain Methods for the due Preserving of every Particular; yet it is expedient to shew the bad Accidents that may befal them, and the manner of applying proper Remedies:

The most usual Inconvenience is, that wet Sweet-meats are subject to sour, and puff, which proceeds from the moistness of the Fruit, which not having sufficiently cast their natural Juice, or the Liquor they imbib'd, as they were Scalding and Cooling, cause the Sugar to give, in process of time; so that the Sweet-meats grow mouldy, and throw out a kind of Scum. This ill Accident is soon perceived in frequently visiting the Store-house, or Repository, and it ought to be immediately remedied, whilst an Opportunity offers itself; otherwise, by neglecting a Matter, which at first might be easily reduc'd to good order, you'll run the hazard of rendering it desperate, and of utterly spoiling your Sweet-meats. To prevent this Disaster, it is requisite to put them into a Copper-pan, over the Fire; causing the Sugar, or Syrup to give a little, with a cup full of Water: Then let all boil together, taking of the Scum, that rises on the top, and having brought them again to the Pearled Boiling, remove the Pan, and put your Fruit into Pots, or Glasses as at the first; by which means they'll be thoroughly free'd from their sourness, and in a condition to keep to the end, provided they be not laid up in too moist a Place. Otherwise, the Syrup alone may be set over the Fire, at first, with a little Water, and after having scumm'd it, as before, the Fruit may be slipt in; which are to boil till the Syrup has attain'd to the Pearled Degree, and then they are to be disposed of in the usual manner. Thus the sourness may be taken away from all sorts of Fruits preserv'd liquid, particularly Walnuts, Plums, Orange and Lemmon-slips &c.

The Inconvenience incident to preserv'd Fruits, is, that they sometimes candy: but this is not properly a Defect, as being only occasion'd by giving the Syrup too strong a Boiling; so that there are grounds to fear, least such an Accident should do your Sweet-meats any Injury; on the contrary, you are assur'd, that they will keep very well, and that the Sugar was good. To repair this slight Damage, you need only put all that part which is candied into a Pan, with a little Water, and when it is brought again to the Pearled Quality, mingle it with the rest; or else let all have a few Boilings together. When the sweet-meats are only candy'd on the Surface, such as Jellies, this Candy may be taken off, by passing hot Water over them, which will easily disperse the Candy and render the Sweet-meats as fine, as they were in the Beginning. These Jellies of Gooseberries, Currans, or other sorts of Fruit, being stale, may also be renew'd, by setting them over the Fire, in a Copper-pan, with a little Water, to dilute and cause them to give: So that as soon as they return to their former Degree of Boiling, which is Pearled, or between Smooth and Pearled, they are to be pour'd, into a Sieve set over an earthen Pan, and afterwards put again into the Pots or Glasses.

There are certain Fruits which are apt to grow greasy, more especially green and ripe Apricocks, and in that Condition, they cannot be well dried. The proper Remedy is, to boil them in new Pearled Sugar, after they have been drain'd from their former Syrup. If the same Cost were bestow'd upon all other sorts of Fruits, they might be much more easily dried, and would become finer, than when the Confectioner, or Officer contents himself according to the usual Method, only to drain them from the Sugar with which they were preserv'd, and afterwards to dress them upon Slates, or little Boards, in order to be dried in the Stove strew'd with Sugar.

Dry Sweet-meats, that are kept for a considerable time, ought to be laid up in a Place free from all manner of Moisture, that is to say near the Stove, or else in some Closet, into which a little Fire ought constantly to be put, from time to time, during the Winter-season: and in regard, that Fruits preserv'd dry, are apt to lose their Ice, when kept for too long a time; it is expedient to dry them Occasion requires; by which means they will also be secur'd from another Accident, that is to say, from being shrivell'd and wrinkled; altho' both may be remedied, by causing those Fruits to be boil'd again over the Fire, in the like Syrup, or other new Sugar, in order to be dried again, after they have been boil'd in it to the Pearl'd Degree, and set by to cool.

CHAP.

CHAP. XXXVI.

The Way of Ordering and Setting-out a Defert, or other Regalio of the like nature, to the best advantage, with some Models of such Entertainments.

After having treated of every Thing that may give Satisfaction to the nicest Palates, the preparing of which is the peculiar Province of Confectioners, Butlers and other Officers; it is expedient to conclude the whole Work, with the Method of serving up all those respective Messes, in due Order, either for a Desert, or some other Entertainment of the like nature.

To that purpose, it ought to be observ'd, That a Banquet of Fruits, as well Raw, as Preserved, with it's Appurtenances, may be dress'd either upon a Level or in a Basket: This last Way is only us'd in preparing Entertainments for certain Fraternities, or particular Societies; where as many little Baskets are serv'd up at first to Table, as there are Guests: These Baskets are usually adorn'd with small Ribbands, and Taffety-covers, according to the allotted Expences, and fill'd up with all forts of Sweet-meats, Biskets, March-panes, Orange and Lemmon-faggots, dried Fruits, &c. so as the most delicious Comfits may lye on the top: At last, after all have been set in good Order, and contributed much to the Decoration of the several Courses; every individual Person shuts up and takes away his Basket, to treat his Family and Friends at home; contenting himself only to eat the liquid Sweet-meats, such as Compotes and Marmelades, or else the raw Fruits, which were provided, to serve for the Out-works.

A Banquet of Sweet-meats is said to be dress'd upon a Level, when disposed of upon *China*-dishes, and Machines made of Wood, or Osier-twigs, having a great Board in the middle, in form of a Square, or Hexagon, that is to say, with six Panes in length, or of any other Figure: This Board is encompass'd with divers other Works of different Shapes, *viz.* That of a Club at Cards, round, oval, or otherwise, and several *China*-dishes are set upon these Boards, by the means of certain small wooden Leggs, or Cups; so as the Oval may contain

two,

two, and the Clubs three; whilst the Oval serve for Compotes, and the Middle-board for a large Pyramid of Fruit, with *China*-dishes round about, fix'd, as before: Or else it may be fill'd up altogether with *China*-dishes; that in the middle being rais'd higher than the others; upon which several small Pyramids are to be erected, of an exact Proportion; so that the same sorts of Comfits, and the same Colours may appear on every side, at the opposite Angles. Lastly, a Row or Border of raw Fruits may be made round about the Dishes, upon every Board to garnish the top, and the whole Desert is to be set out with Flowers, Greens, and other Ornaments, according to the Season.

For the more clear Illustration of this Method, it will not be improper here to produce some Examples, or Models of such Deserts, or Banquets of Sweet-meats, according to which, Measures may easily be taken, for the dressing of those of a greater, or lesser Size.

The Model of a Desert, for an Oval Table of twelve Coverings.

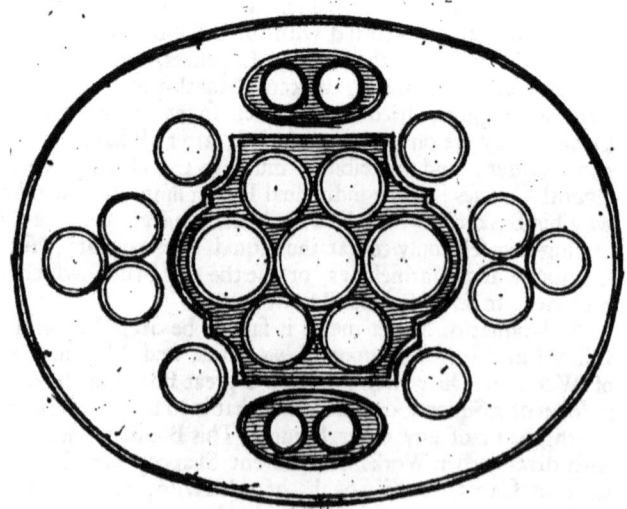

The

The Explication.

The Board in the middle is usually made of Osier-twigs, in form of a Basket, and may be gilt, silver'd over, or painted like fine earthen Ware, with this convenience, that they may be clean'd by Washing. There is also a thin Board, that lyes almost at the Entrance, over-against the Border, to serve for a Ground-plot for the Sweet-meats which are to be dress'd upon it, the Ledge of the Osier-basket, or Board being indented; so that besides the Ornament, to which it contributes, it serves also to keep in the Fruit, with which a Border may be made round about the *China*-dishes: Seven of these Dishes are express'd in the above-specified Model, and the Order of them may be clearly discern'd; but that in the middle ought to be a little larger, and rais'd somewhat higher than the rest. For want of *China*-dishes, certain Tin-moulds of the same shape may be substituted in their room, the Quality of which is not so easily discover'd, in regard, that before any Thing is dress'd upon them, the bottom ought always to be cover'd with Leaves, or Paper: These round Moulds may also be fasten'd upon the Leggs, and by that means the Desert will become more solid.

Those Persons who have no mind to make use of Wicker-boards according to the Model even now describ'd, may cause some to be made, of the same Form, or otherwise, that consist only of a wooden Bottom, supported by little Knobs, or other sorts of Feet, with a Ledge round about, to keep in the Fruit, as before, and this Ledge may be gilt, or done over with Silver. The same Thing may be observ'd, with respect to the other Boards which are added to the greater, as so many Out-works, and upon these wooden Bottoms the several Leggs are to be fix'd, for the *China*-dishes, in which the Sweet-meats are laid in order.

As for a common Desert prepar'd for few Persons, the Confectioner or Officer may content himself, only to make use of the middle Board, without the Out-works, and in disposing those Out-works otherwise, may find Means to diversifie the Service at another time, or for other Tables; as it appears from the following Model.

The

The Model of a Defert, or Banquet of Sweat-meats, for a round Table.

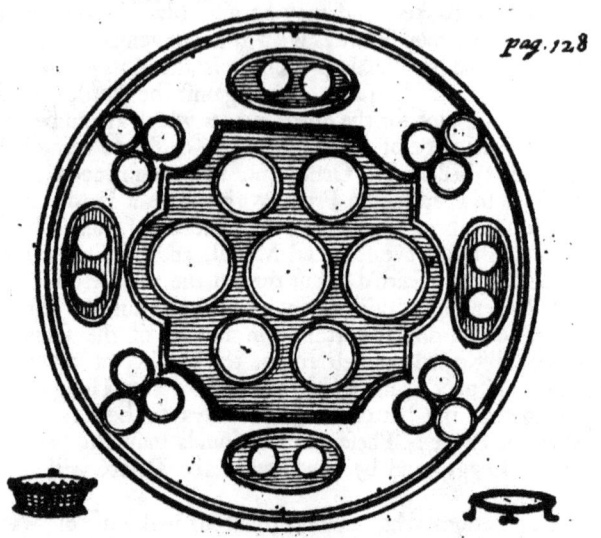

The Explication.

This Defert contains two Oval Out-works more than the former, and the round ones are abfolutely retrench'd: In this cafe, the Compotes may be fet upon the Clubs, and certain fmall Pyramids of Biskets, March-panes, or other Comfits may be rais'd upon the Sides that remain empty and naked. If it be perceiv'd, that the Figure is not fufficiently round, by reafon that the Machine in the middle is not fo broad, as it is long, the Round Out-works may be introduc'd again, or elfe two Ovals with their Ends plac'd inwards; garnifhing the whole Defert, as it may be obferv'd, with real *China*-difhes, or Tin-moulds reprefenting their Figure, upon which the Fruits and Sweetmeats are to be drefs'd in fmall Pyramids: Neither are there exprefs'd in this Model above feven of thefe Difhes for the middle Board, altho' for the moft part, a greater number is admitted, when it is requifite to provide a fomewhat larger Defert.

A

A square Machine set in the middle of such a Table, will render the Figure more round; placing the Oval and Club-Out-works in the same situation: But forasmuch as in such a square Piece, the *China*-dishes leave a void Space, at the four Corners, they may be fill'd up with as many *China*-cups, into which other fine Fruits are to be put, or only some of the same, and the same thing may be done with the other Intervals; garnishing the rest with lesser sorts of Fruit, the thickness of which does not exceed the height of the *China*-dishes: And in a simple Desert, for four Persons, these four Corners may be taken up with little Cups of iced Waters, or other Liquors, according to the Season.

One of the two separate Figures that appear at the Bottom of the Model, or Scheme above delineated, denotes the Form of the above-mention'd Wicker-baskets, either round, or oval, and the other, the simple wooden Machines, with Feet, which may supply the Place of the others, as it has been already intimated. The Clubs, and the Board in the middle are also of the same Construction, and in the little Basket is to be seen the thin Board that lyes on the top at the Entrance, upon which the *China*-dishes are usually rais'd : This Board ought to be cover'd with marbled, or painted Paper, and always set out with Leaves and Flowers, or other Ornaments, according to the Season; more especially in the void Spaces, and Intervals, caus'd by the Indentings on the top of this Wicker-machine. And indeed, very convenient Boards are made for little Tables, where the several Pieces of the like nature, with their whole Contexture is form'd, are all fasten'd together; so that the Desert may be readily serv'd up to Table, all at once, without any manner of trouble, or impediment, and without running the hazard of confounding or spoiling the Sweet-meats; provided a little Care be taken in the ordering of the Machines.

For greater Tables, other Machines of proportionable Dimensions, may be prepar'd at Pleasure, and upon any emergent Occasion, when all these Instruments are wanting, a Desert may nevertheless be very neatly dispos'd of upon the ordinary Table-furniture; after having taken a particular account of the Size and Number of the Dishes, Basons and Plates, which are necessary for that purpose; so that as many *China*-dishes, or Cups may be set in order upon them, as shall be judg'd requisite, to contain the Sweet-meats and Fruits, accordingly as an Opportunity may serve, or the Diversity of Seasons may require.

Upon the whole Matter, it were to be wish'd, that exact Models were produc'd of all the sorts of Materials, with which Deserts might be prepared for different Tables: But considering, that these Circumstances depend upon the Abilities and Inclinations of particular Persons, and the Conveniencies of Houses; such Models would be of no great use, when the Managers are not in a condition to act conformably to those Measures: A certain Officer, for example, thinks fit to serve up *Switzerland*-cheese, cut into Quarters, or Slices; whilst another makes use of Parmesan, or Cheese-curds, during the Festival of *Easter*, with a *Caramel*-embellishment: Another in like manner, judges it expedient only to present a Service of iced Cherries, whilst others are employ'd in preparing a Banquet of more costly and delicious Sweet-meats. Therefore it is sufficient, that we have already given some Account of the several sorts of Comfits and Fruits, which are proper to be serv'd up to Table, in every Month throughout the whole Year: So that recourse may be had, as Occasion serves, to the Rules before laid down in this Treatise; and as for those Persons, who are desirous to be farther instructed in the Method of Dressing an entire Desert, or Banquet of Sweet-meats, to the best advantage; they need only cast an Eye upon the following Model, neatly engrav'd upon a Copper-plate; wherein Endeavours have been us'd, to represent as exact and intelligible a Draught of it, as possibly could be done within so small a Compass.

In this Figure, the middle Board is a Hexagon, consisting of six Angles, or Corners, and the Out-works are of the same nature, as those express'd in the first Model: The Club-figures, at the two Ends, are for iced Waters; the Round ones adjoyning, for *Compotes*; and the Oval on both Sides, serve each to hold a Couple of *China*-dishes, for two small Pyramids. Thus the Quantity of those contain'd in the principal Machine may be very well distinguish'd, and supposing, this Desert were provided for the Month of *July*, you may easily find out, of what Materials it ought to consist, by turning back to Page 12. of this Treatise, in which is contain'd a Description of all sorts of Sweet-meats and raw Fruits, that are proper for that Season: The same thing may be done at any other time, accordingly as Occasion shall require.

NEW

NEW INSTRUCTIONS FOR LIQUORS;

SHEWING

How to Prepare several Sorts of WATERS and DRINKS that are proper for every Season of the Year.

CHAP. I.
Of the iced Waters of Flowers.

THat nothing may seem to be wanting for the compleating of this Work, it is only requisite here to add a few plain Directions relating to certain Liquors and Syrups usually prepar'd by Confectioners, which are of two sorts, *viz.* some cooling to be us'd in the Spring and Summer, and others strong for Autumn and Winter, more especially proper to revive and cheer the Spirits during that rigorous Season, some of which are very particular and remarkable.

Violet-water.

Having provided two good Handfuls of Violets for every two Quarts of Liquor, let them be pick'd and put into Water with

with a quarter or half a Pound of Sugar: When all have been well infused from Morning till Night, at least, for five or six Hours, strain the Liquor thro' a Linnen-cloth, or only thro' a Sieve, and set it by to be iced, according to the Method for all sorts of Waters in general, hereafter explain'd in the last Article of this Chapter.

Another Way.

Whenever you have not leisure enough to let the Ingredients infuse, as before, the pick'd Violets may be thrown into a convenient quantity of Water, with the Sugar, and soak'd as long as it is possible: Then pour off the Liquor out of one Pot into another, as it were beaten Water, till by this continual agitation, it has acquir'd the smell of Violets, which may be farther improv'd with Orrice-powder: Lastly, strain your Liquor; and set it by to cool.

Orange-flower Water.

Take only the Leaves of a Handful of Orange-flowers, without the Yellow and Green, those being sufficient to give the Smell and Tincture: Let these Flowers be infused in a Quart of Water, with a quarter of a Pound of Sugar, in order to be strain'd, cool'd and iced, as occasion requires. Otherwise, if you would make a quick dispatch, beat up your Water, with the Flowers and Sugar, by pouring them several times out of one Vessel into another, and finish the Work after the same manner as in preparing Violet-water.

Jonquil-water.

Let a good Handful of these Flowers be well pick'd and infus'd in Water, with Sugar, from Morning to Noon, or from Noon till Night; and one Hour before the Liquor is serv'd up let it be cool'd and iced, after having strain'd it thro' a Sieve, or a Linnen-cloth. The Work may also be more speedily done, by beating up the Water, with the Flowers and Sugar, after they have been steept, as long as the time will admit: Then strain off the Liquor and pour it into the Cistern to be iced.

Musk-

Musk-rose Water.

Take, as before, only the Leaves of your Roses, and let them infuse in two Quarts of Water, with a quarter of a Pound of Sugar; otherwise beat and pour them out of one Ewer into another: Then straining all set them by to cool, and it will prove a very delicious Liquor.

Pink-water.

Having pick'd the Leaves, throwing away the White and the Green, let them be soak'd in the Morning, or during the Afternoon, with a quarter of a Pound of Sugar, in two Quarts of Water, in order to be strain'd and iced: Otherwise pour off the Liquor out of one Pot into another, till it has imbib'd the Scent of the Pinks, after they have been steept therein for a quarter of an Hour: Lastly, strain it thro' a Sieve, or a clean Napkin, and set it by to cool.

Tuberosa-*flower Water.*

The Leaves of these Flowers are to be taken likewise, without the Yellow and the Stalks, and infus'd from the Evening till the next Morning, or for the space of half a Day; with a sufficient quantity of Sugar. Otherwise, if it be requisite to prepare it sooner, the Liquor may be beat up, as before, by pouring it out of one Pot into another, till it be well impregnated with the *Tuberosa*-flowers: Then it must be strain'd thro' a Sieve, or a Linnen-cloth, and well iced.

Jessamin-water.

Take two Handfuls of *Jessamin*-flowers, and let them infuse in one or two Quarts of Water, with a good quarter of a Pound of Sugar: For a quicker dispatch, the Liquor may be beat up, strain'd and set by to cool.

Thus such Waters as these may be easily made after the same manner, of all kinds of Flowers that have a sweet and pleasant Smell.

How to ice all sorts of Waters and Liquors.

For that purpose, a kind of Cistern in form of a Box is to be provided, which may be of any convenient size, but set out on the inside with Tin-moulds, into which the Liquors are to be put. These Moulds or other Vessels being fix'd in order on this Cistern, and cover'd with their respective Lids, the remaining void Spaces are to be fill'd up with broken Pieces of Ice, as also with several Handfuls of Salt strew'd up and down everywhere and laid over the Moulds; by which means, the Liquors will effectually congeal: A Hole ought also to be made in the Cistern, about the middle of its height, to give passage to the Water, into which the Ice dissolves by degrees, left it should over-flow the Moulds: Then care must be taken from time to time, to break the Ice, that is first made on the Surface, and to put Salt again quite round about the Moulds, to cause the rest to freez: Lastly, when the Liquors are ready to be serv'd up to Table, the *China*-dishes and other Cups, are to be fill'd with these little Pieces of Ice.

CHAP. II.
Of the iced Waters of Fruits, &c.

Cherry-water.

HAving made choice of Cherries that are very ripe, let them be clear'd from their Stones and Stalks, bruis'd, and steept in Water; allowing a Quart for every two Handfuls of Fruit, with a quarter of a Pound of Sugar: If they are not set by to infuse for some Hours, the Water must be beat up, by pouring it several times out of one Pot into another; then it may be strain'd, and iced in the Cistern.

Strawberry-water.

After the Strawberries have been well pick'd and bruis'd, let the Juice be mingled with such a quantity of Water and Sugar,
as

as may be sufficient to make a pleasant Liquor: Then let all be clarified and strain'd, squeezing out the gross Substance strongly, to give the Water a red Colour. If you have no mind to ice this Liquor it must be made clear, by passing it thro' the Straining-bag, or thro' a Napkin folded into three or four Doubles.

Rasberry-water.

This Water is made after the same manner as the former; the proper Tincture and Smell may also be given to both sorts, without the Colour, by making use of white Strawberries or Rasberries.

Curran-water.

Let the ripest Currans be bruis'd, squeez'd and infus'd in Water, with Sugar for five or six Hours; then strain the Liquor thro' a Sieve, if you would have it iced: Otherwise if it be design'd for a cooling Drink, you need only clarifie it, by passing it thro' the Straining-bag.

Apricock-water.

Let very ripe Apricocks, that have been pared, ston'd, and cut into Pieces, be put into Water that has boil'd for some time; adding a quarter of a Pound of Sugar to every Quart of Water: After the Fruit has infus'd for some time, the Work may be finish'd according to the preceeding Method, by often beating and pouring the Liquor out of one Vessel into another: Then it may be strain'd or made clear, in order to be iced, or cool'd.

Peach-water

Is prepar'd after the same manner as that of Apricocks; but 'tis observable, That all these sorts of Liquors, made of Fruits, that have no great smell, may be perfum'd with Amber or Musk, at discretion.

Orange-

Orange-water.

Squeez out the Juice of three or four *Sevill*-Oranges, into two Quarts of Water, and steep the Pulp and Zests in the same Water, during some Hours, with a good Piece of Sugar. This Liquor for a quicker dispatch, may be beat up by pouring it often out of one Pot into another; and then it may be strain'd thro' a Bag or Sieve, in order to be cool'd or iced: The Juice of a Lemmon added, will give it a more agreeable tartness.

Lemmon-water.

Having in like manner squeez'd out the Juice of three or four Lemmons into two Quarts of Water, let the Pulp and Zests be soak'd therein, with a quarter of a Pound of Sugar, during some Hours: Then strain the Liquor, as before and set it by, to be iced or cool'd.

Orangeade.

To make this Liquor, a greater quantity of Oranges is requisite than for the common Orange-water; that is to say, six Oranges and two Lemmons, for every Quart of Water. The Juice of these is to be squeez'd out, and the Zests left to steep for some time; or else the Water must be beat up by pouring it out of one Pot into another: Then pressing the Oranges, the Liquor may be strain'd and set by to cool.

Limonnade.

A very good sort of Limonnade may be prepar'd, by allowing three Lemmons to a Quart of Water, with a quarter of a Pound of Sugar, and these Ingredients may be proportionably augmented, according to the Quantity designed: After having squeez'd out the Juice of your Fruit into the Water, leave the Pulp and Zests to infuse for a considerable time; then press the Lemmon-pulp and Peel, strain the Liquor, and set it by to cool. Several sorts of sweet-smelling Flowers may be added to this Limonnade, to heighten its Scent and Flavour; which may also be done with Amber or Musk, beaten before in a Mortar, with a little Sugar, or Sugar-candy, and afterwards put into the Liquor.

Ano-

Another sort of Limonnade.

Let two Quarts of Wine, one Pint of Water, with the Juice and Zests of two Lemmons, be put into an earthen Pan, adding nine or ten Ounces of Sugar, more or less, according to your own inclination and the Quality of the Wine: Afterwards having left these Ingredients to infuse about half an Hour, pour the Liquor thro' the Straining-bag, and dispose of it in Bottles.

Another sort.

Having provided *Cedres*, *Citrons*, or large Lemmons, take all that part which contains the Juice, and separate them from the Kernels; cutting them into Quarters, or otherwise: In the mean while, let some Sugar be boil'd up to its Blown Quality, that is to say, a Pound for every douzen of Citrons, or Lemmons, and when it has attain'd to that Degree, throw in the Juice; leaving all to boil together, till it return to the Pearled Degree: Then pour the Syrup thro' a Sieve set over an earthen Pan, and keep it in Glass-bottles for use: This Liquor is very delicious and cooling, when a small quantity of it is mingled with Water beaten and pour'd several times out of one Vessel into another, that it may be well diluted.

A *Limonnade* may also be made even with the Leaves of the Citron-tree; which are very odoriferous and full of a pleasant and cooling Juice; but it can only be put in practice in Countries, where such Trees are more common than in these Climates. Lastly, a kind of Liquor may be prepar'd without any Citrons or Lemmons, which nevertheless has the taste of *Limonnade*; by the means of a few drops of Spirit of Salt; being no less useful and wholesome; for the Virtues of this Spirit are very particular and well known; upon which account, it is sometimes used instead of Verjuice in Sauces and Ragoos.

White Water, or Virginal Water.

Take as much Milk as may be sufficient to whiten the quantity of Water you would have prepar'd, and to give it a tincture or relish; adding a quarter of a Pound of Sugar to every Quart, and squeezing in the Juice of a Lemmon, which will much

much promote the pleasantness of its taste: Then pour it thro' a Sieve as other Liquors of the like nature, to clear it from the dross of the Sugar; but if you do not design to ice it, only let it pass thro' the Straining-bag.

Chocolate-water.

This Water, as well as the former, may be us'd in the Winter, and at any time when the above-mentioned Flowers and Fruits are wanting. It is prepar'd only by grating some Chocolate into Water, accordingly as the quantity requires, and adding a good quarter of a Pound of Sugar to every Quart: Afterwards, all being well steept and infus'd for some time, the Liquor must be strain'd in order to be iced or cool'd.

Rosade

Is a pleasant Liquor made of pounded Almonds, with Milk and clarified Sugar; but it will not keep long; because it is soon apt to grow so greasie and unctuous, that it afterwards becomes very disagreeable to the Palate, and consequently fit only to be thrown away.

CHAP. III.
Of Liquors that are proper for the Winter-Season.

SOme of the Liquors above-described, as Orangeade, Limonnade, Rosade, Chocolate-water, Milk-water, &c. may also be used in the Winter; but those that more properly belong to this Quarter, which may likewise reciprocally take place in the other Seasons, are the particular Waters of Cinnamon, Coriander, Anis, and Juniper, several sorts of Hippocras, Ratafiaz, &c.

Cinnamon-water.

Take the best Cinnamon well beaten, and infuse it for the space of three Days in a Vessel of double Glass, with Rose-water, or common Water, a Pint of White-wine, and Sugar
pro-

proportionably to the quantity: To that purpose, the Vessel must be set upon hot Embers, or in a warm Place, and well cover'd; then the Liquor may be strain'd and kept for use.

Another Way of Preparing it.

Upon any urgent occasion, some beaten Cinnamon may be taken, that is to say half an Ounce for every Quart of Water, and boil'd together with Sugar, till it be half consum'd: Then strain your Liquor and it will be very pleasant.

The Water may also be boil'd alone, and when it is taken off from the Fire, the beaten Cinnamon is to be thrown in, with a quarter of a Pound of Sugar; as soon as the Liquor is cold, it must be strain'd as before.

Another more simple Water may be made only by causing the Cinnamon to be steept in it at Night till the next Morning, or from Morning to the Evening of the same Day: Then it must be strain'd and set by to cool after the same manner as the above-mentioned Liquors.

Coriander-seed Water.

Let a Handful of Coriander-seed taken out of its Husk or Cod, be put into a Quart of Water, with a quarter of a Pound of Sugar; leaving all to soak, till the Water tastes strong of the Seeds, and the Sugar is dissolved: Afterwards, having beat up the Liquor, by pouring it out of one Pot into another, let it be strain'd and cool'd, or iced, accordingly as occasion serves.

Anis-seed Water.

Take a Handful of Anis-seed well cleansed, and infuse it in a Quart of Water, with a quarter of a Pound of Sugar: As soon as the Water is sufficiently impregnated, strain it off, and if you think fit, add a little Brandy, to enrich it, when it is not design'd to be cool'd or iced.

In the Summer, a sort of Anis-water may be made, by causing the Leaves only of that Plant, especially the tops of them, to be steept for a considerable time. The same thing may be done with another sort of Herb call'd *Burnet* ; so that these two Liquors may well be added to the others that have been before described and appropriated to the Summer-Season.

Clove-

Clove-water.

This Water is not made of Cloves alone, because its Scent would be too strong and offensive to the Brain; therefore some Cinnamon is usually intermixt, and eight or ten Cloves may be sufficient for a Quart of Water, with a good Piece of Sugar: After all has been infus'd for some time over hot Embers, or in a warm place, the Liquor may be strain'd, and it will prove very pleasant.

Juniper-water

Is prepar'd by infusing a Handful of Juniper-berries in two Quarts of Water, with some Sticks of Cinnamon and Sugar: Then the Work may be finish'd as before; unless you have a mind to add a little Brandy, to render the Liquor more pleasant and efficacious.

Kernel-water.

Having pour'd two Quarts of good Brandy into an earthen Pitcher, put in two Ounces of the Kernels of Cherries well pounded, or else an Ounce and a half of Apricock-kernels likewise well pounded, with the Skin; as also, almost a quarter of a Dram of Cinnamon, two Cloves, as much Coriander-seed as may be taken up between two Fingers, nine or ten Ounces of Sugar, and about two Glasses of boil'd Water, after it is become cold: Then the Pitcher must be well stopt and all the Ingredients left to infuse for the space of two or three Days: Afterwards pour your Liquor thro' the Straining-bag, till it be clear and put it into Bottles, which must be kept close stopt.

CHAP. IV.
Of Hippocras and some other Liquors.

THese Liquors are generally prepar'd for Entertainments during the Winter-season, among them the different sorts of Hippocras are more especially remarkable, viz. White

White Hippocras.

Take two Quarts of good White-wine, with a Pound of Sugar, an Ounce of Cinnamon, a little Mace, two Grains of whole black Pepper and a Lemmon cut into three quarters: Let all infuse together for some time; and afterwards pass thro' a Straining-bag, which is to be hung up in a convenient place, with a Vessel underneath to receive the Liquor, and kept open by the means of two little Sticks: The Liquor must be strain'd thus three or four times; but if you perceive upon such Occasions, that it does not pass freely, pour in half a Glass or a whole Glass of Milk, and that will soon produce the desired effect. The smell of Musk or Amber may be given to this Hippocras, by using a Grain of either pounded with Sugar, and wrapt up in Cotton, which may be fasten'd to the end of the Bag through which the Liquor is strained.

Pale Hippocras.

Let half a Pound of Loaf-Sugar broken into small Lumps, with half a Lemmon, three or four Cloves, a little Cinnamon, three or four Grains of white Pepper and Coriander-seed, and a few Almonds cut into pieces, be infus'd for an Hour or half an Hour in a Quart of pale Wine: Then having caus'd all to be stirr'd about and well mingled together let the Liquor pass thro' the Straining-bag, as before.

Red Hippocras.

Having pour'd two Quarts of good red Wine into an earthen Pan, take half a Dram of Cinnamon; a Grain and a half, or two Grains of white Pepper; a little long Pepper; half a Leaf of Mace; and about a Spoonful of Coriander-seed, all beaten separately; 'tis also requisite to provide a Pound or a Pound and a quarter of Sugar only bruised in a Mortar and six sweet Almonds likewise bruised, with half a Glass of good Brandy. Let all these Ingredients be steept in your Wine, for the space of an Hour, taking care that the Vessel into which they are put, be well cover'd and stopt; and let it be stirr'd a little with a Spoon, from time to time, to cause the Sugar to dissolve: Then strain the Liquor according to the usual method,

and

and if you pleafe, give it a fweet fmell; but the firft Liquor that diftills from the Straining-bag, muft be put into it again two or three feveral times, till it become very clear: Afterwards, fet a Bottle with a Funnel underneath, and when it is full, keep it clofe ftopt.

Hippocras made more fpeedily.

Take any fort of Wine that you fhall think fit, with the requifite quantity of Loaf-Sugar broken into pieces; adding fome beaten Cinnamon, a few Grains of Coriander-feed, three or four Grains of Pepper, and a piece of Lemmon, the Juice of which is to be fqueez'd in. Otherwife inftead of all thefe Ingredients, only ufe a little Cinnamon-effence, if you have any at hand, and having ftrain'd your Hippocras through the Bag with a little Milk, it will very well anfwer your expectation.

Hippocras without Wine.

Let half a Pound of fine Sugar and a little Cinnamon, with the other Ingredients above-fpecify'd, be put into one or two Quarts of Water; and let all infufe from Morning to Noon, or from Noon till Night; the Veffel being well covered: Then let the Liquor pafs thro' the Straining-bag five or fix times, and give it the fmell of Musk, or Amber, at difcretion.

Befides this variety of Hippocras, feveral Difhes of burnt Wine and burnt Brandy are alfo ferv'd up at Entertainments; the particular manner of preparing which is every where fo well known, that it needs no defcription.

A delicious fort of Wine.

Put two Lemmons cut into flices, and two Pippins cut in like manner, into a Difh, with half a Pound of Powder-Sugar, a Quart of good *Burgundy*-Wine; fix Cloves, a little beaten Cinnamon and Orange flower Water; let all be well cover'd and infus'd for three or four Hours: Then ftrain it thro' the Bag, and give it a tincture of Amber or Musk, as either is moft agreeable to your Palate.

CHAP.

Chap. V.
Several sorts of Ratafiaz.

THis Liquor is at present very much in vogue, and may be made of Cherries, Apricocks and Muscadine-grapes, according to the following Instructions.

Ratafiaz of Cherries.

Let your Cherries be bruised together with their Kernels, and put into an earthen Jarr, or into a wooden Barrel; but a Cask that has held Brandy, is more especially proper for that purpose: To twenty Pounds of these Cherries add three Pounds of Rasberries likewise bruised, with five Pounds of Sugar, three Penny-worth of Cinnamon, a Handful of white Pepper in grain, a few Nutmegs, twenty Cloves, and ten Quarts of good Brandy: Leave the Vessel unstopt during ten or twelve Days, then stop it up, and let it continue untouched for the space of two Months: Thus a greater quantity may be made, by mingling the Ingredients proportionably, and the whole may be enrich'd with some Drops of Essences and sweet Scents. When the Ratafiaz is fit for drinking, the Barrel must be pierc'd above the Lees, as the Wine-casks are; but if it be kept in an earthen Jarr, it must be strain'd thro' the Bag, and put into other Vessels carefully stopt up, to be us'd as occasion serves.

Another Way of making Cherry-Ratafiaz.

Having provided ten Pounds of Cherries, let them be bruised and put into earthen Pitchers with two Quarts of Brandy; then let the Vessels be well stopt, and set by for five or six Days, at the end of which, the Cherries must be press'd in a Linnen-cloth to get out all their Juice: In the mean while, let five Pounds of large Currans be boil'd with three Pounds of Sugar, and press'd as the Cherries; so as both sorts of Juices may be mingled together, allowing for every Quart of that Liquor, a Quart of Brandy, and a quarter of a Pound of Sugar. Then add the Kernels of your bruised Cherries, with half a Pound of Coriander-seed, a little Mace, Cloves, Cinnamon and long Pepper,

per, all pounded together, and fill your Pitchers or other Vessels with the Liquor; leaving it to infuse for the space of six Weeks: Afterwards it must be pass'd thro' the Straining-bag, and put again, with the Kernels of Apricock-stones or Cherry-stones, into the Pitchers, which are to be kept close stopt, and the *Ratafiaz* may be drawn off clear, upon all occasions.

To give the *Ratafiaz* a tincture of Rasberries, or Strawberries, some of it may be prepar'd separately, with Brandy, Sugar and Cinnamon; or else the Juice of these Fruits may be infus'd at any convenient opportunity in part of the *Ratafiaz*: Orange-flowers may also be preserv'd, which will give it a very pleasant smell; and to improve its colour, the Juice of Mulberries may be us'd mingled with Brandy, and clarified by straining it thro' the Bag. Those that are prepar'd with Strawberries and Rasberries may also be order'd after the same manner; and a great variety may be produc'd even out of one sort of *Ratafiaz*: Mulberries likewise serve to bring it to a good consistence, and make a very sweet Liquor, when infus'd with the other above-mentioned Ingredients.

White Ratafiaz.

Take a Gallon of Water, a Pound of Sugar, an Ounce of Cinnamon, with Cloves, white Pepper and Ginger tied up in a Rag; as also some Nutmeg and Mace, and put these Ingredients into a Copper-pan set over the Fire: To clarifie the Sugar, throw in the White of an Egg, clear it well from the Scum, and let all boil together, till at least one third part be consum'd; if you perceive that the Liquor has not sufficiently acquir'd the taste of the Ingredients: Then take it off from the Fire, adding a Quart of Brandy, and let it pass thro' the Straining-bag, or only thro' a fine Sieve; you may also give it a fragrant smell, with the Juice of white Strawberries or Rasberries, provided separately in a Pot, as upon other occasions, or else it may be done with Orange-flowers. If for want of the red sorts of *Ratafiaz*, above-described, you are minded to give this the same tincture, it may be coloured by the means of Mulberry-juice; or else with thick *Orleans*-Wine, or some other of the like nature; or lastly, with prepared Cocheneal.

Moreover it is expedient for the making of the like white *Ratafiaz*, to keep in a Pot, the Kernels of Cherries and Apricocks

cocks steept in Brandy, which will serve to enrich it by putting in a little at discretion.

Apricock-Ratafiaz

May be prepar'd two several Ways, viz. by causing the Apricocks cut into pieces to infuse in Brandy for a Day or two; at the end of which Term the Liquor must be strain'd thro' the Bag and impregnated with the usual Ingredients. Otherwise, the Apricocks may be boil'd in White-wine, and by that means more easily made clear, adding to every Quart of such Liquor, a Quart of Brandy, and a quarter of a Pound of Sugar, with Cinnamon, Cloves, Mace, and the Apricock-kernels: After all have been well steept during eight or ten Days, the Liquor must be strain'd again, and put into Bottles or earthen Pitchers, to be kept for use.

Muscadel-Ratafiaz.

Having made choice of the best Muscadel-grapes, that are very ripe, let them be well press'd; allowing for every Quart of their Juice a Quart of Brandy and a quarter of a Pound of Sugar: Then this Liquor must be pour'd into earthen Pitchers, with Cinnamon, Cloves, Mace, and a few Grains of Pepper, and left to infuse for the space of two or three Days; afterwards let the *Ratafiaz* be clarified by passing thro' the Straining-bag, and conveniently put into Bottles; adding a Grain of Musk, if it be not sufficiently perfum'd.

CHAP. VI.

Of the Syrups of Flowers.

WE are now come to an Article, that has a nearer relation to the Confectionary Art, than the preceding; altho' some of the Syrups contain'd therein, are more commonly prepar'd by Apothecaries, &c.

Syrup

Syrup of Violets.

Take a Pound of pick'd Violets, and beat them in a Mortar, with half a Glass of Water, to moisten them a little; whilst four Pounds of Sugar are brought to the Pearled Quality: Then taking the Pan off from the Fire, as soon as the Boiling sinks, throw in your Violets and let all be well stirr'd together: Afterwards you are to press them thro' a fine Linnen-cloth, so as the Syrup may be receiv'd into an earthen Pan, and put into Bottles, when cold.

The gross Substance that remains may likewise be slipp'd into two Pounds of Pearled Sugar, after the Boiling is settled: Then let all be well mingled together, and pour'd into a Pot; to be us'd in the making of Pastes and Conserve of Violets, according to the Instructions elsewhere laid down. The best Violets for this purpose, are such as are of a dark Purple-colour, not pale, and of a very sweet scent; they ought to be gather'd in the Morning, when no Rain has fallen, and before the Sun has impair'd their Virtue.

Another Way.

Syrup of Violets may also be made by an Infusion of the Flowers, according to the following Method: Having caus'd fifteen Quarts of hot Water to be pour'd upon six Pounds of these Flowers, let all soak during eight Hours in an earthen glazed Pot, that has a straight Mouth, which must be close stopt, so as the Virtue and Smell may not exhale: Then the Liquor being heated again, and squeez'd out, add the like quantity of fresh Flowers, which are to be left to infuse in the same manner for eight Hours, and to be strongly press'd again: Afterwards Sugar may be put in, as it shall be hereafter shewn in the Article of *Clove-gilliflowers*; or this Infusion may be kept, according to the common practice of Apothecaries.

Syrup of Roses.

This Syrup may be well prepar'd after the two manners but now explain'd for that of Violets, or else according to the following particular Way. Take entire Roses, put them into a Pot, as before, and pour in as much warm Water; then cover
the

the Pot, and let all infufe for eight Hours on hot Embers: Afterwards, fet them in a Copper-Pan or in the fame Pot over a clear Fire, till the Liquor be ready to boil, and fqueez it thro' a new Linnen-cloth: Laftly, pour this ftrained Liquor, on the fame quantity of other frefh Rofes; let them infufe again, and continue to do fo for nine Days, changing the Rofes every time. This Infufion may be kept a whole Year, without being fpoil'd in Glafs-Viols, provided they be well ftopp'd with Cotton and double Paper, to the end that its Smell and Virtue may be preferv'd.

Syrup of Violets may be made after the fame manner; but the Infufion will not keep fo well.

Syrup of Clove-gilliflowers.

Having provided the beft fort of Clove-gilliflowers of a lively red colour, weigh out three Pounds of thofe that are well pick'd, and put them into an earthen Veffel with a ftraight Mouth, varnifh'd on the infide: Then pour in nine Quarts of Spring-water boiling hot, and dip the Flowers in the Water, with a wooden Spatula: Let the Pot be well cover'd, and fet over hot Embers for the fpace of an Hour; at the expiration of which the Infufion muft have a little Boiling, in order to be ftrain'd and fqueez'd; it muft alfo be heated again, and pour'd hot on three Pounds of frefh Flowers put into the fame Veffel: This Liquor is to be mingled with fix Pounds of good Sugar boil'd till it become Pearled, and clarify'd with the White of an Egg: Afterwards, the whole Mefs muft be pour'd into a Sieve fet over an earthen Pan, or elfe ftrain'd thro' a fine Linnencloth.

This Syrup is of admirable efficacy againft any Infection of the Air and malignant Feavers, and is a great Reftorative for Weaknefs of Body; more efpecially ftrengthening the Heart and Brain, when taken alone in a Spoon, or in ordinary Drink.

CHAP.

Chap. VII.
Of the Syrups of Fruits, &c.

The remaining sorts of Syrups are no less advantagious than the former, and of singular use in private Families.

Syrup of Mulberries.

After having caus'd two Pounds of good Sugar to be boil'd till it has acquir'd its Blown quality, let a Pound of Mulberries be thrown in, and give them eight or ten Boilings: Then pour all into a Sieve set over an earthen Pan, and put the Syrup into Bottles, to be kept as long as you shall think fit and us'd as occasion serves.

It may also be made by pressing the Mulberries to get their Juice, which is to be put into a Pan with a Pound of Sugar, and the whole boil'd till it become Pearled. This Syrup is well known to be a Soveraign Remedy for Distempers of the Throat and other Indispositions of the like nature.

Syrup of Cherries.

Let two Quarts of the Juice of Cherries be first pass'd thro' the Straining-bag, to cleanse it, (which is also requisite to be done in all other cases) and then put to a Pound and a half of Sugar: Afterwards having brought the Syrup to the Pearled Degree of Boiling, as before, let it be set by, and put into Vials, when cold; to be mingled with beaten Water, in order to make a cooling Drink, upon any emergent occasion.

Otherwise (according to the first Method for the ordering of Syrup of Mulberries) you need only to bruise the Cherries and throw them into Sugar that has attain'd to its Blown Quality; so that after ten or twelve Boilings, all may be pour'd into a Sieve, set over some Vessel, to receive the Syrup.

Moreover having caus'd the Cherries to cast their Juice by pressing them in a Copper-Pan over the Fire, this Juice likewise may be put into Blown Sugar, and left to boil till it becomes Pearled.

Syrup

Syrup of Currans and other sorts of cooling Fruit.

Having provided Curran-juice clarify'd by passing it thro the Straining-bag, let as much Sugar be made almost Crack'd, Then mingle both together, and you'll perceive, that the Syrup has attain'd to the necessary degree of Boiling. This syrup may also be prepar'd after the same manner, as that of Mulberries already explain'd; as well as Syrup of Pomegranates, and others of the like nature that are proper for cooking.

Syrup of Apricocks.

Forasmuch as this Syrup is apt to grow greasie, it ought only to be made for present use, according to one of the two following Methods. Let very ripe Apricocks be cut into pieces and thrown into Blown Sugar, with Kernels bruised, so as they may have eight or ten Boilings between Smooth and Pearled: Then pour all thro' a seive, and let the Syrup that runs thro be put into proper Vessels; allowing a Pound of Sugar for every half Pound of Fruit. The other way is as follows; Having par'd and slit your Apricocks in the middle, set them in order upon little sticks laids a-cross an earthen Pan, and put Powder-Sugar on every Bed and Row; making use of the above-mentioned Quantity; thus they are to be left in a cool place, till the next Day: Afterwards slip the Apicocks into a little hot Water, and turn all out upon a Linnen-cloth to drain without pressing the Fruit; so that this Juice together with that which the Apricocks have already let fall into the Pan, will serve to make the Syrup, by causing them to boil, with the usual Precautions, to the Pearled Degree.

Syrup of Quinces.

This Syrup may be made with the Pulp of Quinces grated or cut into small slices, and squeez'd in a Linnen-cloth, to get their Juice, which is to be clear'd by leaving it to settle in the Sun, or before the Fire: In the mean while, having caus'd a Pound of Sugar to be brought to its Blown Quality, let it be mingled with four Ounces of this Juice; but if the Sugar should by that means be too much depress'd, it may have a few Boilings afresh, till it returns to the Pearl Degree; and the Syrup, when cold, may be put into Bottles.

Syrup

Syrup of Bell-grapes, and others.

Syrup of Bell-grapes is made with their Juice clarified after the same manner as that of Quinces, and four Ounces of it are likewise sufficient for a Pound of Sugar, which must attain to its Blown degree of Boiling, before the Juice is incorporated with it. If the Grapes are more ripe, a Syrup may be made of them, according to the Method before laid down for Mulberries.

Syrup of Lemmons may also be prepar'd conformably to these Instructions.

Syrup of Sugar.

Pour Spirit of Wine upon Sugar-candy to the height of a Finger's breadth, and set all over the Fire, till it comes to the Consistence of a Syrup; which may be us'd to very good purpose in promoting the Cure of Distempers of the Lungs and Coughs.

The Juices of all sorts of Fruits.

To get the Juice of Cherries, Currans, Mulberries, Rasberberries, Strawberries, &c. you only wrap them up in a new Linnen-cloth, and cause them to be well press'd: The Juice of Oranges, Lemmons, Pomegranates, Quinces and other Fruit of the like nature is usually extracted by cutting them first into pieces or round slices, and then squeezing or pressing them, as before. Afterwards, take care to clarifie these Juices by putting them into Bottles to settle in the Sun for several Days, and when the gross Substance sinks to the bottom, pour off the Liquor by degrees, in order to be pass'd thro' the Straining-bag. Then the Juices may be us'd for Syrups, or kept in Bottles, covering their Surface with Oil of Olives, which as occasion serves is to be gently taken away with Cotton. Lastly, In the Winter-season these Juices are to be preserv'd in a warm Place to prevent them from freezing; and by this means, they'll be always ready at hand for present use.

F I N I S.

You may also be interested in these titles:

Townsends is please to make available a growing list of rare and valuable books from the 18th and early 19th centuries, including those listed below. Be sure to visit our website for a complete list of titles.

Cookbooks

The Art of Cookery by Hannah Glasse (1765)

The Domestick Coffee-Man by Humphrey Broadbent (1722) and *The New Art of Brewing Beer* by Thomas Tyron (1690)

The Complete Housewife by Eliza Smith (1730)

The Universal Cook by John Townshend (1773)

The Practice of Cookery by Mrs. Frazer (1791 & 1795)

The London Art of Cookery by John Farley (1787)

The Complete Confectioner by Hannah Glasse (1765)

A New and Easy Method of Cookery by Elizabeth Cleland (1755)

The English Art of Cookery by Richard Briggs (1788)

18th & Early 19th-Century Brewing by multiple authors

The Lady's Assistant by Charlotte Mason (1777)

The Experienced English Housekeeper by Elizabeth Raffald (1769)

The Professed Cook by B. Clermont (1769)

The Cook's and Confectioner's Dictionary by John Nott (1723)

The Modern Art of Cookery Improved by Ann Shackleford (1765)

The Country Housewife's Family Companion by William Ellis (1750)

A Collection of Above Three Hundred Receipts by Mary Kettelby (1714)

England's Newest Way in All Sorts of Cookery by Henry Howard (1726)

Biographies & Journals

The Hessians by multiple authors

Travels Through the Interior Parts of North-America in the Years 1766, 1767, and 1768 by Jonathan Carver (1778)

The Women of the American Revolution, Volumes 1, 2, & 3 by Elizabeth Ellet (1848)

The Backwoods of Canada by Catharine Parr Traill (1836)

Travels into North America by Peter Kalm (1760)

New Travels in the United States of America. Performed in 1788 and *The Commerce of America and Europe* by J.P. Brissot De Warville (1792 & 1795)

The Journal of Nicholas Cresswell, 1774–1777 by Nicholas Cresswell (1924)

An Account of the Life of the Late Reverend Mr. David Brainerd by Jonathan Edwards (1765 & 1824)

Travels for Four Years and a Half in the United States of America During 1798, 1799, 1800, 1801, and 1802 by John Davis (1909)

Travels through North and South Carolina, Georgia, East and West Florida by William Bartram (1792)

A Tour in the United States of America, Volumes 1 & 2 by John F. Smyth Stuart (1784)

Townsends
www.townsends.us

www.ingramcontent.com/pod-product-compliance
Lightning Source LLC
Chambersburg PA
CBHW071655170426
43195CB00039B/2195